This   rly
Han
  A   cs.
This   nt
as i: of
corp   er-
purg   a
syste
  As   he
cour   he
cour   he
divis   ce
to th   as
the t

PAU   ly,
New

Cambridge Studies in Early Modern British History

Series editors

ANTHONY FLETCHER
Professor of History, University of Essex

JOHN GUY
Professor of Modern History, University of St Andrews

and JOHN MORRILL
Reader in Early Modern History, University of Cambridge, and Vice Master of Selwyn College

This is a series of monographs and studies covering many aspects of the history of the British Isles between the late fifteenth century and early eighteenth century. It includes the work of established scholars and pioneering work by a new generation of scholars. It also includes both reviews and revisions of major topics and books which open up new historical terrain or which reveal startling new perspectives on familiar subjects. All the volumes set detailed research into broader perspectives and the books are intended for the use of students as well as of their teachers.

For a list of titles in the series, see end of book

For A. L. H.

DISMEMBERING THE BODY POLITIC

Partisan Politics in England's Towns, 1650–1730

PAUL D. HALLIDAY

PUBLISHED BY THE PRESS SYNDICATE OF THE UNIVERSITY OF CAMBRIDGE
The Pitt Building, Trumpington Street, Cambridge, United Kingdom

CAMBRIDGE UNIVERSITY PRESS
The Edinburgh Building, Cambridge CB2 2RU, UK
40 West 20th Street, New York NY 10011–4211, USA
477 Williamstown Road, Port Melbourne, VIC 3207, Australia
Ruiz de Alarcón 13, 28014 Madrid, Spain
Dock House, The Waterfront, Cape Town 8001, South Africa

http://www.cambridge.org

First published 1998
First paperback edition 2002

Typeface Sabon 10/12 pt.

A catalogue record for this book is available from the British Library

Library of Congress Cataloguing in Publication data
Halliday, Paul D. (Paul Delaney), 1961–
Dismembering the body politic: partisan politics in England's towns, 1650–1730 /
Paul D. Halliday.
p.   cm. – (Cambridge studies in early modern British history)
Includes bibliographical references and index.
ISBN 0 521 55253 2
1. Great Britain – Politics and government – 1603–1714.   2. Great Britain – Politics and
government – 1714–1760.   3. Political culture – Great Britain – History.   4. Municipal
corporations – Great Britain – History.   5. Boroughs – Great Britain – History.   6. Central–local
government relations – Great Britain – History.   I. Title.   II. Series:
JN191.H34   1998
306.2′0942′09032–dc21   97-18472   CIP

ISBN 0 521 55253 2   hardback
ISBN 0 521 52604 3   paperback

CONTENTS

Preface   xi
List of abbreviations   xvii

Part one   Corporate ideal and partisan reality

I The paradox of partisan politics   3
   From "party" to partisan politics   5
   The rhetoric of "party" and the paradox of partisan politics 11
   Partisan politics in the borough corporations   18
   Partisan politics and the law: stability in a dynamic society 24
   Dismembering the body politic   28

2 "The best of polities"   29
   The body politic   30
   The charter   33
   The body's members and functions   41
   Rules of order   47
   The crown, the courts, and the corporate person   54

3 From purge to purge: Civil War, Interregnum, and Restoration
  in the corporations   56
   Division and dismissal, 1642–58   59
   Mandamus   67
   Restoring the boroughs, restoring the King, 1658–60   73
   Passing an "Act for the well-governing and regulating of
   corporations"   85

Implementing the Corporation Act 92

Purge and counter-purge 104

4 Partisan politics, 1663–1682 106

The failure of the Corporation Act 109

Partisan conflict in the 1670s 117

The Corporation Act revisited: 1680 124

"Left to the law" 131

Perpetuating and moderating partisan conflict 143

Part two   The King and his corporations, 1660–1688

5 The corporations and their charters, 1660–1682 149

Charters in the 1660s 151

The search for a royal policy, 1660–82 161

Partisan politics and corporate charters in the 1670s 177

Charters and charter policy, 1660–82 187

6 Quo warranto and the King's corporations, 1682–1685 189

The interpretive legacy 192

Quo warranto revived 196

The Worcester and London quo warrantos 201

The development of a charters policy, 1682–83 212

Partisan politics and the corporations' charters, 1682–85 223

The King and his corporations 234

7 Revolution in the corporations, 1685–1688 237

"Regulated according to the new mode" 240

Purge by charter 251

Ignoring partisan verities 260

Part three   Partisan conflict and the law in a dynamic society

8 The legacy of the 1680s 265

1689–90: The struggle to define the 1680s 268

Problems: partisan politics in the 1690s   276

Solutions: King's Bench and Parliament   291

Enduring partisan verities   302

9 Partisan conflict and political stability, 1702–1727   304

Corporate politics in the age of Anne   306

Queen's Bench and parliamentary statute   313

The corporations and the house of Hanover   322

Partisan conflict in a dynamic society   339

10 1660, 1688, 1727, and beyond   342

Appendix A   Royal charters of incorporation, 1660–1727   350
Appendix B   Enforcement of the Corporation Act, 1662–1663   354

Select bibliography   362
Index   383

PREFACE

.

... and every city or house divided against itself shall not stand.
Matthew, chapter 12, verse 25

From the 1640s on, England's cities divided against themselves, yet they stood. That is the point of this book.

This book answers two questions about the transformation of political culture. Where and how did partisan politics evolve? And what was its impact? The answers are as simple as these questions. Partisan politics evolved in England's borough corporations in the wake of the Civil Wars. And the impact of partisan conflict was not to create instability but to create the means for achieving stability. Throughout, a third question constantly arises. What was the relationship between center and locality, that is, between the crown and the borough corporations? The answer: each needed the other because each was made of the other. The most significant change in this relationship was the rapid development of one royal institution, the court of King's Bench, in response to the demands of hundreds of other royal institutions, the corporations governing 200 towns.

The genesis of political parties has long fascinated historians, but the historiography has been vexed by the problem of definition. No one has given a compelling reason to choose one definition of party over another, nor do I imagine that anyone could. What counts as a party keeps shifting so the desired object slips from our grasp. This might be because there was no such object at all, certainly not in the seventeenth century. Before there could be a thing we could call a "party," there had to be a kind of behavior that did not in its earliest manifestations create such things. Rather than look for parties, or for a model or system of party, I propose that we look for an activity: a politics characterized by the division of communities into competing groups, each of which endured from one episode of conflict to the next. Such groups often had very different labels over time and they frequently denied that they were groups at all since contemporary rhetoric insisted that division was sinful. But such groups did exist, and their principal aim was to exclude their foes from public life in order to restore unity. It is this activity of dividing and excluding that I call partisan politics.

I have arranged the book in three sections because three basic insights help us understand the development of partisan politics. Part One explores the law and rhetoric governing life in the borough corporations across the period 1650 to 1730 (chapters 1 and 2), and more specifically from the 1640s to the early 1680s, when the corporations were first dismembered by partisan purges (chapters 3 and 4). The crucial point throughout is that the desire for unity generated in the wake of Civil War promoted purgation. The rhetoric of corporate wholeness conflicted with the reality of a society divided by religious sympathies and personal angers. A traditional insistence on unity pushed seventeenth-century minds to only one conclusion about how to preserve it: purge the body politic. But given the passions generated by political and religious differences after the Civil Wars, and given that one's foes also felt the impulse to create unity by the same means, those threatened by purgation fought back in kind. This is what I call the paradox of partisan politics: the attempt to restore unity fostered disunity as each of the divided sides in towns everywhere sought to exclude each other with the same vigor. Purges of the 1640s and 1650s begat counter-purges in the 1660s, and so on throughout the succeeding decades.

Part Two examines the relationship between the corporations and the crown that created them. Indeed, to speak of center and locality is to miss a crucial point, that king and corporation relied upon each other. Nothing makes this more clear than the texts of hundreds of royal borough charters and the controversies throughout the period over how to interpret charters and when to rewrite them. As we shall see, such controversies arose more from the needs of townsmen than from the needs of the King, for it was generally they who prompted the grant of new charters. Provincial demand drove developments in another branch of royal government, the courts. It was to King's Bench that corporate partisans increasingly turned to settle their differences. Given the significance throughout the period of such local initiative, historians' concern with "absolutism" or "arbitrary government" begins to look misplaced. We must appreciate just how much of the growth of royal institutions resulted from the needs of persons, groups, and communities in the provinces. There was one exception to this: 1687–88. In those years, James II's efforts to recreate the corporations to do his bidding failed because he interfered with long-prevailing norms. The collapse of local, then national, regimes in late 1688 is the greatest testament of all to just how exceptional his efforts were in the context of developments in the generations before and after.

Part Three explores the corporations after 1688, when two major developments of the period before 1688 were consolidated: the genesis of partisan politics, and the evolution of King's Bench to contain partisan politics' worst tendencies. Partisan conflict sharpened as control of the corporations increasingly meant control of parliamentary seats; it sharpened too as new circumstances made it easier for Protestant dissenters to infiltrate corporate bodies from which they were barred by law. In response to conflict, King's Bench developed new uses for old legal devices that helped the court address the problems posed by endemic partisan competition. By means of the court's involvement, conflict did not create instability.

As with any project like this, my search for the origins and impact of partisan politics was shaped by some decisions taken at the outset. I should thus explain three decisions, before recounting an accident: the discovery that to understand the transformation of political culture, one must understand the law.

Decision number one: to search for the origins of partisan politics in the borough corporations. Partisan politics requires organization, and organization requires regular, constant contact among partisans. Only in borough corporations did those with formal rights of participation see one another, and the people they governed, constantly in the conduct of both official business and their private affairs. Corporate status and chartered privileges contributed to the members' collective identity and tied them together in perpetuity. Only in the corporations can we see a rhetoric of oneness that unwittingly stoked partisan angers and retributive behavior. The central paradox of partisan politics' development was not only that it arose in an institution where language and law stressed unity, but that it was the need for unity that compelled people to behave in ways that actually promoted conflict. Regular contact among corporation members, their constant contact with those they governed, and the rhetoric and law of corporations all point to an institutional environment where we would most likely find the kind of new political activity whose origins I have explored.

Decision number two: to study the three generations after the Civil War. This study is bounded by the years 1650 and 1730, years of little significance themselves, but years that suggest the period in which we should look. We will cross a number of important divides: 1660, 1678–81, 1688, 1714–15, and 1722. As we pass them, we shall see how events in those years left their mark on corporate politics and, more so, how politicking in the corporations shaped the way those events unfolded. But more important will be the story of incremental development that runs quickly past these milestones. For the development of partisan politics was part of a process in which these moments played less of a role than did constant competition in hundreds of towns and constant litigation in King's Bench. Partisan competition and purgation was touched off in the wake of the Civil War and immediately picked up a religious sectarian character which was perpetuated by statute in the coming years, only to be transformed in the end by more statutes that effectively withdrew the religious element from partisan difference. Though the initial impetus was gone, a durable form of political practice – partisan politics – remained. Throughout, from the 1640s and 50s to the 1720s and 30s, borough corporations were riven by partisan divisions created and perpetuated by a cycle of purge and counter-purge that was moderated when corporation members went again and again before King's Bench for a hearing of their differences.

Decision number three: to study all the corporations rather than any one or few of them. The historiographical logic of recent decades suggests that the way to explore the questions I have posed would be to write a book called *Corporate Politics in (fill in the blank), 1650–1730*. Such an approach illuminates the blank but leaves more questions in the shadows cast around it. Local studies of the 1960s, 70s, and 80s have helped us understand much about a nation unwittingly approaching civil war. Given the relative dearth of local studies post-1649, the decades following clearly await their school of local history. But central and local, royal and provincial, partake of one another, and they did so even more after 1660 than before 1640. More important, the corporations governing the towns existed only at the behest of the King. The governments of England's towns had no being in law nor in rhetoric without constant reference to the being that made them. By looking at many places, and by moving our eye constantly back and forth between the heart of the royal polity and its distant limbs, we can see how the limbs influenced the heart. We can see how partisan politics could evolve in the provinces and move inward to infect the vital organs of the King's government. By looking at local institutions in all their variety, we can see clearly how important to them was their dependence on and interaction with institutions far beyond them.

This leads me to an accident. I initially explored King's Bench affidavits in hopes of finding good stories of political conflict in the towns. Only by reading the affidavits did I realize that they not only contained stories, but that they were signs of a larger, more important story: the introduction of the law into local political life in a way that was utterly new in the second half of the seventeenth century. This prompted me to look more deeply into the workings of the court itself. What I found there surprised me.

When historians of seventeenth-century England think about the law, they think about "constitutional" developments or about this or that legalist "discourse." My concern here is at a more humble level, one where thousands of forgotten litigants came and went from King's Bench, compelling it to be something it had not been before: the extra-corporate authority that decided who belonged in office and how it was they should behave there. The rolls and order books of King's Bench in the seventeenth century have received scant attention, but by looking at them, and by studying scores of towns involved in litigation from the 1650s onward, we can see the development of a little understood but crucially important legal device – the writ of mandamus – into one of the key instruments for maintaining political stability during a period of rising partisan struggle. Mandamus was joined in this role after 1688 by the information in the nature of quo warranto, a surprising development considering that before 1688, quo warranto was condemned by some as an instrument of royal tyranny. At the end of the day, the key institutional player for settling controversies in the provinces was neither the King, nor his Council, nor Parliament, but the court of King's Bench.

It was the court's success in this role that I believe explains the origins of stability. Though I use the word "stability," I do so reluctantly. In some ways, an analysis in terms of stability compels us to look through the wrong frame of reference: one focusing our eyes on instability. Though much of the analysis below concentrates on episodes of conflict, this is not to say it is about instability. Throughout this work, I want to uncouple the connection we make in our minds between conflict and instability. This was a society marked by constant conflict in politics, and this touched many aspects of many people's lives. But is a society marked by conflict necessarily an unstable one? Might we not also call it a dynamic society? Only in a dynamic society could partisan politics and stable politics emerge simultaneously.

The pages below have taken a long time to cobble together. You may well find some points to quibble with. But this is not for a shortage of people who spotted problems in earlier versions of this work and who have helped me in countless other ways. The bibliography is a testament to the knowledge and good humor of hundreds of archivists. Limited space prevents me from thanking them individually; the list of record offices in the bibliography must serve as a guide to those to whom I am indebted. My thanks go as well to librarians at the Regenstein Library of the University of Chicago and at Widener and Houghton Libraries of Harvard University. In particular, I would like to thank the special collections staff of the Harvard Law School Library and the interlibrary loan staff at Union College. I also owe thanks for financial support to the University of Chicago, Harvard University, the Andrew W. Mellon Foundation, and to the American Philosophical Society for its Henry M. Phillips Grant in Jurisprudence. My gratitude also goes to the Duke of Westminster for permission to quote from the Grosvenor family papers held in the Cheshire Record Office.

Many friends have helped my thinking over the years. Edward M. Cook introduced me to a Colonial American historiography that inspired me to ask some of the questions I have asked of English political culture during the same period. Charles Gray assisted my entry into the intimidating world of legal scholarship. Dan Beaver, David Bush, Tim Harris, Mark Knights, Susan Lively, Steve Pincus, Roy Ritchie, Tom Slaughter, and Robert Wells have read all or part of what follows; their comments have sharpened the arguments made below. Charles Donahue guided me through some of the trickiest legal arcana. Larry Wallace and Richard Linenthal have provided gracious hospitality on more occasions than they probably care to remember.

Four people I can thank now, but this does little to repay all the support they have given. John Morrill read this work in its most ragged form – draft thesis chapters – and encouraged me to produce the book you hold. Catherine Patterson's research on borough politics and elite patronage in the generations before the Civil Wars is a touchstone to which I constantly return; her generosity in sharing her thoughts and friendship has been vital to my progress. I also want to thank Mark Kishlansky. No one I know has a better ability to cut from the margins straight to the heart of an idea, laying bare its strengths and weaknesses. I also know few who are more warm with praise and support. Finally, the dedication is far too little thanks for everything I have been given. Thank you.

A NOTE ON STYLE

In quotations from seventeenth- and eighteenth-century materials, spelling and punctuation have been modernized. Dates are in old style, though the year has been taken to begin on 1 January.

ABBREVIATIONS

BL	British Library, London
Bod.	Bodleian Library, Oxford
CCRO	Chester City Record Office
CJ	*Journals of the House of Commons*
CSPD	*Calendar of State Papers, Domestic Series*
CTB	*Calendar of Treasury Books*
EHR	*English Historical Review*
Eng. Rep.	*The English Reports*, vols. 77–93. London, 1907–09; reprint, Abingdon, 1979–86 (references are made to volume and page number, and, in parentheses, to reporter name and page number according to traditional legal usage)
Hastings Letters	Huntington Library, *The Aristocracy, the State and the Local Community: The Hastings Collection of Mss. from the Huntington Library.* On microfilm, Brighton, 1986
Henning	Basil Duke Henning, ed., *The House of Commons, 1660–1690*, 3 vols. London, 1983
HJ	*Historical Journal*
HMC	Historical Manuscripts Commission, Reports
JBS	*Journal of British Studies*
LJ	*Journals of the House of Lords*
Newdigate LC	Newdigate Newsletters, Folger Shakespeare Library, Washington, DC
PRO	Public Record Office, London
RO	Record Office
Sedgwick	Romney Sedgwick, ed., *The House of Commons, 1715–1754.* 2 vols. New York, 1970
TRHS	*Transactions of the Royal Historical Society*
VCH	Victoria County History
Whitley Diary	Bod., MS Eng. Hist. c.711: Diary of Col. Roger Whitley, 1684–97

Part One

CORPORATE IDEAL AND PARTISAN REALITY

——————————— ≪ 1 ≫ ———————————

The paradox of partisan politics

Queen Elizabeth made Preston's governors "one body corporate and political."[1] Nearly a century later, the divided body struggled to heal itself after two decades of repeated political woundings. The worst strife came in the year or so after the King's return to his kingdom in 1660. Two groups within the corporation competed for local control, each directing at the other the most damaging charges they could contrive. The "honest party" momentarily gained the upper hand and then attempted to restore unity the only way they knew how: they purged their foes.[2] Next, to prevent further dissensions and to tighten their grip on power, those remaining in the corporation made rules.

Debates in all common councils ought still to be had and observed with great moderation, gravity, and modesty, and likewise without the least reflection, or reviling of any person or persons, being members and partners at such consultations, the contrary whereof doth ever occasion great animosities and much distraction amongst the councillors at such public meetings and likewise tendeth much to the great prejudice and disquiet of the weale public.[3]

Following this opening blast against political schism came a detailed code of behavior, made to prevent these "mischiefs and evils." For they *were* evils: "party" divided the social body created by God and the corporate body created by the monarch. If heresy were a crime against the lord in heaven, then party was a crime against the lord at Whitehall. Partisanship was the political kin of religious sectarian identity in an age in which such identity meant social and political exclusion as well as damnation.

Division had not been unknown before 1640, but never had it been so dangerously persistent as in the decades since. Difference of opinion had its place in the life of England's centuries-old borough corporations, whose

---

[1] J. Lingard, *The Charters Granted by Different Sovereigns to the Burgesses of Preston* (Preston, 1821), second pagination, p. 15.
[2] *CSPD 1661–62*, pp. 93, 102, and 229; *CSPD 1660–70*, Addendum, p. 663. PRO, SP29/42/ 8, 59, and 60, SP29/46/55i, and SP29/48/125. PRO, PC2/55/212v, 231v, and 235v–36.
[3] William Alexander Abram, *Memorials of the Preston Guilds* (Preston, 1882), p. 53.

3

members after all were "councillors," each properly bringing his own counsel about the "weale public" to assemblies. Through temperate discussion, conflicting ideas were to meld into one that could be spoken by the singular voice of the corporate body. One voice might be found by unanimous acclamation, or, if need be, a poll of members. In either case, debate and disagreement ended with the decision. In rare instances, members opposing a resolution might subscribe their dissent in corporation records, but tongues were to be still in public once the question was settled. Preston's leaders in 1662 made explicit their requirements of one another:

All sides and parties, after the question is once over, shall in silence acquiesce and submit to such order, and not offer to show or produce any further reason, or use any reflections or reproachful terms, towards any of the council; . . . [and] no person or persons of the council aforesaid shall contrive or combine together with any other secretly, refractorily, and resolutely to make a party against the next meeting, nor shall carry on any private design for any interest whatsoever.[4]

The great political sin was not disagreement, but continuous, "contrived" division, maintained by the secret whisperings of small groups outside of formal meetings. Small parts of the whole body, meeting separately to concert their political activities, were no better than political conventicles. "Sides and parties" represented to the good of the polity the same threat that their religious counterparts did to the good of the church: both broke apart what could only be unified wholes.

Preston's leaders tried to legislate internal unity by outlawing the fractious activities and "reflections" of those who sought "resolutely to make a party" in defiance of the general good. But political reality upset their intentions.[5] While a new charter temporarily restored peace in 1662, "private designs" persisted. Partisan rather than corporate interests dominated members' thoughts, words, and deeds. There was no longer any one common good, but competing ones represented by competing groups in the corporation. The extent and careful definition of Preston's rules testify to the state of division in which they found themselves and to their desire to end it. Despite their rules, partisan competition did not end. Ultimately, rule making led the way out of their bewilderment by establishing the means for accommodating and absorbing conflict, if not, as hoped, for ending it. Over time, Preston's leaders, and those in towns all over England, came to appreciate how a divided polity did not necessarily lead to "the disquiet of the weale public," to see that partisan politics was not the politics of instability.

[4] Ibid.
[5] For conflict at Preston, see Michael Mullett, "'To Dwell Together in Unity': The Search for Agreement in Preston Politics, 1660–1690," *Transactions of the Historic Society of Lancashire and Cheshire*, 125 (1974), pp. 61–81.

Civil war in the 1640s and non-monarchical rule in the 1650s dismembered both national and local political bodies. Well-organized groups did political battle in communities throughout England, throwing one another from office with unprecedented virulence and frequency. Diverging religious identities, personal recriminations and political animosities, extensive purges and counter-purges: town political life in the 1640s and 50s sowed the seeds of feuding between coherent urban groups that flourished in the decades following. In a society that stressed political unity and made rules to protect it, a new politics emerged based on competition between organized, continuous opposing groups. Though universally condemned for the instability it seemed to threaten, partisan politics gradually became the political norm, and nowhere more clearly nor more pervasively than in the boroughs.

Partisanship – which is about division – and corporateness – which is about unity – are inimical to one another: this was the problem faced by borough corporations in the generations after the Civil War. In law, corporations were fictional persons with most of the same legal capacities as real ones. Images of the human body invoked one flesh and one mind, creating a moral and legal imperative for unanimity.[6] In dealing with the outside world, whether granting leases or petitioning the King, corporations had somehow to find one voice for many tongues. Thus corporations like Preston's tried to control the process by which decisions were reached. This was important, for all members were bound by the corporate will, whether or not as individuals they had concurred in a corporate resolution. No problems arose so long as the questions in difference were of little ideological, personal, or spiritual significance. Everything about the idea of corporateness denied division, but everything about the political circumstances of the post-Civil War world promoted it.

Corporations had long known occasional conflict. As Catherine Patterson has demonstrated, in an earlier age, they had ended such conflict through mediation, often with the help of noble patrons.[7] But divisions cutting across the corporations in the wake of civil war took on a new quality, a persistent, partisan quality. Partisan groups were identifiable by their durability and coherence from one conflict to the next, by the

---

[6] On anthropomorphism in corporate law, see C. T. Carr, *The General Principles of the Law of Corporations* (Cambridge, 1905), chapter 10.

[7] Catherine F. Patterson, "Urban Patronage in Early Modern England: Corporate Boroughs, the Landed Elite, and the Crown, 1580–1640" (Ph.D., University of Chicago, 1994). See also Patterson, "Conflict Resolution and Patronage in Provincial Towns, 1590–1640," *JBS* (forthcoming).

organization that gave such groups shape and impetus, and by the leadership that made organization possible. Leadership brought such groups together around shared interests, especially those concerning the role religious identity should play in determining one's fitness to participate in political life. Conflicting religious/political agendas, and the more general revulsion of political division felt by all, meant that competing groups denied the legitimacy of one another's existence. Partisan politics did not set two mutually recognized groups *within* government against one another – this is our modern notion – it pitted one group *claiming to be* the government, against an illegitimate group they argued should be excluded from government. This brings us to the essence of partisan politics: it was fundamentally negative; it was less about joining friends than about excluding foes, though accomplishing the latter required doing the former.

Political animosities first gathered themselves into partisan groups in the towns. These groups were not political parties. They had no consistent group names, no dues nor membership cards; nor were they tied together into any kind of national network. In our quest for the origins of party, we look unwittingly for institutions, models, or "systems" that are identifiably party, even as we remind ourselves not to apply modern standards or to look for national organizations. By concerning ourselves not with party, but with partisan politics – with a type of political practice, not with coherent organizations – we can understand better why political life after 1660 came to be dominated by division rather than concord, despite everyone's hopes for union. Actually, as we shall see, partisan politics was born and grew not despite the desire for union, but because of it. This is the paradox of partisan politics. The impulse to recreate corporate unity after the Civil War was strong, but the only way seventeenth-century minds could imagine doing so was by excluding those perceived to be "factious," "malignant," or otherwise illegitimate as participants in public life. But those threatened with exclusion, to protect themselves and to restore unity on their own terms, were driven by the same impulse. Thus exclusions begat exclusions, purges begat more purges. The paradox of partisan politics was that the search for unity ended up provoking more disunity.

Partisan politics in the corporations predated the rise of coherent political parties in Parliament and was the result of an evolution from consensual to competitive political norms in English society. As Mark Kishlansky has shown, competition only became a regular part of English political life during the Civil War and the decades following.[8] As competition became more fierce, partisan politics appeared, giving shape to competition by

---

[8] Mark Kishlansky, *Parliamentary Selection: Social and Political Choice in Early Modern England* (Cambridge, 1986): see especially chapters 1, 5, and "Conclusion."

organizing political actors to work together against their foes, not only in one instance, but continuously over time. Organization and continuity is what made partisan politics so new and so alarming and differentiated it from the episodic conflict experienced in the centuries preceding.

Because of the primacy they accord Parliament, historians have always assumed that parties formed there first and then reached out into the provinces. But in seeking the origins of party – to find the first rumblings of partisan politics – we must turn this view on its head. We must redirect our gaze from Parliament, parliamentary elections, and county elites to the incorporated towns: boroughs with royal charters detailing collective rights and governmental responsibilities. By 1660, there were at least 190 corporations, and 18 more by 1727.[9] County benches, the Privy Council, Parliament, the royal courts at Westminster: no other major magisterial, administrative, nor law-making institution existed in such profusion as borough corporations, and none possessed such extensive written codes of procedure.

The corporations provide the perfect context for studying the origins and implications of partisan politics and for understanding how a society that reviled the very idea of such a politics came to accommodate it so that it would not destabilize the polity. Each of the hundreds of corporations nationwide were in uninterrupted session, most for centuries. Their thousands of members saw one another virtually every day. Though by no means democratic institutions, the corporations touched directly the daily lives of a large part of the English population, both those whose families lived in town for generations, as well as those who came now and then to attend a market, or who passed a few years there learning a trade, finding a mate, and earning an income before moving on.[10] Each town's permanent population constantly rose and fell as visitors and short-term migrants momentarily subjected themselves to the apprentice regulations, market tolls, and justice administered by corporate leaders. Institutional continuity and the close contact among governors – and between governors and the governed – suggest the possibility that a political practice based on regular personal contact, organization, and group continuity would have developed sooner in the towns than in Parliament, where such conditions would not pertain until after 1689, and that this new political practice would affect

[9] This count is made from the list in Martin Weinbaum, *British Borough Charters, 1307–1660* (Cambridge, 1943).

[10] On "large-scale movement into towns," see David Souden, "Migrants and the Population Structure of Later Seventeenth-Century Provincial Cities and Market Towns," in Peter Clark, ed., *The Transformation of English Provincial Towns, 1600–1800* (London, 1984), p. 161. See also Peter Clark's "Migration in England during the Late Seventeenth and Early Eighteenth Centuries," in Peter Clark and David Souden, eds., *Migration and Society in Early Modern England* (Totowa, N.J., 1988), pp. 213–52.

many more people in hundreds of towns than if it developed in some far away place like Westminster. Lingering Civil War animosities and divided religious loyalties provided the personal and ideological reasons for partisan activity; the corporations provided the environment in which partisan groups could spawn and grow.

Given the emphasis previously placed on Parliament, "national issues," and "ideology," a brief review of the historiography is in order before considering what is to be learned from the corporations about the origins and impact of partisan politics. David Hume applied various meanings to "party." "Party rage" was born of "bigoted prejudices." At first, it was simply a part broken from the whole: a Presbyterian "party" arrayed against church and crown. They were the first, Hume said, to manipulate electoral processes for their own ends. This provided the foundation for a "country" party opposing a "court" one. Court and country, after the elections of 1679, became tory and whig.[11] While Hume condemned parties, Macaulay celebrated them, tracing an evolution of language and purposes from the conflict between crown and Parliament. He dated the origins of party precisely, when Parliament reconvened in October 1641: "From that day dates the corporate existence of the two great parties which have ever since alternately governed the country." They may have worn different labels at different times, but the ideological poles around which they gathered never changed: first they were Cavaliers and Roundheads; after the Restoration, court and country; in the Exclusion years, they became the enduring tory and whig. Rejecting Hume's cynical view, that party was the organization of bigotry, Macaulay portrayed it as the organization of the two great ideas of the polity. Parties were competing "confederacies of statesmen, a confederacy zealous for authority and antiquity, and a confederacy zealous for liberty and progress."[12] From their interplay over the years arose the finest regime on earth.

Keith Feiling took the notion of ideological descent found in Hume and Macaulay a few generations back.

The first germs of Whig and Tory in England may be dated . . . from a wedding – the sacrament which united Henry VIII to Anne Boleyn . . . Having then the same nativity with Queen Elizabeth, the embryo parties grew in accord with the actions and reactions of the Elizabethan age, at the close of which two twin schools of thought may be discerned, decisively opposed to each other on the causes which most divide mankind – on religious truth and political power.[13]

[11] On bigotry, the Exclusion era origins of party, and the conflation of tory and whig with court and country, see David Hume, *The History of England*, 6 vols. (Indianapolis, 1983), vol. VI, pp. 353, 356–57, and 381.
[12] Thomas Babington Macaulay, *The History of England from the Accession of James II*, 3 vols., (London: Everyman's edition, n.d.), vol. I, pp. 82–84, 161, and 201.
[13] Keith Feiling, *A History of the Tory Party, 1640–1714* (Oxford, 1924), p. 13.

Feiling and others drew lineages of toryism and whiggery, each with a line of begats of near biblical proportions: reformers begat puritans, begat roundheads, begat the country, begat whigs. All culminated in the Exclusion Crisis, when, as David Ogg put it, "a birth has to be recorded – that of the modern party system." Like his predecessors, Ogg saw court and country begetting tory and whig, which would become the modern parties contending with each other in the nation's legislature and on the hustings over the following centuries.[14]

An historiography based on ideological genealogies is a venerable one. But ideology, while the core of partisan identity, is too slippery for careful analysis of the origins and development of partisan politics. Genealogies suggest a coherence and continuity present more in the minds of historians than in the line of parents and progeny they try to draw. More recent work, while continuing to give important place to ideology, does so by stressing the role of organization, the leadership that made organization possible, and the arena in which such leaders worked: Parliament. J. R. Jones highlighted the role of leadership. The Earl of Danby's parliamentary organization supporting royal policies in the 1670s served both as model for and cause of subsequent whig organization in opposition to him. To some, Danby's policies threatened Protestantism and society; their response was to rally round their own leader, the Earl of Shaftesbury, who successfully manipulated the so-called "Popish Plot" to galvanize a potent political force.[15] Andrew Browning looked back to the 1660s and the Earl of Clarendon's attempts at parliamentary control, itself resulting from even earlier forces.[16] Each of these interpretations stressed the role played by prominent individuals in creating a party. Parties were clearly more than competing sets of ideas; they were people organized around certain ideas, organized by one or more leaders' coordinating efforts.

Since Hume, this has been an historiography driven by modern notions of party: two national organizations whose efforts focus on Parliament as the only institution where party goals would have any meaning and the only one where partisan organizations could be developed and directed toward achieving those goals. Recently, a renaissance in Restoration studies has produced a number of challenges to these ideas about the origins of party and even whether we can find parties at all between 1678 and 1681. Jonathan Scott has assaulted older interpretive verities most directly. The "Restoration crisis" did not generate "'parties,' but polarities

---

[14] David Ogg, *England in the Reign of Charles II*, 2nd edn. (Oxford, 1984), pp. 606–08.
[15] J. R. Jones, *The First Whigs: The Politics of the Exclusion Crisis, 1678–1683* (Oxford, 1961), pp. 20–21.
[16] Andrew Browning, "Parties and Party Organization in the Reign of Charles II," *TRHS*, 4th ser., 30 (1948), p. 21.

of belief."[17] Mark Knights makes a similar point: "We should look for the community of sentiment rather than the structure of party."[18] By their studies of politics at court and Parliament between 1678 and 1681, Knights and Scott have largely dismantled Jones's argument that one can find coherent parties forming at Westminster.

Then where shall we look for these more elusive "polarities of belief" and "communit[ies] of sentiment"? Scott has suggested that perhaps to search at all is to chase a mirage: "in the absence of evidence for the existence of such 'parties' what is presently taking its place is the assumption that although such organization does not 'appear on the surface', it may be taken to be operating out of sight."[19] But perhaps our eyes are pointed in the wrong direction. The "surface" appears to be Parliament and the court in the years 1678 to 1681. Looking beneath Parliament, and looking beyond these years, has made other scholars more hopeful of finding something. Knights is one of these, who, while reluctant to use the word "party" to discuss extra-parliamentary politicking, has helped us understand how the nation became politicized through pamphlet wars and petitioning campaigns in 1678 to 1681.[20] Tim Harris, who even more than Knights has looked to the world beyond Whitehall and Westminster, has been more bold, consistently arguing that by looking outside of Parliament, we can see that "party" remains useful for understanding these years.[21] Harris not only looks to the local level; he suggests that we search further back in time as well because the rise of party was a *"process,"* not an event.[22] Likewise, Mark Goldie has argued that we should look earlier than we have for "party," and well beyond Westminster too: "our notion of party should not be allied too closely with parliaments and electorates, nor with the new party labels that appeared in 1679 . . . the many institutions that made up the wider society beyond Parliament had long provided arenas for sharp contests."[23] If Parliament is the "surface," looking beneath offers possibilities for further insights into the origins of partisan politics. And happily, this world beneath the surface may be closer to view than a

---

[17] Jonathan Scott, *Algernon Sidney and the Restoration Crisis, 1677–1683* (Cambridge, 1991), p. 14.

[18] Mark Knights, *Politics and Opinion in Crisis, 1678–1681* (Cambridge, 1994), p. 143. Chapter 1 contains an excellent overview of the historiography of "party."

[19] Scott, *Sidney and the Restoration Crisis*, p. 21.

[20] Knights, *Politics and Opinion*, part two.

[21] Tim Harris, "Party Turns? Or, Whigs and Tories Get Off Scott Free," *Albion*, 25 (1993), p. 582. See too Tim Harris, *London Crowds in the Reign of Charles II: Propaganda and Politics from the Restoration until the Exclusion Crisis* (Cambridge, 1987).

[22] Tim Harris, *Politics under the Later Stuarts: Party Conflict in a Divided Society, 1660–1715* (London, 1993), pp. 6 and 109.

[23] Mark Goldie, "Danby, the Bishops and the Whigs," in Tim Harris, Paul Seaward, and Mark Goldie, eds., *The Politics of Religion in Restoration England* (Oxford, 1990), p. 78.

more pessimistic assessment might allow. By looking for partisan politics rather than anachronistically conceived political parties, and by looking where partisan politics was "operating out of sight" – in England's hundreds of borough corporations – we will find local leaders dividing, organizing, and competing.

THE RHETORIC OF "PARTY" AND THE PARADOX OF PARTISAN POLITICS

To understand a transformation of political culture, to understand how partisan politics evolved, we need to understand how people talked about politics. Only then can we see the paradox of partisan politics: how the desire to end conflict, and the language used to condemn competition, were actually the most potent forces driving the creation of partisan politics after the Civil Wars. We must begin by looking at language not only because it reflects something about the beliefs and ideas of those using it, but because the words, and especially the figurative language people used, shaped the world in which they lived. As we shall see, language was used to mark those who were politically suspect and in turn to cut them out of politics altogether. The hope was that by doing so, it would create union. It did not.

Tim Harris has drawn a distinction between political organizing around ideology and organizing around other interests: "Unity based on 'professed principles' distinguished parties from 'factions' . . . party was something more than mere faction."[24] But a distinction between party and faction is based more on our notions and language of party than those current three centuries ago. Thus Mark Kishlansky finds that as "party" came to acquire its modern political meaning in the 1640s, its use was often synonymous with "faction." And Mark Knights, in looking at the common phrase, "the factious party," notes that "the two elements of this label were, for contemporaries, interchangeable in a way no longer acceptable to modern definitions."[25] Party did not come in two forms, one more acceptable because it was ideologically rather than instrumentally motivated. This is a modern construct, one in which we grudgingly respect our partisan foes for their commitment to their cause while opposing the cause itself. We admire the desire to win and consider it legitimate when directed toward some ends, not others: ideological rather than self-interested ones. This distinction was not made in the seventeenth century, when the desire to win, for any reason, was condemned as divisive and dangerous. The political

---

[24] Harris, *Politics Under the Later Stuarts*, p. 5.
[25] Mark Kishlansky, "The Emergence of Adversary Politics in the Long Parliament," *Journal of Modern History*, 49 (1977), pp. 625–26. Knights, *Politics and Opinion*, p. 145.

process was supposed to compose differences, not produce winners and losers.[26]

Even as late as 1740, "party" and "faction" were conflated in David Hume's movement back and forth between them. While Hume recognized the existence of non-ideological parties, he differentiated between two types of party *or* faction, not between party *and* faction. "Factions may be divided into PERSONAL and REAL; that is, into factions founded on personal friendship or animosity among such as compose the contending parties, and into those founded on some real difference of sentiment or interest . . . a party may be denominated either personal or real, according to that principle which is predominant."[27] Hume's language slips between "faction" and "party" to condemn both as one. Townsmen in the generations before Hume also elided party and faction into a single notion equated with sedition and political ruin. From Gloucester in 1670 came news of "a seditious faction . . . a Presbyterian party."[28] In Thetford, the "fierce and factious proceedings of the triumphing party" in choosing a new recorder was part of a larger "design to unsettle the corporation."[29] Party or faction was as great an evil in the minds of those who challenged strict ecclesiastical uniformity as among Anglican "loyalists." William Prynne decried the corporations bill debated in Parliament in 1661 from fears it would perpetuate "divisions, contentions, factions, and parties."[30] "Party," "faction": both signified the illegitimate formation of groups within the whole which threatened the life of the whole by breaking it into parts.

Organized division of any kind – faction *and* party – was an evil and it remained an evil in political rhetoric for generations, long after political reality had changed. Benjamin Calamy accused those breaking off from the whole of the sin of pride: "pride is always the cause of the quarrel that makes the breach and forms the party."[31] Condemnations of the evils of division rang through sermons preached before corporations on mayoral election days and other civic occasions: "the wars and fighting among ourselves can proceed from no other cause, but those lusts that war in our

---

[26] For this point in the early seventeenth-century urban context, see Patterson, "Urban Patronage," chapter 3. More generally, see Kishlansky, *Parliamentary Selection*, part one.

[27] David Hume, "Of Parties in General," in Eugene F. Miller, ed., *Essays Moral, Political, and Literary* (Indianapolis, 1987), p. 56.

[28] *CSPD 1670*, pp. 419–20.   [29] Ibid. *1668–69*, pp. 571–72.

[30] [William Prynne], *Summary Reasons, Humbly Tendered to the Most Honorable House of Peers . . . against the New Intended Bill for Governing and Reforming Corporations* [London, 1661]. For another conflation of faction and party, see Roger North, *Examen; Or, An Enquiry into the Credit and Veracity of a Pretended Complete History* (London, 1740), pp. iii–iv.

[31] Quoted in John Spurr, *The Restoration Church of England, 1646–1689* (New Haven, 1991), pp. 265–66.

members."[32] This was Satan's work. "All contentions and factions come from the devil, and gratifie him, whose nature is spiteful and malicious."[33] John March made much the same point before Newcastle upon Tyne's corporation: "Though Satan be the principal cause of schisms and divisions, yet he employs the lusts and passions of men as instruments to raise them."[34] Following this oft-used formula, Edward Fowler identified partisan division as an "evil spirit, when 'tis gotten into societies, tendeth mightily to the debauching of them."[35] He targeted not a specific party or parties, but the phenomenon of partisanship. Preachers regularly referred to the Book of Matthew (12:25): "Every kingdom divided against itself is brought to desolation; and every city or house divided against itself shall not stand." Across the political/religious spectrum, everyone agreed that unity was both a social necessity and a Christian duty. Gilbert Burnet saw little reason to belabor so common a theme: "I shall not enter into a Panegyrick of unity, or a declamation against discord; a man may as well praise light or commend health or show his eloquence in disparaging the gout or stone."[36]

But unity of what? Unity of all, to be gained through forgiveness, or unity of some – of the "righteous" – to be gained through exclusion of the unrighteous? In other words, two potential solutions to party existed: bring in political apostates or cut them off. Some preachers touched upon Gospel themes of forgiveness, and, like Burnet, hoped that all might be comprehended in a single community of believers. John Griffith reminded his listeners at Reading of the Thessalonians, who "were a people too prone to be turbulent, and . . . apt to create factions and disturbances." So he suggested that "all men should endeavor to promote love and unity in the town or place of their abode."[37] Others asked their congregations to remember Psalms 122: "Pray for the peace of Jerusalem."[38] Of course this really just avoided the main issue: if one prayed for peace, how would peace be achieved? By turning the other cheek, or by destroying the damned?

[32] Thomas Long, *The Original of War: Or, The Causes of Rebellion* (London, 1684), p. 1.
[33] John Griffith, *A Sermon Preached at St. Lawrence Church in Reading . . . [on] the Day on which the Mayor was Sworn* (London, 1693), p. 21.
[34] John March, *Sermons Preach'd on Several Occasions* (London, 1699), p. 109. For the same theme, see ibid., pp. 36–38, 107, and 109–12.
[35] Edward Fowler, *A Sermon Preached at the General Meeting of the Gloucestershire-Men* (London, 1685), p. 26.
[36] Gilbert Burnet, *An Exhortation to Peace and Union: A Sermon Preached . . . at the Election of the Lord-Mayor* (London, 1681), p. 3.
[37] Griffith, *A Sermon Preached at Reading*, pp. 3 and 7.
[38] Martin Blake, *An Earnest Plea for Peace and Moderation in a Sermon, Preached at Barnstaple* (London, 1661), p. 4. Clement Barksdale, *A Sermon Preached upon the Fifth of November, 1679, in the Cathedral Church at Gloucester* (Oxford, 1680). Henry Glover, *An Exhortation to Prayer for Jerusalem's Peace. In a Sermon Preached at Dorchester* (London, 1663).

Most sermons turned on texts promoting divine retribution instead of charity. Their authors played on strains of righteous magistracy that echo through St. Paul's letters. "The punishment of unjust men," John Jeffrey reminded Norwich corporation, "is a vindication of the just God, and demonstrates his providence and his equity."[39] It is in this appeal to divine justice, wielded to maintain Christian unity, that we hear the shrill language that drove the partisan paradox, that imposed retribution in the name of unity.

There was a suspicion, an abhorrence, of unity with the evil. William Williams, in the pulpit at Haverfordwest, which had endured years of partisan ejections from the corporation and plenty of litigation to reverse them, celebrated a newly made local peace in 1682. But Williams also warned of potential dangers in readmitting the refractory: "There are some unions [that] look more like conspiracies, than peace."[40] Similarly, ministers like Richard Wroe could easily in one breath explain that "everything in our religion is an argument to unity . . . there is one Body, and one Spirit, and one Hope of our calling; one Lord, one Faith, one Baptism, one God and Father of all." Then, in the next breath, Wroe lashed out, reminding his hearers of "The caution [St. Paul] gives to the Romans . . . 'Mark them which cause divisions and offences, and avoid them'." Wroe, preaching to Preston's corporation, continued: "I mean not a mark of private grudge and revenge, but . . . a mark of shame and disgrace . . . a mark of infamy and reproach . . . a mark of distinction, which the laws set upon them . . . let the magistrate know that in this respect he bears not the sword in vain."[41] Like so many others, Wroe invoked Romans, chapter 13: "For he beareth not the sword in vain."[42] Following this logic, another clergyman goaded Grantham's leaders to excise sin: "The way for you to cure the wounds of and breaches of the body politic is to cleanse out the rotten and corrupted humors thereof . . . It is sin that opens not only a gap between God and

---

[39] John Jeffrey, *A Sermon Preached in the Cathedral Church of Norwich, at the Mayor's Guild* (London, 1693), p. 15.

[40] William Williams, *The Necessity & Extent of the Obligation, with the Manner and Measures of Restitution, in a Sermon, Preached . . . Before the Corporation of Haverford-West* (London, 1682), p. 29. The use of "restitution" may well refer to the fact that a writ of mandamus was often called a writ of restitution. Six members had recently been restored to the corporation by mandamus. PRO, KB21/20/32a.v, 63, 66v, and 97v.

[41] Richard Wroe, *The Beauty of Unity, in a Sermon Preached at Preston* (London, 1682), pp. 13 and 31–32. Joshua Richardson used the same text from Paul's epistles: *A Sermon Preach'd before the Right Honourable the Lord Mayor and Aldermen of the City of London* (London, 1682), p. 16.

[42] For this usage, see B. Rively, *A Sermon Preach'd at the Cathedral of Norwich upon . . . the Mayors Admission to his Office* (London, 1679), pp. 1 and 6; Nathanael Ellison, *The Magistrates Obligation to Punish Vice: A Sermon Preach'd before . . . the Mayor . . . of Newcastle upon Tyne* (London, 1700), pp. 4–5 and 11; and Samuel Bradford, *A Sermon Preach'd . . . At the Election of the Lord Mayor* (London, 1700), especially pp. 14–15.

man, but between man and man too . . . [Magistrates must] cut it off with the sword of justice."[43] York's magistrates heard the same message: "Physicians of the body politic, as well as natural, sometimes are constrained to make choice of corrosives, and cut off members."[44] In their actions, corporate partisans took heart from their pastors' words, and damned rather than redeemed the opposition. "Loyalists" at Stafford observed of their foes that "they stink for want of amputation."[45] Dismembering corrupted flesh would once again make whole, make one, the body politic for both man and God.

Amputation and purgation: the impulse to exclude remained strong for decades after the Civil Wars. But exclusion only encouraged more of the same. This was the paradox of partisan politics. The intolerance of any opposition and the imperative to destroy it only made conflict more virulent. Partisan strife persisted as the efforts of each local party to gain control, expel its opponents, and recreate a unity of the righteous cancelled one another out. The rhetoric of unity compelled each side to seek the total victory by which party would be eradicated; as each sought victory with equal vigor, neither could win for long. Purges of the 1650s were met by purges in the 1660s, followed by more of the same in the 1680s, and again in the decades after 1688; orgies of purgation, intended to end partisan division, invariably made it worse.

Separating the righteous from the unrighteous – the legitimate from the illegitimate – was the first step to cutting evil out of politics. Given this, we should not be surprised to see the art of the political label coming into its own, both reflecting and constituting political reality in the corporations. Except for "the loyal" or "the Church party," party labels were always negative, worn not with pride to describe one's own affiliations, but used by foes to tar their opposition. The label defamed those on whom it stuck and by implication, marked off its user and the rest of the world as its opposite. Those who successfully termed others "the factious party" were by this reflexive property "the loyal." That labels were almost always used negatively suggests the deep mistrust of party and faction, and of the idea of organized, collective political action. This was something in which only those with malign intent would participate; the "loyal" – those who formed the legitimate political nation – need not concert their actions for truth was their cause. Those who applied labels to others sought not to portray themselves simply as the larger, more just, and thus prevailing party, but to

[43] Bod., MS Eng.th.f.63, f. 106: Sermon of Henry Knewstubb, preached at Grantham in 1665 and Newark in 1685.

[44] Christopher Jackson, *The Magistrate's Duty in a Sermon, Preached . . . in the City of York . . . Immediately after the Reception of the Charter* (York, 1685), p. 11.

[45] *CSPD 1682*, p. 456.

cut their opponents off from political participation altogether by calling attention to their illegitimacy.

Urban preachers understood how labels created and nourished partisan animosities. Edward Fowler at Gloucester took his text from the Book of Psalms: "who so privily slandereth his neighbor, him will I cut off."[46] "Those who invent slanders are the greatest pests and plagues to a body politic. They are constantly stirring up strife and contention, animosities and emulation . . . One of these is sufficient to set a whole neighborhood together by the ears, and a few of them are enough to enflame a whole city."[47] Implicit in Fowler's analysis is the understanding of how language constitutes as well as reflects political reality. The rhetoric of personal and partisan hatred created such hatred. William Strengfellow condemned the "sarcastic invectives, the direful slanders, and infamous libels" he heard at elections each year.[48] John Williams made a similar point about "a multitude of words, a troop of exaggerations."[49] Partisan politics was as much a linguistic activity as it was one of secretly concerted efforts to capture the tools and ensigns of government. Each of these activities was crucial to the success of the other.

In the decades after 1660, we find three kinds of "party" labeling: expressed in terms of loyalty or its inversion, personal connection, and religious identity. Unsurprisingly, the three were often mixed together to describe the same group. In the early years after the Restoration, "party" was nearly always pejorative, either with an adjective – "factious," "disloyal" – or alone. No adjective was needed with a term that by itself carried connotations of dishonesty and sedition. Those claiming to be the champions of King and Church described themselves as the only legitimate political force and all others as tainted political separatists. While they were simply "honest" or "loyal and understanding men," their opponents were the "factious party" who broke away to pursue private ends rather than the public good.[50] Over time, "party" gradually became a term one took for oneself. Beginning in the late 1670s, and more so after 1680, "loyal party" appeared in increasing use.[51] But negative uses of "party" predominated well into the eighteenth century. Thus Roger North, during

---

[46] Edward Fowler, *The Great Wickedness and Mischievous Effects of Slandering* (London, 1685), p. 1. The text is Psalms 101, verse 5.

[47] Ibid., p. 8.

[48] William Strengfellow, *A Sermon Preach'd before the Right Honourable the Lord Mayor, Aldermen and Livery-men . . . At the Election of the Lord Mayor for the Year Ensuing* (London, 1693), p. 19.

[49] John Williams, *A Sermon Preached at St. Lawrence Jewry . . . At the Election of the Lord Mayor* (London, 1695), p. 13.

[50] *CSPD 1682*, pp. 543–44.

[51] Thus one could observe that the Duke of Monmouth's "adoring party" at Coventry in 1683 defied "the loyal party here." BL. Add. 41,803, f. 45.

Anne's reign, could still comfortably contrast "party" with "the established religion and government." North was, after all, "on the side of truth and sincerity, which cannot properly be termed a party, but a duty."[52]

Personal partisan tags were common too, and always negative. Identifying a group's interests with anyone but the King by its very nature suggested sedition since the King's interest was the only legitimate interest in the land. At Rye in the early 1680s, a variety of epithets applied to the same group: the mayor and "his partisans," the "fanatical mayor and that gang," "Mr. Tournay [the mayor] and his faction."[53] "Wimbledon . . . and seven other of his confederates" made an illegal mayoral election at Andover.[54] By identifying parties with particular persons, observers called attention to the leadership that made organization around dissenting interests possible. Leadership turned a set of beliefs into a partisan force. Political conflict in the towns, though usually charged by religious difference, was typically identified, fought, and feared because of the power of particular individuals to give shape to inchoate goals. Partisan politics and the labels of party thus depended in part on the identification of the important players.

Wimbledon, Tournay, and other corporate party leaders were also identified by their religious sympathies. In the early 1660s, many had hoped that there could be one political and religious community in the land comprehending a broad spiritual and political middle. But the policies of exclusion in church and state, pursued with more vigor by local governors than by royal masters, ultimately prevailed. Self-imposed purges in the corporations in 1659–61, further purges wrought by local gentry under the Corporation Act, and the new borough charters of the early 1680s contributed to division by exclusion. Such exclusions were typically based on a religious test, as in the Corporation Act, or on suspicions about religious sympathies and the corrosive political impulses they might generate. Thus Mark Goldie notes, "We soon discover that the predominant language of politics was overwhelmingly the language of religious parties and civil war wounds . . . The new names tory and whig were not only numerically limited, but conceptually subordinate to the language of church politics."[55] "Tory" and "whig" were slow to catch on, especially in the provinces.[56] "Whig" and "tory" in the early 1680s, and long afterward, were largely the terms of London and parliamentary

---

[52] North, *Examen*, pp. iv and v.
[53] *CSPD 1680–81*, p. 439; *CSPD 1682*, p. 368; and East Sussex RO, Rye 1/17/97.
[54] Bod., MS Tanner 290, f. 234.
[55] Goldie, "Danby, the Bishops and the Whigs," in Harris, Seaward, and Goldie, *Politics of Religion*, p. 79.
[56] See for instance examples from Chester, Macclesfield, and Wigan: *CSPD 1682*, pp. 280, 459, and 525–26.

politics. Even in Anne's reign, when hundreds of King's Bench affidavits survive from borough political litigation, the terms tory and whig rarely appear in the testimony of local witnesses describing corporate partisan feuding.

Even without "tory" and "whig," borough partisans had plenty of ugly things to call one another. All the language they heard – from the pulpit, in corporate charters, when they referred to each other as "brethren" – insisted that they be united. Thus they created labels to identify and cut off the "factious." But one person's "factious" was another's "righteous." Each side looked at the other in mutual disgust and fear; each side tried to exclude the other by the same means; each side failed when confronted by the efforts of the other. It was in the pursuit of unity that partisan conflict endured.

PARTISAN POLITICS IN THE BOROUGH CORPORATIONS

This experience of division, name calling, and exclusion first became widespread in the corporations in the 1640s and 50s. Bell-ringing euphoria upon Charles II's return in 1660 signaled a brief rejection of the politics of mutual revulsion. But restoring the corporations also required rejecting all who had profited from the turn of events during the Civil War and Interregnum. Dismissals of personnel in the 1640s and 1650s by internally-managed purges, Cromwellian charters, and parliamentary ordinances, and the replacement of those dismissed by new men, left bitter jealousies behind in 1660. From Maidstone "the King's loving subjects" complained they had endured "the tyranny and slavery of a sectarian party who in the late sad times usurped the power into their own hands."[57] Revenge and envy in towns everywhere overwhelmed hopes for peace through comprehension of a broad religious/political middle. Restoration in the boroughs ultimately rested on acts of exclusion, casting out those who had come in during the preceding decades.

The basis for exclusion came to be defined overwhelmingly in terms of religious sympathies. The Corporation Act of 1661 – requiring the expulsion of dissenters – and other efforts to purge the boroughs produced one of two results in each town. If thorough, purges left an angry rump outside the corporation with the incentive and the political experience to coordinate their efforts to recapture the heights they once held. This they did by exerting pressure from outside, for instance by controlling other town institutions such as charitable feoffments. The other possible result – and one more common than a full purge – was an ineffective, partial one. Many

---

[57] BL, Add. 37,157, f. 65.

of those who came to power in the 1650s were not dismissed, including some with dissenting beliefs or a tolerance of people holding them. The lapse of the Corporation Act commissioners' powers in 1663 only enhanced dissenting strength within the corporations; now dissenters were able to re-elect many just removed or to appoint others who should have been barred by the act's provisions. In the mid- and late 1660s, dissenters and those sympathetic to their cause gained ground in corporate assemblies. Then, with his Declaration of Indulgence of 1672, many thought the King had given royal approval to the involvement of moderate dissenters in all aspects of public life. By the mid-1670s, dissenting successes were apparent all around the country. With their success came rising corporate division. A few years later, the scare over the illusory "Popish Plot," and the struggle in Parliament over the Duke of York's political fate, stoked urban partisan energies. The string of parliamentary elections, 1679–81, and the interaction of elections to Parliament with elections to corporate office, promoted further partisan organizing in the towns.

The dissenting interest in the corporations reached the high-water-mark during the Exclusion years; in the years of the "tory reaction," 1682–85, those in the towns who called themselves "the Church party" and "the loyal" soon turned the tide with help from royal officials. Charles II's remodeling of county benches was matched by an investigation of borough personnel nationwide, followed in the years 1682 to 1685 with the most comprehensive rechartering of the corporations ever undertaken. In the process, Charles purged the personnel of England's borough corporations and recast the terms by which they would exercise power. After two decades of attempting to deny or overlook political division in the corporations, the King had now favored one side against the other, and in doing so, turned the towns upside down.

But another revolution soon followed. With greater powers in the new charters of 1682 to 1685 permitting the King to remove whomever he pleased from corporate office, James II in 1687 and 1688 threw out the allies his elder brother had so carefully put in control of the towns a few years earlier. James then granted more new charters favoring his brothers' old foes. More astonishing, James's charters dispensed all members from taking the oath of supremacy or from receiving the Eucharist according to the rites of the Church of England. The result was a flood of Catholics and dissenters into the corporations in 1687–88. James's complete reversal of political allegiances, pursued at all levels of administration, was nowhere so prominent as in his removal of thousands from corporation offices; nowhere else did it create such deep resentment in so many people. This left him with the shakiest of political foundations in the towns when his strength was tested by the Prince of Orange's invasion in November of

1688. Many borough leaders expelled by James II supported the foreigner when his arrival meant their own return to local power.

Political division in the boroughs not only continued after 1688, it deepened. With Parliament now in near constant session, partisan politics became a permanent feature of life at Westminster, as it had been in many towns since 1660 and before. Partisan organizing in Parliament and in the towns interacted more and more, each dependent on the other as victory in corporate elections became ever more important for winning parliamentary ones, and vice versa. Bishop Burnet noted in 1708 that, "the parties are now so stated and kept up, not only by the elections of parliament-men, that return every third year, but even by the yearly elections of mayors and corporation-men . . . and in every corner of the nation the two parties stand, as it were, listed against one another."[58] Making matters worse, frequent changes in personnel and reversals in policy from 1680 to 1688 left chaos in the corporations. Urban partisans now exploited legal confusion created in many towns by the receipt of one or more new charters in the 1680s to attack their foes in court. Many successfully dislodged their opponents and gained control for themselves by their courtroom assaults. Quo warrantos and writs of mandamus abounded in the decades after 1688 as winning legal battles became the only way to win local political wars.

Contentions arose not only from efforts to control corporate offices in order to win parliamentary elections. Geoffrey Holmes characterized local officials as "pawns in the national party game," reading all local partisan maneuvering as preparation for the next parliamentary contest.[59] But this relegates borough governments to the status of electoral colleges and slights their importance in local administration.[60] Borough offices were sought for the many real benefits they provided their holders, the parliamentary vote rarely being the most important of these. Partisan conflict was no less frequent nor fierce in the 1700s and 1710s in non-parliamentary boroughs than in parliamentary ones: witness the bloodshed, rancor, and litigation following the choice of a new recorder of Macclesfield in 1716.[61] Historians recently have surveyed more of the political landscape, but they still tend to stand at Westminster or Whitehall and look outward, rather than

---

[58] Burnet, *History of My Own Times*, vol. VI, p. 224, quoted in B. W. Hill, *The Growth of Parliamentary Parties, 1689–1742* (London, 1976), p. 17.

[59] Geoffrey Holmes, *British Politics in the Age of Anne*, revised edn. (London, 1987), p. 25; see also pp. 312–14.

[60] For a compelling argument that corporate administration remained effective throughout the eighteenth century, see Elizabeth June Dawson, "Finance and the Unreformed Borough: A Critical Appraisal of Corporate Finance, 1660 to 1835, with Special Reference to the Boroughs of Nottingham, York, and Boston" (Ph.D., University of Hull, 1978).

[61] See below, pp. 333–35.

going forth to the provinces for a closer look. Examining the towns from within the towns yields a very different view of the nature and import of local partisan conflict. Parliamentary electoral politics in the years of "the rage of party" did not create urban partisan groups; it worked with those already established there.[62] The movement of pawns determined the moves available to the knights and bishops.

Borough residents in the 1720s would have been surprised to learn from historians that political division became less acute with the end of the Stuart dynasty and the ascendancy of Walpole, when J. H. Plumb and others contend the first age of party met its demise. For Plumb, division was ended by the destruction of one of the parties, the tories: "single-party government . . . helped to bring about political stability."[63] W. A. Speck followed this view, noting that by the time of the first election under the Septennial Act in 1722, "the struggle between Tory and Whig had been decided."[64] But this view depends on studying Parliament and elections to it rather than a fuller analysis of politics in countless local jurisdictions. Even at Parliament, recent work suggests that the "political stability" ostensibly attendant on "single-party government" after 1715 was more fractious and contentious than previously thought. Linda Colley's tribute to tory defiance demonstrates their survival as a vital force in Parliament, at court, and in the provinces. Kathleen Wilson's look at the "sense of the people" beyond Westminster finds the same vitality and conflict in the political nation and well beyond it. Other studies of popular politics stress the vigor of opposition.[65] And as we shall see in part three, the amount of litigation brought before King's Bench by borough partisans against each other only grew over the course of the 1720s, and this trend appears to have continued well beyond. Everywhere we look, partisan conflict was alive and well long after its supposed demise.

This is important not only for what it suggests about the continuation of conflict, but for what it says about how society came to accommodate such conflict. Colley and others have challenged the stability argument by contending that political *competition* continued after 1715. But is that the

---

62 The quoted phrase is from J. H. Plumb's *The Growth of Political Stability in England, 1675–1725* (London, 1967), chapter 5.

63 Ibid., p. 172.

64 W. A. Speck, *Tory and Whig: The Struggle in the Constituencies, 1701–1715* (London, 1970), p. 8. Geoffrey Holmes seems to accept Plumb's judgment that the tory appeal dwindled after 1715, and with it, party strife: *British Politics in the Age of Anne*, p. 405.

65 Linda Colley, *In Defiance of Oligarchy: The Tory Party, 1714–1760* (Cambridge, 1982). Kathleen Wilson, *The Sense of the People: Politics, Culture and Imperialism in England, 1715–1785* (Cambridge, 1995). On popular Jacobitism, see Paul Kleber Monod, *Jacobitism and the English People, 1688–1788* (Cambridge, 1989). On corporate politics in the southwest, see John M. Triffitt, "Politics and the Urban Community: Parliamentary Boroughs in the Southwest of England, 1710–1730" (D.Phil., University of Oxford, 1985).

same as saying that *instability* continued? More important, had instability ever existed? For Plumb, in the decades before 1715, "party division was real and it created instability."[66] All discussions of politics in the era assume that division and instability are the same thing. But are they? Recent students of the Restoration era would all appear to answer "yes." Indeed, "crisis" – a close kin of "instability" – has been found everywhere in English politics after 1660. Even though there is some disagreement over the nature of the "crisis" of the years 1678 to 1681, all seem to agree that these were years of crisis of some kind.[67] And this crisis has spawned others as we have searched for its antecedents. We now have crises in the early 1660s and the late 1660s to the early 1670s as well.[68] It would appear then that the entire period post-1660 was one of constant crisis.

But this cannot be, for three reasons. First, "crisis" appears only by concentration on a few people, institutions, or sources. We dote on Shaftesbury, Halifax, and Sidney, all of whose writings make their authors, their friends, and their enemies the principal cast in a drama revolving around themselves. We focus on Parliament, especially the House of Commons, as the heart of politics, though it was a good day indeed when even a simple majority of members appeared.[69] We look at the press, cranking out pamphlets promoting partisan purposes that were often best served by creating an impression of impending doom. Taken together, these have generated an historiography of "crisis," one that focuses on what did not happen – rebellion – rather than on what did happen: peace. We are told that many pamphleteers raised fears of another war, but "Forty-one is come again" was propaganda, not reportage.[70] Given how recent was the cataclysm of mid-century, we should not be too surprised to find warfare and civil strife providing some of the richest language for people writing about their fears for the future. But for a political writer of 1681 with pronounced ideological leanings to employ images of civil war is not the same as saying civil war was likely. After all, we have the best evidence possible that this was not the case: there was no civil war.

Second, if "crisis" characterizes the age, then how do we explain the

---

[66] Plumb, *Growth of Political Stability*, p. 157.

[67] Both Jonathan Scott and Mark Knights have demonstrated that the "Exclusion crisis" was about more than exclusion, though they differ on exactly what we should call it. Scott suggests it was a crisis of "popery and arbitrary government": *Sidney and the Restoration Crisis*, pp. 8 and 20. Knights terms it a "succession" crisis and a crisis of "politics and opinion": *Politics and Opinion*, p. 29 and title.

[68] Gary DeKrey, "The First Restoration Crisis: Conscience and Coercion in London, 1667–73," and Richard L. Greaves, "Great Scott! The Restoration in Turmoil, or, Restoration Crises and the Emergence of Party," both in *Albion*, 25 (1993), pp. 565–80 and 605–18.

[69] Knights, *Politics and Opinion*, p. 118.

[70] On rhetoric making parallels to the 1640s, see Harris, *London Crowds*, pp. 134–35.

continuous operation throughout these crises of hundreds of local governments that affected many more lives much more powerfully than did
Shaftesbury or L'Estrange? Townsmen followed conflicts at Whitehall and
Westminster with interest, but this had little effect on their management of
day-to-day affairs. There is one crucial exception: 1688, when James II's
purges of thousands of members from scores of corporations momentarily
undermined effective urban government. But the interruption in assembly
meetings and record keeping in many towns in 1688 is the exception that
proves the rule, the break in governance that stands out in sharp relief
against a background of constant governance in the decades before and
after. The experience of 1688 in the towns points to a real crisis and the
real impact it must have had on very many people. This was not crisis in
the abstract: not simply arguments in a distant parliamentary debating
chamber or London tavern. This was crisis. But it was soon over. At all
other periods, in the vast majority of places, we see the same thing: amidst
the strife of supposed crisis, government worked.[71]

Third, if "crisis" and "instability" are the key historiographic devices for
understanding the generations between the Civil Wars and the Walpolean
ascendancy, then how do we explain another powerful current running
through the historiography of this period? This was the age of an "urban
renaissance," of the "making of the English middle class."[72] It was an age
in which the "sinews of power" were strengthened, an age when Britons
began "forging the nation."[73] Here, instead of "crises," we have images of a
confident society, an expanding state, a growing nation: all this creates an
impression of success. The historiography of the late seventeenth and early
eighteenth centuries thus appears struck by schizophrenia. There is an
historiography of fears – "crisis" – and there is an historiography of
"renaissance" – of change, of movement toward what is implicitly a better
future.

How shall we bring "crisis" and "renaissance" into the same analysis?
What we find in the generations after the Restoration is not an unstable
society. It is a society bubbling with conflict, but somehow not only
accommodating that conflict, but apparently channeling it productively.

---

[71] For instance, Peter Clark notes both the party conflict and administrative continuity in
Gloucester, with the exception of 1688. "The Civic Leaders of Gloucester, 1580–1800," in
Transformation of English Towns, p. 327.

[72] Peter Borsay, *The English Urban Renaissance: Culture and Society in the Provincial Town,
1660–1770* (Oxford, 1989). Peter Earle, *The Making of the English Middle Class: Business,
Society and Family Life in London, 1660–1730* (London, 1989). See too E. L. Jones and
M. E. Falkus, "Urban improvement and the English Economy in the Seventeenth and
Eighteenth Centuries," in Peter Borsay, ed., *The Eighteenth-Century Town: A Reader in
English Urban History, 1688–1820* (London, 1990), pp. 116–58.

[73] John Brewer, *The Sinews of Power: War, Money and the English State, 1688–1783* (New
York, 1989). Linda Colley, *Britons: Forging the Nation, 1707–1837* (New Haven, 1992).

This was not an unstable society, it was a dynamic one. Dynamism helps us explain conflict and the fears it created in the minds of contemporaries, as well as a burgeoning economy stretching round the globe, a strengthening state, and a growing consumer society capable of beautifying public spaces in dozens of towns. Dynamism also helps us understand the coexistence of partisan politics and stable politics.

PARTISAN POLITICS AND THE LAW: STABILITY IN A DYNAMIC SOCIETY

J. H. Plumb contended that stability was achieved only with the creation of one-party government. But he offered another test of stability: "the acceptance by society of its political institutions, and of those classes of men or officials who control them."[74] By this standard, stability was achieved decades before 1715. How? Quite simply, through the law.

"Party" in seventeenth-century usage, as now, not only suggested a part broken away from the political whole, but a person or group involved in a legal action.[75] After 1650, corporation political parties increasingly became parties to law suits in order to settle their differences. Historians know the seventeenth-century's leading cases well: Bushel's case, the Magdalen College case, the case of the seven bishops. We appreciate the political repercussions of these legal *causes célèbres*. But hard cases make bad law. By concentrating on these extraordinary moments, we have overlooked thousands of less extraordinary ones which, taken collectively, were of greater significance. We have missed the more subtle, though more profound, creep of the law into political life at a less exalted level, a process pushed from below rather than from above, a process with significant implications for the changing way in which politics would be played.

Something extraordinary happened at the same time partisan groups evolved: the courts – especially King's Bench – replaced the Privy Council as the overseer of all subsidiary administrative jurisdictions, especially the corporate boroughs. By the ready allowance of successive monarchs, by the pronouncements of judges, and by the constant pleas of litigants, King's Bench became the institution that society accepted for adjudicating political disputes, making partisan conflict a part of political life in a stable polity. By constantly turning to the court for redress of their grievances, borough partisans drove the creation of the rules that permitted a dynamic society to contain – in both senses of the word – conflict.

Four things stand out about this development. First, it came from below,

---

[74] Plumb, *Growth of Political Stability*, p. xvi.
[75] On uses of "party," see Kishlansky, "Emergence of Adversary Politics," pp. 624–26.

or from the periphery, to use another, perhaps more appropriate, image.[76] Thousands of provincial litigants from the 1650s, and especially after 1660, drove the court to develop in this way. Second, royal courts are royal institutions every bit as much as the Privy Council or the great offices of state. Historians of the Stuart age tend to read crown relations with the provinces in terms of encroachment, as the imposition from the top-down of an alien authority reviled by feisty, independent-minded locals. But by watching the development of King's Bench as the supervisor of local government, and by appreciating how this was driven from the margins rather than from the heart of the polity, we can see better the development of national institutions in non-antagonistic terms. We can appreciate the possibility that the development of state powers that monitored provincial governance may have evolved because of, not against, the wishes of people on the periphery.[77] So third, an institution of royal government – King's Bench – became the solution to rather than the cause of a problem: "instability." The creativity of corporate litigants brought them back to court again and again, and each case, by differing slightly from the last, contributed to the court's ongoing generation of rules regulating partisan competition. Fourth, this process happened without anyone intending it to happen. The growth of the state, and especially King's Bench's expanding influence in provincial administration, occurred because thousands of corporation leaders, lawyers, and judges examined the problems before them one at a time. Rarely, if ever, did they look up to consider how their collective actions contributed to the integration of provincial and royal administration. This is a development we can see happening elsewhere too, perhaps most vividly when we look at how the American colonies were drawing themselves ever more into the culture and political structures of the metropolis. Jurisdictional integration and state building were being driven by myriad people and forces; the later Stuart Kings – those quintessential "absolutist" state builders and purveyors of "arbitrary government" – were only bit players we can barely find on stage among a cast of thousands.

That this kind of integration happened between crown and corporation,

[76] The image of periphery and center has been developed by Jack P. Greene in his analysis of relations within Britain's transatlantic empire: *Peripheries and Center: Constitutional Development in the Extended Polities of the British Empire and the United States, 1607–1788* (New York, 1990).

[77] For a thoughtful consideration of the importance of provincial involvement in state development, see Michael Braddick, "State Formation and Social Change in Early Modern England: A Problem Stated and Approaches Suggested," *Social History* 16 (1991), pp. 1–17. For a look at the same issue in colonial America's relations with Britain, see Jack P. Greene, *Negotiated Authorities: Essays in Colonial Political and Constitutional History* (Charlottesville, 1994), chapter 1.

that it happened through King's Bench, and that the court thereby provided
the basis for stability, depended on the evolution of two legal instruments:
the writ of mandamus and the information in the nature of quo warranto.
Mandamus – the writ by which King's Bench ordered a subsidiary administrative authority to perform a task it was required in law to perform – came
into its own after 1660, largely as a result of actions brought by corporation members illegally removed by their brethren. By granting and enforcing writs of mandamus, King's Bench curtailed the more excessive
tendencies of partisan behavior, preventing those who captured majority
control of a corporation from effecting an illegal exclusion of all their foes.
While this prevented excess, it also perpetuated partisan politics. The fear
of party conflict encouraged borough leaders to do all they could to destroy
party by purging all opposition, but court decisions prevented them from
doing so without sound legal reasons. Mandamus made purgation ineffective by restoring those illegally removed and compelling a grudging retention of partisan enemies within the local polity. The law thus forced
political foes to remain together within the corporations. As mandamus
perpetuated partisan politics, it also protected stability by defining the
terms in which urban partisans would compete, terms they recognized by
their increasing recourse to King's Bench.

Quo warranto, the judicial means for enquiring into the use of a royal
franchise, also came to prominence. The process took the form of a
question: by what warrant – quo warranto – do you claim to be a
corporation or to exercise a certain privilege granted by the King? As
Blackstone wrote in the eighteenth century, when a corporation neglects or
abuses its responsibilities and privileges, "the law judges that the body
politic has broken the condition upon which it is incorporated, and
thereupon the incorporation is void." By quo warranto, the King inspected
and corrected those who misused corporate powers that derived from the
King.[78] Quo warranto saw only fitful use in the 1660s and 70s and had
little real political or legal impact then since few cases produced conclusive
judgments from the bench. But in the Worcester case – brought on local,
not royal initiative – and then the London case of 1681–83, the crown and
others, for the first time in centuries, fought quo warrantos all the way to a
final judgment. In the case of Worcester, the court's judgment forced the
expulsion of over two dozen from power; in the case of London, the

---

[78] William Blackstone, *Commentaries on the Laws of England*, 15th edn., 4 vols. (London,
1809; reprint, Abingdon, 1982), vol. III, pp. 262 and 480–84. See also *The Law of
Corporations: Containing the Laws and Customs of All the Corporations and Inferior
Courts of Record in England* (London, 1702), p. 300. See also Sir Matthew Hale's
comments: *The Prerogatives of the King*, ed. D. E. C. Yale, Selden Society, vol. 92 (London,
1976), p. 179.

corporation forfeited its existence altogether when its privileges were seized after judgment.

At the time, the London decision was more controversial for its political than for its legal import, for it marked the beginning of an unprecedented effort by the crown to reshape borough corporations nationwide by threatening them with quo warrantos. Parliament reversed the immediate effects of the London decision in 1690. Nonetheless, in the decades and centuries following, the legal thinking behind the court's decision endured.[79] Innumerable cases on quo warranto in the eighteenth century, brought not by the crown but by borough partisans, attest to the vitality of the doctrine confirmed by the London decision. Thus a 1702 work on corporations included chapters on quo warranto and the causes of forfeiture, recounting at length the arguments in the London case. Misuse or usurpation of a franchise entailed a failure of justice; where a corporation permitted such a failure in its most important public duty, "by judgment of the law, the city or village shall be restored to the government or jurisdiction of the common law, by the seizure of [the] franchise into the King's hands."[80] Quo warranto remained good law after 1688, and was used as such by scores of corporations in their internal legal battles. With quo warrantos common in the early eighteenth century, corporation members everywhere began to pay better attention to how they followed the terms of their charters in order to avoid losing their places or privileges. This in turn promoted a more precise legalism in the way they performed their duties and in the way corporate enemies conducted their battles.

Like the growing use of writs of mandamus, cases on quo warranto after 1688 contributed to the court's rise as the overseer of local administration and as the enforcer of the corporations' obligation to perform their public duties. Mandamus and quo warranto developed quickly because they were the means for a respected outside authority – the court of King's Bench – to monitor and adjudicate corporation politics using a tool revered by all parties: the law. The law provided a political safety valve; in turn, rising corporate litigation compelled changes in the law. In the evolution in this period of a law for the review of local administration, we see the intertwining of legal and political practice in a way that was critical to both and in a way we have not fully understood before because political historians have spent little time exploring the records of King's Bench. As it grew, partisan politics created the means by which its worst tendencies would be contained. There was no instability waiting to become stability;

---

[79] See Jennifer Levin, *The Charter Controversy in the City of London, 1660–1688* (London, 1969), chapter 5, especially pp. 60 and 68.
[80] *Law of Corporations*, p. 326.

stability was maintained throughout, however much competition there may have been among local partisans all over a dynamic society.

DISMEMBERING THE BODY POLITIC

Thomas Hobbes branded corporations "many lesser commonwealths in the bowels of a greater, like worms in the entrails of a natural man."[81] Organic imagery came readily to seventeenth-century observers of state and society, but Hobbes demonstrated powerfully that annelid metaphors would now serve better than the traditional human ones. If corporations were worms slowly disemboweling the nation, they were also worms in their incredible ability to divide and live as two bodies. As the century wore on, it would become more difficult to envision the body corporate as a human one, for dismemberment rather than unity now characterized corporation politics. One purge, one amputation after the next tore political bodies first one way and then another in the decades after the Civil War. Try as corporators at Preston and elsewhere might, "sides and parties" became political reality in the midst of England's lingering unitary corporate ideals.

We can no longer speak in the later seventeenth century of the resolution of conflict. Owing to the paradox of partisan politics, conflict between organized local teams was endemic. But we may speak of the accommodation of conflict. Borough corporations not only survived the rise of partisan politics, they remained effective institutions of government in a dynamic society. In all but the worst cases of local conflict, governance continued: lands were leased, courts settled commercial disputes and convicted petty criminals, and charities and other public services were maintained. This was the great success of the English polity in the generations after civil war rent the nation in two for good. The new politics of competition may well have been reviled, but it was peacefully absorbed by the body politic, which, though dismembered, continued miraculously to live.

[81] Thomas Hobbes, *Leviathan*, ed. C. B. Macpherson (London, 1968), p. 375.

2

"The best of polities"

"Charles the Second, by the grace of God King of England, Scotland, France, and Ireland, Defender of the Faith . . . ": the overture trumpeted the name and titles of the author of Kingston upon Hull's charter. The initial bore the King's portrait, with birds flitting and flowers bowing round about him, set off with the royal arms, all encircled by the garter. Engrossing the whole required a half-dozen parchment skins, from the last of which hung the great seal of England.[1] This was a striking piece of work.

For corporation members who understood Latin, royal graciousness resounded throughout their charter. For those who did not, Hull had lawyers enough to explain. Charles proclaimed that Hull would have "of our special grace and of our certain knowledge and mere motion . . . one body corporate and politic, in thing, fact, and name." By a wave of his hand, the King created a being alive in law if not in flesh. Lawyers imputed moral and theological, as well as legal and political, meaning to corporateness: "The best of polities is that invention whereby men have been framed into corporations . . . Although art cannot altogether arrive at the perfection of Nature, yet has it in this showed a fair adumbration, and given to man the nearest resemblance of his maker, that is, to be in a sort immortal."[2] Invoking God the singular rather than God tripartite, the leap from deity to corporation was a short one. God made Adam and Eve in His image; in corporations the King mimicked God, fashioning "a fair adumbration" of his own God-like form. In corporations, individuals became part of an immortal body. Legally, politically, spiritually: much was at stake in the proper definition and operation of borough corporations.

The corporation was unitary, many people acting as one person in law.

---

[1] J. R. Boyle, *Charters and Letters Patent Granted to Kingston-upon-Hull* (Hull, 1905), p. 152.

[2] William Shepheard [sic: Wing catalogue and all commentary uses "Sheppard"], *Of Corporations, Fraternities and Guilds* (London, 1659), prefatory letter. For an opinionated analysis, see Amasa M. Eaton, "The First Book in English on the Law of Incorporation," *Yale Law Journal*, 12 (1903), pp. 259–86 and 364–79. A more balanced assessment is in Nancy Matthews, *William Sheppard, Cromwell's Law Reformer* (Cambridge, 1984), pp. 133–43.

The King embodied this incorporeal person so "that the town . . . may be and remain a town or borough of peace and quietness, to the dread and terror of the evil, and for the reward of the good, and that our peace and other deeds of justice may there without further delay be maintained."[3] Royal charters appointed the terms of good rule, defining the proper methods for electing officers, the days for holding fairs and markets, and specific powers for keeping the peace. The King's charters also permitted the corporations to make by-laws for protecting corporate unity by regulating the behavior of its individual members both in and out of assembly meetings.

But self-regulation did not prevent political conflicts from dismembering the corporate person. Corporations were also franchises, the King's privileges granted to others to be exercised in his name. This status would be their salvation in the face of division. According to Sir Matthew Hale, "a corporation . . . hath its original from the King, so in some respects it hath its preservation."[4] As franchises granted by charter, the King, through his courts, could inspect and correct corporations when they erred. At the behest of partisan litigants, King's Bench became the principal monitor of corporate political life, and thus the means for preserving local government by checking the excesses of partisan politics. The power of the court to adjudicate the corporations' disputes would help maintain each as "one body corporate . . . for the good rule and government of the people."

THE BODY POLITIC

To understand politics in English towns in the generations after the Civil Wars, and in particular, to see how and why partisan politics first appeared in the towns, we must understand what a corporation was, why it existed, and how it functioned. For the idea and the law of corporations created the rhetorical and legal environment in which the paradox of partisan politics operated. It was in the corporations that the impulse to purge in order to protect unity was strongest because it was in the corporations that the idea of unity was most keenly felt. But purges inspired counter-purges, thereby creating opposing political groups, each attempting to exclude the other in the name of peace. Mutually excluding purges might have threatened corporate stability, but corporations, as legal beings, had recourse to legal institutions for settling the effects of their internal differences. Thus corporate status helps us understand not only how and why partisan politics arose in the towns, but how and why developments in the law would make partisan politics into stable politics.

[3] Boyle, *Charters to Hull*, p. 154.   [4] Hale, *Prerogatives*, ed. Yale, p. 243.

The corporation was a fiction made real; in fact it was a concept, in law it was a person. Paradoxically, the idea of the *persona ficta* gave legal *reality* to a corporate person.[5] As Hale noted, the corporation was a liberty from the King giving individuals acting together a capacity distinct from their natural one.[6] An anonymous student of corporations wrote in 1702 that "a corporation or incorporation is a body framed by policy or fiction of law, and it's therefore called a body politic . . . [It is] a capacity to take, hold, and enjoy, and act as a natural body."[7] Each living person, distinct in fact and law, when in his corporate capacity, was subsumed in a collective legal person possessing the same powers as any natural one. But in the formulation of Sir Edward Coke, the corporate body "is invisible, immortal, and rests only in intendment and consideration of the law."[8] Seventeenth- and eighteenth-century lawyers followed Coke's lead: "A corporation aggregate is a thing in imagination only, having no body, nor soul, nor conscience." As a notional rather than a breathing person, there were certain things the corporation could not do: it could commit no crime nor appear in person to answer a summons or to plead its own cause; with no soul, it could not enter into any engagement requiring an oath.[9] There was something unmistakably other-worldly about this "body in fiction of law."[10]

Nonetheless, it was a body carefully dissected by lawyers with very worldly needs who emphasized what the corporation could do rather than what it could not. "A corporation is something more than a mere name or

---

[5] Thus in English law, the fiction theory of corporateness serves only as explanatory device, not as legal ground. In law, the corporate person was real, not fictional. See Jethro Brown, "The Personality of the Corporation and the State," *Law Quarterly Review*, 21 (1905), pp. 365–79. Frederick Pollock, "Has the Common Law Received the Fiction Theory of Corporations?," *Law Quarterly Review*, 27 (1911), pp. 219–35. On the relationship between fiction and realism in the law, see Carr, *Corporations*, chapters 10, 11, and 16. See also F. W. Maitland, "Moral Personality and Legal Personality," in H. D. Hazeltine, G. Lapsley, and P. H. Winfield, eds., *Maitland: Selected Essays* (Cambridge, 1936), especially pp. 225–26; and John P. Davis, *Corporations: A Study of the Origin and Development of Great Business Combinations and of their Relation to the Authority of the State*, 2 vols. (New York, 1905; reprint, Buffalo, 1986), vol. II, chapter 7, especially p. 242.

[6] Hale, *Prerogatives*, ed. Yale, pp. 240 and 243. Hale wrote this in the 1640s or 50s: ibid., pp. xxiv–xxv.

[7] *Law of Corporations*, pp. 1–2.

[8] *Eng. Rep.*, vol. 77, p. 973 (10 Co. Rep. 32b). This is Coke's report on the Case of Sutton's Hospital, the single most influential writing on corporations in the seventeenth and eighteenth centuries. The analysis and language used in this report appears prominently in the case law and in theoretical writings.

[9] *Law of Corporations*, p. 6. Sheppard, *Of Corporations*, p. 109, follows the same line, which comes from Coke's report on Sutton's Hospital. On the problem of corporate criminal liability see Carr, *Corporations*, pp. 72–93; Levin, *Charter Controversy*, pp. 45–46 and 73–76; and L. H. Leigh, *The Criminal Liability of Corporations in English Law* (London, 1969), chapters 2 and 3.

[10] Sheppard, *Of Corporations*, p. 1.

notion ... It is a capacity framed to be and act as one person." It was "a body politic ... [with] members, all which together are able, by their common consent, to grant, give, receive, or take anything within the compass of their charter, or to sue and be sued, as any one man may do or be."[11] Writers like these moved blithely from metaphor, to simile, to reality: in law, the corporation was not just the analogue of a person, it was one. A corporation might not be able to swear fealty, but it could "give and grant, have and take, sue and be sued" like any individual.[12] As the King put it in his charter to Leeds, the members acting collectively were to be "one body corporate and politic in thing, fact, and name ... capable to have, take, receive, and possess ... enabled to implead and be impleaded, to answer and be answered ... in such like manner and form as other our subjects of this our realm of England, being persons able and in law capable."[13] By acting *like* a person, Leeds corporation would *be* one.

As Coke put it, "none but the King alone can create or make a corporation."[14] Even William Sheppard, writing during the Interregnum, stressed the exclusive creative power of the sovereign, once the King, now the Lord Protector.[15] Corporate status had been granted by other means, namely by prescription and by Parliament. But arguments that a corporation existed by prescription presumed the prior grant of a royal charter now missing. Sir Robert Atkyns, by no means a friend of the crown, put it this way: "[a corporation has] its essence by charter, or prescription, which presupposes a charter ... a corporation is a mere creature of the charters that does [*sic*] constitute it, and gives it its being."[16] Neither antiquity nor tradition could make a corporation without a royal letter patent. Nor could Parliament. In his report on the case of Sutton's Hospital, Coke recognized that Parliament had passed an act for the creation of the hospital. But he explained that the act did not create the corporation, it simply permitted the establishment of one, which the King then made.[17] Hale concurred,

---

[11] *Law of Corporations*, p. 2. Sheppard, *Of Corporations*, p. 4.

[12] Sheppard, *Of Corporations*, p. 109.

[13] James Wardell, *The Municipal History of the Borough of Leeds* (London, 1846), Appendix, pp. lxiii–lxiv. The language in all charters was virtually identical.

[14] *Eng. Rep.*, vol. 77, p. 975 (10 Co. Rep. 33b).

[15] Sheppard, *Of Corporations*, p. 45. Sir William Blackstone agreed a century later: the "King's consent is absolutely necessary to the erection of any corporation, either impliedly or expressly given": *Commentaries*, vol. III, p. 471. C. T. Carr called this the "concession theory" of corporateness: corporations exist only at the behest of the state, not simply by many individuals acting as a group. *Corporations*, pp. 159 and 163, and chapter 13.

[16] *Eng. Rep.*, vol. 87, p. 8 (3 Mod. 12). Atkyns was a justice of Common Pleas, 1672–80, before his removal for his political views; the quote is from 1682. Even Thomas Hunt, in his often extreme argument against the quo warranto by which London's charter was seized in 1683, stated clearly that corporate powers come only from the King: *A Defence of the Charter, and Municipal Rights of the City of London* (London, [1683]), pp. 1–3.

[17] *Eng. Rep.*, vol. 77, pp. 962–63 (10 Co. Rep. 24b).

though suggesting the monarch could delegate this creative power: "It remains that the King or those to whom he confers it have the power of erecting . . . corporations."[18] Other authorities such as the counties palatine granted a few corporate charters under their own seals, though at the King's sufferance, not by their own original authority.[19] Throughout the seventeenth and eighteenth centuries, all commentators recognized the sole power of the sovereign to make corporations. Thus a chartered liberty was a franchise: "a royal privilege in the hands of a subject."[20] The ancient franchise theory of corporate origins proved persistent. One could still gush to the King in 1726 that "Your throne is . . . the fountain from whence those municipal liberties have flowed which cherish and enliven the cities."[21] As with the ideal of corporate unity, this idea of franchises granted to corporations had a spiritual as well as a legal aspect. One cleric explained to a corporate congregation: "in all civil polities there is the original of power in God, who next unto himself confers it upon Kings, and they convey it unto others that are sent by them. This is that golden chain that cannot be broken without the manifest ruin of all."[22]

God to King to corporators. The powers, privileges, and responsibilities of governing were handed down, finally granted to a group of individuals embodied as one for better local government and the maintenance of the King's peace.[23] Remaining as one was vital for preserving the "golden chain" unbroken. The most important link in that chain was the charter, the King's license for corporate existence and the constitutional foundation of all the corporation's actions in his name. Violating the terms of that charter – dividing the "one body corporate" – would break the chain and destroy the corporation by uncoupling it legally, politically, and morally from its creator.

THE CHARTER

The corporation was not an independent being within the state; it was a crucial organ of the state, beholden to the King for its life and subservient to his needs, the chief of which was preserving the King's peace. Peace

---

18 Yale, ed., *Prerogatives*, p. 242.
19 On the delegation of the King's power, see Carr, *Corporations*, pp. 114–15. For instance, Liverpool's charters of 1677 and 1685 first passed the King's privy seal, before being granted under the seal of the Duchy of Lancaster, not the great seal. The Bishop of Durham also exercised this delegated authority. Weinbaum, *Borough Charters*, pp. 33–35.
20 *The Case of the Charter of London Stated* (London, 1683), p. 4.
21 Thomas Madox, *Firma Burgi, or an Historical Essay Concerning the Cities, Towns and Buroughs of England* (London, 1726), dedication. See also Hale, *Prerogatives*, ed. Yale, p. 201, and Sir Francis North's comments at BL Add. 32,520, f. 67.
22 Bod., MS Eng.th.f.63, f. 104.   23 See also, *Law of Corporations*, p. 2.

would be ensured by giving clear expressions to the "undoubted manner and form of government" in corporate charters.[24] Coke and those writing after him suggested that creating a corporation required no particular incorporating language.[25] But throughout the seventeenth century, the author of corporate charters consistently used one form to signify a corporate foundation, as at Nottingham, where the King ordained "a body corporate and politic in thing, deed, and name by the name of the Mayor, Aldermen, and Burgesses of the Town of Nottingham."[26] The name was crucial since it conferred personality. Just as any legal document referred to an individual by a name, first and last, its full name was the proper and only way to address a corporation. Thus its forename was something like "the Mayor and Aldermen . . . " or "the Bailiffs and Burgesses . . . ", with the place added as an integral component of the personal title: " . . . of the town of x in the county of y." In all pleadings and other legal actions, the corporate name would have to be fully stated or the action might be judged void. There could be no corporation without a name, and a suit by an improper name would be no suit at all.[27] Many corporation names changed in charters after 1660. Those once called "the Bailiffs and Burgesses" now became "the Mayor and Aldermen." This was an accession of dignity as well as a change of name, requested by a corporation in imitation of larger, more prominent towns.[28] Most name changes came in the 1680s, when the crown rechartered scores of towns not only to gain more political control, but to homogenize the chartered titles and privileges granted to England's towns.

After this preface in which the King created and named the corporation and explained his gracious purposes, the charter outlined the five general features of corporateness: perpetual succession, the capacity to sue and be sued as one, and powers to hold lands, to have a common seal, and to make by-laws.[29] Likewise, all other powers and privileges – governing

---

[24] William Robert James, *The Charters and Other Documents Relating to the King's Town and Parish of Maidstone* (London, 1825), p. 131.

[25] *Eng. Rep.*, vol. 77, p. 969 (10 Co. Rep. 30a); Sheppard, *Of Corporations*, p. 13; *Law of Corporations*, p. 11.

[26] W. H. Stevenson, ed., *Royal Charters Granted to the Burgesses of Nottingham* (London, 1890), p. 89.

[27] Madox, *Firma Burgi*, p. 115. *Law of Corporations*, p. 13. Sheppard, *Of Corporations*, pp. 17–18 and 126.

[28] For instance, Stamford's charter of 1664 changed the title of the corporation's head officer from alderman to mayor, and with it, the name of the corporation from "Alderman and Burgesses" to "Mayor, Aldermen and Capital Burgesses." This brought Stamford into line with most other corporations. PRO, IND1/4227/165.

[29] Sheppard and others contended that charters need not state these powers for they were "incident" upon corporateness. Nonetheless, all thought it advisable to state them. Sheppard, *Of Corporations*, pp. 41–42 and 52–58, and *Law of Corporations*, pp. 16 and 209.

structures, election procedures, judicial powers, fairs, markets – were detailed at length to preclude disputes that might otherwise arise over the terms of corporate authority. Charters included lengthy recitals of fairs and markets the corporation could hold, the days on which they could be held, the tolls and other duties collectable on those days, and the officers and courts of piepowder that would handle commercial disputes arising during them. And new charters to old corporations confirmed all lands previously owned. By granting fairs and markets and by confirming property, the King ensured the corporation's means of subsistence. This also provided the income from which the corporation could pay the annual fee farm rent to the crown for the enjoyment of its chartered privileges.[30]

Certainty of magisterial form, and thus of function, was the foundation of local peace. The longest, most detailed, and most important section of the charter was "the governing part," defining the corporation's composition, its procedures, and its administrative and judicial authority. Decision-making power was typically conferred on a senior body – usually called the aldermen or the capital burgesses – and a junior body – the common council or the burgesses. A head officer – a mayor in most cases, or at Yarmouth and a few others, two bailiffs – presided over the whole, chosen for a one-year term by means of electoral processes that varied from one town to the next according to local customs and charter provisions. The mayor summoned assemblies and controlled the agenda when they convened. Many decisions were made by the senior officers, and much of the day-to-day managerial work was conducted by small committees. But the full assembly of the aldermen and common councilmen possessed the final authority by which leases were granted, corporate property managed, by-laws passed, and by which all other decisions concerning public welfare were made.[31]

The charter spelled out the size, powers, and means of admission to the two chambers in the heart of the corporate body. Leicester's specified that twenty-four serve as aldermen and forty-eight as councilmen; Grantham's appointed twelve to each, though a smaller senior body by about half was common.[32] Charters specified the manner of electing new members to replace those who died, without which provision the corporation could not perpetuate itself. In most cases, the King also granted corporators power to

---

[30] Madox, *Firma Burgi*, p. 242.

[31] For instance, Winchester kept two books, one for entering matters considered by a senior group of corporation members for later consideration by the full assembly (called the Proposal Books), and another book recording the approval of the full assembly (called the Books of Ordinances). Hampshire RO, classes W/B1 and B2.

[32] Helen Stocks, ed., *Records of the Borough of Leicester, 1603–1688* (Cambridge, 1923), p. 80, and G. H. Martin, *The Royal Charters of Grantham, 1463–1688* (Leicester, 1963), p. 177.

dismiss members for misbehavior and many charters included clauses permitting the corporation to fine or even imprison those who refused to serve when elected and to fine members absent from meetings. Such clauses appeared with even greater frequency in new charters as mounting partisan tensions made such rules all the more necessary. As we shall see, the use of such powers, though intended to heal divided corporations, often had the reverse effect in the decades after 1660.

Most important of the charter clauses controlling admission to office were those concerning the election of the mayor. Charters always specified the day of election, often a saint's day or a day expressed in terms of one: the Monday before or after Michaelmas or St. Matthew's were common. As a result, September and October were hectic months given the partisan planning before the vote, and frequently the partisan recriminations and litigation after it.[33] Especially after 1688, provisions appointing the day assumed increasing importance and created serious problems as divided corporations often failed to elect a new mayor on "the charter day." Unintended disruptions during a contested choice, or intended disruptions by corporate partisans who stopped at nothing to defeat their foes, might prevent an election altogether. Depending on the charter, inability to elect on the proper day could mean either the continuation of the previous mayor for another year or the forfeiture of the charter when it made no provision for continuing the preceding mayor. In such cases, the corporation no longer had a mayor, and a body without a head was dead; charter forfeiture typically followed.[34]

Throughout the late seventeenth and early eighteenth centuries, charter clauses concerning elections became more detailed in order to avoid disputes and their sometimes serious consequences. In Hull's charter of 1661, the election clause only directed that they proceed "according to the ancient custom heretofore used." The charter of 1685 was more precise, requiring the nomination of two aldermen by their brethren; these two were then to stand in election before the burgesses at large, who would choose one of them to serve for the year.[35] This served two purposes. First, it limited the options available to the more popular body of burgesses. Second, by spelling out clearly the method of election, it diminished the possibility of disputes arising from disagreement over the exact terms of "the ancient custom." Royal charters increasingly included clauses detailing election procedures which before had been governed by local traditions. In election provisions, as in everything in charters of this period, the tendency

---

[33] Michaelmas term was particularly busy in King's Bench, especially after 1688: PRO, KB21, passim.

[34] For examples of this problem, see below, pp. 313–15, 327–28, and 333–36.

[35] Boyle, *Charters to Hull*, pp. 160 and 198–99.

was for more words, more definitions, more precision: the peace would be maintained by the thoroughness of legal language.

Assisting the deliberative heart of the body was a small group of officers and servants. Most prominent of these was the recorder, often a well-known lawyer, who gave legal advice and sat on the borough's bench. Increasingly, corporations chose noblemen to be recorder, while they in turn appointed deputies with legal training to perform the work required. The town clerk was usually the hardest working local official, updating assembly minutes and drawing up the leases, conveyances, contracts, and other legal documents through which the inanimate corporate body conducted business with the animate world. The clerk also maintained records of the town's courts and handled corporation correspondence. Mountains of neat records survive in many towns as a testament to their industry. In larger cities like Chester, it was a job consuming most if not all one's time. While neither the clerk nor the recorder had any legal right to vote on questions before the corporation – unless they had separate appointments to one of the conciliar bodies – they exercised enormous influence over decision making and administrative activity. Serving in some cases for decades, their views frequently carried more weight than the mayor's, who served only one year at a time. Their experience provided an important source of continuity from one year to the next. Corporate charters also appointed the lesser servants, most important being the serjeants-at-mace, who acted as messengers, served legal process, summoned councilmen at the command of the mayor, and carried the mace and other regalia on ceremonial occasions.

The most important clauses in the charter defined judicial powers. Nearly all towns had at least one civil court of some kind, variously called a court of record, court of pleas, or sheriff's or mayor's court. These courts determined all common law pleas arising within the borough concerning debts and contracts, deceits and trespasses. Charters appointed the presiding officers – typically the mayor, the recorder, and two or more bailiffs or senior aldermen – and when and how often the court would convene. Charters nearly always set a monetary limit on the matters the court could hear. Sudbury's court of record could hear disputes involving amounts up to £10 in value, but by their charter of 1664, their jurisdiction doubled to £20.[36] This increased purview was a common feature of Restoration charters, resulting from desires for greater self-determination in commercial disputes. Town merchants thus had a better venue for redress without the expense of an action in the courts at Westminster.

---

[36] *The Charter of the Borough of Sudbury of Charles II* (Sudbury, 1830; reprint, Sudbury, 1989), p. 15.

Corporations guarded their commissions of the peace even more jealously than their civil jurisdictions. A few towns still had benches appointed
by occasional royal commission, just like those in the counties, but the vast
majority had benches appointed in their royal charters.[37] Typically, a
charter named the mayor, the recorder, the deputy recorder, and one or
more aldermen; the final size of the bench varied from town to town, but
correlated roughly to town size. The aldermen appointed usually sat by
virtue of having previously held the mayoralty or by some other seniority
standard. In a few cases, the corporation itself was permitted to elect
justices each year.[38] With most borough JPs holding the posts *ex officio* by
virtue of the charter, the crown had much less control over who sat on the
corporate bench than it did over the county benches.

Borough benches possessed the same powers wielded by their county
counterparts. In what was typical language, Preston's charter declared their
"full power and authority to keep therein our peace, and that of our heirs
and successors, and to do and execute therein all other things, which in any
of our counties of England belong to be done and executed by a justice of
our peace."[39] New charters of the Restoration era tended to broaden the
size, powers, and independence of borough benches. The inclusion in most
charters of a general *non-intromittant* clause barred entry to the borough
of any outside official, most importantly, the county sheriff and justices.
This gave borough JPs exclusive jurisdiction in their precincts and allowed
only borough sheriffs, bailiffs, or serjeants to serve writs.[40] Townsmen
guarded this privilege more jealously than any other as it was the one most

[37] Towns with benches by occasional commission were: Bedford, Buckingham, Cambridge,
Oxford, Poole, Ripon, Saffron Walden, Thetford, and Woodstock. New commissions were
granted on request. For requests for commissions, see Cambridgeshire RO, Shelf C/8,
passim, and Woodstock Town Hall, 76/1, f. 63. See PRO, C181/7, passim, for dockets of
such commissions. For background, see Elizabeth Kimball, "Commissions of the Peace for
Urban Jurisdictions in England, 1327–1485," *Proceedings of the American Philosophical
Society*, 121 (1977), pp. 448–74; and Weinbaum, *Borough Charters*, pp. xviii–xix.

[38] For instance by charters to Macclesfield (1666) and Hertford (1680): J. P. Earwaker, *East
Cheshire: Past and Present*, 2 vols. (London, 1887–80), vol. II, p. 461, and Lewis Turnor,
History of the Ancient Town and Borough of Hertford (Hertford, 1830), pp. 99–112.

[39] Lingard, *Preston Charters*, part two, pp. 74–75. In a rare clause, Preston's mayor was also
made a county JP. Wigan's charter of 1662, Liverpool's of 1677, and Lancaster's of 1684
contained the same provision. This probably had something to do with the role of the
Duchy of Lancaster, which influenced the choice of Lancashire's JPs. Lionel K. J. Glassey,
Politics and the Appointment of Justices of the Peace, 1675–1720 (Oxford, 1979), chapter
10.

[40] A few charters explicitly omitted the *non-intromittant* and permitted county JPs to act
within the borough, continuing pre-1660 practices peculiar to the towns concerned:
Warwick (1664 and 1693), Chesterfield (1680), and Boston (1685). A handful of others
showed greater innovation, as when the crown appointed county JPs to the town bench by
charters granted after some act of town justices displeased the crown: Taunton (1677),
Newport, Isle of Wight (1684), Newcastle under Lyme (1685), and Berwick (1686).

clearly setting the corporation apart from the world around it. They were quick to complain, and quicker still to litigate when their exclusive powers were violated.

In the towns as in the counties, JPs represented the clearest and strongest link between crown and locality. Thus it is not surprising that one of the most common features in post-1660 charters was the appointment of more justices.[41] Other towns received peace commissions in their charters for the first time.[42] Preston's 1685 charter increased more dramatically than most the number of town JPs; while previously only the mayor had been a justice, now he was joined by the preceding mayor, another senior alderman, and the recorder.[43] This gave the town enough JPs on its own to perform those tasks requiring more than one justice without having to call in county JPs, an important accession of authority to the corporation. Increasing the number of JPs resulted from desires of both crown and borough for fuller, more powerful, and better defined urban magistracies. The crown's enduring interest in urban benches, its desire for closer ties to the locality, and its concern for better enforcement of an increasing number of statutes for which the justices were responsible, were all well served by enlarging the borough benches and widening their powers. Towns were delighted by this trend as it gave them more authority and greater protection from the encroachments of county justices.

While there was still much variation owing to local customs – many ancient, others only allegedly so – and to special privileges granted to certain towns by English monarchs centuries before, the provisions outlined above formed the bulk of all borough charters. Beginning especially in Elizabeth's reign, and during each of her successors', English charters increasingly followed standard forms. As the number of grants rose over the years, the crown gradually articulated a clearer, more uniform code of corporate privilege. By cutting back on the peculiarities and increasing the likenesses between them, borough corporations were tied more tightly to the crown whence their powers originated. The charters of the Restoration era carried this evolution toward its logical end. Charters of Charles II's reign reveal a great attention to detail: defining procedures for electing and swearing members of the corporation, widening the powers of civil courts and increasing the number of borough JPs, and granting new fairs, markets, and more valuable licenses of mortmain, thereby making it easier

---

[41] For instance, charters to Leeds and Hull (1661), Beverley (1663), Lichfield (1664), Gloucester (1672), Hertford (1680), Maidstone (1682), Canterbury (1684), and Grantham (1685). On crown interest in borough benches, see Weinbaum, *Borough Charters*, p. xviii.

[42] For instance, Sutton Coldfield and Newcastle under Lyme, in 1664: W. K. Riland Bedford, *History of Sutton Coldfield* (Birmingham, 1891), p. 28; T. Pape, *The Restoration Government and the Corporation of Newcastle-under-Lyme* (Manchester, 1940), p. 26.

[43] Lingard, *Preston Charters*, pp. 64–94.

for the corporations to fund their various public responsibilities. This culminated in the 1680s with what the principal student of borough charters has termed a "universal and uniform system of chartered rights," a system whose basic outlines were well established before 1660, only to be drawn more precisely in the decades following.[44] The increasing similarity between borough charters resulted as much from borough desires for increased powers like their neighbors', as from a crown desire for a more uniform set of rights accorded to corporations nationwide. The corporations gained broader jurisdiction and more clear definitions of procedure at the same time that changes in their charters – by making each corporation more like the next – drew them closer to the King who created them. Thus Boston's charter of 1685 was ordered to be drawn just like Salisbury's, granted only days earlier; Ludlow's, granted days later, was drawn according to the examples of both Boston and Salisbury.[45] Each grant followed on and borrowed from those preceding, creating a coherent set of chartered rights applied to all.

As we shall see in part two, reincorporations after 1660 should not be examined solely, nor even primarily, in the context of the political and religious conflicts of the age, as most analysts of Restoration charters have done. We must also consider them against this background of a less sensational but no less important institutional history, one exploring the changing legal and governmental nature of corporations and the evolving needs of a sovereign concerned to apply uniform norms nationwide. This need arose less from a desire for more power over the towns than from an interest in increasing the effectiveness of magisterial authority in the localities, and in integrating those who wielded that authority more fully into the ever neater workings of an incipient national state. Defining more thoroughly the authority of borough corporations was a critical part of that effort, for corporations were not independent governments, but an integral part of that state. This tendency also developed in response to the desires of townsmen everywhere for clear statements of their legal status and administrative procedures after the chaos of Civil War and Interregnum.

Those speculating on the nature of corporations liked to say that the exact form of words in the charter was unimportant to establishing the corporation or to defining its privileges. But in the decades after 1660, charter terms were more thoroughly defined in "words sufficiently ample."[46] Extra attention was paid to smaller details to ensure the legal

---

[44] Weinbaum, *Borough Charters*, p. xii.
[45] See the warrants for Boston's and Ludlow's charters: *CSPD 1685*, pp. 49–51. This practice, of ordering that a charter include the same terms as another, was common. Martin Weinbaum, *The Incorporation of Boroughs* (Manchester, 1937), p. 23.
[46] Stevenson, *Charters of Nottingham*, p. 87.

propriety and administrative usefulness of every new clause. Charters created united corporate bodies. They also established the terms of the body's existence and clarified procedures for coping with divisions. These terms would provide the crucial points of reference for lawyers and justices when corporate litigants went to the law to settle their differences. In court more than anywhere else, exact charter clauses assumed enormous importance as partisan contentions grew. As Sir Robert Atkyns put it, "the charter gives the only rule."[47]

THE BODY'S MEMBERS AND FUNCTIONS

Historians typically see corporations as part of the "unreformed" political world, institutions whose only imaginable historical end was destruction by progress. A tone of contempt echoes through much of the writing about them. From the report of the corporation commissioners of 1835, to Beatrice and Sidney Webb, to our own day, critiques of oligarchy dominate the analysis.[48] Those who expect early modern corporations to look and behave like modern town councils are bound to be disappointed. But one of the most thoughtful students of corporate governance notes that "the typical municipal corporation during this period [1660–1835] had no conception of itself as a local government authority in the modern sense."[49] They had their own sense, one characterized by a paternalistic concern for the public good and informed by an ever clearer notion of public duties. This concern for public duties in part explains how otherwise bitterly divided corporations continued to perform crucial administrative and judicial business.

Corporations were private bodies with public functions. Their original purpose was to promote and regulate local commerce, but by the second half of the seventeenth century, their briefs bulged with other matters. Corporations of the late seventeenth century became the executors of the principal modern public duties: to determine questions affecting individual rights, to provide services for the public welfare, to enforce the law, and to

---

[47] *Eng. Rep.*, vol. 87, p. 8 (3 Mod. 12).

[48] See for instance Joan Kirby, "Restoration Leeds and the Aldermen of the Corporation, 1661–1700," *Northern History*, 22 (1986), pp. 123–74. The epic work of Sidney and Beatrice Webb on local government included impressive volumes on corporations: *English Local Government from the Revolution to the Municipal Corporations Act: The Manor and the Borough* (London, 1908; reprint, Hamden, Conn., 1963). But they relied heavily on the often flawed researches of the corporation commissioners of 1835, whose work was ordered on the view that borough government had become unworkable by then. But they assumed that if that were the case then, it must always have been so. Municipal Corporation Commissioners, *Report of 1835* (Parliamentary Papers, vols. 23–26).

[49] Dawson, "Finance and the Unreformed Borough," p. 68. Dawson also questions reliance on the 1835 commissioners and on the Webbs: ibid., pp. 69, 97–98, and 216.

perform in accordance with and to protect the local constitution by conducting legal elections and keeping appropriate public records.[50] They executed justice, civil and criminal; administered schools, almshouses, and other charities; passed and enforced by-laws to keep the streets clean, lit, and safe; controlled access to markets and fairs; maintained public works such as water cisterns and harbor facilities; and held elections and passed ordinances regulating public life according to the terms of their charters.

As a private body funding public works from its own resources on some occasions, and on others, by drawing revenues from the wider citizenry, the differences between public and private rights, goods, and responsibilities were blurred. The confusion about the corporation's public or private status was mirrored in the dual status of the corporation's individual members, who, as William Sheppard pointed out, possessed a "double capacity," natural and legal.[51] In their natural capacity, members were private individuals like anyone else; in their legal capacity, their private individuality was subsumed in the collective, unitary whole with public duties. Complicating matters was the property theory of corporate office: office was a freehold, a form of personal property. But that property was a place in a body with public obligations that predated and outlasted the life of any private member. The law's tendency to treat the corporation as much as possible like a single person de-emphasized the interests of separate members, stressing instead the unitary interest of the corporate whole. This had the effect of reducing the importance of the private interests of individual members while expanding the importance of the public responsibilities of the collective body. As we shall see, this stress on the public aspect of the corporation would be enormously important in promoting King's Bench's development as the supervisor of proper corporate governance.[52]

Like most governing bodies and organizations, borough corporations included a handful who did most of the work, a majority who appeared regularly to support them, and a minority that rarely came to meetings. A study of attendance figures from 1,483 meetings in four towns over the period 1660–1727 shows that on the whole, rates of participation were better in the two larger towns, Chester and Leicester, than in the two smaller ones, Henley and Woodstock.[53] Overall, 54% of Woodstock

---

[50] A. J. Harding, *Public Duties and Public Law* (Oxford, 1989), pp. 28–31.

[51] Sheppard, *Of Corporations*, pp. 109–10.

[52] As Chief Justice John Holt noted, mandamus only lay where a public office was in question, not a private one: *Eng. Rep.*, vol. 87, p. 782, and vol. 91, p. 795 (6 Mod. 18 and 3 Salk. 232).

[53] Henley and Woodstock kept attendance records in their assembly books, Oxfordshire RO, A.V.6, 7, and 8 (Henley), and Woodstock Town Hall, 76/1 and 2, 86/1, and 87/1. At Chester, attendance records were made in the notes taken by the town clerk during

members appeared at meetings there; 59% in Henley; 66% in Chester; and at Leicester, an impressive 74%. In all likelihood, the differences correlate to the varying degrees of gentry membership in each corporation, ranging from Woodstock, with the highest number of gentlemen members, to Leicester, with almost none.[54] Gentlemen rarely lived in town, and even when resident nearby, were often occupied with other matters. Their attendance at meetings tended to be sporadic. Some of Woodstock's gentlemen corporators went months or years between meetings, appearing with only slightly greater frequency in times of increased political turmoil, such as the years 1679–81. On the other hand, the core of inhabitant members in each town attended faithfully, doing the bulk of the regular work. From place to place, and from one year to the next, overall, about three-quarters of resident members came to meetings.

The Restoration, the years of the Exclusion debacle, 1714–15: controversy in national or parliamentary politics was not evinced in widely fluctuating rates of attendance, with a few exceptions from which generalizations are difficult to make.[55] Likewise, meeting agendas had little impact on turnout. Meetings when new leases were granted, almshouse places were filled, or decisions were made about dung heaps drew virtually the same numbers as those when controversy erupted, members were removed, or debates flared over the wisdom of renewing the town's charter. The one important exception was elections, especially those for the head officer, when levels rose to or above the three-quarters mark.[56] Elections to the council or to the aldermancy also proved a larger attraction than more mundane matters, except at Leicester, where attendance was always good.

Corporation business kept active members hard at work; for the mayor and other senior leaders, it was nearly a full-time job. One needed wealth not only to uphold the public dignity of a corporation member, but to

meetings: CCRO, AF. Leicester's attendance records are in the Hall Books and Hall Papers, Leicestershire RO, BRII/1 and BRII/18.

[54] Leicester corporation pushed out, or readily accepted the resignations, of those who moved from town. Leicestershire RO, BRII/18/32, f. 346, BRII/18/33, f. 24, and BRII/18/35, f. 88. The first two of these were the dismissals of Robert Turlington and William Nutt, in 1669 and 1671 respectively; both had been appointed by the Corporation Act commissioners. Leicester experienced similar attendance problems with others appointed by the Corporation Act. They too were later dismissed. See ibid., BRII/18/31, f. 420.

[55] In Woodstock, participation rose a bit during the reign of Queen Anne, and then began a slight decline in the 1720s. Chester members attended in slightly larger numbers in the early 1660s than in the rest of the period. At Henley, where half the meetings held between 1660 and March of 1663 did not have a quorum, levels of participation were markedly lower then than at any other time in the decades following.

[56] Chester and Henley rates only. Attendance at mayoral elections was not recorded at Woodstock. At Leicester, attendance survives for only three elections, when the average rate was 91%.

afford the cost members paid in foregone attention to private affairs.[57] The diary of Colonel Roger Whitley, mayor of Chester in the 1690s, records vividly the daily round of public business.[58] Assembly meetings were only the tip of the iceberg. Whitley arbitrated in disputes within and between the various trade companies, especially involving apprenticeships. Frequent meetings of committees appointed by the assembly were held to consider matters ranging from gate repairs to viewing corporation property before granting a new lease. Small groups of aldermen met weekly or more often to conduct business.[59] Crown orders to attend to impressment and quartering had to be implemented, and fears of citizens about the same had to be allayed. Taxes and tolls, local and royal, were assessed and collected. Frequent courts were held. And whether at dinner or at bowls, social occasions included largely if not entirely other corporation members. Life was little different elsewhere.[60]

Managing corporation lands commanded the lion's share of assembly attention as well as time spent outside of meetings. Most towns required an assembly vote upon the grant of every lease. In some, as at Henley, all leases were not only approved, but were later sealed before the full body. Careful attention was paid to the regular care of ditches, fences, and buildings to protect property values. This was important, because rents on corporate properties paid for the majority of services provided by the corporation, from maintenance of market places, bridges, and other public facilities, to charities and public entertainments. Hospitals, almshouses, schools, and doles of woolen cloth, bread, or firewood were managed by the corporations.[61] The same hand that gave also chastised the poor, setting them on work or confining them to houses of correction.[62] In times of plague, corporations built "pest houses" to quarantine the sick, and passed

---

[57] As Elias Hartell said when resigning at Leicester, he was "obliged to be frequently abroad in the country, and [when] at home [was] engaged in such business that the leaving of it unfinished is very prejudicial." Leicestershire RO, BRII/18/39, f. 97.

[58] Bod., MS Eng. Hist. c. 711.

[59] See for instance CCRO, MF/110, ff. 36–38 and passim.

[60] Kirby notes the same of Leeds: "Restoration Leeds," p. 140. Leicester's Hall Papers create the same impression of constant and varied activity. Leicestershire RO, BRII/18/30–39, passim.

[61] Oxfordshire RO, A.V.6, f. 322. Henley minutes are filled with references to the accounts of various charities managed by officers appointed and overseen by the corporation. Alms recipients were often chosen by corporate vote. Gloucestershire RO, GBR, B3/4, pp. 57–59, 67, and passim. Kingston upon Thames: Surrey RO, KB1/1, pp. 21, 22, 34, and passim; one could be expelled from an almshouse by the same process: ibid., p. 39.

[62] At Henley, the poor were not allowed to come into the market on market days to beg corn. Oxfordshire RO, A.V.6, f. 296. Woodstock tried to set the poor to work: Woodstock Town Hall, 76/1, ff. 73v and 74. Chester continued its house of correction though the results were poor: CCRO, AB/2, ff. 153v and 156v.

rules barring strangers from town. And in times of public danger, when fears of sectarian or "popish" plotting ran wild, they posted watches.[63]

Land rents and other regular incomes from tolls, freemen's fines, and fines imposed on members for non-attendance of meetings or other misbehavior, covered operational costs. Some charters granted power to tax inhabitants, like Grantham's, where the corporation could "assess and tax such reasonable sums within the said town . . . for the public and common good or utility of the said town."[64] But for the most part, corporations were self-financing, paying for their activities from the rents and fees they were entitled to collect, rather than taxes on the citizenry. When debts mounted, corporations typically paid them by loans or subscriptions from their own members.[65] Taxes on the general population went largely for what would now be called public works: water systems, payment of scavengers, road repair, and, later in the period, street lighting.[66] But the corporations undertook many maintenance programs solely on their own charge. Leicester's annual accounts show large expenditures on road and bridge repairs every year, and most corporations paid from their own funds to maintain the town hall and other buildings and public spaces in their care, such as market places.[67] The "weale public" was surprisingly a private concern, promoted largely by the corporation's own revenues.

The corporation attended to interests beyond town as well as within it. This took many forms, including defense of local privileges and economic well-being, and the promotion of new schemes to bring trade to town. They managed petitions to the King for permission to build or extend port

[63] For plague regulations, see Oxfordshire RO, A.V.6, ff. 301–02 and 328 (Henley); Stocks, *Records of Leicester*, p. 496; and Leicestershire RO, BRII/18/31, ff. 664–65 and 681. For examples of watches, see ibid., f. 283 and CCRO, AB/2, f. 133.

[64] This privilege was granted in charters of 1631 and 1685. Martin, *Charters of Grantham*, pp. 134–35 and 190–91.

[65] Though not obligated by their charters to provide for the general welfare from corporation funds, a sense of responsibility weighed on corporators' minds, and grew over time. Dawson, "Finance and the Unreformed Borough," pp. 68–69, 98, and passim. Kirby, "Restoration Leeds," pp. 137–38.

[66] As at Woodstock for its water system: Woodstock Town Hall, 76/1, f. 62v and 76/2, f. 13. Leicester levied a tax by ward to pay for well repairs: Leicestershire RO, BRII/18/32, f. 157. At Chester, a general rate paid for a nightly watch in 1661–62, and for a scavenger: CCRO, AB/2, ff. 133v, 139v, and 184; AB/3, ff. 10 and 13. Woodstock's bellman also served as a scavenger: Woodstock Town Hall, 86/1, May 28, 1712.

[67] For paving costs, see Leicestershire RO, BRIII/2, passim. The corporation spent over 10% of its budget on road and other repairs in a typical year, 1663–64: BRIII/2/86, ff. 143–45. Henley too covered most of the costs of bridge and road repair from corporation accounts: Oxfordshire RO, A.V.6, ff. 270–72v, 276v, 279v, and 354v–56v. Orders for householders to clean the street before their homes were common too. CCRO, AB/2, f. 172, and Woodstock Town Hall, 86/1, Nov. 2, 1713. Dawson, "Finance and the Unreformed Borough," chapters 7–10.

facilities, and later in the period, shepherded legislation through Parliament for building canals or dredging rivers to promote trade.[68] Frequent disputes erupted between townsmen and county gentlemen appointed to make tax assessments, and someone had to handle these matters as well.[69] Corporations were just as assiduous in protecting their magisterial jurisdiction from the gentry, and always acted quickly when a county sheriff or justice acted within borough limits. Both in making arrests within the town's liberties and in handing out ejectments concerning borough lands, Windsor castle's court and officers overstepped the bounds on more than one occasion. The immediate response in each instance was litigation or the threat of it.[70] Corporations also protected their interests against other corporations.[71]

Borough corporations of the later Stuart age may not have looked much like modern urban governments, but the care and commitment with which they did their work shows a growing consciousness of their public duties. The benefits of corporate membership – power, dignity, the enjoyment of various perquisites – were real enough, but so too were the responsibilities. Detailed corporation account and minute books testify to the seriousness with which public duties were discharged. When political divisions threatened the lives of many corporations after 1660, a sense of stewardship and of paternalistic concern for the common good, as much as anything else, kept the corporations working. Many members found themselves tugged one way by partisan interests, and the other way by community interests. Rarely did the particular so override the general as to damage the common weal by splitting and killing the corporate body. Corporators did all in their power to ensure that all minded general interests rather than partisan ones in order to maintain the health of the one body corporate and the "weale public" that depended on it. This they did by making rules.

---

[68] See for instance H. Robinson, "Cheshire River Navigation with Special Reference to the River Dee," *Journal of the Chester Archaeological Society*, 55 (1968), pp. 63–87.

[69] Chester clashed with the county over the royal aid between 1669 and 1672. This is covered well in CCRO, ML/3 and MF/87–90, passim.

[70] Shelagh Bond, ed., *The First Hall Book of the Borough of New Windsor, 1653–1725*, Windsor Borough Historical Records Publications, vol. 1 (Windsor, 1968), pp. 17 and 20. Woodstock prevented the county sheriff from executing writs within the borough, though they stopped short of commencing a court action on this occasion. Woodstock Town Hall, 76/2 unfol., Sept. 8, 1684. Northampton sued the county sheriff for making arrests within the borough. Northamptonshire RO, 3/2, p. 197.

[71] Leicester joined Northampton, Warwick, and others in the early eighteenth century to prosecute Coventry for withholding charity funds meant for their use. Coventry released the moneys after lengthy Chancery proceedings. Leicestershire RO, BRII/18/39, ff. 177, 195, 203, and 240; BRII/1/4, f. 68. Most charters dictated that freemen were free of tolls in other towns. Macclesfield and Chester spent five years in court after Macclesfield freemen were distrained for tolls at Chester. Macclesfield ultimately won. CCRO, AB2/194v, 197, and 199; Cheshire RO, LBM/1/1/93.

RULES OF ORDER

Consistent attention to accounting and to managing property were aspects of a broader concern for the careful conduct of all business. Regularity was the hallmark of corporate life; interruptions to it often serve as the best indicators of conflicts below the placid surface of most town records. Observance of local customs and ordinances directing the time and manner for conducting corporate business and for maintaining records was often the best defense corporations had against the threat to political stability posed by worsening partisan divisions. One of the most remarkable aspects of the first age of party was the degree of continuity most corporations maintained in their administrative responsibilities through some of the ugliest internal feuds. Adherence to traditional calendars for conducting elections, and regular attention to matters of general concern such as maintaining property and operating charities and courts, helped to prevent partisan animosities from destabilizing the local polity. The importance of these common interests compelled the continuing conduct of vital business while opposed sides fought for control of the corporation. The regularity in the audits of Gloucester's accounts in the years 1670–74, when the corporation was wracked by a succession of expulsions, disputed mayoral elections, and a controversial new charter, bears witness to the power of routine to carry governance over the roughest patches.[72]

Corporations operated on annual calendars running from the swearing of one mayor to the next. The outlines of that calendar were drawn by the terms of the charter, which set the dates for the mayor's election and for his swearing. Michaelmas to Michaelmas, or St. Matthew's to St. Matthew's, the corporate year in most towns began and ended in autumn. The annual cycle set a tempo for all other activity. Most corporations held meetings on an irregular basis, according to the summons of the mayor. But others met on a regular timetable: bi-weekly meetings, as at Rochester, or monthly ones, as at Evesham. A 1717 ordinance at Henley requiring monthly meetings met a common fate: enthusiastic endorsement and inconsistent application.[73] Even in their failures, the corporations did all in their power to impose order and predictability on their proceedings.

The power to make by-laws was granted in every charter, though it was considered one of the "incidents" of corporateness – a power implicitly held by all corporations without statement in their charters – "For as reason is given to the natural body for the governing of it, so the body corporate must have laws as a politic reason to govern it."[74] Nowhere was

---

[72] Gloucestershire RO, GBR/F5/15–18.   [73] Oxfordshire RO, A.V.7, Sept. 20, 1717.
[74] *Law of Corporations*, p. 209. See also Sheppard, *Of Corporations*, pp. 81–82.

"politic reason" more carefully pronounced than in by-laws governing elections and meetings. At Evesham, the mayoral election process began with a formal summons of the corporation to the election meeting, which the outgoing mayor made six days ahead of time. Election day began with a sermon followed by a dinner for the corporation. Then they proceeded to the choice, beginning with the nomination by the full council of two to stand, and ending with a final round in which one of the two was elected. St. Albans also required six days' summons before proceeding in two stages: nomination of two by the mayor and aldermen, followed by the final choice between them by the assistants and free inhabitants. If the new mayor could not be chosen by a clear acclamation, the two sides stood in different parts of the hall while polled by the mayor, recorder, and aldermen. If for any reason the mayor could not attend, St. Albans made detailed arrangements for conducting a legal election in his absence in order to avoid any lapse in authority for a failure to hold the election on the appointed day. Failure to do so might well endanger the charter.[75] In all cases, the choice of the mayor was to be by a free election, without any prior orchestration of voting. At Rochester, the first and most prominent by-law passed in 1673, during a period of local political turmoil, imposed fines and dismissal on any alderman or councilman who dared to "solicit a freeman to give his voice for any particular alderman to be mayor."[76] Each person eligible to vote was to make his own determination about the fittest person to succeed to the chair, unswayed by any making of parties for one or another candidate.

A related mortal sin was "soliciting" members or non-members to act in concert together in other matters. Secrecy rules attempted to prevent disclosure or discussion of corporate counsels outside the assembly room. While corporations were to serve the "weale public," this did not mean that the public should have any influence on proceedings. Fines for disclosing corporation business ranged from 20s at Barnstaple, to £40 for guilty aldermen at Liverpool; at Abingdon, a loose tongue could mean dismissal.[77] By outlawing public discussion of corporate business, corpora-

---

[75] William Tindal, *The History and Antiquities of the Abbey and Borough of Evesham* (Evesham, 1794), appendix, pp. 335–36. E. Farrington, *The Charter and Also the Constitutions Granted to the Inhabitants of the Town of St. Albans* (St. Albans, 1813), pp. 37–43.

[76] *An Authentic Copy of the Charter and Bye-Laws of the City of Rochester* (London, 1809), part two, p. 31. Chester had a similar by-law against "soliciting" votes passed in 1613 and reiterated in 1685: CCRO, AB/3, f. 4.

[77] J. R. Chanter and Thomas Wainwright, eds., *Reprint of the Barnstaple Records*, 2 vols. (Barnstaple, 1900), vol. I, p. 99. James A. Picton, *City of Liverpool: Selections from the Municipal Archives and Records* (Liverpool, 1883), p. 246. Bromley Challenor, ed., *Selections from the Municipal Chronicles of the Borough of Abingdon* (Abingdon, 1898), p. 157.

tions sought to prevent party making outside of meetings. Evesham's corporation made unusual allowance for public involvement in corporation debates, though it placed clear restrictions on the expression of political opinions.

No person of the common council of this borough, or any other inhabitant thereof
. . . shall by any means speak against, or go about to break off, overthrow, or impugn any such order or agreement that shall happen to be so conferred of or agreed upon, unless by due and orderly course in the council-chamber, by showing forth his or her reasons how the same may be prejudicial to the government of this borough.[78]

Use of the word "her" suggests an unusual readiness to consider the views of the unenfranchised. But as in all towns, the corporation would always have the last word, with fines for any, inside the corporation or out of it, who presumed to speak further of a matter officially closed. Likewise at Preston, fines were imposed on those "combining, confederating, or making parties in the council, or not acquiescing in the determination of the question."[79] Resolution of any question precluded further discussion.

The line between defamation of character and the expression of a political opinion was perilously thin. Regulations forbidding "reproachful words" against the corporation or specific members, in meetings or on the street, circumscribed the speech of corporators and inhabitants alike. Fines for reviling language, "whereby the King's peace or brotherly love may be broken or impaired," were a commonplace in corporation rule books.[80] Outraged corporate leaders quickly prosecuted any verbal affront. Two residents of Sudbury were presented at quarter sessions for calling the corporation "rogues," "drunkards," and "a pitiful company."[81] Speech in the council chamber was even more closely monitored. The mayor chaired all meetings, determining who could speak, when, and for how long. Most towns, like Barnstaple, set fines on anyone who interrupted one of his brethren. Some limited the number of times one could speak on any given issue. Though a Preston councilman could air his views on any subject up to four times per session, at Abingdon, once was all without special permission from the chair. Quality as well as quantity was controlled. A

---

[78] Tindal, *Evesham*, appendix, p. 338.
[79] Removal was required for the third offense. Abram, *Preston Guilds*, p. 54. In St. Albans, anyone who tried "to break over, through, or repugne" any resolution made when absent from a meeting was to be fined. E. Farrington, *The Charter and also the Constitutions Granted to the Inhabitants of the Town of St. Albans* (St. Albans, 1813), p. 54.
[80] This quotation comes from St. Albans, Farrington, *Constitutions of St. Albans*, p. 54. The other towns discussed above had similar rules.
[81] Suffolk RO (Bury St. Edmunds Branch), EE501/2/8, p. 161. King's Bench decisions curtailed corporate powers to punish those whose words challenged their dignity: *Eng. Rep.*, vol. 86, p. 711 (1 Mod. 35).

Preston member was to "stand up uncovered, and direct his speech only to the mayor, and . . . [was not to] use any opprobrious, reproachful, uncivil, or reflecting words or language of, unto, or concerning either the mayor or any other of the council." While speaking, all were to listen in silence, and were "not to use any whisperings privately."[82] Preston dictated that matters introduced at one meeting should not be discussed until the next, to give time for each member to consult his own mind about the town's good, and to prepare his thoughts for temperate presentation when they met again.

At the end of discussion came time for a decision. Uncontroversial decisions were made by acclamation, as when approving a new lease to a good tenant or when allocating 10s for repairs to the water conduit. Minutes books declared simply that it had been so agreed and ordered. Often, the words "by unanimous consent" or "nemine contradicente" were entered as well, to present an image of a united body in action. Many decisions were not so easy, and required a poll of members; in such cases, a simple majority would win the day. But the need for majority procedures was by definition a sign of division, and, on difficult questions, could lead to more dispute, especially if not carefully regulated. By charter, by-law, or both, the mayor's vote counted double in cases of a tie, as at Colchester, "so that faction and division among voters, as far as can be done, may be removed."[83] Voting was typically conducted openly, by voice. Rules dictated the order, based on seniority: "if upon passing the question the votes [of] each party be so equal, as that the mayor cannot decide it without going to the poll, then the mayor shall begin with the junior common councilman, and so in order to the senior alderman, marking each man's vote as he passeth."[84] Balloting was rare, though in 1680, Leicester corporation ordered that "for the future, all elections of members to be chosen of either of the companies shall be elected and chosen by ticket only and no otherwise." At Pontefract, balloting was not only secret, but all ballot papers were to be burned after counting. Amidst controversy in 1656, Winchester developed a system for each member "privately" to drop colored bullets into a box, "for the better continuance of love and unity amongst themselves."[85]

A few towns made a point of polling every question, including the most mundane, even when unanimity was evident. Draft minutes and other notes from meetings survive at Gloucester and Chester.[86] Numbers of votes

---

[82] Challenor, *Abingdon*, p. 179. Abram, *Preston Guilds*, p. 53.

[83] This language was in charters of both 1635 and 1663. *The Charters and Letters Patent Granted to the Borough [of Colchester]* (Colchester, 1904), p. 115.

[84] Abram, *Preston Guilds*, p. 53.

[85] Leicestershire RO, BRII/18/35, p. 8; Stocks, *Records of Leicester*, p. 554. PRO, SP44/108/203v–05v. Hampshire RO, W/B1/5, ff. 98–100v.

[86] Chester draft minutes are in the Assembly Files, CCRO, AF; final minutes are in Assembly

on each side of a question were noted in draft minutes in nearly every case; the names of those casting each vote were not. But such tallies were not for the final record. In both towns, final minutes only told the outcome of the vote. At Chester, the assembly books record whether a decision was reached "by unanimous consent," or by majority, but no numbers were recorded. Though functionally the same, majority and unanimous decisions were always differentiated, the former being morally and politically suspect. As Lord Guilford said, "Great things should not depend upon major vote of great assemblies. Many times that is the minor vote of people, and it is flitting and various. The major vote will change in a day."[87] At Gloucester, all matters and votes were recorded in the draft minute books, but only questions resolved in the affirmative appeared in the final minutes; questions resolved in the negative had not happened at all, according to the official record. In both towns, and in assembly books everywhere, clerks and the corporations they served put a seamless appearance on corporation decisions, creating an image of unity – even in the face of discord – one they hoped might become reality itself.

Fines were imposed to protect the corporation's dignity. At St. Albans, two aldermen and four assistants were required to attend the mayor publicly to church every Sunday and feast day. And nearly every town required corporation members to acquire and maintain gowns which they were to wear to all meetings and on all public occasions, whether feasting or walking the market.[88] Colchester's charter of 1663 required gowns in church, where corporation members were to go each Sunday, led by the mayor, who was preceded by the mace, "because the dignity of that place is wholly lost when whatsoever conduces to decorum is not observed."[89] At Henley, fines for not wearing gowns might be levied by distress; at Kingston, fines were not enough, as removal was threatened against those not buying gowns.[90] Gown regulations, like voting regulations, were meant to impose an outward appearance of uniformity and thus of unity.

As a body existing only in law, leases, minute books, charters, and other records were critical to the corporation's well-being. Without them, the corporation could not prove what they owned, what in law they could and could not do, and what others owed to them. Corporations lavished great

Books, CCRO, AB. At Gloucester, draft minutes are in Gloucestershire RO, GBR, B3/4; final minutes are in GBR, B3/3.

[87] BL, Add. 32,518, f. 36.

[88] Farrington, *Constitutions of St. Albans*, p. 50. Gown regulations may be found everywhere. See for instance Bod., MS Top. Berks. c.20, ff. 39 and 40 (Abingdon), and Edward Griffith, *A Collection of Ancient Records Relating to the Borough of Huntingdon* (London, 1827), pp. 117–20.

[89] *Charters [of Colchester]*, p. 114.

[90] Oxfordshire RO, A.V.6, ff. 277–78v. Surrey RO, KB1/1, pp. 83–85.

care on their records, imposing fines for defacing them, and regularly sorting, cataloguing, or securing them.[91] If possession is nine-tenths of the law, then holding the corporation's records was an important political asset. Documents often became one of the first targets of each side when partisan disputes erupted; capturing them permitted one side to control the terms of the legal and political debate that might determine which side would emerge triumphant.[92] Thus many towns had two or more locks on the chests and rooms where records were stored, their keys remaining in separate hands to prevent any one person or group from gaining such a powerful advantage. Andover, like other corporations experiencing internal division after 1660, added a third lock to the door behind which they kept their records and seals.[93]

On the surface, most by-laws looked innocuous enough. Voting rules, quorums, conventions in record keeping: clearly defined procedures created the appearance if not the reality of unity. Passed by the corporation according to powers given them in their charters, by-laws were intended to regulate activities in the interest of peaceful and effective government, their strictures ostensibly restraining all members equally. But not all by-laws had such neutral effects, nor were they intended to. Though meant to preserve unity, new by-laws were often an important part of partisan conflict. Increased fines on refusing office might be imposed to harass dissenters or their sympathizers who preferred to refuse office rather than receive the sacrament regularly or take the oaths mandated by the Corporation Act. The sudden resurrection of long-dormant rules fining absentees, or, more often, the raising of such fines, could be an attack on a corporation group dependent for support on the occasional attendance of non-resident members. Most of all, by-laws reforming election procedures were frequently passed to serve partisan ends. Lymington corporation made just such a new rule not long before a by-election in 1677. In mayoral and parliamentary elections, colored tags would be distributed to all voters, each candidate having announced the color signifying his own name. Then the voters would "privately" put the appropriate colored ballot slip in a box, proceeding in reverse seniority order. In case of a tie, the mayor would

---

[91] Chesterfield kept a register of documents going in and out of their muniment chest. Philip Riden and John Blair, eds., *History of Chesterfield*, Records of the Borough of Chesterfield and Related Documents, 1204–1835, vol. 5 (Chesterfield, 1980), pp. 229–33. For committees appointed to catalogue records, see HMC, Report 11, appendix 7, pp. 196 and 201 (Reading, 1668 and 1687); Cambridgeshire RO, Shelf C/8, f. 221v (Cambridge, 1668); and Leicestershire RO, BRII/19/20 and 21, and O.S.88.

[92] This was an especially common problem after 1688. King's Bench responded by granting numerous writs of mandamus ordering one officer to relinquish records to another. See below, p. 294.

[93] C. Collier and R. H. Clutterbuck, *The Archives of Andover*, part 2 (Andover, 1889), p. 26.

have the deciding vote. Whether because of this stipulation or the unusual secret ballot requirement, the order was rescinded before it could be used. John Button, a former parliamentarian who lost the ensuing by-election, had wanted the new rule, probably to bolster his own chances; Sir Richard Knight, his victorious foe, signed the order canceling it. Only three of the sixteen approving the original rule acquiesced in its demise, underscoring its partisan origins.[94]

With the attention given detailed rules regulating corporate life, big issues were often fought as conflicts over procedure: defining it, controlling it, disputing the meaning of rules delimiting it. After a disputed election at Marlborough in 1714, a number of corporation members complained how an election by-law there "had been made use of to evil purposes."[95] Frequently, local contests involved one group manipulating a local by-law to their political advantage, while their foes called them to account for their alleged abuse of it. Interest in charter clauses and adherence to customs or by-laws arose from and contributed to a spirit of legal precision and a tendency to litigate whenever proceedings went awry, especially when by-laws and charter clauses contradicted one another, as was all too often the case.[96] In court actions on writs of mandamus in the Restoration era, and on quo warrantos in the years after 1698, legal and thus political argument revolved around careful readings of the corporation's constitutions: its charters, its by-laws, and its customs. Lawyers and judges encouraged this tendency. The justice or injustice of one's removal from the corporation, or of a group's claim to have exclusive legal right to govern, depended on the ability to make a case based on precise readings of these constitutions and on arguments addressing the requirement of the corporation to fulfill its public duties. The attention to detail fueled a niggling interest in the niceties of corporation proceedings: political opponents never failed to exploit the least oversight of charter provisions, oversights which, in law, put their political power in jeopardy. But the attention to detail also saved the corporations. Even the smallest corporation conducted business according to clear forms established in its charters and by-laws. These forms helped maintain an image of continuity and unity during periods of strife. More important, these forms provided the means by which stability was maintained and by which corporations continued to perform their public duties through the worst bouts of partisan rivalry.

---

[94] Hampshire RO, 27M74/DBC2, ff. 86v–87v. Three of those signing the original by-law had been removed by the Corporation Act commissioners: compare with 27M74/DBC283. Henning, vol. I, pp. 249 and 757–58.

[95] PRO, KB1/1, affidavit of John Fowler, *et al.*, Jan. 31, 1715.

[96] Such a contradiction was exploited dramatically at Chester in the 1690s. See below, pp. 280–88.

When corporations split apart, their constitutions gave partisans something more benign to fight about – rules – and being based in law, a safer place to fight about them – in court.

THE CROWN, THE COURTS, AND THE CORPORATE PERSON

The corporations were often seen as independent entities within the kingdom, by definition in an antagonistic relationship with the crown. Many shared the view of the Marquess of Newcastle, who condemned corporate liberties in 1660: "every corporation is a petty free state against monarchy."[97] Corporations tended to usurp powers properly belonging to the sovereign; from this, chaos ensued. Such a view insisted on the inevitability of town/crown conflict, an insistence inherited by latter day historians. But stressing antagonism does not help us understand actual relations between crown and town or the role of the corporations as parts of a greater body. Symbiosis rather than antagonism describes relations between the King and his corporations during most of this period, for borough corporations were not political atoms, but extensions of crown government itself, created by the monarch to maintain the public welfare and the King's peace. Crown and borough shared goals and needs and throughout the period worked in concert to obtain them: witness the interest both sides showed in negotiating charter terms extending the size or powers of the borough bench.

Despite all the changes in political needs and fortunes over the period 1650 to 1730, the views of jurists and theorists on the nature of corporations remained remarkably consistent, stressing their franchisal nature and the need for internal unity to maintain their legal personality and magisterial effectiveness. This was to be achieved by self-regulation in obedience to charter clauses and by-laws governing what corporation members could and could not do. But self-regulation alone would not suffice for maintaining corporate unity in the face of Civil War divisions and the political and religious angers they generated. As partisan tensions pulled corporations apart in the decades after 1640, and especially after 1660, townsmen turned ever more frequently to the King for their protection, to the King sitting in King's Bench in the person of his justices. It made sense that townsmen should seek settlement of their differences by legal means since corporations were bodies that had their being through the law. By appealing to the law for help, the corporations in turn tied themselves ever more tightly to their royal creator. Summoned again and again by borough

---

[97] Quoted in Ian Roy, "The English Republic, 1649–1660: The View from the Town Hall," in H. G. Koenigsberger and Elisabeth Müller-Luckner, *Republiken und Republikanismus im Europa der Frühen Neuzeit* (Munich, 1988), p. 213.

partisans to settle their differences, King's Bench became the means for maintaining stable government in the midst of conflict, thus ensuring that even corporations divided by partisan politics would remain "the best of polities."

From purge to purge: Civil War, Interregnum, and Restoration in the corporations

Music, speeches, a bonfire for the inhabitants, and a large dinner for the corporation: the bailiffs, magistrates, peers, and headboroughs of Kingston upon Thames begrudged no expense celebrating the King's restoration in May of 1660. Three pounds went to the trumpeters alone. Another pound paid the ringers at the bell tower.[1]

The joyful peals of 1660 must have grated on the ears of those who had created the political discord of the last decade. Kingston's corporation had begun to fall apart in 1653 with the removal of one headborough and the refusal to swear another into office. By the following year, well-defined factions, hardened in their opposition to one another, struggled for control. In August 1654, members unsympathetic to the Protectorate tried but failed to dismiss bailiffs Theophilus Colcock and Obadiah Wicks. Colcock and Wicks countered two days later, dismissing from the corporation six of those who had just voted for their ouster. Then Colcock, Wicks, and their partisans elected three new men "to make strong Colcock's faction."[2] By purging their foes, Colcock and Wicks could now feel confident in their hold on authority.

But even in the mid-1650s, officers wrongly removed had some recourse in the courts. Those dismissed turned to the Upper Bench – once the court of King's Bench – where they sued for writs of mandamus. The court complied, directing that the corporation "restore, or cause to be restored [those removed], or do signify to us the cause thereof to the contrary." Colcock, Wicks, and their corporate friends chose the last option, refusing restitution and making a return to the writ which justified the dismissals. The judges then referred the dispute to the mediation of Sir Richard Onslow and Colonel Robert Ward, who, after hearing both parties, again ordered the restoration of all removed and the dismissal of those who had

---

[1] Surrey RO, KD5/1/2, ff. 162–66.
[2] *Scandal on the Corporation: Royalists and Puritans in Mid-Seventeenth-Century Kingston* (Kingston, 1982) [A transcription of Surrey RO, KB16/7/1–59], pp. 1–6 and 17.

replaced them. But these efforts too failed to leave "the said parties united and reconciled in love and amity as they were before the said differences." The parties returned to court again in Michaelmas term, 1655.[3]

Colcock's and Wick's charges against those dismissed were serious:

at a court held for the town . . . there was like to be a tumult and uproar . . . whereupon the bailiffs that held the court did adjourn the court and commanded all persons there to depart, and then they [Colcock and Wicks] with the rest that were of their party went away. But the other parties on the contrary side, whereof . . . [those] that were disfranchised were a part, stayed still in the town hall, and said the court was not dissolved, and did affirm they were a court, and did thereupon make divers orders or acts of court, and caused them to be entered in the court book.

This they said was "a setting up of government against government."[4] Partisan politics did not set two groups within government against each other; it set one group claiming to be the government against a group they said should be excluded from government. No one questioned the assumption that unity among members – conceived as individuals, and, metaphorically, as parts of the body politic – was necessary to the well-being of the corporation.

The judges took seriously these allegations against those dismissed. But they had more questions about the return to the writ, concluding that it did not establish clearly the corporation's right to expel its own members. So they again ordered restoration, but Colcock, Wicks, and their partisans, with the connivance of Major General Kelsey, suppressed the court's new writs. Only one out of six of those ordered restored by the court regained his place.[5] Ironically, the failure of those expelled to receive justice in 1655 quieted Kingston for the next five years. One party in the corporation had succeeded, for now, in cutting off the other from all involvement in local governance, and in so doing, imposed a temporary end to partisan conflict.

The King's restoration in May of 1660 must have heartened those excluded from the corporation. In September, they petitioned the King, explaining that "many that were well affected to your Majesty's interest in your absence [were] for that cause discorporated." Charles referred the matter to the Earl of Manchester, Attorney General Sir Geoffrey Palmer, and Viscount Mordaunt, lord lieutenant of Surrey.[6] In December 1660, they wrote to the corporation:

---

[3] Ibid., pp. 11–42. PRO, KB29/303/88–89v, and KB29/304/85.
[4] *Eng. Rep.*, vol. 82, p. 877 (Style, 478).
[5] Ibid., pp. 878–79. *Scandal on the Corporation*, p. 17.
[6] *Scandal on the Corporation*, pp. 16 and 18–21. *CSPD 1660–61*, p. 455. Charles ordered the corporation to forgo its annual elections; he soon wrote again, permitting an election of two bailiffs, and naming those he preferred, who were chosen. Surrey RO, KB12/1/3. *Scandal on the Corporation*, pp. 35–36.

We assure you it is no pleasure to either of us to hear you reproaching, and laying open the weaknesses and former miscarriages of each other, which tend to nothing in the end, but the bespattering and defaming of one another, and the damage and prejudice of the whole town and corporation . . . [we] should be glad to see you join hand in hand as brethren and members of one body corporate for the common good of the town and preservation of the privileges thereof, which you have all sworn to maintain.

Manchester, Mordaunt, and Palmer suggested that reuniting the brethren would require forgiveness, "as his Majesty hath been pleased to be your example in forgiving."[7] Kingston's leaders tried. But new charges were soon heaped on old recriminations.[8] Twice more in response to requests from one party at Kingston, the King ordered the corporation to remove those illegally elected and to restore those removed in the 1650s. Finally, in May 1661, they made the long-awaited personnel changes.[9] Kingston's corporation was restored as one party again succeeded in excluding the other, thereby reversing the exclusions of 1653. But would restoration by purgation recreate political unity and peace?

In English towns during the 1640s and 50s, an unprecedented number of expulsions from corporations spawned and fed the beast of party. Novel political circumstances propelled new groups to the fore by extra-legal means. The success of local factions around the country rested not on their ability to work with or around opposition in local government, but on their ability to exclude it. Arguments on the Kingston writ show the inability of the mid-century political imagination to envision a peaceful partisan politics: it was a "setting up of government against government . . . done to eradicate the whole government of the town."[10] Legal and political necessity made real the metaphorical body corporate; competing parts within it were life-threatening. Ascendant groups tried to preserve the body by excising malignant opposition. As they did so, faction itself ended and the body was healed by being made one again. At least that was the ideal. In reality, exclusion begat more of the same, tit-for-tat rounds as the power of competing groups rose and fell, a cycle begun in the conflicts of the 1640s and 50s, and perpetuated in the decades following. This was the paradox of partisan politics: all the efforts of first one side and then the other to end opposition by removing it invariably made partisan angers worse. In May and June of 1660, bells rang and bonfires burned in

---

[7] *Scandal on the Corporation*, p. 37.

[8] Charges of illegal sales of corporation property and misappropriation of funds were added to earlier charges. Ibid., pp. 36–41.

[9] *CSPD 1660–61*, p. 515. *Scandal on the Corporation*, pp. 43 and 45–47. That the long desired changes were made is evident in the records of the Corporation Act's implementation: Surrey RO, KB13/1/1.

[10] *Eng. Rep.*, vol. 82, p. 877 (Style, 478).

hundreds of communities.[11] Beneath the merriment, misgivings abounded, as all knew that purges of old would be met by purging anew.

DIVISION AND DISMISSAL, 1642–58

From 1642, borough corporations were dismembered by forces within and far beyond them. Both warring sides of the mid-1640s cleaned out local governments in the areas they captured and in so doing broke apart provincial communities. Before the war, these communities, however awkwardly at times, had conducted their politics according to consensual norms.[12] In the 1640s and 50s, and in the decades to come, the *rhetoric* of consensus would endure as would the visual manifestations of the ideal of unity: for instance, corporate gown wearing and processing. But the *reality* of politics had been forever fractured by the angers generated during Civil War. This is not to say that there had been no conflict before. But then it had been handled by composition and mediation.[13] Comprehension, not exclusion, was the means for recreating unity prior to 1640. The dismissal of corporation members had been rare indeed.[14] Now the visits of competing armies, and their tax collectors and governing committees, would undo the politics of unity. The mid-1640s would give many towns in England their first serious experience of purgation. It was an experience they would not forget.

The King ordered purges in towns he captured, and was assisted by his local supporters. He began at Oxford, his capital during the war, where he ordered expulsions from the council in 1643.[15] Purges favoring urban royalists continued as his control of the countryside spread into the southwest.[16] But overall, royal purges of the corporations were minor compared

---

[11] Bonfires, beer, or bell ringing figure in every town's celebrations of the King's return, as indicated by corporation accounts. Suffolk RO (Bury St. Edmunds Branch), EE501/2/7, and David Underdown, *Fire from Heaven: Life in an English Town in the Seventeenth Century* (New Haven, 1992), p. 231.

[12] On pre-war political practices, see Kishlansky, *Parliamentary Selection*, especially chapter 1. On politics in the towns before 1640, see Patterson, "Urban Patronage."

[13] See Roger Howell, *Newcastle-upon-Tyne and the Puritan Revolution: A Study of the Civil War in North England* (Oxford, 1967), chapter 2, on oligarchy and the kinds of conflicts it generated, which did not produce purges.

[14] Patterson, "Urban Patronage," pp. 171–77, recounts the experience of a divided Yarmouth corporation in the 1620s where there was an attempt to expel foes, though this was prevented by the Earl of Dorset's mediation.

[15] Ian Roy, "The City of Oxford, 1640–1660," in R. C. Richardson, ed., *Town and Countryside in the English Revolution* (Manchester, 1992), p. 154. See also Roy, "The English Republic, 1649–1660: The View from the Town Hall," in H. G. Koenigsberger and Elisabeth Müller-Luckner, *Republiken und Republikanismus im Europa der Frühen Neuzeit* (Munich, 1988), pp. 218–22.

[16] Exeter lost some members this way: Mark Stoyle, *From Deliverance to Destruction: Rebellion and Civil War in an English City* (Exeter, 1996), p. 96. On royal purges in

to what Parliament wrought as its forces gained the upper hand. Parliament acted decisively even before the start of hostilities, imprisoning the mayors of Salisbury, St. Albans, and Hertford for reading the King's Commission of Array.[17] But by late 1644, the circumstances of war inspired bolder measures. The Northern Committee received orders "to consider of the civil government of the town of Newcastle, how a mayor and aldermen may be there settled." On the Committee's recommendations, Parliament dismissed the mayor, recorder, and five aldermen; more dismissals followed in 1645.[18] In 1646, a similar ordinance sent Chester's mayor, the recorder, seven councilmen, and half of the aldermen into the political wilderness.[19] Oxford, after the King lost control of it for good in 1646, endured a wave of Parliament-ordered purges in 1647 and 1648, reversing the changes made by Charles I.[20]

But parliamentary purges at Oxford had not simply fallen from above on to the heads of hapless councillors. They resulted from efforts orchestrated within the city for parliamentary intervention. The importance of ordinances and the arbitrary commands of parliamentary committees notwithstanding, local pressure and local information was the crucial force inducing the purges of the 1640s. More important, many purges were made from within. In the 1640s, corporation members, long inhibited by their consensual ideals from dismissing their own, overcame their reluctance, and for the first time, undertook their own dismemberment.

Internally ordered purges began immediately after the first shots were fired in 1642. At Maidstone, the "sectarian party" – as they were labeled in 1660 – convinced members of the county committee to summon the mayor, recorder, five jurats, and a dozen of the common council before the committee in October 1642. The day for their appearance was also the town's mayoral election day. With their foes thus occupied, those in the corporation who favored Parliament's interest easily controlled the election and voted to dismiss four jurats, twelve councillors, and the recorder.[21] At

the southwest, see Nicholas Marlowe, "Government and Politics in the West Country Incorporated Boroughs, 1642–1662" (Ph.D., University of Cambridge, 1985), chapter 3.
[17] *CJ*, vol. 2, p. 696.
[18] *CJ*, vol. 3, pp. 700 and 714–15. *LJ*, vol. 7, p. 395. See also Howell, *Newcastle-upon-Tyne*, pp. 169–70.
[19] Parliament tinkered with Chester personnel again in 1647 and 1651, as well as making removals at Bristol. *LJ*, vol. 7, p. 673; and vol. 9, p. 490. *CJ*, vol. 7, p. 12. C. H. Firth and R. S. Rait, eds., *Acts and Ordinances of the Interregnum, 1642–1660*, 3 vols. (London, 1911), vol. I, pp. 801–02 and 876–79. A. M. Johnson, "Politics in Chester during the Civil Wars and the Interregnum, 1640–1662," in Peter Clark and Paul Slack, eds., *Crisis and Order in English Towns, 1500–1700: Essays in Urban History* (London, 1972), pp. 215–22.
[20] Roy, "Oxford," in Richardson, *Town and Countryside*, p. 156.
[21] BL, Add. 37,157, f. 65. The recorder was Thomas Twisden, who became a justice of King's Bench in 1660.

Norwich, where the freemen had an unusual power to dismiss aldermen, the aldermen's bench was purged by more popular means.[22] At Norwich and elsewhere, long-standing religious differences provide a guide to the lines drawn across corporate bodies. Other old cleavages were clear too. At Bristol, corporate purges in 1645 appear to have been based on one's view of the Merchant Venturers' monopoly control of commerce: those connected with this traditional elite were largely identified with the King's cause and were now dismissed.[23] But while pre-war animosities help explain the differences dividing the corporations, it remains significant that it was only now, in the midst of war, that such differences could lead to a new kind of political behavior: mass dismissals. Religious difference, social and economic conflicts of long-standing: these played their part. But only the fury of war and the recriminations it generated could break what David Scott, studying wartime York, has called the "traditional political consensus" in pre-war city government.[24]

With the first Civil War over, Parliament began a more ambitious program of corporate purgation. In September 1647, letters were sent to all towns ordering that no one who had taken arms against Parliament could hold corporate office and requiring the election of new mayors where "delinquents" had been chosen. Then on October 4, Lords and Commons confirmed this command in a general ordinance barring all delinquents from voting or office holding.[25] More now lost office. At Bath, this included six councillors and the recorder, Serjeant Robert Hyde, who was replaced by William Prynne.[26] Despite these broad measures adjusting corporate membership, Parliament continued to pass acts reordering membership in specific towns, especially after Charles I's execution, but such commands met with only mixed success. An ordinance of March 1648 barring anyone of suspect loyalty from office at Norwich proved typically unequal to the task. Corporation elections there a few days later returned a number of conservative Presbyterians and others sympathetic to the royal cause. This led to a petition to Parliament from Norwich's anti-royalists. A riot broke out and scores died when Parliament sent a messenger to arrest the conservative mayor, John Utting. Only purges enacted by the corporation

22 John T. Evans, *Seventeenth-Century Norwich: Politics, Religion, and Government, 1620–1690* (Oxford, 1979), pp. 54 and 124–27.
23 David Harris Sacks, "Bristol's 'Wars of Religion'," in Richardson, ed., *Town and Countryside*, pp. 118–19.
24 David Scott, "Politics and Government in York, 1640–1662," in Richardson, *Town and Countryside*, p. 53.
25 The ordinance was to remain in effect for five years. It was then renewed until September of 1655. *CJ*, vol. 5, pp. 292, 317, 320, and 326. Firth and Rait, *Acts and Ordinances*, vol. I, pp. 1023–25, and vol. II, pp. 620–21.
26 Bath City RO, Council Book 1, December 13, 1647.

itself in early 1649 settled city government in the hands of those supporting the Commonwealth.[27] Another ordinance remodelled the corporation at Winchester. And Hull required not one, but three acts adjusting corporate membership in 1650 and 1651.[28] Measures like these, correcting lapses in general policy in specific cases, suggest how the corporations, even those with many predisposed to support the new order, were unhappy with meddling from without.

Even with all these dismissals, town leaders' loyalty remained in doubt. Parliament passed a succession of acts requiring tests of allegiance: oaths were required of all freemen (February 1649) and then of corporation officers upon entry to office (September 1649, just before annual elections in most towns). Most important was the Act for Subscribing the Engagement, to be signed by all holding any public trust (January 1650).[29] The Engagement in particular forced many corporators who opposed the new regime to quit their places. Nonetheless, the mayor elected at Chester in 1651 had to be ejected by parliamentary command for refusing the Engagement, suggesting how some remained in office despite these comprehensive measures.[30] In 1655, one week before a second ordinance barring delinquents from office was set to expire, Cromwell proclaimed its continuation indefinitely, and defined more extensively than ever the faults disabling one from office or from voting. Now added to the list of negatives – having been sequestered, imprisoned for delinquency, or in any way having aided the King – was the requirement that those who might vote or serve in office "shall be such as are of pious and good conversation."[31] At no time before had the qualifications for holding corporate office been so narrowly defined.

The Interregnum regimes thus set not only the precedent for the removal and appointment of town officers by extra-corporate authority, they also set the precedent for tests – oaths, subscriptions, and sufficient piety – for

---

[27] Evans, *Norwich*, pp. 172–86. Parliament passed another act "for preventing the election of ill-affected persons" at Norwich in March 1649 (*CJ*, vol. 6, pp. 153 and 158), though by then, the corporation had purged itself.

[28] *CJ*, vol. 6, pp. 464, 472, and 530–31. The ordinance for Winchester, passed September 13, 1649, ordered the mayor, two aldermen, and seven benchers removed. Orders for the following meetings there were torn from the corporation's Book of Ordinances: Hampshire RO, W/B1/5, f. 19. Those favored at this time lost their offices later in the 1650s.

[29] Firth and Rait, *Acts and Ordinances*, vol. II, pp. 2, 241, and 325–29.

[30] *CJ*, vol. 6, p. 619, and *CJ*, vol. 7, p. 1. For more on obstruction of the Engagement, see David Underdown, *Pride's Purge: Politics in the Puritan Revolution* (London, 1971), pp. 304–05.

[31] The text of this proclamation is in J. H. Round, "Colchester during the Commonwealth," *EHR*, 15 (1900), p. 655. See also S. R. Gardiner, *History of the Commonwealth and Protectorate, 1649–1656*, 4 vols. (London, 1903), vol. IV, pp. 49–50. Gardiner discusses other cases of magistrates' removal: ibid., pp. 50–54. On the major generals' influence, see Thomas Birch, *A Collection of the State Papers of John Thurloe*, 7 vols. (London, 1742), vol. IV, pp. 197, 216–17, 224, 241, 273, 330, and 396.

determining fitness for office. The inversion of these tests by new tests after the Restoration would be the enduring legacy of such novel measures imposed from above and would fire much of the partisan effort in the decades after 1660. Aware of the novelty of what they did, the Commons declared that the dismissals they ordered should not serve as precedents nor do any "prejudice to the charter" of the towns concerned.[32] This was both an admission and a protestation: an admission of the extra-legal nature of the proceedings, and a protestation of innocence of any designs on the sanctity of corporate liberties, a protestation that extraordinary times legitimated extraordinary measures. But no borough charter had ever included provisions for the removal of corporation members by any extra-corporate authority: Parliament, court, or King. Dismissals by parliamentary order were nothing if not prejudicial to chartered privileges, and served as a precedent that would return again and again to haunt the corporations in the decades after 1660.

Recomposition of corporate councils in the 1640s and 50s occurred by less spectacular means too, as many simply stopped showing up at assembly meetings, or even resigned their places, disgusted by the turn of events. Fluctuations in chamber attendance at Exeter reveals the split of the corporation into two camps. First, while under parliamentarian control, a royalist group abandoned the council meetings. They then reappeared and their foes stepped aside when the King captured the city. The parliamentarian portion of the corporation returned in triumph when parliamentary soldiers seized Exeter for good in April 1646. They then purged the council, thus reversing the purge made by the King.[33] At tiny Berkhamsted, in Hertfordshire, many corporators likewise stopped attending meetings, opening the way for their foes to dismiss them for neglect and replace them with men amenable to the ascendant political interest.[34] Such absences and resignations only increased during the 1650s. Seventeen councilmen and five aldermen quit at Worcester in the mid-1650s. This mass withdrawal from the chamber created a majority for those willing to work with the Cromwellian regime and permitted them to remove those holding out against them, as four more councilmen found in 1656 when they were expelled "in respect of their disaffection . . . unto the present government."[35]

---

[32] See orders remodeling Hull and Chester: *CJ*, vol. 6, pp. 464, 472, 530–31, and 619.

[33] Mark Stoyle charts partisan loyalties by examining attendance patterns: *From Deliverance to Destruction*, pp. 62–63, 87–90, 99–101, and 140, and tables on pp. 224–26. David Scott has found a similar voluntary withdrawal at York: "York, 1640–1662," in Richardson, *Town and Countryside*, pp. 50 and 54.

[34] Hertfordshire RO, D/EX/652/22, pp. 29, 30, 34, 38, 41, and 50.

[35] Hereford and Worcester RO (St. Helen's), Shelf A.14 (chamber order book, 1650–1676), ff. 8v–9, 9v, 10, 15v, 16, 20, 22, and 24v. See the effect of purges and natural attrition at Norwich: Evans, *Norwich*, pp. 184–85.

Resignation, withdrawal, removal: all created voids that could then be filled by men of a different cast of mind, committed to the interests pursued by the various regimes of the 1650s. Newcomers to ancient corporations now rose through the traditional *cursus honorum* of office holding with unprecedented speed. But this by no means entailed any significant change in the social composition of England's urban leadership, nor does it appear that those promoted were political radicals, leaning toward republican forms of government that subverted a world predicated on hierarchy and status. As John Evans has noted, new magistrates at Norwich, like those in London in the 1650s, "were advanced Puritans but not social or political radicals."[36] Nonetheless, they created a world that played a different kind of politics, one that permitted, or even encouraged, the exclusion from government of some of those with the proper social credentials because their political loyalties or religious sympathies made them suspect. It was a world that would be dominated by the paradox of partisan politics.

Colchester provides an especially vivid example of how partisan angers generated purges and counter-purges. Essex's most prominent town had endured an ugly siege in the summer of 1648. Immediately afterward, those in the corporation that looked favorably on the army's political ascendancy took the opportunity to purge thirteen from their ranks. But this purge, like most, did not remove all the "malignants." There remained a large group that objected to what had happened and now opposed those who had promoted the purge. Partisan sides evolved in the years following, each with clear leadership, each looking back to allegiances formed in the wake of the first purge to determine their current political allegiances and behavior. By 1654, those who had opposed the purge had gained enough strength to elect their leader, Thomas Reynolds, as mayor. Reynolds's first act as mayor was to summon a meeting during which he convinced the corporation to expel three men, including Henry Barrington, the man who had led the purge of 1648. Purge had been met with counter-purge. Petitions to the Lord Protector condemning and justifying this new purge soon followed from the opposing sides, each accusing the other of "tumultuous proceedings" and "malignant design." More disputed elections and appeals to the Protector followed until Cromwell appointed Deputy Major General Hezekiah Haynes to handle the matter. Haynes obliged by vetting the list of those eligible to vote in corporate elections. But he also recommended the grant of a new charter to bolster the "honest men" there. Thus a new charter followed in 1656, effecting yet another

---

[36] Evans, *Norwich*, p. 192. For more on newcomers and rapid promotion, and on the stable social composition of urban leadership after the purges, see Underdown, *Pride's Purge*, pp. 318–20; Scott, "York, 1640–1662," pp. 47 and 55; Evans, *Norwich*, pp. 189–93; and Roy, "View from the Town Hall," pp. 223–27.

purge in favor of Barrington's supporters, who had proved themselves loyal to Cromwell's regime.[37] Internal purges had begotten more purges. At Colchester, the paradox of partisan politics compelled each side to seek help from central government to win total victory by one more purge of their foes.

Despite the concern demonstrated by successive Interregnum regimes to control corporation membership in a comprehensive way, few suggested that this should be done by a nationwide policy of charter remodelings. There are signs though that as early as 1650, a parliamentary committee for corporations was at work. Two years later, Parliament ordered the committee to "take into consideration how corporations may be settled, as may be suitable to, and agreeable with, the government of a common-wealth, and how their respective charters may be altered and renewed, to be held from and under the authority of this Commonwealth."[38] Nothing came of their efforts. Though many towns later brought their charters to Cromwell's government for renewal, little advantage was taken on such occasions to make sweeping changes in the terms of corporate governance. Indeed, corporations came seeking charters, or, more precisely, parts of corporations did. As at Colchester, the grant of new charters was driven by local needs and requests; urban partisans of the 1650s sought new charters to consolidate their hold on local power and to confirm the exclusion of their foes. Thus both Reading and High Wycombe corporations petitioned for new charters after those sympathetic to the Protectorate had won local control by expelling their opponents. Norwich too desired a charter and nearly succeeded until Oliver's death brought the effort to a halt; this was certainly not a central government effort to impose on a reluctant corpora-tion.[39] At no time did Cromwell's regime encourage boroughs to surrender their charters in order to renew them on terms central government might favor.[40] Various major generals proposed new charters for certain towns late in 1655. But one added that "the consideration of charters [should] be

---

[37] Round, "Colchester," pp. 641–64. Underdown, *Pride's Purge*, pp. 324–25. VCH Essex, vol. IX, pp. 115–16. James R. Davis, "Colchester, 1600–1662: Politics, Religion and Officeholding in an English Provincial Town" (Ph.D., Brandeis University, 1980), chapter 4.

[38] *CJ*, vol. 6, pp. 351 and 384; vol. 7, p. 178. B. L. K. Henderson, "The Commonwealth Charters," *TRHS*, 3rd ser., 6 (1912), p. 129. Little else survives about the committee.

[39] Reading began work for a new charter in April 1656, though it is not clear they received one: Berkshire RO, R/AC1/1/6, f. 38, and HMC, Report 11, appendix 7, pp. 192–93. Henderson examined Reading and emphasized central government pressure, but the impetus apparently came from the corporation. The same was true at High Wycombe and Colchester. Removals from the corporation in High Wycombe occurred before a new charter, not as a result of its being granted: L. J. Ashford, *The History of the Borough of High Wycombe from its Origins to 1880* (London, 1960), pp. 138–40; R. W. Greaves, ed., *The First Ledger Book of High Wycombe*, Buckinghamshire Record Society, vol. 11 (1947), pp. xiii–xiv. Evans, *Norwich*, pp. 214–16.

[40] Pace Henderson, "Commonwealth Charters," p. 129.

timorously taken up."[41] Timorous they were. Few corporations received new charters; those that did received them as a result of local rather than central government initiative.

Though the government showed little interest in promoting new charters, a process developed by which old charters were reviewed and proposed new ones scrutinized. By May of 1656, the Council of State had formed a committee "on renewing charters" to consider petitions from the towns. A "council-at-law," composed of lawyers interested in corporations – including William Sheppard, author of the first extensive work in English on the law of corporations – served as an advisory panel. As Sheppard wrote a few years later, "a corporation is a body politic, authorized by the Lord Protector's charter . . . There must be a good and lawful authority and warrant for the erecting of it."[42] At no time during the Interregnum was there any suggestion – from townsmen, charter committee members, or from others in Cromwell's government – that corporate rights resulted from voluntary association. Even after Civil War, corporations petitioned for new charters on the unquestioned assumption that their privileges derived from the sovereign authority once embodied in the King, and now in the Lord Protector. The Council of State and its committees answered such petitions aware that it alone determined the nature of chartered authority. Such authority was now in disarray and many towns sought clarification of their privileges. Marlborough needed a new charter not simply for clarity's sake, but to replace one seized by royalist forces.[43] Corporate life without a charter wracked the nerves of borough officers who had barely survived more than a decade of strife and felt all the more vulnerable with no documentation of their privileges.

Colchester presents one of the few cases in which the body politic underwent major surgery by the charter committee. Colchester's council of assistants was entirely abolished by their new charter and the number of remaining aldermen and councillors reduced from forty-two to thirty-four; fifteen were expelled.[44] Corporation size was also reduced at Marlborough and Salisbury; at High Wycombe, it was increased.[45] Sudbury's new charter required parliamentary approval of mayors and bailiffs after each

[41] Birch, *State Papers of John Thurloe*, vol. IV, p. 216.
[42] *CSPD 1655–56*, pp. 330 and 370. *CSPD 1656–57*, p. 224. Matthews, *William Sheppard*, pp. 49–58. Sheppard, *Of Corporations*, pp. 4 and 6.
[43] *CSPD 1656–57*, pp. 208 and 241.
[44] Round, "Colchester," p. 657. Gardiner gives a different account: *History of the Commonwealth*, vol. IV, pp. 55–76.
[45] James Waylen, *A History, Military and Municipal, of the Town of Marlborough* (London, 1854), p. 275. Hubert Hall, ed., "The Salisbury Commonwealth Charter," *Camden Miscellany*, 11 (Camden Society, 3rd series, vol. 13, 1907), pp. 163–64. "Cromwell's Charter, High Wycombe," *Records of Buckinghamshire*, 7 (1897), p. 511.

election.[46] Such examples notwithstanding, there was no grand design to remodel the nation's borough constitutions.[47] The Council of State and its charter committees reacted to situations as they came before them, and then only with deliberation. Throughout the 1650s, as during the Civil War, parliamentary and Protectoral regimes preferred to keep the lid on potential borough disorders by dismissing and appointing corporate personnel directly, not by imposing new charters. Little advantage could be gained by making the dangerous political mix even more volatile by altering the corporations' legal formulation.

In corporate dismemberments sanctioned from above and wrought from within during the years of war and those following, we can see the creation of the mutual hatred and envy that would produce retribution in the years ahead. The whole had been broken as parts within it were identified as "usurpers" or "malignants" and as such identities were used as the basis for determining who belonged in the local polity and who did not. We can also see how the rise of partisan politics inspired corporate combatants to appeal more than ever to various organs of national government for support, thus making it more involved in provincial government. But the Lord Protector, his council, and his other representatives were not the only agents of central government that competing locals could use in their quarrels.

MANDAMUS

Many lost office in the 1640s and 50s, some even gave it up voluntarily, but not everyone went away quietly. Even in these turbulent years, there remained one authority looked to for some measure of impartiality in determining corporate disputes and correcting unprecedented dismissals from office: the Upper Bench, once known as the court of King's Bench. It was to the Upper Bench that those who lost their places at Kingston upon Thames turned, asking for writs of mandamus to compel their return to office. And they were not alone.

A person aggrieved by an official act – usually a dismissal from office – went to King's Bench requesting a writ of mandamus.[48] The writ first issued in an "alternative" form: ordering that the action complained of be

---

[46] Suffolk RO (Bury St. Edmunds Branch), EE501/2/8, pp. 1 and 13–14.
[47] There is no foundation for Ronald Hutton's claim that by 1660, "most towns were governed under charters conferred by Interregnum regimes": *The Restoration: A Political and Religious History of England and Wales, 1658–1667* (Oxford, 1985), p. 159.
[48] The court acted by virtue of the King's power to correct any wrong, a power long devolved upon the courts. Many still referred to any royal order as a "mandamus." But this general usage of "mandamus" should not be confused with the writ of the same name.

reversed or that the recipient of the writ "show cause" why it should not be. Actually, the alternative writ typically issued three times: the original mandamus, an "alias" mandamus requiring a return on pain of a £40 fine for failure to do so, and a "pluries" mandamus, returnable on pain of an £80 fine. It was often only after the last of these that the writ's recipient made a return either announcing that the deed had been performed as ordered, or explaining why it had not been done. Once filed, the court was obliged to accept the truth of the return, unless the complainant then brought a separate action on the case for a false return to challenge it. If the return were found false, then a "peremptory" mandamus would issue, requiring restoration of the plaintiff with no option for further returns or arguments from the recipient. Failure to comply at this stage would put one in contempt of court, which could lead to imprisonment.[49]

The writ of mandamus was still something of a novelty, a legal remedy that had seen little use by the time the Civil War broke out. It had first appeared in 1606, but it only gained prominence after James Bagge's case of 1615.[50] Sir Edward Coke may not have invented the writ by himself, but in his report on Bagge's case, he provided a broad justification of the new authority he and the other justices of King's Bench accorded themselves when they ordered Bagge's restoration to the corporation at Plymouth, from which he been dismissed for ugly language and other misbehavior. Coke declared the court's power to use mandamus "not only to correct errors in judicial proceedings, but other errors and misdemeanors extra-judicial, tending to the breach of peace, or oppression of the subjects, or the raising of faction, controversy, debate, or to any manner of misgovern-ment."[51] In other words, Coke imagined mandamus as a catch-all device for correcting any perceived wrong that pre-existing legal remedies did not cover. He justified this on two grounds. First, King's Bench was in theory the King dispensing justice, and there could be no limit to such an authority; if there were no device for correcting a given wrong, the King's court could invent one. Second, a corporate office was also a freehold, a bit of property; dismissal was thus a disseising, and if done illegally, there was no other remedy available to right the wrong. Because Bagge had not been properly summoned and heard in response to the charges against him, he

---

[49] Procedure on mandamus is derived from examining cases in *Eng. Rep.*; from a study of King's Bench rule books, PRO, KB21; from Edith G. Henderson, *Foundations of English Administrative Law: Certiorari and Mandamus in the Seventeenth Century* (Cambridge, Mass., 1963), pp. 62–65; and Blackstone, *Commentaries*, vol. III, pp. 110–11.

[50] Henderson, *English Administrative Law*, pp. 46–50. For a discussion of the writ's development, see chapters 2 and 4.

[51] For Coke's report on Bagge's case, see *Eng. Rep.*, vol. 77, pp. 1271–81 (11 Co. rep. 93b); the quotation is at pp. 1277–78 (98a).

had been illegally deprived of his office and his property. Thus we can see why in the first half of the seventeenth century, the writ of mandamus was usually called a writ of restitution: a writ by which one had a property restored.[52] "Restitution" would be supplanted by "mandamus" in the coming decades, especially after 1660, as new uses were found for it in addition to restoration to office, and as lawyers' arguments, even in cases of restoration, depended less on ideas of private property and more on notions of public responsibilities.

Bagge's case remained the touchstone as mandamus began its fitful development. Prior to the Civil Wars, there were relatively few occasions for contributing to this development. Given the political norms of the day, dismissal from office was rare indeed; when it happened, everyone involved preferred to mediate rather than litigate their differences. Recourse to the courts was always a last resort. Even in the few cases when a writ was sought before 1640, matters rarely went as far as a return from the corporation and a court contest on its merit. Thus Richard Sharman lost his place in Worcester's corporation in 1618 for "opprobrious words" and brought his writ of restitution. This in turn induced the corporation to seek a settlement with him that consisted of a public apology from Sharman in return for his restoration. Both sides then dropped their legal actions.[53] As corporations continued to settle differences on their own or with the help of noble mediators, the court had little role to play and few occasions to declare when and how the device might be used.[54]

But the struggles in the towns during the 1640s and 50s made wreckage of such practices as the corporations experienced dismissals on a previously unimagined scale. Though one dismissed corporate officer informed his friends as he sought a writ of restitution in 1657, "there [has] been not there business of this nature before any judges in Westminster these twenty years," he was quite wrong. Given the number of comings and goings from borough corporations in the 1640s and 50s, the bench suddenly had a number of opportunities to hear arguments for the writ. While charting developments is complicated by the fact that the single most important source for the study of the Upper Bench – its rule and order books – are missing for most of the Interregnum, court records that do survive tell us

---

[52] Thus in Warren's case of 1619, the denial of his writ turned on property arguments: *Eng. Rep.*, vol. 79, p. 463 (Cro. Jac. 540), and Henderson, *English Administrative Law*, p. 78.

[53] A similar case occurred in 1636. Hereford and Worcester RO (St. Helen's), Shelf A.14/1, Book II, ff. 61v, 63v, 64, 91, 94v, 99, and 99v. My thanks to Catherine Patterson for these references.

[54] On noble patrons settling corporation disputes in the early seventeenth century, see Patterson, "Urban Patronage," chapter 3, and Catherine Patterson, "Leicester and Lord Huntingdon: Urban Patronage in Early Modern England," *Midland History*, 16 (1991), pp. 45–62.

plenty, especially when complemented by published case reports and records available in town archives.[55]

Corporate dismissals of the 1640s and 50s fell both on those who were suspected of not supporting the ascendant regime, as well as on those who had been promoted by those regimes though they were considered unworthy by neighbors who thus removed them. Thus at Winchester, a parliamentary ordinance of September 1649 had made John Woodman an alderman. But he apparently made the corporation uncomfortable. When Woodman was found to have made unflattering comparisons between the mayor and a well-known local fool in early 1651, he was dismissed. Woodman's name actually appeared on corporation lists on a few occasions in the following years, but in September of 1656, the corporation repeated its original dismissal order.[56] Woodman looked outside for help, and quickly brought back court orders for his restoration. These accomplished his aim.[57] The process was not quick, and as other litigants learned, it had probably not been easy, but it worked.

Aldermen, burgesses, and town clerks all won restoration by mandamus in the 1650s.[58] And litigant pressure helped create new uses for mandamus too. In the 1650s came the first successful efforts by litigants to use mandamus not only to regain office, but to require admission to office after an election. Though in 1651, Chief Justice Henry Rolle had denied a request for a mandamus to order the swearing of Bossiney's new mayor, saying that there was no precedent for such a thing, he granted a similar request from Colchester the next year.[59] By the time of the Kingston case of 1654–55, the court was ready to grant mandamus to command new officers' admission without hesitation.[60] Officers of merchant companies and fellows expelled from All Souls had the writ as well, though after 1660, there would be questions raised about the court's authority in such cases.[61] Thus business for the writ rose throughout the decade as the court broadened its purview in response to pressure from litigants able to

---

[55] Controlment rolls survive (PRO, KB29); they contain full entries of writs (though it is unclear whether all were recorded here), as well as the returns to them.

[56] *CJ*, vol. 6, p. 294, and Hampshire RO, W/B1/5, ff. 19, 20, 31v, 94v–95, and 96–97v.

[57] PRO, KB29/305/100. He reappeared on corporate lists the following September: Hampshire RO, W/B1/5, f. 118.

[58] For instance at Hereford, Sudbury, and Yarmouth: PRO, KB29/303/93 and 122; KB29/304/80.

[59] *Eng. Rep.*, vol. 82, pp. 726 and 773 (Style 299 and 355). There was at least one pre-war precedent of an unsuccessful use of the writ for this purpose: Henderson, *English Administrative Law*, pp. 80–81.

[60] *Eng. Rep.*, vol. 82, pp. 876–79 (Style 477). A similar writ went to Monmouth to swear the mayor in 1657: PRO, KB29/306/93.

[61] PRO, KB29/304/13 and KB29/307/22v, 72, and 107v.

imagine and articulate arguments for such new uses.[62] Litigant demand would push the court in its further development after 1660 too.

Colchester corporation was riven by partisan divisions between a group led by Henry Barrington, the leading local Cromwellian and the mayor in 1648–49, and another led by Thomas Reynolds. Barrington was followed in office by his partisans for the next three years, but this provoked a reaction against them in 1652. In 1654, Reynolds gained the mayor's chair and immediately set about dismembering his foes. At his first meeting presiding, he convinced the corporation to expel Barrington, his son Abraham, and Recorder Arthur Bernardiston. They went to court.[63] Serjeant Thomas Twisden – who would be a justice of King's Bench after 1660 – and Serjeant John Maynard – who would become one of the leading barristers in corporation cases for the next thirty-five years – argued the corporation's case explaining the reasons for Bernardiston's dismissal. But they failed to prevail in the face of arguments that the office "is a freehold" and that he had not been duly summoned to answer the charges against him. So the Bench ordered Bernardiston restored to his place in Trinity term, 1655.[64]

Reading corporation removed their steward, Daniel Blagrave, in the following spring, and replaced him with Richard Bulstrode. Two months later, Blagrave's son appeared at an assembly bearing a mandamus for his father's restoration. Like Colchester, Reading corporation turned to Serjeant Maynard to make their arguments against Blagrave's restoration before the Upper Bench. But the judges found the corporation's return to the writ insufficient, and made a final order for Blagrave's reappointment.[65] Bulstrode thought he saw the hole in the arguments they had made: that they had failed to explain in their return that the corporation possessed the power of removal by charter. He and Serjeant Maynard now appreciated that one of the hallmarks of all proceedings on mandamus was the great precision required in any return attempting to justify non-compliance with the writ. The court was wary, and would remain wary in the coming decades, about any failure to explain in great detail not only what the person expelled had done wrong, but also how it was that the corporation possessed the authority to expel him for such a wrong. The corporation obeyed the peremptory writ and restored Blagrave; but confident now that

---

[62] *Eng. Rep.*, vol. 82, pp. 773, 850–51, and 1225 (Style 355 and 446, and 2 Sid. 6).

[63] Round, "Colchester," pp. 645–49. PRO, KB29/303/87.

[64] *Eng. Rep.*, vol. 82, pp. 850–51 and 855–56 (Style 446 and 452). The Lord Protector and his council heard the matter too and reached the same conclusion. What if any connection there was between the proceedings before court and council is unclear. It appears Henry Barrington won restoration too, though the fate of Abraham Barrington is unclear: Round, "Colchester," pp. 649–52.

[65] Berkshire RO, R/AC1/1/6, ff. 34v, 36v, and 39; R/AC1/1/7, f. 41v. PRO, KB29/305/27.

they knew how to win the next round, they just as quickly dismissed him again. Again Blagrave brought his writ, again the corporation made its return – though more carefully worded this time – and again the bench heard their arguments. Now the corporation prevailed, though Blagrave's counsel contended that the corporation had acted from a "poisonous and malicious will" in dismissing him a second time. Thomas Twisden and other counsel arguing on the corporation's behalf convinced the justices that by their charter, the office was at the corporation's pleasure to bestow – and to revoke.[66] As we shall see, a corporation's pleasure was a fickle thing. The new steward, Richard Bulstrode, would lose his office in just as peremptory a manner as Blagrave did when the wheel of partisan fortune turned again in 1659.

The mandamus cases of the 1650s were important for a number of reasons. In the first place, there were enough of them over a short period to give the court the opportunity to clarify the ways in which the writ might be used. Though authorized by a "usurping power," the judges sitting on the Upper Bench were legal conservatives, careful to interpret the cases brought before them in terms of the legacies left them from before 1640. Thus they delivered opinions that would remain useful guides for decades after the King returned.[67] The arguments and judgments in Bernardiston's and Blagrave's cases would be among those most frequently cited by lawyers well into the eighteenth century. Second, a number of key players on the bench and before the bar after the Restoration were the same lawyers who figured most prominently in court during the 1650s. Among these was Thomas Twisden, whose pronouncements as a justice of King's Bench after 1660 would be among the greatest influences shaping the subsequent development of mandamus. In addition to his general skill in the law and the experience that came with a successful practice in the 1650s, his experience as recorder of Maidstone made him well acquainted with corporate legal issues and thus an obvious choice as counsel for other corporate litigants. Likewise, Serjeant John Maynard had served as counsel to Exeter corporation since 1638 and as recorder of Plymouth and Totnes. As we have seen, he was also called upon to represent other corporations in mandamus matters. He would be one of the most prominent of barristers throughout his long life (he died in 1690) and active throughout in arguing corporation cases. The 1650s provided both bench and bar with important

---

[66] *Eng. Rep.*, vol. 82, pp. 1225, 1250–51, and 1264 (2 Sid. 6, 49, and 73). Berkshire RO, R/ AC1/1/7, ff. 85 and 88; R/AC/1/1/8, f. 93v; and HMC LI 65.

[67] Concerning continuity in legal thinking in the Interregnum, see Alan Cromartie, *Sir Matthew Hale, 1609–1676: Law, Religion and Natural Philosophy* (Cambridge, 1995), chapters 4–8, especially p. 65.

experience in using mandamus, experience that would be put to extensive use after 1660.

Divisions, dismissals, and the partisan contentions of the 1650s encouraged recourse to the courts at Westminster to a degree that was unprecedented in the generations before. The writ of mandamus developed as a result, and in so doing, provided the basis for the development not only of partisan politics, but of stable politics too. Despite the expense of time and money, extensive use of the writ points to its effectiveness for those who felt they had just cause for return to office. Using a writ that in the first half of the century had more foundation in Justice Coke's imagination than in precedent, the court, through its decisions of the 1650s, forged an effective instrument for unmaking the dismissals wrought in the heat of partisan conflict. By the time of Charles II's return, King's Bench had become a powerful arbiter of corporation disputes and the means by which a developing partisan politics would be prevented from destroying the governing bodies in which it obtained.

RESTORING THE BOROUGHS, RESTORING THE KING, 1658–60

Extensive removals and appointments of corporation personnel since 1642 and new charters granted in the 1650s meant that most towns faced legal and political chaos by the time Oliver Cromwell died and was succeeded by his son Richard in September of 1658. Cromwell's death touched off the start of efforts for a restoration of corporation members and constitutions, a process that began in earnest long before it became clear the King would return, a process that would provide the local foundations on which Charles's own restoration would be laid. The effort to throw the "malignant" out of doors in the 1640s and 50s was now reversed as some corporations, on their own initiative, started readmitting those dismissed previously.[68] Others used mandamus to get back into old offices.[69]

After two former aldermen were restored at Reading by such means in 1659, the aldermen there proceeded to expel eight aldermen and six assistants for their obstreperous behavior at a meeting the previous December and their subsequent illegal seizure of the corporation's documents and mace. New members were elected to replace them in the weeks ahead; when they finished, over one half of the corporation's places

---

[68] On locally initiated corporate restorations from late 1658 onward, see W. A. H. Schilling, "The Central Government and the Municipal Corporations in England, 1642–1663," (Ph.D., Vanderbilt University, 1970), chapter 4.

[69] See for instance a mandamus for an alderman at Stratford: PRO, KB29/307/166v, and Shakespeare Birthplace Trust, BRU2/4, p. 23. Mandamus was also used to compel the swearing of new bailiffs elected amid conflict generated in the rapidly changing political climate, as at Buckingham and Tewkesbury: PRO, KB29/307/168, and KB29/308/27.

had changed hands. Reading also removed Richard Bulstrode as their steward and replaced him with none other than his nemesis Daniel Blagrave. Blagrave would soon bolt the country: having signed Charles I's death warrant, it seemed prudent to live out his days in Aachen rather than Berkshire.[70] Thus as restorations of a few old members occurred, the political balance in many corporations began to shift, making way for still more changes.

The Act of Indemnity and Free Pardon, passed by the revived Rump Parliament in July 1659, hastened this process of local change. As an important side-effect to the general pardon granted to all who served the Protectorate, the act prompted the restoration of more corporate officers. It acquitted "all and every person and persons, bodies, politic and corporate" who, between April 1653 and June 1659, had acted by virtue of any authority derived from any "assembly called or reputed a Parliament . . . or from any person or persons titled, reputed, or taken to be Lord Protector." The conflation here of bodies sole and aggregate was crucial, as it meant that not only warrants to single persons, but those to collective legal persons – corporations – were of no effect. The act explicitly did not "confirm the grant of any office or place of trust given or granted, or pretended to be given or granted, by patent, charter, or otherwise." All such offices were "in the disposal of this Parliament."[71] Corporate offices were now up for grabs, but it was the corporations, not Parliament, that undertook the restorations now allowed by statute.

Corporations rechartered since 1653 reverted to their former constitutions. Parliament also passed separate acts granting specific towns the authority to operate under their pre-1653 charters, to turn out members elected since then, and to readmit those dismissed. On July 18, Parliament directed that Colchester govern under its former charter; likewise, Salisbury was ordered two weeks later to bring their Cromwellian grant to the House "to be cancelled." Former members of both corporations quickly resumed their places in accordance with their ancient charters. The following January, Barrington and his partisans were once again dismembered from Colchester's corporation.[72]

But like all regimes since 1642, the restored Rump Parliament also indulged the impulse to purge. In September, the Commons sent a bill for

---

[70] PRO, KB29/307/167 and Berkshire RO, R/AC1/1/9, ff. 1–5v. Those dismissed from the corporation used mandamus to get their places back; they also tried mediation, to no avail: PRO, KB29/308/28–31, and Berkshire RO, R/AC1/1/9 and 10, passim.

[71] Firth and Rait, *Acts and Ordinances*, vol. II, pp. 1299–1304. Hutton, *The Restoration*, p. 50.

[72] *CJ*, vol. 7, p. 745; Round, "Colchester," pp. 659–60; HMC, *Various Collections*, vol. IV, p. 243.

the better government of Newcastle upon Tyne to a committee empowered "to offer to this House fit qualifications of persons to govern the several corporations within this Commonwealth." Parliament also "dissolved and disincorporated" Chester corporation and created a committee to consider how best to settle its government. This act was reversed by the following February. With their charter restored, Chester's governors reconvened their assemblies, and a few weeks before the King's return, began remaking the corporate body. While none were yet restored to positions lost long ago, five were removed and two resigned in recognition of the rapidly changing political situation.[73]

Removals, resignations, and reappointments occurred on local initiative throughout 1659 and 1660. On the day Charles landed at Dover, High Wycombe's leaders entered the following order in their ledger book: "Whereas for the composing of the present animosities and differences occasioned between several members . . . it hath been proposed unto us the said mayor, aldermen, bailiffs, and burgesses, that we should surrender and resign our said several offices . . . [and we] do resign, surrender and release . . . our offices or places." The mayor, six aldermen, the two bailiffs, and twenty-seven of the thirty-one burgesses signed the order for their own dismissal. Five days later, with little or no corporation left to do the job, a new mayor was elected. Of the four signing the election order, one had just resigned and would not be re-elected for another month. Despite the irregularity of a non-existent corporation electing a mayor and non-members signing orders, there appear to have been few qualms about the corporation's quitting all at once and then reconstituting itself.[74] Aware of the need to compose "present animosities," other corporations followed High Wycombe's example with voluntary resignations and restorations. In April 1660, in Norwich's annual elections, freemen elected sixteen fresh faces to the council. In June, the recorder was forced out in order to restore his predecessor. Two weeks after Charles's restoration, Abingdon corporation removed those "unduly elected" since 1648, and chose a host of replacements.[75] In July, twenty-three gave up their places at Yarmouth; most of their replacements were men dismissed in the preceding decades. At Sudbury, the corporation restored the mayor and others ousted by their Cromwellian charter of 1658, then began efforts to gain a new charter

[73] *CJ*, vol. 7, pp. 780 and 854. CCRO, AB/2, ff. 127, 128v, 130, and 130v. Johnson, "Politics in Chester," in Clark and Slack, *Crisis and Order*, especially pp. 227–29.

[74] Greaves, *High Wycombe Ledger*, pp. 162–70.

[75] All but one of Norwich's Commonwealth aldermen held out for now. Evans, *Norwich*, pp. 226–29. Berkshire RO, T/F41, ff. 186v–90. Three of those signing the first removal order at Abingdon were also removed by the corporation in September 1661.

from the returned King. And at Maidstone, in October, a jurat and seven
councilmen put out between 1644 and 1651 were readmitted.[76] Locally
induced resignations, removals, and restorations suggest that many
townsmen sensed the passing of their political moment – temporarily at
least – and yielded the field, fearing they would soon lose their places
anyway; others were pushed out by brethren eager for revenge or to prove
their loyalty to the new King.

Numerous towns voluntarily readmitted ejected officers from mid-1659
onward. But some of those dismissed during the 1640s and 50s needed
stronger measures, and the court that was once again called King's Bench is
where they found them. Mandamus activity quickened in the wake of the
Act of Indemnity of July 1659, and even more so immediately before and
after the King's return. Thirty-six complaining of wrongful dismissal
received the writ in Easter term 1660; another fifty-eight did so in Trinity
term.[77] This was nothing short of an explosion in the use of mandamus.

These were mandamuses of two sorts: for those dismissed in the 1640s
and 50s and now desiring a return, and those dismissed in 1659–61 as
corporations undertook their own restorations. Those making claims of the
first kind tended to succeed more readily in King's Bench during 1660 and
1661 than those seeking mandamuses of the latter kind. Thus Norwich
aldermen John Andrews and William Davy failed to be restored after their
ouster from the corporation in early 1661, apparently on the argument that
their original elections were illegal, based as they were on the unjustifiable
removal of those whose places they took in 1649 and 1650.[78] Two recently
dismissed at Canterbury "for their disaffection to his majesty and to his
government" met the same fate.[79] And though expelled before 1659,
Cornelius Hooker also lost his bid for restoration as Winchester's recorder.
Elected in 1652, Hooker had apparently been the main source of contentions there. In 1657, the corporation had dismissed him after resolving that
he was "the principal occasion of the manifold differences that hath been in
the corporation."[80]

Most suing writs to reverse dismissals made in the 1640s and 50s appear
to have won their places back with mandamus unless there were special

---

[76] Perry Gauci, *Politics and Society in Great Yarmouth, 1660–1722* (Oxford, 1996),
pp. 102–03, and Schilling, "Central Government and the Corporations," pp. 151–52.
Suffolk RO (Bury St. Edmunds Branch), EE501/2/8, pp. 23–24. K. S. Martin, ed., *Records
of Maidstone* (Maidstone, 1926), pp. 115, 116, 122, 123, 128, and 144.

[77] PRO, KB21/14/3–16v.

[78] PRO, KB21/14, ff. 37v, 44a.v, and 46v. Evans, *Norwich*, pp. 231–33.

[79] Canterbury City and Cathedral Archives, CC/AC/5, ff. 33v–34, 40, 41, and 45v–46v. PRO,
KB21/14/42v, 51v, 60, and 62v, and KB29/310/44 and 66.

[80] Hampshire RO, W/B1/5, ff. 50v, 119–23v, and 161v, and PRO, KB21/14/4.

allowances in local customs or charters permitting arbitrary removals by the corporation. Prominent recorders did especially well. Sir Harbottle Grimston succeeded at Harwich. Sir Robert Hyde was restored at Salisbury, and at Bath too "according to his writ of restitution . . . he being first displaced by the power of the then times and no otherwise." Hyde later declined the place at Bath and William Prynne, who had received it when Hyde had been removed, was again installed. Three members of Bath's council removed at the same time as Hyde in late 1647 had restoration by mandamus as well.[81] The use of multiple writs at Bath points to an important aspect of the use of mandamus in 1660: many from one town joined together to pursue their grievances collectively, though each by law needed a separate writ. Thus five from Leominster, ten from Bristol, eleven from Hereford, and twelve from Worcester sought their writs together. Each group had their complaints represented at the same time and by the same barrister.[82] Use of mandamus was not just to return a disgruntled individual to the body, but to restore whole groups who acted collectively to achieve their common purpose: undoing the order of the 1650s and restoring the order of old. These were people whose common experience as purge victims gave them an appreciation of their shared interests and a sense that they would best be pursued in concert.

Not all succeeded, but this typically involved unusual local circumstances. Torrington's steward, removed by Major General Desborough in 1656, failed because his replacement had been elected each year since according to local custom. But an alderman and a capital burgess removed there by the same arbitrary power had their places back again since the same custom did not pertain in their cases. At Lincoln, a mandamus failed when the corporation showed that the alderman concerned had been absent in 1647–50, so according to their charter, they had had to replace him.[83] Such disappointments notwithstanding, scores made use of the writ to regain their places in 1660. The rate of corporate readmissions picked up after Charles's entry into London on May 29, 1660, but by then, townsmen had already been restoring their corporations for more than

---

[81] Bath City RO, Council Book 2, pp. 242 and 245–47; PRO, KB21/14/7 and KB29/309/ unfol. (two writs and return explaining restoration). Restoring the three councilmen meant removing three others from the corporation. Rather than simply remove those chosen to the places in 1647, or those with the least seniority, the corporation instead held three votes to choose those who would lose their places. One of these dismissed got a mandamus for himself, but failed in the end: PRO, KB29/309 and KB21/14/14.

[82] PRO, KB21/14, passim.

[83] Ibid., ff. 7v, 8v, and 20; PRO, KB29/309: writs and returns for William Halse, James Smith, and John Dennis, and two writs and the return for William Bishop.

eighteen months. The King's Restoration followed on and participated in the local restorations nationwide that preceded it.

Restoration entailed not only putting a king back on his throne and aldermen back on their benches; it also required re-establishing the proper relationship between the King and the corporations which his authority alone created and sustained. It had been no small matter when in 1651 Parliament ordered the replacement in all towns of the King's arms with those of the Commonwealth. Maces, arms, and other regalia served as vivid representations of the relationship between the boroughs and royal government, the source of corporate authority. Having been at their own charge in 1651 to change the arms, towns like Leicester now bore the costs of erecting the King's arms once again in 1660. At Hull, the corporation went one loyal step further, ordering the Cromwellian arms hanged, then burned.[84] Silversmiths around the country were busied re-engraving maces, swords, cups, and other corporate plate.[85] The corporations quickly restored the King's fee farm rents, once paid to the crown according to terms in corporate charters, but sold off to the towns by the Interregnum regimes to raise cash. In presenting them to the King, most towns made certain to mention, as Nottingham did, that they had been "constrained to purchase [the rents] for £500 ready money, to preserve our charters and liberties, rather than become farmers to the unjust power that had so long deprived you of your birthright."[86] Surrender of the rents became universal as one town imitated the deeds of the next. Townsmen besieged the crown with fulsome addresses of thanksgiving for the Restoration and with gifts for the King.[87] Corporations also elected prominent royalists to their most important offices, those of high steward and recorder. Lords lieutenants were common choices. Boston asked Montagu Earl of Lindsey, Lincolnshire's lord lieutenant, to be their high steward, and Dorchester asked the Duke of Richmond. The Earl of Clarendon was an especially popular choice given his position near the King; he became high steward of numerous towns, including Abingdon, Cambridge, Yarmouth, and Salisbury. Selecting such noblemen evinced a corporation's desire to

---

[84] *CJ*, vol. 6, p. 531. Stocks, *Records of Leicester*, pp. 472–73. Leicestershire RO, BR III/2/86, f. 29. James Joseph Sheahan, *History of the Town and Port of Kingston-upon-Hull* (Beverley, 1866), p. 178.

[85] Kingston spent nearly £38 for new maces: Surrey RO, KD5/1/2, pp. 162–66. See also Bond, *Hall Book of Windsor*, p. 9; and Stocks, *Records of Leicester*, p. 469.

[86] *CSPD 1659–60*, p. 437. For other examples, see *CSPD 1660–61*, pp. 4, 48, 49, 66, and passim.

[87] For example, see John F. Bailey, *Transcription of the Minutes of the Corporation of Boston* 5 vols. (Boston, 1980–93), vol. III, p. 326. Numerous addresses are mentioned in *CSPD 1660–61*, passim, and published in *The Kingdoms Intelligencer of the Affairs Now in Agitation in England, Scotland, and Ireland* (London, 1660–63).

enhance its position with the crown, to re-establish traditional relationships with prominent local families, and to coopt those same grandees in hopes they would view the town as a friend, not as a hostile force to be subdued. Thus Yarmouth would put their connection with Clarendon to good use when negotiating a new charter on favorable terms in 1663–64.[88]

Restorations of borough members and the election of leading royalists to high corporate office continued throughout 1660. The crown took little action in these early months to promote the return of dismissed members or the election of its most loyal servants. In law, it could not require such actions. But the King did write to some requesting that certain persons be returned to office, and many corporations complied. Two points stand out about these royal letters: they were obtained at the initiative of townsmen, not crown officers, and they were usually written in order to restore someone to an office lost in the 1640s and 50s, not to add a newcomer. Thus a few members of Preston corporation petitioned the King for his letter to the corporation ordering the removal of some elected in the 1650s and the restoration of those they had replaced. A number of Tewkesbury corporation members removed in the 1650s by Major General Desborough simultaneously petitioned the King for his letter and sued writs of mandamus. By one means or the other, they won back their old places.[89] The crucial element in these and other cases was the request from the locality for the King's letter.

Though the King could write all the letters he liked, no charter permitted the crown actually to make changes in personnel; only the corporations could order dismissals, and not all did. At Maidstone, Charles asked that they appoint Thomas Brewer, a victim of sequestration, as recorder. This they did, seven years later. Two others held the coveted post in the interim. Early in 1661, Canterbury had complied with a royal request to restore members dismissed before 1660 and to remove the disaffected. But the corporation went its own way later. Canterbury's recorder, Francis Lovelace, requested the King to write the corporation ordering the re-election of the mayor for another year. Charles did so, but Lovelace and others then ignored his letter and elected another. They reported that their choice, as a

---

[88] Two years later, Boston elected Attorney General Sir Geoffrey Palmer as their recorder. Bailey, *Minutes of Boston*, vol. III, pp. 334–35 and 383. Underdown, *Fire from Heaven*, p. 233. Challenor, *Abingdon*, appendix, p. lii; H. Swinden, *The History and Antiquities of the Ancient Burgh of Great Yarmouth* (Norwich, 1772), p. 584. HMC, *Various Collections*, vol. IV, p. 244. Cambridgeshire RO, Shelf C/8, f. 127v. Gauci, *Yarmouth*, pp. 109–10.

[89] *CSPD 1661–62*, pp. 102 and 229; *CSPD Addendum 1660–70*, p. 663. PRO, PC2/55/17 and KB21/14, f. 4. Daniel Beaver, "Symbol and Boundary: Religion, Family and Community in Northern Gloucestershire, 1560–1690" (Ph.D., University of Chicago, 1991), p. 223.

loyal man, served the same purpose as the mayor originally desired by Lovelace and recommended by the King. Charles could not count on automatic compliance with his letters, even when they were requested by those who then disobeyed them. Against the mayor of Salisbury's wishes, the rest of the corporation replied to a royal letter that they were all well-affected so changes desired by the King were unnecessary. York's leaders made the same argument when refusing to comply with Charles's desires.[90] Such towns snubbed the King's requests despite the good will that might be won by compliance, arguing all the while that this was in no way inconsistent with loyalty.

At Maidstone, the royal request called for innovation: the appointment to office of a person who had never held it before. But in most cases, the King simply desired the restoration of those turned out in the Interregnum and the dismissal of those who had taken their places, especially those appointed by order of Parliament or the Protector.[91] Royal letters to the towns in 1660 and 1661 were intended to recreate the status quo ante; they were not an attempt to remodel the corporations. Unlike the dismissals ordered by Parliament and Protector since 1644, Charles did not, and could not, effectively command changes in corporation personnel. The restorations and removals of 1660–61 were thus essentially the result of local efforts. Even when they were desired by the King, there was little he could do to gain their enactment except send the implicit warning that the corporation might thereby lose his good graces. Given the crown's unsure footing in these years, some corporations apparently believed this threat amounted to little.

With the municipal elections of the autumn of 1660, it became clear that the crown would need to become more involved in settling local disputes, even if this did not entail a request for removals or restorations. From Newcastle, the Earl of Clarendon received notice of a "tumultuous assembly" on election day, "forcing them to an election contrary to our charters." Sir John Marley and others, restored there after their dismissal by a parliamentary ordinance of 1644, were accused of fomenting the trouble. The case quickly came before the Privy Council, which then sent two of the King's serjeants-at-law to compose the differences, so "that all

---

[90] *CSPD 1660–61*, pp. 246 and 552. Martin, *Records of Maidstone*, pp. 154 and 271. *CSPD 1661–62*, pp. 70 and 90. Scott, "York, 1640–1662," in Richardson, *Town and Country-side*, p. 61. Lincoln hesitated in the face of repeated royal orders and leading corporators were brought before the Privy Council after they reluctantly complied, but no further action against them followed. *CSPD 1660–61*, p. 246. J. W. F. Hill, *Tudor and Stuart Lincoln* (Cambridge, 1956), pp. 171–72. PRO, PC2/55/132.

[91] At Worcester, the corporation restored ten, eight of whom had been dismissed in 1652, and expelled their replacements, according to a royal order. Another order to remove four more does not appear to have been obeyed. Hereford and Worcester RO (St. Helen's), Shelf A.14, Chamber Order Book, ff. 38 and 41.

former animosities will be forgotten and buried."[92] The mediators in this instance were none other than Sir John Glynn, former chief justice of the Upper Bench, and Sir John Maynard, prominent in arguing corporation cases in the 1650s.

Charles made extensive use of such mediators to handle contested mayoral elections and other corporation disputes brought before his council in 1660 and 1661. This reliance on mediators arose not only from the crown's weak position, but also from a royal belief that political settlement nationwide might best be achieved by moderate measures, drawing upon ancient political assumptions that stressed unity and the leading role to be played by those of the highest social status to create and maintain that unity. Rather than operate by means of exclusion, as Interregnum regimes had done, the restored King sought comprehension of moderate members of competing local groups and the dismissal only of the recalcitrant. Use of men like Maynard, Glynn, and others who showed pronounced Presbyterian leanings, as well as noblemen and gentry with strong traditional connections to the areas where they served in this capacity, points to the middle ground the King hoped to find for settling the corporations on stable political foundations.

The King reproached extremists at both ends of the political spectrum. When the mayor of Wallingford petitioned the King in November 1660 for an order to restore those ejected from the corporation by parliamentary soldiers in 1647, the King, rather than simply sending a letter making the standard request, referred the matter to the deputy lieutenants of Berkshire with orders to procure a peaceful composition of differences. The following March, the Privy Council considered a complaint from the same mayor that he had been unduly ejected by the deputy lieutenants. After further Council enquiries, the King wrote to the deputy lieutenants expressing his indignation that they should exceed their authority "concerning the redressing some irregularities in our town of Wallingford in an amicable way." He countermanded their decisions and ordered that they restore the mayor. Similarly, the Council heard complaints from Christchurch, Grantham, and Newark, that disaffected persons entering those corporations "in the late usurped government" continued in their places. In each case, the King and Council ordered local gentlemen to arbitrate a settlement by which those removed might retake their places and those who had come in illegally would be put out. But Charles had to reprimand two mediators at Christchurch for using severe, divisive measures. Power from the King to settle a borough dispute was just that; it was not *carte blanche* given to local magnates to remodel towns at will. Charles wanted

[92] Bod., MS Clarendon 73, f. 241. PRO, PC2/55/22 and 25.

to avoid partiality in deciding disputes to heal torn corporate bodies, and he expected his agents to do the same, though he had frequent cause to be disappointed.[93]

At Bath, those who thought of themselves as the King's loyal subjects employed especially dangerous tactics in their effort to gain the mayoralty in 1661. Earlier that year, Sir Thomas Bridges had written to Secretary Edward Nicholas seeking help to win a parliamentary seat for himself and another royalist against William Prynne and Alexander Popham. Bridges hoped the Privy Council would order the dismissal of Mayor John Ford – who favored the latter pair – and the installation of one of his own allies. But after an examination of the matter, the Council dismissed Bridges and his tendentious complaints against Mayor Ford. Prynne and Popham then won the parliamentary choice with ease.[94] But this did not deter Bridges and his friends.

In the next mayoral election in September, Bridges did all he could to gain victory for Henry Chapman, who had been restored to the corporation by a mandamus in 1660. Chapman and "his confederates" on the city council and among the county's deputy lieutenants called in the militia four days before the vote to arrest four aldermen and seven councilmen who opposed them. At the election, Recorder William Prynne damned these measures, "informing [the corporation] that a city divided against itself cannot stand," and warning of the dangers of military power used this way.[95] Chapman won the voices of eleven gathered there; his foe, John Parker, received only ten. But Parker, Prynne, and their partisans added the votes of eight of the jailed corporators based on a signed and sealed statement declaring their votes for Parker, who was then with them in their confinement. Though Chapman was initially noted as the winner in the council book, his name was crossed through and Parker's was inserted instead.[96] With the vote over, both sides rushed to the Privy Council with

---

[93] *CSPD 1660–61*, pp. 373 and 550. PRO, SP29/33/51, and 52. Similarly, the King intervened after the Earl of Derby showed his partiality in settling differences at Wigan. PRO, PC2/55/15v, 28, 44, 47, 74v–75, and 89v.

[94] *CSPD 1660–61*, p. 544. PRO, PC2/55/93v and 100–100v. Henning, vol. I, p. 370.

[95] Bath City RO, Council Book 2, p. 276; pp. 266–86 contain an account of the election, minutes of meetings where its aftermath was considered, and entry of corporate orders condemning Chapman and his friends.

[96] Norrey suggests that there were two elections, one on September 19, the other on the 23rd. The 19th was the day of quarter sessions, and the day the corporation members were arrested, but there was no election then. The election was on the 23rd (the Monday before Michaelmas, as in other years). Ticks in the council book suggest it happened in two stages: first, the votes of those present were counted; and second, Prynne's group added the eight votes of those in prison. P. J. Norrey, "The Relationship between Central and Local Government in Dorset, Somerset and Wiltshire, 1660–1688," (Ph.D., Bristol University, 1988), pp. 119–21. See Bath City RO, Council Book 2, p. 275, for an account of the sessions on the 19th, and p. 266, for the election on the 23rd.

charge and counter-charge. The King in Council declared his displeasure "that his militia should be any way employed to strengthen a faction and to disturb the civil government." Charles proclaimed Parker duly elected and suggested that if Chapman were disappointed, he could turn to the law for redress, advice Chapman never took because he probably knew his legal arguments were so weak. As a final punishment, Charles ordered the Duke of Ormonde to withdraw Chapman's militia commission. The corporation had already exacted its own revenge by dismissing Chapman from their number.[97]

Throughout 1660 and 1661, King and Council promoted moderate measures, hoping as few changes in personnel as possible might restore local unity. When those ostensibly acting in the King's name over-stepped the bounds of his policy, countermanding orders issued and those responsible received notice of the royal ire. Charles agreed with Prynne's assessment: divided cities cannot stand. Forced elections promoted "faction," and would thus "disturb the civil government." The royal reaction in these cases demonstrated the King's belief that successful government was unified government. Unity could only be obtained by restoring those unduly dismissed and no more, and by squelching faction in whatever guise – "loyal" or "disaffected" – it might assume. Charles's desire for unity differed from that of the 1640s and 50s in one crucial respect: the way it would be achieved. In the months following the Restoration, the King hoped to achieve unity through composition between feuding parties, not by favoring one and excluding the other.

Charles faced two related questions in encouraging the corporate restorations begun long before his return to England: how to restore displaced personnel with as little commotion as possible, and how to re-establish municipal corporations on firm legal ground? The corporations had done much on their own to answer the first question. But the second problem remained: what of the corporations' legal status? Purges by parliamentary ordinance, by parliamentary committees, by the Protector and the major generals, or by the corporations themselves, had all been illegal. As such, officers appointed to the places of those removed acted illegally. Any actions such officers performed, including elections of new members, were thus illegal too. Surrender of royal charters and the receipt of new ones from the Lord Protector only compounded the problem. And it is not clear that either the Act of Indemnity or the Act Confirming Judicial Proceedings released the corporations from the potential legal problems: certainly neither act addressed the corporations directly.[98] In theory then, most if not

---

[97] PRO, PC2/55/214v. Bath City RO, Council Book 2, p. 270.
[98] Stats. 12 Charles II c. 11 and 12. The Corporation Act of December 1661 (Stat. 13 Charles II, st. II, c. 1) protected all charters from legal dangers posed by deeds done before 1661.

all corporation charters had been abrogated in countless ways during the 1640s and 50s, and a good argument could be made that in law, such corporations were dissolved.

Actions by Parliament and the Protector in the 1640s and 50s furnished ample reason for strong measures to correct these problems; actions by Parliament and the Protector also furnished the precedents for any steps the crown might take. The legal confusion town governments now faced resulted from the dismissals, appointments, and recharterings of the years of war and Interregnum. A comprehensive rechartering of all towns presented one possibility for settling personnel and re-establishing corporate constitutions at the same time. Many around the King and around the country anticipated just such measures and numerous towns looked forward to an opportunity to put their legal status beyond reproach. Others saw in these legal problems an opportunity to redefine the relationship between crown and towns across the kingdom. The Marquess of Newcastle suggested that as towns were "the common seminaries of faction, sedition, and rebellion, so now to uphold your Majesty in peace and wealth, your Majesty's care and labor must be to reduce and keep them in their due subjection which may be done by removing the great distance which is between sovereignty and vulgarity." That some good might come of the "late, horrid" rebellion, he proposed that Charles

take the forfeiture not only of charters and privileges, but also to seize unto your Majesty's hands and become landlord of all houses and lands in or belonging to any of the aforesaid places . . . because . . . landlords do more than any other power own the people and lead them after their own humor and so into faction, whence followeth sedition and rebellion.[99]

Newcastle's argument is unusual both for its extreme perspective on corporation politics, and for the way he connects control of property to political power: lessees are tenants of borough corporations rather than of the King, so that is where their political loyalties lie. This not only creates political divisions within the population at large, but of greater consequence, between the nation and its sovereign. By transferring control of corporate properties to the King, "all interposing powers between your Majesty and the people will be removed excepting such as are immediately derived from your Majesty, whereby they shall look upon your Majesty as their only master for livelihood, law, and religion." Views like these occupied the far end of a broad spectrum of advice about settling borough governments. But the sentiments regarding the origins and results of partisan politics were not peculiar. Concerns about "faction" mirror those expressed in the Kingston case before the Upper Bench in 1654–55.

---

[99] Bod., MS Clarendon 73, f. 359.

Regimes of the 1650s and the 1660s shared equally a fear of division in any form and by any name. Newcastle argued that from "faction . . . followeth sedition and rebellion"; lawyers of the Interregnum feared that "party" entailed "a setting up of government against government, and this is corrupting . . . done to eradicate the whole government."[100] Worries abounded that in the corporations existed the prospect of division and political chaos without end. While in many corporations during 1660 it may have appeared to local leaders that order was being re-established, among some at Whitehall, doubts remained. Less severe proposals than Newcastle's gained a more sympathetic hearing but operated under the same assumptions: settling the nation required the eradication of division, an end most easily gained by excluding from the political nation all whose loyalty to the restored regime was still suspect.

While rechartering all corporations might have been the obvious simultaneous solution to the persistent problems of loyal corporate leadership and sound legal status, there appears to have been little interest in doing so. This may have been due to the anticipated difficulty of such a task. The length and complexity of a process involving hundreds of towns must have boggled even the most ambitious bureaucratic minds in 1660–61. More likely, a comprehensive charter policy was not pursued as it did not serve the crown's principal concern: ensuring stable local government in the hands of trustworthy persons. Charles and his advisors appeared willing, temporarily at least, to overlook the obvious legal weakness if not legal death of most corporations. Ideas of comprehensive measures against borough charters were thus dropped in the early years after the Restoration. But other measures to ensure the loyalty of corporate personnel were not.

PASSING AN "ACT FOR THE WELL-GOVERNING AND REGULATING OF CORPORATIONS"

Local initiative, writs of mandamus, and royally appointed mediators went a long way toward restoring the corporations, but by mid-1661, firmer and broader measures were pursued. Little is known of the origins of a corporations bill introduced in the House of Commons in June 1661, but the idea of a law requiring further adjustments in corporation personnel must have surprised few people. The Commons worked quickly, taking only three days to approve amendments calling for commissioners named by the House to conduct a purge of borough corporations. In little more than a week, commissioners' names proposed by the MPs for each county

---

[100] Ibid. *Eng. Rep.*, vol. 82, p. 877 (Style, 478).

were inserted in the bill; only those to enforce the bill in London would be left to the King's discretion. On 5 July, the bill passed its third reading and moved to the House of Lords.[101]

The bill's quick passage through the Commons belied the opposition it faced there. William Prynne, angered by its success, rushed an anonymous broadside through the press detailing reasons why the Lords should dismiss it.[102] Using language similar to that he used to condemn the conflict at Bath, Prynne emphasized principally the lack of due process: corporation members would lose the freehold they possessed in their offices without proper trial as required by Magna Charta. The commissioners conducting the purges would be bound by no oaths to behave fairly and there would be no appeal of their decisions. These were arbitrary powers that could only be compared to those of their predecessors, the sequestrators, county committees, and major generals. Prynne noted that at least if informations of quo warranto were brought against the charters of all the kingdom's corporations, they would be able to answer the charges against them in a proper court proceeding. Underscoring the arbitrary nature of the bill, Prynne noted that peers too could lose their corporate offices. Second, Prynne highlighted the threat posed to corporate charters. The commissioners might dismiss half or all a corporation's members. In doing so, the body would be too small to conduct legal elections. Without legal elections, the corporation would cease to exist. Third, Prynne argued from necessity, or rather the lack of it. Given that most of those ejected from corporations in the preceding decades had now regained office, what point could the bill now serve? Those not yet returned to office could be restored by writs of mandamus, as so many had already. The bill would "prove a remedy far worse than any disease it pretends to cure," serving as yet another precedent for arbitrary powers bestowed by act of Parliament.

Most interesting is the issue raised throughout by Prynne concerning the divisive effect of purges. By reviving "former marks and names of distinction between his subjects" and the memory of "forgotten crimes," the proposed bill would abrogate the Act of Oblivion and Indemnity and other declarations of pardon made by the King. By not requiring oaths of the commissioners, the act might allow "corruption, malice, rancor and revenge" to direct their actions; this would stir up "divisions, contentions, factions and parties."[103] Previous acts of restoration – by mandamus, by

---

[101] *CJ*, vol. 8, pp. 275, 279, 285–88, and 291. Hull City RO, BRS/9/5, is a list of names proposed for the Yorkshire commission by the county's MPs. It contains 123 names, nearly twice as many as appointed in the final commission, which is at ibid., BRS/9/4, and HMC, Report 8, appendix 1, p. 275.

[102] [Prynne], *Summary Reasons*.

[103] [Prynne], *Summary Reasons*. Prynne had attacked the "disofficing" of corporation members in 1656 as well: *A Summary Collection of the Principal Fundamental Rights,*

royal recommendation, or by local initiative – operated piecemeal to reunite corporations dismembered by two decades of political division. Wholesale ejections imposed from without would threaten this incremental process. Prynne pointed to the paradox of partisan politics: persecution and division would chase one another in a vicious circle; the effort to destroy faction by excluding the supposedly factious would only perpetuate faction.

For a House of Commons looking for a purge, arguments of illegality, arbitrariness, or even partisan dangers would not override their intentions. Prynne, discovered as the author, was forced to make an abject apology to the House.[104] Worse still, Prynne's words fell on deaf ears in the Lords where the bill was being changed in ways even more chastening.

The Lords' amendments chastened the remainder of the Commons too. Their original bill had been transformed from one implementing a purge of corporation personnel into one destroying most if not all borough autonomy. By their version, the Lords would have had all charters voided if not brought to the crown for renewal. The King would appoint all recorders and town clerks henceforth. Each year, all corporations would submit a list of six mayoral candidates. The King would then "nominate or prick" his choice: use of the word "prick" drew the parallel between crown selection of county sheriffs and what the Lords proposed should be a similar control over mayors. In addition, county JPs would be empowered to act in all towns.[105] The corporations' magisterial independence, their most cherished privilege, would be destroyed. The stunned Commons rejected nearly all the amendments and appointed a committee to prepare a rejoinder to present to the Lords in conference.

Solicitor General Sir Heneage Finch reported to the Commons on the objections drawn up by this committee. First, the Lords' bill struck out the commissioners appointed by the Commons, thus destroying "the powers given to remove ill members, and [to] restore those who are unjustly removed." "Nothing enacted by their Lordships seems to us to provide for present safety" by permitting a careful vetting of membership.[106] Of equal concern were the provisions forcing charter renewals and limiting cor-

---

Liberties, Properties of all English Freemen (London, 1656). See Matthews, *William Sheppard*, pp. 48–49.
[104] *CJ*, vol. 8, pp. 299 and 301–02.
[105] Ibid., pp. 310–11. In his treatise of advice, Newcastle had proposed the idea of royal control of mayoral appointments. Bod., MS Clarendon 73, f. 359v. What influence he had in crafting this amendment, if any, is unknown.
[106] *CJ*, vol. 8, p. 312. John Miller notes this difference between the Commons and Lords, stressing that while the former sought a one-time purge of the towns, the latter hoped to impose a permanent royal control over the corporations without a purge: "The Crown and the Borough Charters in the Reign of Charles II," *EHR*, 100 (1985), pp. 60–61.

porate independence. Allowing county justices into the towns "may occasion a clashing of jurisdictions, and a disturbance of government." Finch carried these concerns to the conference the following day, explaining that the Commons' bill "establisheth all corporations' charters; your Lordships' put us in another course, that all shall renew whether defective or no, whether innocent or no." While the Commons wanted a purge in order to place the corporations' traditional powers in loyal hands, the Lords bill skipped the purge in favor of a permanent diminution of those powers.[107] One or both sides had to yield. Each finally did, apparently after Finch settled tempers and worries in both Houses, for which service he received the thanks of the King and his brother. With attendance "growing thinner and thinner," Parliament dropped the matter until after the impending recess.[108] Upon reconvening in December, the Lords backed away from their previous stand, quickly approving an amended bill presented by Attorney General Sir Geoffrey Palmer. The Commons had won the struggle over whether the bill should purge the corporations or reduce their powers. With all differences overcome, both Houses approved the bill which then gained the royal assent on December 20, 1661.[109]

Generations of historians accepted with little comment J. H. Sacret's analysis of the Corporation Act's legislative history. In the act, as in all other crown/town dealings, Sacret saw malevolent crown ambitions at work. As the Lords' committee assigned to consider the bill in July met at the Duke of York's lodgings, Sacret felt that the changes they proposed represented a royal policy.[110] In challenging this assumption, John Miller has pointed out that most committees met at York's quarters, and suggested that Sacret mistakenly assumed that the Lords' amendments designed to curtail corporation autonomy were meant to expand rather than supplant the Commons program of a short-term purge.[111] By Miller's reading, Charles's government knew it was on far too unstable ground to try anything resembling what the Lords desired. More recently, Paul Seaward has returned to Sacret's argument, claiming that the Lords' initial amendments "seem to have had wide ministerial backing." Seeing a connection to the court in the Earl of Portland's and the Earl of Southampton's involve-

---

[107] Bod., MS Clarendon 75, f. 48. These minutes of the conference, in the hand of Lord Privy Seal Annesley, agree in large measure with the note of objections in *CJ*, vol. 8, p. 312. Similar notes of the Commons' objections are at BL, Harleian 6846, f. 255, and at Hull City RO, BRS/9/2.

[108] *CJ*, vol. 8, p. 313. Finch's role is reported here, and in BL, Add. 23,215, f. 40v.

[109] *LJ*, vol. 11, pp. 346, 349, 353, and 358. House of Lords RO, MS5/H/3/1, p. 87. Miller, "Borough Charters," p. 61. Paul Seaward, *The Cavalier Parliament and the Reconstruction of the Old Regime, 1661–67* (Cambridge, 1989), p. 155.

[110] J. H. Sacret, "The Restoration Government and Municipal Corporations," *EHR*, 45 (1930), p. 249.

[111] Miller, "Borough Charters," pp. 60n. and 62.

ment in the Lords' proposals, Seaward felt that "the government" or "prominent ministers" must have supported if not initiated these measures.[112] But this makes the crown more monolithic and purposeful than it was or could have been. Portland reported both the more severe version of the bill in July and the moderated version accepted in December; he also managed joint conferences during each of these very different stages of the bill's life.[113] It is difficult to infer from this thin evidence in which Portland pointed one way, then the other, that he was part of any ministerial program. Similarly, Lord Treasurer Southampton only seems to have played a significant role when it came time to dampen fears in the Commons by moderating the Lords' proposals. There is little to suggest that Southampton was trying to sell any particular version of the bill.

If any evidence of a crown policy exists, it is in the actions of the attorney and solicitor generals. Finch was a leading crown spokesman in the Commons, particularly in legal matters. Both Finch and Palmer were knowledgeable in corporation law from their courtroom practice. Most matters before the Privy Council concerning the corporations were referred to them for advice; when new charters were sought or old ones confirmed, the attorney or solicitor general prepared the draft and recommended all changes required. In short, these were the King's experts on the law of corporations. In addition, Solicitor General Finch was the most active crown officer in the Commons and usually the leading figure in conferences between the Houses. Finch played the leading role in formulating and presenting the Commons' objections to the Lords' amendments in July, and Attorney General Palmer submitted to the Lords the version of the bill that was ultimately approved.[114] The content of the act, explicitly protecting charters as it does, points as well to the influence of officials concerned to prevent the legal chaos that would have ensued had the Lords been victorious in requiring hundreds of corporations to send in their charters before June of 1662. As all charters would have passed through their offices during the renewal process, they knew well how impossible it would have been for their departments to handle this deluge of work. These two legal officers, directly involved in proposing the changes which brought the bill

---

112 Seaward, *Cavalier Parliament*, pp. 152–54. Ronald Hutton adopts this line too, suggesting that Charles was behind the Lords' amendments of July 1661: *The Restoration*, pp. 158–61.
113 *LJ*, vol. 11, pp. 318, 349, and 356.
114 Henning, vol. II, pp. 317–22. D. E. C. Yale, ed., *Lord Nottingham's Chancery Cases*, 2 vols., Selden Society Publications, vols. 73 and 79 (London, 1957–61), vol. I, pp. xiv–xx. Palmer sat in the Lords by writ of summons. Finch had recently argued a mandamus: PRO, KB21/14/46v. Seaward calls Finch "the most prominent of court spokesmen": *Cavalier Parliament*, p. 83. On the importance of crown lawyers in parliamentary management in general, see ibid., pp. 79 and 82.

to its final form, had a clear interest in defining the act's provisions, whether in accordance with their own views or as representatives of a "ministerial" policy. If such a policy existed, these men defined, pursued, and achieved it.

The "Act for the well-governing and regulating of corporations" followed the Commons' original hopes in large measure: it permitted a purge while protecting the corporations' chartered privileges. The preamble, written by the Lords, laid out clearly the reasons for the act:

Whereas questions are likely to arise concerning the validity of elections of magistrates . . . as well in respect of removing some, as placing others during the late troubles, contrary to the true intent and meaning of their charters and liberties; and to the end that the succession in such corporations may be most probably perpetuated in the hands of persons well-affected to his Majesty . . . it being too well known, that notwithstanding all his Majesty's endeavors and unparalleled indulgence in pardoning all that is past, nevertheless many evil spirits are still working.[115]

These lines addressed the government's and the Commons' two central concerns: that loyal men should govern and that corporations should stand on firm legal ground. Implicit in the concern about the validity of elections made contrary to charters was the understanding that a corporation's illegal acts could make the charter void, thus killing the body corporate. So charters would now be confirmed by re-establishing the legal corporate succession that had been broken by illegal removals. The Commons also added a provision indemnifying all charters from legal challenge for any corporate actions taken before the first meeting of the present Parliament in 1661. Thus by means of the Corporation Act, both the loyalty of personnel and the safety of chartered privileges would be confirmed.

The act's punch came in the clauses appointing commissioners to implement the purge. In the last days before its passage, the Commons conceded to the Lords' demand that the crown, not the Commons, should appoint the commissioners. Commissions would issue under the great seal by February 20, 1662, empowering those appointed to enforce the act until March 25, 1663.[116] The commissioners were to visit the corporations and hear all corporation members swear the oaths of allegiance and supremacy and an oath against taking up arms against the King. Each corporator would then subscribe a declaration disavowing the Solemn League and Covenant. Persons refusing any of the oaths or the declaration were removed *ipso facto*, "as if the said respective persons so refusing were naturally dead." The commissioners thus had no discretionary power to

---

[115] Stat. 13 Charles II, st. II, c. 1.
[116] Thus the commissioners were to have thirteen months to act, not three years, as Seaward suggests, *Cavalier Parliament*, p. 155.

save the positions of those whom they might favor if on grounds of conscience an officer refused the declaration against the Covenant. But the commissioners did have broad discretion in ordering if not preventing ejections from office. The act gave them power to remove anyone, whether or not he took the oaths, if they should "deem it expedient for the public safety."

What had been wrought by the Interregnum oath acts would now be undone by similar means. Interregnum oaths and removals provided both the reason for the act and suggestions for its contents; it could have surprised no one that new oaths would be used again as a test of fitness for office. A clause requiring the exclusion from office of all admitted since 1642 had been struck from the bill in its earliest form: there would be no blanket removals of Civil War and Interregnum appointees.[117] But the present government could not be expected to permit persons who had once sworn allegiance to a "usurping power" to rule in the localities without requiring that they reassign that allegiance to their returned King. Some test would be needed to remain in corporate office, and better the oaths than a date of election, which would lead to the arbitrary removal of the majority of those presently serving, many if not most of whom were quite prepared to support the restored monarch.

Removals from office would create vacancies. Commissioners received full authority "to restore such person or persons as have been illegally or unduly removed." They also had power to appoint to vacancies any other inhabitant of the town. With an eye to upholding the validity of the corporations' charters, all appointed by the commissioners would serve "as if they had been duly elected and chosen according to the charters and former usages" of the town. Thus by statute, such appointments were made part of the corporation's legal succession. While the presence of three or more commissioners would suffice to certify that a person took the requisite oaths, five or more were to be present to remove or appoint.

After the commissioners' powers expired in March of 1663, all elected to borough offices in the future were to take the same oaths and declaration and certify that they had received the sacrament within the year prior to election. Each corporation was to maintain records showing that all subsequently admitted to office observed these provisions. Parliament thus created a permanent set of legal qualifications for office holding that would continue at the heart of partisan conflict in the corporations for decades to come. In the early years, the declaration against the Covenant would produce a broad exclusion of Presbyterians, though many of them were political conservatives who had assisted in the restoration of old corporate

[117] *CJ*, vol. 8, p. 288.

bodies and thus of royal government. In later years, the importance of the declaration as a test would fade as those who had originally sworn the Covenant died. But the sacramental barrier would remain. While corporations had known conflict within them between different degrees of Protestants, never before 1640 had one group of Protestants been formally excluded from politics; it is this that differentiates occasional conflict pre-1640 from constant partisan conflict post-1660. Now the exclusion of certain sorts of people – borrowing from precedents of the 1640s and 50s – had been carved in statutory stone. The passage of the Corporation Act marks a watershed in the genesis of partisan politics: here we see a particular class of persons defined; defined in religious terms; defined in order to set them apart and to exclude them from participating altogether. Little wonder that spiritual sympathies would provide the center around which the purgative impulses driving partisan politics would revolve in the years ahead. The Corporation Act, more than anything else, transformed religious identity into partisan identity: it created "divisions, contentions, factions, and parties."

IMPLEMENTING THE CORPORATION ACT

Little is known about the process of selecting and appointing the commissioners who were to oversee the purge. The act required the King to name the commissioners within two months of its passage. The only surviving reference to their selection is in a note passed from Clarendon to Charles during a Privy Council meeting: "I have appointed a meeting at my chamber this night to prepare an account for your Majesty concerning the bill [sic] of corporations, it being time those commissions were dispatched."[118] The mention that the time approached for sending out the commissions suggests a date of sometime in late January or early February 1662, as the first commission granted, that for London, passed the great seal on February 8.[119] As Clarendon appointed the meeting and its purpose was to prepare a report for the King, we may assume that Clarendon oversaw the selection of commissioners and that perhaps Charles vetted his final list for each county before it passed the great seal.

Commissions went to each of the English and Welsh counties, with separate ones to London, Bristol, Nottingham, and Southampton. Commissions issued on the 8th for London and Bristol; the others passed the seal

---

[118] W. D. Macray, ed., *Notes Which Passed at Meetings of the Privy Council Between Charles II and the Earl of Clarendon* (London, 1896), p. 79. The "bill" by now was an "Act."
[119] PRO, C231/7/156.

on February 19, one day before the deadline for granting them.[120] Social station was the crucial criterion for appointment. Many were probably appointed entirely owing to their social position, with little expectation that they would act. Lords lieutenant were evidently named to all commissions; JPs and deputy lieutenants were prominent throughout. The principal student of the act's implementation, William A. H. Schilling, suggested that the lords lieutenant played the leading role in recommending the others who would serve in each county, but no evidence exists to confirm this. On the other hand, holding county offices such as a deputy lieutenancy or a place on the bench did not mean automatic inclusion.[121] Thus the crown apparently exercised some discrimination in selecting commissioners rather than simply appointing all county leaders, some of whom may not have been appropriate for the work.

A look at the names of those enforcing the act in the Staffordshire boroughs of Walsall and Newcastle under Lyme reveals the expected sprinkling of JPs and deputy lieutenants: seven out of fifteen.[122] Most resided in Staffordshire; the others held property there and lived in adjacent counties. All knew well the county whose corporations they regulated. Unsurprisingly, they knew one another well too: marriage or blood connected eight of them. Of these fifteen active commissioners, four endured imprisonment or sequestration during the late troubles; but they were offset by five commissioners who, by serving on assessment and militia committees or as JPs or sheriffs in the 1650s, had been complicitous with the "usurpers." In short, the commissioners who visited Newcastle and Walsall were a closely tied bunch, well aware of the political situation in the area, and balanced in their political experience and outlook. The commission for Shropshire appointed a group more clearly affiliated with the royalist cause. Like those acting in Staffordshire, Shropshire's commissioners had a good deal of political and administrative experience at Parliament and in the county. Most were Anglicans. But the crown had not gone out of its way to select ardent royalists to conduct the most extensive

---

120 Dockets for the commissions may be found in PRO, C231/7/158, 165, 174, and 177. Names of commissioners are not given here and no copies of full commissions exist in the PRO, though a few exist in local record offices.
121 Schilling, "Central Government and the Corporations," pp. 194–95.
122 These are the commissioners identifiable by having acted, not the entire county commission, the list of which does not survive. The fifteen were: Sir Edward Bagot, Sir Hervey Bagot, Sir Brian Broughton, Walter Chetwynd, William Chetwynd, Rowland Cotton, Randolph Egerton, Samuel Hinton, John Lane, Sir Francis Lawley, Robert Leveson, Sir Edward Littleton, Robert Milward, William Sneyd, and Sir Walter Wrottesley. Ernest James Homeshaw, *The Corporation of the Borough and Foreign of Walsall* (Walsall, 1960), pp. 43–53; Pape, *Newcastle-under-Lyme*, pp. 16–18; Ruth Kidson, "The Gentry of Staffordshire, 1662–63," *Staffordshire Record Society*, 4th ser., vol. 2 (1958), pp. 1–41; and Henning, passim.

purge possible. Religion and past royalism aside, social prominence and local knowledge were still the most important qualities required for appointment.[123] Local knowledge was so important that corporation members served on numerous commissions in their own towns. Mayors at Bristol and Chester, recorders at Pontefract and elsewhere, and aldermen at Woodstock were all appointed. At Southampton, the mayor and twenty aldermen served in the commission for their city.[124]

Appointment to a county commission was one thing, acting quite another. Of the counties studied here for which are available both full lists of the county commission as well as a record of who implemented the act in each town, rates of participation ran from a low of 10% to a high of less than one third. Only six of Yorkshire's sixty commissioners appeared at Pontefract; six of Shropshire's thirty-four enforced the act at Shrewsbury; eight of Lancashire's thirty-nine made it to Liverpool; and at Kingston upon Thames, commissioners achieved the highest level of participation, ten out of thirty-six on the county's commission. In many towns, commissioners barely managed to gather the five required for making ejections or appointments. At Abingdon, only four commissioners appeared and at Maidenhead, only three came on one occasion, and just two on another, both clear contraventions of the act.[125] On average, in the twenty-six towns studied where the number of commissioners acting may be ascertained, only eight commissioners appeared, though most counties had scores in their commissions. While appointment to the commission was a fillip to the honor of local gentlemen, doing the dirty work was less attractive. Most did not run off to the towns to impose their will or seek revenge for deeds of years gone by. Time and travel – simply the bother of serving – must have dissuaded some. But for many, serving might have been seen more as a threat to one's local standing than as a support to it. Some commissions had their zealots, but many who acted, and even more so, those who stayed home, had little stomach for potentially ugly work.

Those who did act took their time. Visits to the boroughs began in late spring 1662, peaking in August and September, with another flurry of activity – mostly repeat visits – in the last weeks before the commissions expired in March of 1663. At Newcastle under Lyme, commissioners came to town on two consecutive days in September but only implemented the

---

[123] Schilling, "Central Government and the Corporations," pp. 199–209. At least fifteen of the seventeen commissioners acting in Oxfordshire were county inhabitants. A similar proportion applies for Berkshire. Henning, passim. Jeremy Geere, *Index to Oxfordshire Hearth Tax, 1665*, Oxfordshire Family History Society (Oxford, 1985).

[124] HMC, Report 11, appendix 3, p. 55, and BL, MS Egerton 868, f. 49.

[125] Challenor, *Abingdon*, p. 149. Berkshire RO, T/F41, ff. 190v and 192v–93, and A/AOza and b (Abingdon); M/AC1/1/1, second pagination, pp. 49 and 51 (Maidenhead).

dismissals they ordered then in another visit the following March.[126] In some towns, commissioners tendered the oaths and made removals as required, then permitted the corporation to elect the replacements rather than appoint new members themselves.[127] Commissioners at Warwick made sure to record their magnanimity: "though by the act the commissioners had power to have placed others in the rooms of those that did refuse, yet they were so civil to the principal burgesses that they gave them leave to choose others into the said places." Other towns were similarly permitted to fill the openings left by the purge.[128]

Previous accounts of the commissioners' actions retail the numbers of officers ejected from their places without considering the percentage of each corporation dismissed. These accounts thus assume the quality of a catalogue, listing highs and lows, but providing little basis for conclusions about the act's impact.[129] Commissioners' actions in thirty-six towns have been analyzed for the extent of dismissals and the reasons given for them.[130] Of the 1387 persons serving on these thirty-six corporations, 919 (66.26%) were left unaffected by the commissioners' visits; 468 (33.74%) yielded their places. Of these 468, commissioners left behind clear evidence of their reasons for dismissing 263 of them. In this group of 263, 53% lost their places for refusing to subscribe the declaration against the Covenant; another 19% lost them for refusing either one of the oaths or the declaration, the distinction not being made clear; and another 3% for not appearing upon the commissioners' summons. Of the group refusing either the oaths or declaration, the vast majority probably refused the declaration, not the oaths. All but the most recalcitrant were prepared by 1662 to swear basic oaths of allegiance to the King. Anyone losing office for refusing either the oaths of allegiance or supremacy was immediately suspected of

126 Pape, *Newcastle-under-Lyme*, pp. 16–23.
127 This happened at Abingdon and Chesterfield. At Liverpool, commissioners appointed new aldermen, but allowed the corporation to replace the seven councilmen removed. Ramsey Muir and Edith M. Platt, *A History of Municipal Government in Liverpool* (Liverpool, 1906), p. 101.
128 Philip Styles, "The Corporation of Warwick, 1660–1835," *Transactions of the Birmingham Archaeological Society*, 59 (1935), p. 30. Bath City RO, Council Book 2, ff. 325–26.
129 See for instance, Hutton, *The Restoration*, pp. 160–61; Sacret, "Restoration Government and Municipal Corporations," pp. 252–54. Schilling gives a list of numbers removed in 107 towns, but no comparison to numbers serving according to the charter of each town. "Central Government and the Corporations," Appendix II, pp. 235–56.
130 See below, Appendix B. The towns are: Abingdon, Banbury, Barnstaple, Bedford, Beverley, Bewdley, Boston, Bristol, Bury St. Edmunds, Cambridge, Canterbury, Chester, Chesterfield, Coventry, Devizes, Exeter, Gloucester, Henley, Kingston upon Thames, Leicester, Liverpool, Maidenhead, Maidstone, Maldon, Marlborough, Newcastle under Lyme, Norwich, Plymouth, Reading, Shrewsbury, Stratford-upon-Avon, Wallingford, Walsall, Warwick, Windsor, and Woodstock.

treasonous designs and should thus be easily identifiable in surviving records: in those few cases where one of the oaths was refused, the refuser was imprisoned or bound over. Thus in most cases where it is unclear whether the oath or declaration was refused, the declaration against the Covenant was probably the stumbling block. Thus at Abingdon, Plymouth, Bristol, Warwick, Barnstaple, and Maidstone, all losing office did so for refusing the oaths or the declaration. At Chester, Liverpool, Chesterfield, and Kingston upon Thames, all but one giving up office in each town did so for the same cause.

Thus most relinquished their positions, the commissioners did not remove them.[131] Of those for whom we have evidence of the reason for their dismissal, probably three-quarters lost office owing to their own unwillingness to perform what was required of them: over one half for refusing to forswear the Covenant, another 19% probably for the same reason. Three Aldermen at Durham, "showing present dislike [of the declaration], returned answer that they desired not to continue longer." As the act stipulated, any person refusing the declaration was "*ipso facto* removed and displaced . . . [as if they] were naturally dead." Refusal, not the commissioners, made the removal: the commissioners served only as witnesses to the refusal and as guarantors that the office was vacated. Nor could commissioners prevent removal if they wanted to. At Colchester,

the commissioners summoned the mayor, of whom they had some hopes, built, perhaps, upon their desires to keep him in because they knew him a civil person, but having already taken the oaths, he, after many earnest persuasions from the commissioners, would by no means be drawn to subscribe, so put himself out, much against the commissioners' desire.[132]

Refusing the declaration resulted from clear and unavoidable commitments that gave those holding them a collective identity, especially now that they suffered for those commitments. Such commitments, and such common identity, provided the bedrock on which partisan groups lay their foundations.

Only in one quarter of removals could the commissioners be said to have exercised discretionary power: those in which a dismissal was ordered for "public safety." Most commissioners took care to publicize the moderate exercise of their discretionary authority and the alleged intemperance of those who, despite all entreaties, forswore their places rather than the

---

[131] Nicholas Marlowe also finds the declaration much more significant than commissioner discretion: "Government in the West Country Boroughs," pp. 283–85.

[132] *Kingdoms Intelligencer*, number 33, Aug. 11–18, 1662, pp. 542–44, and number 34, Aug. 18–25, 1662, pp. 550–51.

Covenant. At Colchester, commissioners "turned out none but such as turned out themselves by refusing to subscribe," and in Devon, they "made no use at all of any arbitrary power, turning out none but such as refused the oaths or subscription."[133] Commissioners at Aldeburgh gave corporators extra time to consider what they would do.[134] At Lyme Regis, a wholesale purge was prevented by "the almost incredible conversion of this town . . . [which] evidenced their unfeigned resolution to deserve their share of the Act of Oblivion."[135] Conscience permitting, most officers preserved their places by conforming to the terms laid down in the Corporation Act.

Few patterns emerge to explain why some towns experienced more removals than others. Ronald Hutton's contention that the north and the east Midlands suffered less than other regions falters under scrutiny, as Boston lost 52% and Leicester 53%; Liverpool and Beverley each lost 40%, and Chesterfield, 62%. Neither geography nor attempts to connect the act's impact with regions of political proclivity during the Civil Wars explain what happened. One factor does: the extent of readmissions to office prior to 1662 of those ejected before 1660. Corporations with the highest numbers of members elected in the 1650s, and with the fewest personnel changes immediately before and following the Restoration, suffered the greatest losses in 1662. Walsall, Boston, Chester, and Leicester each lost more than 50%, none having made significant changes in corporation composition since 1660.[136] All six removed at Pontefract had been "forcibly introduced in the late times of rebellion." All but two of the fifteen dismissed at Maldon had been elected between 1646 and 1659; the three persons chosen since 1660 retained their places. The boroughs of the southwest, where few changes in personnel were made after 1660, also suffered more than the national average.[137]

---

133 Ibid., number 33, Aug. 11–18, 1662, p. 542, and number 36, Sept. 1–8, 1662, p. 593.
134 Suffolk RO, Ipswich Branch, EE1/C5/3.
135 *Kingdoms Intelligencer*, number 42, Oct. 13–20, 1662, pp. 696–97.
136 Hutton, *The Restoration*, p. 160. At Walsall, eight of the fifteen removed had been parliamentarian soldiers or on the county committee: Homeshaw, *Walsall*, pp. 36–37. At Chester, nearly all dismissed had come into office as a result of the parliamentary purges of 1646 and 1652. CCRO, AB/2, ff. 135–37v. Record of the commissioners' work at Leicester does not survive, but may be inferred from other surviving evidence. See Stocks, *Records of Leicester*, pp. 606–07, showing corporation lists of 1660 and 1662. These lists compare perfectly with attendance lists from the last full meeting before and the first meeting after the commissioners' visit: Leicestershire RO, BRII/18/30, f. 244 (May 19, 1662) and BRII/1/3, ff. 774–76. References to their visit are at BRIII/2/86, ff. 65, 66, and 68.
137 *Kingdoms Intelligencer*, number 39, Sept. 22–29, 1662, p. 649. Bod., MS Top. Essex.e.6/11, ff. 75v–79. Marlowe calculates that 136 of 292 (47%) in the corporations of the southwest were removed in 1662: "Government in the West Country Boroughs," pp. 252–56, on the lack of changes 1660–62, and p. 280 on removals in 1662.

Towns that had already undergone extensive changes since 1660 were largely passed by. At Kingston, where members dismissed in the 1650s regained their places in 1660, fewer than one fifth of the corporation lost their positions in 1662. Leeds, having recently received a new charter making extensive changes, escaped a visit altogether, as did Preston, where the corporation purged itself in 1661 before receiving a new charter.[138] The same appears to have occurred at High Wycombe where thirty-six resigned *en bloc* in 1660, and at Bury St. Edmunds. Much the same happened at Bristol, Norwich, and Worcester where changes under the act were few after those corporations had already remodeled themselves.[139] In these towns, the commissioners' work was essentially done for them, just as in those where corporation members in large numbers refused the oaths or the declaration and thus automatically lost office. In either case, the commissioners had few decisions to make.

Some commissioners did impose their will with all the rigor allowed by law. At Lymington, they removed nearly the entire corporation.[140] At Gloucester, where three-quarters of the corporation was removed, 12.5% of them lost their places for refusing the declaration, and an extraordinary 87.5% were removed by the commissioners' arbitrary command. Lord Herbert, who led the effort, seemed to believe he acted with exemplary moderation. Days before the expiration of their powers, Herbert exhorted his fellow commissioners to conduct one last visit:

if you do commit an error, let it now be on that safest hand, for a thing cannot be left too clean that hath never the means more to be cleansed, and I think the axiom among physicians, that the body doth every day gather something of ill humor that at length needs to be purged away, is not more true of a natural than a politic body . . . I descend to none in particular, for truly I may safely say I am as impartial as to persons in that town as a judge ought to be.[141]

Cooler counsel prevailed among Lancashire's commissioners, despite the Earl of Derby's call to apply the law with equal vigor. Writing to Secretary Nicholas, Derby proposed "that all such as ever had been against the King,

---

138 *CSPD Addendum, 1660–70*, p. 663. See below, pp. 153–55.
139 Greaves, *High Wycombe Ledger*, pp. 162–63; Suffolk RO (Bury St. Edmunds Branch), D10/3/(5), p. 2 and D14/1. R. C. Latham, ed., *Bristol Charters, 1509–1899*, Bristol Record Society, vol. 12 (Bristol, 1947), p. 39. Francis Blomefield, *An Essay Towards a Topographical History of the County of Norfolk*, 11 vols. (London, 1805–10), vol. III, pp. 403–05. Hereford and Worcester RO (St. Helen's), Shelf A.14 (Chamber Order Book), f. 38, and Shelf A.10, Box 3, unfol., 1662.
140 Hampshire RO, 27M74/DBC283.
141 Roland Austin, "The City of Gloucester and the Regulation of Corporations, 1662–63," *Transactions of the Bristol and Gloucestershire Archaeological Society*, 58 (1936), pp. 265–66.

and had given no testimony of their loyalty before his Majesty's happy restoration, should, notwithstanding they be willing to subscribe or take the oaths appointed by the act, be turned out." But Derby's commission colleagues objected that such harsh measures had not been used elsewhere; some felt they owed leniency to the corporations in return for past political support. They appreciated that allowing Derby's vindictiveness free rein would only contribute to the more precise delineation of the party lines they hoped might now be erased. In writing Secretary Nicholas, Derby hoped for a response interpreting the law as he did: a royal letter to inspire the commissioners to a more severe purge before the act ran out. What he received was a peremptory order to attend the King, probably to be reprimanded for his obstructive behavior in settling the militias of the northwest, but perhaps also to lower the feverish heat firing his vengeful feelings toward the towns.[142]

The lack of encouragement Derby had from the King was in keeping with the apparent royal policy of keeping a good distance from the commissioners as they performed their chores. Most of what the Council did see came in the form of unsolicited reports of the commissioners' actions in various towns. In anticipation of the commissioners' visits, a few petitions came into the crown from local persons scavenging for a lucrative place or from corporations arguing for light treatment. Responding to such petitions, the King granted letters to the commissioners at Devizes and Newcastle upon Tyne, recommending town clerks in both cases. Requests from Bristol and Hull for freedom from outside interference in enforcing the act were also granted. Of greater interest are the few reports of corporation officers refusing the oath of allegiance or that against taking up arms against the King, for behind these refusals, greater dangers might lie. From Lord Lovelace at Newbury and from others at Chard came word that refusers of the oaths were bound over.[143] The Privy Council ordered the disarming and binding over of oath refusers upon similar reports from Arundel and Taunton, where almost all of both corporations refused.[144] But scattered, unsolicited reports like these do not point to any royal effort to monitor commissioners' work.

Implementation of the act varied from place to place and depended on the personalities involved. This might explain why some of Berkshire's corporations were so hard hit. Reading lost over one half and Wallingford over two-thirds of their members. On the other hand, Abingdon lost less than one third and Windsor under 10%. Perhaps at Wallingford the

[142] PRO, SP29/61/45. Bod., MS Clarendon 77, ff. 292 and 380.
[143] *CSPD 1661–62*, pp. 286, 319, 411, 419, 485, and 539.
[144] PRO, PC2/56/80 and 95v.

commissioners included some of those who had received a royal rebuke after their earlier attempt to remodel the corporation. This might have been an opportunity for retribution, or for conducting unfinished business.[145] Lord Lovelace, who visited each of the towns as the head of the commission, may have been the crucial factor in determining the extent of purges in Berkshire. At Reading, nearly twice as many were removed by commission discretion than by refusal of the oaths or declaration. Conversely, the much milder action at Windsor might be explained by the mediating presence of John Viscount Mordaunt, the castle governor and the town's high steward. Unlike Lovelace, who came to town then left, Mordaunt had a continuing interest in a stable Windsor.[146] Just to the north, in Oxfordshire, the story was quite different. Oxford itself fared better than the average English town, though worse than the others in the county, with just under one third forfeiting their places. Woodstock did better, with 24% meeting the same fate. The commissioners apparently saw no reason to bother Henley with a visit, and at Banbury they came calling, witnessed the taking of oaths and subscribing of the declaration, and then left, disturbing no one's hold on office.[147]

Leniency and lack of thoroughness meant that many with close connections to Parliament's or the Protectorate's cause went unscathed. Nor did all dissenters lose their places if they swallowed conscience with pride and subscribed the declaration against the Covenant. At Coventry, at least four dissenters remained on the corporation after the commissioners' visit. At Bristol and Cambridge too, known parliamentarians and dissenters survived. Two of those favored by local Cromwellians to enter Chester's corporation after Booth's rebellion remained after 1662; a third was promoted by the commissioners to the aldermen's bench. Four sequestrators at Beverley retained their places while 40% of their brethren lost theirs. At Yarmouth, at least four prominent supporters of the Cromwellian regime remained to support dissenters in the years ahead.[148] In addition to

[145] See above, p. 81. George Purefoy, one of those reprimanded by the King, acted in the commission at Reading and Abingdon. The commissioners acting at Wallingford, besides Lord Lovelace, are unknown.

[146] Berkshire RO, M/AC1/1/1, second pagination, pp. 49 and 51; J. H. Sacret, "The Corporation Act Commissioners at Reading," *The Berks, Bucks and Oxon Archaeological Journal*, 30 (1926), pp. 18–42; John Kirby Hedges, *The History of Wallingford*, 2 vols. (London, 1881), vol. II, p. 220, and Berkshire RO, W/AC1/1/1/2, ff. 25v–27; Bond, *Hall Book of Windsor*, pp. 11–12.

[147] J. S. W. Gibson and E. R. C. Brinkworth, eds., *Banbury Corporation Records: Tudor and Stuart*, Banbury Historical Society, vol. 15 (Banbury, 1977), p. 211; M. G. Hobson and H. E. Salter, *Oxford Council Acts, 1626–1665*, Oxford Historical Society, vol. 95 (Oxford, 1933), pp. 293 and 305–06; and Woodstock Town Hall 76/1, ff. 4–6. No record survives of any visit to Henley. Oxfordshire RO, A.V.6, passim.

[148] Judith Hurwich, "'A Fanatick Town': The Political Influence of Dissenters in Coventry, 1660–1720," *Midland History*, 4 (1977), p. 19. Latham, *Bristol Charters*, p. 39. W. M.

those remaining, many appointed were little different from those they replaced. At Newcastle under Lyme, two appointed by the commissioners neglected the oaths and one never took his place on the corporation. In Reading, one of those appointed declined the honor; another dropped it within a year. At Boston, where many elected in the 1650s remained, two of the newly named aldermen never took their oaths of office. Two others had to be dismissed later in the year, they not having received the sacrament. Of four appointed at Leicester, three were ultimately removed by the corporation without incident "in regard they have failed in their several callings and absented themselves from the town"; the fourth resigned, claiming he was too poor to serve. Commissioners in these cases do not seem to have been terribly concerned to appoint prominent royalist Anglicans. Others appointed, like the new mayor of Poole, never acted.[149] The results were mixed indeed.

Dust stirred up by the commissioners settled quickly in most towns as corporations returned their attentions to the matters of greatest interest: managing property, regulating trade, and providing local services. But some did not take their ejections quietly. The act not only provided no means of appeal but discouraged it with a clause charging treble costs in unsuccessful suits. Nonetheless, some hoped to invent a remedy by requesting writs of mandamus from King's Bench. This made the court the final arbiter of the act's extent, not the commissioners, whose powers lapsed in March 1663. Canterbury's attorney of the town court regained his place this way, though the justices split their decision when first hearing the case. After considering it again a year later, they ruled that the office was "but a private profession," and thus not one in which the commissioners had "a power to intermeddle."[150] Others were not so lucky: when mandamuses went out ordering their restoration, returns came back explaining their removal by the commissioners, and the judges were not about to contradict powers exercised according to statute.[151]

Palmer, "The Reformation of the Corporation of Cambridge," *Proceedings of the Cambridge Antiquarian Society*, 17 (1912–13), pp. 75–136. CCRO, AB2/135–37v. J. Dennett, ed., *Beverley Borough Records, 1575–1821*, Yorkshire Archaeological Society Record Series, vol. 84 (Wakefield, 1932), pp. 103–04. PRO, SP46/134/159 and 163. Gauci, *Yarmouth*, p. 103.

[149] Pape, *Newcastle-under-Lyme*, pp. 16–23. Sacret, "Reading," p. 40. Bailey, *Minutes of Boston*, vol. III, pp. 386–87. Leicestershire RO, BRII/18/31, ff. 420 and 427. John Sydenham, *The History of the Town and County of Poole* (London, 1839; reprint, Poole, 1986), p. 199.

[150] *Eng. Rep.*, vol. 82, p. 1027, and vol. 83, pp. 31, 51, 304, 990, 1010, 1111, and 1179 (1 Sid. 152; T. Raymond 56 and 94, 1 Lev. 75, 1 Keble 354, 387, 558, and 675). Canterbury City and Cathedral Archives, CC/AC/5, ff. 57, 89v, and 96v–97. PRO, KB21/15/27, 39v, and 40; and KB29/315/unfol.: writ and return for Edward Hurst.

[151] See for instance the failure of Woodstock's town clerk, though at one point the mayor was threatened with an attachment for not making his return to the writ: PRO, KB21/15,

The most interesting case involved none other than William Prynne, who lost no time suing his writ following his dismissal as recorder of Bath. The return made by the remodeled corporation explained that Prynne was dismissed for "the public good." Prynne raised a host of objections. Foremost of these was that "the commissioners being made hereby judges . . . may hereby remove for other causes than at common law, but they must show some [cause] or else this inconvenience would follow, that the King's best friends may be turned out, and [the commissioners'] private friends induced. Also these commissioners are without appeal." Prynne's counsel condemned the contention that he had been removed for the public good as "a judgment on effects without cause, for they ought to show for what cause [he] was so dangerous."[152] Nor had Prynne been summoned; referring to language in the act's preamble, he had no opportunity to show whether or not he was "well-affected." Finally, the argument from property law was made: that the recordership being a freehold, Prynne could not be deprived of it by parliamentary act or otherwise without a hearing.

These arguments borrowed their reasoning from Prynne's *Summary Reasons* against the act. Likewise, the response those arguments met outlined his fears of an arbitrary authority whose actions would be beyond appeal. Counsel for the commissioners pleaded the act, contending that it "reposed a trust in the commissioners, for breach of which the party is remediless . . . here were secrets of state in this act, and they intended not a judicatory, as at common law." While the judges leaned in the direction of this argument for a narrow construction of the act, they ordered a consultation with the House of Lords. Upon resuming the matter the following term, disagreements arose between the justices over the proper nature of a return to mandamus under the act. Ultimately they agreed that cause need not be shown for dismissal by the commissioners who had performed the deed. As the return had come from Bath's mayor, not the commissioners, Prynne ultimately won another mandamus. But the court privately advised the commissioners that they need only make a new return

---

ff. 46, 53, 55v, 66, and 68v, and Woodstock Town Hall, 76/1. See too the failure of Barnstaple's town clerk: PRO, KB21/15/6v and 12; KB29/313/113 and KB29/315/1, second foliation and return at end of roll. Also Bideford: PRO, KB21/15/17v and 34v; KB29/313/184 and KB29/315/unfol.: writ and return for John Hill. A small crowd attempting their restoration at Richmond probably met the same fate: PRO, KB21/15/8 and 10; KB29/313/31 and KB29/315/1.

[152] *Eng. Rep.*, vol. 83, pp. 1100–01 (1 Keble 539). A friend of the King's was removed in the manner Prynne suggested: the Earl of Clare was ejected as recorder of Nottingham, but reinstated on the King's order to the commissioners there. *CSPD 1661–62*, pp. 540 and 553.

that the dismissal was expedient according to the terms of the act. Prynne would not regain his place after all.[153]

Prynne's case served as a precedent in later years.[154] In upholding his dismissal, in restoring Canterbury's attorney, and in other cases, the court followed a strict reading of the act. While mandamus had shown itself an effective remedy for wrongful removal, there was little the writ could do given the act's broad terms. The Corporation Act gave to temporarily appointed officers hitherto unheard of discretion to recreate hundreds of governing bodies nationwide. That relatively few cases on mandamus were brought in response to removals under the act – and that so few of these succeeded – suggests both the wide sweep of the act's language and the limited use made by the commissioners of their arbitrary authority.

Though its implementation is typically represented as an opportunity for the crown, the gentry, or both to scour the corporations, the majority of dismissals resulted from the delicacy of corporators' consciences, not gentry zeal, and certainly not crown meddlings.[155] Three-quarters dismissed under the act had probably refused to forswear the Covenant. The declaration, added to the bill by the Lords in December 1661, made the act essentially one for the exclusion of conscientious Presbyterians. If the vast majority *lost* their places rather than being taken from them; and if those who lost their places did so because they refused to renounce the Covenant, the embodiment of Presbyterian ambitions; and if the corporations suffering the greatest hemorrhage were those with the most elections to their bodies in the 1650s and the fewest removals since 1660; then a high correlation between adhering to the Presbyterian cause and gaining borough office during the Interregnum becomes clear. Presbyterian hopes of comprehension in the local polity, as well as in a national church, had been dashed by 1663. As many of those elected to corporations in the 1650s were of that persuasion, the act finished the process begun in 1659 of removing those who came illegally to office and of restoring those removed in the 1640s and 50s.

The commissioners' powers ceased in March 1663. Ironically, the act

---

153 Twelve others removed at Bath used mandamus, with the same result. PRO, KB21/14/93v; *Eng. Rep.*, vol. 83, pp. 1100–01, 1131–32, 1140, and 1186 (1 Keble 540, 594, 608, and 686). Henderson, *English Administrative Law*, pp. 138–39. The commissioners replaced Prynne with Francis Lord Hawley, but the corporation still considered Prynne their recorder. When Prynne died, they elected a new recorder. This prompted Hawley to seek a mandamus for his restoration, which failed. PRO, KB21/14/93v; KB21/15/9, 19v, 35v, 37v, and 49; KB21/17, passim; and KB29/315/7v–8. Bath City RO, Council Book 2, pp. 359 and 512. *Eng. Rep.*, vol. 84, pp. 503–04 (2 Keble 796), and vol. 86, pp. 98–99 (1 Ventris 143).

154 *Eng. Rep.*, vol. 83, p. 1237 (1 Keble 777).

155 Pace Sacret, "Restoration Government and Municipal Corporations," especially, p. 251; and Hutton, *The Restoration*, pp. 160–61.

would prove an even greater source of contention than it had while they exercised their authority, for in the continuing requirement of the declaration, and even more so, the sacrament, lay the seeds of partisan conflict in the towns for generations to come. The Corporation Act shows the paradox of partisan politics in its most vivid colors. A law meant to restore unity by declaring certain people beyond the political pale instead united and energized those left out. Loss of eminence and fears of persecution gave those who once enjoyed the fruits of office powerful reasons to join together to get back into their places.

PURGE AND COUNTER-PURGE

More than any other single measure, the Corporation Act attempted to undo the changes wrought in the years of Civil War and Interregnum. Hundreds had been forced from or had come to power in England's borough corporations in the troubled years before 1660. New men swore new oaths to new regimes. With the repudiation of those regimes begun at the end of 1658, a long process commenced, begun in the corporations themselves, and culminating in the act, that meant to reverse the orders and decrees by which so many had lost or abandoned municipal office. The dismissals and oaths of the 1640s and 50s provided reason, precedent, and prescription for the actions taken at the Restoration. In the early 1660s, fire was fought with fire: purges with purges, oaths with oaths.

The restoration of borough government was a national effort to eradicate political difference, to eliminate faction in all forms, and to create unified corporate bodies on the unquestioned assumption that divided bodies were dead bodies. The crown, weak from its sojourns abroad, hoped by conciliation, limited removals, and comprehension of a broad middle to reunite a country rent asunder by the sword and by political recriminations. But decisions made by individuals in the towns, not by the crown, proved the crucial ones, and these emphasized exclusion. Many simply resigned their positions when it became clear that their days were done. Others were forced out by the courtroom actions of those they had supplanted. Still others gave up office in the face of requirements they could not meet, defined in an act passed by a Parliament consisting largely of representatives from the corporations. While some under the Corporation Act swallowed hard, swore softly, and remained in the polity, others could not. In many towns, the potential for revived partisan rivalries persisted within the corporations and would only be promoted by the body of less moderate opinion now left out of doors by its refusal to come in.

The great mistake of the borough restorations was the belief that excluding the obdurate and those who gained office illegally in the 1640s and 50s would make them politically neuter. It did not. The comprehension within many corporations of those who would later be known as occasional conformists, and even more so, the exclusion from the corporations of groups still politically potent, would keep alive the politics of partisan competition created in the Civil War years. The one hope to come from this period may be found in the courts. In the 1650s and early 1660s, King's Bench developed quickly – using the writ of mandamus – as an institution capable of arbitrating partisan disputes. As a partisan political practice developed, and as attempts were made to destroy it with purges, the institutional arrangements were evolving by which partisan competition would become a type of political practice that did not endanger state and society. This was crucial, for in the end, Prynne proved correct. The Corporation Act and the entire process of restoration in the boroughs did not destroy faction as was hoped, but encouraged it. Even in corporations touched little if at all by the act, "former marks and names of distinction" kept alive the memory of "forgotten crimes" and perpetuated "divisions, contentions, factions, and parties."[156] Here Prynne identified the paradox of partisan politics: that the impulse to create unity through exclusion only provoked more disunity. Those who had just lost their places would see to that.

[156] [Prynne], *Summary Reasons.*

4

Partisan politics, 1663–1682

The Corporation Act left behind two groups in Northampton: the corporation and a disgruntled rump expelled from it.[1] In March of 1663, the third parliamentary by-election in eighteen months set the corporation against "the secluded members." Mayor John Brafield's choice, Sir William Dudley, challenged Christopher Hatton. Hatton won with the help of those expelled.[2] The "secluded members" showed elsewhere that their political vigor remained as they attacked Brafield and his corporate friends with law suits. Within the corporation, the political weight began to shift with the choice of William Vaughan – a foe of Brafield – as mayor and Vaughan's allies as JPs and coroners.[3] But March 1664 brought another by-election. This time, ardent Anglican Sir John Yelverton prevailed against Vaughan's candidate, Sir John Bernard. So Vaughan, to shore up his damaged base, tried to expel Yelverton's supporters from the corporation but was prevented by a letter from the King, sent in response to pleas to help "the loyal party."[4]

The electoral struggle of 1663 set the corporation against those excised from it, but in 1664, the corporation began dividing within as partisans of those left out tried to expel their foes and to restore their ousted friends. The center of political gravity then shifted again as Francis Pickmer, "loyal" Brafield's ally, followed Vaughan as mayor in 1664. Tradition dictated that when Pickmer's year ended, he should preside at his successor's election. But Pickmer left town on the appointed day, aware that "the house [had] crossed him in his design of choosing a man he intended." So six of the

---

[1] BL, Add. 34,222, f. 33. Bod., MS Clarendon 77, f. 66. No record of the corporation commissioners' work survives. The assembly book gives the names of the remodeled corporation: Northamptonshire RO, 3/2, pp. 167–70. Bod., MS Top. Northants. c.9, p. 113, says fifty-seven were removed.

[2] Henning, vol. I, p. 340. Kishlansky, *Parliamentary Selection*, pp. 174–80.

[3] Northamptonshire RO, 3/2, pp. 179–82.

[4] This election was occasioned by Richard Rainsford's appointment as an Exchequer Baron. Rainsford seconded the request for the King's letter to Northampton. *CSPD 1663–64*, p. 603. Henning, vol. I, p. 340.

eight aldermen, along with forty-five of forty-eight councilmen, broke into the hall and elected John Friend mayor. Pickmer later refused to swear Friend and then had him arrested, "upon pretence that he was grown a fanatic." Though Friend was freed after several aldermen posted a £1,000 bond, Pickmer still would not swear him. Friend finally took his oaths from the recorder, former parliamentary general the Earl of Manchester.[5] Little more than a week later, Manchester obtained a Privy Council warrant to imprison Brafield and Pickmer, the "loyal" pair.[6] Meanwhile, Pickmer, Brafield, and four of their partisans entered charges at the Council that Friend had scorned a royal letter to Northampton in order, it was said, to rally the "factious and fanatic party." Friend and some of his supporters were now arrested too.[7]

If Brafield's partisans hoped to stir the fears of the King and his Council with charges against the "fanatic party," they failed. The Privy Council ordered that Pickmer and Brafield apologize, surrender the mayor's mace to Friend, and that they then be dismissed by the corporation.[8] Friend had won a complete victory, despite the charge that he favored the "factious." King and Council showed greater interest in a legal corporate succession than fear of those who ostensibly strengthened a dissenting faction. But more dismissals did not end the struggle. Brafield now turned to King's Bench for his mandamus, though the corporation prevailed in arguments before the justices.[9] Friend continued as mayor, and was chosen again in 1669, after which he was succeeded by William Spencer who had been dismissed by the Corporation Act commissioners in 1662. Brafield, the commissioners' appointee, remained outside the corporation while the "factious" strengthened their hold over it. Brafield only regained his place in 1672 after an unusual case in the court of Exchequer, but by then, the balance of power was irretrievably tipped against him.[10]

5 Northamptonshire RO, 3/2, p. 190. Christopher Markham and John Charles Cox, eds., *The Records of the Borough of Northampton*, 2 vols. (Northampton, 1898), vol. II, p. 35. Bod., MS Top. Northants. c.9, pp. 115 and 116.
6 PRO, PC2/58/130v and 132.
7 They were soon released on bond. PRO, SP29/134/97; *CSPD 1665–66*, p. 15.
8 PRO, PC2/58/139. Ironically, Brafield had been instrumental in gaining the 1663 charter which gave the corporation the power of dismissal. Markham and Cox, *Northampton Records*, vol. I, pp. 137–42. The Earl of Manchester, Friend's supporter, was a Privy Councillor, but was not present at any meetings when the matter was discussed.
9 *Eng. Rep.*, vol. 86, pp. 14–15 (1 Ventris 19) Rex v. Braithwaite [*sic*], and vol. 84, p. 307 (2 Keble 488). PRO, KB21/16/67, 74v, 78, 83v, 98v, and 101v; KB21/17/4v, 54v, and 86; and KB29/320/65–68 and KB29/324/63 and 89v.
10 Markham and Cox, *Northampton Records*, vol. II, p. 36. Brafield's suit was an action for a false return. Most such actions were brought before King's Bench. But there was no reason why such an action – legally distinct from the original writ – could not be taken before other common law courts. Brafield won a large award, but the Exchequer suit could not order Brafield's return to the corporation. For that he had to get another mandamus from

Given the extent of corporate purges after the Restoration, we should not be surprised to see a partisan politics based on conflict between those in the corporations and those left out. More surprising is that partisan conflict should also be so virulent *within* corporations. John Brafield detested the idea of a foe succeeding him as mayor, so he subverted the election process. On the other side, John Friend's crew could not suffer Brafield and Pickmer in their midst, and gained their expulsion by royal order. But Brafield kept picking away at his enemies in court until he had his place again. The most prominent quality of corporate partisans was their tenacity, their ability to spring up when knocked down. Borough partisans worked to remove their opponents; their opponents, made as they were of the same stuff, rarely succumbed. Opposing efforts for total victory canceled one another out and perpetuated rather than ended conflict: this was the paradox of partisan politics at work.

In the towns, partisan struggle had a continuous history since the Civil Wars. The years following saw men of one persuasion, then another, gain local control. The factors at work when they traded places were many: intervention by Interregnum or royal regimes, statutes, court rulings, sneak tactics by local partisans. Only a well-orchestrated effort could bring off a local purge or prompt outside institutions like the Council or King's Bench to intervene. The use made of Council and court by Northampton's partisans illustrates how partisan conflicts arose in the provinces and then worked their way to the center. Divisions flowed inward from the peripheries rather than the other way around. Organized competition in corporations like Northampton's thus lay the foundations for the development of partisan politics at Westminster. For "Exclusion" did not create partisan politics, certainly not in the boroughs, where partisan competition long pre-dated the "Crisis."

Northampton's troubles also reveal the shifting roles of Council and court as adjudicators of political conflict. Judgment by the Council came quickly, but it was not final; only in the courts were final resolutions achieved. Feuding townsmen quickly learned this. As they did, the center of provincial administrative supervision shifted from the King's Council to the King's Bench. A crucial change in the workings and in the location of authority in the state thus occurred because countless people in the towns needed it to change. The King did not mind this movement of jurisdiction from Council to court, even when the court's decisions reversed the Council's. Local order and effective governance were the chief concerns of

---

King's Bench. The corporation did not oppose this last writ. Brafield and Pickmer were restored in February 1672. Northamptonshire RO, 3/2, pp. 214–15, 219, 221, and 223–25.

the crown in its interaction with the boroughs through the 1660s and 70s, so angry partisans were simply "left to the law."

THE FAILURE OF THE CORPORATION ACT

Why the ugly turmoil in Northampton, so severe that it required outsiders to end it? The simple answer is that the Corporation Act failed. Northampton politics cast the shortcomings of the act in sharp relief: persons later disapproved of by the King had been appointed by the commissioners; those removed found their way back into office, even with royal approval. The act was not the only means by which the Restoration, and restoration, operated in the boroughs. But the act, and the entire process of restoration, failed on two counts: it neither excluded all who sympathized with dissent, nor did it deny political power to those it did exclude. The political potential of those excluded persisted, especially when they could use other local institutions as alternative power bases from which to take on the corporation. School, hospital, and other charity trusts became important political prizes in themselves. So too did feoffments of town lands.

Legal title to Bury St. Edmunds's corporate lands was actually in the hands of feoffees: a group of named individuals who held the lands in trust for the corporation.[11] In 1630, the corporation granted their properties to two feoffees. These two in turn reconveyed the same to the members of the corporation severally by name, and to three others.[12] Thus people who in one legal guise were corporation members, in another, held the corporation's property in trust as a legally distinct panel of individuals. The same people acted "sometimes as feoffees and sometimes as members of the said corporation." The feoffees were said to hold the property "to the use of" the corporation: they were expected to manage it in the corporation's interest. As long as the feoffees and the corporators were the same people, dispute between the two groups – distinct in law, but identical in personnel – was out of the question. This continued to be a workable arrangement until 1660, when the corporation and the feoffment suddenly found themselves composed of different people with opposed purposes.

---

[11] There were two reasons a corporation might do this. Enfeoffing property avoided limitations on corporate land-holding imposed by charter terms and medieval mortmain statutes. Second, it protected corporate properties from any danger of loss if the corporation committed some wrong or were otherwise judged forfeit. Thus in the 1680s, many corporations placed their properties in feoffments before surrendering their charters to ensure their property would not be lost by surrender. See below, p. 219.

[12] The following account of troubles at Bury is from Suffolk RO (Bury St. Edmunds Branch), D10/3/(5), (11), and (14). For more on feoffments, see J. H. Baker, *An Introduction to English Legal History*, 3rd edn. (London, 1990), chapter 14, and Carr, *Corporations*, chapter 5.

At Bury, Restoration exclusions from the corporation were self-imposed. By the time they were finished, only nine of the thirty-three living feoffees remained in the corporation. So suit and counter-suit between corporation and feoffment commenced in the court of Chancery to decide who would control the property.[13] The corporation's case turned on the contention that it had never been intended that feoffment profits should be out of corporate control; with most of the feoffees dismembered from the corporation, the present situation was untenable since the feoffees refused to do the corporation's bidding. Raising the specter of factiousness, the corporations also charged the feoffees with appointing ministers "who are not conformable to . . . the Church of England"; they named ten feoffees as "disaffected" or of "the Independent persuasion." Charges of greed rounded out their complaints: that feoffees employed funds for private uses. For these reasons, the corporation asked the court to return feoffment properties to corporate control.

The feoffees responded by explaining that the feoffment had been created to perform certain duties that "could not so well be performed by them in their body politic as by some of the corporation, and inhabitants not of the corporation, in their private capacities." As trustees, they, not the corporation, held exclusive power over the properties in their care. Further diminishing corporation claims, they contended that their trust "concerned the benefit of the inhabitants as much if not more than the corporation," so they could not reconvey lands to the corporation without the "consent of the inhabitants." Responding to the religious charges, the feoffees defended their ministers and noted that if anything were improper, it was for church, not lay, authorities to judge. For the corporation to pass judgment was "to invade the bishop's office" – an ironic charge, coming as it did from those who allegedly defied ecclesiastical unity. Despite the valiant effort, the court ordered the feoffees to reconvey all properties to the corporation and to account for all their profits to one of the masters in chancery, whom the judges instructed to allow no payments to "nonconformable ministers."[14] The feoffment they had used to maintain partisan coherence had been destroyed. One party in Bury had now succeeded not only in excluding, but in destroying the other. The outcome was what was always desired yet so

---

[13] The corporation commissioners had only one person to remove since so many had quit in early 1661. PRO, PC2/55/66v, and Suffolk RO (Bury St. Edmunds Branch), D14/1. Corporations had probably anticipated the purges of 1661: while still in charge of the corporation in October of 1660, they ordered that all feoffment documents should be separated from corporate documents and stored in locked chests. They thus quit the corporation with everything necessary for defending their control of town lands. Suffolk RO (Bury St. Edmunds Branch), D4/1/2, ff. 27, 35v, and 37.

[14] After examining the accounts, the eighteen feoffees named were charged £225, which they paid in August 1662. Suffolk RO (Bury St. Edmunds Branch), D4/1/2, f. 42.

rarely achieved: the end of party. With the matter settled by late summer 1662, Bury corporation passed the next two decades in comparative calm.[15]

The complete exclusion of one group was rare, but the effort to use the feoffment to control local life suggests how dismembering one's corporate enemies did not necessarily end their political potency.[16] More common than such a complete exclusion was a more muddled result that left some of the "factious" untouched. This happened less as a result of corporation commissioners' leniency than as a result of the malleability of the act's terms in corporators' hands. The political tests written into the statute – the oaths of allegiance and against taking up arms against the King – presented no obstacle to the country's corporation officers: nearly all took them. It was the declaration against the Covenant and the sacrament that separated adherents of the established Church from those of the "factious" sects. Or did they? While exclusion may have been the act's purpose, in the end, it achieved an awkward combination of exclusion and comprehension.

Sympathy and doctrinal flexibility proved the problems that the act could not solve. Among some corporators who attended only the established Church, sympathy for others of "tender conscience" meant they forbore prosecuting conventicling neighbors. Many urban magistrates apparently protected nonconformists.[17] Some went even further, allowing dissenters to participate in local governance. Thus by 1673, Bewdley's corporation contained nineteen who had not received the sacrament.[18] The allowance of illegal political participation arose from friendships, family connections, and business relationships that crossed the ecclesiological divide. Belief was not a wedge, black on one side and white on the other, splitting the worthy from the unworthy. For those of dissenting tendencies, the declaration, and even the sacrament requirement, proved remarkably flexible. Many subscribed without compunction, received communion, and

---

[15] Those left out of the corporation formed the core of a group that tried, unsuccessfully, to influence both parliamentary elections in 1679. Henning, vol. I, p. 397.

[16] For similar partisan conflict between feoffment and corporation, see the case of Walsall in Paul D. Halliday, "Partisan Conflict and the Law in the English Borough Corporation" (Ph.D., University of Chicago, 1993), pp. 208–13.

[17] Reading corporation dismissed Alderman Samuel Howse in 1670 for doing so. He was readmitted after getting a mandamus and a recommendation from the dean of Bangor: Berkshire RO, R/AC/1/1/14, ff. 33–34, 42, 42v, 44v.–45, 71, and 73; R/AC1/1/15, ff. 6v, 20v, 22v, 23, and 27; PRO, KB21/17/50v, 99, 110, 115v, and 127; KB21/18/23; KB29/323/ 217; and KB29/325/91 and 149. Widespread leniency in enforcing the conventicle acts has been well established. Anthony Fletcher, "The Enforcement of the Conventicle Acts, 1663–1679," in W. S. Shiels, ed., *Persecution and Toleration* (Oxford, 1984), pp. 235–46. Hurwich, "'A Fanatick Town'," pp. 21–23.

[18] Philip Styles, "The Corporation of Bewdley under the Later Stuarts," in *Studies in Seventeenth-Century West Midlands History* (Kineton, 1978), p. 48.

perhaps attended the parish church on Sunday mornings; but they could still easily hear an excluded minister later that afternoon. This then makes it easier to understand the "incredible conversion" of the leaders of Lyme Regis in subscribing the declaration when the commissioners visited.[19] Such conversions were not so miraculous after all as they were probably neither true nor full ones. Occasional conformity was born the moment England's corporators began swearing the oaths and signing the declaration. In towns around the country after the Corporation Act ostensibly settled the political and religious loyalties of corporation members, men with a wide range of personal and religious sympathies retained their corporate dignities; others soon regained them.[20] No act, and certainly not that implemented in the towns, could sort through such subtleties to impose a lasting political settlement.

Some MPs tried to pass a more extensive act to remedy these failings. In May of 1662, before most commissioners had made any borough visits, a new bill for corporations received two readings in the Commons, then disappeared. On March 6, 1663, less than three weeks before the commissioners' powers were to expire, the Commons appointed a committee to "examine whether the [act] be defective." A bill was read in July. Though approved for a second reading, it too disappeared. Another corporations bill received two readings and was committed the following April, only to die once again.[21]

The text of a "bill for the reviving the act for regulation of corporations," produced on one of these occasions, expressed the political hopes, fears, and disappointments left by the Corporation Act among Anglican loyalists. The commissioners had done their best "to purge . . . corrupt members." Nonetheless, many who gained office in the "late rebellion and usurpation" had concealed their true principles and "colorably and deceitfully" took the oaths, subscribed the declaration, and thereby retained their places. Now they "continue their evil and unsound principles and prove factious," electing as new corporation members parliamentary committeemen and sequestrators just ejected by the commissioners. To keep out the rebellious, the bill proposed reviving the Corporation Act; new commissioners would be empowered to deny office to all complicitous in the usurping regime, as well as those "notoriously disloyal," even if they took all oaths and

---

[19] *Kingdoms Intelligencer*, number 42, Oct. 13–20, 1662, pp. 696–97.
[20] At least four dissenters remained at Coventry: Hurwich, "'A Fanatick Town'," p. 19. At Yarmouth, four prominent corporators of the 1650s also remained to support dissent: Gauci, *Yarmouth*, pp. 103–04. Preston wanted to elect men who refused the declaration, but whose loyalty they guaranteed: *CSPD 1668–69*, pp. 371 and 373. For readmissions of those put out and the election of persons unfit by the act's terms, see Underdown, *Fire from Heaven*, pp. 236–40.
[21] *CJ*, vol. 8, pp. 424, 426, 445, 517, 551, and 553–54.

subscriptions.[22] No mention was made of changing the religious formulation of the oaths and declaration, but the real test would now be one's history. Oaths would play little role in an exclusion based on past affiliations because oaths had been so unequal to the task in the first round. As vague a test as "notorious disloyalty" may have been, it promised to be effective because it was so broad. It would certainly mean many more removals since so many serving in the 1660s had served in the 1650s too. Most important, the new commissioners would retain their powers until one year after the present King's death so they would have a continuing authority to prevent readmission to office of those expelled. But the bill never had a final reading. This would be Parliament's last effort concerning the corporations until 1680: the act of 1661 would remain the law defining eligibility for corporate membership.

Old act, new act, or no act, England's towns continued to endure spasms of partisan conflict. Exclusions from office, by whatever means, necessarily left an irate rump outside; another more thorough act would only have enlarged and enraged that group. Those excluded found many points at which their interests intersected. Their exclusion, based largely on the declaration, or increasingly, on the sacrament, points to their shared religious concerns. And these were necessarily political concerns too because they formed the basis for a formal exclusion from public life and raised the threat of persecution. Those excluded also shared the disappointment of losing something they valued: office. Corporate membership conferred dignity on its holders and confirmed one's social standing. Membership allowed one to preside over the choice properties and extensive moneys corporations controlled. From these flowed leases at favorable rates, cheap loans, and charitable support for a son setting up in his trade. Those who once tasted such fruits could only want to return again to the tables where they were served.

Getting back to the table was easy enough if those still sitting there were willing to make room for you. As the proposed "bill for reviving the act for regulation of corporations" noted, the original act was undermined by remaining corporators who revealed "the secret purposes of their disloyal principles . . . by choosing in of others of like principles," including those expelled by the commissioners and others complicitous with the usurping regime.[23] Perhaps the most amazing thing about the Corporation Act was that there was nothing that could be done to stop them. The act contained an impressive hole: nothing in it barred the return of any dismissed officer who received communion and was re-elected, swore the oaths, signed the

---

[22] The text of the bill, at PRO, SP29/440/93, was identified by Miller in "Borough Charters," p. 63. Miller dates this document to the April 1664 effort.

[23] PRO, SP29/440/93.

declaration, and thus fulfilled the Act's requirements. It was a glaring oversight in legislative drafting.

Across the country, many expelled by the commissioners found their way back through this opening. Dorchester corporation declared its intention to re-elect anyone removed who would subscribe the declaration.[24] The courts and the Privy Council seemed helpless, perhaps even uninterested in stopping it. In 1664, Chief Justice Robert Hyde "doubted whether one turned out by the commissioners may in futuro [be] elect[ed] by the mayor etc., into any other vacant place," but no judgment against the legality of such an election may be found in the law reports.[25] Even as late as September 1681, Secretary of State Sir Leoline Jenkins recognized that there might be no way to plug this hole in the act. While admitting that a person removed by the commissioners might later qualify himself by fulfilling the act's terms, he nonetheless believed "the true meaning [of the act] to be otherwise, for the law . . . never intended that men once removed as dangerous to the government should come in by a back door, whether the [corporate] government would or no."[26] But this was politically wishful rather than legally precise thinking. The Privy Council continued to make little serious effort to prevent the re-election of those formerly turned out, reflecting collectively Jenkins's confusion in confronting the hole in the act.

Some towns, like Warwick and Bewdley, made even easier such returns to office, as well as the election of new members whose consciences were troubled by disavowing the Covenant: they struck the phrase from the declaration stating that the Covenant imposed no obligation "on any other person."[27] This allowed younger persons who never swore the Covenant to forswear it themselves while respecting those who could not. Other corporations loosely enforced the requirement that one had to have received the sacrament within one year before election. At Coventry, new members qualified by taking communion after election.[28] Those seeking corporate office did not take the sacrament regularly in order to be prepared in case of election; they did so only if elected. After all, many of a flexibly dissenting persuasion must have reasoned, why compromise any more than necessary? This subverted the provision's purpose: that all corporation members should be in full communion with the church. In such loose local variations on the act's rigid themes were the origins of occasional conformity.

From the start, those who lost office after the Restoration, especially as a result of the Corporation Act, made their way back into their old places. Some still tried to use mandamus. Most failed, though Stephen Welsteed,

---

24 Underdown, *Fire from Heaven*, p. 237.   25 *Eng. Rep.*, vol. 83, p. 1237 (1 Keble 777).
26 *CSPD 1680–81*, pp. 463–64.   27 Styles, "Corporation of Bewdley," p. 49.
28 Hurwich, "'A Fanatick Town'," p. 23.

Winchester's clerk in the 1650s, regained his place in 1671 after an assize jury found his original expulsion illegal; he duly subscribed the declaration when readmitted.[29] More often, one returned to office with the connivance of those currently in authority rather than by judicial force. Though long powerless by November 1667, Kent's Corporation Act commissioners reported the mayor of Maidstone for readmitting those turned out and for refusing to accept the votes of those appointed by the commissioners. This tended "to the promotion of faction."[30] Elsewhere, those looking to return conspired with a few comrades still in the corporation who orchestrated surprise elections to gain their ends.

Complaints to the courts and to the Privy Council quickly multiplied. At the head of Bridport's corporation were two bailiffs rather than a single mayor; such a constitution provided ample opportunity for serious divisions all the way to the top. In 1664, one of Bridport's bailiffs, Thomas Ellis, and numerous burgesses, petitioned the Privy Council, announcing their disfranchisement of two principal burgesses – done they said to suppress conventicles – and their election of two new ones. They had not gone unopposed. Henry Browne, the other bailiff,

combined with divers of the schismatical party . . . [to] defeat if it were possible the said elections, and to bring in again such members as were formerly ejected for their disaffection to his Majesty's government by the commissioners for regulating corporations, by which means the petitioners are likely to be involved in great suits of law to their undoing, the town will be divided into factions, and the charter itself in danger of being forfeited.[31]

The petitioners looked to the Council to save them from the "schismatical party," composed of those removed by the Corporation Act and their friends still in the corporation. The Council sent a copy of the petition to the recalcitrant bailiff, Henry Browne, with an order that he respond in writing. Browne not only neglected to reply, he soon led his faction in holding their own election of bailiffs, choosing two "persons disfranchised for their crimes notorious." Bailiff Ellis and the loyal group meanwhile elected their own pair.[32] With two separate elections held to fill the same offices, Bridport's corporation was in danger of becoming two bodies, each

---

29 Welsteed's case is one of the few that may be traced in assize records: PRO, ASSI24/38: Aug. 10, 1671. Hampshire RO, W/B1/6, ff. 69v–70v. John Coe, who refused to subscribe the declaration in 1662, tried to regain his town clerkship at Maldon. PRO, KB21/17/24v, 31v, 48v, 60, 62v, 66, and 82; KB29/322/224; KB29/323/52 and 221; KB29/324/224.

30 PRO, PC2/60/27v. Other corporations admitted occasional conformists, for instance, at Norwich: Evans, *Norwich*, pp. 249–51.

31 PRO, PC2/57/121. Both Ellis and Browne had been appointed by the Corporation Act commissioners. Basil Short, *A Respectable Society: Bridport, 1593–1835* (Bradford-on-Avon, 1976), p. 21.

32 PRO, PC2/57/140. This led each side to sue writs of mandamus: PRO, KB21/15/74 and 91, and KB29/314: writs for Henry Browne, Thomas Ellis, Joseph Bishop, and William Burt.

denying the other's legitimacy. Given the increasingly shrill cries coming from each side, the Council at last held a hearing and ordered Browne to join Ellis in swearing the bailiffs elected by Ellis's group.[33] With clear guidance from the crown, matters stood settled. Local peace was promoted by the receipt of a new charter the following year, and by an agreement made between the competing sides to lay aside all disagreements. A tacit understanding appears to have been reached as well, giving corporate control to local Anglicans, while permitting dissenters to go about the practice of their faith unharmed.[34]

The Privy Council resolved controversies at Bridport, but in most cases, the Council abdicated its responsibility for settling local disputes occasioned by the election of those who were to be excluded by the Corporation Act. But the Council did take momentary, if ineffective notice of the act in 1668. Upon reports from Marlborough, the Council suggested that the corporation not choose someone previously removed by the act. At Oxford, such elections had already occurred. Dr. Peter Mews, who reported the news, proposed that the Council issue a proclamation forbidding such elections unless candidates gave clear testament of their loyalty. Whether owing to this suggestion or to its own initiative, the Council sent letters five days later to county sheriffs and lords lieutenant across the country with orders to reacquaint all corporations with the terms of the act and to instruct them not to elect those who did not qualify. Though Mews was pleased, the Council's order was a particularly weak one given the loopholes in the act, and because it required no reports of compliance, either from the sheriffs and lieutenants, or from the corporations.[35]

Corporations duly read the royal letter; they did little else. The usual local informers made their reports from towns where lapses had occurred or the letter was ignored. But few of these elicited any official reaction.[36] At Sudbury, the entire corporation resubscribed the declaration to be certain all were in full compliance. Tiny Aldeburgh did much better about recording subscriptions after 1668; so too did Devizes and Stratford. But in most places, the 1668 effort made no impression: corporations continued to violate the act's provisions for swearing officers, for taking the sacrament before election, and for keeping a record of each new officer's compliance with these requirements. Cambridge copied the royal letter into their town book and then continued their practice of only occasionally recording the

---

[33] PRO, PC2/58/7.   [34] Short, *A Respectable Society*, pp. 21–22.

[35] PRO, PC2/61/24v and 26v; *CSPD 1667–68*, pp. 589 and 611.

[36] *CSPD 1668–69*, pp. 10–11: the report of Yarmouth's self-appointed "loyal" vigilante, Richard Brower, met the usual silence. PRO, PC2/61/112: county JPs were instructed to prosecute Romsey's mayor at assizes if reports that he did not take the oaths of supremacy and allegiance were found to be true. This was one of the only responses to the 1668 enquiry from the Council.

taking of the oaths and declaration by new officers.[37] Wallingford defied the act unabashedly, declaring that they chose Thomas Norton as alderman, notwithstanding his removal in 1662; Norton was then elected mayor in 1671.[38]

The crown quickly reverted to its inconsistent enforcement of the act as well after issuing the 1668 order. At Colchester, attorney of the town court, Thomas Lucas, who had been removed from his post by the commissioners, demanded readmission in 1669, though he still refused the declaration. He appeared before the Privy Council, where the King ordered that he not be allowed into his old post. But one year later, Lucas petitioned the Council to be restored, having made his apology and proved his loyalty. The Council left it to the corporation's discretion whether or not to admit him.[39] No explicit dispensation from the act by the King has been found. But the crown's tendency to overlook lapses suggests a frequent *de facto* dispensation. When Charles II granted Gloucester a charter in 1672, royal officers ignored the fact that the corporation had appointed John Dorney as town clerk in 1667, five years after the commissioners removed him. Not only did the King's charter confirm Dorney, it appointed two councilmen dismissed in 1662 as well.[40]

While excluding some troublesome members, the Corporation Act failed to exclude the potential for political trouble. And the crown did nothing to plug the hole in the Corporation Act through which many of those dismissed in 1662 re-entered the corporations in the years following. Local partisan energies and crown passivity meant that partisan foes fought on after purgation had ostensibly settled England's bodies politic.

PARTISAN CONFLICT IN THE 1670S

The animosities of the Civil War years and persistent religious bigotries had not been washed away by even the most draconian self-imposed corporate purges nor by seemingly far-reaching legislation. Partisan struggle continued after 1660 and 1663, diminishing slightly in the mid- to late-1660s, but rising again in response to two opposing forces: the Conventicle Act of 1670, giving Anglican zealots an opportunity to enforce their will, and the improving fortunes of dissenters and their sympathizers as they continued

---

[37] Suffolk RO (Bury St. Edmunds Branch), EE501/2/8, p. 132. Suffolk RO (Ipswich Branch), EE1/D1/1; Wiltshire RO, G20/1/18; Shakespeare Birthplace Trust, BRU2/4, ff. 189ff; Cambridgeshire RO, Shelf C/8, ff. 225v–26; and Styles, "Corporation of Bewdley," pp. 48–49.

[38] Hedges, *Wallingford*, vol. II, p. 221.   [39] PRO, PC2/61/171 and 177v, and PC2/62/93.

[40] Dorney subscribed when elected in 1667, and is thus an example of one who, though dismissed in 1662, qualified himself later by the act's terms: Gloucestershire RO, GBR/C8/1, f. 24. *CSPD 1672*, pp. 444–45.

to circumvent the strictures in the Corporation Act. Many read Charles's Declaration of Indulgence, effective from 1672 to 1673, as tacit royal approval of the return of moderate dissenters to positions of local authority. Dissenters now turned the political tide in many towns. Corporations around the country soon found themselves with a large minority, if not a preponderance, of those who saw little need to support a strict religious uniformity.

As a result, by the end of the 1670s, the frequency of contested mayoral elections increased dramatically, especially in the explosive combination of parliamentary, religious, and local politics during the years 1678 to 1681. Rumblings in various towns throughout the 1670s foretold these later eruptions. As the life of the Cavalier Parliament dragged on, parliamentary by-elections interacted with local political divisions in an increasingly combustible mix. At Dover, disputes arose after the 1670 mayoral election when two men were chosen by different franchises, each arguably customary as both franchises had been used at various times during the last century. Each of the contending mayors had backing from one of the men vying for Dover's then vacant parliamentary seat: one favored the dissenting interest, the other the cause of uniformity. Both mayoral contestants complained to the Privy Council, where the King ordered a new election, though he was careful to dictate that they follow the older, more restricted franchise, "as tending to the peace and quiet of that place."[41] Dissenter Richard Barley won the mayoral vote; Lord Hinchingbroke, his backer, then easily carried the parliamentary contest that followed.

Barley's two-year mayoralty was an unhappy one, and opposition to him gathered not only around his religious foes, but among those he should have counted with his supporters. Captain Richard Jacobs, of a prominent Huguenot family, captured the mayoralty in 1672 and then turned it to good effect a few months later by making over fifty new freemen the day before another by-election. All those newly enfranchised gave their votes for Sir Edward Spragge, Jacobs's candidate, against the favorite of local dissenters, Thomas Papillon.[42] Control of the mayoralty, in order to control admissions to the freemen, had proved crucial in both parliamentary elections. Contending interests organized themselves to capture these prizes; strong leadership made organization possible. Around such organization and leadership, Dover's parties coalesced, in pursuit of prizes in town and at Westminster. Likewise at Eye, in Suffolk, new freemen were made and four corporation leaders were removed by "the faction" in the weeks before a parliamentary by-election in 1675. Then came writs of

---

[41] PRO, PC2/62/149v, and *CSPD 1670*, pp. 441 and 444–45.
[42] On Dover parliamentary elections, see Kishlansky, *Parliamentary Selection*, pp. 163–71.

mandamus, but restoration by the writs could not happen quickly enough to undo the results of a parliamentary election long since past.[43]

The number of contested parliamentary elections resulting in petitions to the Commons increased over the 1670s; so too did contested mayoral and other corporate elections producing petitions to the Privy Council or cases in court. All over England, corporate partisans understood the cynical advice of Lord Guilford: "set up a false mayor, make disturbance, and the case will be disputable."[44] Though High Wycombe's corporation regulated itself in 1660, political peace had not followed. In 1664, two petitions were presented to the Privy Council, each from a group claiming to have elected the legal mayor. One group said Henry Elliot was chosen, the other, Edward Bedder. The Council referred the petitioners to the arbitration of Sir Robert Hyde, chief justice of King's Bench. Hyde ordered that Elliot be sworn and the Bedder group readily acquiesced. Then Elliot's partisans immediately consolidated their position and revealed their biases. Charges were brought against local conventicles and at least three of Elliot's opponents were expelled from the corporation, though they regained their places using mandamus. Elliot's costs in defending these actions were paid by the corporation, in a vote subscribed by the same persons who had earlier supported him before the Privy Council; none who opposed him in his election signed the order for paying these legal bills. Elliot had the support of a clearly defined group, a group interested in curbing dissent and removing its sympathizers from the corporation. He was opposed throughout by an equally well-defined group. Despite their efforts, Bedder had the last laugh when he succeeded Elliot in the mayor's chair.[45]

Bedder held the mayoralty, though not without dissensions in his own ranks. Richard Lucas, by all other indicators a supporter of Bedder's, sued for a mandamus to command Bedder to swear him mayor in the autumn of 1666. Nothing was done to install Lucas then, but apparently some accommodation was reached and Lucas became mayor in 1667. At the same time, the differences between the Bedder and Elliot groups subsided in the late 1660s, as the selection of a new high steward and of a new school teacher – the sorts of occasions when partisan loyalties were often clearest – passed in quiet agreement. But the choice of Dr. Martin Lluelyn as a burgess in 1671, and then as mayor only three weeks later, would spark renewed conflict. Lluelyn's leadership galvanized the loyalist group formerly led by Elliot. Conventicles again came under attack. Prominent

---

[43] Suffolk RO (Ipswich Branch), EE2/D5/1 and EE2/I/2, f. 9. PRO, KB21/18/119 and 129v; KB21/19/16v, 17, and 32v; and KB29/332/39.
[44] BL, Add. 32,518, f. 36v.
[45] PRO, PC2/57/123 and 125. Greaves, *High Wycombe Ledger*, pp. 177–79. PRO, KB21/15/105v, 110v, 116, and 118v; KB29/316/81.

local dissenters were further harassed when they were repeatedly elected to office, which they just as repeatedly refused to accept because of the requirements of the Corporation Act, for which refusal the corporation, according to its by-laws, could repeatedly fine them. Tensions rose still higher when MP Sir John Borlase died in August of 1672. His son hoped to fill his place, but Lluelyn accused him of receiving support from the "fanatic" part of town.[46] With a parliamentary seat on the line, and the annual mayoral election fast approaching, there was bound to be trouble.

Happily, the mayoral election of September 26, 1672 went without a problem; unhappily, the victor died an hour later. The Bedder group reacted immediately, choosing Henry Bigg to replace him. Lluelyn's partisans complained to the Privy Council of this snap election, alleging Bigg had been chosen with the help of aldermen disqualified by the Corporation Act, including Bigg himself, who they said had not received the sacrament. The King declared Bigg's election void, and ordered that another be held, "wherein no person is to intermeddle who is not duly qualified thereunto by the said act." The Lluelyn group, believing that this third election would be held on December 9, was surprised to learn two days before that Richard Lucas had just been chosen by "the fanatic party." Again they cried foul, claiming that they legally chose Thomas Gibbons on the appointed day. Nonetheless, Lucas quickly set about electing new aldermen and naming over 100 new freemen before the upcoming parliamentary contest between his candidate, the second Sir John Borlase, and Sir William Egerton, supported by Lluelyn and his partisans. Though Lucas and Borlase easily prevailed, a double return was made. Bigg, Bedder, Lucas, and their friends retained corporate control throughout, despite protests from the other side, and Bigg succeeded Lucas in the mayoralty the following year. "The fanatic party" was now firmly ensconced. The next May, finding himself ineligible for office owing to his negligence of the sacrament, Bigg was ceremoniously removed by his partisans; he then received the Eucharist, after which the corporate majority supporting him instantly reinstalled him.[47] It was a vivid demonstration of the uses of occasional conformity and of the approval of such uses by Bigg's partisans. The momentary political peace of the late 1660s had been broken at Wycombe as parties competed more fiercely during the 1670s, goaded by frequent contests for the mayoralty and for a parliamentary seat. Religious

---

[46] PRO, KB21/16/25v, 27, and 29v; KB29/317/157 and KB29/318: writ to swear Richard Lucas, and return from Edward Bedder. PRO, PC2/63/72. Greaves, *High Wycombe Ledger*, pp. xv, 184–85 and 190–94.

[47] Greaves, *High Wycombe Ledger*, pp. xv–xvi and 195–205. PRO, PC2/63/174v, 178v, and 183. *CSPD 1672–73*, pp. 576–77. Borlase was seated. Henning, vol. I, pp. 142–43.

proclivities provided the poles around which they organized; strong leadership guided each group as it pursued victory over the other.

Illegal admission of freemen was just as likely to precede a mayoral election as a parliamentary one.[48] In Rochester, local partisan activity increased at a time when no by-elections were in sight. Aware perhaps of the potential for trouble, new by-laws for controlling the election of officers and admissions to the freemanship were passed in 1673 on the advice of Recorder Francis Barrell.[49] Nonetheless, Mayor Arthur Brooker tried to remain in office another year, "as a design to maintain faction." To do so he illegally made new freemen before the mayoral election, which he then won. When called before the Privy Council, the King ordered Brooker to quit making freemen and to hold a new election. In addition, Brooker's opponents – Recorder Barrell and "others of his party" – began legal proceedings against him.[50] Contests like Rochester's were no less vigorous for occurring in boroughs without MPs: Walsall did not need parliamentary elections to spur partisan conflict between current corporation members and former ones controlling the local feoffment of town lands.[51] Borough corporations, even those that chose MPs, were not primarily parliamentary electoral bodies; they were local governments, concerned most of the time with affairs in town. Before 1679, elections to Parliament were intermittent, held unpredictably when a member died or was promoted to the Lords or a judgeship. Little could be done in the corporations to prepare for such contingencies, so contests were brief if sharp. Corporate politics usually looked inward for the most serious, ongoing sources of contention, rather than to Parliament.

Elections to corporate office created the most serious problems. Mayors commanded the local magistracy and thus had the strongest influence over how laws against dissent were used: witness Mayor Henry Elliot's use of these powers at High Wycombe. Mayors also presided in civil cases, enforcing debts and contracts and assigning damages where wrong was done. The mayor held his hand on the tap from which flowed the considerable *largesse* at corporate disposal. While he could rarely act alone, he exercised enormous influence over the use of corporate cash, and in many towns, could assign small funds at his own discretion. Unsurprisingly, misappropriation of funds was one of the charges frequently made in the heat of partisan battle. The mayor controlled the agenda in assemblies.

---

[48] For instance, see Picton, *Liverpool Records*, pp. 247–48.

[49] *An Authentic Copy*, part two, pp. 31–36.

[50] The outcome is unknown. PRO, PC2/64/276, 278, and 377. Brooker failed in an earlier effort – against the wishes of most of the corporation – to get a new charter, probably to purge the corporation.

[51] Halliday, "Partisan Conflict and the Law," pp. 208–13.

Many charters also gave him the casting vote whenever a tie occurred. The trappings of authority were scarcely less important. Wherever he went – at church, in public processions, in the town hall – the mayor assumed the pre-eminent place. A mace or sword of office was borne before him, symbols of his headship over the town, and with the royal insignia engraved upon them, of the royal sanction for his authority.

If mayors' places were desirable for so many reasons, so too were aldermancies: the latter led to the former. Membership of the common council was thus coveted since getting on to the corporation was the first step for anyone hoping to reach the top. For those already in the corporation, controlling who came in after them or who advanced ahead of them determined their own political futures. The dignities and powers that came with corporate office were not new in the Restoration era, nor was occasional political dispute. But the energy with which office was sought and dispute carried on was new. Office was desired in and of itself, and as the means for advancing particular political/religious agendas in the locality. Success required support, support required organization, and organization required leadership. That partisanship grew in the heat of political competition in the towns attests to the peculiarity of corporate politics: that community leaders were in daily contact with one another and thus the issues over which they struggled were always before them. With no breaks between sessions and no exodus from town between meetings, urban political life enjoyed – or endured – a continuity that made Parliament seem a disjointed affair. Whether borough politics created neat groups of ins and outs – as at Bury – or more complex in-fighting within corporations – as at Northampton – the story was the same. Membership in and control of a borough corporation was coveted, and the only way to get it was to act consistently in concert with others, to work with partisans.

Concerted action became more important during the 1670s as dissenters or those sympathizing with them achieved increasing prominence in many corporations.[52] Dissenting successes, and the Conventicle Act of 1670 and the Test of 1673, catalyzed those who opposed them. The rising number of by-elections, by bringing the most sensitive issues and strongest loyalties to the fore, heightened the friction. Then the rapid succession of parliamentary elections in 1679–81 brought the issues and contentions into their

---

[52] Canterbury corporation split as dissenting strength grew in the 1670s, leading to extensive litigation over various offices, and ultimately to a quo warranto brought against the corporation by the cathedral. Canterbury City and Cathedral Archives, CC/AC/6, opening leaf and passim. PRO, KB21/18/74; KB21/19, passim; KB29/331/159v; KB29/332/25 and 171. PRO, PC2/65/388, 394, and 395. *CSPD 1676–77*, pp. 444–45. *CSPD 1680–81*, pp. 479 and 505–06. *CSPD 1682*, pp. 337–38. *Eng. Rep.*, vol. 84, pp. 1174–75 (Jones, T., 116). Henning, vol. I, pp. 276–77. *The Case between the Mayor and Aldermen of Canterbury, and Mr. Serjeant Hardres their Late Recorder* (1681).

sharpest focus yet. The disputes in those years involved not only capturing parliamentary seats, but all available positions of influence in the corporations. In countless towns, partisan competition had become a permanent state of affairs. Struggles for urban and parliamentary office cut both ways: victory was sought in parliamentary elections in order to strengthen one's hold on local office, as much as one sought local office in order to control access to parliamentary seats.

In Andover, struggles within the corporation had begun in the months prior to a by-election in October 1678. The following January, in preparation for the upcoming general election, Bailiff William Wimbledon led a *putsch*. First, he and his partisans chose a new steward, William Withers. Less than two weeks later, Wimbledon's group chose a new approved man (what other corporations termed an alderman) and a new burgess. The following day, with Wimbledon's faction thus strengthened, new MPs were chosen: Withers was elected along with Francis Powlett, both of whom feared for Protestantism if the Duke of York should become King. Withers died later that year, but Powlett was returned to parliament in August 1679, accompanied by another who disliked the Duke of York's religion, Sir Robert Henley.[53] The annual bailiff's election followed less than three weeks after the parliamentary vote. Wimbledon controlled the outcome in favor of his ally, William Barwick. Or so he thought. Wimbledon's and Barwick's foes petitioned the Privy Council, claiming that they had chosen "loyal" Thomas Westcombe instead. Westcombe charged that Wimbledon was "confederating with . . . [others] turned out for their disloyalty" by the Corporation Act; "the confederates are disaffected persons, encouragers of conventicles, and many of their families frequenters thereof." But discounting the votes of the "confederates," Westcombe claimed eleven legal votes for himself to Barwick's eight. Westcombe then provided a list of the opposing parties, easily distinguishable as they were by their spiritual/political leanings. After hearing the allegations, the Privy Council ordered Barwick to surrender the bailiwick to Westcombe. In December, the crown also appointed a commission of association to Robert Noyes. Noyes was a corporation member and a supporter of Westcombe's, but he was not by charter a JP. By this commission, he now received special royal appointment to the bench. Use of this device suggests that magistracy was the principal concern both to the parties in Andover and among the King's advisors.[54]

---

[53] Henning, vol. I, pp. 245–46. Hampshire RO, 37M85/4/MI/3.
[54] Hampshire RO, 37M85/4/MI3. Bod., MS Tanner 290, f. 234. PRO, C231/8/17. A commission of association had also been appointed for Andover in 1674. Circumstances suggest it was gained by local gentlemen who sought greater authority in the town to protect dissent. See Paul D. Halliday, "'A Clashing of Jurisdictions': Commissions of Association in Restoration Corporations," *HJ* (forthcoming, 1998).

With Noyes's participation in the magistracy, and with the replacement of two of the burgesses chosen by Wimbledon's group, Westcombe's partisans were now ascendant.[55]

The intermittent discord in towns around the country during the 1660s and 70s became constant in 1679–81 as loud clashes sounded again and again in one parliamentary and borough election after another, each clash heard against a background din of political and religious debate at Westminster and in the provinces. Corporate partisans had much of their own to fight about in the 1660s and 70s. Frequent parliamentary electoral contests now drew upon and in turn fired long-standing corporate conflicts. In the Exclusion years, occasional partisan hostility became a permanent fixture, especially as "loyalists" sought to impose the laws against dissent with greater vigor.[56] The noise was now deafening, even in Whitehall. The once passive King could not ignore it any longer.

THE CORPORATION ACT REVISITED: 1680

The frenzy created by a so-called "Popish Plot," the battle waged in Parliament over the Duke of York's political fate, and the rhetoric and tactics of parliamentary electioneering in 1678–81 dramatically altered the political stakes for crown and corporations. The King's casual attitude toward political and religious dissent since 1660 could no longer be sustained. The problem of political loyalties in the corporations was part of a larger problem of the dependability of magistrates around the country. In 1680, crown officers scrutinized lists of current and prospective county JPs and then remodeled the county benches. This undertaking in the counties marked the start of a comprehensive involvement in local affairs by central government administrators without precedent since the 1640s and 50s.[57] Its impact on the corporations would be even more powerful than it was in the counties.

In the boroughs, the crown's initial impulse was to work with what it had. The Corporation Act, whatever its shortcomings, provided the basis for an inspection of corporate personnel on a case-by-case basis. At the

---

[55] PRO, PC2/68/206, 216, and 269. Hampshire RO, 37M85/2/JC/2, unfol. J. E. H. Spaul, *Andover Archives: The Bailiwick, 1599–1835* (Andover Local Archives Committee, 1971), pp. 9–10. M. J. Darrah and J. E. H. Spaul, *The Corporation of Andover, 1599–1835* (Andover Local Archives Committee, 1970), p. 15. Henning, vol. I, p. 246.

[56] Attacks against dissent in the towns increased after the dissolution of the Oxford Parliament: Newdigate LC 1109, 1110, and 1117.

[57] Lionel K. J. Glassey, *Politics and the Appointment of Justices of the Peace, 1675–1720* (Oxford, 1979), pp. 45–47. John Miller notes this transformation of the royal regime, though he sees it beginning in 1681. "The Potential for 'Absolutism' in Later Stuart England," *History*, 69 (1984), p. 203.

same time that the county benches were being reviewed, the Privy Council wrote to all the corporations asking about their performance under the Corporation Act. Learning perhaps from the ineffectiveness of the effort in 1668 to enforce compliance, the circular letter of March 12, 1680 required each corporation to return a report to the Council. The lieutenancy was charged with seeing that reports were made and that they were accurate.[58] Then the Privy Council – or a "committee for corporations" – considered each report and gave approval or wrote back to those corporations where they found problems.[59] By such means, the crown would gain a comprehensive picture of the political loyalties of corporate personnel nationwide.

The reports could hardly have heartened their readers. Many corporations could honestly claim to have observed the terms of the act regarding the oaths, the declaration, and the annual taking of the sacrament, but few had kept the records required by the statute. Some were exemplary: Bury and Gloucester had each kept registers of oath taking and subscriptions against the Covenant. Bury, careful to allow no lapses, wrote out the declaration in full on every occasion a new officer was sworn; the entire corporation had also made a special subscription of the declaration in 1666 in order to ensure that all were in compliance. Chesterfield's leaders kept a roll for their subscriptions. Other corporations, like Boston's, carefully recorded subscriptions annually in their assembly books.[60] Most corporations were less careful. Some, like Banbury and Chester, started off well enough, but by the mid-1660s their record keeping had faltered.[61] Leicester, an otherwise loyal corporation, was lackadaisical in recording subscriptions though it answered honestly when it said there had been no problems, except for a flap in the mid-1660s when three had avoided office by refusing to subscribe. Chester too had permitted no lapses in the act, except for patchy documentation.[62] Smaller corporations were less likely to have maintained proper records; no mention of the act survives in Macclesfield, Sudbury, or Lymington. Northampton, never the model of peace, had failed

---

58 Letters went out in March. For a copy, see Greaves, *High Wycombe Ledger*, pp. 213–215. For the lieutenancy's involvement, see Leicestershire RO, BRII/18/34, f. 169, and CCRO, ML4/512.

59 Three references to a special committee survive in the Privy Council register; little else is known about it: PRO, PC2/69/32, 45v, and 66v. Knights, *Politics and Opinion*, p. 261. Only problem cases earned mention in the Council. Word formally or informally was returned to the corporations of the Council's approval of their reports. See for instance Leicestershire RO, BRII/18/34, f. 169.

60 Gloucestershire RO, GBR/C8/1; Suffolk RO (Bury St. Edmunds Branch), D11/11/2; Riden and Blair, *Chesterfield*, vol. V (Chesterfield, 1980), pp. 206–07; Bailey, *Minutes of Boston*, vol. II, passim.

61 Gibson and Brinkworth, *Banbury Records*, pp. 211ff; CCRO, AB/2.

62 Halliday, "Partisan Conflict and the Law," pp. 218–19. Leicestershire RO, BRII/18/34, ff. 169, 175a, and 214–16. Stocks, *Records of Leicester*, pp. 552–53. CCRO, MF98, April 19, 1680.

as well. In many of these cases, the neglect probably lay in an honest laziness in record keeping. But as Col. John Strode reported from Sandwich, "I fear there have been designs as well as neglect."[63] Sandwich may not have been alone.

Most lapses probably resulted from inattention rather than intention. The mayor of Winchelsea expressed bewilderment when he found that neither he nor any of his brethren were duly qualified. This only happened through "inadvertancy," he said. But others described Winchelsea as having "two parties, one for the King, the other for the country." The mayor, eager to make amends, proclaimed "their unanimous consent to the established government . . . both in church and state." Though they had neglected the declaration and had no sacrament certificates, they were all "constant receivers" of the Eucharist, "there being not one dissenter among us."[64] Little if any punishment was meted out against Winchelsea or other towns. As Leicester's recorder reported, "I do not hear that any proceedings has [*sic*] been against any [corporation] upon this business, only the mayor and aldermen of Bedford were sent for to the Council board . . . but they are dismissed again, the information not being proved." Bedford's officers were the only ones brought before the Council. All but the deputy recorder and town clerk were found in compliance there. These two were referred to Chief Justice Francis Pemberton and Attorney General Sir Creswell Levinz; everyone else was sent home.[65] Mayors in Newcastle and Huntingdon received praise from Secretary Sir Leoline Jenkins and advice that they continue making their subscriptions "with solemnity . . . [so that the] trouble that one or two corporations . . . [will] be involved in may never befall yours." Jenkins exhorted Canterbury's leaders to obey the act with similar care to avoid the informations he threatened against the three removed there who were found to have disregarded the act.[66] Beyond such praise and warnings, crown officers did little else.

In most towns reporting lapses, those who still refused the declaration were expelled. Worcester tried to make up for its extensive failings by ordering all corporation members to take the oaths and subscribe the declaration, but this sudden display of zeal was not enough to prevent Worcester from being a precedent-setting political victim. By means of an information in the nature of quo warranto, brought by a group of 'loyal'

---

[63] Cheshire RO, LBM/1/1; Suffolk RO (Bury St. Edmunds Branch), EE501/2/8; Hampshire RO, 27M74/DBC2; and Northamptonshire RO, 3/2. *CSPD 1679–80*, p. 479.

[64] *CSPD 1679–80*, pp. 487–88 and 507; PRO, SP29/413/154.

[65] Stocks, *Records of Leicester*, p. 553. PRO, PC2/68/471 and 487. Avoidance of the Corporation Act continued in Bedford. Michael Mullett, "'Deprived of our Former Place': The Internal Politics of Bedford, 1660 to 1688," *Publications of the Bedfordshire Historical Record Society*, 59 (1980), pp. 17–18.

[66] *CSPD 1679–80*, pp. 433–34, 438, and 479–80.

corporation members against twenty-six members found ineligible under the act, Worcester provided the first real test of the legal instrument that would ultimately undermine scores of corporations nationwide in 1683–85.[67] Here as elsewhere, the key was local, not royal, initiative. Warwick removed four who refused the oaths; three others who had been hesitant now received the sacrament, subscribed the declaration, and retained their places. The town clerk and four councilmen lost their places at Ludlow; but the clerk as well as two of the councilmen later reappeared on the corporation by virtue of their appointment by the crown in Ludlow's charter of 1685.[68] Marlborough found all their corporation in compliance, except for Francis Penstone, whom they dismissed for refusing the sacrament. These and other towns showed signs of making amends and promised to do better.[69] The Council accepted their pleas of reformation and pursued the matter no further.

But others would not let the matter rest. The Council depended entirely on the honesty of the corporations and the energy of those responsible for observing them in making their reports, though the entire experience with the Corporation Act since 1662 suggested that neither should be trusted. The grand survey would necessarily be flawed.[70] Stalwarts in or near the boroughs sent in charges of false returns. Col. John Strode and Robert Hall picked over the returns from the Cinque Ports. Hall was the one who extracted from the mayor of Winchelsea his shamed acknowledgment of that corporation's complete disability under the act. And Strode's report to the Privy Council about Dover contradicted the report of compliance submitted by the corporation. Though two jurats and twenty-five councilmen had been removed as a result of the enquiry, the Privy Council was not amused by the discrepancy between Strode's and the corporation's accounts, so Secretary Jenkins sent a sharp letter to the mayor. The mayor waxed incredulous in response, stunned that Strode could have complained, he having been with them when they prepared their return. By September, more disqualified councilmen had been smoked out. Strode did not act alone in gaining these dismissals. He was assisted by allies in the corporation. One faction in town used Strode's influence to gain the crown's

[67] Hereford and Worcester RO (St. Helen's), Shelf A.14, Box 2, p. 91, and Shelf A.10, Box 4, 1680 accounts. On Worcester's court case, see below, pp. 201–04.

[68] Styles, "Warwick," pp. 33–34 and 122n. Shropshire RO, LB/1/18 and LB2/1/2, ff. 340–41.

[69] B. Howard Cunnington, *The Orders, Decrees and Ordinances of the Borough and Town of Marlborough* (Devizes, 1929), pp. 44–45. Wiltshire RO, G22/1/23, f. 63, and G22/1/91. Penstone failed to get his place back with a mandamus: PRO, KB21/20/48, 77v, and 88. Beverley removed two on their own, and then a third according to a royal request: Dennett, *Beverley Records*, p. 166.

[70] P. J. Norrey has suggested that deputy lieutenants in the southwest were inactive in policing the enquiry, "Relationship between Central and Local Government," pp. 248–49.

assistance against their corporate foes. The result was a thorough partisan purge.[71] Likewise at Dunwich, removals for non-compliance with the Corporation Act permitted a partisan reconfiguration of corporate membership.[72] Elsewhere, corporations made the removals of those found ineligible; then they immediately elected them again after they had qualified by taking the sacrament.[73] Occasional conformity, by its very nature, was a resilient, durable practice and the hole in the Corporation Act was as large as ever. Even now, those dismissed for non-compliance could be reappointed if they received the Eucharist and subscribed the declaration.

Partisan use was made of the Council's enquiry elsewhere. In May, Hull corporation approved by a narrow vote a certificate to the Council stating that all were in compliance, except Alderman Daniel Hoar. But the corporation excused him, saying that though he did not have a certificate showing he took the sacrament the year before being made an alderman, he had received it annually since then. Less than one week later, with Hoar and others of his friends absent, the mayor – who signed the first certificate – and eight aldermen, composed a new certificate, stating that since Hoar had not been qualified when made an alderman in 1671, his place was now void. A few days later, Hoar appealed to his brethren; the mayor, reversing himself once again, wrote yet a third certificate stating that Hoar had been in compliance all along. The corporation now refused to restore him. Hoar petitioned the Privy Council, the King ordered his restoration, and the corporation promptly obeyed, but it also asked the Council to revoke its order. Despite testaments to Hoar's loyalty, the King reversed his earlier order according to the corporation's request. That lengthy notes about Hoar's case exist in the archive of Eye corporation suggests how carefully corporators everywhere watched developments in the rest of the country.[74] Many were aware that but for the grace of God – and King – Hoar's fate might well have been their own.

By 1682, despite efforts in King's Bench, Hoar remained outside the

---

[71] *CSPD 1679–80*, pp. 519 and 529; *CSPD 1680–81*, pp. 2–3. Colin Lee underscores the partisan uses of the 1680 enquiry and shows how informers like Strode were aided by one corporate party in its bid to overpower the other. "'Fanatic Magistrates': Religious and Political Conflict in Three Kent Boroughs, 1680–1684," *HJ*, 35 (1991), pp. 45–46.

[72] Suffolk RO (Ipswich Branch), EE6/1144/13, ff. 29–32v. HMC, *Various Collections*, vol. VII, p. 103.

[73] Canterbury removed three, but one was re-elected; the record notes he received the sacrament. Bedford removed two and reinstalled them later. Canterbury City and Cathedral Archives, CC/AC/6, ff. 123 and 126. Mullett, "Deprived of our Former Place," p. 17. At Ludlow, four were removed and later readmitted. This same courtesy did not extend to Town Clerk William Charlton, whom the corporation excluded now that it had legal pretext for doing so, but the King chastised them for their partiality and commanded his reappointment. Shropshire RO, LB/1/18.

[74] Suffolk RO (Ipswich Branch), EE2/K/5/22.

corporation. So he printed a broadside making his case before the court of public opinion. He argued, with some justification, that if all corporation officers in England were required to prove they had received the sacrament years earlier, then at least half of them would be turned out. Hoar stated emphatically that he had received it before being made an alderman, and that even if he had not, the "King's act of pardon" of 1672 – presumably the Declaration of Indulgence – exonerated him. The intention behind the Corporation Act was to keep dissenters from office, Hoar contended, not to remove those loyal persons who "had not the spirit of divination to know before-hand when they should be chosen into offices, and so take the sacrament purposely to qualify them for such elections."[75] Hoar's indignation was understandable, but his argument wandered on to shaky ground. The point of requiring the sacrament within one year *before* election was to keep people in constant communion with the church. One was not supposed to divine just beforehand that they were to be elected, and thereby receive the sacrament at the last moment, as Hoar suggested.

The emphasis in Hoar's case, and throughout the returns to the 1680 enquiry, on the sacrament and not the declaration suggests a shift in corporate personnel and the uses of the act. As the years passed, new men entered the corporations who had never sworn the Covenant, and who thus felt little compunction in forswearing it, even if they sympathized with it. The declaration had become irrelevant as a test of dissenting views and fitness for office. On the other hand, the sacrament was the ultimate symbol of the established Church's divine authority. Receiving it not only meant accepting the church's Eucharistic theology, it meant coming into communion with a spiritual authority that most dissenters held anathema. By 1680, many who might subscribe the declaration would still balk at the sacrament. Others who did not accept the church's doctrine might stomach the bread and wine on an annual basis if it would give them political legitimacy, but they saw little reason to do more. Hoar may well have been one of these, an occasional conformist. His words disclose a view of the sacrament as a chore to be performed no more than necessary. That so many others apparently felt the same and thus lost their offices or were pushed into an after-the-fact receipt of the sacrament in 1680 suggests the extent to which occasional conformity had invaded the corporations. From 1680 on, the sacrament would be the great divide between those in and out of office; the declaration against the Covenant – expressing long dead hopes for a national Presbyterian church – ceased to be relevant. Hoar did not regain his place by the town's new charter of 1685, but he was

---

[75] *The Case of Daniel Hoar, Merchant, Alderman of . . . Kingston-upon-Hull* (London, 1682). PRO, PC2/69/16, 32, 52v, and 75; *CSPD 1679–80*, p. 530; and Hull City RO, BRL/977.

appointed mayor in the Jacobean charter of 1688, suggesting that the government of James II saw him as one who would support that King's policy of religious toleration.[76] After 1688, the kind of occasional conformity suggested by Hoar's arguments would provide one of the most contentious issues in corporate and national politics.

As the enquiry of 1680 wound down in late June, the Council considered further measures. It asked the attorney general three questions about the ambit of the Corporation Act. First, did the act extend to members of livery and trade companies; second, did it cover town freemen and trade companies governed by borough corporations? These two questions had implications for London most of all, but the question of turning out freemen could have serious repercussions nationwide. Third, the Council asked about the great hole in the act: could those removed by the commissioners in 1662 qualify later for readmission by fulfilling the act's terms?[77] The attorney general's response to these questions has not been found, but recognizing as he must have the dictates of local practice and of King's Bench judgments, he could not have encouraged pushing the act further. Nonetheless, renewed royal interest in the act provoked concerns in Parliament, where, in December and January 1680–81, a bill to revoke the Corporation Act passed two readings before dying with the session.[78] But parliamentary worries were misplaced: if the returns to the enquiry of 1680 showed anything, they showed that the act had been enforced only to the extent those controlling the corporations cared to enforce it. Many towns – or partisan groups within them – had ignored its provisions and admitted those who were not qualified in law. Revoking an ineffective act could have made little difference.

The 1680 enquiry was at once the most important crown intrusion into the corporations since 1660, an indicator of the strength of corporate dissent, and a failure as an effort to control corporate membership. In towns like Dover and Hull, local partisans, not the crown, used the Privy Council's letter as an occasion to gain advantage over their opponents. By ordering the enquiry, the crown unwittingly contributed to the partisan divisions that had been evident since the Restoration and had grown during the 1670s.[79] Elsewhere, the enquiry resulted in embarrassed admissions of shortcomings, fervent promises to do better, and little if any action. There were some dismissals, and many a town quickly cleaned up its image. But

---

[76] Boyle, *Charters to Hull*, pp. 196 and 226.   [77] PRO, PC2/69/16.

[78] *CJ*, vol. 9, pp. 692, 696, and 700–01. Douglas R. Lacey, *Dissent and Parliamentary Politics in England, 1661–1689* (New Brunswick, 1969), p. 145.

[79] As Colin Lee noted of Dover: "The return to the Corporation Act in 1680 crystallized divisions between [dissenters and loyalists] in Dover which had developed during the 1670s." "'Fanatic Magistrates'," p. 45.

the act had not worked, and if the crown intended to control corporate membership, more serious measures would be required. But such measures were still two years in the future.

"LEFT TO THE LAW"

Throughout the Restoration era, corporators everywhere had plenty to fight about over who legitimately belonged among them. Resignations, removals, elections: each change in the personnel list presented another opportunity for contest. The definitions of suitability for office promulgated in the Corporation Act complicated rather than clarified matters as from one year to the next, a corporation might elect officers based on completely different readings of the act. By such means, the factions created in the 1640s and 50s were perpetuated, and the struggles between them became more severe. As the number of disputes rose over the 1660s and 70s, and as questions about the validity of local elections or the legitimacy of one's claim to office increased, the need for outside adjudicators increased too.

Most went first to the Privy Council. In law, the conciliar courts and the Council's judicial functions ceased in 1641. But after the Restoration, the Council acted in a manner which, while not actually judicial, looked judicial, hearing disputes between parties in hopes of resolving them. The King presided, giving the Council's pronouncements – by "King in Council" – an impressive ring. Suitors to the Council commenced proceedings by petitions rather than by the writs, informations, or indictments of the courts. As in court, the parties in conflict appeared before the Council by attorney. After a few hearings over a period of only days or weeks, a decision would be made. Such expedition stood in stark contrast to the common law courts where actions and counter actions, and pleas and arguments on successive false returns to writs, stretched proceedings over years. But there remained a major drawback to Council proceedings: any case seemingly concluded there could easily be taken to one of the royal courts by one of the parties concerned. Lacking true judicial authority, the Council's decisions were in no way final. Thus after his loss before the King, Northampton's Brafield transformed himself from a petitioner to the King and Council into a litigant in King's Bench. This is one of the great untold stories of political development in this period: the replacement of the Privy Council by King's Bench as the overseer of local government, a development resulting from the rise of partisan politics. As teams divided in the towns, they sought support and arbitration from outside. Increasingly, they sought this from King's Bench. King and Council, as well as litigants and judges, encouraged this development. The Council tended to retreat from rather than embrace the opportunity to dictate the outcome of corporate disputes. Increasingly, the crown concluded its hearing of such cases by declaring that the parties should be "left to the law."

This happened in a fracas at Newtown, Isle of Wight, where the mayoralty was prized in order to control an upcoming parliamentary by-election. Combatants there were "left to the law" after Privy Council hearings. The result put the mayoralty and control of the parliamentary seat in the hands of Sir Robert Holmes, the island's military governor, and thus arguably in the hands of a government interest. But the decision in this case was the result of the Council's lack of interest in a contested mayoralty rather than a considered effort by the crown to support one partisan against another. As the attorney general put it, the case did not concern the military government of the island, and thus should be heard by King's Bench, not the Privy Council.[80] The Council's dismissal of many other complaints brought to it by those ostensibly defending its interests must have disappointed borough partisans who went to the Council with stories told in terms meant to gain royal support.[81]

The first rumblings from Rye came in Robert Hall's and Col. Strode's charges that the mayor had connived with some of the jurats to make a false return to the 1680 enquiry about the Corporation Act. Certain corporation members sought outside support to use the enquiry against their enemies. The corporation's return, reporting all was well, had been prepared by Town Clerk Thomas Tournay because Mayor Benjamin Martin was illiterate. Three jurats who refused to sign Tournay's return seconded Hall's and Strode's charges, saying that few besides themselves were qualified by the act. It was Tournay, they alleged, who had engineered the election of the pliable, unlettered Martin by allowing the votes of seven dismissed by the corporation commissioners in 1662, "the whole seven being fanatics . . . joining with those jurats that are of their party which sit upon the bench now." Tournay was the perfect borough party leader. He had already led his minions in parliamentary and mayoral elections, and in the choice of a schoolmaster "of their own principles."[82] The three jurats who complained of his tactics listed his partisans, detailing their political views and thus what they assumed were their opponents' political liabilities in the eyes of the King. The lines through the corporation were precisely drawn. Now the most serious struggles were joined.

Despite Tournay's political strength, Thomas Crouch, one of his fiercest opponents, was chosen mayor in 1681. Or was he? Crouch claimed election

[80] *CSPD 1676–77*, pp. 401, 431, and 578–79. PRO, PC2/65/369, 371, 382, 432, and 435. Henning, vol. I, pp. 251–52.

[81] See for instance cases at Dover and Canterbury: Lee, "'Fanatic Magistrates'," pp. 46 and 51.

[82] *CSPD 1679–80*, pp. 467, 526, 527–28, 529, and 534; PRO, SP29/413/167, 168, and 168I.

by those who were never "expunged" according to the Corporation Act; Tournay contended that he had been chosen, though his supporters included some expelled in 1662. Crouch and Tournay took the mayor's oaths in separate ceremonies. No town being big enough for two mayors, Crouch's crew complained to the Privy Council. Strode suggested that by charter, the King could remove Tournay from the corporation if he chose. Despite the strong charges and tough political advice, the Council proceeded in the usual course of hearing both parties. Crouch had received only nine votes to Tournay's eleven, but the Council discounted five of Tournay's as cast by freemen disfranchised in 1662. Tournay was ordered to hand over the mace, seal, and all records; if he felt aggrieved by the decision, he could "pursue the due course of law."[83]

Now in control, Crouch and his friends transformed the corporation by making eleven new members. Orders were given to purchase a new edition of *Statutes at Large*, indicative perhaps of an intention to obey scrupulously laws that had previously been ignored. The corporation dismissed Tournay from his clerkship, but realizing how much fight he had in him, they also requested the King, using his power under the Cinque Ports' charter, to order his removal as well, and Charles complied. But despite repeated requests, Tournay held on to the borough's records, aware that the corporation could not conduct most business without them.[84]

More new freemen were chosen in the ensuing months, strengthening Crouch's hand. At the same time, Tournay followed the King's earlier advice and pursued his grievances in court. First, with William Williams, Chester's recorder, as his attorney, he obtained a mandamus for Crouch to swear him as mayor. Crouch, with the help of the attorney general, used the usual delaying tactics, requiring the court to issue a succession of writs to which he and his compatriots ultimately made an insufficient return. Finally, in June 1682, Tournay was sworn as mayor according to a peremptory mandamus from King's Bench. Crouch responded in kind, suing for a mandamus to be sworn mayor himself; the court denied him, and assessed £90 in costs against him.[85] Tournay was again the legal mayor. With this judgment as his warrant, and with a staff in his hand, Tournay summoned the crowds in Rye's market place; 300 marched with

---

83 *CSPD 1680–81*, p. 439. Order was also given for county JPs to see that the laws against conventicles were enforced, with commands to the attorney general to prosecute the notorious Rye preacher, Samuel Jeake. PRO, PC2/69/175, 175v, and 176. *CSPD 1680–81*, pp. 422, 429, 444, and 445. East Sussex RO, Rye 3/22, unfol., entered at Aug. 29, 1681 and Dec. 3, 1681.
84 Ibid, Sept. 19 and Dec. 3, 1681, and Rye 1/17/62 and 66. PRO, PC2/69/196v and 203. *CSPD 1680–81*, p. 583.
85 PRO, KB21/21/27, 31v, 35, 43, 56v, 59, and 67v. *CSPD 1682*, pp. 225–26. *Eng. Rep.*, vol. 84, p. 1224 (Jones, T. 215), Rex v. Turner [*sic*]. East Sussex RO, Rye 1/17/144.

him to take back the town hall. Crouch and his constables stood him down at first, but Tournay returned, gathered another mob, broke into the hall, and sat himself in the mayor's chair to conduct a meeting. As he left the hall, smiths were changing the locks and the bells of Rye rang out his triumph. His foes feared the consequences, especially as Tournay, recently chosen town clerk at Hythe as well, had "the assistance of many places to carry on this design." But Crouch's further complaints to the Privy Council brought no reply. Tournay used his control of the assembly to disfranchise those made free under Crouch and to add his own friends to the freemen's rolls.[86] Rye's revolution had come full circle in under twelve months.

Both sides pulled out all the stops for the next mayoral election. Crouch's group – which continued to act as if they comprised the legal corporation – supported Lewis Gillart, with help from three neighboring JPs. Tournay was bolder, imprisoning some of his opponents and, with "his partisans," making yet more freemen days before the vote. At the election, the visiting county justices condemned Tournay's use of imprisonment and his making of freemen. They then proposed that Gillart and Tournay should make way for a compromise choice, but "the disaffected party would hear of no accommodation." Polling began, from which Joseph Radford, one of Crouch's supporters, emerged the victor. Whispering among themselves, Tournay walked out with most of the jurats and other freemen. While those remaining swore Radford, Tournay was chosen and sworn mayor "by the Whigs." Once again, Rye had two mayors, and, in effect, two corporations. Blame for the energy and success of the "factious" was laid on King's Bench, whose verdict returning Tournay to the mayoralty had heartened them in their cause.[87]

Unsurprisingly, the Privy Council received yet more petitions and held another round of hearings. Tournay again acted as mayor, retaining all the corporation's records. But the Council declared Radford's the legal election. Tournay was ordered to hand over the records and ensigns of office; again, the King said he could go to the law if he liked. True to form, Tournay stalled in relinquishing the records and was arrested. In Rye, another revolution turned one group out and another in. The "loyal" group, now back in authority, elected yet another set of freemen that winter and spring and revoked the freedoms granted by Tournay and his gang.[88]

Tournay now edged toward sedition. When someone commented that the King would destroy him when he supported "the loyal" against "the

---

[86] East Sussex RO, Rye 1/17/71–72 and 144, and Rye 3/22, July 26, and Aug. 22 and 26, 1682. *CSPD 1682*, pp. 225–26 and 234. PRO, PC2/69/260v.

[87] *CSPD 1682*, pp. 366–68. East Sussex RO, Rye 3/22, Aug. 28, 1682.

[88] *CSPD 1682*, pp. 410 and 544. PRO, PC2/69/277v, 283, 294, and 300. East Sussex RO, Rye 3/22, entered at May 21, 1683; and Rye 1/17/80 and 89–90.

dissenting party," Tournay replied that "scepters and crowns must tumble down."[89] Tournay was no master of political poetry, but he continued to master the political situation. That summer, he appeared again in King's Bench as defendant on the riot charge for which he had been held briefly in December. But the issue moved from riot to Tournay's claim to have been elected mayor. The legal question revolved around whether or not the four former freemen who had been removed in 1662, and whose votes for Tournay had thus been discounted by the Council in deciding the election's outcome, had been legally removed by the corporation commissioners. The court ruled that freemen were not removable under the terms of the act, and "that such persons [freemen] as have not taken the oaths, etc. prescribed by that act may however vote." In short, though the "freemen" of Rye were functionally like councilmen elsewhere, they were treated in law as freemen, and thus stood beyond the reach of the Corporation Act. These four had been freemen all along and their votes for Tournay had been good. The court once again delivered a serious blow to the Corporation Act and to conciliar judgment.[90]

Despite the court's decision, Tournay's party did not come back into its own again until 1688, when all made free during his years as mayor were restored, and those made free by Crouch were removed for good.[91] But from 1683 to 1688, the political tide beat against Tournay and his partisans, who were now disfranchised by Radford, Crouch, and company. The loyal remained firmly in control, despite regular chastisement from the crown for their unneighborly treatment of Rye's French Protestant fishing community.[92] The crown had finally taken a firm stand for one side, and as long as it did so, that party held sway.

Combatants at Rye – like those at Northampton almost two decades earlier – found the Privy Council could deliver judgment swift if not sure. In such cases, political disputes that went before the Council moved on to King's Bench.[93] Petitioners became litigants; costs went up and time wore

---

[89] *CSPD Jan.–June 1683*, p. 147.
[90] *Eng. Rep.*, vol. 90, pp. 54–55 (Skinner 116), Rex v. Tolney [*sic*]. "Freemen" in Rye were like councilmen in other towns: part of the corporation's deliberative body, not simply those free to trade. The question thus centered on whether or not they were in law like freemen – which the commissioners could not remove – or councilmen – which the commissioners could remove.
[91] The timing of this case may have been critical, as it was heard only weeks before Sir George Jeffreys became chief justice. His arrival on the bench may have produced a reversal, thus explaining why Tourney did not regain the mayoralty after this decision. Though this decision went for him, it was not for a mandamus, which he would have to sue separately in order to be restored. By then, it may have been too late.
[92] East Sussex RO, Rye 1/17/ 90, 97, and 143–45; PRO, PC2/70/58 and 134, and PC2/71/ 105v.
[93] Many cases may be traced from hearings before the Council to the court. For instance: Canterbury, 1677 (PRO, PC2/65/388, 394, and 395; *CSPD 1676–77*, pp. 444–45; and

on. But such impediments were nothing to those determined, more than anything, to *win*. Increasingly, litigants by-passed the Council and went straight to court. Contestants for corporation control spent more and more time in King's Bench, and in the process, contributed to the creation of a law of administrative review. Subsidiary units of government were knit more tightly into the national state in response to local litigants' desires for the court's involvement. King's Bench thus became the monitor of the performance of local governors. In so doing, the law made partisan politics safe for society.

Four factors explain this movement of ultimate authority from Council to court: royal willingness, litigant desires, the court's interest in broadening its purview, and the involvement of leading members of the bar. The Council seemed wearied at times hearing corporation cases, but its handling of them remained consistent throughout the 1660s and 1670s. One party brought a petition complaining of another; both groups were heard and judgment quickly followed. Arguing from the example of Northampton and other cases in which decisions went against those who would have appeared to be the King's natural allies, the Council's decisions were not motivated by an effort to create or strengthen a "Court party" in any town. But even-handedness diminished after 1680 as the crown became aware of the need to control admission to the corporations. We might imagine then that the Council would make increasing use of its quasi-judicial capacity to direct the outcome of borough battles. But this did not happen. Even in cases when the King in Council delivered a decision – as happened twice in Tournay's visits to Whitehall – he allowed that the losers could always go to court.[94] Frequently, matters did not even go this far, as the Council simply dismissed disputants without a decision; they were thereby "left to the law."[95] This was especially likely when it came out that petitioners to the Council had simultaneously sought redress in the courts. Secretary Jenkins wrote to John Mendham of Thetford, who looked for crown support against his enemies, that the Council would not hear his case as it was already before King's Bench. Jenkins told him that the King desired "that you make the law your rule," especially the Corporation Act, which Mendham said his foes had violated. He added, "I doubt not you'll have all the fairness while you have the law on your side."[96] But once again, the justices of King's Bench ordered a mandamus for someone who

Eng. Rep., vol. 84, pp. 1174–75 [Jones, T. 116]); and Saltash, 1681 (PRO, PC2/68/245, 260, and 303, and *Eng. Rep.*, vol. 83, pp. 225–26 [Raym., Sir T. 431] and vol. 84, p. 1205 [Jones, T. 178]).

[94] See also the case of Eye, 1679: PRO, PC2/68/275.

[95] See the result of hearings involving Newtown, Isle of Wight: PRO, PC2/65/435. Daniel Hoar of Hull was also "left to the law": PC2/69/52v and 75.

[96] *CSPD 1680–81*, p. 558.

was allegedly ineligible by the Corporation Act, and enforced their order by use of their power of attachment.[97] Apparently the law was not on Mendham's side after all.

Second, the rise of partisan politics prompted corporate foes to become corporate litigants. With plenty of precedents of Council decisions nullified in court, those who lost in Council had good reason to try again. Many preferred working through the more expeditious Privy Council, at least initially, but litigants increasingly turned to King's Bench in the first instance. Even when they began with the Council, one of the two parties was certain to be disappointed there. Process on initial, alias, and pluries writs was expensive and time consuming. This might be followed by all new proceedings in an action on the case for a false return, including a jury trial, which would have to wait until the next assizes. But all this effort might in the end produce a peremptory mandamus for the reappointment of the plaintiff, a conclusive result the Council could not produce.

Third, and more speculatively, King's Bench may have promoted this movement of jurisdiction from the Council to the bar. The court's frequent use of attachments to compel obedience to the writ suggests the seriousness with which the justices viewed corporation conflicts and their readiness to make mandamus useful to plaintiffs.[98] Plenty of people stood to profit from a rise in court business, especially the clerks and other functionaries in Westminster Hall. The possibility of increased fees resulting from increased judicial activity cannot have escaped their notice. More important, the justices themselves promoted the move by their willingness to consider a variety of corporation cases on mandamus to correct perceived wrongs in the performance, or lack thereof, of public duties. Not only was King's Bench the great beneficiary relative to other courts in the use of mandamus, it was the beneficiary relative to non-judicial institutions, namely the Council. By encouraging mandamus business, the court became the principal venue for administrative and judicial review, and thus the chief means for superintending local governance. It is no accident that this expanding use of mandamus occurred at about the same time that the writ of certiorari – for calling judgments of lesser jurisdictions before King's Bench for review – was also developing apace.[99] The use of certiorari and mandamus

---

[97] PRO, KB21/21/23, 28v, 32, 33, 39v, 43v, 57v, and 62v.

[98] It may be that King's Bench used attachments more frequently over time, thereby strengthening its own authority. Ascertaining this for certain would require a more comprehensive study of King's Bench practice beyond mandamus than could be undertaken here. See the use of attachments at Woodstock, Reading, and Bossiney, successfully compelling the filing of returns to mandamus: PRO, KB21/15/66 and 68v; KB21/17/127 and KB21/18/20; and KB21/20/10v, 22, and 26v.

[99] On certiorari, see Henderson, *English Administrative Law*, and Norma Landau, *The Justices of the Peace, 1679–1760* (Berkeley, 1984), pp. 345–55.

produced an extraordinary expansion in King's Bench's role, and must have been a development that the justices would encourage given their belief in the primacy of the law as revealed in their own decisions.

Finally, lawyers themselves stood to gain as well from an increase in corporation business. King's Bench's case load generally was in decline after 1660, but mandamus business rose at the same time, thus pointing to the rapid growth in the relative prominence of the device in the court's dockets.[100] It was also an era when the size of the bar was contracting and when a smaller cadre of leading lawyers garnered the lion's share of business. This concentration of work in a few hands may have been especially true in corporation matters, an area of the law that required special expertise. The same names of barristers making motions for mandamus show up again and again at the end of entries in King's Bench rule books.[101] These names belong to some of the most prominent members of the profession; nearly all the most frequently employed barristers in corporation cases would hold major crown legal offices, judgeships, or high political posts. Recorders of London, as the chief legal representative of the leading city, figure prominently here: William Wilde, John Howell, William Dolben, George Jeffreys, and George Treby. Sir Heneage Finch and Sir Francis North each served as solicitors and attorneys general; Finch, as Lord Nottingham, would be one of the century's leading chancellors; North would become Lord Keeper and the Baron Guilford. Both played an active role advising the crown in legal matters and North would be instrumental in developing the crown's policy for rechartering the boroughs in the 1680s, thus building on his years of experience in corporation law.

Other leading practitioners in mandamus included Sir William Jones and Sir Francis Winnington. Jones served as solicitor general in the early 1670s; then Winnington replaced him when Jones was promoted to attorney general. Both left their places in 1679 as their support of Exclusion brought them into conflict with the dominant interests at court. Both also continued to be among the most active members of Parliament. William Williams, another major figure in King's Bench, would be the speaker of the House of Commons in 1680 and 1681 and well known as an ardent whig.[102] In

---

[100] This increase in mandamus was part of a general increase in the use of actions on the case. David Lemmings, *Gentlemen and Barristers: The Inns of Court and the English Bar, 1680–1730* (Oxford, 1990), pp. 167–68.

[101] For general trends in the barristers' profession, see ibid., pp. 124–35 and chapter 7. In his study of the crown side of King's Bench – whence mandamus issued – Lemmings found a clear group of practitioners monopolizing the court's business, especially Henry Pollexfen, William Scroggs, Sir Creswell Levinz, Edmund Saunders, John Holt, Sir George Jeffreys, and William Williams. Ibid., p. 268.

[102] Ibid., pp. 200–04.

the early to mid-1680s, he would also be the most prominent lawyer encouraging corporations to oppose quo warranto. Then, in 1688, as James II's solicitor general, Williams would lead the King's attack on corporate privileges. After 1688, he would continue as a major legal figure, despite what many considered his earlier professional apostasy. George Jeffreys and William Scroggs, men of very different political proclivities, also handled more than their share of work on mandamus in the 1660s and 70s, and would become infamous as justices in King's Bench in the late 1670s and 80s. George Treby and Henry Pollexfen, who would unsuccessfully defend London's corporation in the quo warranto brought against it 1681–83, gained experience in corporation cases in the years immediately preceding, and would go on to judgeships after 1688. In short, the barristers who entered most of the motions in court contests between corporate partisans after 1660 were also the leaders of the profession, and included a number who were among the major political players of the day.

We can thus begin to imagine one of the chief means by which corporate partisan battles worked their way to the center of the polity. Though Pollexfen, with connections in Devon, handled cases mostly from the southwest, most of these other barristers did business from everywhere. They relied less on personal connections to particular areas than on professional eminence, and, increasingly, on partisan connections. These then are in all likelihood the factors that inspired their clients to seek their services. Thus Williams, with roots in Wales and Chester, represented complainants from Rye, Northampton, Richmond, and Woodstock; Winnington, of Worcestershire, took on arguments from York, Reading, Stafford, and Stratford.[103] While further research remains to be done on the legal profession and political connections within and beyond it, we can imagine a process whereby local partisan contests gradually infected the heart of the national polity. In going to court, corporate litigants sought the aid of leading lawyers, who were also leading crown officers and MPs. With their help, partisan angers in the provinces worked their way inward to the political center.

Leading lawyers made arguments before the justices, and in later years, became justices themselves. But what kind of body of law were they making? How did mandamus help the body politic absorb the shocks of partisan conflict?

In decisions in mandamus cases, we can see the court's role and doctrine changing over time. The rising case load on mandamus gave lawyers and the court an opportunity to clarify the law concerning local administrative

[103] PRO, KB21, passim.

propriety. Juries decided matters of fact in actions for false returns, but most arguments in the reports, where we can see justices and lawyers working through their ideas about the law, were made and settled by the judges at earlier stages or in matters that never went to a jury trial. The readiness of corporate litigants to return to the court again and again signaled a growing recognition in the provinces that King's Bench was the place for such matters to receive their definition. The necessity that the court define the scope of statutes like the Corporation Act, and the court's willingness to pass judgments contrary to those handed down in the Privy Council, suggests not only judicial independence, but a growing coherence in the application of a developing body of law detailing the public responsibilities of governors in subsidiary institutions like borough corporations.

Early writs were granted to persons removed from their offices who claimed they had a property right in them: an office was a private thing taken, not a public position from which one was expelled.[104] Property rights were a slender thread on which to hang a device that soon grew heavy with increased use. Nonetheless, the freehold argument remained good through the 1640s and 50s.[105] After the Restoration, use of this argument declined, especially after a number of decisions in cases involving college fellowships established that colleges were private societies with regulations and visitors appointed by their founders. The visitors, not the court, had jurisdiction; that one might claim a freehold in his fellowship was not enough for King's Bench to intercede.[106]

While property arguments would not disappear altogether, the emphasis in mandamus moved from restitution of property to restoration to a place concerned with justice or the public good. Thus the court would grant a mandamus to restore the steward of a court leet, for it concerned the administration of justice, but not to a court baron, which was a private court.[107] Oddly enough, similar thinking applied in the converse case of an

---

[104] In Warren's Case, 1619–20, the court decided that an alderman held a freehold, but a councilman did not, for his office "is a thing collateral to a corporation." *Eng. Rep.*, vol. 79, p. 463 (Cro. Jac. 540). Henderson found no authority outside of mandamus cases in which aldermen were supposed to have a freehold in their office: *English Administrative Law*, pp. 77–80.

[105] See for instance *Estwick v. London*, 1647, and Bernardiston's Case, 1655. Henderson, *English Administrative Law*, pp. 77–78, and *Eng. Rep.*, vol. 82, pp. 850–51 and 855–56 (Style 446 and 452).

[106] Mandamus was granted in 1660 for many college fellowships and even for a teacher in Reading. PRO, KB21/14, ff. 3–4, 13v, 23v, and passim. Such uses of the writ would decline but not disappear. College litigants continued to receive writs after 1688, though whether these were later allowed upon returns from their recipients is unknown. See PRO, KB21/23–32, passim.

[107] Charles Viner, *A General Abridgment of Law and Equity*, 2nd edn. (London, 1793), vol. 15, p. 193; Henderson, *English Administrative Law*, pp. 79–80.

attorney of the corporation court in Canterbury who was removed from his place by the corporation commissioners. Though King's Bench considered his place to be a private one, the court restored him on a judgment that the commissioners were only empowered to remove persons from public, not private places.[108] But the general movement in the court's thinking was away from the writ as an instrument protecting private property rights, toward one for ensuring the proper conduct of public officials. This applied first and foremost to corporation officers, and it was on cases brought by them that the foundations of modern administrative law were laid.

By the early Restoration, King's Bench had drawn a distinction between corporate office as a private right and office as a public responsibility. Though mandamus was used almost entirely by those who sought read-mission to offices from which they had been expelled, their success in winning restoration depended on their claim that a public wrong had been committed by their expulsion – that the charter had been violated – and that government and the administration of justice suffered thereby. More and more hearings on returns to mandamus prompted King's Bench to articulate a clearer notion of the public responsibility of corporate leaders. Partisan battles in the corporations were not the wranglings of private men; they represented the division of a vital public institution. As Justice Wadham Windham noted, mandamus lay only "where the office concerns some public or necessary work of government or administration of justice."[109] This emphasis on public duty was perhaps made even more clear with the use of mandamus for other ends besides restorations, for instance, to require the swearing of the new mayor or the handing over of records from one officer to his successor, each of which helped provide for the orderly transfer of authority.[110] Neither use of mandamus concerned property claims. As such uses of mandamus increased, especially after 1688, the court moved ever more clearly in the direction of compelling the corporations to perform the public trust committed to them.

Though Chief Justice Matthew Hale was the brightest luminary of the Restoration bench, it was Thomas Twisden who figured most prominently in the clarification and expansion of the use of mandamus. Appointed to the bench two days after Charles's arrival in London in 1660, Twisden remained

[108] *Eng. Rep.*, vol. 83, pp. 31 and 51 (Raym., Sir T. 56 and 94), and 1179 (1 Keble 675).
[109] Ibid., p. 1153 (1 Keble 631). As a recent student of public law notes, "the law of public duties has developed around the prerogative writ of mandamus, in which the public-law/ private-law distinction is, and always has been, fundamental." Harding, *Public Duties*, pp. 3–4.
[110] Writs of mandamus were granted to force a departing office holder to relinquish records to his successor, but they were not allowed in precedency fights, for instance, when one alderman claimed seniority over another. *Eng. Rep.*, vol. 82, p. 951 (1 Sid. 31); vol. 83, p. 327 (1 Lev. 119); and vol. 84, p. 155 (2 Keble 250).

there for the next eighteen years, until age finally compelled his departure.[111] As a serjeant-at-law in the 1650s, he had been involved in the principal corporation cases of the day, and thus came to the bench well aware of the issues at stake.[112] Twisden accepted the freehold view of office.[113] This view was rapidly falling out of favor, but Twisden's arguments for the broad power of mandamus proved significant elsewhere. He argued successfully that the writ should apply for restoring officers dismissed for speaking ill words of another corporation member, as when a councilman of Eye was removed for calling an alderman "a knave." Twisden suggested that one could only be turned out for words spoken to another that "related to the duty of his place," not to his personal reputation.[114] Rudeness was no grounds for dismissal. Nor was it grounds for "suspension." Guildford corporation "suspended" a member for saying of another that he was "a lying knave." When he sought a mandamus to regain his place, the corporation returned that he had not been removed, only "suspended," until he should apologize. Twisden argued "with his whole force to the contrary" that suspension was removal by another name; for the court to allow it "would open a great gap for oppression." Following Twisden's logic, the suspension ploy was found untenable and restoration was ordered.[115]

In considering mandamus cases, King's Bench showed a preference for restoring those expelled, a preference derived from its essentially conservative instincts. These instincts insisted on the maintenance of things as they stood: corporation personnel should remain in place unless removed for some egregious wrong. King's Bench typically supported the claims of the officer dismissed against those of the corporation that dismissed him unless two factors were demonstrated: justifiable cause for removal and the power to dismiss their own stated in the corporation's charter. Furthermore, these points had to be explained fully and precisely in the corporation's return to the writ. Anything short of this tended to lead to the readmission of the officer removed. Thus removal would not be allowed simply for defying the majority of the corporation. When a corporation member in Ripon refused to contribute his two pound share

---

[111] A. F. Havighurst suggested that age may only have been a pretence, and that he may have been removed. "The Judiciary and Politics in the Reign of Charles II" (Part II), *Law Quarterly Review*, 66 (1950), pp. 230–31.

[112] See for instance the Kingston case of 1655 and Bernardiston's and Blagrave's cases: *Eng. Rep.*, vol. 82, pp. 876–79 (Style 477), 850–51 and 855–56 (Style 446 and 452), and 1225, 1250–51, and 1264 (2 Sid. 6, 49, and 72).

[113] Ibid., vol. 83, pp. 1010 (1 Keble 387) and 329 (1 Lev. 123).

[114] Ibid., vol. 86, p. 195 (1 Ventris 302). This view was followed after 1688: ibid., vol. 92, pp. 18–19 and 184–85 (2 Ld. Raym. 777 and 1029).

[115] Ibid., vol. 83, pp. 349 (1 Lev. 162), 1290 (1 Keble 868), 1297 (1 Keble 880), and 81 (Raym., Sir T. 151); vol. 84, p. 1 (2 Keble 1).

for renewing the charter, his brethren expelled him. The court found that this might be good cause for an action for debt, but they could not dismiss on these grounds.[116] For those of a carefully legal turn of mind, the will of the majority appeared arbitrary and was insupportable against the precise restrictions of charters, traditions, and legal propriety.[117] The mandamus process thus gave an advantage to the complainant rather than the corporation, and in so doing, forced many a corporate majority to swallow its more vengeful urges.

But the court's conservatism did not lead it to promote royal interests in borough politics. King's Bench worked out its understanding of this developing writ with an impressive degree of independence.[118] As seen above, Privy Council decisions were effectively reversed in suits from Rye and Northampton. And the attorney general, the King's legal representative, lost numerous mandamus cases in the 1660s and 70s.[119] This happened in the suit of Lord Hawley, dismissed as recorder of Bath for his five years' absence, and because he was not "learned in the law," as required by charter. Despite Attorney General Sir Heneage Finch's arguments that Hawley had been appointed by the corporation commissioners, Twisden noted that their appointment could not make Hawley learned in the law contrary to reality. Bath's charter, not the commissioners, must be supreme. The King's attorney general lost his case, a prominent royalist lost his place, and the corporation commissioners had yet another of their decisions reversed.[120] King's Bench was the final arbiter.

PERPETUATING AND MODERATING PARTISAN CONFLICT

Edith Henderson put it this way when comparing the methods of King's Bench and the Privy Council: "The Council came in as mediator rather

---

[116] Ibid., vol. 82, p. 1107 (1 Sid. 282).

[117] Thus the court was disappointed that it could not order the readmission of Stratford's town clerk in 1670, who had been dismissed according to their charter's provision that he held his place at the corporation's pleasure. The court admitted the dismissal was within corporate powers, but they added that the charter should be revoked "as unreasonable." Ibid., vol. 83, pp. 98–99 (Raym., Sir T. 188) and 413 (1 Lev. 291); vol. 84, pp. 404 and 412–13 (2 Keble 641 and 656); vol. 86, pp. 54 and 57 (1 Ventris 78 and 82). See below, p. 176.

[118] A. F. Havighurst argued that Restoration judges were more independent than traditionally thought, especially before 1680: "Judiciary in the Reign of Charles II," pp. 249–52.

[119] See Attorney General Sir William Jones's failure on behalf of Thomas Holt, who desired restoration as Abingdon's recorder in 1676–77. *Eng. Rep.*, vol. 89, p. 330 (1 Freeman 441), and vol. 84, pp. 964 and 980 (3 Keble 706 and 734).

[120] *Eng. Rep.*, vol. 84, p. 487 (2 Keble 770), and vol. 86, pp. 98–99 (1 Ventris 143). PRO, KB21/17/30, 37, 56v, 61, 65v, 66v, 68, 71, 74, and 93v; KB29/323/54; and Bath City RO, Council Book 2, p. 512. Sir William Jones, a future attorney general, represented the corporation.

than judge, with a primary interest in keeping the peace and therefore in settling the whole controversy, rather than in doing justice to a petitioner who claimed to have been disfranchised unjustly."[121] Councillors had traditionally acted as arbitrators, either on their own, or in many cases by referring a matter to persons nearer the scene whom they charged with reaching a compromise.[122] In court, two sides argued to establish which was right. Only one could be. The adversarial assumptions of the legal process were well suited to the new politics of partisan competition. That disputants over the decades following the Restoration gave up on the Council and moved their disagreements before the bench is telling: they sought not settlement, but victory. By offering decisive results, the court both fueled the flames of political anger, and gradually tempered the processes of political competition so that partisan politics would not destroy the polity.

The justices adhered to a strict reading of legal propriety in deciding mandamus cases. By doing so, did they actually encourage partisan conflict by returning to corporate office those a majority preferred to see removed? Was doing justice for the individual deprived of office contrary to settling local political peace? Yes on both counts. In an age when the reality of partisan conflict had not yet been accepted – and thus the legitimacy of one's opposition was not yet accepted – any procedure that restored persons anathema to most of the group was bound to produce contentions. Divided corporations tried to heal themselves by eliminating the cause of pain, obstreperous members. The courts acted like some demented physician, prescribing the retention rather than the purgation of vile humors. This was strange medicine indeed.

The slowness of the courts to diagnose and prescribe in each case only exacerbated these problems. Finally gaining restoration on a mandamus was time consuming; litigants on both sides employed all available means to win the point, and this dragged out the proceedings. As Bristol's recorder noted when deploring the mayor's illegal prevention of the election of an alderman:

If it be said, that in case the mayor unreasonably defer [an election] we may complain to this court, viz. the King's Bench, and have a mandamus . . . to compel him to proceed to an election, who will be at so great a charge and trouble? And that course is not so speedy; [the court] may chance to be in vacation; but let it be as speedy as can be, the mayor in the mean time has obtained his ends and gained his opportunity.[123]

By such means, a minority could circumvent legal processes and thus win

121 Henderson, *English Administrative Law*, p. 74.
122 See Patterson, "Urban Patronage."   123 *Eng. Rep.*, vol. 87, p. 12 (3 Mod. 20).

significant political advantages while the matter languished at law.[124] Why then so much activity in court? Because in the end, it worked. Those who went to King's Bench for justice sought total victory over their opponents. So it was at Rye, where the attempt to choose a compromise candidate in the 1682 mayoral election or to settle matters in the Privy Council were rejected. Tournay knew he could muster the necessary legal arguments to win his point and thereby reimpose himself on those who hoped they had seen the last of him. By returning him to the corporation, the court helped perpetuate partisan struggle. In so doing, King's Bench slowly established the principle that one could not be removed from a governing body for his political allegiances. By enforcing writs of mandamus, King's Bench helped create and protect the legitimacy of partisan politics, and thereby prevented the stifling of partisan competition by those who sought the complete elimination of their opponents. In short, by forcing competing partisans to remain together in the polity, King's Bench chipped away at the paradox of partisan politics in the generations after 1660.

Through all this, the crown remained largely aloof until the political forces bearing down on it during the controversies of 1678 to 1681 woke the King from his passivity. Opening his eyes and looking out onto the towns, he saw that he had little of the political leverage there that he would now need. As the King belatedly tried to reimpose his will after 1680, the tools he had – principally the Corporation Act – were unequal to the task. It would be some time before more effective measures were devised. In 1682, the crown began using new charters in a haphazard effort to shore up its position. Slowly, a policy was formulated that redefined the relationship between crown and town and transformed the personnel of corporations nationwide. It was not until 1684 that this policy achieved any coherence and comprehensiveness. Once it did, the political situation in the towns would be altered dramatically. The number of court cases would decline as the crown took direct control of who was in and who was out of the corporations by means of new charters.[125] From the King's grant, there could be no appeal.

---

[124] New statutes in the reigns of Anne and George I were written with these problems in mind, and helped to expedite procedure in mandamus and quo warranto. See below, chapter 9.

[125] Mandamus cases almost disappear in the mid-1680s. The granting of new charters put an end to most mandamus actions by defining anew who the corporations' members were. Once a new charter appointing certain persons had been granted, any argument to be in or out of a corporation based on actions before that charter was granted would be useless.

Part Two

THE KING AND HIS CORPORATIONS, 1660–1688

5

The corporations and their charters, 1660–1682

It was the spring of 1661. Leicester's senior aldermen carried their charters to London for "the manifesting of the liberties of the corporation."[1] If they were not nervous, they should have been. Like aldermen across England, Leicester's had acquiesced in the destruction of monarchy in the 1640s and 50s when they sold off the fee farm rents long paid to the crown in return for the privileges granted to them by Charles II's ancestors. This and other sins provided ready grounds for forfeiting their charters. Leicester's corporate life hung from a slender thread, one that could be broken by the slightest legal tug.

But in the first years after the Restoration, the King was more concerned with good behavior than with good law. The question of Leicester's legal status was put aside while the Corporation Act commissioners did their work. With new members in place by the autumn of 1662, Leicester's corporation again tended to its legally suspect charters. Work proceeded slowly; not until the following June did a corporate committee recommend "the renewing of the town charter with such liberties as formerly and such other additions as Mr. Recorder shall advise." Despite this intention, continued dithering over the charter ultimately provoked crown impatience. Word arrived in town that if they did not hasten their efforts, an information in the nature of a quo warranto would be sued against them, forcing them to renew the charter on less favorable terms.[2] But no quo warranto was needed to inspire the corporation; the prospect of clarifying old privileges and perhaps gaining new ones gave incentive enough. The corporation issued regular orders to their solicitor to pursue the charter, but delays piled on delays. Cash ran short as well. But at last, on January 20, 1665, Leicester's charter passed the great seal.

Along the way, the attorney general had picked up £20, the lord chancellor £30; £12 went to the secretaries of state, and £52 to the clerks

---

[1] Leicestershire RO, BRII/18/30, ff. 115 and 209.
[2] Ibid., 18/31, ff. 307–08 and 386. Stocks, *Records of Leicester*, p. 487.

149

and functionaries wielding the seals passed along the way.[3] Hundreds more spilled from corporate coffers as the charter went back and forth between lawyers and bureaucrats. Clearly pronounced legal privileges were a costly but prudent investment. Leicester's document was short, a simple confirmation of all charters conferred on the town by previous monarchs. This was precisely what towns wanted in the 1660s: an explicit statement re-establishing their corporations on solid legal ground after the chaos of the preceding decades. Leicester's charter also included a non-intromittant, a clause barring interference by outside officials, including county justices and sheriffs. This was the most coveted of chartered liberties, the means by which the corporation's magisterial sanctity was preserved. Two novel clauses appeared as well. The first required all members to take the oaths of allegiance and supremacy when entering office, as already dictated by the Corporation Act. More interesting was the requirement that all future recorders, stewards, solicitors, and town clerks receive the King's approbation before serving. Impressive as this new power seemed, the King refused none of the corporation's choices during the succeeding decades. Finally, as in most seventeenth-century charters, Leicester's contained the all-important general indemnity clause, releasing the corporation from any liability for deeds committed before the date of the new charter.[4] The corporation now stood absolved of all sins, free to proceed without legal worry.

Like the other charters of the 1660s and 70s, Leicester's was granted in response to local initiative arising from a corporation's desire to solidify its weak legal position. Like most, it was short and to the point: a formal statement of the corporation's legal status, referring to and confirming previous charters, with few additions. Towns gained a host of new powers and privileges, and the King gained a better regulated, more closely monitored magistracy. A process of direct negotiation between the corporation's lawyers and royal officials produced a charter that benefited crown and town in equal measure. Things would be very different in 1684, when Leicester returned to Whitehall for another charter. Then it would be extorted from them, by a crown eager to gain more control of corporate government, and by a prominent nobleman seeking his own advantages. But in the 1660s and 70s, new charters resulted from and served the interests of the corporations themselves, or at least, part of each corporation. Requests for new charters often arose from partisan divisions as they

---

[3] Leicestershire RO, BRII/18/31, ff. 539, 570, 615, and 618; BRI/2/48/5; BRII/5, f. 141; and BRIII/2/86 and 87. Leicester's accounts, barely balanced in 1660–63, turned downward in the years following. Only the controversial sale of £900 worth of corporation properties in 1670–71 put them in the black again. Ibid., BRIII/2/86, f. 161, and 88, ff. 11–14.

[4] The 1665 charter is in Stocks, *Records of Leicester*, pp. 499–503. The same indemnity clause was in their 1609 charter: ibid., p. 88.

sharpened over the years. The 1670s thus saw more attempts by corporate partisans to use charters to effect a purge of local government. The 1670s also saw a variety of new charter policy ideas considered by the King's legal advisors, but for now, the King did little to assist or promote partisan purges by granting new charters, even when the "loyal" begged for his help. It would only be after 1682 that novel royal policies and virulent partisan energies in the corporations would combine to unleash a flood of new charters cleansing the "factious" from the corporations.

CHARTERS IN THE 1660S

At Whitehall and in the towns in 1660, most people were too wrapped up with the question of who should govern the corporations to give much thought to legal niceties. Borough leaders ousted during the 1640s and 50s moved quickly to regain their places, with little or no help from the King. In some corporations, those who had replaced them acquiesced in their return; writs of mandamus forced the restoration of others. What these means did not accomplish, the Corporation Act did. By March of 1663, the work of restoring the corporations' members was done, but the more complicated problem of restoring their legal foundations remained.

Townsmen were well aware of their predicament. They could hardly be blamed if in the interest of self-preservation they had gone along with the reigning powers of the 1650s. But in doing so, England's corporations had broken the legal ties to the crown that created them. Many had even accepted new charters from the Lord Protector, only to burn, hang, or hide them in 1660 in mildly hypocritical displays of attachment to the restored house of Stuart.[5] By receiving Cromwell's charters, by selling off fee farm rents once paid to the crown, by dismissing members illegally, and even by continuing to govern under a usurping regime, all corporations had arguably forfeited their charters, and with them, their very being. The Act of Indemnity and Oblivion of 1660 perhaps settled some worries: "all and singular bodies in any manner or wise corporated . . . are by the authority of this present Parliament acquitted, pardoned, released, indemnified, and discharged . . . of and from all manner of treasons, misprisions of treason, felonies, offences, contempts . . . and of and from all arrearages of tenths and first fruits, fines, post fines."[6] This was vague, sweeping language. But charters were delicate things; any breach could endanger them. Illegal removals and irregular elections were part of corporate lives in the

---

[5] Henderson, "Commonwealth Charters," pp. 144–49.
[6] J. P. Kenyon, *The Stuart Constitution, 1603–1688* (Cambridge, 1969), pp. 367–68.

preceding decades and were the stuff of which charter forfeitures were made.

Efforts to gain new charters to correct for the peculiarities of the last twenty years began immediately in some towns. Just weeks after Charles's return, Doncaster's mayor and others carried a loyal address to the King; their corporation also instructed them to enquire "if anything be done, and what, by other corporations in relation to renewing of charters." But, they added, "[you are] not to meddle at all with our own until [you] receive further instructions."[7] Legal jitters inspired both a desire for new charters and a fear of proceeding. While a few stepped forward to request new letters patent, others lagged behind to judge the results. Hull's solicitor in London, William Lister, only began work when ordered to by the corporation; otherwise, "I should not have hastened you in it 'till I had seen some other corporations had effected, to their advantage, their new grants." Royal officers proceeded no more hastily in these early years, as Lister soon found: "Our charter goes as slowly on as the rest. We may spend a great deal of time."[8] Confusion clouded townsmen's intentions, and for the time being, clogged the King's administrative machinery.

Some pressed ahead nonetheless. In November 1660, three petitions for new charters arrived at Whitehall, the first of scores to follow in the next five years. Doncaster was one of these, despite earlier hesitation. So too Bury, where corporators pleaded for a new charter to indemnify them for improper elections.[9] But conflicts for local control put Bury's corporation off their initial efforts; they did not achieve their goal for another eight years. At Sudbury in September of 1660, the corporation reinstalled the last mayor to have served in the 1640s. Having reverted to the pre-Interregnum order, they then decided to "solicit" a new charter.[10] Despite their desires, Sudbury waited four more years for it. Doncaster too remained without a new charter until 1664. Delays like these arose from two sources. First was the pre-eminent concern with personnel rather than charters in those years. Especially while the Corporation Act was at work, charters were not among the royal officials' priorities. In addition, the crown had no policy for new charters – though some efforts were made to articulate one – and no system to handle the administrative work. In the meantime, chartering was a hit-or-miss affair.

Only seven charters passed the great seal before the expiration of the corporation commissioners' powers in March 1663. Each differed from the

---

[7] Joseph Hunter, *South Yorkshire: The History and Topography of the Deanery of Don-caster*, 2 vols. (London, 1828–31), vol. I, p. 27.

[8] Hull City RO, BRL/652 and 657 (May 28, and June 15, 1661).

[9] The third came from Denbigh. *CSPD 1660–61*, p. 372.

[10] Suffolk RO (Bury St. Edmunds Branch), EE501/2/8, pp. 23–24.

others, thus revealing the lack of coherent crown purpose while the corporations were occupied with the purges then under way.[11] The first was an oddity, a new incorporation transforming the village of Smithwick into the corporation of Falmouth.[12] The next began the work of confirming old charters. Leeds's was one of a handful in the 1660s prompted by local efforts to settle partisan scores. A group of former corporation members petitioned the King to purge the corporation 'and to grant a new charter reinstalling themselves. Corporation members remaining from the 1650s submitted a counter-petition, alleging that their foes pursued the charter only "to out us and to bring in themselves." Precisely: no one promoting it intended the charter to be politically neutral. After perusing the petitions, Attorney General Sir Geoffrey Palmer recommended a new charter since in law, the old one was void. The new charter would restore those illegally removed and resuscitate the legally dead body in one step.[13] The charter expelled over one half the corporation, but the purge was conducted only in part along the factional lines drawn by the competing petitions. All but three who opposed the new charter were removed; but only three of the five excluded in the 1640s, and who now favored the new grant, were named in it. In keeping with its other efforts to mediate differences in the early 1660s, the crown tried to use Leeds's charter to end partisan divisions by uniting representatives of each group instead of giving free rein to one or the other. By the charter, the King gained new power to appoint all town clerks and recorders, a provision unprecedented in royal borough patents. The corporation also won new privileges: power to fine those absent from meetings and those refusing office, a freedom for townsmen from serving on county courts, and, most important, an expanded bench.[14]

Hull's charter followed in December 1661, one month after Leeds's, and was the first to require the oaths of allegiance and supremacy of all corporation members, a clause that would appear in charters throughout Charles's reign. As at Leeds, the crown retained the right to name recorders and town clerks and the power not only to appoint high stewards, but to remove them too. Little else changed.[15] Newport, Isle of Wight's charter came along days later, and in March of 1662 followed Preston's, where the King would only have the right to approve or disapprove of those the

[11] For a chronological listing of charters, see below, Appendix A.

[12] R. Thomas, *History and Description of the Town and Harbour of Falmouth* (Falmouth, 1827), pp. 58–60.

[13] *CSPD 1660–61*, pp. 475, 503, and 505. J. G. Clark, *The Court Books of the Leeds Corporation: First Book, January 1662 to August 1705*, Thoresby Society, vol. 34 (Leeds, 1933), pp. 199–202. Kirby, "Restoration Leeds," pp. 123–29.

[14] Wardell, *Municipal History of Leeds*, appendix, pp. lxii–lxxxii.

[15] Boyle, *Charters to Hull*, pp. 152–89. Leeds's charter required only the oath of allegiance, and of the mayor only, not of other corporators.

corporation chose as stewards, recorders, or clerks; the corporation thus retained the initiative in naming them. In these early charters, the crown was casting about for a policy for limited control over officer selection, but had not yet settled on one.

The King granted Preston's charter, like Leeds's, to close fissures in the corporation. Two groups in the corporation traded recriminations with one another throughout 1661, each charging the other with complicity with the regimes of the 1640s and 50s. A locally inspired purge preceded a disputed mayoral election in September.[16] Those supporting the victorious candidate then carried the corporation's records to London seeking a new charter to confirm the corporation's privileges and their own dominant position. King and Council ordered the attorney general to examine whether the conduct of the election violated Preston's charter. Everyone in Preston saw the writing on the wall; both parties quickly began efforts to control the contents of the anticipated new charter. Each side in town had a noble patron: the winners of the mayoral contest supported by Charles Lord Brandon, and their opponents by the Earl of Derby. Brandon and Derby submitted very different lists of proposed members for the restored corporation. Brandon's, countersigned by other prominent gentlemen, was adopted in its entirety; Derby's was dismissed with a notice of the illiteracy, poverty, and disloyalty of those he championed.[17] While it removed some and left in others active in the corporation during the 1650s, the new charter represented a victory for the group that had won the last election and had successfully used Brandon's support.[18]

At Preston and at Leeds, the paradox of partisan politics was quite in evidence as opposing sides competed to control the contents of their new charters in order to oust their foes. Local, not crown initiative prompted the pursuit of new charters for partisan gain. Wigan's charter, passed two months later, may well have been tangled up in some of the same gentry conflicts and, like Preston's, was intended to resolve struggles in the corporation from before 1660. Like others, Wigan's charter excluded

[16] Those making the removals had requested the King's permission, but then made the removals before permission arrived. *CSPD 1661–62*, pp. 102 and 229, and *CSPD Addendum, 1660–70*, p. 663; PRO, SP29/42/59 and 60, 46/55, 48/125, and 446/50.

[17] The victorious mayor, James Hodgkinson, had been mayor the previous year, and had led the effort to gain royal sanction for removing some and restoring others to the corporation in 1661. PRO, SP29/446/50, and PC2/55/212v, 231v, and 235v–36. Derby's and Brandon's lists are at PRO, SP29/26/30. *CSPD 1660–61*, p. 454.

[18] Lingard, *Preston Charters*, part 2, pp. 35–63. Michael Mullett recounts the charter's passage, but misdates it to 1663 rather than 1662, the date in all printed versions and in the great seal docket: PRO, IND1/4227/95. This puts the charter after the implementation of the Corporation Act, which creates confusion about the timing and nature of dismissals there. It appears that the commissioners did nothing in Preston since the corporation had already been purged by the charter. "Preston Politics," pp. 66–67.

county JPs from town limits, though it added an unusual clause permitting town JPs to act on the county bench.[19] On the other hand, the crown returned to the requirement that the King could nominate future recorders and town clerks, rather than simply approving those chosen by the corporation, as at Newport and Preston. The crown had still not fixed its intentions regarding royal control of the appointment of corporation officers. With all these changes in these first six charters, the last granted before the expiration of the Corporation Act did nothing but change Maidenhead's market day while confirming its traditional liberties.[20]

The new clauses in these first seven charters – clarifying election procedures, creating new courts, and expanding urban benches – benefited crown and town alike. By giving broader purview to local judicial bodies and by defining more clearly charter terms which had proved contentious, townsmen hoped for greater order at home. The charters of 1661–63 – in their moderation, in their origin in local initiative, in their greater clarity and their confirmation of traditional liberties, and in their expansion of crown involvement in the selection of leading officers – would serve as models for those granted over the next two decades. In particular, in clauses enlarging benches or granting JPs new powers, we see signs of the most prominent royal concern for the towns throughout the Restoration: that they should have loyal and effective magistrates. But still, no charter policy had emerged. With royal attention diverted by other concerns in the early 1660s, and with royal willingness to let the Corporation Act run its course, there was little to encourage the crown to take the lead.

In the preceding two centuries, the number of charters granted had risen dramatically in the first three years of each reign as towns asked the new monarch for new privileges.[21] Confusion, removals, restorations after 1660, and the implementation of the Corporation Act postponed the usual rush for new charters at the start of Charles II's reign. But with their personnel lists settled by mid-1663, many corporations were momentarily more unified than they had been for years; scores now asked the crown for a guarantee of old liberties and for the grant of new ones, just as their ancestors had done at the start of new reigns past. Over the next two years, the number of new charters shot skyward – granted at the same rate

[19] David Sinclair, *The History of Wigan*, 2 vols. (London, 1882), vol. II, pp. 86–92.
[20] All remaining in Maidenhead's corporation after the Corporation Act was implemented were confirmed. Berkshire RO, M/IC5 and M/AC1/1/1, second pagination, pp. 49 and 51.
[21] Since 1500, two to five new charters were granted in a typical mid-reign year. The numbers increased greatly in the years following the accession of a new monarch. From 1509 to 1512, fifty-one charters were granted; sixty in 1547–49; forty-seven in 1553–55; thirty-nine in 1558–60; and forty-nine in 1603–05. The years immediately after Charles I's accession did not see this marked increase. Charters per year have been counted from lists in Weinbaum, *Borough Charters*.

experienced in the early years of any new ruler – reaching a peak in 1664 that would not be matched for another twenty years. While only seven charters had been granted between 1660 and March 1663, forty-eight more passed the seals by the end of 1665.[22] The reason was simple: England's corporations relied on the crown for their lives. All could see the benefits of a new charter that put their powers beyond legal doubt.[23] The corporations, not the crown, would lead the rechartering effort, forcing the crown to develop administrative procedures to handle the demand they created.

Some in Whitehall appreciated the need for a comprehensive charters policy. The Marquess of Newcastle suggested that in all new charters, the King should reserve to himself the appointment of all mayors. Permitting corporate election of mayors only encouraged plebeians in the "fanatic and groundless opinion that kings ought to be chosen by and be account[able] unto the people, whereas they, being abridged of choosing inferior magistrates, their other higher thoughts will quickly perish."[24] Mayors, he argued, differed little from county sheriffs and justices of the peace; there was no reason why they, unlike county officers, should be chosen locally. Though his logic was sound, implementing the proposal would have lit a political firestorm, in all likelihood destroying much of the support the King enjoyed in the boroughs after the Restoration. Such ideas were not the stuff of which royal policy would be made.

The first attempt to spell out a policy came in May of 1661, when a royal warrant proclaimed four clauses to be added to all new charters. First, the King would name the initial aldermen, recorder, and town clerk. By long-standing practice, charters of reincorporation already named all appointed to the new body, so this was no innovation. Second, common council positions would be filled henceforth by freemen only. Similarly, most corporations, by custom or by previous charter, permitted only freemen to serve, thus this would attract little notice. Third, the election of MPs would be by the common council alone, excluding all other franchise forms.[25]

---

22 Sacret's contention that "the number of new charters . . . far exceeds that of any such period before" is thus incorrect. "Restoration Government and Municipal Corporations," p. 259.

23 All charters after 1660, like those before, included a general indemnity, freeing the corporation from any quo warranto enquiry into deeds done before the new charter's passage. Some historians assumed this meant the new charter was granted after a quo warranto. They thus believed they had found an instance of the crown attacking borough privileges with quo warranto. Sacret, "Restoration Government and Municipal Corporations," p. 258. But this clause had long been added for corporations' benefit, for it would preclude any suits brought by any party for any deed done before the date of the new charter.

24 Bod., MS Clarendon 73, f. 359v.

25 *CSPD 1660–61*, p. 582; John Miller assumes this last provision would restrict the franchise to common councillors, excluding the mayor and aldermen. But by charter, the mayor and aldermen were part of what was usually referred to as the "common council" or

This was a dramatic proposal, but it would not be added to a borough charter until the 1680s.[26] The fourth proposal – that in all charters, the King would retain the nomination of future recorders and town clerks – touched corporate autonomy most directly. But during the two years before this policy was explicitly revoked, the nomination clause was used in only three of the seven charters granted. Hull's charter contained the provision in diluted form; so too did those of Leeds and Wigan. The warrant for Warwick's charter of 1664 originally required the King's "nomination," but the final charter only called for his "approbation" of those selected by the corporation.[27] Wallingford's charter warrant also employed the more limited approbation clause, "and not the nomination of them as was heretofore directed."[28]

Policy as proclaimed and as implemented were very different things. After reviewing the situation in June 1663, the King declared that the nomination clause "may beget obstructions in the settlement of corporations, the peace and well-ordering whereof is and was our principal aim and desire."[29] He thus canceled the policy. While historians have made much of the original declaration of May 1661 as the sign of an ambitious regime, they have overlooked the two most important results that followed from it: the lack of implementation and its revocation.[30] Instead, the crown opted for the approbation requirement: that corporations elect their recorders and clerks, who were then subject to the King's approval. Approbation imposed some restrictions, but these were not as severe as if the crown had the nomination of all major officers. In addition, approba-

---

"assembly," terms that encompassed councillors *and* aldermen and the mayor. "Borough Charters," p. 58.

[26] Evesham's charter of June 1684 was the first of many in the mid-1680s to change the franchise: PRO, SP44/66/348–51. Newark's charter of 1673 granted the franchise to the borough for the first time, so this was a newly enfranchised borough rather than one with a changed franchise.

[27] *CSPD 1663–64*, p. 519; PRO, SP44/16/73; and VCH Warwickshire, vol. VIII, p. 497. The warrant was the royal order to the attorney or solicitor general to engross the charter on parchment. This then went to the great seal. The warrant detailed the charter's contents and included a list of those to be appointed. But charter terms occasionally changed between the warrant and the final charter.

[28] PRO, SP44/15/55–56.

[29] *CSPD 1663–64*, p. 169; PRO, SP44/14/10. As John Miller notes, this revocation mistakenly refers to the original order by a date of August 3, 1661, not the correct date of May 7, 1661. "Borough Charters," p. 65.

[30] Thus John Evans and Ronald Hutton make much of the May 1661 memo, without mentioning its cancellation. Evans, *Norwich*, p. 239. Hutton, *The Restoration*, p. 159. Sacret's contention that the nomination provision "was generally insisted upon" is incorrect. He confuses nomination with the more widely used approbation clause. The distinction is critical. Sacret, "Restoration Government and Municipal Corporations," p. 242.

tion was almost never denied, and not once before 1680, when the crown's view of the boroughs did indeed become more menacing.

Royal officers expected a flood of requests for new charters upon the conclusion of the work of the Corporation Act commissioners. Little more than two weeks after he nullified the nomination policy, Charles promulgated a new set of guidelines after being "informed that divers cities and corporations . . . do intend and humbly desire our confirmation of their former charters and privileges." Finding the traditional process – draft charters, followed by bills and warrants, before engrossing the charter – unwieldy, the King ordered it simplified. Those charters requested with only "such alterations and additions as are usual" were to move straight from the attorney or solicitor general to one of the secretaries for a warrant under his signature, without need for the sign manual, before proceeding to the great seal. Only in instances where extensive changes were desired would further review be required; in these cases, the King would reserve to himself the approbation of recorders, stewards, and town clerks. In practice, the approbation clause would appear in nearly all future charters, because most towns desired a variety of new clauses in addition to a simple confirmation. Few if any changes in personnel would be made by the charters to come: "the present officers and members [shall] continue and be confirmed in their respective offices and places unless we shall give any particular order to the contrary."[31] The charters of the 1660s would not be instruments of purgation.[32] But perhaps the most important part of this statement came at the beginning: this was a system created in response to anticipated demand, not the result of crown intentions to encourage towns in large numbers to take new charters.

As expected, charter business picked up dramatically over the next two years. Despite the statement of what appeared to be a systematic policy in June 1663, clauses for each charter, especially the approbation clause, continued to be considered on a case-by-case basis.[33] Some towns avoided the approbation requirement altogether. The solicitor guiding Yarmouth's charter through the various offices reported with relief: "I thank God I have effected your desires, and the exception or restraint [the approbation] inserted in your charter, is rased out of the bill, in the presence of his Majesty and by his special command."[34] Little more than a week earlier,

---

[31] *CSPD 1663–64*, p. 185; PRO, SP44/14/38.

[32] Of the sixty-four charters granted after Preston's until Gloucester's in 1672, the membership under old and new charters of thirteen have been compared, and no changes may be found: Norwich, Coventry, Beverley, Yarmouth (1664), Windsor, Hedon, Newcastle under Lyme, Woodstock, Stratford, Leicester, Bridport, Macclesfield, and Yarmouth (1668).

[33] For instance, at Stamford, Havering, and St. Albans: *CSPD 1663–64*, pp. 500, 575, and 657.

[34] Swinden, *History of Great Yarmouth*, p. 581n.

the corporation had petitioned the Earl of Clarendon, their high steward, to block this, the only clause to which they objected. Clarendon reported the town's good behavior and requested the change, noting that the King had omitted the clause in charters recently given to Norwich and Bristol.[35] Colchester too gained its 1663 charter without the approbation requirement; Ipswich did as well.[36] Nonetheless, most charters granted in the period included the approbation clause, and as such, this was the one clear sign of an expanded crown power in the boroughs during the 1660s and 70s.

As with supposed Restoration era innovations like oaths of loyalty and externally imposed dismissals from office, the approbation clause also had its Commonwealth precedent: Sudbury's charter of 1658 had required Parliament's annual approval of mayors and bailiffs.[37] Now this power would apply to the corporations' leading legal officers. Corporations, as beings that existed only in law, relied on their recorders and town clerks for legal advice. Recorders were JPs and town clerks were usually clerks of the peace. Both were critical to the operation of local magistracy and the approbation policy gave the crown a limited oversight of them. Just as was revealed by the expanded corporate benches and clarified judicial powers added to Restoration charters, and by the new device of commissions of association, approbation was the policy of a government whose concerns in the towns were focused first and foremost on the administration of justice.

But approbation was a weak policy even more weakly used. The King's new power was only to vet, not to appoint, and on no occasion before 1680 did the King reject any corporation's choice. Of the seventy-five requests for the approbation of a new officer found among the state papers or in the Privy Council's registers, the results in sixty-eight are known. Of these, sixty-three were approved and five denied, the first after the election of a town clerk in Ludlow in June 1680.[38] Approbation was a power of which little advantage was taken, and none before 1680, when the crown's approach toward the boroughs became more aggressive. Approval appears to have been granted as a matter of course. Even after a disputed town clerk's election in Windsor in 1669, the crown's concern in approving the corporation's choice focused not on his political leanings, but on the legality of the election. Thus Windsor's clerk was approved with little ado

[35] Yarmouth's petition and Clarendon's notes are in ibid., pp. 581–82n. Gauci, *Yarmouth*, pp. 109–10. For the Norwich and Bristol charters, see: *The History of the City and County of Norwich* (Norwich, 1768), pp. 273–80, and Latham, *Bristol Charters*, pp. 175–78.

[36] *Charters [of Colchester]*, pp. 104–26. Suffolk RO (Ipswich Branch), HD36/A/290, and Richard Canning, *The Principal Charters which have been Granted to the Corporation of Ipswich* (London, 1754), pp. 30–48.

[37] Suffolk RO (Bury St. Edmunds Branch), EE501/2/8, pp. 1 and 13–14.

[38] *CSPD 1679–80*, p. 531. Shropshire Records and Research Service, LB/1/18.

after Prince Rupert, governor of Windsor castle, examined the proceedings.[39] Nonetheless, the crown was clearly wedded to the approbation policy, repeating in 1675 its original order that the approbation be included in all charters.[40]

The King's pronouncement of June 1663 that all charters should include the approbation clause was his one definitive statement of intent concerning charters. There are other indications that approbation was the only concession he sought. Chester's solicitor reported in 1664 that the principal reason the crown wanted new charters was to put this provision in them.[41] But given that only about one third of all corporations received new charters in the 1660s, and that most were granted on petitions from the towns themselves, the approbation clause apparently provided little incentive to pursue a comprehensive rechartering of England's corporations. As stated in the royal memorandum promulgating the policy, it was simply something that would be done when a corporation requested a new charter.[42] As we shall see, despite occasional talk of quo warranto at Whitehall and in some towns, little effort was made to force renewals on the towns in the 1660s in order to impose a restricted set of liberties.

Other policy goals are apparent, even if never publicly articulated. The charters of the 1660s accomplished three things besides imposing the approbation requirement. First, they protected the life of each corporation by restoring the legal relationship between the corporations and the crown after the troubles before 1660. Second, they granted a host of new privileges, including extra fairs and markets and increased licenses in mortmain: a permission to the corporation to own lands up to a certain annual value without the restrictions imposed by medieval mortmain legislation. With inflation over the centuries, old mortmain limits had eroded the value of corporations' income since they often precluded the acquisition of more profit-generating land. Increasing the license was one of the most common and coveted of new privileges: Reading's 1667 charter doubled the amount of land the corporation could hold, from £500 to £1,000 of annual value; Newark's license quintupled to £200; and Maidstone's went from £20 to £300. This helped secure the financial welfare of each corporation.[43] Another prominent component of charters in the period was the grant of new fairs and markets or changes in the days they could be held. This contributed to the inhabitants' well-being by promoting local commerce, and to the corporation's by creating more occasions for collecting market tolls.

[39] PRO, PC2/62/4v and 8v. *CSPD 1668–69*, p. 531.
[40] PRO, PC2/64/467.   [41] CCRO, ML3/400.   [42] PRO, SP44/14/38.
[43] PRO, IND1/4227/248 and 387–88. *CSPD 1672–73*, p. 520; PRO, SP44/34/221. James, *The Charters of Maidstone*, p. 151. Blackstone, *Commentaries*, vol. III, pp. 478–79.

Third, the charters clarified and widened the powers exercised by individual towns. Among these were provisions defining in greater detail the proper days and methods for electing officers, clauses appointing fines and other punishments corporations could impose on persons refusing office, and other measures designed to lessen the potential for conflict when choosing members. Even more important were provisions increasing the size and purview of the bench and other courts, and those protecting urban jurisdictions from encroachments by county officers. Thus nearly all charters contained a non-intromittant barring county JPs, and many expanded the size of the bench, thereby permitting easier enforcement of those statutes requiring the involvement of more than one justice.[44] Increasing the number of JPs in new charters resulted from the needs of both crown and town for more powerful borough benches. In the use of approbation, and in the granting of these privileges, Charles's charters show a remarkable consistency and benignity throughout the 1660s.[45] Both town and crown were gainers by the new charters.

THE SEARCH FOR A ROYAL POLICY, 1660–82

The crown responded to rather than created a desire for new charters, but was it always so passive? Was local initiative the only force at work? Was there no one near the King thinking about redefining the proper relationship between the corporations and the King?

Previous analyses of crown/corporate relations in the 1660s and 70s have been strongly influenced by our knowledge of what happened with borough charters in the last years of Charles II, when the crown formulated and pursued an aggressive policy. Historians have read these events back on the preceding decades, assuming that the crown had the same desires and intentions from 1660 onwards, but only realized them fully in 1683–85; thus they have found a "systematic effort" throughout the Restoration to control the corporations with new charters.[46] But this is to miss the point of what both crown and town wanted in the first two

---

[44] This was usually done by adding more aldermen to the bench. Beverley's 1663 charter increased the number more than most, from two to twelve. George Poulson, *Beverlac: Or the Antiquities and History of the Town of Beverley*, 2 vols. (London, 1829), vol. I, pp. 382–83. Other towns received peace commissions for the first time, for instance, Sutton Coldfield, in 1664: Riland Bedford, *History of Sutton Coldfield*, p. 28.

[45] Ronald Hutton distinguishes between the charters of 1663 and 1664 to show the King's increasingly malign intentions. *The Restoration*, p. 213. My examination of all charters granted in both years shows no important differences between them. Throughout the decade, new charters confirmed old privileges and granted the usual new ones, most upon corporate request.

[46] Sacret, "Restoration Government and Municipal Corporations," p. 259. See also ibid., p. 233. Robert Pickavance, "The English Boroughs and the King's Government: A Study of

decades after 1660: clarified corporation privileges and expanded powers for corporate magistrates. We must appreciate the limited nature of the crown's interest in the boroughs in the 1660s and 70s. By doing so, we can see how new and dramatic was the crown's use of quo warranto after 1682 to impose new charters making extensive changes in the corporations' personnel and constitutions.

What policy or policies – if any – did the crown have for governing relations with the towns in the 1660s and 70s? The crown did not develop a comprehensive policy for supervising urban government, but the 1660s, and even more so the 1670s, saw a few quiet innovations in policy thinking. To see this, we must look in three areas: the use of quo warranto, the development of commissions of association – by which county JPs were appointed to the bench in certain towns – and proposals made for regulating Irish corporations.

Quo warranto – "by what warrant" – was the judicial device by which the usurpation or abuse of a royal franchise might be examined in court. Sir Francis North explained that public franchises, such as corporations, "are all but parts of the King's ordinary government, detached and entrusted to particular persons, for his ease and the people's convenience." Attached to them was a duty to use them in the public interest. This was the condition of the franchise of being a corporation and of all the franchises attendant on it, such as the power to make by-laws, to operate a market, or to hold a court:

These are all forfeitable either by nonuser [or] abuser, because there is a condition in law tacitly annexed to them, that if they be so used as to turn to the public prejudice, against the end of their institution, or are discontinued, whereby the public hath not the benefit of them, they are forfeited, and the reason is strong, because such are not erected for the sake of the persons, but of the public interested in the administration.[47]

Since the franchise was the "King's ordinary government" in other hands, when "reseized, there follows no chasm or defect of government, only the ordinary takes place instead of the extraordinary, being as sufficient for all the necessary ends of government." But the point of seizure was not for the King to exercise direct government, but to put the franchise "into other hands that will not abuse it."[48] One did not need to be an unabashed proponent of the royal prerogative to take this view. Sir Matthew Hale put

---

the Tory Reaction, 1681–85" (D.Phil., University of Oxford, 1976), pp. 11 and 41. John Miller effectively questioned these ideas: "Borough Charters," especially pp. 53–56.

[47] BL, Add. 32,518, f. 182, and 32,520, f. 66–v. Here North distinguishes between the use of quo warranto against public, not private, franchises, thus paralleling the sharpening public/private distinction made in mandamus cases.

[48] BL, Add. 32,520, f. 67.

it in much the same language: "when those conditions in law which are annexed to [a corporation] are broken, that franchise as well as others may be forfeited or by seizure suspended."[49]

Quo warranto was the means by which the King – represented by his justices in King's Bench – could ascertain if an abuse had occurred. Quo warranto had begun its life in the thirteenth century as a writ returnable in special eyres. By the sixteenth century, action by information superseded that by writ: hence the contemporary technical term, "an information in the nature of a quo warranto."[50] The distinction here was important. First, the medieval writ had been a general order to appear and show one's warrant – the charter – for exercising a franchise. Informations were neither so vague nor so easily answered. They detailed specific abuses, misuses, or non-uses of a franchise. Precise charges, based on precise charter provisions, required precise answers. Second, an information required no previous finding by a grand jury; the King, via his attorney general, simply filed the information with the master of the Crown Office in King's Bench. Though strictly a royal device, others who could convince the attorney general to act in the King's name could use quo warranto as well. This explains how local initiative could be so important in the use of quo warranto throughout the period. Third, a judgment reached on an information rather than a writ, to use Blackstone's words, was "not quite so decisive."[51] A finding against the defendant on a writ automatically dissolved the franchise. But a finding on an information could have a variety of consequences, including a fine, the ouster of one or more of those exercising the franchise, the seizure of only part of the franchise (such as the power to hold a certain market), or the seizure of the entire franchise (such as a corporate charter). As we shall see in the next chapter, it was of great importance in the London decision of 1683 that the judges resolved that the corporation be seized into the King's hands, not dissolved. Dissolution posed the possibility of the corporation's death, and with it, the demise of all its properties and powers, which could not then be granted elsewhere. Seizure on the other hand meant that in law, the corporate body lived while it was held in the King's hands, so he could grant it again to

---

[49] Hale, *Prerogatives*, ed. Yale, p. 244.

[50] On the evolution from writ to information, see J. H. Baker, *An Introduction to English Legal History*, 3rd edn. (London, 1990), pp. 167 and 578; Harold Garrett-Goodyear, "The Tudor Revival of Quo Warranto and Local Contributions to State Building," in Morris S. Arnold, *et al.*, eds., *On The Laws and Customs of England: Essays in Honor of Samuel E. Thorne* (Chapel Hill, 1981), p. 241; Blackstone, *Commentaries*, vol. I, p. 484, vol. III, pp. 262–64, and vol. IV, pp. 307–12; and Hale, *Prerogatives*, ed. Yale, pp. 179 and 201–03.

[51] Blackstone, *Commentaries*, vol. III, p. 263. This distinction between proceeding by writ and by information was highlighted in the first report of a quo warranto case post-1660, concerning the Trinity House. *Eng. Rep.*, vol. 82, p. 986 (1 Sid. 86).

others as he wished.[52] Lack of clarity about this distinction prior to 1683 may well be one of the reasons that quo warranto was used so fitfully in the two decades after 1660. Many apparently feared the possibility of a corporation's dissolution and all the legal chaos that would ensue.

To appreciate just how different were the goals and methods in the use of quo warranto before and after 1682, we must examine the one body of sources that can tell us about its use, the one body of sources that has not previously been explored by students of the period: the records of King's Bench. The threat of quo warranto was generally seen as an effective means for compelling a corporation to seek a new charter, thereby providing an opportunity to redefine the terms of crown/town relations. But spotty use of the information after 1660 suggests that the crown had very little interest in changing this relationship. The first information of the reign, issued less than a week after Charles returned, concerned not a corporation, but a private franchise in Northamptonshire.[53] Given the nature of the franchise and the speed with which it was prosecuted, this certainly resulted from the initiative of someone in the county rather than from any effort of a King who had plenty else on his mind. From the start then, we must appreciate the importance of local initiative in the use of this royal device.

After reports of seditious behavior in Taunton in the spring of 1661, the Privy Council ordered the attorney general to "call in question their charter by a writ of quo warranto."[54] Nothing came of the command. Dorchester too faced quo warranto in 1661; again, the threat proved toothless.[55] But in Trinity term 1661, informations were introduced in King's Bench against London and York, the first actual court proceedings against any urban jurisdiction since the Restoration. Certainly at York, quo warranto resulted from local efforts: in this case, in response to a petition from citizens there for changes in the magistracy. The quo warranto against York, and that against London, were later dropped: because the corporations bill was then making its way through Parliament, and this could be expected to take care of York's personnel troubles, and because both cities soon began efforts to receive new charters.[56]

Quo warranto lay dormant while the Corporation Act commissioners did their work. But in March 1663, the Privy Council received reports of "disaffection" at Rye and Arundel, and in response ordered quo warrantos prosecuted against each. Not content to stop there, the Council also

[52] On the distinction between dissolution and seizure, see Hale, *Prerogatives*, ed. Yale, p. 245.
[53] PRO, KB21/14/6v, 7v, and 11v.   [54] PRO, PC2/55/119.
[55] Underdown, *Fire from Heaven*, pp. 233–34. Charles Herbert Mayo, *The Municipal Records of the Borough of Dorchester, Dorset* (Exeter, 1908), p. 87.
[56] PRO, KB21/14/49, 49v, 51, 52, 54, 56, and 65. David Scott, "Politics and Government in York, 1640–1662," in Richardson, *Town and Countryside*, pp. 62–63.

commanded the attorney general to "prosecute the like quo warrantos against such other corporations . . . who have not renewed their charters since his Majesty's Restoration."[57] Certainly this was a blanket policy, requiring the rechartering of all the nation's corporations. Or was it? King's Bench did see a flurry of activity in 1663, though oddly enough, this began in Hilary term, *before* the King's order. The attorney and solicitor general may well have had good reason to anticipate the royal command, or they may have begun efforts on their own authority before later enlisting the King's support. Either way, sometime in January or February 1663, quo warrantos were brought into King's Bench against the corporations of Rye and Arundel – as ordered by Charles the following month – and against Oxford, Shrewsbury, Stafford, Newbury, Berwick, and Southampton. A handful more followed during the next year.[58]

Three things stand out about these quo warrantos. First is their number: a total of twelve informations were entered in the Crown Office in the year following the King's 1663 order. This left over 180 more to prosecute. If this were to be a comprehensive program, much remained to be done, and at the current rate, would require about fifteen years to complete. Second, of these twelve towns, only five received a new charter. Of the other seven, six appear to have kept their charters. This brings us to the third point. Though pleadings began in many of these cases, only one went all the way to a final judgment resulting in the seizure of privileges. Berkhamsted lost its charter when it failed to appear to answer the lengthy catalogue of charges against it.[59] Why these corporations were attacked and not others is unclear, though again, information from the locality was probably the key. Berkhamsted, for instance, may have run into trouble in September of 1662 prior to the annual bailiff's election, which in turn, may have inspired complaints to the King.[60] Berkhamsted would be the only corporation to lose its privileges by quo warranto between 1660 and 1683.

Quo warranto's appearance in court was limited: in the actual number of informations commenced, in the legal consequences for the towns concerned, and in the number of new charters it inspired. Of course, the mere mention of quo warranto may have been enough to accomplish crown

[57] PRO, PC2/56/173v.
[58] The first eight of these were enrolled together at PRO, KB29/313, 14–v. The others, against Gloucester, Hemel Hempstead, Hadleigh, and Berkhamsted, are at KB29/313/92, 134, 159, 161, 164–v. For other orders in these cases, see KB21/15/83, 85, 85v, 93, 95, and 102; KB21/16/7v; and KB29/314/111 and 184.
[59] Hertfordshire RO, D/EX/652/32, 33, 34, and 35. PRO, KB29/313/164v. The corporation petitioned for a new charter and were told they would receive one, but none followed. Thin town records prevent learning any more. Hertfordshire RO, D/EX/652/13 and 15–17.
[60] The corporation minute book is missing at least three leaves – which had been written upon – at this point. Hertfordshire RO, D/EX/652/22, pp. 58ff.

goals – whatever they were – thus court proceedings in many cases may have been unwarranted. But again, in cases where we know that the attorney general was ordered to begin quo warranto proceedings or where a corporation received threats of one, the record is spotty. A quo warranto ordered against Barnstaple in early 1664 – "in order to the calling in of their charter" – led to no new charter, nor did one against Maidstone in 1666. Canterbury corporation considered renewing its charter when they heard a quo warranto was pending against them, but no charter followed.[61] As with the nomination clause, use of quo warranto occurred rarely, and then to little effect. Strong pronouncements – as in the King's order of March 1663 – and comprehensive policy implementation were still very different things.

Threats did compel a few towns to receive new charters, though on terms no less favorable than those granted to towns that were more forthcoming. Grantham's 1664 charter, gained after a threatened quo warranto, was nothing more than a simple confirmation of all its previous grants, adding only the usual clauses requiring the oaths and the approbation of future recorders and town clerks.[62] Woodstock confronted the threat of quo warranto that same year, but the King ordered its withdrawal before it went to court. That summer, the corporation negotiated a new charter that made no changes in personnel, nor any other changes of note, except the addition of the usual provisions.[63] Newcastle under Lyme also prepared to respond to a quo warranto in April of 1664. A new charter arrived in August, which, like Woodstock's, contained the approbation and oath clauses, while it also expanded the powers of the borough's civil court.[64]

News of the Privy Council's March 1663 order to sue quo warrantos spread nationwide and inspired a few towns to act though there was no direct threat. Stratford-upon-Avon began working for a new charter after hearing of the policy in April and received one sixteen months later, much

---

[61] PRO, PC2/57/13v. Martin, *Records of Maidstone*, pp. 153–54. Canterbury City and Cathedral Archives, CC/AC/5, f. 146. There is no sign of Canterbury's quo warranto in King's Bench.

[62] Martin, *Charters of Grantham*, pp. 20–21 and 157–69.

[63] The charter is at Woodstock Town Hall, #149. The quo warranto episode may have inspired or resulted from internal controversy, as two pages were cut from the assembly book, and another pasted in, covering January–September 1664: ibid., 76/1, ff. 13–14. Events may be traced in Bod., MS Top. Oxon.c.351, ff. 89–92, which suggests that the quo warranto was brought by Clarendon, who had been angered when he was not chosen high steward. VCH *Oxfordshire*, vol. XII, p. 374, cites this source, but says the quo warranto came in 1667–68, though the cited item clearly says 1664. There may have been another quo warranto then, for there is notice of an order to enter a nolle prosequi in a quo warranto against Woodstock: *CSPD 1667–68*, p. 218. Given Clarendon's political problems culminating in his exile later in 1667, the thought that he would have or could have issued a quo warranto against a small borough that year seems unlikely.

[64] Pape, *Newcastle-under-Lyme*, p. 26.

to their advantage.[65] Sir William Doyley wrote Yarmouth of the King's intentions, and the corporation immediately appointed a committee to gain a favorable renewal. Liverpool also started efforts for a new charter upon receiving similar news, but soon lost interest, aware perhaps that little would come of the seemingly aggressive policy; no charter followed.[66] As before March 1663, most towns asking for new charters did so on their own initiative, aware of all they could gain by them. As Michael Mullett notes of Lancaster's request for a charter at this time, it was "a prudential measure to clarify relations with the crown." Lancaster's new charter enlarged the bench; otherwise the charter was a full confirmation of ancient liberties.[67] Beneficial new clauses and greater clarity were inducement enough to inspire most towns to act.

In fact, corporations had ample reason to want new charters in the 1660s, and many that applied were disappointed. Devizes petitioned in 1665, but failed.[68] Leicester and Sudbury each sought new charters in 1660, only to be put off for four years before succeeding.[69] Cambridge solicited a charter in 1664 to gain a provision prohibiting those who had not served a proper apprenticeship from trading in the town, but no charter appeared. Bath too failed in its efforts for a charter that would have required county sessions to meet there.[70] Thetford desired a charter to clarify the jurisdictional problems created by the fact that their town straddled the line dividing Norfolk and Suffolk.[71] Dozens of other towns petitioned for and won new charters in the 1660s with quo warranto nowhere in sight. Charters granted extra fairs and markets, broadened the authority of civil courts, increased land-holding privileges, enlarged benches, created new offices and clarified corporate independence from county authorities, and conferred other important benefits. As Recorder

---

[65] The new charter raised the monetary limit on cases the borough's court could hear, made no changes in personnel, and appointed extra JPs, all desirable provisions. Shakespeare Birthplace Trust, BRU2/4, pp. 80, 82, 85, and 90. VCH, Warwickshire, vol. III, pp. 250–51.

[66] Swinden, *History of Great Yarmouth*, p. 584. Picton, *Liverpool Records*, pp. 241 and 243.

[67] Michael Mullett, "Conflict, Politics, and Elections in Lancaster, 1660–1688," *Northern History*, 19 (1983), p. 66. T. Pape, *The Charters of the City of Lancaster* (Lancaster, 1952), p. 57. The nomination clause was originally ordered for Lancaster, but by the warrant of June 21, 1663 (eight days after the cancelation of the nomination policy) the approbation clause was inserted instead. PRO, SP44/15/61. The charters of the southwest also resulted from local initiative: Norrey, "The Relationship between Central and Local Government," p. 134.

[68] CSPD 1665–66, p. 145.

[69] Suffolk RO (Bury St. Edmunds Branch), EE501/2/8, pp. 24 and 58. On Leicester, see above, pp. 149–51.

[70] Cambridgeshire RO, Shelf C/8, f. 180. Bath City RO, Council Book 2, p. 526.

[71] CSPD 1668–69, pp. 549–50.

John Sicklemore of Ipswich wrote to his neighbors of the new charter he was about to bring home in 1664:

I make no question but the charter will please beyond our expectation; the advantages are besides confirmation of former grants and usages, a recorder to be a justice of peace, and the town clerk and he to officiate by deputies and the election of them to be as formerly [without the approbation], the bailiffs, justices, and recorder to hear and determine felonies, etc., and a gaol delivery.[72]

The towns were the winners by the new letters patent of the 1660s and 70s, and as long as this was so, the initiative in the rechartering of England's corporations would remain with them.

Berkhamsted's quo warranto produced the one judgment for a seizure of corporate liberties found for the period 1660 to 1683. Since this happened on the default of appearance by the defendant, there had been no occasion in court for lawyers and judges to consider what quo warranto could really do. As such, lingering doubts about the information's legal utility may well have curbed any effort to use it to compel more corporations to do the royal bidding. The information in the nature of quo warranto, seemingly the most powerful weapon in the crown's legal arsenal, was perhaps its weakest, having endured few real court tests since the reign of Henry VIII.[73] Quo warranto had seen some use in the 1610s, 20s, and 30s, but only one – Southampton's – apparently ended with a judicial decision for seizure of liberties. Most other prosecutions were dropped or were concluded by default of appearance.[74] The case law on quo warranto was perilously thin so its effectiveness for controlling the corporations remained in question. This could hardly be the means then for making all towns bow before the King. More to the point, it does not appear that the King wanted the corporations to bow to him. He simply wanted loyal keepers of his peace sitting on the benches of England's towns and cities. For this, quo warranto was both too blunt and too weak an instrument. Other devices were used instead.

John Sicklemore had made much of the clauses concerning the magistracy in Ipswich's new charter. More corporation members were added to the bench, they were given new powers, and the town's traditional independence from county justices and sheriffs was maintained by a non-intromittant clause. The crown's enduring interest in urban benches, its desire for closer ties to the locality, and its concern for better enforcement of the many statutes for which JPs were responsible were all well served by

---

[72] Suffolk RO (Ipswich Branch), HD36/A/305.

[73] Even then, the result typically favored the corporation. Only in one case was a franchise seized. Garrett-Goodyear, "The Tudor Revival of Quo Warranto," pp. 242–43 and 290–94.

[74] Levin, *Charter Controversy*, pp. 11–12.

enlarging urban benches and widening their powers. So it is significant that one of the most common features in charters passed after 1660 was the appointment of more corporate justices. But what about monitoring their performance and correcting abuses when they occurred? County JPs could simply be dropped from the commission, but town JPs could not since charter terms defined who participated in the magistracy. Quo warranto could be used to force towns to receive new charters on terms curtailing the bench's authority, but, as we have seen, quo warranto was used to little effect. Quo warranto and new charters were too clumsy for handling minor lapses in the work of urban magistrates. The King needed a more limited measure, a supplementary judicial commission that could be granted quickly and easily, permitting specific county justices to act in a *particular* town to correct *particular* troubles in the execution of justice: in short, commissions of association.[75]

Between 1664 and 1688, the crown granted commissions of association naming county JPs to sit on the bench in twenty-one towns after reports had been received of some failure by each town's own justices. The associated justices were thus empowered to act in jurisdictions from which they were normally barred in order to supervise erring urban JPs. The same theory of franchises that justified granting and seizing corporate privileges also justified modifying them by these means. Sir Francis North gave this explanation: a corporate charter's non-intromittant excluded county JPs "as to their ordinary commission. But the King may for his service empower other justices, notwithstanding such clauses, by commission of association, because the King is not bound without express words [in the charter] to exclude him."[76] Tellingly, North likened this special appointment of powers by commissions of association to commissions of gaol delivery and of oyer and terminer, which the King could grant whenever and wherever he thought best.

Though granted according to royal powers, local initiative was the key to the use of this device for monitoring urban justice. In the 1660s, all commissions were granted after reports from local gentlemen about alleged disorder in the area, especially disorder they said arose from dissent. Thus Reading and nearby Newbury received commissions in 1664, and it was probably owing to similar allegations that more went to Wallingford and Abingdon later in the year. But dissent was not the only factor. At Windsor, Castle Governor Lord Mordaunt gained a commission of association to attack a local foe.[77] Gentry initiative explains the grant of these early

---

[75] The following paragraphs follow the analysis in Halliday, "'A Clashing of Jurisdictions'."
[76] BL, Add. 32,518, f. 155v.
[77] The dockets of these commissions are at PRO, C231/7/223, 232, 234, 237, and 272. See also Halliday, "Clashing of Jurisdictions."

commissions giving gentlemen near the towns greater powers within them. In the 1670s, commissions were increasingly used to serve the King's needs, which concerned enforcing the excise more than anything else. Commissions were recommended for Worcester, Chester, Stratford, and other towns in the 1670s when urban JPs showed too much favor for brewers and too little for excisemen.[78]

Commissions of association thus provided a limited means for inspecting and correcting lapses in the execution of justice without imposing new charters. And this is what the crown wanted: a supervisory power over the magistracy, and a reminder to errant urban leaders of where their authority originated and of the King's perpetual power to correct them when they had wronged him by a misuse of their authority. But the use of commissions of association was a policy with more bark than bite: surviving judicial records for the towns concerned reveal little to no activity by associated JPs. Most town benches went on unmolested after their appointment. Ineffective though it may have been, the use of associated justices represented a policy nonetheless. Commissions of association saw more frequent and consistent use in the 1660s and 1670s than quo warranto, and provided the principal means – and a limited means – for overseeing corporate governance. But developments in one other area must be considered if we are to understand how and what crown advisors were thinking about when they examined the relationship between the King and his corporations in the first twenty years after the Restoration.

Corporations created by royal letters patent governed Irish towns as well as English ones, and their legal status was just as vexing after 1660. Given the history of English rule in Ireland, we should not be surprised to find more drastic measures used there to regulate the corporations. But it was not until 1666 that a clear policy was first promulgated, when the King ordered all Irish towns to renew their charters. Those which "refuse to accept of our grace and favor hereby intended" would face quo warranto. The King spelled out the reasoning: all Irish charters were forfeit as a result of the late rebellion, thus providing sound legal pretext to "seize their rights and franchises." The lord lieutenant, the Duke of Ormonde, was ordered to review all charters and to regrant them as he saw fit.[79] But the process moved slowly, and before it went far, another tack was taken. The Act for Settling Ireland, passed by the Irish Parliament in 1665, had authorized the lord lieutenant to make what rules he pleased for regulating Ireland's corporations. In August of 1668, he issued the first such set of rules, for

---

[78] PRO, C231/7/337 and 411, and PRO, PC2/66/186.
[79] The lord lieutenant was also given authority to void charters of towns he considered too small to continue enjoying chartered privileges. *Calendar of State Papers, Ireland, 1666–69*, pp. 172–73.

Drogheda. All corporation members there would be required to take the oaths of allegiance and supremacy and to receive the sacrament twice yearly, an imposition more extreme than any made on English corporation members. As in English charters, the rules required the lord lieutenant's approbation of future recorders and sheriffs. Going a long step further, the corporation's choice of mayor would need the lieutenant's annual approval as well.[80]

In 1670, the Treasury Board and the Committee for Irish Affairs in England again considered renewing all Irish charters. Acting on a report from Attorney General Sir Heneage Finch, they recommended granting new charters which would include a provision appointing county justices to serve in the corporations.[81] This would be the application of commissions of association – used on a case-by-case basis in England – on a comprehensive and permanent basis in Ireland. The committee also ordered the lord lieutenant to prepare a draft standard charter form to be used in all towns. In August, Charles ordered the renewal of all Ireland's borough charters according to these recommendations. In addition, new charters would require the usual oaths, and not only approbation, but the appointment of all town clerks and recorders by the lord lieutenant. Most important, each corporation would be required to surrender all previous charters before the grant of a new one, "without which a new charter will never abrogate an old privilege, and if any corporation refuse to surrender, we suppose the King's learned counsel there may avoid their charters by due process of law."[82] This proposal marked a turning point in thinking about chartered privileges. Surrender would clean the legal slate, wiping away all privileges enjoyed before, leaving only those enumerated in the new charter. Here then was the first comprehensive charter policy articulated by crown advisors in England, though it was intended for Irish towns. Each town would be tied to the crown by exactly the same terms as the next and the administration of justice in urban and rural areas would be fully integrated. This was a far cry from the policy – or lack thereof – pursued in England in the 1660s and 70s, though it certainly showed what could be imagined.

But again, little happened, and it was not until the winter of 1671–72 that the Irish Council finally set to work.[83] Then, with the administrative

---

[80] The lord lieutenant exercised this power at least once, when Drogheda's mayoral choice was rejected in 1674. T. Gogarty, ed., *Council Book of the Corporation of Drogheda, 1649–1734* (Drogheda, 1915), pp. 17–18 and 163.

[81] *CTB 1669–72*, pp. 486–87 and 632.

[82] PRO, PC2/62/136, and *Calendar of State Papers, Ireland, 1669–70*, pp. 224–25.

[83] And this only after a repeat order from the King and a second proclamation from the lord lieutenant for charter renewals. Youghall corporation ordered their mayor to appear about their charter; Kinsale's corporation for the second time in ten years began raising funds for a new charter. *CSPD 1671*, p. 432. Richard Caulfield, *The Council Book of the Corpora-*

machinery finally building up some steam, the King ordered a halt to all enquiries into Irish charters in April 1672.[84] This sudden retreat was accompanied by a return to the policy begun in 1668, then quietly dropped, of passing new rules regulating corporate governance. In late September 1672, the Irish Council issued more regulations. While they varied from town to town, most or all included provisions requiring the lord lieutenant's approbation of future clerks, sheriffs, recorders, and mayors.[85] Less than six weeks after promulgating the new rules, the King ordered these suspended too until he and his Council could examine them. The rules were then reimposed the following July.[86] While the crown had abandoned the effort to create a uniform system of chartered privileges by requiring all towns to surrender, a comprehensive policy was now in place that would have the same effect by different means.

No indication survives that English officials saw Ireland as a testing ground for policies that might later be turned on England's corporations. But the successes and failures of these proposals cannot have been lost on English Privy Councillors, the attorney general, and others who reviewed these plans before approval for use in Ireland. Irish policy was consistently more aggressive and ambitious, and in the end, more comprehensive in its impact than English urban policy. Policy for Ireland was directed toward curbing local authority, not enhancing it as in England, where the powers of urban benches were in many cases enlarged. The requirement that every Irish town submit its mayoral choice for the lord lieutenant's approval every year was especially ambitious. Given the numbers involved, this may have been a workable policy for Ireland, but it is difficult to imagine how Whitehall's bureaucracy could have vetted mayoral choices from 200 English towns, most being submitted at around the same time annually. Most remarkable was the unimplemented proposal that all Irish corporations surrender their charters, thereby extinguishing ancient privileges so that all corporate liberties could be expressed in a single document of recent vintage. Nothing like this had been attempted before. In short, policy makers considered erasing centuries of incremental local constitutional development. This would allow them to refashion the relationship

tion of Youghall (Guildford, 1878), pp. 336–38; idem, *The Council Book of the Corporation of Kinsale, 1625–1800* (Guildford, 1879), p. 124.

[84] *CSPD 1671–72*, p. 299. Further orders stayed the quo warrantos brought on behalf of private suitors against Dundalk and Belturbet. *CSPD 1671*, pp. 218 and 447; *CSPD 1671–72*, pp. 125, 254, and 299; and *CSPD 1672*, pp. 486–87, 497, 515, 521, 540, 580, and 596–97.

[85] Ireland, *Statutes at Large*, 13 vols. (Dublin, 1786), vol. III, pp. 205–34.

[86] *CSPD 1672–73*, pp. 64–65, 74, 116–17, 129–30, 225, 226 and 301; and *CSPD 1673*, 456–57; PRO, PC2/64/62–63. Rumors that the rules were issued to harass Catholics prompted this review.

between the King and his corporations from the ground up, applying uniform codes to all. In the end, the new rules promulgated by the lord lieutenant replaced plans for surrenders and new charters, but the rules would have the same effect. Nonetheless, the proposal of blanket charter surrenders must certainly have been on many minds at Whitehall a decade later when consideration was being given to the problem posed by what was then seen as the undue independence of England's corporations.

Vacillation more than anything else characterized Irish policy in the 1660s and 70s, and in this it mirrored English policy, if "policy" is even the right word to describe measures lacking coherence, continuity, or clear long-term purpose. Perhaps then it would be best to say that the crown had no policy toward England's corporations, though there was an erratic search for one, a search led as much or more from the provinces than by leaders at Whitehall. This search produced weak supervisory efforts – the approbation requirement, commissions of association – but no program to recharter the towns.

But even non-policies have their policy makers, and we should consider who was behind the efforts that were made to monitor the corporations. Unfortunately, there are few signs pointing to any one or two guiding minds: of course this helps explain the overwhelming appearance of vacillation in crown/town relations. Clarendon may have had some in-volvement in the quo warrantos of 1663–64.[87] He might also have promoted commissions of association: he proposed that one be used at Coventry, though in the end, it was not.[88] But Clarendon's name appears surprisingly little in mail going to or from Whitehall, in Council orders, or in any other evidence one might consult concerning the royal view of corporations.

A few advisors though did leave their imprint on royal efforts: the attorney general and the solicitor general and others near them. These offices changed hands a number of times in the 1660s and 70s, but by tracing the succession of the King's leading legal advisors, and by noting the timing of various developments, we can see where policy suggestions may have originated. More important, we can begin to imagine how legal and political experience was acquired that would be put to such different use after 1682. The attorney and solicitor generals were the leading royal advisors in all matters corporate. Of necessity, one or both was involved in determining the provisions written into new charters and then in seeing

---

[87] It was alleged at his impeachment in 1667 that Clarendon had promoted new charters as a way of making money from the fees paid during the process, but we must be wary of such testimony intended to smear one who was disliked for other reasons. *CJ*, vol. 9, p. 16, and Miller, "Borough Charters," p. 67.

[88] Bod., MS Clarendon 77, f. 154.

them through the seals. While the attorney general was the senior of the two, they often worked as equals, especially in passing charters. As Roger North noted a few decades later, the solicitor general "in some respects, is coordinate with the attorney, that is in drawing up and passing royal grants, which are to go to the great seal."[89] Attorney General Palmer may actually have stayed in the background to let his solicitor general and others carry the administrative and courtroom load, especially as his health declined in the later 1660s.

Two figures stand out: Solicitor General Sir Heneage Finch and Palmer's young protégé, Sir Francis North. North held no official post during most of the 1660s, when he was building his legal practice with the support of his highly placed mentor. While he did much work in Chancery, "his home was the King's Bench."[90] Here he increasingly argued briefs that he prepared for the attorney general, to the point that he was generally known as "Mr. Deputy Attorney."[91] There exists no direct indication of North's involvement in corporation policy discussions in the 1660s, but the combination of his courtroom experience and his professional connections are powerfully suggestive. He would be brought formally into the King's service in 1668 when he was made King's counsel.[92] Even if North did not influence crown policy at this stage, he was gaining extensive experience of the political and legal questions raised by problems in the corporations, experience he would put to good use first as solicitor and attorney general in the 1670s, and later when he would write the most extensive analysis by any royal advisor of quo warranto, charter surrenders, and crown powers over the corporations.[93]

If the 1660s and 70s were largely a time for North to gain skill and knowledge in the law, it was a period for another man to have a more direct impact on royal actions toward the towns: Sir Heneage Finch. As we saw in chapter 3 when examining the passage of the Corporation Act, Attorney General Palmer, and even more so, Solicitor General Finch, had been the key players in determining the act's final form. Finch remained solicitor until Palmer's death in May of 1670, after which Finch succeeded to his late superior's post. Both as solicitor general, and in his private practice, Finch had extensive experience in corporate litigation in King's Bench, including delivering the threat of attachment against the mayor of Bristol and the lodging of a quo warranto against the corporation in Hilary term 1664.[94] As an MP, Finch was one of the most important voices pronouncing royal policy in the Commons, especially in legal matters.

[89] Roger North, *Lives of the Norths*, 3 vols. (London, 1826), vol. I, p. 148.
[90] Ibid., p. 183.   [91] Ibid., p. 63.
[92] Ibid., pp. 65–69. Henning, vol. III, p. 151.   [93] BL, Add. 32,518 and 32,520.
[94] PRO, KB21/15/47v. For biographical background on Finch, see Henning, vol. II, pp.

Legal expertise and political clout make him a prime suspect as a leader in policy discussions about the corporations.

More telling evidence of Finch's importance concerns the timing in the use of quo warranto. As we have seen, there was a spate of activity on quo warranto in 1663–64, followed by a lull in the years following. Then beginning in the summer of 1670 – just after Finch's appointment as attorney general – another slew of informations were presented against numerous holders of the King's franchises. Though the action had commenced a year before Finch moved to the attorney's office, it was only afterward that the quo warranto brought by some Kent fishermen against James Herbert's claim to an oyster monopoly was actively pursued in court.[95] A number of manorial and other non-corporate franchises were attacked in 1670 and 1671, each probably having its story, like Kent's oystermen, of some disgruntled local party turning to the government for help. They received it in the form of a device sued in court, in the King's name, that could only be used by the attorney general. Again and again, it was the attorney general himself making the motions in court that pushed these proceedings forward.[96] It was in these months too that the Privy Council ordered Finch to prosecute a quo warranto against the Stationers' Company, apparently to encourage the stationers to monitor the presses more carefully.[97] If it is no accident that so many quo warrantos were begun immediately after Finch came to office, it can be no accident either that it was in the same months that the attorney was consulted about the best means for regulating the Irish boroughs. Finch's answer: the surrender of old charters to be followed by the grant of new ones containing restricted powers.

A handful of English towns found themselves targeted by quo warranto at the same time as these other franchises, including Totnes, Bodmin, Newbury, and Much Wenlock.[98] Finch began proceedings against Bristol

---

317–22, and D. E. C. Yale, ed., *Lord Nottingham's Chancery Cases*, 2 vols., Selden Society Publications, vols. 73 and 79 (London, 1957–61), vol. I, pp. xiv–xx.

[95] PRO, KB21/17/5 and KB29/324/110v. HMC Finch, vol. II, p. 1. Herbert reportedly had a quo warranto brought against him in 1664, but there is no sign of this in King's Bench. Henning, vol. II, p. 534.

[96] These include informations brought against non-corporate franchises in Shropshire, Yorkshire, Warwickshire, Leicestershire, Middlesex, and Surrey: PRO, KB21/17/52, 56, 61v, 62, 64v, 71, 73, 74v, 75, 77, and 78; KB21/18/48v, 107v, and 115; KB21/19/30, 32v, 43, and 85v; and KB29/324/20, 84, and 94.

[97] Finch was soon ordered to drop the effort. PRO, PC2/62/139 and 153, and HMC Finch, vol. II, pp. 1–2.

[98] PRO, KB29/323/154, 158v; KB29/324/97, 111, 116, and 141. The Wenlock case may have been connected to another quo warranto brought in Shropshire, involving the private franchises of Sir John Weld, among others, who served as Wenlock's MP in 1679: Henning, vol. I, pp. 366–67.

too after a disputed mayoral election in September 1670.[99] Despite all the activity, none of these towns forfeited their charters or received a new one. Quo warranto, once again, did not produce the dire results generally associated with it. Nor did any other of the quo warrantos commenced later in the decade lead to new charters, with one intriguing exception.[100] Stratford-upon-Avon gained a new charter after a quo warranto was brought against them. They had dismissed their town clerk, Thomas Dighton. The judges were perplexed and annoyed when hearing Dighton's request for a mandamus, for "although [the justices] confessed they knew the merits of the person," they had to admit that Stratford's charter gave the corporation power to dismiss him at their pleasure. Thomas Twisden and the other justices were united in their disgust that the corporation should have such an authority, and recommended that it would be proper to repeal their charter. Attorney General Finch took up their suggestion and began quo warranto proceedings in Hilary 1671. King's Bench issued no judgment on the information, but a new charter arrived at Stratford in 1674.[101] An episode like this suggests vividly how careful we must be in assuming that royal malevolence explains the use of royal powers, as is so often the case in analysis of quo warranto. Here, politically temperate judges – including Twisden – prompted the attorney general to action, showing that many across the legal/political spectrum might be shocked by the wrongs corporations could commit and might feel that the solution to them was a redefinition of corporate powers.[102]

Finch's fingerprints appear everywhere on the quo warrantos issued after his move to the attorney general's office. He would later rise to the lord keepership in 1673 and to the Chancery in late 1675. Throughout these later years until his death in 1682, we can only imagine the impact he may

[99] *CSPD 1670*, pp. 441–42 and 450. PRO, PC2/62/152, 155, 184, 187v, and 194; KB29/324/116.

[100] The Privy Council ordered a quo warranto against Northampton, but it never went to court. Informations were entered against Maldon, Canterbury, and Stockbridge in 1675–76, but no judgments nor any new charters followed. PRO, PC2/63/173v; KB21/18/96v; KB21/19/2v, 8v, and 15; KB29/331/7, 78, and 159v; and KB29/332/25.

[101] *Eng. Rep.*, vol. 83, pp. 98–99 and 413; vol. 84, pp. 404 and 412–13; and vol. 86, pp. 54 and 57 (Sir T. Raymond 188 and 1 Lev. 291; 2 Keble 641 and 656; and 1 Ventris 77 and 82). PRO, KB29/324/6 and 94; KB21/17/34, 35v, 41v, 75v, and 87v. The chartering process may be followed in Shakespeare Birthplace Trust, BRU2/4, passim, and BRU15/11, #36 (copy of the quo warranto and notes of the corporation's answers) and BRU15/14, #57. A detailed account of costs (just over £240) in the quo warranto and the charter effort is at ibid., BRU15/7, #65. VCH Warwickshire, vol. III, p. 251. *CSPD 1671–72*, pp. 81 and 177.

[102] Other outsiders could use quo warranto to threaten a corporation, as Canterbury's dean and chapter did against the corporation in the 1670s: Canterbury City and Cathedral Archives, CC/AC/6, ff. 47, 49v, and 74v. PRO, KB21/19/2v and 8v; KB29/331/159v and KB29/332/25.

have had on crown relations with the towns. But Finch had certainly seen and experienced the possibilities in 1670–71, and though the use then of quo warranto had produced no overwhelming results, he had learned what might be done – and what obstacles there might be – if and when the crown had the will to do more. Only dramatically different political circumstances would create that will. But the experiences of the 1660s and 70s of commissions of association, Irish proposals, and quo warrantos provided royal lawyers like Finch and North with the ideas that would revive the crown's control of the corporations after 1682. Until then, partisan contentions rising within the corporations themselves gave crown legal officers a few opportunities to try out some of these policy ideas in isolated instances.

PARTISAN POLITICS AND CORPORATE CHARTERS IN THE 1670S

The surge in rechartering from 1663 to 1665 had been prompted by the desires of temporarily united corporations. The Corporation Act had left behind a tenuous, brief unity in some towns. And if there was one thing most members could then agree on, it was the weakness of their legal status and the support it could be given by a confirmation charter. So dozens of corporations solicited new charters in those years. After 1665, the number of charters granted dwindled again to the pre-Civil War norm of no more than three per year.

More than just the numbers changed. The reasons behind requests for new charters began to change too. A charter in the mid-1660s was a good sought by the whole corporate body in order to confirm privileges. But as the political temperature rose during the late 1660s and 1670s, charters increasingly became objects of partisan contention. A new charter, since it appointed each corporation member by name, offered an opportunity for effecting a purge by those who could control the composition of the list of members inserted in the final document. Indeed, a new charter offered the surest means for excluding foes. No one could claim illegal dismissal if left unnamed to a corporation by the King in a new charter. No interminable hearings on mandamus would follow. Petitions and counter-petitions to Whitehall show well how the specter of a new charter thus heightened local partisan contentions as one side tried to gain a grant excluding their foes, and the other tried to stop them.

In 1674, Anthony Brooker, mayor of Rochester, petitioned the King for a new charter; at the same time various aldermen and councilmen submitted a counter-petition asking the King not to grant it. After hearing both sides in the Privy Council, Charles ordered the mayor's request dismissed, finding Brooker had made it without the consent of his brethren. Partisan conflict continued in Rochester, and while he could do little to stop it, Charles was certainly not going to countenance it by his own letter patent.[103] This did not keep partisans elsewhere from trying.

The expulsion of three-quarters of Gloucester's council by the Corporation Act had failed to settle that city's politics. When selected as town clerk in 1668, John Dorney subscribed the declaration against the Covenant and resumed the place from which the commissioners had removed him in 1662.[104] Dorney's restoration underscored the shortcomings of the Corporation Act – its inability to prevent the re-election of one removed who later abided by its provisions – and signaled trouble as those sympathetic to dissent gradually wormed their way back into the corporate body. Tempers flared in early 1670, when "loyalists" led by Mayor John Wagstaffe first tried to remove Alderman Robert Fielding, a leader of the "factious." The narrow margin by which Fielding retained his place on this occasion, nineteen to sixteen, demonstrated the nearly equal strength of the contending parties.[105]

This was just a prelude to more serious contentions over the mayoralty. By seniority customs, Henry Fowler was to advance to the mayor's chair in 1670, but the "Presbyterian party" intended to install a junior alderman, William Bubb. After the first nominating round in August, Bubb seemed well on his way to a precedent-setting victory. "The royal interest" cried for help to halt "the rise of faction," and the King responded by commanding the corporation to elect Fowler.[106] Fowler was indeed declared the winner of the next nominating round, though "disorders and animosities" fired by "reproachful words" forced an abrupt end to the meeting. In reporting events to Secretary Sir Joseph Williamson, Recorder Sir William Morton highlighted the leadership of the "factious" Fielding and four other aldermen in defying the King's letter promoting Fowler. Though victorious, Morton bemoaned his failure to quiet them; he thought a purge was now the only way to settle the corporation. Meanwhile, Fielding and the other "dissenting" aldermen petitioned the King, who again ordered them to choose Fowler.[107] In the third and final round on the Monday after

---

103 PRO, PC2/64/244 and 250.

104 Gloucestershire RO, GBR/C8/1, f. 24. See also Peter Clark's article on Gloucester in VCH Gloucestershire, vol. IV, pp. 113–14.

105 Gloucestershire RO, GBR/B3/4, p. 196. The pretext for removing Fielding was his alleged promotion of the trade of non-freemen.

106 Ibid., p. 212 and GBR/B3/3, p. 446. According to custom, the first nominating round was held by the aldermen only, who cast seven votes for Bubb to Fowler's four. CSPD 1670, pp. 419–20, 428, and 431; PRO, PC2/62/145v.

107 Gloucestershire RO, GBR/B3/3, pp. 449–50, and GBR/B3/4, pp. 219–21. Balloting in the second round was among the aldermen and councilmen. The vote was thirty-seven to five in favor of Fowler, no abstentions. The quotations from the record, apparently made on the spot and broken off in mid-sentence, are from the draft minute book (B3/4). The account of the meeting by Morton, who was a justice of King's Bench, is in CSPD 1670,

Michaelmas, Fowler won unanimous backing from the twenty-four electors, including the five aldermen who had "dissented" against him before.
Those originally opposed, aware that they had been outmaneuvered, saw
no reason to endanger their positions by continuing to disobey the King,
and thus acquiesced in choosing Fowler.[108]

A calm settled over Henry Fowler's mayoralty in 1670–71.[109] But as his
year drew to a close, Fowler and his friends began the purge they had long
sought by voting again on the disfranchisement of Robert Fielding, this
time winning his ouster by the same margin by which they had failed
before. Though Morton believed Fielding would seek a mandamus for his
restoration, he remained optimistic: "now the great spring of our dissension
being stopped, we hope to be more quiet."[110] Eliminating its leadership,
Morton believed, would eliminate "the party."

Contentions in the mayoral election process ended celebrations by the
"loyal." Fowler opened the first nominating meeting by suggesting that
they should elect a new alderman to replace Fielding. But his opponents,
unwilling to acknowledge Fielding's removal by choosing a successor,
refused. Fowler and his friends paraded out while the "factious" remained
and conducted their own nominations, and again, they chose William
Bubb. Fowler now asked the crown for a clean sweep of the corporation by
means of a new charter. He put a legal justification on his partisan plans,
reasoning that without a new alderman to replace Fielding, they were "a
maimed body"; without all the aldermen, no mayoral nomination could be
made; without a new mayor, the charter was in abeyance. Two, then three
weeks passed, and no reply to these arguments came from Whitehall.
Morton and Fowler complained that royal dithering hampered their efforts
to suppress faction.

Election day arrived and chaos prevailed. Mayor Fowler and his forces
emerged from the cathedral after the usual pre-election service to the sound
of bells celebrating the choice of a new mayor; while Fowler and his
partisans were in all likelihood being exhorted from the pulpit to cast votes
for "loyalty," Bubb's supporters had pulled off an electoral coup. Twenty-
four votes had been given for Bubb, and none for anyone else. Fowler and

p. 448; PRO, SP29/278/204. Both the draft minute of Fowler's selection and Morton's
letter use "dissenting" to describe the five aldermen opposing Fowler. This appears to refer
to their dissent from the vote of the majority rather than to their religious views, though it
is a telling choice of words. The petition of Fielding and the other four is at PRO, PC2/62/
154.

[108] Gloucestershire RO, GBR/B3/3, p. 457, and B3/4, pp. 236–43. By tradition, the twelve
aldermen and the twelve senior councilmen voted in the final round of mayoral elections.
All twenty-four were present.

[109] Note the unanimity in assembly voting. Ibid., pp. 224–92, passim.

[110] Ibid., pp. 286–92. *CSPD 1671*, p. 419; PRO, SP29/292/28. There is no sign in PRO,
KB21/17, that Fielding sought a mandamus.

eighteen others then tried to hold an election of their own, but were chased off by Bubb's champions. There was little left to do but sign a protest against Bubb's election and send it to the King. As hoped, Charles at last intervened, asking Lord Herbert, now the Marquess of Worcester, to maintain calm in the city; Fowler was directed to continue as mayor until the Privy Council could hear the case. Though Fowler summoned two assemblies, none but a few friends appeared. Bubb too acted as mayor, presiding over meetings of his own faction. Two bodies claimed corporate status, competing claims that canceled one another out. If the corporation were not legally dead before, as Fowler had claimed, it was now. Attorney General Finch agreed: failure to hold the mayoral election according to the charter's terms amounted to a forfeiture. Within weeks, Gloucester's charter had been surrendered into the King's hands and jockeying had begun on both sides to determine the terms of its successor. Meanwhile, those faithful to Bubb continued to attack Fowler's authority as regally appointed interim mayor.[111]

The Privy Council named Sir Thomas Clifford, Lord Keeper Sir Orlando Bridgeman, and the Archbishop of Canterbury as a committee to consider who should be in or out by the new charter. They pored over lists of old corporation members, who were divided into three groups: twenty "who disobeyed the King's letter and were the irregular electors" in the 1671 mayoral election; seven who disobeyed the King but were "of more moderate principles"; and nineteen "that opposed the irregular election and obeyed the King's letter." The "loyal" nineteen, who protested Bubb's election, were secure. But the fate of those who voted for Bubb was not, though seven were still being considered for the new corporation, despite their behavior. While it would have been easy enough to cut them off based on a simple test of voting behavior, those creating the new corporation would be more discriminating, for two reasons. One was that they may have feared the difficulty of finding better replacements: Fowler himself lamented the problems he had had only a few months earlier in filling empty places with loyal men.[112] Second, these seven were probably to be saved from political damnation by their willingness to bend. They would be joined with those who opposed Bubb's election to form the core of the new corporation. Still, the committee had many decisions to make.

The Marquess of Worcester, attempting to exert his influence over the

---

111 Gloucestershire RO, GBR/B3/4, pp. 302–08. *CSPD 1671*, pp. 429, 456–57, 469, 517, 521–22, 525, 526, 531, and 587; *CSPD 1671–72*, pp. 2–3, 7–8, 11, 23, 24, and 41. The draft minute book and the final minute book stop abruptly after the record of the disputed election and the protest against it. Each then contains 12–13 blank pages. No entries were made again until after the new charter was received in April 1672. PRO, SP29/292/52, and PC2/63/53, 53v, and 55v.

112 Bod., MS Add. c.303, ff. 225–28. *CSPD 1671*, pp. 411–12; PRO, SP29/292/6.

outcome, proposed his own list. By late January, both the committee and the Marquess had finished lists that agreed on only eighteen of the fifty-seven persons proposed in them.[113] Worcester's list displayed a marked leaning toward those considered disloyal by the archbishop and his companions. In the end, virtually all first approved by the archbishop's committee were appointed, with the important exception of William Bubb – whom they had thought to rename as an alderman – and Nicholas Webb, another considered for an aldermancy despite his dismissal from the corporation in 1662. Otherwise, the final corporation was named entirely from the list settled on by the committee. Of the thirty-four Worcester had proposed, only sixteen appeared in the charter. In all, eight of twelve aldermen and nine of thirty-six councilmen lost their positions by the new charter, though most of those left out of the junior body had lost their positions not for their imputed disloyalty but because the size of the common council was reduced from thirty-six to twenty-eight.

Many of those favored by Worcester may not have passed the committee's muster, but the committee did not pursue a strict partisan purge in creating the new corporation. John Dorney, the town clerk removed in 1662 and who had returned to his post five or six years later, was now confirmed. Evidently the testimonials to his loyalty outweighed complaints that "he flies from the organ as from the face of a serpent," a dark suggestion indeed. The committee also considered appointing four expelled by the corporation commissioners, and in the end, two of these were named in the new charter. William Bubb, the central object of contentions during the 1671 mayoral election, was not only considered, he was actually named in the charter warrant, the last step before the charter itself was engrossed; but somewhere along the way, he was replaced by a local gentleman, Duncombe Colchester.[114] In the end, Bubb's removal may have had less to do with his loyalty than with a rumor of his death.[115]

According to a prior agreement between the cathedral and the corporate

113 These lists are at Bod., MS Add. c.303, f. 58, and PRO, SP29/302/133 and 134.

114 *CSPD 1671–72*, pp. 32 and 33. Colchester and William Cooke, another gentleman made an alderman by the charter, were close associates of the Marquess of Worcester (my thanks to Molly McClain for this information). But it was the archbishop's committee, not the marquess, who proposed their inclusion in the corporation.

115 The two removed in 1662 who were named in the charter were John Perks and John Webb; the other two considered were Daniel Lysons and Nicholas Webb. Compare the prospective list of personnel in Bod., MS Add. c.303, f. 180, with the final charter list in Gloucestershire RO, GBR/B3/3, p. 498. The warrant is at PRO, SP44/34/138. Dean Vyner wrote Williamson in April that some thought that Bubb was removed from the list owing to rumors of Bubb's death, though he hoped Bubb would not be removed. Why Vyner should support Bubb is unclear, though he apparently resented what he called the Marquess of Worcester's "undue practice." *CSPD 1671–72*, p. 322. The replacement by Colchester of Bubb is the only change made between the approval of the warrant and the engrossing of the charter.

group promoting the new charter, the dean and chapter gained all they wanted regarding protections of their jurisdiction. In addition, the mayor, recorder, and aldermen would be joined as JPs by the bishop, the dean, and two prebends: this was in essence a commission of association by other means, appointing outsiders to sit on the corporate bench.[116] Those seeking the new charter in order to expel their foes did not mind abdicating authority to clerical allies if it contributed to obtaining their partisan ends. Reducing the committee's size was another provision probably sought by Fowler's party; having fewer places to fill diminished the necessity of appointing unfit persons. In addition, election procedures were clarified in the new charter, as was the power to fine, gaol, or disfranchise those who refused office.[117]

Gloucester's charter marked two firsts: the first granted after a surrender of the corporation's previous charters, and the first since Leeds's to make an extensive purge of the corporation. Both were important. By enrolling a charter surrender in Chancery, the corporation's legal past was erased. A new charter could then be granted without the danger that its terms might be contradicted by the liberties and duties outlined in earlier charters.[118] No evidence survives to explain why Gloucester made this surrender, though the fact that the charter was sought by one group to damage another in the corporation suggests that the idea might have been promoted by those seeking the charter. Surrender made a purge by charter the most effective kind; those not included in the new charter would have no basis for claiming corporate membership by earlier charters voided by surrender.[119] Just over one third of the old body was now gone. Though extensive, the crown, acting on the recommendations of the archbishop's committee, did not simply purge those whom the "loyalists" wanted out and appoint all those they preferred. While the crown was apparently willing to countenance a corporate purge in keeping with the wishes of local loyalists by 1672, it would still not order a complete cleansing based on their recommendations. It would be another ten years before that could happen.

---

[116] For a copy of this agreement, see Bod., MS Add. c.303, f. 60.

[117] A translation of the charter is in Sir Robert Atkyns, *The Ancient and Present State of Glostershire* (London, 1712; reprint, Wakefield, 1974), pp. 94–119.

[118] The charter surrender, enrolled at PRO, C75/6, was the first on the surrender rolls for Charles's reign.

[119] Surrender did raise the fear of a hiatus in corporate governance, thus it was important that it not be enrolled until the new charter was granted. Attorney General Finch went out of his way to assure the nervous corporation of Stratford that they had not actually surrendered their charter in 1671, and thus their old powers subsisted until the new grant arrived. Nonetheless, the corporation indemnified their officers for continuing to perform their duties at a time when they feared there might not actually have been a corporation: Shakespeare Birthplace Trust, BRU2/4, pp. 247, 255, 258, 259, and 271.

Changes in charters over the 1670s reflected changes in the corporations – namely increasing partisan division – rather than changes in crown policy, or for that matter, the existence of any crown policy except the consistent use of the approbation clause. Quo warranto continued its fitful career. After Northampton corporation removed the Earl of Peterborough from the recordership in 1672, the King ordered a quo warranto against them to force a charter renewal. But as so often in the previous decade, the information went nowhere. Likewise, a quo warranto ordered against Stratford in 1677 was dropped one month later. Another brought against Plympton was put aside as well after they petitioned the crown.[120] Quo warranto remained a non-policy throughout the 1670s. The surrender procedure, copying proposals made around the same time for charter surrenders in Ireland, would only be required of English corporations in the 1680s.

Taunton's 1677 charter yields further insights into how policy suggestions generated in the Irish effort may have influenced affairs in England. The Privy Council had ordered a quo warranto against Taunton as early as May of 1661; in 1662, corporation commissioners noted the "notorious disaffection" of the members there, nearly all of whom refused the declaration. No indication of a quo warranto against Taunton survives, nor of any revocation of its charter. But the corporation did go into abeyance after the commissioners removed most members without replacing them. In 1669, the late corporation's members petitioned the King for a new charter to revive their defunct body, and a draft charter was prepared along the lines of those granted elsewhere in the 1660s. Later, the usual approbation clause was replaced in the charter warrant by the nomination clause, a provision seen in no English charter since 1662. In an even more novel suggestion, Attorney General Palmer also recommended that the King retain power by the charter "to dissolve the corporation or disfranchise any member at pleasure."[121] For unknown reasons, all work on Taunton's charter again ceased in December 1669. While the crown did not employ such extreme measures in English charters for another dozen years, the clauses proposed for Taunton in late 1669 marked a clear and important shift in what crown officers thought might be relevant, legal, useful – and possible – in the future.

In early January of 1676, the King approved another warrant for a charter to Taunton. The terms it enumerated were common to nearly all charters since 1660: a confirmation of all previous liberties, reserving to the King the approbation of future recorders and town clerks. Again, obstacles

---

[120] PRO, PC2/63/169 and 173v; PC2/66/164, 184–87, and 200–01. *CSPD 1679–80*, p. 194.
[121] PRO, PC2/55/119 and 56/95v, and SP29/263/55 and 55 I–VII. *CSPD 1668–69*, pp. 420–21.

arose, raised this time by the town's MP, Sir William Portman, who objected to the approbation provision. Secretary Henry Coventry was annoyed that Portman had not voiced his concerns earlier, when the charter's terms were still under negotiation. Coventry suspected it would be difficult now to get the King to retreat from his declared intentions. But he did; once again, Taunton's charter efforts miscarried.[122]

By early the next month, the Privy Council's Committee of Foreign Affairs resolved to pass yet another warrant for Taunton, now amended in two unusual ways. First, recorders and town clerks would serve during the King's pleasure; not only would they need the King's approval, they could be removed by him at any time. Second, the King would have authority to create new freemen by royal order under his sign manual, to make it easier "to place such artificers which shall according to several proclamations come over and bring manufactures with them." Local gentlemen proposed instead that the privy seal rather than the sign manual should be used to make such foreigners free, an attempt on their part to water down the effects of the clause by raising dramatically the cost of freemanship.

Both of these provisions were new to English borough charters. According to Secretary Coventry, Portman and Finch – now the lord chancellor – promoted these novel clauses, and the Committee of Foreign Affairs was ready to approve them. Coventry warned against opposing the charter in this new form; to do so would suggest that "the gentlemen that pursue this charter intend not to increase the King's authority to govern the town, but to create an authority to the town to oppose the King." Disliking these provisions, the area gentlemen who originally sought the charter now let it lie; other "loyal gentlemen" in Somerset actively opposed granting any charter at all to Taunton.[123] Coventry was right. Taunton's controversial charter had clearly been pursued less as a means of resurrecting an urban corporation, or of broadening crown powers, than as a device promoting the ends of one county faction against another. The imposition of gentry needs on borough political conditions was a telling sign of the shifting political terrain during the 1670s.

Coventry too had supported the proposal to allow the King to remove recorders and clerks at pleasure: "this is no more than the patents of the judges are resolved to be hereafter." Coventry now imagined the possibility that *durante bene placito* could become comprehensive policy, equally applicable to the bench in Westminster Hall and to corporate leadership.

[122] PRO, SP44/40A/126. This and the following paragraph are based on letters from Coventry to the Bishop of Bath and Wells, in BL, Add. 25,125, ff. 3–5. Revocation of charter warrants for Taunton in 1669 and 1677 are two of very few examples of such revocations during the Restoration.

[123] BL, Add. 25,125, ff. 4–5.

This would not come to pass for another half-dozen years, when the crown's political needs and concerns, transformed by events in the years of the Exclusion controversy, would promote the imposition of tighter controls. Thus Chipping Sodbury's charter of 1681 would be the first in which the town's legal officers – its clerk, recorder, and deputy steward – served during the King's pleasure.[124] Coventry's analogy – likening judges and corporate court officers – seemed sensible enough; more to the point, it boded ill for the magisterial independence of England's corporations. While he did not mean to prophesy, Coventry foretold developments of the 1680s.

In July of 1677, one last warrant for a Taunton charter was approved, this one reverting to the standard approbation policy and mentioning nothing of the royal appointment of freemen. Like other towns of the period, Taunton would receive a charter requiring approbation and strengthening the magistracy while also dramatically increasing the amount of land the corporation could own. But it did something not seen before, nor since, in an English charter. As suggested in earlier proposals to impose county justices by new charters in Ireland, Taunton's charter named county JPs to serve alongside those of the corporation. Six county gentlemen were to be on the borough's bench at all times, to be appointed by occasional commissions of association passed under the great seal.[125] Though this clause was one of a kind in England, the twisted history of Taunton's charter was portentous. It signaled increasing local division, and the likelihood that new charters would become the means by which local factions would contend for increased power at the expense of their rivals. It suggested too that the concern of many local gentlemen was less to win terms increasing royal authority than their own.

While the addition of county justices to the borough bench was in all likelihood a concession to gentry desires for more control in town, it provides a clear view of Charles II's principal concern regarding borough governance: the condition of the magistracy. Chesterfield, Chipping Sodbury, and Hertford, like dozens of towns in the two decades before them, had extra JPs appointed to their benches by charters of 1680 and 1681.[126] Approaches to strengthening urban benches differed from town to town, but rarely did the solution involve according extra powers to outsiders. Unlike most, Chesterfield's 1680 charter empowered any county justice to act there, without any other special commission. Tiny Corfe in Dorset was made a new incorporation by a charter of 1679 that appointed the mayor as a justice, but required him to hold "petty sessions" with a

---

124 PRO, SP44/51/384v.
125 *CSPD 1677–78*, pp. 260–61; PRO, SP44/40A/210.
126 Riden and Blair, *Chesterfield*, p. 97. PRO, SP44/51/383–85. Turnor, *History of Hertford*, pp. 99–112.

county JP.[127] Typically, new justices were found among the corporation's own members, often by simply adding more aldermen to the list of those already appointed to the bench by previous charters. Most charters of the 1670s, like those of the 1660s, continued to contain non-intromittant clauses barring county JPs or sheriffs from acting in town.[128] Charters also continued the tendency of the 1660s to define more precisely the proper method of holding elections. As in the rules for Irish corporations promulgated in 1672, Oswestry's charter of 1674 limited the franchise in corporate elections to the mayor, aldermen, and councilmen, "the popularity excluded for the prevention of bloodshedding and other great disorders."[129] Nonetheless, the hope of using charters to end partisan rivalries by clarifying procedures did not always work. Saltash's charter of 1678 failed to prevent contentions in the mayoral election the following year, leading to a string of complaints to the Privy Council and legal action before King's Bench.[130]

Chartering activity slowed to a trickle between 1666 and 1682; few provoked the troubles caused by Gloucester's or Taunton's. Most, like Pontefract's of 1677, passed without controversy. Though it took three years to arrive, the two new fairs granted made the charter worth the wait.[131] Newark's 1677 charter, passed only three years after their previous one, omitted the approbation clause, giving the corporation full latitude to appoint their recorders and clerks.[132] Newark's two charters of the 1670s also permitted the town to choose MPs for the first time, a much more controversial development. But it is hard to see this singular use of a charter to enfranchise a town as "an experiment," as Carolyn Edie suggests, in preparation for a broader enfranchisement of other towns by charter. No evidence exists either before or after the grant of Newark's charters of any discussion of enfranchising boroughs by charter. What was imputedly the King's "experiment" was more probably the Earl of Shaftesbury's experiment. Like others of the 1670s, Newark's charter was desired by, and one whose terms were determined by, local interests and those of a nobleman who saw something to gain by the new grant.[133]

[127] PRO, IND1/4228/36.

[128] For instance Newark (1674) and Daventry (1675): PRO, IND1/4227/387–88 and 466.

[129] S. Leighton, "The Records of the Corporation of Oswestry," *Transactions of the Shropshire Archaeological Society*, 4 (1881), pp. 4–47. PRO, SP44/40/95.

[130] PRO, PC2/68/245, 260, and 303, and *Eng. Rep.*, vol. 83, pp. 225–26, and vol. 84, p. 1205 (Raymond, Sir T. 431 and Jones, T. 178).

[131] PRO, PC2/64/463. *CSPD 1673–75*, pp. 180 and 389; *CSPD 1675–76*, pp. 97 and 113.

[132] C. G. Parsloe, "The Growth of a Borough Constitution: Newark-on-Trent, 1549–1688," *TRHS*, 4th ser., 22 (1940), pp. 194–96; William Dickinson, *The History and Antiquities of the Town of Newark* (London, 1819), pp. 376–86.

[133] Carolyn Edie, "Charles II, the Commons, and the Newark Charter: The Crown's Last Attempt to Enfranchise a Borough," *JBS*, 10 (1970), p. 54. Edie's contentions are built on assumptions that the crown wanted to increase its power in Parliament, and that any

Experimentation was not the point in the crown's dealings with English towns in the 1670s. Charters granted in those years, with the exception of Gloucester's, Taunton's, and Newark's, show little variation from the procedures and terms used in charters in the 1660s. Charters included the clauses requiring the oaths and approbation; otherwise, their terms reflected local, not crown wishes. County gentlemen at Taunton and corporation leaders at Gloucester gave the vital impetus in seeking and defining the terms of royal charters. But the experience gained in the 1670s in both England and Ireland proved critical in the end, providing the background of policy discussion against which policy practice developed in the decade following.

CHARTERS AND CHARTER POLICY, 1660–82

Talk and action are very different things. The 1670s were the days of talk, the 1680s the days of action. Finch, North, and other royal lawyers saw a variety of possibilities in the 1670s, but neither the need nor the will existed to transform policy thoughts into policies. The back and forth over what to do in Ireland – force universal charter surrenders, if need be by quo warranto; write new rules restricting corporate powers; impose county JPs in all towns – provides the most vivid example of the consideration of various options. The possibilities were certainly imagined. In England, individual charters like those to Taunton and Gloucester – suggesting closer control of the urban bench and the use of charter surrenders – and words dropped by crown officials – like Coventry's likening the tenure of judges and corporation officers – reveal glimmers of what some hoped might come to pass. But for now, such thoughts or isolated usages reflected nothing more than wishful thinking, not blueprints for comprehensive action.

Throughout the 1660s and 70s, the crown had only one consistent policy regarding English corporation charters, and that was a passive one, left unexploited until 1680: approbation. With the exception of the Newark case, no effort was made to change a borough parliamentary franchise before 1684, despite the policy intentions stated in 1661. The crown did have important interests in the towns, but these had less to do with controlling them than with ensuring order. These interests revealed themselves in the frequent charter clauses defining local court powers and election procedures more precisely and those increasing the capacity of corporations to hold land and thus perform the services expected of them. Most of all, the expansion of borough benches and the requirement that

changes made in franchises would necessarily be directed toward that end. Shaftesbury's personal associates were chosen to the new seats. Henning, vol. I, p. 353.

recorders and town clerks receive the King's approbation suggests that the crown's paramount interest was with the magistracy, not in determining the electoral franchise or the outcome of corporate deliberations. This concern with magistracy is highlighted as well by the use of commissions of association: a policy aimed directly at specific problems with the magistracy without requiring the complicated work of granting a new charter.

The initiative remained with the corporations themselves from the Restoration until the early 1680s. Quo warranto was still a long way from striking the kind of terror in corporate hearts that it would in the mid-1680s. Both the rush to gain new charters in the mid-1660s and the trickle that followed over the next fifteen years point to the absence of any effort, or desire, on the crown's part to recharter towns nationwide. Most reasons for a new charter served town not crown interests. But controversial Parliaments, fears of "Popery," and challenges to royal authority in 1678–81 began to change the crown's calculations about what it needed to do to make real its theoretical control over the exercise of authority in the towns. Calls in the 1670s for more direct royal intervention from partisans in places like Rochester or Gloucester would be met with more decisive action in the 1680s. A policy for controlling the corporations would evolve slowly in the early 1680s out of the scattered ideas of the 1670s. Once a few critical courtroom tests had been survived, and once the King had found there were plenty in the corporations ready to work with him to remodel their charters, the political will and means were at last created for undertaking a radical restructuring of the relationship between corporate bodies and the sovereign who gave them life.

Quo warranto and the King's corporations, 1682–1685

The Earl of Huntingdon shook a stick over Leicester's head, but he also dangled a carrot: "All corporations of England have surrendered and even the most factious, and all are generally subject to the quo warrantos and it is probably such writs will issue against the refusers with greater disadvantage and if Leicester do surrender, if they desire any enlargement of privileges, I believe they may be obtained."[1] By September 1684, Leicester corporation was tangled in the same legal and political net cast by the crown over all the nation's boroughs. Willing county gentlemen and nobles like Huntingdon were crucial to the effort. Once one of the Earl of Shaftesbury's chief lieutenants in the Exclusion effort, Huntingdon had "kissed his majesty's hand" in October 1681, and quickly rose to prominence at court. He then set about persecuting dissenters with the same zeal he once showed in attacking the Duke of York.[2] To demonstrate his loyalty and to restore his family's ancient influence over the town, Huntingdon prodded Leicester to follow the lead set in scores of other towns surrendering their charters and receiving new ones in the mid-1680s.

Huntingdon stayed away from town throughout the delicate proceedings by which surrender and regrant were arranged, all the while keeping a tight hold on strings that should not be seen reaching back to himself. John Geary, rector of a living in his gift, monitored the "several cabals" in the corporation as they pondered what to do in the face of the quo warranto threatened against them. The earl requested Geary to report "who agrees and who opposes, and what the parties are," all the while counseling subtlety: "What relates to me I would rather should seem to be the town

---

[1] Quoted in R. W. Greaves, "The Earl of Huntingdon and the Leicester Charter of 1684," *Huntington Library Quarterly*, 15 (1952), pp. 376–77.

[2] Narcissus Luttrell, *A Brief Historical Relation of State Affairs from September 1678 to April 1714*, 6 vols. (Oxford, 1857), vol. I, p. 138. Huntingdon was one of those who tried to present York as a Catholic in 1680. HMC, Report 7, appendix, p. 479; HMC Ormonde, vol. V, pp. 339–40. By early 1683, Huntingdon promoted a Catholic to county office, hoping he would attack conventicles. Hastings Letters, 6017.

acting than mine."[3] Leicester's corporation had been a model of quiet loyalty since the corporation commissioners purged half the body over twenty years earlier. Even so, many balked at throwing away their cherished liberties. But the fear of quo warranto proved greater than the fear of surrender; assurances from Geary and Huntingdon of improved privileges in a new charter and the example of scores of other towns provided extra encouragement. At last, a majority in Leicester voted to yield their charters to the King. Only four of the nearly fifty members present voted against surrender; it was a sign of the issue's importance that this was one of the only occasions when the names of those dissenting from the majority were noted on record. At the same time, the corporation conveyed their property into the hands of trustees as a hedge against their greatest fear of surrender, that it might somehow lead to the loss of their properties along with their charters.[4]

Now two issues had to be confronted: the personnel of the new corporation and the terms of the charter by which they would serve. Huntingdon proposed cutting the total in half by attrition. In the end, probably on Geary's advice, the number of aldermen remained the same – at twenty-four – while the council was reduced from forty-eight to thirty-six. Some removals were thus inevitable, but Geary warned against a thorough purge, noting that if some were removed because they were "presbyterially inclined," then others would have to go too given complaints against them. This would only provoke further differences.[5] Rumors abounded in town, prompting fears that "some juniors [will be] brought over the heads of seniors and those juniors much less deserving if deserving at all." To dampen such concerns, Huntingdon and Geary made as few alterations as possible: "as they were not very factious, they might become good men and unite the town thereby."[6] All who voted against surrender were removed, along with a handful of others. There was little reason to do more at this stage: "there will be less exactness in this new choice because there will be a clause in the charter that if at any time the King shall dislike any of the members of the corporation, upon signification of such dislike, the mayor shall proceed to a new election and the others removed."[7]

Huntingdon intended to become Leicester's recorder and sought the appointment of associated justices to the borough's bench by the new charter. The first he achieved, but Geary warned unequivocally against the second: "I perceive a perfect averseness and great dislike amongst them all against any country gentlemen to be joined with them, and they all

---

[3] Hastings Letters, 3968 and 6034.   [4] Leicestershire RO, BRII/18/35, f. 131.
[5] Greaves, "Leicester Charter," pp. 384–85 and 389–91.
[6] Hastings Letters, 3973 and 6042.   [7] Greaves, "Leicester Charter," p. 387.

seriously declare they had much rather their corporation were totally destroyed than such a thing done . . . it may oblige four or five gentlemen, and disoblige 500 inhabitants."[8] Huntingdon backed away from this unusual request. Throughout, Geary emphasized proceeding by means of the least innovation possible. As his trusted observer on the ground, Huntingdon followed Geary's advice. Only the obdurate were to suffer, and in Leicester, they were few: "The townsmen have not carried themselves with faction. Elections went easily, conventicles [were] suppressed, and all the magistracy [are] frequenters of divine service. They all voted to a surrender except those who are now left out."[9]

The progress of Leicester's charter of 1684 could not have differed more from the corporation's experience in 1665. Most evident this time around was the significant role of intermediaries between town and crown. Before, Leicester had handled negotiations directly with crown officers through their own solicitor. The charter negotiations of 1665 had given no extra influence in the town to county gentlemen, who remained largely aloof from borough affairs for the next two decades. But in 1684, the Earl of Huntingdon controlled the process from beginning to end. It was on his recommendations – based on the advice of his clerical dependent – that the names of those removed were selected, and that other of the charter's terms decided. In addition, the charter appointed Huntingdon the town's new recorder, demoting their former recorder to the rank of deputy, though he would continue to do all the work associated with the office. But while Huntingdon performed no official role, his unofficial one would be of paramount importance. Over the next four years, Leicester would endure a degree of outside interference – largely directed by the earl – that it had not and would not experience in the years before and after.

Leicester corporation surrendered its charters to the crown against the will of some, but well aware that the consequences of not doing so would be much worse. A few recent critical court cases had transformed the information in the nature of quo warranto from an empty threat into a legal device of enormous power. Nearly all the nation's borough corporations now bowed before it, relinquishing their charters to the crown for new ones, the terms of which would be largely beyond their control. After 1682, the crown moved beyond its efforts to control urban magistracy by the weak and indirect methods, so little used, of approving the election of clerks and recorders and appointing associated JPs. By new charters, the King now took on a complete power to remove any corporation member at

---

[8] Huntingdon believed that associated justices were appointed in all the new charters of the 1680s, but no sign of associated justices has been found in them. Ibid., pp. 387–91.

[9] Hastings Letters, 6042.

any time. This signaled the King's new intention to control corporate membership and decision making as well as magistracy.

Of course, many in the corporations also promoted the King's new project because it meant promoting their own partisan interests. As we saw in chapter 5, urban foes understood well how a new charter could be the perfect instrument for effecting a thorough partisan purge, but in the 1660s and 70s, the crown had proved reluctant to use charters this way. Now, in the changed political climate in the years after the Oxford Parliament, the King was quite ready to make the most of local partisan energies. The "loyal" – now called "tories" in a few places – came from scores of towns to surrender their charters and to request new ones. Their foes, knowing well this would mean the end of their public careers, fought such efforts tooth and nail. Thus the surrender of corporate powers and the grant of new charters from 1682 to 1685 mark an epoch in which partisan conflict in the corporations reached fever pitch as for some, new charters meant absolute victory, and for others, political death.

THE INTERPRETIVE LEGACY

Leicester received its new charter in the midst of an unprecedented program to remodel England's corporations. From 1660 to the end of 1681, the crown had granted eighty-five borough charters; from early 1682 to early 1687, another 134 passed the great seal.[10] Not only the rate changed. The initiative and motivation behind the new charters was now quite different too, as were the terms written into them. In the 1660s and 70s, the crown's relations with the towns had been largely reactive, granting charters when requested or assigning commissions of association in specific cases of trouble. But the political dangers confronted in the wake of the "Popish Plot" and the vexed Parliaments of 1679–81 prompted the crown to take a more stern view of the corporations. Though the political climate was changing, new charters in 1681 and 1682 were still granted in response to local initiative. Crown lawyers remained uncertain about whether they should promote new charters, and if so, how. But by mid-1683, a royal policy was in place to encourage charter renewals nation-wide. This transformation of intentions resulted from an appreciation of what quo warranto could do, for it was only in 1683 that the instrument finally proved its effectiveness for compelling a corporation to surrender itself back into the King's hands. The towns gave the lead in 1681–82, but the crown soon took it up, hitting on a policy to force charter surrenders

---

[10] See below, Appendix A.

and renewals and making effective use of the assistance of urban tories, local gentry, and noblemen like Huntingdon to do so.

The charters of the 1680s have received more attention from historians than any other aspect of corporation politics after 1660. For good reason: these charters represented the most extensive assertion of crown control over borough government since the first Stuart ascended the throne. Pursued consistently, the rechartering effort of Charles II's last years proved enormously successful in reminding the corporations where their authority originated and in checking some of the more threatening political rumblings emanating from them. But consistency ultimately proved the problem. By an extraordinary reversal in 1687–88 in methods and persons favored, James II undid all that his brother's legal advisors accomplished in the years before. So while we must recognize the fundamental shift in policy in 1682–83 away from the measures pursued since 1660, we should also note another sudden transformation of charter policy in 1687. The years from 1682, until the last of Charles II's charters passed the great seal two years after he died, mark a separate era in crown/town relations characterized by different goals and different methods from what came before and what would follow.

J. H. Sacret offered the classic whig reading of Charles II's charters. While Sacret focused on relations between crown and town before the 1680s, he did so to stress what he saw as the continuity of crown efforts and intentions across the whole of Charles's reign, not to contrast what was done in the 1660s and 70s with what happened in the 1680s. The Corporation Act and the new charters of the 1660s and 70s were different manifestations of the same intentions, argued Sacret, and precursors to the more ambitious effort to use quo warranto to force charter surrenders *en masse* in the 1680s. From 1660 to 1688, Charles II, then his brother James, pursued a consistent effort to control the boroughs at the expense of cherished ancient liberties and in the face of constant opposition in the towns, an effort that became stronger and more extreme with each passing year. Most of all, Sacret contended, the crown hoped to control Parliament by controlling the corporations: "The primary object of the policy . . . was that securing control over elections to future parliaments."[11] Sacret thus established two orthodoxies about Restoration charters: the consistency of intentions, 1660–88, and the desire to control the Commons.

Two scholars in the 1970s challenged Sacret's view about controlling Parliament. Rather than a purge of "whig strongholds," Robert Sinner argued that the charter effort of the 1680s began as part of a general restructuring of the corporations, regardless of their partisan leanings and

---

[11] Sacret, "Restoration Government and Municipal Corporations," p. 232.

with no intention to influence corporations' choice of MPs. Only in late 1684 did the crown become interested in controlling parliamentary elections. Still, "Charles's intention was not so much to seat loyal Tories as it was to make municipal officers in general subject to his will, regardless of their party loyalties."[12] By analyzing the boroughs remodeled and the elections that followed, Sinner concluded that the charter effort had little impact on the outcome of the elections of 1685, thus countering older assumptions that the charter effort was intended to aid the "packing" of Parliament and that it had succeeded in doing so.[13]

Robert Pickavance went further than Sinner when he argued that it was corporators' role as JPs, not as parliamentary electors, that convinced the crown to take stricter measures against them in the 1680s.[14] This identification of the importance of magistracy advanced our understanding of the importance of local administration, and served as a challenge to historians to look beyond Parliament for the full story about the transformation of political culture. Pickavance's suggestion takes on broader relevance given the crown's emphasis on magisterial concerns in charter provisions concerning borough JPs in the 1660s and 70s, and in the use of commissions of association, both of which were examined in the previous chapter.[15] Developments in the 1680s, and their connection to an interest in the magistracy, make greater sense viewed against this wider backdrop. Pickavance explored three other issues, reaching surprising conclusions given the emphases in the previous historiography. He stressed the importance of local initiative and support for new charters in the 1680s; he contended that the crown acted moderately in passing new charters so as not to alienate urban allies; and he highlighted the resurgence of gentry interest in the corporations:

the government's borough policies was Whitehall's response to local pressures for reform . . . it should not be supposed that the policy was arbitrarily imposed on an unwilling nation. The campaign would have been unworkable in any case without a large measure of cooperation from the boroughs themselves. The fact is that the boroughs, or a faction within them, pleaded for invasion.[16]

New charters were, after all, the ultimate means by which one local partisan group could purge their foes.

John Miller developed some of these themes further by tracing policy

---

[12] Robert John Sinner, "Charles II and Local Government: The Quo Warranto Proceedings, 1681–1685" (Ph.D., Rutgers University, 1976), chapter 4, especially pp. 179–81 and 191.

[13] Ibid., pp. 26 and 37–38, and chapter 5. Sinner compared the outcome in corporations with new charters and those without, and found little difference in the members returned.

[14] Pickavance, "English Boroughs and the King's Government," pp. 17–18 and chapter 2.

[15] On commissions of association, see Halliday, "'A Clashing of Jurisdictions'."

[16] Pickavance, "English Boroughs and the King's Government," pp. 216–17, and chapter 5.

developments from 1660 forward. Miller emphasized change, and in so doing, challenged Sacret's argument about consistent crown ambitions, 1660–88: "If it is difficult to discern a consistent royal policy towards the boroughs in 1682–85, it is even harder to see such a policy over the whole reign."[17] Sinner and Pickavance had accepted Sacret's assumption of a continuity in crown goals from 1660 to 1685.[18] For Miller, "A new 'charter policy' began to emerge in 1681–82 in response to requests by local Tories for new charters and to the King's anger at disorders or denials of justice in certain boroughs."[19] Miller thus added an important component to the analysis by looking across the entire reign to see how and why the crown's approach to the boroughs changed in the early 1680s. Like Pickavance, Miller stressed the moderation of crown policy and its tendency to react to pressure from the localities rather than to take the lead.[20] More recently, Colin Lee has underscored this local dimension in his study of three Kent towns by showing how local partisans prompted the receipt of new charters in order to gain an advantage over their foes.[21]

Pickavance, Miller, and Lee all emphasized the importance of local initiative. But we may now go one step further to show how local initiative not only produced charter surrenders, but also prompted those around the King to formulate an aggressive, comprehensive policy for remodeling England's corporations. One previously unexplored case in particular – the use of quo warranto by one faction at Worcester against their corporate opponents – charted the legal course royal lawyers ultimately followed. Local initiative had driven the crown since 1660 to grant new charters and commissions of association, though the King consistently ignored the more extreme demands of borough partisans in the 1670s. After 1680, such demands were heard more sympathetically. As urban tories sought quo warrantos against their foes in 1681–82, they encouraged the crown to take bolder measures. After a period of exploring various policy options in 1682, the crown began to do just that. By 1683, crown advisors had a policy in place, and by year's end, they began to implement it. This policy would effect a partisan purge on a scale unseen since the early 1660s. The political events of the years 1678–81 gave the crown the reason to look for a new approach; encouragement from borough tories gave it the inspiration and assistance to act aggressively; policy discussions over the preceding years gave it the options from which to choose; but it was the success of quo warranto that brought these elements together into an effective policy

---

[17] Miller, "Borough Charters," p. 84.
[18] Sinner, "Charles II and Local Government," chapter 2. Pickavance, "English Boroughs and the King's Government," pp. 11–16 and 41.
[19] Miller, "Borough Charters," p. 74.   [20] Ibid., pp. 79–82.
[21] Lee, "'Fanatic Magistrates'."

to recraft the relationship between the King and the most numerous and important of subsidiary jurisdictions, the borough corporations.

QUO WARRANTO REVIVED

The strife nationwide following the "Popish Plot," the chaos left by the quick succession of parliamentary elections, and the parliamentary attack on the King's brother transformed calculations in Whitehall about the strength of royal government. Charles began to respond in 1680 with an ambitious remodeling of county benches and a nationwide enquiry into the loyalty of borough personnel based on the terms in the Corporation Act.[22] This was the start of a comprehensive effort to recast the King's relationship with the principal organs of government, nationally and locally. By dissolving the Oxford Parliament in 1681, Charles proved to even the most recalcitrant MPs that, despite all their arguments to the contrary, they met only at his grace. By purging the county bench and lieutenancy, Charles further undermined his opponents in their communities and imposed his will on the enforcement of law in the bulk of England that was still rural. Such actions were impressive displays of resurgent royal confidence. But the effort to enforce the terms of the Corporation Act in the spring and summer of 1680 was too little too late. Royal *diktat* humbled Parliament and refashioned county government, but it did not bring the corporations to their knees.

Potential remedies for the King's urban headaches abounded. Any solution needed to pass three tests: legality, comprehensiveness, and effectiveness. The Corporation Act had been pushed to the limit and had failed to produce the desired results in 1680. But other familiar measures merited further consideration. Commissions of association appointed to all corporations, or at least all deemed "factious," was one possibility. By naming county justices of known political temperament to act in the towns, the King could monitor more closely the behavior of corporate magistrates. With the crown now anxious to impose the laws against dissent with greater rigor given the political connection between dissent and parliamentary assaults on the King's brother, associated justices could push borough magistrates to enforce those laws or they could enforce them themselves. New commissions of association passed the legality test and could be used comprehensively. But would they be effective for shoring up the crown's weak position in the towns?

Experience suggested they would not. Associated justices had a spotty record. Few had appeared at the sessions of those towns their special

---

[22] See above, pp. 124–31.

commissions ordered them to watch. The crown continued to name associated justices on an irregular basis throughout the 1680s, but commissions of association did not provide the basis for an effective program to control the boroughs. This was in part owing to the limited success of the commissions in achieving what they were created to do. But it was also in part because the crown's ambitions now went well beyond monitoring corporate leaders and imposing laws against dissent more vigorously. The King wanted to control, and even change, corporate membership. For this, commissions of association would be useless.

Attempts to purge and control corporate membership by external authorities had a long history by the early 1680s. Beginning in the 1640s and 50s, and again in the Corporation Act, a succession of Parliaments sanctioned the removal of corporation members on the basis of one loyalty test or another. No Parliament was in session now, and none could be expected to countenance new purges if it had been. The sessions of 1680–81 had even seen a failed bid to repeal the Corporation Act.[23] Purges without parliamentary sanction would not pass the legality test, an important one given that whatever was done, it had to be seen to be legal in order to do as little political damage as possible to anyone but the King's enemies. Even if a new test – a new corporation act – could be passed, experience with the old one suggested it would accomplish little.

Policy developments in Ireland during the 1670s presented other possibilities. The lord lieutenant had promulgated comprehensive rules governing elections in municipal corporations and giving him authority to remove and appoint new corporate officers at will. Commissions of association had been proposed as well, but powers to remove and appoint to the corporation were far more effective. The rules imposed in Ireland had no precedent in England and had been written with the sanction of the Irish Parliament, a condition that would not pertain in England. Rules like these were not the answer in England, for they did not pass the legality test, though the Earl of Arran did propose their use in 1683.[24] Ireland also provided examples of the use of quo warranto to force corporations to surrender their charters. But as in England, quo warranto had been used with hesitation, never confronting the courtroom test which, if victorious, would have made it a much more powerful device.

Ideas abounded closer to home. Charters like Gloucester's of 1672 suggested the effectiveness of gaining a charter surrender to cancel the legal meaning of previous charters, followed by a new grant purging the "factious" from the corporation and imposing new restrictions on those remaining. But Gloucester's charter had been possible owing to the

---

[23] *CJ*, vol. 9, pp. 692, 696, and 700–01.   [24] HMC Ormonde, vol. VII, p. 56.

initiative and assistance of corporation members who knew they would gain by it. The crown could not always count on such local aid, at least not in towns where the greatest changes would be desired and where the greatest opposition could be expected. For a process like Gloucester's to work elsewhere, important new inducements for surrender and rechartering would have to be found.

Events in the towns in the 1670s and early 80s suggested to many in the provinces what these inducements might be. Though the crown had not resorted to quo warranto to gain Gloucester's surrender, corporation members seeking a new charter had proposed its use to force a surrender on their local foes. Rochester's mayor had unsuccessfully sought a quo warranto against his own corporation in 1674.[25] Throughout 1680, then in the backlash against dissent begun after the Oxford Parliament, connections were increasingly made in the minds of local loyalists between corporate disloyalty, nonconformity, and the need to eradicate both by forcing recalcitrant corporations to surrender their charters. Devon deputy lieutenants complained in June of 1680 of conventicles and faction in Tiverton. They suggested that only the King's prerogative to inspect and dissolve corporations could correct the situation. Their arguments were bolstered by the opinion of Henry Pollexfen, a prominent lawyer with extensive experience in corporate litigation. Pollexfen suggested that since most of the corporation had not taken the oaths prescribed by the Corporation Act, their offices were void; if over half the *de facto* corporation were in this condition, then the remaining rump would be legally insufficient to hold new elections to replace them. In short, the corporation was dissolved. The King ordered the attorney general to bring a quo warranto against Tiverton's charter, but nothing was done at this stage.[26] Complaints against the meetings of "disaffected persons" in Berwick also inspired crown threats of quo warranto in 1681, but again, threats came to little.[27] From Ludlow in late 1680, Sir Job Charlton called first for a quo warranto, and then a scire facias – a similar Chancery procedure – after the corporation failed to elect his son town clerk. Ludlow was finally compelled to elect William Charlton, but threats against their charter dissolved.[28] Provincial partisans – those calling themselves "the loyal" –

---

25 PRO, PC2/64/244 and 250.
26 *CSPD 1679–80*, pp. 499–500, and PC2/69/20v. No sign of a quo warranto process against Tiverton has been found in King's Bench rule books. It is interesting to see Pollexfen arguing that a corporation was dissolved in this manner when three years later, in defending London from quo warranto, he would argue that corporations are immortal.
27 PRO, PC2/69/133.
28 Shropshire Records and Research Service, LB2/1/2, ff. 340–41 and 342b.; LB2/1/3, ff. 6–7. *CSPD 1679–80*, pp. 514, 531, 602–03, 606–07, 615–16, and 628; *CSPD 1680–81*, pp. 23 and 158.

had plenty of thoughts about what the crown might do to help them, but further action would have to wait a few more years until events bolstered royal confidence in its legal powers over the corporations.

Charlton's suggestion of a scire facias is intriguing. Scire facias was the writ brought in the court of Chancery to revoke any royal patent which should not have been granted in the first place or when the recipient of a patent had done something amounting to a forfeiture.[29] Scire facias did have a successful court outing in 1680, used then to void a patent granting to Sir Oliver Butler the franchise to hold a market at Rochester. As young Heneage Finch – son of Sir Heneage Finch, the lord chancellor – argued, "every patent which wrongs the subject dishonours the King, whose great prerogative it is not to be able to do wrong."[30] Certainly, many felt the same applied to borough patents as well as private ones and might be cause for their revocation. But fears existed that a finding against a corporation on a scire facias might utterly dissolve it. This would cancel any debts owed by or to the corporation and would lead automatically to the reversion of all corporate properties to their donors or their heirs. The corporation would cease to exist; were the corporation revived later, its lands and debts could not be revived with it.[31] Scire facias would not do. The crown's purpose in checking corporate independence was not to destroy them, but to control them, not to eradicate franchises, but to seize and regrant them in order to circumscribe their use.

This left quo warranto. By quo warranto, one, some, or all members of a corporation could be ousted from the corporation, which would then be seized into the King's hands; he could then regrant the legally subsisting body to others. The effects of dissolution – corporate death, the loss of all lands, the cancelation of debts, the destruction of charitable trusts managed by the corporation – would be avoided. Throughout the 1660s, 70s, and early 1680s, the crown proved hesitant to use what many in the provinces believed was its best weapon against the corporations. Its reluctance was well justified. When used previously in the seventeenth century, threat alone had been enough to encourage surrender in most cases; in others,

---

[29] Blackstone, *Commentaries*, vol. III, pp. 260–61.

[30] D. E. C. Yale, ed., *Lord Nottingham's Chancery Cases*, 2 vols., Selden Society Publications, vols. 73 and 79 (London, 1957–61), vol. II, p. 790. *Eng. Rep.*, vol. 86, p. 477 (2 Ventris 344). Butler brought a writ of error to be heard in the House of Lords, who did not hear it until 1685, when they confirmed the decision on the judges' recommendation that "the King has an undoubted right to repeal a patent wherein he is deceived or his subjects prejudiced." *Eng. Rep.*, vol. 83, pp. 659–61 (3 Lev. 220). Finch the younger would later argue the King's case in the quo warranto against London.

[31] Jurists from Coke, to Hardwicke, to Blackstone, agreed with this view of the effects of dissolution. See William Holdsworth, *A History of English Law* (London, 1903–66; reprint, London, 1982), vol. III, p. 489 and vol. IX, pp. 62–69. See also Hale, *Prerogatives*, ed. Yale, p. 246.

proceedings ended without a decision owing to the defendant's failure to appear or to a cessation of the prosecution by the crown. In the time of Edward I, when quo wárranto had its first use, judgment for the King resulted in fines, not seizure of franchises. During the reign of Henry VIII, when the writ was revived in a new process by information, judgment against the defendant rarely even resulted in fines.[32] Legal scholars produced sound arguments why corporations could be seized into the King's hands upon a judgment against them in quo warranto, but the lack of sufficient precedent made even the most thorough reasoning seem weak.

Quo warranto was a royal device that could be sued only in the King's name, though if one presented the right arguments, the attorney general might be convinced to use the King's authority to support your cause.[33] Various Bermuda islanders convinced the attorney general to do just that. As early as July 1679, the Committee of Trade and Plantations began to consider proceeding against the Bermuda Company charter, by scire facias or quo warranto, based on allegations by islanders of illegal taxes and seizures of property made by the company. By year's end, they had decided to pursue a quo warranto. The information was lodged in Trinity term, 1680, but Attorney General Sir Robert Palmer apparently made mistakes in his pleading and the case collapsed in 1682.[34] It can hardly have been a heartening example to those who may have been harboring hopes of using the process elsewhere.

Given such problems, no crown policy for using quo warranto was even contemplated in 1680–81. In the Privy Council's inner core, the committee of intelligence, there was no mention of the problem posed by the corporations, and no discussion of possible solutions that might be found by reference to policy in Ireland or to local calls for quo warranto and scire facias.[35] But local leadership would show the way. The first major courtroom test of the information since the Restoration resulted from the persistence of partisans in one city who used it against their foes. By late 1680, twenty-six corporation members in Worcester, sued by their local tory opponents, learned they would be the first victims of a revived quo warranto. It would not be until the end of 1681 that the crown – frustrated by the

---

[32] Donald W. Sutherland, *Quo Warranto Proceedings in the Reign of Edward I, 1278–1294* (Oxford, 1963), pp. 136–38. Harold Garrett-Goodyear, "The Tudor Revival of Quo Warranto," pp. 242–43 and 252–54.

[33] On the justices' reiteration of the attorney general's sole authority to commence an information, see Newdigate LC 1671 (June 1686).

[34] John Henry Lefroy, *Memorials of the Discovery and Early Settlement of the Bermudas or Somers Islands, 1511–1687,* 2 vols. (London, 1877–79), vol. II, pp. 466–91. Another information was brought against the company; a verdict against them came in July 1684. Ibid., pp. 512–26.

[35] A register of the committee of intelligence's meetings from May 1679 to February 1681 is at BL, Add. 15,643, and contains no mention of the boroughs.

defiance of the City of London, and inspired by the example of Worcester – would take the lead and issue its infamous quo warranto against the City.[36]

The quo warranto brought against London is well known, but it was not the only quo warranto case that went all the way to judgment in the 1680s, nor was it the first. That honor belongs to Worcester. The Worcester quo warranto had a very different basis and effect in law than its later counterpart against London, brought as Worcester's was against individual members of the corporation by personal name instead of against the entire corporation by its legal name. By attacking individuals instead of the full body, a successful quo warranto action would purge a selected group rather than lead to a seizure of the corporation. As the campaign against the corporations picked up steam, the crown ultimately opted for the example set by the London case: for quo warrantos against full corporations rather than named individuals. The crown thereby sought to seize the corporation – or compel it to surrender – in order to start all over again with a new charter, rather than remove a few persons and replace them without changing the terms of corporate governance too. As we shall see, the London case provided the clearer precedent for proceeding in the 1680s. But the Worcester example would have a longer term legal and political impact, as after 1688, corporate partisans increasingly brought quo warrantos against one another by personal name in an effort to oust their enemies without forcing royal seizure of the corporation. Examining both cases closely will help us understand the political significance of quo warranto over the long run.

Both parliamentary elections in Worcester in 1679 returned Thomas Street, one of the King's serjeants, and Sir Francis Winnington, the former solicitor general who had been dismissed only weeks before the first election of 1679 for his political apostasy in Parliament: it is telling that the first major use of quo warranto would involve two of the land's most prominent lawyers, each with courtroom experience with the law of corporations on his resumé. Street remained firmly in the King's camp, for which he was rewarded in April 1681 by promotion to the Exchequer bench. Meanwhile, corporate politics had divided leaders in Worcester. It was probably Street who suggested solving problems there by commencing a quo warranto against twenty-six of the corporation's seventy-two members. Quo warranto was by definition a royal device; it could only be brought in the King's name. But it could be sued at "the relation" of others.

[36] Levin, *Charter Controversy*, p. 23.

In this case, as in so many in succeeding decades, the quo warranto exhibited against the defendants – alleging that since November 1680, the defendants "did usurp upon the King" by occupying offices they did not legally hold – was brought at the instigation of the local opponents of those charged. Quo warranto would be the mirror image of mandamus. Rather than restore victims of a partisan purge, it would be the means for effecting one.

Proceedings began as early as the autumn of 1680 and were certainly under way by the following spring, by which time the city had endured a riotous parliamentary election returning Winnington and another exclusionist, Henry Herbert.[37] Meanwhile, legal delaying tactics put off the day of reckoning for Mayor James Higgins and his twenty-five co-defendants. The corporation also voted to send an address to the King in March of 1682 expressing their "abhorrency" of the association.[38] Despite the delays and the public relations efforts, *Rex* v. *Higgins et al.* finally came to trial in the winter of 1682–83. All the defendants made their separate pleas to the charge that they had not subscribed the declaration against the Covenant when first chosen to office, in which case their offices were void. Once the jury gave its verdict against them, the defendants' counsel made several objections to the jury's makeup and to the manner of its summons, aware perhaps that whiggish juries in London had been answered by a tory one in Worcester. But these complaints failed. The defense requested leave to enter a bill of error, which was allowed, though with Parliament not then in session, it was not clear they could be saved before judgment was finally entered against them.[39]

Worcester's tories became increasingly impatient awaiting this last judicial act which would give them complete control in town. The Earl of Plymouth joined their efforts to see judgment entered, complaining that delays had already spun the matter out for over two years. Someone in Whitehall scribbled his agreement on Plymouth's notes, recommending to move for final judgment; then the remainder of the corporation could voluntarily surrender their charter to the King.[40] This was a new development. While Worcester tories had brought the information to oust their

---

[37] In 1683, the Earl of Plymouth suggested the quo warranto had begun in Michaelmas, 1680, but the first venire facias summoning the defendants is on the rolls for Trinity term, 1681. *CSPD Jan.–June 1683*, p. 183; PRO, KB29/340/135; and Luttrell, *Brief Historical Relation*, vol. I, p. 85. Henning, vol. I, p. 467.

[38] Hereford and Worcester RO (St. Helen's), A.14, Box 2, p. 102. It is a sign of the vote's significance that it was the first occasion since 1660 that the number attending (39) was noted.

[39] *Eng. Rep.*, vol. 83, pp. 253–54, vol. 86, p. 236, and vol. 90, p. 43 (Sir T. Raym. 485, 1 Ventris 366, and Skinner 91).

[40] *CSPD Jan.–June 1683*, pp. 183–84.

partisan foes, somebody near the King now had other plans. The following term, when the defense moved to arrest judgment, the attorney general moved that it be entered. And so it was at last.[41] The twenty-six convicted, from the mayor down to a number of common councillors, were removed and quickly replaced with more reliable men. Fines totaling £282 were imposed, moneys the crown then gave to the remodeled corporation, "all in regard of their loyalty and good affections, they having been instrumental in reducing that city to its former good government." This covered at least some of the expenses incurred by those who brought the quo warranto against their enemies. Corporate funds paid the remaining costs. Special thanks were given by the corporation to Sir Thomas Street for his care in the case against the "late delinquents."[42]

The Worcester quo warranto was carried on from start to finish by local initiative. This was no small matter; it signaled a confidence in the efficacy of quo warranto among the legal advisors of a borough faction, a confidence that had been lacking among crown lawyers throughout the 1660s and 70s. Given the time it took – well over two years – the costs involved, and the doubts surrounding the final outcome, Worcester loyalists displayed impressive legal judgment, not to mention patience and tenacity. After the fact, the crown happily turned over the fines paid by the "ringleaders of the factious party" to the "honest party that have disbursed their money so freely in removing the illegal mayor and sheriff."[43] Worcester's "honest party" achieved its goal – expulsion of "the factious party" – without damaging the legal position of the corporation at large. Personnel changed, not the charter. Nonetheless, Worcester's loyalists joined the rush for new charters that soon followed, freely surrendering theirs the next year to demonstrate their unhesitating faith in the King.[44]

Though the outcome of the Worcester case would not be known for over another year when an information was lodged against London in December 1681, it may well have provided encouragement to try the same against a greater target. After a year in which the City corporation petitioned the King to call a new Parliament and elected a succession of whiggish sheriffs, who in turn impaneled a string of juries whose verdicts freed some of the most notorious anti-court leaders, the King and his advisors had had quite enough of London. The time had come to bring the corporation to heel, and no way would be better than by a new charter revising its privileges, responsibilities, and personnel. To do this, its old charters would first have

---

[41] *Eng. Rep.*, vol. 90, pp. 48–50 (Skinner 101 and 105).
[42] *CSPD Jan.–June 1683*, pp. 249–50. *CTB 1681–85*, part 2, p. 871. Hereford and Worcester RO (St. Helen's), A.14, Box 2, pp. 108–10.
[43] *CSPD Jan.–June 1683*, pp. 343–44.
[44] Hereford and Worcester RO (St. Helen's), A.14, Box 2, pp. 123–28.

to be voided. Crown lawyers took up the policy suggested by the proceedings then under way against Worcester. On December 21, 1681, City leaders received an information asking them by what warrant they claimed to be a corporation.[45]

The London quo warranto differed in important ways from its Worcester cousin. It was brought against the corporation as a whole, by corporate name, rather than against private persons. This had two important consequences. First, it simplified the legal case: there would be only one set of charges and one set of pleas in response, rather than dozens of separate cases to be made against individuals. More important, a successful quo warranto against individuals entailed their ejection from the corporation, while the corporation itself continued untouched. This was precisely what was intended at Worcester, where one faction used the information not to destroy the corporation, but to expel their foes. But an attack on individuals would not have the sweeping effect desired in London. Now the intention was to seize the corporation, then to give it to new persons by new terms written in a new charter.

As in any information, the London quo warranto contained detailed charges for the accused to address. The central charge was that the corporation ceased to exist when they committed certain crimes: collecting illegal market tolls and sending a petition to the King charging he had been wrong to dismiss Parliament.[46] Continuing to act as a corporation after committing such crimes only compounded them: members of the defunct corporation usurped on the King. London's response to these charges worked on a number of different levels. First, they denied the illegality of their market tolls and claimed that the petition to the King had been to encourage recalling Parliament so it could investigate the "Popish Plot" and thereby protect the King's person. More ambitiously, they claimed that an act of the common council was not actually an act of the corporation. Even if the council passed illegal by-laws or approved a repugnant petition, they did so in the council's name, not that of the corporation; if such acts were wrong, individual members of the council were punishable, not the corporation itself. None other than Sir Francis Winnington, former solicitor general and the leading legal figure defending against the Worcester quo warrantos, helped to compose the plea.[47]

---

[45] For events leading up to the quo warranto, see Levin, *Charter Controversy*, pp. 17–24. Newdigate LC, 1156 and 1164.

[46] This raises the issue whether a corporation doing some wrong committed an act *ultra vires* – outside the purposes for which it was established – or committed a crime. Blackstone considered quo warranto a criminal procedure: *Commentaries*, vol. III, p. 263, and vol. IV, p. 312. The London case was cited in the nineteenth century to show that a corporation can have malice. Carr, *Corporations*, pp. 64–99.

[47] Levin, *Charter Controversy*, pp. 46–47. T. B. Howell, *A Complete Collection of State*

Arguments ultimately revolved around the principal questions about the nature of corporations. Did the King have exclusive authority to create, monitor, and destroy? Could a corporation commit a crime; if so, how could it be punished? Did the decisions of the common council bind the whole corporation? More troubling, could the vote of a majority bind the minority, making them liable as well for any wrongs committed in the name of the whole? London's fate hung on the answers. This was nothing less than a legal contest to determine where sovereignty lay in the growing national state: as a singular power located in the monarchy or a power divided between national and local jurisdictions. The outcome would help determine the course of relations between central and local administrative authority in the centuries to come.

In two separate rounds, Solicitor General Heneage Finch – son of Heneage Finch, the recently deceased Lord Nottingham – argued the King's case against Sir George Treby, and later, Attorney General Sir Robert Sawyer confronted London's Henry Pollexfen. Arguments for the King were grounded firmly in a view of corporate privileges as franchises, a view lawyers at most points on the political spectrum had held for centuries. As Finch noted, "the King is the head and original of all corporations and franchises."[48] Implicit in the grant of franchises was the condition that they not be abused; to do so was to incur an automatic forfeiture. "Suppose a corporation under their common seal should authorize a rebellion, would any man say that were no forfeiture?"[49] The corporate person should be subject to the same laws as any natural person for a criminal deed. Finch pointed out the extraordinary quality of this case, for no corporation had ever challenged the authority of the King to seize a franchise when an act had been done that amounted to a forfeiture. If legal precedents were wanting to illustrate the King's powers, Finch suggested, it was only because quo warranto had never been pushed to this extreme in court before. Corporations had always met it with submission and surrender, including occasional submissions made without trial on quo warrantos in the 1660s. Having made his case that corporations could be seized for misbehavior, Finch now had to show what such misbehavior might be. This meant showing that an act of the majority of the common council bound the whole body. Such an act, he said, was symbolized by the use of the corporation's seal in validating their acts. When the common council imposed an illegal tax or

---

[48] *Eng. Rep.*, vol. 89, p. 930 (2 Show. KB 263). As diverse a group as Coke, Hale, and Sheppard propounded such views. Arguments in the case are also in Levin, *Charter Controversy*, chapter 3.

[49] Howell, *State Trials*, vol. VIII, pp. 1088–89. Finch cited a number of authorities, including Coke. Finch's arguments for the royal power of seizure echo those he made in the scire facias brought against a market franchise in 1680.

approved a seditious petition under their seal, it performed an illegal corporate act, which, by its nature, left the corporation forfeit.

Treby used on the City's behalf some of the same authorities to which Finch appealed. Citing Coke, Treby's corporation was an amorphous, abstract thing, a "capacity," not a person. Corporations did not live, so they could not die. Though corporations had surrendered before, this did not mean they could be forfeit, nor could they commit a crime; even if they could, they could not be punished. His best argument was much less abstract. The quo warranto had been brought against the corporation by name, but the King's case also claimed that the corporation no longer existed owing to its allegedly illegal deeds: "[the quo warranto] supposes them to be a corporation, or else they could not be defendants; and then it comes and falsifies that supposal, by assigning that they are no corporation, nor ever were, or if they had been, they had forfeited it." The attorney general "brings us into court, and when he has brought us here, he quarrels with us for being here."[50] It was a ludicrous situation, a case made against a body that the very same case contended no longer existed. Attorney General Sawyer later turned this argument aside, claiming that the corporation continued to subsist until judgment was entered against it.[51]

Leaving the higher ground of abstraction on which corporation law spent so much time, Treby answered the specific charges. He then argued that no crimes could have been committed: crimes require evil intention; intention requires a mind; a corporation has none. If any case were to be made, Treby concluded, it had to be brought against individuals who did the acts complained of, for only they could imagine and perpetrate a wrong. Though it had not been decided at the time, Treby cited the Worcester case, among others, to prove that quo warranto might lie against individuals, though not against a corporation. But Treby's argument exasperated the bench. Chief Justice Edmund Saunders wondered, "can your corporation do any corporate act? According to your notion, never was one corporate act done by them."[52] For Saunders, like so many of the age, corporations were very real persons. The actions of many persons in their corporate capacities became the action of one person, the corporate person: this was the same point made by Finch in his discussion of the meaning of the corporate seal. If Treby were right, then all so-called corporate acts were only the actions of many individuals behaving from one occasion to the next as a different group, not as a true corporation, living and acting as one over time. If there were no single entity to act, there could be none to monitor or punish, none accountable for its deeds.

---

[50] Ibid., pp. 1116 and 1119.   [51] Ibid., p. 1154.   [52] *Eng. Rep.*, vol. 89, p. 935.

Treby's argument amounted to there being no corporate body and thus nothing the sovereign could control.

This conclusion to the first round of oral argument did not bode well for London and the abstract view of corporateness on which its life depended. The following term, in April of 1683, Attorney General Sir Robert Sawyer picked up where Finch left off. In court and in the press, arguments had been made that a conviction on the quo warranto would devastate the corporation and the people of London. London's supporters predicted that if the corporation were seized, no new one could be made, its debts would be extinguished, and all property it held would revert to its donors or their heirs. They hoped that by raising the greatest possible fears of the consequences of corporate seizure, public outcry and legal jitters would compel crown lawyers to rethink their stance. But Sawyer remained unconvinced:

This quo warranto is not brought to destroy, but to reform and amend the government of the city, by running off those excesses and exorbitancies of power, which some men . . . have assumed to themselves under color of their corporate capacity . . . Herein the politic body of [the King's] subjects resembles the natural, that the disaffected members are best cured by laying on the King's hands upon the body.[53]

Sawyer now took apart Treby's earlier arguments one-by-one after first reviewing the franchise theory of corporations. Since corporations existed for better government, they should be judged according to that standard. As Treby cited Coke, so too did Sawyer, pointing to the case of Sutton's Hospital to show that while Coke could think about corporations in the abstract, in practice, he treated them as very real beings. Countering Treby's claims that corporations could not be forfeit, Sawyer brought forth a number of examples of seizures of corporations forfeit for wrongdoing. He made an analogy to a trust. Corporations are "subordinate governments," whose trust consisted of a number of public duties, which if unfulfilled or wrongly executed, violated that trust.[54] It simply remained for the trust to be seized and granted to others who would honor the purposes for which it had been created.

Then Pollexfen stepped forward to answer Sawyer by resurveying much of the ground covered by Treby before him, contending that none of the precedents showed a corporation had been or could be forfeit. Any charges of wrongdoing lay not against the corporation, but against individuals: "there is no offence but the actors will be punishable in their private capacities."[55] Pollexfen also rejected the idea that a simple majority could

---

[53] Howell, *State Trials*, vol. VIII, p. 1148.   [54] Ibid., pp. 1158–66 and 1178.
[55] *Eng. Rep.*, vol. 89, p. 937.

bind the body, for those in the minority would then be subject to – and liable for – any wrong committed in their names without their consent. To punish the corporation as one would be to punish innocent individuals.

> We know assemblies determine their acts by the major vote, and great struggling there is, as we too frequently see in their debates and resolutions, and carried by majority of one or two votes, sometimes by surprises and undue management, sometimes by fear and terror: suppose an evil act so carried or managed, is it reason that all the whole corporation should be thereby forfeit?[56]

At bottom, the City's arguments depended on a reading of corporations that in law, they were not persons, but only *like* them: "A body politic is but a person created by law in resemblance of a natural person."[57] Corporate status was simply a legal "capacity" to certain persons to do certain things together: grant and purchase land, sue and be sued collectively. An immortal capacity was not something that could be given away, by forfeiture for illegal acts, by surrender – even if unanimously agreed – nor by seizure into the King's hands after judgment against them. Pollexfen then enumerated the ill consequences he said would attend seizure: reversion of land to their donors; loss of debts owed to and by the City; the loss of liberties enjoyed by freemen and inhabitants; and the demise of numerous charities and public works. Even if the King created a new corporation by the old name, it would not be a recreation but a new body; all ancient liberties and properties would be lost with no chance of reviving them. London would be reduced to the status of a village. For one who argued corporations were immortal, the consequences of death were impressive.

Pollexfen, like everyone, saw the writing on the wall if the decision went against London: if London were forfeit, so too were all the corporations of England. "Is there any corporation in England that hath not offended or transgressed?"[58] Chief Justice Saunders appreciated this potential difficulty, but was more concerned with the alternative. "If a corporation be not dissolvable, then you oust the King of his quo warranto and you likewise set up so many independent commonwealths as there are corporations in the kingdom." He went on: "surely we are not to be guided altogether by what is convenient or what is not convenient; what we are to look at principally is what the law is . . . we presume and know that the law is wiser than we are."[59] Justice would have its day, even if it worsened the political situation in the towns.

By the end of April 1683, when arguments concluded, the King and the

---

[56] Howell, *State Trials*, vol. VIII, pp. 1241–42.   [57] *Eng. Rep.*, vol. 89, p. 938.
[58] Howell, *State Trials*, vol. VIII, p. 1256.
[59] *Eng. Rep.*, vol. 89, p. 938, and Howell, *State Trials*, vol. VIII, p. 1266n.

judges still hoped what they had hoped all along: that the corporation would surrender before final judgment had been given and entered.[60] Despite all the effort expended in building its case, the crown still preferred that this occasion not be used to set a landmark precedent clarifying the nature and status of corporations as "subordinate governments." This would deny the crown the final glory of establishing by judicial precedent that the King could indeed take away a corporation's life for the commission of a crime. Nonetheless, the crown hoped that London would, like all corporations threatened before it, surrender its charters to the King's mercy and that others would follow London's lead. In the end, the City refused to yield and judgment came down from the bench: "that the franchise and liberty of London be taken into the King's hands."[61] Still, only entry of the judgment would produce a royal seizure, and this too was put off in hopes that the City might still make its submission. But it would not.[62] With the entry of judgment, care was taken to distinguish between dissolution and seizure, by which the King took a still subsisting corporation back into his hands and retained it in himself or granted it to others. Hale had made this distinction, noting clearly that upon dissolution "all prescriptions and lands [are] gone," as London had argued. But a seizure, Hale added, "is not thereupon a dissolution of the corporation, but if the King do restore it again though of grace, they stand incorporated."[63] By seizing, not dissolving, the King's lawyers obviated the concerns that ancient liberties and properties would be lost with no chance of their resurrection. The King put City government in commission, where it remained until 1688, the corporation meanwhile in limbo, though not actually dead. City property remained legally intact; corporate debts, contracts, and other obligations remained good.

The London case represented a victory for the realist view of corporations – that in law, corporations *are* persons – over the fiction view, that they are only *like* persons, a "capacity" to do certain things living persons do. London's argument was simply too abstract to answer the legal and political needs corporations were meant to serve. If corporations were immortal, if they could commit no crimes, if they could not be punished, if

---

[60] As Saunders noted, "I do believe [that] nobody here wishes this case should come to judgment." Howell, *State Trials*, vol. VIII, p. 1266n.

[61] Ibid., p. 1272n.

[62] The City asked Finch, Sawyer, Treby, and John Holt whether to surrender or allow judgment to be entered. They received very different replies. The City followed Treby, who warned the consequences of surrender would be worse, as it would dissolve the corporation. But the example of surrenders soon showed otherwise: that corporations could surrender and have the same regranted, without the demise of obligations made before surrender. Levin, *Charter Controversy*, pp. 50–55.

[63] Hale, *Prerogatives*, ed. Yale, pp. 245–46.

majority votes would not bind the whole, then corporations acted as sovereigns beholden to no other authority. As Sawyer suggested, London borrowed their arguments from the "Jesuits' school to encourage subjects to rebel against their princes."[64] The judges rejected London's view of corporations. Though politically charged, the decision was nonetheless built on a clear conception of the corporation found good in law then and since.[65]

The debate on the nature of corporations had been as extensive in the press as in the courtroom. The writ, pleas, and rejoinders were printed in full so that a wider public could follow the legal give and take. On both sides, pamphleteers rehearsed the lawyers' arguments, with extra political invective thrown in for good measure. It was not enough to repeat London's contention that individuals, not corporations, commit crimes. One also had to be sure that all understood that the anti-City party were "manifest declared Papists."[66] Predictions of anarchy and the reduction of London to the status of "country villages" made the rounds. Again and again, the City's defenders foretold the death of ancient liberties and the irrevocable loss of property supporting corporate charities.[67] Arguments and fears like these travelled quickly around the country in print, slowing the surrender process just then getting under way, even in compliant corporations ready to do the King's bidding.

Thomas Hunt made the most ambitious arguments in support of the City, arguments bordering on sedition in their hints of republicanism, arguments that spelled out clearly the partisan implications of the judgment.

> To what a madness and frenzy hath our heats and animosities brought us that one party of Protestants should practice to get the government over another part in such sort and manner as will infallibly bring up the Papists into all governments in cities and corporate towns, and in consequence thereof give us at the next turn, a parliament of Papists and red coats.[68]

Like Treby and Pollexfen, Hunt argued an anti-majoritarian line in the matter of corporate dissolution: "A greater number cannot dissolve a body politic; every man hath a negative against a dissolution of that body whereof he is a member." Majorities do not make decisions in the state of nature; as all must consent to come into a society, so too must they consent

---

[64] Howell, *State Trials*, vol. VIII, p. 1149.
[65] On the impact of the case, see Carr, *Corporations*, pp. 81–82 and 91–93, and Levin, *Charter Controversy*, chapter 5.
[66] *Reflections on the City-Charter, and Writ of Quo Warranto* (London, 1682), pp. 5 and 22.
[67] *The Citizen's Loss when the Charter of London is Forfeited, or Given Up* (London, 1683). Reprinted in *Somers Tracts*, 13 vols. (London, 1812), vol. VIII, pp. 387 and 391.
[68] Hunt, *A Defence of the Charter of London*, p. 6.

to leave it. At most, the majority could simply "dismember themselves," leaving the minority to continue the society.[69] Hunt conceded that the King created corporations, but he could not change nor seize them. The implications of Hunt's arguments, and those of the City, were that corporations had a life over and above any other sovereign, that they existed at the consent of all in them, and that they lived and acted according to a body of natural rights. His arguments flew in the face of the concession theory of corporateness, that corporations exist only at the sufferance of the sovereign, not simply by the group act of a collection of individuals.

Responses to the pro-City publication campaign rested on the idea that corporations were franchises existing only at the King's behest. The idea of corporate immortality only meant that a legal corporation enjoyed a perpetual succession of its properties as members came into the body and later died. The coming and going of individuals had no impact on the body so long as the body behaved itself. When the body did not behave, the King was free to seize the corporation and to grant it again to others. Both the Worcester case, brought against individuals and ending in their ouster while the corporation survived, and the London case, brought against the whole body and resulting in corporate seizure, were based on the same basic principles: "his majesty may proceed against [corporation members] in their politic capacity, and so to a forfeiture of their corporation and franchises; or in their natural capacities against any particular persons of the corporation which are offenders."[70] Each case arose from the King's undoubted right to inspect the actions of his corporations and their members as holders of his franchises, and each underscored his authority to seize the one or eject the others, as the case might be, when crimes had been committed.

Taken together, the London and Worcester cases were a legal triumph for the King with wide-reaching legal and political consequences, as we shall see later when we follow quo warrantos post-1688. For now, quo warranto had at last survived the serious courtroom test so long avoided, emerging considerably stronger as a result. The information in the nature of a quo warranto stood as the indisputable device by which the King monitored, and if need be, seized corporate franchises. In the two years following these

---

[69] Ibid., pp. 41–42. Hunt was answered by Roger L'Estrange, who accused Hunt of attacking the King himself, condemned his "republican maxims," and connected him to the political dangers posed by dissent. *The Lawyer Outlaw'd; or a Brief Answer to Mr. Hunt's Defence of the Charter* ([London], 1683).

[70] *The Case of the Charter of London Stated*, p. 19. This was reprinted as *The Power of the Kings of England to Examine the Charters of Particular Corporations and Companies* (London, 1684). The anti-London pamphlet writers did more with satire than their opponents. See *The Charter: A Comical Satire* (London, 1682), and *The Last Will and Testament of the Charter of London* (London, 1683).

two judgments made in the spring of 1683, the mere rumor of a quo warranto would suffice in nearly all cases to compel a corporation to surrender its charter without further fuss. All now bowed before the King their creator, who, angered by the political impudence of whigs and dissenters, and emboldened by the new clarity given to the law of corporations, went about inspecting, seizing, adjusting, and regranting corporate privileges with a vigor never before seen.

THE DEVELOPMENT OF A CHARTERS POLICY, 1682–83

Initiative from the towns, or from factions within them eager to show their loyalty by surrendering, continued to play its part while the Worcester and London cases wound their way through court. But local initiative was no longer the greater part of the rechartering story as in the 1660s and 70s. Tentatively at first, the crown's legal officers developed a corporations policy in 1682–83. In January 1682, Secretary of State Sir Leoline Jenkins could still say that the only addition the King desired in new charters would be the clause requiring his approbation of recorders and town clerks, thus continuing the policy in place since the early 1660s.[71] Terms varied from one charter to the next through 1682–83, revealing hesitation as crown officers worked out their vision of what corporation charters could and should include. But by March 1683, the crown had clearly articulated its desires to recharter the nation's corporations, its method for doing so – by charter surrenders, gained by quo warranto if need be – and its reason for doing so – to control corporate office holding more carefully. Robert Pickavance recounted the circumstances behind the charters granted early in the effort. Nonetheless, it will be useful to re-examine these to clarify how a royal policy developed in 1682–83, and to show how royal policy development combined with local agitation for new charters – and ultimately with the decisions in the Worcester and London cases – to create a campaign serving the interests of the crown and urban tories.[72]

From the beginning, the new charter policy would arise from and favor certain partisan interests in the towns who sought the crown's aid to gain power over their local foes. In October of 1681, Mayor John Mendham of Thetford sent charter excerpts to Secretary Jenkins to substantiate his charge of illegal conduct in the late mayoral election, carried on by his political enemies in his absence. Mendham refused to swear their choice, Wormley Hethersett, even after receiving a mandamus to do so. But having

[71] *CSPD 1682*, p. 6.
[72] Pickavance, "English Boroughs and the King's Government," pp. 157–71.

already made his return to Hethersett's mandamus – with the advice of some of London's leading legal talent – Jenkins rejected Mendham's request for a hearing before the Privy Council. He and others in Thetford were "left to the law."[73]

Following the usual course in mandamus, Mendham received a succession of writs ordering him to swear Wormley Hethersett mayor, culminating in a "mandamus absolute." Mendham's allegations that Hethersett was disqualified both by an illegal election and by not having taken the declaration against the Covenant had not convinced King's Bench.[74] But Mendham continued in his refusal; so the judges imprisoned him in February 1682 for his contempt of their orders.[75] Finding himself stymied, Mendham pursued more drastic measures, forcing a surrender of the town's charter so he could get a new one purging his foes.

Doing so was not easy, and was made more difficult by confusion in Whitehall about what exactly comprised a legal surrender. In December, reports circulated that Thetford corporation had brought their charter to the King in Council.[76] In all likelihood, Mendham and others had simply grabbed the charter from the town chest and taken it to London, ready to hand it over. But legal surrender would not be accomplished by moving a few sheets of vellum from one place to another. What was needed was a clear document spelling out the corporation's surrender of its charters and liberties into the King's hands. Preparing such a document required approval by a majority of the corporation, a majority that could only be created by a purge or by procedural deception. By the end of January, Mendham got the vote he needed, though by allegedly unsavory means.[77] The surrender, granting all "powers, privileges, liberties, and immunities" back to the King, was in London early in February, where negotiations on

[73] *CSPD 1680–81*, pp. 518–19, 552, and 558. Mendham's expense accounts are highly detailed and assist in charting his movements. Among others, he consulted Sir George Jeffreys, [Roger?] North, Heneage Finch the younger, and Attorney General Sir Robert Sawyer. Thetford Town Hall, T/C2/6, p. 64.

[74] *CSPD 1680–81*, p. 552. Mendham suggested that Hethersett and others had made a false return to the Privy Council's 1680 enquiry about their conduct under the Corporation Act.

[75] PRO, KB21/21, ff. 23, 28v, 32, 33, 39v, 43v, 57v, and 62v; KB29/340: initial, alias, and pluries writs to Mendham.

[76] The report, in a newsletter in *CSPD 1680–81*, p. 612, said the charter was delivered on the "last council day." This may mean it was on the day of a council meeting, but not done before the council itself. No record of any visit from Thetford in December has been found in the council's register, PRO, PC2/69. But corporation accounts suggest Mendham was in London at the time.

[77] According to an account given in 1690, the surrender required accepting the votes of Mendham's son – a minor – and an excommunicate, while denying the votes of opponents. His foes protested against the surrender, to no avail. This account gives a date of January 30, 1682 for the surrender vote: *CJ*, vol. 10, p. 140. PRO, SP44/66/60, a record of the vote, confirms the date. Luttrell reported in March of 1682 that the surrender was "against the mind of some of the inhabitants." *Brief Historical Relation*, vol. I, p. 169.

the terms of the new charter had proceeded over the last month.[78] The King ordered the surrender kept in the petty bag office, where care was taken not to enroll it. Enrollment only happened on March 6, the same day Thetford's new charter – with no changes except the addition of the approbation requirement – passed the great seal.[79]

Thetford's charter was the first granted after a general surrender of a corporation's previous letters patent since Gloucester's ten years earlier. Knowing what would come in the years following, we could see it as the first charter in the crown's new effort, extorted from an unwilling corporation, as previous analyses have done. But crown legal officials probably did not see it that way in early 1682. By now they had brought the quo warranto against London – signaling that a decision had been taken that *something* must be done – but they were still trying to figure out *what* should be done and *how*. No policy was in place for promoting and handling surrenders or for defining new terms applicable to all charters. Thetford's charter looked just like those of the past twenty years in its addition of nothing more than the approbation clause. It also looked like those earlier charters in the role played by local initiative. Indeed, local initiative had been the key. Mayor Mendham had been hard pressed to fight off the orders and imprisonment imposed by King's Bench. The only way he could win control at home was to turn to the crown for help in the form of a new charter effecting a purge giving him control in Thetford. And this is what he got: all appointed in the new charter had signed the surrender with him; Mendham was again mayor, and Sir Joseph Williamson was the new recorder. Mendham's chief foe, Wormley Hethersett, had been excluded, and the new corporation was left on its own to fill the vacancies left unfilled by the King.[80] Mendham had moved for the charter, and he and his party in Thetford were the chief beneficiaries when it arrived. Thetford's new charter was the perfect example of the use energetic partisans could make of crown powers.

---

[78] Charter clauses were apparently prepared in January. The warrant, noting the surrender and the charter terms, was dated (though not sealed) February 11: *CSPD 1682*, pp. 50 and 72; PRO, SP44/66/61.

[79] The surrender was enrolled at PRO, C75/7, March 6, 1682. It had been sealed only two days earlier.

[80] Thetford Town Hall, T/C2/6, pp. 1–13 and 15–17. Pickavance suggests that the surrender was extorted from Mendham in exchange for his release from imprisonment on the court's attachment, basing this on the account of events given to Parliament in 1690: *CJ*, vol. 10, pp. 139–40, and Pickavance, "English Boroughs and the King's Government," pp. 153–57. The dating of the December submission, the January surrender, and the early February warrant, as well as events in King's Bench, suggest this analysis is incorrect. There is nothing in Mendham's extensive contact with Sir Leoline Jenkins suggesting he would have opposed surrender; everything about his desires to overpower local opponents, as well as the contents of the new charter, suggest he promoted it.

Hereford's charter followed three weeks later. William Gregory, the deputy steward, and MP Herbert Aubrey – the foe of the city's other MP, exclusionist Paul Foley – were probably behind the preparation of a list detailing the merits and demerits of current corporation members. They alleged that the majority of the corporation were "such as have been and are suspected to be factious and disaffected to the present government in church and state." With only a minority of the body allegedly fit by the terms of the Corporation Act, the corporation was legally void.[81] Based on these charges, the corporation faced the threat of a quo warranto soon after London received theirs, but Hereford chose to surrender rather than fight. Or at least part of the corporation did.[82] On February 14, two weeks after Thetford, Hereford corporation voted to surrender; on March 3, the mayor and town clerk knelt before the King.[83] Again, as in the Thetford case, merely presenting the old charter did not suffice. So the mayor returned home, and on March 14, read to the assembly an instrument of surrender of all charters and liberties, drawn on the advice of Attorney General Sawyer. Care was taken once again that the surrender not be enrolled in Chancery until the new charter was ready. The new charter, granted on 28 March, went beyond Thetford's to require not only the approbation of the high steward and town clerk, but of all the aldermen as well.[84] While this was the first time a charter mandated that members of the corporation's deliberative heart should receive a royal nod before serving, this was just a stopping-off point on the way to greater things.

Hereford's charter was a partisan weapon, just like Thetford's, used by local tories to purge their foes. Supporters of Hereford's whiggish MP, Paul Foley, were missing from the list of new corporators. An anonymous apologist for the new charter admitted that those removed, like those remaining, were largely "favorers of the church." But why should the King not have a power "which every steward of a leet hath in making up of a jury": any reader would appreciate the meaning of the direct connection made here to "ignoramus-juries." To protect against injustice in the towns, the King merely exercised his undoubted prerogative in choosing loyal local leaders. What's more, the pamphlet's author noted, the charter confirmed all the town's ancient privileges, and added a new fair to the list, an

---

[81] Henning, vol. I, pp. 264 and 568–69; PRO, SP29/417/187; *CSPD 1680–81*, p. 659. Pickavance, "English Boroughs and the King's Government," pp. 157–59.

[82] BL, Add. 28,875, f. 202, is a letter from "H. A." to unknown, dated January 16, 1682, describing efforts to gain a new charter, including offers of local assistance with a quo warranto, if needed. H. A. is in all likelihood MP Herbert Aubrey.

[83] The following account is given in *The Proceedings of the Citizens of Hereford in the Delivery up of their Charter and Renewing of it* (London, 1682).

[84] John Duncombe, *Collections Towards the History and Antiquities of the County of Hereford* (Hereford, 1804), pp. 360–61.

important addition. The broader political context of Hereford's charter and the legal basis for it were spelled out:

At this time some considerable charters are upon the point of trial, and . . . many more are in ill circumstances, and willing to surrender. At this time, to render the King inconstant in his promises, severe in taking advantages of his subjects (that were willing to own their omissions, and to sue for pardon and a renewal of their forfeited franchises, and to lay their charters humbly at his Majesty's feet (which are already under his power) in hopes of being restored to the same if not greater privileges), is to make the best of Kings odious, and the submissive subjects stubborn . . . and rather fond to espouse and contend for a mistaken right to the uttermost.[85]

The syntax was tortured but the message was clear: surrenders were nothing more than the proper submission of the King's corporate subjects to his mercy.

Two points were now evident in the wake of the charters to Thetford and Hereford: that the crown wanted to proceed by a surrender of an old and the grant of a new one, and that it would threaten quo warranto to do so. Surrender was important to cancel all previously granted privileges, thus providing a smooth legal surface on which to re-erect the corporation. Some corporations would surrender without fuss; in others, surrenders would be produced by factions within them anxious to prove their loyalty to the King. Some, like Hereford, would take a bit of prodding. The crown's willingness to use quo warranto in this way signaled the end of the passivity that marked its posture toward the boroughs in the 1660s and 70s.

Though quo warranto's efficacy remained in doubt until the outcome of the London and Worcester cases, the threat of quo warranto was clearly seen as having an important part to play early on in the effort. Hereford thought better of challenging it more than a year before the London decision. We may also see here that the point of quo warranto was not to destroy the corporation, but to gain its surrender. This would be the hope with London, that surrender would simply follow on the threat of quo warranto, as had happened so often in previous centuries, and as it did at Hereford. No one intended at the outset of proceedings against the City that a precedent-setting court battle should be waged. Still, it was, with what would be important benefits for the crown's effort in the corporations. But in early 1682, the exact methods and terms of surrender as well as the scale of the contemplated effort remained undetermined and local initiative still dictated what happened in the corporations.

Thetford and Hereford surrenders had not been enrolled immediately for

---

[85] The charges of partisan considerations in the dismissals were made by Richard Janeway in *The Impartial Protestant Mercury*, number 114, and were answered in *The Proceedings of the Citizens of Hereford*, pp. 3–4, from which the quoted passages come.

good reason. Enrollment was the point at which the surrender became legally effective, the moment when previous charters expired. Thus Ludlow corporation asked in their surrender in early 1684, that "to the intent there may be no vacancy in the government of the said borough we do likewise humbly beseech that the enrollment hereof upon record may be forborne until such regrant may be also ready for the seal."[86] Sir Francis North advised that surrenders not be enrolled "until the new grant is ready to pass, that so in the mean time they may carry on the government and other affairs of the corporation."[87] By waiting to enroll the surrender until after the new charter had passed, there would be no lapse in government; new and old corporations would overlap, ensuring that public order and corporate business would continue and that debts would not lapse nor corporate property revert to its former owners or their heirs owing to a momentary death of the corporation.

In fact, few surrenders would be enrolled at all.[88] This might create the opposite problem: not a hiatus between corporations that could destroy corporate property and create a gap in local governance, but two competing corporations, each with good claims to legal existence. One Turner, an attorney of Derby, figured this out and charged that the surrender had destroyed the corporation's property, so he owed it no rent for the lease he had from it. At the same time, he contended that since the surrender had not been enrolled, it was not good in law, thus old corporation members retained their places by the old charter and the new charter was invalid. Never mind that Turner's two positions were logically at odds: on the one hand, by surrender the defunct corporation owned no land and could demand no rent from him, and on the other, the surrender was worthless and the old corporation subsisted still. Turner's "factious practices [made] a great disturbance."[89] Arguments about the legality of surrender and which charter was the governing charter after all the grants of the 1680s would give corporate partisans competing for local control plenty to use against

---

[86] PRO, C75/7, surrender dated January 19, 1684 and enrolled November 5, 1684. The Earl of Huntingdon pointed out to Leicester that their surrender would not be enrolled until the new charter was finished in order to prevent a lapse of corporate government. Greaves, "Leicester Charter," pp. 380–81.

[87] BL, Add. 32,518, f. 184v. On the role of the King's legal advisors – Attorney General Sawyer, Solicitor General Finch, and of North especially – see Pickavance, "English Boroughs and the King's Government," pp. 120–21. In early 1682, North was still chief justice of common pleas. He would become lord keeper in December of 1682, and created Lord Guilford in 1683.

[88] Surrender enrollments have been found for Thetford, Nottingham, Bridgwater, Ludlow, Bewdley, Beverley, and Tewkesbury in Chancery surrender rolls: PRO, C75/7. Full copies of the Nottingham and Beverley surrenders are at PRO, C203/5, September 18, 1682 and August 11, 1684. No enrollment date is given for Bewdley or Tewkesbury; of those with a date, only Ludlow's enrollment predated the grant of a new charter.

[89] *CSPD 1683–84*, p. 126.

one another in court. Turner's arguments, and others' suggestions about the effects of surrender and, worse, the effects of not enrolling them, foretold the legal and political battles to come in the 1690s and beyond as competing partisans argued about what corporation, and what personnel, by what charters, governed in the towns.

For now, the King's law officers took care that each new corporation was alive in law before the old one died to prevent the calamities later predicted in London's arguments, namely, reversion of property to its donors and the cancelation of all debts. North contended that doing so required not only postponing enrollment; it also required a broader form of surrender. Thetford and Hereford, and Derby in mid-July, surrendered "all charters, letters patents, powers, privileges, and immunities."[90] But in Andover's surrender, made six weeks later, the corporation not only handed over its charters and liberties, but its lands and other properties as well.[91] The shift in the terms of surrender had not happened according to local accident. North noted that "care must be taken of the good corporations that they first surrender and grant to the King all their lands and goods and chattels, and the king regrant them to the new corporation, that there may be no escheats."[92] Properties and debts would only survive the surrender and regrant process if they were first surrendered in their entirety into the King's hands. If not, they could not be regranted in a new charter, and if not regranted, the new corporation could not assume them. The new corporation would be propertyless and debtors to the old could have no satisfaction. Surrender of lands and other properties, prior to a regrant, would solve this potential problem.

From the summer of 1682 until 1684, all surrenders included corporate property as well as charters and liberties. Then, in 1684, lands were again dropped from the surrenders, which now only specified "the governing part" of the corporation: of the powers "by letters patent, custom, or prescription in, for, or concerning the electing, nominating, consulting, being, or appointing of any person or persons to or for the several and respective offices and places."[93] Even after the shift to surrenders of "powers of election" only, some surrenders continued to come in that included lands throughout 1684 and 1685.[94] This acceptance of varying

---

[90] From Derby's surrender, PRO, SP44/66/109.   [91] PRO, SP44/66/134.

[92] These notes are at PRO, SP44/66/88.

[93] This language is from Beverley's surrender of August 11, 1684. PRO, C203/5. Ludlow's surrender of January 19, 1684 contained the same language. PRO, C75/7. Doncaster's was the same: John Tomlinson, *Doncaster from the Roman Occupation to the Present Time* (Doncaster, 1887), p. 168n. Compare to Nottingham's of September 18, 1682, including all "manors, messuages, lands," etc.: C203/5.

[94] Including those of Canterbury, Colchester, and Helston, whose charters were granted in late 1684, and Kendal, Newark, Launceston, Plympton, Godmanchester, Chichester, and others

surrender forms perhaps demonstrated a growing royal confidence that regardless of forms, the King could seize, grant, or regrant liberties and properties as he pleased, without fear of the demise of properties and debts. On the other hand, the loyal borough of Kingston upon Thames ended up making two surrenders. Its first of the "governing powers" only, made according to advice from the attorney general in January of 1685, was followed by another in June, again drawn according to the attorney general's directions, this time including corporate properties as well. It took repeated assurances from Judge Jeffreys, as well as a bit of nudging by a threatened quo warranto, that surrender of lands would not harm them.[95] But no one ever made a successful legal argument showing that surrender by either means prevented the King from regranting the same in new charters. No escheats or demise of debts occurred after any surrender.[96]

Still many corporations had serious concerns about the legal survival of their property through the surrender process. Marlborough, after proclaiming their loyalty, put the case against surrender in the clearest terms: "if they surrender their charters by their common seal, they thereby totally destroy the body of that corporation and so lose all their ancient prescriptions, immunities, and privileges, which by their oaths they are obliged to preserve and that all their lands will there also escheat."[97] Some, aware they could not avoid surrender, hedged their bets by granting their lands over to feoffees to hold it in trust separately from the corporation so that whatever happened, the property could still be managed for local benefit. Before surrendering, Newcastle under Lyme corporation handed their properties over to six local gentlemen for 1,000 years, on condition that they permit the mayor and bailiffs to continue disposing of the profits as they saw fit.[98] This was a common arrangement, and an entirely proper trust. Tewkesbury corporation deeded their properties to trustees before approving a surrender, by a margin of one vote. With their lands thus transferred to feoffees, corporate surrender could not harm their property. Still, only a bare majority could be convinced to yield to the King.[99] Fears

---

the following year. Pickavance, "English Boroughs and the King's Government," pp. 174–75, suggests the use by 1684 of a standard form surrendering only the governing part. But variations in form continued throughout 1684–85.

[95] Surrey RO, KB1/1, pp. 65–66 and 72–77, and KA/3/2/1–4. PRO, KB21/22/104v.

[96] Thus King's Bench justices ruled that debts did not lapse with a surrender in a case from Scarborough in 1685. *Eng. Rep.*, vol. 83, p. 668 (3 Lev. 237). Later case law confirmed this view that surrender did not entail dissolution and its consequences. Carr, *Corporations*, pp. 125–27.

[97] Wiltshire RO, G22/1/7.   [98] Pape, *Newcastle-under-Lyme*, pp. 31–32.

[99] Beaver, "Symbol and Boundary," pp. 291–93. Tewkesbury's new charter drastically reduced the corporation's size, purging members supporting a combative local minister forced from his living in 1681. See idem, "Conscience and Context: The Popish Plot and the

of the effects of surrender would slow many loyal corporations in complying.

The method of remodeling corporations – surrender followed by regrant – took shape during the summer of 1682. But the purpose of doing so was still not clear. The terms granted in the charters of 1682 differed little from their predecessors of the 1660s and 70s; the crown seemed unsure what to do with the corporations once it had them in its hands. But Tavistock's charter of July marked a critical departure from previous usages. For the first time, a charter provided the King with unfettered authority to remove any corporation member or officer at will.[100] Portsmouth's, granted the following month, included the same provision.[101] The King's new power represented an impressive step forward; but the crown now took a few steps back. Andover's charter, coming two weeks after Portsmouth's, permitted the King to displace only the steward, deputy steward, and town clerk. In Derby's, three days later, the crown returned to the approbation provision of the 1660s and 70s, though it also permitted the King to remove any JP at will. And Nottingham's, passed in late September, included only the approbation clause. The next month, Maidstone's charter combined the strictures of Andover's and Derby's: empowering the King to remove the recorder, the town clerk, any JP, and the mayor too. But no other corporation members were under this royal threat, as in the charters of Tavistock and Portsmouth.[102] Nonetheless, Maidstone's charter represented a return to the offensive. But in these charters granted since Thetford's, most of the impetus for the new grants came from within the corporations themselves. By late 1682, despite the initiative of corporate partisans in towns like these, the crown was still casting about for an effective, uniform clause for controlling all corporate personnel.

What did the crown intend to gain by new charters as it increasingly used local partisan energies and suggestions to craft a royal policy for granting new charters to all towns? Why encourage surrenders in order to grant new charters if they were to include no important changes? To some extent, the

Politics of Ritual, 1678–1682," *HJ*, 34 (1991), pp. 297–327. My thanks to Dan Beaver for sharing his notes and thoughts on Tewkesbury.

[100] G. H. Radford, "Charter of Tavistock," *Transactions of the Devon Association*, 46 (1914), pp. 176–80. *CSPD 1682*, p. 108; PRO, SP29/418/130 and PC2/69/267v–68 and 269v.

[101] Robert East, *Extracts from the Records in the Possession of the Municipal Corporation of the Borough of Portsmouth* (1891), p. 607. Pickavance, "English Boroughs and the King's Government," p. 159, says this was the first charter with the clause permitting a broad displacement of members by the King. But Portsmouth's followed Tavistock's by three weeks.

[102] PRO, SP44/66/134–35 (Andover). Robert Simpson, *A Collection of Fragments Illustrative of the History and Antiquities of Derby*, 2 vols. (Derby, 1826), vol. I, pp. 117–55. Stevenson, *Charters of Nottingham*, pp. 86–123. James, *Charters of Maidstone*, pp. 130–52.

charter effort of the 1680s may be seen as the logical extension of efforts of the preceding two decades. Since 1660, in charters expanding the number of justices of the peace in many towns and broadening the purview of civil courts, and in the novel policy of appointing commissions of association, the crown had exhibited an overriding concern with the quality of urban justice. This concern echoes throughout notes about corporations and the King's control of them written by Sir Francis North in the late 1670s or early 1680s. North made the common observation that all jurisdictions originate in the King and are exercised on the condition that justice be done or "it is cause to resume, and the King may either annex them again to the ordinary judicatures or use them himself."[103] Monarchs created corporations to administer justice and maintain peace in populated areas where it might be inconvenient for county justices and sheriffs to act. If corporate justices behaved in an inappropriate manner, it was the King's place to make adjustments with new charters, by commissions of association, or both. From here, North moved easily to thoughts about quo warranto, by which the King could examine whether justice had been done. In one brief document, North pulled together the disparate elements of the King's mastery of all jurisdictions – by charters, by special commissions, by quo warranto – into a single coherent explanation of royal authority. That all these aspects could be arranged together in this way suggests the degree to which crown legal officers saw the connections between them, and points to the central place in their concerns occupied by magistracy.

North stressed magisterial matters in other notes, written sometime in early to mid-1682.[104] His chief interest was in the "government" of the corporation – the judicial functions and officers – as opposed to the "private affairs" – the concerns of the council's deliberative bodies, the aldermen and common council. What mattered were the mayor, recorder, town clerk, justices, and the sergeants or bailiffs who ran local courts and served writs and other process. North was adhering here to a clear public/private distinction, concerning himself with the corporation's public duties, not its private rights. Any rechartering effort needed to address itself to the former, not the latter. He noted the problems in impaneling disinterested juries "in small corporations [where there is] perfect knowledge and acquaintance" that might pervert justice. Appointing county JPs by commission of association was one way to correct some of the abuses of

---

[103] BL, Add. 32,518, ff. 155v–56. Pickavance prints the text in "English Boroughs and the King's Government," pp. 429–31. The dating is speculative, but BL, Add. 32,518, f. 184 contains a discussion of surrender that points to composition in the first half of 1682.

[104] PRO, SP44/66/88. Pickavance discusses this document: "English Boroughs and the King's Government," pp. 134–35 and 138–42. He calls it the "May 1682 memo," based on its placement in the state papers. Internal evidence suggests it could have been prepared any time in the first eight months of 1682, though probably in the spring or summer.

borough justices acting in the interest of neighbors rather than the King. But the real solution could only be achieved with new controls over members and officers written into new charters. North suggested that in charters, Charles should retain power to remove any mayor or sheriff: in other words, the chairman of the corporate bench and the officer who returned and executed writs. North also advised that the King be able to appoint any county gentlemen, judges, or Privy Councillors to act as JPs in any town, and that he continue to have approbation of the recorder and town clerk, the bench's two other principal officers. Otherwise, North took a very limited view of new charters, and did not envision creating new royal powers to effect local purges at whim. North's overriding concern was not to control corporation legislators – aldermen and common councillors – but its judicial officials: the mayor, recorder, the other justices, the town clerk, and the sheriff.

As a former solicitor and attorney general, and now as a judge whose primary contact with the corporations came while on circuit, it is unsurprising that North should have been concerned principally with magisterial matters. Many shared his concern, and the charters of the 1680s continued to expand corporate benches and to widen the purview of civil courts as before. While this was important, others around the King soon developed an interest in more than just the exercise of justice. North was ready to let the "private" part of the corporation go on unrestricted, but this suggestion was not taken up in the end as new charters ultimately subjected all corporation members to full crown powers of removal.[105] By arrogating full power to remove any member, the crown now showed that it wanted to do more than control justice, it wanted to control decision making in all matters. From 1683 to 1685, all charters would grant the King complete power to dismiss corporation members. Charles II would rarely make use of this power. But his brother would, with extraordinary consequences. Perhaps North foresaw such consequences for he soon became dismayed as the charter policy veered off the moderate course he had set.[106]

The next charter after Maidstone's did not pass the seals until late the following March, a hiatus in activity that apparently allowed for further discussion of the purposes of new charters, and for the taking of firm resolutions about what these were. Norwich's March 1683 charter marked

---

[105] North's suggestions empowered only the corporation to make removals. In proposing a royal approbation power over the mayor, North did suggest that the King be allowed to appoint the mayor if the corporation presented three unacceptable choices in a row. The same would apply to sheriffs. PRO, SP44/66/88. A royal appointive power was not granted by any charter before 1688.

[106] The importance of magistracy to North – and his disgust with more extreme measures – was stressed in the apologia of his behavior written more than twenty years later by his brother North: *Examen*, p. 624.

the new start many had anticipated, bringing a comprehensive surrender of all charters, liberties, and properties together with a clause in the new charter that permitted the King to remove any corporation member or officer at will. All charters to follow in the next four years, with one exception, would include the same provision.[107] By March 1683, the crown at last had both reason and method for renewing corporate charters. With the London and Worcester decisions following a few months later, it also had an overawing power to act, power conferred by a revived quo warranto. The effort could now begin in earnest.

PARTISAN POLITICS AND THE CORPORATIONS' CHARTERS, 1682–85

In court, Henry Pollexfen had foretold the political consequences of the London decision better than the legal: "what divisions and contentions hath [quo warranto] already produced, some for surrendering, others for defending, what animosities are about it? The end of the law is to preserve the peace and quiet. Divisions and dissensions frequently end in the destruction of both parties."[108] Local initiative played an important role in the early charter surrenders, and would in those to come. This was not the initiative of whole corporations, but of corporate parties seeking an advantage over their enemies. They would organize their forces by fair means and foul to win corporate votes for surrender, as Mendham allegedly did at Thetford. They would call in local gentlemen and nobles well placed at court to assist them. When all else failed, they would provide the information about the abuse of franchises on which a quo warranto could be based. The crown's success in the London quo warranto gave added strength to corporate partisans seeking new charters to show their loyalty and to purge their foes. Partisans on one side could threaten quo warranto to force their foes to capitulate. Those who lost would then find themselves dismembered when the new charter arrived.

Norwich's charter epitomizes what would become the norm over the next few years. The desire for surrender originated within the corporation, among a tory group eager to submit to the King in order to purge their foes, who naturally opposed surrender. Nonetheless, two forces brought

107 William Hudson and John Cottingham Tingey, *Records of the City of Norwich*, 2 vols. (Norwich, 1906–10), vol. I, pp. 50–51. The exception was Buckingham's 1684 charter, which permitted the King to remove major officers, not the aldermen. See Browne Willis, *The History and Antiquities of the Town, Hundred and Deanery of Buckingham* (London, 1755), pp. 96–106. This provision created trouble for the government prior to the 1685 parliamentary election when some hoped that Charles could remove an alderman to promote Viscount Latimer's election. Kishlansky, *Parliamentary Selection*, p. 221.
108 Howell, *State Trials*, vol. VIII, p. 1257.

enough of those initially opposed to support surrender: the threat of quo warranto and the intervention of a leading nobleman who settled worries and twisted arms. Corporate leaders concerned about the effects of surrender slowed the process as best they could. But when talk of quo warranto arose, and when the Earl of Yarmouth began assisting the local tories who managed the project, they at last quit their delaying tactics. The new charter dropped ten aldermen and sixteen councilmen from the old corporation, most having opposed the surrender.[109] The charter represented a major victory for corporate tories, and the earl.

Nottingham had been badly divided since a contested alderman's election in May of 1681, when John Sherwin – an alleged frequenter of conventicles – was apparently chosen. Despite this, the tory faction there swore William Toplady into the place. So Sherwin went for his mandamus. There is perhaps no better sign of the nature of the partisan split at Nottingham than to note that William Williams – Chester's whiggish recorder – was one of Sherwin's counsel, and that Sir George Jeffreys advised his foes, including Toplady. But before Sherwin could finish his business before King's Bench, local tories had begun efforts to surrender their charter in return for a new one that would purge their foes. They were just as energetically opposed by a group led by William Sacheverell, a man well known for his parliamentary attacks on the Earl of Danby, the French, and "Popery."[110]

Fourteen voted in favor, fourteen against, and one abstained in the surrender vote in late July 1682. The casting vote of the new mayor, Gervase Wild, settled the matter in favor of submission. So he hoped. Those opposed shot back with mass petitions, caveats in the offices of the lord chancellor and the signet and privy seals, and with a printed plea to the public. The pamphlet, published in August of 1682, explained what had happened.[111] In late July, Mayor Wild had convened the common council with no notice – except to those "of his own party and confederacy" – that he intended to present the question of surrender. The mayor, twenty-two councilmen, and five aldermen appeared to the summons, including William Toplady, the "*de facto*" alderman currently occupying the place anti-surrender forces claimed belonged to John Sherwin. After

---

[109] This account follows Evans, *Norwich*, pp. 280–96. In their first charter petition, the tory corporate group asked the King to give himself power to remove all personnel by the new charter, much to Yarmouth's surprise. This request was not repeated in their second petition, though the clause was included in its charter. The Earl of Yarmouth was also instrumental in gaining Yarmouth's charter: Gauci, *Yarmouth*, pp. 151–62.

[110] PRO, KB21/21/23v, 32, 40v, 56v, 59, 68, and 74; KB29/341/75. HMC Finch, vol. II, pp. 169–70. Henning, vol. III, pp. 371–74.

[111] *The Case of the Burgesses of Nottingham, in Reference to the Surrendering of their Charters* (London, 1682). The following is from this pamphlet, except where noted.

conducting other uncontroversial business, the mayor suddenly put the question of surrender, provoking immediate complaints against the proceedings. The mayor polled the question, accepting the votes of the aldermen over complaints that aldermen did not have the right to vote in corporate councils. References to ancient charters and customs meant little to Mayor Wild, who wrapped up the poll and gained the victory he needed: a very narrow one, but a victory all the same.[112]

In their public account, anti-surrender forces listed the names on each side of the question, making a point of honor of opposition to surrender of the borough's ancient privileges at the same time that they undermined the time-honored tradition of conciliar secrecy by publishing assembly proceedings. Prefiguring suggestions made later in the pamphlet war on the London case, they argued that with or without aldermen's votes, the council had no legal right to surrender the privilege of being a corporation.[113] Neither these arguments nor petitions signed by 300–400 freemen impressed the mayor or the lord chancellor, and the surrender moved ahead.

But upon examination, royal lawyers found the surrender insufficient. Though drawn according to a draft surrender sent from London by means of "an honorable person in Nottinghamshire" – in all likelihood the Duke of Newcastle – the surrender did not include the corporation's lands.[114] A second surrender would be required. Given the trouble with the last one, Mayor Wild could not be bothered with another council vote, so he forced the triple-locked corporate chest and set the corporation's seal to a new instrument. "If the putting of the town seal to an instrument without the consent of the body corporate should be said to be sufficient in law to give away the lands and rights of any body corporate, then any thief that can but steal the corporate seal will have it in his power, though he be no member of the corporation."[115] The outraged anti-surrender party made the familiar arguments about the consequences of surrender: that lands would revert to their donors, and that rights by prescription, such as access to commons, would die with the old corporation.

These arguments fell on deaf ears at Whitehall, where the King's advisors pressed ahead: the second surrender was approved on September 18, the warrant followed on the 21st, and the charter passed the great seal one week later. All this effort for a charter whose only new terms were the

---

[112] The anti-surrender group said that aldermanic participation in corporate councils was an innovation sanctioned neither by charters nor by prescription.

[113] Thomas Hunt argued that no majority could vote to surrender, though he did say that they could by a unanimous vote. *A Defence of the Charter . . . of London*, p. 41.

[114] Sir Leoline Jenkins reported soon after the fact to the Earl of Yarmouth, then preparing Norwich for surrender, that Nottingham's first surrender had failed for want of including the corporation's lands. *CSPD 1682*, p. 431.

[115] *The Case of the Burgesses of Nottingham*, p. 2.

cancelation of one fair, the addition of two new ones, and a clause requiring the standard fare of the 1660s and 70s, royal approbation of recorders and clerks. The real fuss arose not over the terms, but the personnel. It was a straight party split: none of those opposing surrender survived, while all supporting it did, with the addition of Ralph Edge, who abstained in the surrender vote.[116] A partisan purge reminiscent of the days of the Corporation Act commissioners had been made by charter.

Crown lawyers had rushed to finish the charter in time for Nottingham's Michaelmas mayoral elections. The charter, with the wax barely cooled, arrived in Nottingham at eleven in the morning of election day, the day after it had passed the great seal.[117] Mayor Wild immediately summoned the new corporation, swore them into office, and commenced the voting. At the same time, the anti-surrender party gathered in St. Mary's church and then sent an ultimatum to Mayor Wild that if he did not join them, they would choose a mayor according to the old charter. They then marched to the town hall shouting "a Greaves, a Greaves; no new charter, no new charter." Seizing corporation records and the sheriff's mace, the "dissenters" forced Mayor Wild to retreat from the hall. Having captured the seat of government, the anti-surrender party proceeded to fill it by electing Alderman William Greaves as mayor along with a full slate of other officers which they proclaimed at the cross. Meanwhile, Wild conducted an election according to the new charter and then proclaimed none other than William Toplady their choice for the coming year, but he was shouted down by more cries against the new charter. Nonetheless, the new corporation prevailed while those of the old were soon convicted of a riot that Chief Justice Jeffreys characterized as "next door to rebellion."[118] The defendants, including Sacheverell, Alderman Greaves, John Sherwin, and sixteen others, were assisted in their defense by London's lawyer, Henry Pollexfen, a man becoming ever better known for his counsel in corporate litigation, especially to those who leaned toward whiggery or "faction." Only the presence of the Duke of Newcastle the following year prevented a repeat of the fracas of Michaelmas 1682.[119]

Nottingham corporation had readily sent a loyal address to the King after the dissolution of the Oxford Parliament in 1681, indicating that many were ready to put past struggles behind them. But the rechartering effort that took shape in 1682 presented to one local party the possibility of

---

116 PRO, SP44/66/139. Stevenson, *Charters of Nottingham*, pp. 86–123.
117 PRO, IND1/4228/56. *CSPD 1682*, pp. 437–38.
118 Newdigate LC, 1531 and 1549.
119 Ibid., and *CSPD 1683–84*, pp. 6–7. Sacheverell was fined 500 marks for his part in the riots; the others were fined less. Luttrell, *Brief Historical Relation*, vol. I, p. 307. PRO, KB21/22, ff. 2–v, 6, 12v, 14, 20v, 23v, 25, 27, 39, and 43v.

destroying their foes, a possibility they fully exploited. The paradox of partisan politics drove developments throughout. One party employed the powers of the crown in an effort to destroy their foes, who responded with court actions and everything else they could think of to protect the old charter and thus their places. Even after they had been expelled from the corporation, they continued to battle it from the outside. The imputed connection in Nottingham between dissent and those defending the charter would be played out around the country. In corporation politics in the 1680s, efforts by local party leaders to gain new charters, now assisted by the crown, would do more than anything to raise partisan temperatures, widening the political and rhetorical distance between the "loyal" and the "factious." Tables would be turned in 1688 when James II, pursuing a very different political agenda, would restore the losers of 1682 to their old places and expel their foes.[120] But for now, borough tories prevailed.

Local conflicts only worsened as those on each side in town called in outside forces to aid them in their struggles. Borough tories readily worked with crown officers, nobles, and county gentlemen to gather information for quo warrantos or otherwise to compel surrenders in order to dismember their partisan foes.[121] In 1682, the possibility of gentry intrusion in the towns had made the crown nervous. As Secretary Jenkins warned, "Tories of the neighboring counties are, and ought to be, very sparing in their discourses of the quo warranto. There will be designs to draw speeches from them in order to subject them to challenges."[122] But local gentlemen were eager to get involved. The dean of Chester and the castle governor offered early on to provide information for a quo warranto against the city's corporation.[123] Major noblemen brought in multiple surrenders from whole counties or regions, like the Earl of Bath in Cornwall and Devon. Less impressive figures like Huntingdon gained surrenders from only one or two towns, though in aggregate, such efforts were crucial to the project.[124] Noblemen and gentlemen could even have a moderating effect on personnel changes and new charter terms, as at Leicester by Huntingdon's influence, or at Coventry and Warwick, where dissenters remained in each corporation by Lord Brooke's intercession.[125] They might also obstruct the project

---

120 PRO, PC2/72/72, and J. R. Jones, "James II's Whig Collaborators," *HJ*, 3 (1960), p. 67n.

121 For instance activity at Leeds and Preston: Kirby, "Restoration Leeds," p. 151; Mullett, "Preston Politics," p. 75. For similar stories from Kent, see Lee, "'Fanatic Magistrates'." Pickavance develops this point, "English Boroughs and the King's Government," pp. 177–78.

122 *CSPD 1682*, p. 302.   123 Ibid., p. 439.

124 Newdigate LC, 1594, 1610, and 1617. Pickavance, "English Boroughs and the King's Government," chapter 6. On Bath, see ibid., p. 270, and on those of lesser consequence, see pp. 283–307.

125 Hurwich, "'A Fanatick Town'," p. 25. Styles, "Warwick," pp. 33–36. See also BL, Add. 41,803, ff. 33 and 39.

as they competed to control it in specific towns. At Hull, the Earls of Dartmouth and Plymouth slowed negotiations by their haggling.[126] By force or favor, local gentlemen and nobles became the key players in gaining surrenders and new charters. This disturbed Francis North, now Lord Guilford. While he had promoted the grant of new charters, the proposals outlined in his notes on jurisdictions had called for only moderate changes in their contents. But in the last year of Charles II's reign, North condemned the charter effort as "a devil raised, which could not readily be laid." In particular, he was disgusted by the zeal various gentlemen displayed as they humbled the towns, though he reserved special condemnation for Jeffreys's "trade of procuring charters."[127] In 1684 and early 1685, a royal policy to grant new charters with more restrictive terms had been driven further than originally intended by nobles and gentlemen with their own agendas.

Despite noble and gentry pressure and threats of quo warranto, a number of corporations resolved to test their strength. Dunwich corporation initially voted to contest the quo warranto against them in May of 1684, though by another vote two weeks later, they reversed themselves.[128] Berwick proved more defiant and resolved to contest the action against them. Agitation by garrison leaders there ultimately forced a surrender, and town government was placed in commission while it awaited a new charter.[129] York too decided at one assembly to answer quo warranto, and at the next, not to. Nevertheless, the struggle went on. Those who lost the second vote continued preparations to answer the information, but the majority of the corporation finally stopped them by convincing King's Bench to disallow their pleas. York's government, like Berwick's, was also put into a special commission for just over a year until a new charter was granted in July of 1685.[130] Inhabitants of Calne sent a delegation to London to surrender, only to discover later that they had instead entered a

126 A superb series of letters charts events there and gives a clear view of the charter process at work, and of Dartmouth's and Portsmouth's differences. Hull City RO, BRL.

127 Roger North, *Lives of the Norths*, 3 vols. (London, 1826), vol. II, pp. 15 and 67. Idem, *Examen*, pp. 624–27. These remarks about North, by his brother Roger, must be taken with a grain of salt as they were written to defend his brother's reputation. But these remarks are lent credence by North's more moderate views about policy goals in his notes on corporations, in BL, Add. 32,518.

128 Suffolk RO (Ipswich Branch), EE6/1144/13, ff. 51 and 52. HMC, *Various Collections*, vol. VII, p. 103. PRO, KB21/22/39v. Bristol and Oxford also resolved initially to answer the quo warrantos against them: Pickavance, "English Boroughs and the King's Government," pp. 146–48, 177–78, and 293–97. Newdigate LC, 1481.

129 BL, Add. 41,803, ff. 98–99. John Scott, *Berwick upon Tweed: The History of the Town and Guild* (London, 1888), pp. 218–21. See below, pp. 237–40.

130 Newdigate LC, 1510, 1512, 1525, 1526, 1555, 1568, and 1577. Francis Drake, *Eboracum: or The History and Antiquities of the City of York* (London, 1736), pp. 209–10. PRO, C231/8/103. For York's quo warrantos, see PRO, KB21/22/18 and 19.

plea to the quo warranto.[131] Despite such efforts, each case ended in capitulation, though battles within the corporations over whether or not to surrender or over whether or not to answer a quo warranto continued to sharpen partisan conflict.

As early as May of 1682, the Duke of Beaufort was trying to win a surrender from Leominster's corporation.[132] A year later, after the decision against London, Leominster tories asked Beaufort to help them get a quo warranto to encourage "the fanatics" to submit; Secretary Jenkins directed Attorney General Sir Robert Sawyer to prepare the information on Beaufort's order.[133] But "the whigs of Leominster," led by exclusionist MP, John Colt, would not be so easily cowed. When the corporation met to consider surrender in July of 1683, Colt and the councilmen "of his principles" presented a loyal address for members to sign. But the "loyal party" refused to sign unless the others would first join in the surrender. Warnings were sent to the King not to countenance the address from Colt "and the rest of his gang," they being "men of factious, anti-monarchical, dissenting, rebellious principles."[134] Their address, cast in "loyal" terms, nonetheless signaled no intention to surrender. The following February, Colt appeared at a corporation meeting with a letter of attorney naming a solicitor to appear to answer the charges in the quo warranto. The "royal party" would have nothing to do with such measures, and left the meeting. Then Colt and the bailiff sealed the letter of attorney. None other than William Williams of Chester – who had assisted the "factious" Tournay at Rye a few years earlier – now helped Colt's group prepare the corporation's defense.[135]

But by October, the corporation was forfeit, thus obviating the need for quo warranto proceedings to do the job, and negating any effort Colt and Williams may have planned to appear against it in court. Local tories used a ploy that would become common in serious corporation disputes after 1688: they refused to appear at meetings. The common council, consisting of twenty-five members, required a quorum of thirteen to conduct business, especially the annual bailiff's election at Michaelmas. With the death of one of the "fanatic party" and the imprisonment of Colt for a *scandalum magnatum* against the Duke of York, his party could only muster twelve for meetings. The "loyal party," though only eleven in number, could thus stymie any effort to conduct corporate business if all simply stayed away. Most important, the "loyal" only needed to prevent the election, for if it did not occur on the day appointed by charter, the charter itself would be void. At Michaelmas, the twelve "fanatics" waited all day in hopes of the

---

[131] Newdigate LC, 1553.   [132] *CSPD 1682*, p. 219.
[133] *CSPD Jan.–June 1683*, p. 323, and *CSPD July–Sept. 1683*, p. 33.
[134] *CSPD July–Sept. 1683*, pp. 179–80.   [135] *CSPD 1683–84*, pp. 280 and 396.

arrival of one more to make a quorum, to no avail. No vote was held, thus the old charter died with the day. The "loyal party" was now free to proceed for a new one.[136]

William Williams was crucial elsewhere in doomed efforts to stop the onslaught of quo warranto. The labels of national parties had arrived in Chester earlier than in most towns. Efforts to prosecute dissenters, a riot-provoking visit by the Duke of Monmouth, and increasing intervention in city politics by county gentlemen turned Chester upside down in the 1680s. A city jury, infected by a "London contagion," returned "ignoramus" on the Monmouth riot, but Sir George Jeffreys came to preside at assizes in September 1682 with a commission of oyer and terminer appointing a number of county gentlemen to hear the matter again. Williams, then in Chester, denied the legality of the commission, and in court "addressed himself to the people in a very factious harangue." But the people were not the commissioners of oyer and terminer, who this time returned guilty verdicts.[137]

Two weeks after assizes came the mayor's election. Colonel Roger Whitley was confident of victory with the support of "the mobile." But Whitley found himself one vote shy of Alderman Peter Edwards in the final round of voting, a result that revealed the sharp division among the corporation's aldermen.[138] Edwards's win was a victory for the "loyal." They now pushed their advantage and sought a quo warranto to purge the corporation of their foes. But it was not until the following July that the Privy Council ordered the attorney general to bring a quo warranto against Chester to force the recalcitrant to join in surrender.[139] Still, the stalemate continued through the autumn and winter of 1683–84. Meanwhile, Alderman Street, an ally of Williams and Whitley and a known friend of dissenters, was elected to the mayoralty after voting that showed partisan

---

[136] Ibid., p. 89, and *CSPD 1684–85*, pp. 168–70, 173–74, 182, 183, and 186.

[137] Letters describing efforts to prosecute dissent, and the visit of Monmouth, are in *CSPD 1682*, passim. The quotations are at ibid., pp. 280, 434, and 438–39.

[138] Descriptions of the election are in ibid., pp. 471–72. Shakerley reported that Edwards won by two votes, but the original record of the election shows a split of 9 to 10. CCRO, AF/41g/14.

[139] *CSPD July–Sept. 1683*, p. 188. No record of the decision may be found in the council register, PRO, PC2/70. Williams and Sir Geoffrey Shakerley prepared different addresses for the King in response, the first omitting any mention of surrender, and the latter promising surrender. A vote on August 3, 1683 shows the corporation refusing to seal an address to the King, by a vote of 26 to 1, though to which of these addresses is unclear. CCRO, AB2/197 and AF/41h/9. Shakerley's address was signed by area gentlemen and clergymen, as well as various citizens. Williams submitted his address, under some form of corporate seal, though perhaps the mayor's seal, not that of the common council, which would be required to signify a corporate deed. The King accepted Shakerley's address, but refused to entertain Williams's. *CSPD July–Sept. 1683*, pp. 265 and 293–94. Chester's quo warranto is at PRO, KB21/22/32v.

divisions running through the corporation and the freemen. Street won the election with backing from the freemen, though with the support of less than half the aldermen and even fewer of the common council.[140] Street might have won the election, but he would have a harder time controlling corporate decision making.

Williams, reaching once again beyond the corporation for support, gave a stirring speech at the annual festivities for the setting of the mayor's Christmas watch. He reminded his listeners that when Henry VIII brought a quo warranto against Chester, the city stood him down. "Shall we be afraid of the name and sound of the writ?" Better to challenge in court and lose the charter by judgment than to surrender, he advised. Williams warmed to his theme of sacred city privileges, which by their oaths, all freemen were sworn to protect. Giving up their charter would destroy the support of the poor, of widows and orphans, even the unborn, "who had by freedom and charitable dependencies an interest" in the charter. Surrender would lead to the loss of debts and lands, and the end of their representation in Parliament. He ended with a "passionate peroration," and the cry "God save the King and preserve the city."[141] Williams's words hit their mark. Just days later, at the city sessions, the grand jury suggested that the corporation should do what few corporations since London had dared to do, fight quo warranto in court.[142]

The following month, in a more sober mood, the corporation in full assembly voted not to challenge the information against them; apparently only Mayor Street himself wished to struggle on.[143] Street and Williams were nothing if not tenacious. Having regaled the people with the glories of their ancient city and corporation, Williams could hardly be expected to drop the matter simply because of a clear and overwhelming loss of heart

---

[140] The mayoral election process began among the senior aldermen, progressing through five more rounds, each polling a larger group than the last, until the penultimate round when the freemen "housed" two nominees to stand in election before the aldermen in the final round. In each round except the last, everyone had two votes. Voting among the freemen shows clear partisan divisions, Street and Whitley being housed together by a similar number over their rivals: Whitley 331, Street 327, William Wilson 248, and Sir Peter Pyndar 295. Pyndar and Wilson, the "loyal," enjoyed a convincing majority in each of the early rounds within the corporation, and lost just as convincingly before the freemen in the fifth round. Thus for the final round, two of the anti-surrender group stood together to be chosen, so it mattered little to their party which of the two won. CCRO, AF/41h/12 and 13.

[141] Two reports of the speech, one by Whitley and one by Shakerley, survive and are remarkably similar. *CSPD 1683–84*, pp. 165–66 and PRO, SP29/435/81 and 82. Newdigate LC, 1472.

[142] *CSPD 1683–84*, p. 200, and PRO, SP29/436/11.

[143] CCRO, AB2/197v and AF/41i/2. The latter item is the note of voting and is badly damaged. The tally appears to have been 34 to 1. Mayor Street is noted as polling "yes" to the question of whether to make an appearance.

among those who might once have supported him. Using the mayor's rather than the corporation's seal, Williams and Street sealed a letter of attorney to appear on the city's behalf. Meanwhile, thirty-nine corporation members – just over one-half the body – petitioned Chief Justice Jeffreys not to admit any appearance to the quo warranto by Williams. King's Bench obliged, denying that Williams could appear on the corporation's behalf by a warrant only under the mayor's seal. Without any other legal means for gaining the right to plead on the city's behalf, Williams, Whitley, Street, and their dwindling number of supporters had reached the end. Williams could only watch in silence when King's Bench gave the order to enter judgment against their charter.[144]

Whitley and Williams, with the freemen's support, led the effort to save the city; Shakerley, and Sir Thomas Grosvenor of Eaton Hall, just outside Chester, with the help now of a majority in the corporation, led the fight against them. Having won the contest over surrender, the terms of the new charter would be theirs to define in negotiations with the crown. Throughout the spring and summer of 1684, this is what they did. Those who "voted honestly" would remain in the corporation. Williams, Whitley, Street, and their compatriots would clearly have to go. Like Huntingdon at Leicester – angling to be recorder by their new charter – Sir Thomas Grosvenor controlled developments in order to be made mayor at Chester.[145] The charter, passed on February 4, 1685, left out thirty of the old corporation, roughly half; a host of gentlemen were added to the aldermen's bench.

New charters were welcomed in towns like Chester with bells, music, bonfires, and feasting. County gentry and prominent citizens waited on horseback at the city's gates to greet the King's letter patent with all due respect. They then carried it into town and read it to the crowds gathered there.[146] The new members and officers, from the mayor down to the mace bearer, were sworn to uphold its terms and the honor and liberties of the town and corporation. Then the speech making began. Sir Thomas Grosvenor explained that the King had graciously regranted to them all their old privileges, only reserving to himself the power to remove any member at will "in case they fall into the same faction and caballing again in choosing persons disaffected to the present government." Grosvenor reminded his hearers of the power of leadership to create and motivate a local party: "you may see how blindfolded you were carried on, to do as you did, by

---

[144] CCRO, G/Mc.9. *Eng. Rep.*, vol. 89, p. 988, and vol. 90, pp. 71–72 (2 Show. KB 365 and Skinner 152). Newdigate LC, 1543, and PRO, KB21/22/32v.

[145] Eaton Hall, Papers of Sir Thomas Grosvenor, 3rd Bart., #8 and 9, consulted at the Cheshire RO.

[146] Newdigate LC, 1563, 1614, and 1617.

underhand dealings, and carrying on parties, the which for the future, your eyes being now opened, I hope you will never fall into again."[147]

Dark warnings about partisan sins were everywhere in such harangues. As at Northampton, no speaker could resist pointing fingers at the "evil men [who] lately crept into authority among you and by their stubborn and seditious practices have abused [the King's] trust." The lessons of the dangers of party – of falling away from the King's grace – were preached over and over. By his charters, the King regranted old privileges, only reserving his power to displace, a paternal power meant to keep them from falling again into the sin of party:

you have heretofore been subject to his correction if you did ill; now he has made it his care (by way of prevention) that you may not hereafter do amiss . . . Is there any among you [that] have been tainted with ill principles, that you revolve often in your minds? Now there is an eye upon you, which will have a respect to justice, as well as mercy.

It only remained for "you of the loyal party [to] be constant and united, and the rather because the seditious have been broken in their measures."[148] With the King's help, the "factious" had been excluded and the corporation made whole again; by his help, it would continue that way. Sir George Pudsey, recorder of Oxford by its 1685 charter, sounded all the same themes: good men sometimes stray from the beaten track; the good master understands and returns them to it. Oxford avoided the fate of London, whose sin was "caballing against the government." When Oxford saw the wrongs they had committed catalogued in a quo warranto, they begged forgiveness by surrendering, and were granted it in the form of a new charter. They would remain safe if they obeyed, but "if they rival kings in their royal concerns, adieu to all privileges and franchises."[149] The surrenders and charters of the 1680s made this lesson ever so clear.

Pudsey and Grosvenor believed that all order had been recreated in the corporations by recreating the corporations themselves. Certainly, many of those who had allegedly opposed the King and his friends at Oxford and Chester were now out of office. But given the enduring power of the paradox of partisan politics, only a slight change of circumstances would be needed to give those ousted ample room to stir up more contentions. For now, the King's urban friends tried to forget this as it appeared Charles had

---

[147] Eaton Hall, Papers of Sir Thomas Grosvenor, 3rd Bart., #10, p. 10, consulted at the Cheshire RO.

[148] *An Account of the Surrender of the Old Charter of Northampton . . . and the Manner of their Receiving their New Charter; Together with an Eloquent Speech made by Robert Clerk* [1683]. Clerk was the corporation's deputy recorder.

[149] Sir George Pudsey, *The Speech of Sir George Pudsey, Serjeant-at-Law, Recorder of the City of Oxford . . . at the Swearing the New Mayor* ([London], 1685).

settled his corporations. But in a few years, James II would undo that peace by his own purges and charters, and in the years after 1688, the charters, purges, and attendant angers generated by the remodeling of the corporations by Charles II would provide much of the fuel firing partisan conflicts in countless English towns. The paradox of partisan politics ensured that purges now would only be met by more purges later.

THE KING AND HIS CORPORATIONS

All examples of gracious majesty and moderation aside, the charter campaign was principally a partisan affair, driven first by factions within the towns themselves. It took Worcester tories to test and prove quo warranto in court. Once they had, the crown then developed a policy for using quo warranto and surrenders to impose new charters on new terms. As Robert Pickavance noted, two qualities in particular marked the charter effort: the initiative of corporate tories coming to the crown for new charters, and the ultimate success of the effort owing to the crown's willingness to adopt their preferences in purging their corporate foes. Pickavance contended that the charter policy's success resulted in part from a willingness to compromise: in the extent of purges in Leicester, in the retention of dissenters in places like Coventry and Warwick.[150] But townsmen at Leominster, Chester, Oxford, Berwick, and Nottingham would have scoffed at the suggestion that compromise had anything to do with the new charters. Local partisan initiative proved crucial in most cases, and as a result, those losing the partisan battle saw little of moderation. In many instances, even in "loyal" corporations, it took the threat or issue of quo warranto to compel surrender. This was hardly a light touch. New charters meant victory for one group and defeat for another in every town, though the impact of such defeats varied.

The difference between a Chester and a Leicester – between broad and narrow purges – resulted from the extent of partisan divisions within the town and the level of concern county leaders and others felt about the quality of the persons in the corporation. At Leicester, John Geary and the Earl of Huntingdon were willing to turn a blind eye to those "presbyterially inclined," aware that they could deal with them later if the need arose by an appeal to the King for an order for removals. At Chester, area gentlemen would not wait to see what reforms a charter might work upon recalcitrant spirits, preferring instead to oust their opponents now by means of the new grant.

---

[150] Pickavance, "English Boroughs and the King's Government," chapter 5. On the theme of compromise, see ibid., pp. 186–88.

In either case, it was the Huntingdons and Grosvenors hovering around England's boroughs who were the winners of the rechartering effort, more so than their friends in the corporations, and even more than the King. By controlling the information running between town and crown that dictated how decisions by each were made, local grandees regained an influence in the towns that they had not enjoyed since before the Civil Wars. The desire by men like Huntingdon to become corporation officers perplexed Sir Francis North: "Why are great Lords ambitious of empty titles to corporation service, as steward, recorder, etc., whereby they make the corporation unreasonably proud and put it in their power to affront them. Other usage would be more prudent."[151] The Duke of Albemarle became recorder of Harwich and Saffron Walden and high steward of Totnes, Barnstaple, and Colchester for his efforts.[152] But the new charters gave Huntingdon, Albemarle, and others an opportunity to expand their influence in corporations they believed were theirs to control, but which since the Restoration may not have been as compliant with their wishes as tradition suggested they should be.[153]

Expanded benches, increased licenses in mortmain, new markets and courts: this was standard fare in the charters of the 1660s and 70s; so too in the 1680s. Promises that towns would be "gratified with new fairs and markets or jurisdiction in civil causes . . . for their profit," in North's words, helped inspire many surrenders.[154] Charters contained other new provisions. The corporate names of dozens of towns changed, eradicating local oddities like the "Mayor, Masters, and Burgesses" of Wells, who became by their charter of January 1684 the "Mayor, Aldermen, and Burgesses," a style used now by most towns. At Kingston upon Thames and Yarmouth, the two bailiffs at the head of each corporation were replaced by a single mayor, thus becoming, on their request, "mayor towns." This added to their dignity, giving the corporation's head the preferred title of mayor, and removed the possibility allowed under old arrangements that divisions in the corporation could go all the way from the bottom to the top, when two bailiffs fought on opposite sides in local partisan contests. In such seemingly minor changes, the crown continued the process under way since 1660 of making ever more uniform the terms by which England's corporations lived. As each borough became more like the next, they were all united more closely to the crown.[155] Similarly, the remodeling of

---

151 BL, Add. 32,518, f. 45v.
152 Pickavance, "English Boroughs and the King's Government," p. 281.
153 Thus Pickavance saw an "aristocratic revival in local politics" as a result of the charter effort. Ibid., chapter 6.
154 PRO, SP44/66/88.
155 For more on this point, see Weinbaum, *Incorporation of Boroughs*, p. 5.

borough charters must be viewed in a wider context of administrative rearrangement then under way. Before he started on the towns, the King purged county benches and lieutenancies.[156] Moving on to the corporations was an extension of a larger effort to bring all subsidiary jurisdictions under stricter royal review and control. Borough corporations were by no means the only ones affected by this larger effort. London trade companies, American colonial charters, and Irish towns were all dragged together by the same bureaucratic net.[157] In all of these efforts, there was a tendency toward increased integration of crown with local or other lesser authorities. This process of standardization and integration was made all the more effective in English towns by adopting the policy proposed for Irish towns in the 1670s of beginning in each with a surrender of previous charters. By doing so, all local oddities were wiped away.

The most important and consistent change in borough charters after 1682 was the addition of uniform clauses permitting the King to remove corporation members at will. They would now be like judges, serving during the King's pleasure. Their performance would be monitored, and if need be, punished. This was in part another sign of the crown's concern with local magistracy, as displayed in charters since 1660 and in the commissions of association. By being able to remove town clerks, mayors, recorders, sheriffs – all local justices and court officers – the crown held more power than ever to superintend the administration of justice. But the additional power to displace aldermen and councillors was a sign of a broader interest to control membership in the corporations' deliberative bodies, and by extension, the outcome of their deliberations. Charles made sparing use of the power in the months remaining to him.[158] In the hands of his younger brother, the displacement power was a partisan bomb waiting to explode. James would light the fuse in 1687, soon blowing apart the loyal corporate bodies his brother's bureaucrats had worked so hard to create. The charter effort of Charles II, so effective in bringing certain persons to local power, and cutting others off from it, contained in it the source of its own destruction when the crown's political leadership, political needs, and partisan alliances changed.

---

[156] See Glassey, *Politics and the Justices of the Peace*, chapter 2.

[157] On trade companies, see Sinner, "Charles II and Local Government," pp. 182ff. On colonial reincorporations, see J. M. Sosin, *English America and the Restoration Monarchy of Charles II: Transatlantic Politics, Commerce, and Kingship* (Lincoln, 1980), and Richard Johnson, *Adjustment to Empire: The New England Colonies, 1675–1715* (New Brunswick, 1981). Charter efforts continued in Ireland too throughout the 1680s.

[158] Removals ordered in the Privy Council according to royal powers in their new charters were directed to Coventry, Bristol, and Colchester, the last only a week before the King died. PRO, PC2/70/182, 266, and 299.

❧ 7 ❧

Revolution in the corporations, 1685–1688

Berwick endured a more painful reincorporation than most. Military leaders in that strategic border town, eager to enforce the laws against dissent with more severity, had long sought to control the corporation. Hopes of doing so by a quo warranto or a commission of association in 1681 and 1683 had come to nothing.[1] But by October 1684, it looked as if local garrison commanders had won over enough of the corporation to gain their ends, though many still resisted, as Chief Justice Jeffreys learned from his informants there: "[They are] resolved to stand trial with the King about their charter; but forty-five of the most loyal of them will by Colonel Widdrington, our lieutenant governor, petition your Lordship to speak with his majesty that since they have always protested against and opposed the factious party, they may not be involved in the common name."[2] To help "the loyal party," the attorney general served quo warranto to compel the intransigent to join them in surrender. Still, a majority voted defiance; these "dissenters" then prepared to answer the King's information, taking counsel with none other than London's lawyer, Henry Pollexfen. But he and John Holt, another prominent lawyer, advised conceding their charter as it would certainly be lost by the quo warranto, with worse consequences. Again the corporation voted, now capitulating by a majority of six.[3]

The mayor lay the charter at Charles's feet and kissed his hand on January 23, 1685. Two weeks later, the King was dead. James II graciously condescended to grant Berwick's desires for a new charter. But for now, according to suggestions from garrison officers, he put the town under a special "commission for executing justice," which appointed the Duke of Newcastle, the Bishop of Durham, local clergymen and gentlemen, and numerous military men, including ensign Ferdinando Forster, who became mayor. Though governing in the King's name, the magisterial commission

---

[1] PRO, PC2/69/133. *CSPD Jan.–June 1683*, pp. 355–56.
[2] BL, Add. 41,803, ff. 98–99.   [3] *CSPD 1684–85*, pp. 212 and 231.

lacked corporate status, so a new charter would still be required, though it would not arrive in Berwick for over eighteen months.[4]

The greeting it received once it did matched the effusions of joy shown elsewhere and speeches were made praising a King so gracious as to grant such liberties. After the usual harangue against "Exclusioners," one speaker reminded his hearers that James not only confirmed ancient liberties; he now permitted the corporation to bear a mace and sword on ceremonial occasions, the symbols of the regal authority given to them for preserving the King's peace. "Thus God" had made the King "to minister judgment and mercy to the people . . . to establish good laws to the people and to command obedience to them, [and] to defend the Church of England in the beauty of holiness against factious sectaries and separatists." The King in turn granted magisterial powers to Berwick's leaders, for "his majesty's service and the welfare of this ancient corporation."[5] Like those granted by James's elder brother in 1682–85, Berwick's charter of September 1686 strengthened the royal alliance with forces in the towns committed to the defense of King and Church. But not for long. In January 1687, the King expelled eight of those appointed by that glorious charter. More lost their places in August the following year.[6] Dismissal by the King's own hand, of those who ranked themselves among his most loyal subjects, must have perplexed all who saw it.

Between the grant of Berwick's charter in September 1686 and the time he ordered the first removals the following January, James began a major reformulation of political means and ends. He cultivated new allies in the localities to achieve a toleration for his Catholic co-religionists by holding out hopes for a statutory toleration to Protestant dissenters as well. Doing this meant undoing the political alliances so effectively put together by his brother over the preceding half-dozen years. Once again, the effort depended on purgation, wrought by royal dismissal orders permitted by clauses in the new charters of 1682 to early 1687. What he started in Berwick in January of 1687 was then pursued nationwide later in the year. The revolution that rolled over the corporations by means of new charters in 1682 to early 1687 was now reversed by a revolution of greater magnitude in 1687 and 1688. Thousands lost their places, most with impeccable royalist credentials, only to be replaced by their partisan foes – many of whom had been dismissed only a few years before by Charles's

---

[4] Scott, *Berwick-Upon-Tweed*, pp. 218–20. PRO, C231/8/122. The charter was granted September 17, 1686, but did not arrive in town for three months. PRO, IND1/4228/106v, and *CSPD 1686–87*, pp. 231–32.

[5] Bod., Rawlinson D.1481, ff. 20–21.

[6] Two of those expelled had also been named in the special commission governing the town before the new charter's arrival. PRO, PC2/71/196v and 72/151.

charters – and by Catholics and dissenters with little if any natural local constituency. Following such widespread revolutions in personnel, corporate government around the country ground to a halt in the summer and autumn of 1688. This was the one period of true crisis in local government in the three generations after the restoration of monarchy. It was not until October 17, 1688 that James admitted his dreadful political mistake and ordered the corporations restored to their previous condition. So Berwick reverted to the government and personnel under its last charter; over 300 made free under the new charter were immediately disfranchised.[7] Yet another revolution in the corporations – which had already seen two revolutions in the last half-dozen years – turned out one group and put another in power.

Berwick's loyal leaders had been sacrificed to one of the most ambitious royal policies of the century, James's effort in 1687–88 to reshape the electorate in order to gain a Parliament ready to grant religious toleration. J. R. Jones has characterized this campaign, and the effort in the boroughs in particular, as proceeding with a clear understanding of political realities: as one that, in the end, may well have worked, had not a revolution intervened.[8] But it would not have worked. We know this because it did not work. When viewed from the corporations themselves, it becomes apparent how unfavorable conditions were for royal intervention of this sort. For nowhere did James's efforts have such a comprehensive effect and produce such disastrous results as in the nation's boroughs; nowhere did the effort show such desperation. No royal policy toward the towns since 1660 showed such disregard of the prejudices of England's urban leadership. No policy depended so little on local initiative and so heavily on alien agents of a suspect royal government. No policy relied so much on those with no natural place in local political life, including many of the reviled sect of Friends. And no policy alienated both whig and tory stalwarts so thoroughly, for no policy so ignored the vast political middle – of either partisan flavor – in an attempt to unite political extremes – namely dissenters and Catholics. Ironically, that alienation ran so deep in the towns was the result of the success, not the failure, of James's purges.[9] For it was the very thoroughness of James's agents in dismissing thousands of urban

---

[7] Scott, *Berwick-Upon-Tweed*, p. 221.

[8] J. R. Jones, *The Revolution of 1688 in England* (London, 1972), p. 138. See also Jones, "James II's Revolution: Royal Policies, 1686–92," in Jonathan Israel, ed., *The Anglo-Dutch Moment: Essays on the Glorious Revolution and its World Impact* (Cambridge, 1991), p. 62.

[9] As Jones argued, the campaign was "more efficient" than any other effort to control local government in the seventeenth century, and this is certainly true. But efficiency in execution is not the same as effectiveness in producing intended results. Jones, *Revolution of 1688*, p. 130.

leaders in towns like Berwick that engendered alienation. Success in this immediate objective – replacing uncooperative urban leaders – ensured the failure of James's larger project – religious toleration – and led to the corporations' acquiescence as their king was driven from his kingdom in late 1688.

"REGULATED ACCORDING TO THE NEW MODE"[10]

Removals ordered by James II in Berwick made fewer changes than similar orders to scores of other towns in the same period. But the message was no less clear: the King was reversing the political alliances made by his elder brother. There had been few intimations of James's abandonment of the "Church party." When he ascended the throne in February 1685, James and most others envisioned a continuation of the policies and personnel favored in recent years. The composition of the Parliament elected soon after his accession appeared to underscore the union between the new King and the Anglican tory interests that were in control nationwide. Few could have foreseen that a few years later, the King would turn for support to the weakest political forces in the land, creating and depending on a previously unimaginable combination of dissenter and Catholic.

When Charles II died, scores of surrendered charters and drafts of renewals lay in the attorney general's office or were awaiting the great seal. But the stalled process started again as towns like Berwick petitioned the new King to finish what his brother had begun. Dozens of charters under negotiation when Charles died were granted in February, March, and early April 1685, each appointing members strengthening the "Church party" in the towns. The pace of regrant then slowed considerably, with the occasional charter, like Berwick's, passing the seals over the next two years. Even those of 1686 and early 1687 were Charles's charters, though passed under a great seal bearing his brother's likeness, based as they were on surrenders to the elder Stuart and containing terms matching those Charles had granted in 1683–85.[11] Though James concluded the work under way at his accession, he encouraged no more surrenders from 1685 to 1687, effectively scuttling what Charles had intended should be a comprehensive rechartering of all corporate towns. The last of Charles's charters went to

---

[10] Luttrell, *Brief Historical Relation*, vol. I, p. 436, describing the effects of a new charter for Norwich in 1688.

[11] For instance, Guildford and Gravesend surrendered their charters in November 1684. Guildford's new charter did not pass until April 1686; Gravesend's passed in March 1687. *The History of Guildford* (Guildford, 1801), p. 203. Robert Pierce Cruden, *The History of the Town of Gravesend* (London, 1843), pp. 376–77. Maldon's March 1687 charter and Lichfield's of July 1686 were also granted after 1684 surrenders: *CSPD 1684–85*, pp. 110 and 255. For the rate of rechartering after Charles's death, see below, Appendix A.

Gravesend in March 1687. James's first charter, granted one year later to Exeter, proclaimed loudly how his intentions and methods differed from his brother's.

Though James showed little interest in the towns during the first two years of his reign, the charters of Charles II left him two important legacies: a clear example of what could be done by granting new charters, and a royal power to remove any corporation member at will encoded in the new constitutions of well over 100 towns.[12] Both the power to remove and the power to grant new charters would play their part in James's policies in the coming years, policies openly directed at creating a Parliament ready to do his bidding. Parliament was the target of James's charters of 1688 as surely as the magistracy was Charles's target a few years earlier. When James finally turned his gaze on to the towns, his vision encompassed very different goals from those of Charles, though pursued by means taught him by his elder brother.

In June of 1686, James used his power of removal for the first time, commanding the dismissal of a Bristol alderman after receiving reports that the mayor and others there had supported mobs that mocked the Virgin Mary and the Catholic host. But this and other dismissal orders in 1686 were still in keeping with royal interventions in the boroughs since 1660: a limited response to local disorder.[13] No more than one or two persons were ousted by these early orders, which, as of yet, were part of no larger reconception of the proper qualifications of borough personnel. In December 1686, James ordered his first broad changes in the county benches; most of the commissions' new names belonged to Catholics.[14] With his ambitious remodelings of county benches, James started throwing over the Anglican tory allies Charles had cultivated since 1680.[15] He then began a very tentative tinkering with corporate officers. Removals of eight at Berwick on January 14, 1687 were the first made of more than an individual or small handful. Four at Grampound and eight at Truro were

---

12 127 charters from Tavistock's in July of 1682 to Gravesend's of March 1687 included a crown power to remove corporation members. The only exceptions were charters to Andover, Buckingham, Derby, Nottingham, and Maidstone, which included more limited powers for royal dismissals.

13 A commission of association was also appointed for Bristol. PRO, PC2/71/145 and 147. John Latimer, *Annals of Bristol in the Seventeenth Century* (Bristol, 1905), pp. 439–41. *CSPD 1686–87*, pp. 94, 116, 118, 136, 137, 152, 156, 159–60, 164, and 184. Newdigate LC, 1654, 1660, 1663–66, 1668–69, and 1671.

14 A few new county commissions had been granted earlier in 1686, but a more ambitious review began in October 1686, with the first major remodelings made in December. Glassey, *Politics and the Justices of the Peace*, pp. 68–77.

15 For more on James's shift in political alliance, see John Miller, *James II: A Study in Kingship*, revised edn. (London, 1989), chapter 12, and Jones, *Revolution of 1688*, chapter 5.

dismissed the same month, but the remaining dismissal orders of the spring and summer of 1687 reverted to the former pattern: limited in number and directed at just a few individuals.[16] The larger reversal of political direction evident in changes to the county benches would not be evident in the towns until year's end.

But evidence of the King's changing political temper mounted throughout 1687. In mid-March, James directed a halt to prosecutions of dissenters:

Nothing can more conduce to the peace and quiet of this kingdom and the increase of the number as well as of the trade of his subjects . . . than an entire liberty of conscience, it having always been his Majesty's opinion, as most suitable to the principles of Christianity, that no man should be persecuted for conscience's sake, which his Majesty thinks is not to be forced.[17]

A few weeks later, he made his declaration for liberty of conscience, thereby permitting forms of Christian observance other than those of the established Church. James's hopes, increasingly clear over the last six months, could no longer be ignored. "We cannot but heartily wish, as it will easily be believed, that all the people of our dominions were members of the Catholic Church."[18]

Efforts were now made to have the corporations send addresses thanking the King for his toleration. Chester voted quickly and unanimously to address the King, perhaps after some prodding from Governor Peter Shakerley. Woodstock took a while longer: four assembly meetings passed until they approved an address.[19] Leicester corporation avoided pronouncing its opinion on the toleration until October. The Earl of Huntingdon had given them a form of address to use, but the mayor, aware of the likelihood of defeat, proposed a watered down version to the assembly instead. Still, "many objected by reason of the word (indulgence) therein"; they rejected even the mayor's moderated text by a vote of thirty-four to nineteen.[20] James ordered the mayor of Totnes removed in June after he was "complained of for discountenancing addressing to thank the King for his declaration."[21] Many shared his discomfort, but most corporations,

---

[16] These included one alderman each at Bristol and Boston, in both cases on the petition of those dismissed, each claiming age or infirmity. They may have asked for a royal removal order since if they had resigned, they would be subject to fines according to charter provisions or town by-laws. PRO, PC2/71/197, 198v, 199v, 202, and 211v; PC2/72/19 and 36. James had made a few other removals of individuals since the removal at Bristol: at Northampton, Canterbury, Worcester, and Harwich. PRO, PC2/71/150v, 161v, 165v, 179v, and 196v.

[17] PRO, PC2/71/210.

[18] J. P. Kenyon, *The Stuart Constitution, 1603–1688* (Cambridge, 1969), p. 410.

[19] CCRO, AB/3, f. 13v. Woodstock Town Hall, 76/2, Sept. 2, 1687.

[20] Leicestershire RO, BRII/18/36, ff. 66 and 71. Hastings Letters, 13,676.

[21] Luttrell, *Brief Historical Relation*, vol. I, p. 405. Newdigate LC, 1805 and 1814. Miller, *James II*, pp. 172–73.

driven more by loyalty than fear of the rising stars of Catholics and dissenters, complied in addressing and in the few removals the King ordered them to make before the autumn of 1687.

The Parliament sent to Westminster in 1685 had been fervent for a strong Church and a strong King.[22] This proved a serious problem as James's goals and political allegiances swung around from the interests of the Church to those of dissent. Winning the statutory toleration he now sought depended on gaining a more malleable Parliament. James at last dismissed his first Parliament in July 1687 after nineteen months of prorogation; work began immediately to make a new one. Such a Parliament would not simply be elected, it would be created to the King's liking by cajoling electors. Few thought the county vote could be manipulated successfully, "yet the King is still assured that by his power in the corporations he shall have a House of Commons to his liking."[23] The towns after all chose many more MPs, with many fewer voters, than did the counties. In addition, given the alterations in corporate membership in the early 1680s, the towns contained many tories known for their zeal for the royal prerogative. Thus the King looked initially to them for support. But even in the King's first, more tentative measures, it quickly became clear that provincial tories were reluctant at best. Thus when "a Romanist produced the King's mandamus to be mayor" at Cambridge in September 1687, the corporation simply refused to do what by law the King could not require. Kingston upon Thames, a place notable for its loyalty in the last reign, rejected the King's choice for mayor too.[24]

If loyal tories would not support him owing to fears for their Church, then the King could turn to Protestant dissenters since they, like Catholics, stood to benefit from the intended toleration. Of course, turning from tories to dissenters would mean removing the former from their corporate places and installing the latter, but this would be easy enough given the power the King enjoyed by the new charters of the 1680s to dismiss corporation members at will. From at least as early as June 1687, "there [was] a talk of purging all the corporations of the kingdom and putting in such as were called whigs."[25] By making a few changes in corporate membership, James would have an amenable electorate that would choose an amenable Parliament. At least, this was what was expected.

---

[22] Charters remodeling scores of corporations before the parliamentary elections of 1685 had little if any impact on their outcome, nor had they been intended to. Robert Pickavance, "English Boroughs and the King's Government," chapter 2, and Sinner, "Charles II and Local Government," pp. 26, 179–81, 193–200, and chapter 5.

[23] *CSPD 1687–89*, p. 66.

[24] Cambridge successfully pleaded that they had already made their choice for the year. Newdigate LC, 1861–62, and 1868.

[25] Ibid., 1834.

Conducting a nationwide purge would require detailed information about the views of current and prospective corporators. Deciding who would stay in the corporations and who should replace those removed required a test: the infamous "three questions." These were simple enough. Will you promote repeal of the sacramental Test and the penal laws against dissent if elected to Parliament? Will you aid the election of those who will? Will you support the King's Declaration of Indulgence and live at peace with dissenters and Catholics? By 1687, such tests were a time-honored tradition in corporate life. The oaths, engagements, and "good conversation" required in the 1650s; the declaration against the Covenant in the Corporation Act; the sacramental test: England's local leaders must not have been surprised to see yet another standard applied by yet another regime.

Testing the loyalty of local governors in 1687–88 became the job of a visiting professional bureaucrat, not a local figure respected within the community. In 1662, the crown had been careful to name persons of high local standing to serve as corporation commissioners. Now the new tests would be given by "regulators" chosen for their sympathy to the cause rather than their prominence in the areas they would visit. One Chester regulator was condemned as a man who "had formerly preached treason, was in the Western rebellion . . . and was one of those fanatics that had frequent consults with the Papists in the Temple."[26] Most were paid lawyers. They did their work with energy if not subtlety. Reports of their canvass of town and country leaders began arriving in Whitehall in the autumn of 1687, and continued throughout the following winter, spring, and summer, providing the basis for a purge of provincial officialdom on a scale unseen since 1662–63.

In mid-November 1687, a new committee of the Privy Council began inspecting the regulators' reports and removing all those who would not support repealing the laws against dissenters and Catholics. Unsurprisingly, both the committee at Whitehall and their minions in the provinces included a host of dissenters and Catholics. None other than William Sacheverell, who had fought so ardently to stop the new charter at Nottingham in 1682, assisted this new purge. Perhaps he would have his revenge after all.[27] At Whitehall, work began in earnest on November 20,

---

26 Whitley Diary, f. 91v.
27 Those removed by the new charter at Nottingham, recounted in the previous chapter, were now restored to the corporation: Jones, "Whig Collaborators," p. 67n. The Council committee included Lord Chancellor Jeffreys, Lords Powis and Castlemain, Sir Nicholas Butler, and Father Petre. Depositions considered in the House of Lords in 1689 also named the Marquess of Powis and Lord Arundell of Wardour: *LJ*, vol. 14, p. 388. Sacheverell reportedly assisted them. Newdigate LC, 1881 and 1883. Jones, *Revolution of 1688*, chapter 6, especially pp. 144–52.

when the Council sent out orders for extensive removals at Gloucester, Tewkesbury, and three other towns. With more removals at Tewkesbury the next month, over three-quarters of the corporation had lost their places. At the same time, the crown sent letters under the sign manual directing the election of their replacements, though by the charters of the early 1680s, the King could not require such elections. Nonetheless, Tewkesbury corporation complied, choosing into the vacancies, at the King's direction, dissenters excluded from their councils since the purges of the early 1660s.[28] As Narcissus Luttrell noted, "it falls heavy on the Church of England men."[29] Catholics, dissenters, and occasional conformists – many removed by the charters of 1682–85 – now replaced the loyal "Church of England men." By early in the new year, about sixty towns had been hit as the committee worked away as fast as the information arrived from provincial regulators. By March, reports were about that most corporations had been remodeled and that a Parliament would be called for May. But reports at the same time of attacks on Catholic chapels must have dampened the spirits of even those most ready to believe that changing corporate personnel lists would solve the deeper problem of the nation's bigotries.[30]

Tories who had benefited by the charters of Charles II and who dominated most corporations because of those charters were now asked by their King to quit their places, remove their peers, or to elect those whose politics and religion they found repugnant. Corporate tories were thus caught between passive obedience to their King and duty to their Church, the two of which they never imagined could be so opposed. Though James received important help from those J. R. Jones has called the "whig collaborators," the irony of James's remodelings was that it relied as much on the submission of tory loyalists – like those at Leicester – at least at first.[31] Newcastle under Lyme corporation received a Privy Council order in December for the removal of just over one half of the corporation along with a royal letter appointing others. The corporation obeyed both commands, dismissing many of the same county gentlemen carefully installed in the corporation by their charter of March 1685. Nine of the fourteen replacements were not new at all, having served in the corporation until losing their places by that same charter. James's order effectively reversed the personnel changes of Charles's charter, and, with it, the partisan qualifications for corporate membership.[32] Here and elsewhere,

[28] PRO, PC2/72/54v–55 and 68. Beaver, "Symbol and Boundary," pp. 293–94.
[29] Luttrell, *Brief Historical Relation*, vol. I, pp. 420–21.
[30] Newdigate LC, 1896, 1904, 1905, and 1924.   [31] Jones, "Whig Collaborators."
[32] Pape, *Newcastle-under-Lyme*, pp. 50–52. PRO, PC2/72/62v.

James's effort initially worked because good tories like Newcastle's leaders did as their king told them to do. Fewer did so over time.

Even in these early months of the effort, the King met plenty of obstruction. In two orders of November and January, the King directed the removal of over 80% of Worcester's corporation. Though the mayor was replaced according to the second command, none of the other removals appear to have been made.[33] In March, the Catholic Viscount Molyneux, lord lieutenant of Lancashire, received a Privy Council order for removing the mayor, the clerk, the bailiff, and ten others at Preston. When he went to serve the order, his forewarned victims had gone to Lancaster for the day.[34] Lancashire tory Roger Kenyon complained of "the extravagant methods practiced by the new magistrates in the ancient loyal corporations, contrary to the express concessions in their charters, to the ruin of the boroughs [and] destructive to the government thereof." Perhaps with his connivance and that of other gentlemen opposed to Molyneux's measures, four Preston aldermen the King had ordered removed in March were either never removed or were re-elected by June.[35] Molyneux did little better in Lancaster. Thirty-one corporation members appeared to answer the three questions when he came to tender them. Eighteen flatly refused to agree to any of them; six or seven responded more evasively. The mayor, three aldermen, ten bailiffs, and the town clerk were later ousted by Privy Council order.[36]

Other problems arose too. At Abingdon, two orders removed the entire assembly in November and December. One of those dismissed by the latter order had been appointed by the former one; one of those appointed refused to join the corporation and another resigned four days later. In short, even those meant to profit by James's measures were wary of them from the outset, especially since the King seemed able to change his mind later about who was fit to serve. At Dunwich, removals were made according to royal command, as well as new appointments ordered by the King, though one of those named to the corporation insisted on taking the oaths of allegiance and supremacy and on subscribing the declaration

---

[33] PRO, PC2/72/58v and 72. One of those ordered removed – Wintour Harris – was only replaced in September after he had died. At least five of those who were to have been expelled were still in the corporation in early October 1688. Hereford and Worcester RO (St. Helen's), Shelf A.14, Box 2, 2nd pagination, pp. 32, 34, and 37.

[34] More removals were ordered in June. Molyneux had been so eager to start that he began asking the three questions in the corporations before ordered to do so and received a reprimand from Sunderland. PRO, PC2/72/98 and 134; *CSPD 1687–89*, pp. 102–03 and 174.

[35] County tories, especially Roger Kenyon, opposed Molyneux. Mullett, "Preston Politics," pp. 76–77. In October, Molyneux reported that Preston had not complied with removal orders. *CSPD 1687–89*, p. 323.

[36] Pape, *Charters of Lancaster*, p. 67. HMC Le Fleming, pp. 205–06. PRO, PC2/72/95v.

against the Covenant required by the Corporation Act: a clear sign of what he thought of James's interest in relaxing those same requirements.[37]

Problems like these arose with ever greater frequency over the winter and spring of 1688. As they did, measures became more drastic. Cambridge corporation disregarded the first Council order sent there in March, commanding the dismissal of the mayor, five aldermen, and twelve of the common council. In April, the regulators visited, noting the negative influence of the University. So they suggested more extensive changes. The first dismissal order was repeated; another order followed later, adding eighteen names to the original list. Perhaps owing to some arm-twisting by the regulators, the corporation at last made the changes commanded by the King. It must have been quite a spectacle to see thirty-six of the forty members quit their places. This did the job: their replacements voted unanimously to send the King an address thanking him for the second Declaration of Indulgence of April 1688.[38] But the question must have arisen: what would be the long-term cost of such thorough purges?

Information on the disposition of Leicester's leaders was gathered with the help of a county Presbyterian, John Oneby. A royal order arrived in February directing the removal of eleven aldermen, sixteen councilmen, and three other officers; the corporation executed the order the next month.[39] Those named to replace them included three aldermen and seven councilmen removed from the corporation by the charter of 1684. Among those appointed for the first time, one begged to be excused from serving, "not having been educated amongst them," and because he was not a freeman.[40] Other new members did nothing at all: "several new aldermen of the dissenting party have refused to act."[41] Two more removal orders to scour the yet unclean corporation followed in April. A full 70% had now been dismissed, including three of those appointed earlier by the King.[42] Even so, this reconstructed body was no more accommodating than its predecessor. In May, only three voted in favor of addressing the King after

---

[37] PRO, PC2/72/58v and 68. Berkshire RO, A/AOzc. Challenor, *Abingdon*, pp. 176–78. Suffolk RO (Ipswich Branch), EE6/1144/13, ff. 61–62v.

[38] PRO, PC2/72/101, 113, and 114v. Cambridgeshire RO, Shelf C/9, pp. 101–07. Sir George Duckett, ed., *Penal Laws and Test Act: Questions Touching their Repeal Propounded in 1687–88 by James II* (London, 1883), p. 223.

[39] Oneby sent lists of those who should be continued to the Earl of Huntingdon: Hastings Letters, 9778. PRO, PC2/72/95v. Leicestershire RO, BRII/1/3, f. 933.

[40] Hastings Letters, 9844.

[41] Ibid., 664, Sir Henry Beaumont to the Earl of Huntingdon, April 1688. Beaumont assisted in Leicestershire out of loyalty, but he expressed doubts about its wisdom in his letters. Ibid., 667–70. There were other reports of reluctant dissenter appointees: Newdigate LC, 1907.

[42] PRO, PC2/72/114 and 114v. Two ordered removed – Tobias Marshall and William Walker – had been appointed by royal orders in February. Both were elected aldermen not long after they should have been removed.

his second Declaration of Indulgence.[43] Those the King appointed to serve had refused the honor; some appointed were quickly removed again by the King when they were found insufficiently compliant; repeated orders were required to gain a friendly corporation; even then, the new group could not be counted on to support the King's project: results in Leicester boded ill for the long-term success of James's program. Problems at Leicester were repeated in scores of towns. Broad resistance to the King's measures by sitting corporation members required broad purges. Continued resistance of remaining members, and even newly appointed ones, required yet more purges. Each act of the Crown seemed to require further, more drastic acts to make them effective. The more effective the regulators were in removing people, the more they lost local control.

James's removals wrought havoc in the corporations and comprised a purge of the towns of greater magnitude than that imposed by the Corporation Act in 1662–63. Dismissal orders went to 103 towns, approximately half of those incorporated. Nationwide, the King directed 2,199 corporation members to quit their places, 76% of all members in those 103 towns. 101 other officers – town clerks, high stewards, and recorders – lost their positions too, as did another forty-two lesser servants such as mace and sword bearers. In some towns, the entire corporation was ousted.[44] In others, the King's commands cleaned the body once, then he returned for another round, ultimately turning out more than 100% of the corporation as later purges removed members recently appointed by James himself.[45] Apparently many of those James named on the advice of his regulators were found wanting upon subsequent examination. Why, in an effort so clearly directed at recasting the corporations in order to control their choices of MPs, the non-parliamentary corporations of Basingstoke, Doncaster, Kingston upon Thames, and Macclesfield also suffered purges is unclear. But as the regulating machine ground through the nation's towns, it is unsurprising that a few hapless bystanders were caught in its maw.[46]

---

[43] Hastings Letters, 1703. Leicestershire RO, BRII/18/36, ff. 86–89. Stocks, *Records of Leicester*, p. 588. Such defiance could be dangerous, as Ipswich found when its corporation was dissolved after it neglected to address the King for the declaration and on the birth of the Prince of Wales. Luttrell, *Brief Historical Relation*, vol. I, p. 457.

[44] For instance Bridport, Evesham, Exeter, Nottingham, Saffron Walden, and Totnes. Numbers removed are taken from the lists of names in the Privy Council registers, PRO, PC2. These numbers have been compared with the number of persons appointed to each corporation by its latest charter. As many later orders contained the names of persons removed by earlier orders, care has been taken not to count them twice. In all, 142 names were sent to the various towns more than once.

[45] For instance Chichester, Ipswich, Newbury, Reading, and Wells.

[46] Basingstoke lost three, Kingston twenty-six of twenty-eight, and Macclesfield, one quarter of its council. PRO, PC2/72/91v, 107, 147v, 149, and 152v. Tomlinson, *Doncaster*, p. 168. *A Calendar to the Records of the Borough of Doncaster*, 4 vols. (Doncaster, 1902), vol. IV, p. 151.

Increasing obstruction produced more desperate measures; each successive order to a given town was more extreme – and more bewildering – than the last. J. R. Jones contended that multiple purge orders to certain towns were planned from the start, not a later response to earlier failures.[47] But multiple orders – a clear sign of initial orders' failure – were the rule, not the exception. In only thirty-six of 103 cases did the crown get it right the first time; all the others required two or more orders to purge them; some took as many as five. Some later removal orders repeated earlier ones in part or in their entirety. But the principal reason for multiple orders to so many towns was the failure of earlier orders to achieve the desired results. In many cases this was because earlier removals were made only in part, if at all; townsmen in places like Worcester quietly ignored the King's commands. In other places, initial orders left untouched some whose support of the King was suspect because earlier information was unreliable. Successive removal orders to the same towns occurred with greater frequency as the King's measures became more desperate and as opposition mounted. Matters grew only worse as James came increasingly to depend on persons from the margins of local society with little if any previous corporate experience. Finding those who had both local clout and the right opinions to provide a new kind of leadership in the towns proved more and more difficult over the summer of 1688. And obstructions increased too. As regulators were told, probably late in the summer of 1688, "weigh well the difficulty of your work and consider that you will meet with all manner of deceit and combination to frustrate your endeavors."[48] Dismissal orders issued unabated as their reports continued to come in.

Though perhaps given to criticism after his removal from government at the beginning of 1687, the Earl of Clarendon accurately foretold the failure of the borough effort soon after it began: "a little time will show us what will be when the corporations are new-modelled, which is the work now executing; and by some of the changes which are already made, it is probable those who are put into those societies will be as averse to what the King would have as those who are put out."[49] Some corporations reluctantly complied in James's measures at first. But as 1688 wore on, Sunderland and other officers received more and more excuses and reports of ignored orders. When ordered to remove *John* Kent, the corporation of

---

[47] Jones made this argument on the basis of a letter by William Blathwayt noting the plan for a second purge of Bristol soon after the first. Thus he suggests later purges of the same town did not result from "an inefficiently planned or executed first attempt." *Revolution of 1688*, p. 149. But this does not appear to have been the case as so many towns received multiple dismissal orders. For instance Barnstaple, Leicester, and Chester required multiple orders, and ultimately new charters, to little avail.

[48] PRO, SP9/247/66.

[49] *CSPD 1687–89*, p. 118. These remarks are dated December 15, 1687.

Wilton responded that there was "no such person in the charter of the borough," without explaining that there was someone called *Richard* Kent. Royal regulators ultimately caught up with Richard and he was removed almost two months later. Thetford corporation simply declared it was not "well satisfied with the reality" of a royal order that they should elect John Mendham – the man behind the grant of their 1682 charter – as mayor for a second year in a row. They elected another.[50] By September and early October, confidence in the King had so eroded that many corporations made the removals as ordered – perhaps because many were no longer willing to serve in the transformed political environment – but then gave creative reasons why they could not choose those whom the King asked them to elect to the empty places. At Fowey and Lostwithiel, the corporations removed those the King named, "but finding they could not with safety to their oaths elect the persons named in the mandate, being contrary to their charters, they chose some of their corporation duly qualified."[51] It was a telling sign when the Earl of Bath reported in early October that these two were the only peaceful towns the regulators had visited. Electing those "duly qualified" by the traditional religious tests preserved peace; royal orders to elect those not so qualified threatened it. Six aldermen in York reported their compliance in dismissing their lord mayor, five aldermen, eight of their "twenty-four men," and ten of the common council, who "all submitted with much willingness." But those the King desired they elect to the vacancies were not freemen; with no mayor, they could make no new freemen; without being freemen, they could not be chosen for corporate office. Besides, the charter dictated the manner of elections, requiring the commons to nominate three to stand in election; results for certain persons could not be ensured without subverting the corporate constitution. When they tried to hold an election, corporate voters declared they could not in good conscience choose those named by the King as it would violate their oaths. Stafford's leaders experienced the same pangs of conscience.[52] In his effort to liberate the consciences of England's religious dissenters, James trapped the consciences of his once loyal subjects, forcing them to choose between duty to King or corporate oath, and between duty to King or Church. By September and early October 1688, the consciences of many forced them to abandon the King to serve their corporate oaths and national Church.

---

[50] Wiltshire RO, G25/1/87, pp. 492–93 and 495. PRO, PC2/72/126 and 148. Thetford Town Hall, T/C2/6, p. 75. Thetford put Mendham's name in nomination, but he lost.
[51] PRO, PC2/72/134, 149, and 155. *CSPD 1687–89*, p. 304.
[52] *CSPD 1687–89*, pp. 300 and 312.

PURGE BY CHARTER

By the charters of 1682–85, the King could order removals, but he could only suggest replacements; corporations had to obey in the first instance, and prudent ones would obey in the second. Like Charles in 1660–61, when he wrote letters to various towns asking them to elect certain persons, all James could do now was ask. Like Charles before him, James found that not all felt obliged to obey. From the beginning of the remodeling effort, it was clear that other measures would be needed to bring the obstinate to heel. This required another round of charters, efforts for which began at about the same time the Council ordered the first removals. A quo warranto was brought against Southampton corporation in late November 1687, days after the first major removal orders. By February, the corporation decided to yield.[53] Soon, in other towns, "the tories [are] turned out and dissenters and papists put in; and quo warrantos are brought and ordered against those that yet refuse to submit to a regulation." By mid-February, fifty-two quo warrantos had issued. More followed in May. The judges were strict and "would not indulge the least favor to the corporations."[54]

Salisbury capitulated quickly enough that no proceedings on its quo warranto were required in King's Bench.[55] But informations brought against nine towns moved forward in Hilary term 1688, and against another thirty-three in Easter term. Twenty-seven Welsh corporations were attacked as well.[56] Most apparently surrendered when assaulted, remembering well the lesson Charles taught them about quo warranto a few years earlier. A few refused, though they would not be so bold in the end as to appear in court to answer the informations against them. Nonetheless, five English corporations and twenty Welsh ones preferred to die at the hands of the law than by their own surrender: their liberties were seized after judgments against them on default of appearance.[57] With Heneage Finch

---

53 H. W. Gidden, ed., *The Charters of the Borough of Southampton*, Publications of the Southampton Record Society, vol. 2 (Southampton, 1910), pp. 166–67n.
54 Luttrell, *Brief Historical Relation*, vol. I, pp. 429, 431, and 439.
55 No mention of Salisbury is found in PRO, KB21/23.
56 In Hilary term: Bishop's Castle, Bridgnorth, Dorchester, Lymington, Monmouth, Queenborough, Southampton, Much Wenlock, and Weymouth. In Easter: Andover, Appleby, Brackley, Buckingham, Colchester, Derby, Doncaster, Dunwich, Godmanchester, Grantham, Gravesend, Grimsby, Harwich, Hereford, Hertford, Hull, Ipswich, Kirby Kendal, Lincoln, Macclesfield, Marlborough, Morpeth, Okehampton, Portsmouth, Ripon, South Molton, Stamford, Tamworth, Thetford, Torrington, Wilton, Winchester, and York. See PRO, KB21/23, ff. 99v, 104v, and 105 for these lists. For the Welsh towns, see ibid., ff. 108v, 109, 112v, and 119v.
57 The five English corporations were Colchester, Hertford, Marlborough, Morpeth, and Southampton. Ibid., ff. 114, 115, and 131.

the younger and Sir Robert Sawyer having resigned as solicitor and attorney generals, a new pair now oversaw the process. Sir Thomas Powys served as attorney general, but it was none other than the champion of Chester's chartered liberties – the recently knighted Sir William Williams – who appears to have led the attack on the charters as solicitor general.

Exeter's charter of March 1688 was the first charter since Gravesend's a year earlier. Two clauses reveal vividly how the King's purposes in granting charters had changed. The first was a new royal power over corporation membership, a power not only to remove, but to appoint as well. Now the corporations would have no choice but to obey the King's orders naming new members. The other was the *non obstante* clause, a dispensation to all present and future corporation members from taking the oaths of allegiance or supremacy, subscribing the declaration against the Covenant, and from obtaining a certificate confirming receipt of the sacrament according to the rites of the Church of England.[58] In short, it was a full permission to Catholics and dissenters to enter the corporations without equivocation or fear of subsequent removal. All thirty-four charters granted after Exeter's until September 1688 contained these two critical provisions; most made no other changes in the corporations' constitutions. A handful of charters did something else new: they changed the parliamentary franchise, narrowing it to the corporation only, a body whose political tendencies could easily be controlled by the King's new power to remove and appoint at will.[59] It was a clear demonstration that James, unlike his brother, would use new charters to shape the Commons to his liking.

Totnes's charter followed Exeter's and more passed in July, but the bulk of James's new charters were granted in August and September 1688.[60] Woodstock had received a quo warranto in January and agreed immediately and unanimously that "a full submission be made." Their charter of August 27, 1688 removed thirteen old members, including the recorder, and appointed eighteen new ones. Only four newly named to the corporation possessed the traditional political and social qualities necessary for election to the corporation again after 1688. But unlike most, Woodstock's 1688 charter did not name a flock of dissenters and Catholics: all sworn on September 3 took the oaths of allegiance and supremacy, and subscribed

---

[58] *CSPD 1687–89*, pp. 160–61. The first *non obstante* clause appeared in the charter of the Distillers' Company in August 1687. Ibid., pp. 54–55.

[59] The following warrants restricted franchises: Newcastle upon Tyne, Woodstock, Barnstaple, Boston, Bridport, Grantham, Hull, Ipswich, Leicester, Marlborough, Norwich, Poole, Southampton, Taunton, Brackley, and Grimsby. *CSPD 1687–89*, pp. 229, 238, 259, 262–64, 268–70, 274, and 275. But the final charters for Hull, Grantham, and Colchester did not contain the provision. Boyle, *Charters to Hull*, pp. 219–55. Martin, *Charters of Grantham*, pp. 214–33. *Charters [of Colchester]*, pp. 149–69.

[60] *CSPD 1687–89*, pp. 182–83. See below, Appendix A.

the declaration against the Covenant, despite the charter's explicit dispensation from doing so.[61] Three named in the charter did not take their oaths as new members, perhaps aware that their affiliation with religious groups that for so long had put them outside the political nation would make it difficult for them to serve now. In all, thirty-one towns received new charters in August and September. About two-thirds went to towns that had already been purged extensively, thus suggesting how new charters were now required in the face of the failure of purges to produce pliable corporations.[62]

Hull surrendered its hard won 1685 charter in June 1688 after a quo warranto was entered against them. The new charter appointed Daniel Hoar as mayor, the same man who had been the object of such controversy after the Privy Council's enquiry into the enforcement of the Corporation Act in 1680 and who had later been imprisoned on suspicion of disloyalty. Only two of the thirteen aldermen serving at the time of surrender in June remained in the corporation by the charter granted in September; two of those now appointed had been ejected from the corporation by the 1685 charter; the others were complete newcomers.[63] Thus the charter did not simply rely on bringing back those who lost favor earlier in the 1680s. It also relied on persons with no political experience at all. In town after town, the new charters of 1688 repeated the personnel changes made by the removals and appointments of the regulators, dismissing tories admitted by the charters of 1682 to early 1687, and appointing dissenters and Catholics who had never held office and others who had been dismissed from corporate places for their lack of fitness as long ago as the Restoration.[64]

Charters were used to make up for the increasingly evident shortcomings of the regulators' purges. The Privy Council had sent orders to Barnstaple in December 1687 and January 1688 directing the removal of twenty-three of the corporation's twenty-five members, as well as the recorder, deputy recorder, and town clerk.[65] But the corporation showed little compliance. Edward Roberts, a Devon regulator, wrote to the mayor that he was "informed of the perverse temper of several of your magistrates." He

---

[61] Woodstock Town Hall, 76/2, January 18 and 20, and September 3, 1688. *CSPD 1687–89*, p. 229. Woodstock's records mention a quo warranto against them. Their quick surrender may have obviated the need for any proceedings on the information, as no mention of the quo warranto was made in King's Bench. PRO, KB21/23.

[62] The eleven towns receiving new charters that had not been purged previously were: Bishop's Castle, Brackley, Gravesend, Grimsby, Hertford, Marlborough, Morpeth, Queenborough, Southampton, Tamworth, and Woodstock.

[63] On Hoar, see above, pp. 128–30. Boyle, *Charters to Hull*, pp. 219–21n.

[64] Bridport's charter removed eleven and appointed all those still living who had been removed by the corporation commissioners in 1662. Short, *A Respectable Society*, p. 26.

[65] PRO, PC2/72/65 and 81v.

threatened the corporation with dissolution and explained that a new charter would go "to those that will pay more reverence and obedience to his majesty's commands."[66] In May, Roberts sent a royal order dismissing the entire corporation and directing the late mayor to consult with regulators about negotiating a new charter. This order was disregarded too.[67] But other more pliable inhabitants petitioned for a new charter and were granted one. The new body included only nine from the old one while adding fifteen new members.[68] Other corporations were dissolved and simply not reincorporated, as at Winchester and Oxford, where the corporations were replaced by governments appointed under special royal commissions.[69] Warwick and Norwich corporations were dissolved after neglecting the King's orders for electing new members. But before work on Warwick's new charter could be completed, the King had reversed his policy.[70]

Like most of the nineteen corporations whose new charters passed the great seal on September 15, 1688, Hull's new corporation never acted.[71] When judicial business was done there later that month, the old bench presided. After that, no affairs were conducted until the old corporation restored itself on November 6.[72] In August, the Privy Council had sent to Chester an order for the removal of virtually the entire corporation. Unsurprisingly, the corporation did not simply quit.[73] A new charter followed on September 15, and was read there one month later, but "none of the company seemed to approve of it; they discoursed of petitioning for their old charter."[74] The charter left out twelve of those appointed under Chester's 1685 charter; three dismissed in 1685 would have served again by

---

[66] Chanter and Wainwright, *Barnstaple Records*, vol. I, p. 76. Regulators who visited sometime shortly before had reported that the corporation only elected some of those named by the King, and otherwise elected persons of their own choosing. Duckett, *Penal Laws and Test Act*, pp. 231–32.

[67] Chanter and Wainright, *Barnstaple Records*, vol. I, p. 77, and PRO, PC2/72/121v.

[68] *CSPD 1687–89*, pp. 221, 261, 265–66, and 275.

[69] Luttrell, *Brief Historical Relation*, vol. I, pp. 438 and 445. The Oxford commission is at PRO, C231/8/193–94.

[70] Luttrell, *Brief Historical Relation*, vol. I, p. 461. Warwick had foreseen the end, voting less than three weeks before to turn corporation lands over to feoffees on a 100-year lease to protect their properties from the perils of dissolution. Styles, "Warwick," pp. 38–39. A warrant was passed, but no charter followed, the King's policy having changed before it could. *CSPD 1687–89*, pp. 271–72.

[71] R. H. George too found little sign that many charters were ever implemented, though many were received in the towns concerned: "The Charters Granted to English Parliamentary Corporations in 1688," *EHR*, 55 (1940), p. 55.

[72] But Daniel Hoar did gain hold of the corporation's records, and as the "late mayor," had to be asked to relinquish them. Boyle, *Charters to Hull*, pp. 221–22n.

[73] PRO, PC2/72/149. No mention was made of the order at an assembly meeting on the 23rd of that month. CCRO, AB/3, ff. 16–17v.

[74] Whitley Diary, f. 97v. The warrant for the charter is in *CSPD 1687–89*, pp. 256–57.

the 1688 grant. But no one ever acted under that charter: the established body showed no signs of relinquishing its control, either in answer to royal removal orders or to new letters patent. Two blank pages followed in the assembly book before meetings resumed again in January.[75]

Leicester's September 1688 charter reveals something about James's intentions. Earlier that year, 70% of the corporation had already lost their places by removal orders, but the King wanted more. The new charter admitted another twenty-three newcomers to the body of sixty-one. Nine were known dissenters, having been prosecuted for non-attendance at church; others probably were as well. Two had been dismissed by the corporation commissioners in 1662. Two others had been removed by the Privy Council earlier in the year but were now returned, while eighteen of those appointed earlier in 1688 were not named to the new body, again suggesting the difficulty throughout 1688 of finding persons amenable to the King's intentions.[76] Those appointed, consisting of hosiers, butchers, and smiths, were noticeably more humble than the mercers and chandlers of Leicester's traditional leadership. Only sixteen had once held or would again hold corporate office: religious identity and social station put them outside the political nation. The personnel list in Leicester's charter showed clearly the quality of the royal program, characterized as it was by repeat efforts, each unsure of the success of the last, putting in and throwing out with little heed to how such dealings might affect the loyalties of individuals and the communities they were meant to lead. Apparently no one in Leicester felt these were people who should govern for the charter was never implemented.

By early September 1688, corporate governance nationwide was rumbling along awkwardly; in many places, especially those sent new charters, it ceased altogether. Word came in from around the country of the reluctance of the few old leaders left untouched by James's purges to act with those he appointed to fill the remade corporations, and even of the reluctance of many of those the King now favored to join in what they apparently saw as his hopeless task.[77] As late as September 9, removal orders issued to fifteen towns, including one to York expelling the lord mayor and forty-four others. Letters recommending parliamentary candidates to various towns went forth from the Earl of Sunderland in the King's name on the 21st.[78] But by then, consideration was being given to

---

[75] CCRO, AB/3, f. 18.   [76] *CSPD 1687–89*, pp. 263–64.

[77] For instance at Banbury, the two corporation members who survived a purge in September refused to act with the new members. Gibson and Brinkworth, *Banbury Records*, p. 244.

[78] For these last removal orders of September 9, see PRO, PC2/72/154–55. The last of Sunderland's recommendations of parliamentary candidates went to Droitwich on September 21: *CSPD 1687–89*, p. 279.

proposals for rolling back the King's efforts to recreate local government. On the 22nd, Sunderland wrote the Duke of Berwick asking for names of those deputy lieutenants and JPs recently removed from their places who should be considered for reappointment. It was the first sign that those around the King had miscalculated the effectiveness of the union they had tried to forge with provincial dissenters and Catholics, and that they now saw the wisdom of turning back to the crown's alienated natural supporters.[79]

By month's end, strong advice came from regional grandees calling for a restoration of the corporations. The Earl of Bath wrote unabashedly of how pleased Cornish gentlemen were with the King's decision to restore the county's JPs and deputy lieutenants; now he recommended the same correction for the towns. Bath complained bitterly of the work of local regulators, especially Edward Nosworthy, whose activities touched Bath's dignity as much as the towns'. In early October, the Earl settled nerves in the towns while he entreated the King, via Sunderland, to "return [them] to their ancient course."

The late regulators themselves have presented an easy method for doing this, with the difference that the corporations may be settled with half the trouble they were disturbed, for if his majesty grant his order in council to turn out persons illegally put in, there will be no need of a mandamus to direct the choice of new members, but it may be left to the corporations to choose.

Exeter, as the region's principal city, and its most divided, needed amendment the most. The powerful cathedral interest there, so ready to show its loyalty to the King, had stood mortified when the corporation's leaders were turned out in favor of dissenters. The changes stupefied townsmen too, who watched the mayor's sword "carried every Sunday before the mayor in state to a conventicle."[80] Bath knew that only the week before he wrote, the King had approved a warrant restoring London's privileges, which, Secretary of State Lord Middleton suggested, had "in a great measure defeated any designs against him."[81] These were telling words, expressing the sense of one of the King's close advisors that James had painted himself into a corner by early autumn 1688, and revealing Middleton's awareness that the only way to open more room for maneuver was by reversing the changes in borough personnel the King had been commanding just three weeks earlier. What London had gained, Exeter and all other towns would require too if James were to settle the land.

[79] *CSPD 1687–89*, p. 280. See also Glassey, *Politics and the Justices of the Peace*, pp. 94–99.
[80] *CSPD 1687–89*, pp. 304–05. See also ibid., pp. 286–87. Bath's reference to a "mandamus" makes use of the term in the general sense – a royal order – rather than in its specific legal sense, referring to the writ from King's Bench.
[81] BL 41,823, f. 77. *CSPD 1687–89*, p. 296.

Many, like Sir Henry Beaumont, a Leicestershire gentleman whose loyalty had prompted him reluctantly to assist preparations for parliamentary elections, suggested "that old friends may still do good service."[82] A similar report came from Hertford, where the corporation had been voided by a quo warranto judgment the previous spring. By mid-August, Hertford's new charter had been granted, though at least one correspondent there was under the impression that it had "not yet passed all the offices, and the old one [still remains] in the hands of either Mr. Brent, or Mr. Solicitor Williams . . . and [is] as yet uncancelled." Thus, he hoped, the previous charter and corporation might be resurrected. After all, "the late aldermen are all loyal, sensible men, and very willing to serve his Majesty." Such men, if restored to power and released from serving with "false brethren," would certainly help the King again.[83] From York, Sir John Reresby wrote Sunderland that some of those recently removed from the aldermancy were more likely to serve the King than those who were to replace them. "It is the opinion of most there that to restore the old charter [then under threat of quo warranto] and the old aldermen would be the best expedient."[84] But before this letter could reach the King's chief advisor, James had decided to respond to "complaints of great abuses and irregularities committed in the late regulations of the corporations." He ordered the lord lieutenants on October 9 to investigate such abuses. The Duke of Norfolk reported the "universal satisfaction" the King's order produced in Norfolk.[85] James may have appointed dissenters and Catholics to the formalities of power, but their position had been utterly untenable as long as the opinion among England's traditional local leadership leaned so heavily against them.

Reality fell hard and fast on the King in late September and early October, waking him from reveries in which he had envisioned acceptance of the Catholic faith by a nation that reviled it as a superstition productive of tyranny. On October 17, James at last dismantled the policy he had pursued so vigorously over the last twelve months, issuing a proclamation canceling all borough charters granted not only during his reign, but as far back as 1679. James thus undid his remodelings and those of his brother too. Charters previously held by the scores of towns rechartered since 1679

82 Hastings Letters, 670.
83 Hertfordshire RO, Hertford Borough Records, vol. 30, #46. For the judgment against Hertford on quo warranto, see PRO, KB21/23/114. They petitioned for a new charter in May, a warrant passed in early August, and the new charter was granted on the 27th of that month: *CSPD 1687–89*, pp. 204 and 246–47; PRO, IND1/4228/128.
84 *CSPD 1687–89*, p. 303. As a sign of how quickly things changed after James's October 17 proclamation, on October 30, York would actually win on the quo warranto against it. PRO, KB21/23/140.
85 *CSPD 1687–89*, pp. 306 and 316, and Hastings Letters, 7165.

were to be restored, except in those few cases where surrenders of previous charters had been enrolled in Chancery. All officers removed from their places in the past nine years, whether by new charters or royal orders, were restored.[86] It was the single most sweeping gesture toward the towns since the Restoration, affecting more towns more quickly than any other royal decision. As such, it marks one of the quickest, most complete policy reversals of that or any reign. But it came too late.

Erstwhile members of decimated corporations acted quickly to reconstitute themselves according to the proclamation. Cambridge corporation reestablished itself without incident on the 22nd; Kingston upon Thames did the same five days later. All in both towns again subscribed the declaration against the Covenant, a telling demonstration of the religious/political loyalties of the restored order. Devizes acted on the 22nd: only three out of twenty-eight from the Jacobean body now remained. Hertford sought the advice of Henry Pollexfen who advised them to revert to their former condition, as if no charter had been granted to them two months earlier.[87] Leicester's old corporation reconstituted itself on October 20 by taking all the oaths the King had so recently been at pains to discard. Thomas Ludlam presided at the meeting as mayor *pro tempore*; he was perfect for the delicate job, possessing the social and political qualifications that made him one of the town's leaders, unlike the men James had tried to foist on Leicester in his abortive charter of September. Ludlam's final act, after overseeing the expulsion of the interlopers imposed on them in recent years, was to conduct the election of a new mayor. The town's bells rang in celebration as William Bentley, a man equal to Ludlam in political experience and social prominence, assumed the mayor's chair and as his brethren retook their proper places around him.[88]

Autumn elections had already occurred in some towns. This could produce awkward results as old corporation members insisted on acting on the King's proclamation. At Northampton, the mayor elected in late September refused to hand over the keys to the town hall. Erstwhile members anxious to reseize their places broke down the doors and elected another mayor. Restoration of the old body followed a few weeks later.[89]

[86] PRO, PC2/72/161v–63.
[87] Cambridgeshire RO, Shelf C/9, pp. 132–37. Surrey RO, KB1/1, pp. 129–30. Wiltshire RO, G20/1/19, unfol.: October 12 and 22, 1688. Hertfordshire RO, Hertford Borough Records, vol. 1, #52.
[88] Leicestershire RO, BRII/18/36, f. 107. John Nichols, *The History and Antiquities of the County of Leicester*, 4 vols. (London, 1795–1815), vol. I, p. 438. Thomas North, ed., *The Accounts of the Churchwardens of St. Martin's, Leicester, 1489–1844* (Leicester, 1884), p. 213.
[89] Bod., MS Top. Northants. c.9, p. 129. This source says John Selby was elected mayor on October 26. Northamptonshire RO, 3/2, p. 310, says Selby's election came at the meeting on November 8, when the rest of the corporation reconstituted itself.

At Coventry, where a dissenter had been chosen mayor the day before James's proclamation, new elections were held nine days later by the restored body, producing a predictably different result.[90]

Lichfield corporation restored itself on October 27, but also took care to ask the King to give his approbation to their choice of a new town clerk.[91] The eagerness of the corporations to undo the damage wrecked upon them by their King did not mean they were ready to abandon the deference due to their sovereign or to neglect the terms of their legal charters. Thus it was with considerable trepidation that corporators around the country received reports of the progress of the fleet of William, the Prince of Orange. Days before the Prince arrived at Torbay, just west of Exeter, that city's corporation restored "the old loyal civil magistrates . . . to their ancient charter," according to James's proclamation. Thousands of citizens cheered when they saw the city sword borne before the restored mayor to the cathedral. The Earl of Bath reported that even many dissenters were pleased to see the world thus righted.[92] Rejoicing quickly turned to worry when news came that Dutch troops were on the road to the city. The old corporation was ready to do what it could with limited resources, but "the common people are so prejudiced with the late regulations, and so much corrupted, that there can be no dependence at present on the militia" to support the King.[93] James's proclamation, while it restored the corporations, and with it the hearts of many regaining former offices, had failed to demonstrate a complete transformation of his intentions to the broader populace, which now went on an anti-Catholic rampage in many towns.[94] It was not long before reports came from Exeter that "for conquered people, we are pretty well used." But the mayor and aldermen would not violate the oaths of allegiance and supremacy they had sworn to the King and Church, though that same King had done all he could to undermine the purpose and meaning of the obligations signified by those oaths.[95]

A few corporations continued to conduct regular business throughout the turbulent months of November and December 1688 and January 1689, as at Kingston upon Thames, where they met frequently to approve leases and pass accounts.[96] But in most towns, common affairs were laid aside to see to the appointment of watches and the mustering of militias. Corporate life momentarily halted – for instance at Ipswich, which had an unusual three-month hiatus in meetings – as members waited anxiously to see the

[90] Hurwich, "'A Fanatick Town'," p. 27.   [91] BL, Egerton 3348, f. 90.
[92] BL, Add. 41,805, ff. 118–19.   [93] Ibid., f. 129.
[94] Newdigate LC, 1944 and 1946.   [95] BL, Add. 41,805, f. 207.
[96] Surrey RO, KB1/1, pp. 131–40. Bath did as well: Bath City RO, Council Book 3, passim.

outcome of events unfolding around them.[97] At Chester, conflict erupted between troops in the castle and the city militia when the former attempted to take up the posts manned by the citizen soldiers. Their neighbors came to join them, "the streets full of the rabble." By mid-December, area gentlemen declared for the Prince and the Protestant religion and thus put an end to such tussles.[98] By then, towns around the country had decided to quit their support of a King who had now quit the country. The revolution in the corporations was complete.

IGNORING PARTISAN VERITIES

The revolution of 1688 in the towns was a true revolution in the seventeenth-century sense of the word, a full turning of the wheel of political change. It was the last of three revolutions that had rolled with devastating effect through the corporations since 1682. First, in the charters of Charles II, hundreds had been expelled from their old places and over 100 borough constitutions rewritten. Then came the most devastating turn, James's undoing of what Charles had accomplished, again reworking corporate charters and removing members by the thousands. By messing with measures *and* men – by promoting religious toleration *and* by rejecting hundreds of England's natural local leaders – James did more than anyone to propel the third and final revolution. The alienation his removals and charters created in 1688 was so powerful that even he could not ignore it; nor could he correct for that alienation by his belated proclamation of October 17. This was only the start of the last revolution that brought a fractious combination of whigs and tories back to local power in a restoration of the partisan political order predating the surrenders of the early 1680s. This final revolution was finished as old corporations reconstituted themselves and then stood aside while the nation, and an invader, expelled their anointed King.

Reaction to James's policies had been hostile throughout 1687 and 1688 and only grew more so with each passing month. The King could exert enormous pressure on the towns through the powers left to him in the charters of Charles II and by granting new charters. But this power did not give James the support of corporate governors or enable him to create an urban leadership that would do his bidding. J. R. Jones's suggestion of corporate complicity in James's measures – "the municipalities had become

---

[97] Suffolk RO (Ipswich Branch), C6/1/7, pp. 148–50. Winchester corporation lay dormant for nine months: Hampshire RO, W/B1/7, ff. 35v–37.

[98] Ever touchy about their independence, Whitley reported that "the mayor and city refused [the gentry's address to William]; [they] resolved to address (as they had acted) apart." Whitley Diary, ff. 99v and 100v.

dependents of the crown . . . the situation in most towns was socially as well as governmentally more favorable to royal intervention" than in the counties – fails to convince when we consider the obstruction James faced in the towns.[99] Certainly, some had gone along, especially at first. At Bedford, removals in March and April had led to a corporation address thanking the King for his Declaration of Indulgence. But when it came time for elections in September, those chosen took the oaths of allegiance and supremacy and subscribed the declaration against the Covenant, proclaiming their adherence to the government in church and state that James tried so hard to undermine.[100] The idea of corporate willingness to help James sounds even less convincing when we consider the hesitation of many of those promoted by his measures to join in them. The success of James's effort was predicated on the ability of men from the social, political, and religious margins to become local leaders overnight. Many shied away from the challenge, aware of the impossibility of such a transformation.

Jones was certainly right though to note that "of all domestic policies, the campaign to pack Parliament was easily the most important in provoking the Revolution, more resented and feared than even the attack on the Church and its leaders."[101] And nowhere did that campaign have such a comprehensive effect as in the nation's boroughs. James's efforts represented the broadest attack on corporate privileges and personnel at any time since 1660. Following on his brother's reign, a time when so many policies, like the commissions of association, were more convincing in theory than in implementation, James's policies were enacted with extraordinary energy and success. The irony then is that it was precisely this success in making good on policy pronouncements that proved James's undoing. His ability to remove over 2,000 corporation members in less than a year, to name their replacements, and to pass dozens of new charters, marks a singular bureaucratic achievement. Perhaps if he had been less efficient in purging the corporations, he may have been more successful in his kingdom at large.

In forcing surrenders and granting new charters in the last years of his reign, Charles II manipulated partisan realities to his advantage. By rewarding the group that represented the prevailing temper of the age, he made for himself a powerful alliance with thousands of local leaders eager to support crown and Church. James defied the political truths that made his brother's efforts so successful. Using the strength of his religious convictions, James took hold of each end of the political spectrum and tried

[99] Jones, *Revolution of 1688*, p. 137.
[100] Mullett, "'Deprived of our Former Place'," pp. 29–33.
[101] Jones, *Revolution of 1688*, pp. 129–30.

to bend it into a perfect circle so that the poles nearly touched; he attempted to bring tory passive obedience at one extreme together with dissent motivated by hopes of toleration at the other. But tories were also motivated by loyalty to their Church; this ultimately took precedence over obedience to their King as his measures became too strong for their stomachs. For their part, many dissenters worried about acting with those who only a few years before had so vigorously persecuted them. Neither could work with the other. As Leicestershire tory Sir Henry Beaumont put it, "it is plain there is false brothers with fanatics."[102] In dissenters' and tories' mutual dislike, the corporate governments that James tried to create by uniting opposites either never came into being, or fell apart under the pressures of 1688. Once James's resolve broke in October, the two immediately sprang back to their natural polar positions. Little wonder too that after the old corporations reconstituted themselves, they then stood aside while the nation, and an invader, expelled a King whose health they had drunk so loyally in 1685.

Revolution brought back the old alignments, the partisan verities that Charles had used so well, but which James had ignored to his undoing. These verities had been created in the years since the Restoration and hardened in the early 1680s. Political developments in the corporations in the 1690s and beyond, constantly interpreted in terms of events of the 1680s, underscored these truths. Partisan fortunes and allegiances in the 1690s would depend a good deal on where one had been and what one had done in the 1680s, just as one's fate in the early 1660s had depended in large part on where one had been in the 1650s: as always, tomorrow's purges looked back to yesterday's for guidance. James had attempted to destroy these verities in his effort to reshape the nation's political/religious temper, manipulating passive obedience to weaken the Church, and the "factious" to strengthen the crown. But their mutual repulsion was far too strong for James to counter; all his efforts in 1688, far from closing the gap between competing sides, only made it wider when corporation politics as usual resumed at the end of the year.

[102] Hastings Letters, 667.

Part Three

PARTISAN CONFLICT AND THE LAW IN A DYNAMIC SOCIETY

8

The legacy of the 1680s

Dunwich had been falling into the North Sea for centuries. By the 1690s, the once bustling borough was a quiet backwater. But Dunwich had a long, proud history of incorporation, and controlling the corporation meant controlling the choice of two members of the House of Commons. For a handful of residents and Suffolk gentlemen, Dunwich politics proved worthy of the most strenuous efforts.

Like the ocean eating away at the sandy bluffs on Dunwich's shore, events of the 1680s crashed again and again on the corporation, leaving nothing but wreckage behind by late 1688. Though the corporation decided to fight the quo warranto brought against them in 1684, they soon thought better of it and surrendered their charter to Charles II and gained a new one not long after he died. According to the power given him by that charter, James II purged most of the new body in 1688. Then, because Dunwich's was one of the few surrenders enrolled in Chancery, it did not benefit from James's proclamation of October 17, 1688, which restored most of England's corporations to their earlier condition. Instead, in one of his last acts as King, James made a special order for Dunwich, dismissing those he had appointed there earlier in the year, and commanding the pre-surrender corporation to reconstitute itself. This they did, and by year's end, it looked as if Dunwich had recovered its fragile status quo ante.[1]

Only weeks later, current and former corporators divided against each other. Elections to the Convention Parliament produced a double return: Sir Philip Skippon and Sir Robert Rich were ultimately seated instead of Roger North and Sir Thomas Allin. Rich, a committed Presbyterian, would sit for Dunwich throughout the decade. Skippon, also inclined toward dissent, died in 1691. Replacing him would produce another contest, with Henry Heveningham prevailing. Whig control of Dunwich's parliamentary seats after 1689 depended on the support of the non-

---

[1] HMC, *Various Collections*, vol. VII, pp. 103–04. Suffolk RO (Ipswich Branch), EE6/1144/13, f. 64. PRO, PC2/72/132, 138, and 186. For personnel in the 1685 charter, see *CSPD 1685*, p. 15.

resident freemen.[2] But the real contentions were fought within the corporation itself, or between what might be better described as two groups, each claiming to be the corporation. Contests were joined to control possession of the town's records. Dismissals from the assembly soon followed. One ousted alderman went so far as to use his power as deputy vice admiral of Suffolk in an unsuccessful effort to impress a current alderman into their majesties' navy.[3]

The competing groups, one composed largely of freemen, many non-resident, and the other currently controlling the corporation, then battled over the charter. Those comprising the current corporation still acted by virtue of James II's charter, since it appeared that neither his proclamation of October 17, nor his separate order for Dunwich, had actually restored their previous charter. But plenty of former corporation members thought there might be a good case for gaining a new charter or a restoration of their old one. In August of 1692, this group consulted the attorney and solicitor generals. Their reply was heartening: the old corporation existed by right of prescription, and persisted still. Based on this understanding, these freemen petitioned the King and Queen for a renewal of their charter of James I. A counter-petition soon followed from the "Bailiffs, Aldermen, and Burgesses of Dunwich" – the name of the corporation by the charter of James II – claiming that they were the legally constituted corporation and thus that no renewal charter should be allowed. As was the common course in such matters, the Privy Council referred the matter to the attorney and solicitor generals, who reported that though the charter of James I had been surrendered in 1684, and the surrender had been enrolled, the old corporation subsisted still because the surrender had been made to Charles II, but it had not been enrolled until after his death. James II's charter, based on a void surrender, was thus void itself. All that remained was to grant a charter that would confirm that of James I.[4]

Dunwich started afresh: the pre-surrender corporation, reborn by a new charter, appointed a clerk to make entries in a new assembly book. But the defunct corporation embodied by James II's late charter continued on as if nothing had happened. They retained the old assembly books, and duly entered the names of those they now removed for refusing to come to the meetings of their deceased body. The new corporation responded in kind, dismissing from their ranks those who pretended the corporation of James II lived on. For another year, the two bodies continued their competing

---

[2] Henning, vol. I, pp. 398–400, vol. II, pp. 541–42, and vol. III, pp. 154–56, 328–29, and 435–36.
[3] HMC, *Various Collections*, vol. VII, p. 105. PRO, PC2/75/2.
[4] BL, MS Add. 34,653, f. 136. PRO, PC2/75/279, 289, 294, 300, 306, 318, and 326. PRO, IND1/4228, f. 186v. *CSPD 1694–95*, pp. 18 and 91–92.

claims to rule Dunwich.[5] The schism culminated in October of 1695 with two choices of MPs. The "Bailiffs, Aldermen, and Burgesses" of the old corporation, along with the resident freemen, returned Roger Wood and John Bence. The old corporators then "openly made protestation against any other corporation or charter than what the bailiffs and aldermen acted under and against all proceedings by any other party on such pretence." Such protests meant little. At the same time, the corporation by the 1694 charter made a unanimous choice of Rich and Heveningham, and they were seated by the Commons.[6] The matter of who controlled the corporation, and who controlled the choice of MPs, was now settled. Rich and Heveningham held their seats for the rest of the decade. James II's corporation disappeared at last. Further complaints in the coming years would be settled by mandamus.[7]

A number of things stand out about Dunwich's troubles, revealing both what was new about corporate conflict after 1688, and what endured from before. First, as in many towns after 1688, corporate contests at Dunwich in large part concerned winning parliamentary contests. Gaining the new charter in 1694 meant being able to determine the outcome of the vote the following year. Indeed, Dunwich politics was tied tightly to politics in two other small boroughs nearby – Aldeburgh and Orford – as competing whig and tory groups tried to capture corporate control in the interest of controlling seats in the Commons.[8] After 1688, the connection between corporate contests and parliamentary contests would strengthen, though, as before, controlling the corporations remained a prize in and of itself. Second, we see at Dunwich how conflicts were defined largely in terms of a legacy left from the 1680s. As in the 1660s, when England's corporators purged their foes according to sectarian divisions and partisan angers left over from preceding decades, corporators of the 1690s did the same, looking back to the 80s for justification for their retributive behavior. As a result of events in the 1680s, Dunwich's corporation faced real confusion

---

[5] Dunwich's two assembly books – indicating the corporation's division – overlap from August 1694 to October 1695. They are Suffolk RO (Ipswich Branch), EE6/1144/13 (old register), and EE6/1144/14 (new register). See also EE6/1144/23/5. Henning, vol. III, p. 154. HMC, *Various Collections*, vol. VII, pp. 105–06.

[6] HMC, *Various Collections*, vol. VII, pp. 105–06. Henning, vol. II, p. 541 and vol. III, p. 328. Luttrell, *Brief Historical Relation*, vol. IV, p. 14. Apparently, earlier in 1695, the old corporation had begun an unsuccessful legal action asserting their right, which Rich helped to block. Folger Shakespeare Library, X.d.451 (131): Rich Papers.

[7] These concerned the restoration of a freeman in 1698, the restoration in 1701 of the town clerk removed in 1695, and the recovery of records and insignia in 1699. PRO, KB21/25/150v and 156v; KB21/26/39; and KB29/357/49 and 97v. Suffolk RO (Ipswich Branch), EE6/1144/14: July 9, 1698 and April 12, 1701. HMC, *Various Collections*, vol. VII, p. 106.

[8] Patricia E. Murrell, "Suffolk: The Political Behavior of the County and its Parliamentary Boroughs from the Exclusion Crisis to the Accession of the House of Hanover" (Ph.D., University of Newcastle upon Tyne, 1982), especially chapters 5 and 6.

about their legal status; related to this were questions about who properly governed there. The people of Dunwich were by no means alone. They were not alone in the use one side made of a new charter to purge their foes. And they were not alone in the failure of the new charter to settle a permanent peace.

The paradox of partisan politics operated as powerfully as ever after 1688. In Dunwich, this meant that those dismembered by the grant of a new charter simply behaved as if nothing had changed. Even when they dropped their pretence of being the corporation, contentions within the legal body continued. Thus we also see at Dunwich the crucial role King's Bench continued to play in the towns by granting writs of mandamus to restore those wrongly removed. More important, the court was expanding its use of the writ. Not only did mandamus restore. At Dunwich, mandamus commanded the transfer of records between officers; elsewhere it compelled the holding of elections. In a 1690s political environment charged by contests referring back to the 1680s, and with the rising political stakes that accompanied an increase in the number of elections to Parliament, King's Bench would become more important than ever. And though Parliament, and especially elections to it, would be a major part of the problem of partisan competition, Parliament would also be part of the solution as its members began to discover the power of legislation to assist King's Bench in making a dynamic political culture a stable one too.

1689–90: THE STRUGGLE TO DEFINE THE 1680S

First the surrenders and charters of Charles II, then the removals and charters of James II, all ostensibly erased by the royal proclamation of October 17, 1688: nothing but legal confusion remained in the corporations, despite the ease and speed with which many restored themselves that autumn. Questions abounded about the legitimacy of the various charters corporations held and about the legal safety of their privileges. Boston corporation worried "that all those persons or corporations who lately made surrenders of their charters or any privileges thereunto belonging [would] . . . be accounted as betrayers of [their] privileges," and feared that the Prince of Orange would revoke their liberties.[9] Just as in 1660, the corporations had to be settled on firm legal ground. As in the 1660s, there would be competition in the towns, and at Westminster, to control the process of settlement. In 1688, whig and tory had momentarily been united by their bewilderment in the face of James II's measures. But in 1689 and 1690, they immediately reverted to their previous positions of mutual

---

[9] BL, Egerton 3336, ff. 146–7.

antagonism and struggled to control the process of explaining what had happened in the years just past, and defining who must now pay the political price for the perceived wrongs committed in those years.

The legislative struggle to settle the corporations began immediately in the Convention Parliament. William Sacheverell, leader of the group ousted by Nottingham's 1682 charter, promoted a bill to repeal the Corporation Act, piloting it through two readings at the same time a bill for religious comprehension wound through Parliament. The comprehension bill's champions hoped to broaden the Church by loosening the terms of participation in it; by trying to repeal the Corporation Act, they worked for a political comprehension too. The effects intended by these bills ran parallel: both would help open the corporations to those who balked at occasional conformity. But motions in the Commons to maintain the annual sacrament requirement in the Corporation Act repeal bill, and provisos in the Lords to prevent occasional conformity, killed such hopes. Churchmen worked to impose even more strictures, so that with or without the Corporation Act, access to the corporations would remain limited. Both the repeal bill and the comprehension effort failed and the statutory toleration granted in 1689 continued to deny dissenters citizenship in the political nation.[10]

Once again, the arrival of a new regime required new oaths. Local leaders swearing new oaths to new rulers had become something of a tradition in English political life. The oaths and declarations imposed since the 1640s, each canceling those that went before, were now rewritten by the "Act for abrogating the oaths of supremacy and allegiance and appointing other oaths" to ensure the adherence of England's governors to their new monarchs.[11] Failure to swear by August 1, 1689 would lead to automatic forfeiture of office. In addition to these new oaths, the Corporation Act's chief strictures remained: the declaration against the Covenant and the receipt of the sacrament. One still had to be in full communion with the established Church, or at least appear to be. Many evaded these provisions in the coming decades and served in countless corporations. With neither a clear proscription of occasional conformity, nor a lifting of the ban on the political participation of dissenters, conflict continued in the corporations over the membership of those occupying the gray area between Church and dissent.

Both Lords and Commons considered further the problems left by the turmoil of the 1680s. The Lords appointed a committee to investigate who promoted the quo warrantos and served as James's regulators. The deposi-

---

[10] *CJ*, vol. 10, pp. 35, 43, and 74. Newdigate LC, 1981. Henry Horwitz, *Parliament, Policy, and Politics in the Reign of William III* (Newark, 1977), pp. 21–26.

[11] Stat. 1 William and Mary c. 8.

tions collected by the committee provide a catalogue of some of the leading players in the remodeling of corporations in the 1680s, but little was done with the information.[12] In the Commons, a proposal to form a committee "to consider of the violations of the liberties and franchises of all the corporations of this kingdom, and particularly of the City of London," passed in the negative. The House voted instead to refer the matter to the Committee of Grievances. Its report of March 5, 1689 concluded that the judgment in the London quo warranto, the regulation of the corporations 1687–88, and the use of the three questions, had been illegal. The Commons then appointed a corporations committee, which soon recommended that a bill be brought in to restore all "bodies politic and corporate" to their condition of May 29, 1660 in order to wipe out the entire Restoration legacy in the corporations.[13]

Various versions of a bill to restore corporations came and went throughout the spring and summer of 1689; another appeared at the end of October, winding its way through Parliament until the Christmas recess. Whig MPs made sure of their organization and appeared in strength after the adjournment, while many tories lingered in the country. Though the idea of undoing all done in the corporations since 1660 had been abandoned along the way, there was talk among the whigs of using the bill to abolish the sacramental test. But ending the test was not their greatest concern. Whig MPs worked quickly in early 1690 to add amendments to make the bill an instrument for the exclusion of corporate tories. On January 2, the Commons approved a "disabling clause" which would bar from office all those, who without consent of a corporate majority, consented to a surrender or solicited a quo warranto in the 1680s. Tories responded by trying to add their own exclusionary clause, disabling anyone who acted as a regulator in 1688, thereby imposing a prohibition hitting whigs as hard as the disabling of "surrenderers" would hit the tories. But the tory clause failed miserably in a division. The whigs then strengthened their disabling clause by striking out the phrase "without majority consent": anyone approving a surrender – even as part of a unanimous or majority vote – would be barred from office. Voting on the successive questions that day showed a well coordinated whig phalanx of approximately 130 votes; tory numbers dropped as candles came in and the evening wore on.[14] On January 10, with many tory members now back in

[12] *LJ*, vol. 14, pp. 331, 381–82, 384, 388, and 394. Horwitz, *Parliament, Policy, and Politics*, pp. 37–38. The Lords also asked the justices of the royal courts to prepare a bill "to regulate *non obstantes*," probably referring to the use of royal dispensations broadly, but perhaps intending as well the *non obstante* clauses in the charters of 1688. The *Journals of the House of Lords* make no other mention of the effort. *LJ*, vol. 14, p. 342.

[13] *CJ*, vol. 10, pp. 35, 41–42, and 51. Newdigate LC, 1983, 1989, 1997, and 2044.

[14] *CJ*, vol. 10, pp. 112, 119–20, 233, 277, 284, 302, 312–13, and 322–23.

town, the whigs' bill did not fare as well on its third reading. The proviso for displacing anyone who voted with a majority for surrender was now removed. Then the entire clause disabling all complicitous in the surrenders, often referred to as the "Sacheverell clause," for its sponsor, was struck from the bill. Twelve hours of debate and voting on the amendments had eviscerated the whigs' bill for excluding tories from the corporations.[15]

Each side now tried to capture the support of the extra-parliamentary audience as the bill went to the Lords. The author of *A Letter Concerning the Disabling Clauses* complained of the whigs' "design . . . industriously concealed," of proposing amendments recasting corporate membership when the House was "thin."[16] The author made clear the partisan nature of the struggle. Excluding those who supported the surrenders in Charles II's reign was a measure to exclude corporate tories; the tory amendment to expel James's regulators was meant to exact payment in kind, as most regulators were identified with whig interests. The analysis of the proposed bill's import drew on an explanation of recent history that tacitly accepted the fact of partisan division in the corporations that had become so clear in the 1680s. According to the *Letter's* author, charter surrenders had been required for "clearing up of the very unquiet and dangerous times; I mean, after my Lord Shaftesbury left England." Charles had behaved moderately, finding "no method so proper and justifiable as that of the law." Proceedings on quo warranto uncovered magisterial abuses in London and elsewhere, abuses for which the only proper response was seizure of corporate privileges so that the King could grant them again to those who would use them properly. By his charters, Charles corrected abuses, removed the ungrateful, forgave the contrite, and rewarded the good with new fairs, markets, and other advantages. Admittedly, some of the gentlemen and noblemen who assisted the King in these "reasonable proceedings" had twisted corporate arms to extract surrenders. But those corporation members who voted for surrenders should not be sacrificed by the proposed bill: "thus far the citizens and inhabitants of corporations, who dreamed not of the inconveniences of these proceedings, are excusable."[17] They acted not from malevolent intent, but out of loyalty to Church and King.

The real villains were not these loyal townsmen who surrendered in the early 1680s, but the "itinerant regulators" who promoted James's radical measures of 1687–88. Those targeted by the whigs' disabling clauses were

---

[15] Ibid., pp. 329–30. Horwitz, *Parliament, Policy, and Politics*, pp. 41–42. Jones, *Revolution of 1688*, pp. 323–24. On the debate's length, see *A Letter Concerning the Disabling Clauses, Lately Offered to the House of Commons, for Regulating Corporations* (London, 1690), p. 5.

[16] *A Letter Concerning the Disabling Clauses*, pp. 3–4.   [17] Ibid., pp. 6–7.

the same who had lost their places for their loyalty to the Protestant religion: "the whole Church of England party. For such they generally were, who consented to surrenders, and yet opposed the torrent of regulators."[18] Replacing them had been those who complied with James's subversive innovations: the whigs. Now the whiggish disabling clause threatened to remove the heroes of the 1680s, leaving the corporations in the hands of one party, "by the name of Dissenters."[19] The purely partisan intent of their disabling clause was evident in the whig refusal to impose the same fate on those complicitous with the regulators. To hide their motives, those promoting Sacheverell's disabling clause had applied new labels to describe the opposed parties: "consenters and non-consenters to surrenders of charters." This "revives a troublesome and scandalous faction which had formerly divided most great towns . . . for what can such a distinguishing character produce as consenter and non-consenter, but the perfection of whig and tory?"[20] The disabling clause recalled the party battles of the 1680s; if passed, those battles would be all the more fierce.

A nameless whig pamphleteer countered immediately with a mirror image of the recent past.[21] The author of *The True Friends to Corporations Vindicated* challenged his tory foe's bid to capture the spiritual/political high ground, condemning those "who usurp or engross to themselves the name of the Church of England Party and would make a faction of the National Church."[22] With venomous wit, the *True Friends'* author assaulted the historical analysis underlying tory thinking and rhetoric. The whig pamphlet challenged the idea that sacrificing ancient charters showed one's loyalty; it mocked "the grants of petty markets and fairs for hobbyhorses and ginger bread, or a mace or rattle for a mayor . . . in lieu of the people's rights of elections to Parliaments." Those who had not complied in trading their charters for such benefits had been "cast to the dogs, as dead in law" by the new charters. The acquiescent – "who would sell their Country for a little place and countenance, but in truth to make them such slaves as they desired, or deserved to be good loyal French Peasants with wooden shoes" – were promoted. Surely it was only by way of irony that the *Letter's* author suggested that those who foisted surrenders benefited the towns. Did they not force locks to get charters; did not tory

---

[18] Ibid., p. 10.
[19] On the lack of due process in such removals, see ibid., pp. 14–20. This recalls Prynne's argument against the Corporation Act in 1662, that those affected would lose their places without trial: see above, pp. 86–87.
[20] Ibid., p. 13.
[21] *The True Friends to Corporations Vindicated, in Answer to A Letter Concerning the Disabling Clauses Lately Offered to the House of Commons for Regulating Corporations* (London, 1690).
[22] Ibid., p. 18.

townsmen provide information for the quo warrantos? "Did a few never pretend to act in the name of the majority?"[23] The *True Friends'* author derided suggestions that the intervention of gentry in gaining charters was a favor and that those who complied only did so under threats from such mighty men. How could his tory foe square contentions that on the one hand, such gentlemen did a favor, and on the other, that most townsmen were to be excused for acting only under duress? The obedience of some townsmen to the vile intentions of certain gentlemen created the trouble in the corporations that the Commons' bill would now punish.

What of the regulators? The whig author suggested that James's regulators only erred because they obeyed their King, as any proponent of passive obedience should have them do. Anyway, the gentlemen of the "Church party" who promoted Charles's surrenders were actually the first regulators, as it was they who decided who would be in and out of the corporations by new charters in the early 1680s. Those same charters then gave James the power of removal that he used in 1688: "Alas! good people! [the tories'] eyes were never opened 'till the power they gave the court was turned against them." More telling, James's regulators had been aided in most corporations by their own tory members. James's removal orders had been supplemented with lists of persons the remaining members were to elect; many corporations, composed of loyal tories appointed in the charters of Charles II, complied in electing men recommended by the regulators in 1688.[24] Whether they did so reluctantly or not, their obedience made them complicitous in the work of the regulators. The whig pamphleteer had given a provocative but accurate reading of the recent past, and if applied to legislation, that reading could have a powerful impact on the future. With those active in the surrenders of 1682–85 exposed as the culprits, the disabling clause was entirely justified, according to the "True Friend" of corporations.

While the rhetorical struggle was joined in print, the corporations bill proceeded quickly through the Lords, who then asked the judges' advice on whether or not surrenders of charters were good in law. If in fact they were, how could those who promoted surrenders be punished for what was entirely legal? On January 22, the judges gave their opinions. The following day, the Earl of Mulgrave reported that the words, "declared and were and are illegal" – referring to the surrenders – would be struck from the bill. Nine peers signed their protest against this important dilution of the intended bill.[25] Nonetheless, surrenders appeared safe and thus the disabling clause appeared in doubt.

---

[23] Ibid., pp. 5 and 10.   [24] Ibid., p. 11.
[25] *LJ*, vol. 14, pp. 410, 419, and 422–24. The nine were Lords Ashburnham, Bedford, Bolton, Herbert, Macclesfield, Montagu, Stamford, Sydney, and Vaughan.

The judges had given mixed opinions about surrenders, reflecting the confusion prevailing over the nature of corporations, a confusion created by an intersection of traditional legal thinking – stressing corporations' franchisal nature – with current political needs, which made surrenders and quo warranto objects of suspicion. Most justices accepted the possibility of dissolution or surrender in some cases and not in others. Henry Pollexfen, who had argued in London's defense in 1683 and was now chief justice of Common Pleas, felt that a corporation might be dissolved if all died, "as by a whole company being sunk in a barge or by the plague."[26] Otherwise, corporation members had a trust signified in their oaths. So if a corporation surrenders, "they are destroyers of the trust and are *felo de se*." A "corporation can no more legally divest itself of its being than a natural body." Peytron Ventris of Common Pleas also employed the corporal metaphor this way. Chief baron of the Exchequer, Edward Atkyns, went further. Members held the corporation not only in trust for their heirs and the town's inhabitants: "Though it is granted to a small town, it is not theirs, it is the whole kingdom's. [The interest of] all the people of England is concerned, and that, it is clear, cannot be surrendered."[27]

Giles Eyre felt lost: "we are all in the dark." The case books pointed neither way conclusively. Then Eyre grew more confident. Why could the members of a corporation not surrender if they all agreed? "A corporation may surrender, for otherwise it is to set up a perpetuity, which the law always avoids." William Gregory of King's Bench also spoke for a power to surrender in some cases. And Sir John Holt, chief justice of King's Bench, pronounced for the same view. Holt's career had taken a number of twists and turns. He had defended Pilkington and the London rioters, Sacheverell and the Nottingham rioters, and Lord Russell against crown prosecutions in the early 1680s. In the same years, he had also declared in favor of the London quo warranto's legality. From this followed appointment as recorder of London in 1686 – the city then being governed under a royal commission – a knighthood, and promotion as a King's serjeant. His ability simultaneously to defend prominent whigs and to support an important element of royal authority enhanced his reputation for integrity. That reputation survived 1688 intact when he became the clear choice for appointment to the senior judicial post.[28] Given his earlier opinion that the

---

26 The following account of the judges' opinions is derived from HMC, Lords Manuscripts, Report 12, appendix 6, pp. 430–32, and notes among Eye corporation's records: Suffolk RO (Ipswich Branch), EE2/K/5/5.

27 Justice Thomas Rokeby of Common Pleas, and Barons John Turton and Nicholas Lechmere, took a similar view. William Dolben of King's Bench suggested there were not enough precedents to support surrender.

28 On Holt, see Edward Foss, *The Judges of England*, 9 vols. (London, 1848–64), vol. VII, pp. 386–95.

King could seize the liberties of London, few must have been surprised when Holt declared "a corporation may surrender." His view fell firmly within the tradition of royal franchises: "I take [the corporation] to be a franchise from the crown and may be surrendered . . . Where is the harm if the King consents and the corporation too?"[29]

Though most of the judges spoke against surrender in most instances, the Lords dropped from their draft bill to restore corporations the declaration of the illegality of surrender found in the Commons's version. Perhaps this was a result of the respect accorded Sir John Holt. Regardless, the controversial bill never became law. But as in so many proposed measures, intentions speak nearly as loudly as results. The bill had opened with an attack on the "wicked design to subvert the constitution . . . and the Protestant religion established by law . . . [by] destroying bodies politic and corporate."[30] It would have voided all judgments on quo warranto and surrenders since 1675, as well as all new charters.[31] To prevent legal chaos, all leases, bonds, and deeds granted by *de facto* corporations since their surrender would be declared good. Two of the most important clauses would have nullified the declaration against the Covenant in the Corporation Act, as well as clauses in pre-1675 charters giving the King either the approbation or nomination of corporation officers and members. The bill had promised much, especially for those who were whiggishly inclined. With the loss of the disabling clause, Sacheverell did not have his revenge on tories; nor did tories have their revenge on Sacheverell and other "regulators." The struggle over the bill showed clearly the partisan divisions at work at Westminster, and the appreciation there of the importance of partisan control in the corporations. Most of all, the debate in Parliament and in the press showed how divisions that had continued in the 1690s would depend on competing readings of the 1680s.

Parliament soon aimed at a closer, better defined target. A bill to reverse the London quo warranto passed the Commons in May 1690. Controversy accompanied it too, centering on whether it should simply "declare void" the 1683 judgment, or "declare void and reverse." Voiding alone implied that the decision had never been good in law; reversal would recognize that it had been illegal until overturned. By "voiding" without "reversing," whigs hoped to gain what they lost in the bill for restoring corporations: a parliamentary declaration of the illegality of quo warranto and charter

---

[29] HMC, Lords Manuscripts, Report 12, appendix 6, p. 429. In denigrating the idea of a corporation as a "capacity," Holt criticized the arguments made by London's lawyers in 1683.

[30] Ibid., p. 422. The text of the bill received by the Lords is at ibid., pp. 422–29.

[31] An important exception here were the North American Colonies, whose charters were voided in the 1680s. Ibid., p. 427.

surrenders. But a combine of churchmen and other tories won over-whelmingly a vote for adding the language of reversal to that of voiding. The final bill passed by a narrow margin: 179 to 171.[32] In the Lords, London's counsel argued: "We would have the word ('reversed') left out of the bill. Now if it be reversed it was a good judgment."[33] But the "Act for reversing the judgment in a quo warranto against London" "reversed, annulled, and made void" the 1683 decision.[34] Including "reversed" represented another loss for whig hopes of making the corporations legally impregnable. Quo warranto remained good law if still bad politics.

Statute provided the terms in which future corporation law would develop, and thus the channels within which corporate partisan conflict would occur. In 1689–90, whig MPs had tried to rewrite the recent past by rewriting the law of corporations. Their attempts to declare the corporations legally invincible had failed. Later statutes would focus on procedural questions concerning the adjudication of corporation battles on mandamus and quo warranto, rather than on the more controversial problems of defining the nature of corporations and the royal power to monitor them. New statutes, by making court procedures faster and simpler, would help King's Bench play all the more effectively its growing role as the overseer of the corporations. After 1688, in debates and acts like these, Parliament admitted the existence and permanence of partisan division in the corporations, and formed a partnership with the court in ameliorating its effects. But with the failure of the repeal of the Corporation Act and of the bill to restore corporations, the situation in the towns remained volatile. As before 1688, the legal propriety of one's claim to office would continue to be the stuff of which partisan conflict was made, and demonstrating one's claim would continue to depend on how people read and replayed the contests of the 1680s.

PROBLEMS: PARTISAN POLITICS IN THE 1690S

Many corporations were buried under legal wreckage left behind when the King fled. Digging out promised to keep alive the troubles they had

---

[32] Horwitz, *Parliament, Policy, and Politics*, pp. 56–57.

[33] HMC, Report 13, appendix 5, pp. 70–72. The Lords consulted the judges on the legality of forfeiture and thus quo warranto. Holt and Eyre declared that corporations could be forfeit upon judgment; Pollexfen, Atkyns, and Ventris declared they could not be. The justices agreed on the different implications of "void" and "reversed," that adding the latter would leave a suggestion that from 1683 to the passage of this bill, the London decision would be viewed as legally sound.

[34] Stat. 2 William and Mary c. 8. *LJ*, vol. 14, pp. 489–91, 495–96, 498, and 504. As in the bill for restoring all corporations, the London Act provided that the actions of the *de facto* corporation remained good. All members at the time of the quo warranto were confirmed in their old places.

endured before 1688. A number of forces continued to divide the corporations in the 1690s. First were the partisan animosities alive since before
1660 and so much strengthened by the charters and purges of the 1680s.
The "loyal" and "factious" of the 1660s and 70s had become "tory" and
"whig" in the 1680s, or, to use the language from the pamphlet exchange of
1690, "surrenderers" and "regulators." Each side in the towns looked back
over the last thirty years and saw a string of wrongs committed by their
foes: whigs saw oppression or exclusion of moderate dissent and the
surrender of corporate charters; tories saw "faction" and complicity with
James II. Each felt it had good reason for wanting to exclude the other now.
Such mutual angers were compounded by the doubts left by the succession
of new charters – some towns had received two in the 1680s – and James's
proclamation of October 17. Confusion abounded over which of the recent
charters currently applied, and thus over who properly belonged in the
corporations. Competing groups could make competing claims to power by
reference to different charters. Corporate partisans used doubts over
charters to capture office, expel opponents, and to win local control. This
control was desired for gaining prizes close to home, and increasingly, for
the leverage it gave over parliamentary elections. The succession of
parliamentary elections from 1689 to 1702 kept the political pot at a
constant boil and enlivened contests for corporate offices.

Partisan disputes within the corporations still occasionally came by
petition before the Privy Council. Where these involved election disputes
and rights to office, the Council continued to leave most cases to the law,
just as before 1688. Nonetheless, disputes involving conflicting claims to
act under different charters kept the Council busy throughout the 1690s.
From Ludlow, the Privy Council received a petition in October 1691 for a
charter to settle differences over who were the legal members of the
corporation. Most of the petitioners had lost their places by the "new and
arbitrary charter" of 1685 but were then restored by James's October 1688
proclamation. They were opposed by "a very few discontented new
chartermen [who would be] disappointed in their designs" if a charter were
now granted that confirmed the restored corporation. But a new charter
was indeed passed in December 1692. It opened by recounting Ludlow's
surrender, the power of removal accorded the King in the charter of 1685,
the use of that power in 1688, and the trouble this had created. All old
privileges were now restored and all those returned to office after James's
proclamation – in other words, all who had lost their places by the 1685
charter – were confirmed in their places. Most important of the clauses in
Ludlow's charter, and in all charters of the 1690s, was the general
indemnity confirming all elections and other affairs conducted by the
corporation under the repudiated charter of .1685, as well as all leases,

deeds, debts, and other contracts. The corporation thus stood protected from any potential legal trouble and freed from any claims by those who lost their places when the corporation restored itself in 1688.[35]

Nottingham had endured an even uglier surrender and regrant than most in 1682. Then in 1688, the entire corporation installed by that charter had been removed by James II.[36] Now in 1692, surviving members of the pre-surrender corporation petitioned for their restoration. Their surrender, as one of the few actually enrolled in Chancery, had put them beyond the saving mercy of James's proclamation of October 1688. The Privy Council referred their problem to Attorney General Sir George Treby, who in 1683 had appeared before King's Bench to defend London's liberties. Treby consulted the judges. Just as when they gave their opinions two years earlier on the legality of surrender, the justices found "great difficulties in point of law," and disagreed whether the old corporation of Nottingham still existed or a new one had to be created. Chief Justice Holt felt the old body subsisted, so a charter was ordered that renewed the corporation's old privileges.[37] The charter noted that "divers doubts, questions, and controversies have arisen of and concerning the liberties, franchises and customs and . . . the election and continuation of certain officers." New charter heads included a general indemnity and made William Greaves – the man whom anti-new charter rioters championed in 1682 – the first mayor and reappointed everyone serving at the time of surrender a decade earlier.[38] Crown and corporation alike hoped the "divers doubts, questions, and controversies" now stood settled.

Colchester and other corporations too received new charters that attempted to answer lingering questions about legal status and personnel. Like others, Colchester's charter appointed the mayor in office at the time of their surrender in 1684 and restored their previous charter of 1663.[39] Charters like these, as well as those to Dunwich, to Plymouth in 1696, and to other towns, arose from the incompleteness of the restoration intended

---

[35] PRO, PC2/74/130 and PC2/75/45 and 49. *Copies of the Charters and Grants to the Town of Ludlow* (Ludlow), pp. 195–212. Shropshire Records and Research Service, LB/1/19.

[36] Henning, vol. I, p. 356.

[37] PRO, PC2/74/169, 171, 186, 216v, and 240.

[38] Stevenson, *Charters of Nottingham*, pp. 129–41. The charter did not settle all problems, as various mandamuses followed in succeeding years. PRO, KB21/24, f. 95; KB21/25, ff. 21, 24v, 25, and 29.

[39] Colchester had continued acting under its 1688 charter until August 1689, when the mayor and eighteen others, not having received the sacrament, stepped aside. This left the corporation without a quorum and thus incapable of acting. Those left, along with some remaining from before the surrender, petitioned for a confirmation of their 1663 charter, which they received in July 1693. PRO, PC2/75/120–21 and 170. *CSPD 1689–90*, p. 225. *CSPD 1693*, pp. 87, 157, and 186. VCH, Essex, vol. IX, p. 117. Bod., MS Rawlinson Essex 1, ff. 109–10. *Charters [of Colchester]*, pp. 170–75. Folger Shakespeare Library, V.b. 294, f. 17.

by James's proclamation of October 17, 1688. In such places, many remained in office after 1688 whose only claim to do so was by their appointment under one of the now abrogated charters of the 1680s. The charters of the 1690s were passed to right this enduring problem.[40] By returning such corporations to their pre-surrender condition, the King and Queen acted quite within their legal powers and followed a strict reading of recent statutes and judicial pronouncements. Nonetheless, the new charters of the 1690s had a distinctly partisan impact, for by removing the "surrenderers" of the 1680s and restoring those in the corporations before they surrendered, these new charters favored whig interests in the towns.

Conflicts continued in these and other corporations over who belonged in them and by what right. Driving the conflict were desires to control corporations in order to exercise power for certain ends within the towns, and increasingly, in order to win parliamentary elections. Corporate contests became all the more common in the last years of William's reign as partisan divisions in the Commons widened. There is perhaps no better sign of this than the sharp increase in mandamus cases in Michaelmas term, 1699, right after most corporations held their annual mayoral elections.[41] But contests went on all year, especially if an incumbent happened to expire mid-term. This is what happened in Banbury's already divided corporation. Like many towns, Banbury had one custom governing the choice of the mayor at annual elections and another governing elections upon a mayor's death. When Mayor William Thorpe died in February 1699, the two groups in the corporation proceeded to vote according to the different usages. Two men now claimed to be mayor. Each then presided at separate elections of their successors the following Michaelmas. These two then fought a "battle royal" to sit in the mayor's "chair of state" in Banbury's church.[42] Mandamuses for new elections and commanding one of them to hand over the records and regalia to the other came and went from town. In the meantime, two mayors presided at two elections of two MPs for the borough's single seat. By deciding in favor of Charles North, the Commons confirmed local tory control for most of the next generation.[43] Of course, such struggles concerned officers below the corporation's headship too. At Andover, in early 1698, Bailiff Isaac Cooper held a surprise election of

---

[40] Plymouth charter was granted to restore all still living who had been left out at the time of surrender in the 1680s. PRO, PC2/76/207v, 270, and 285v. *CSPD 1696*, pp. 423–24.

[41] In this term alone, cases concerning mayoralties came from Dartmouth, Abingdon, Newport, Bossiney, and Derby. A host of court contests for offices in other towns were ongoing or were initiated. PRO, KB21/25/176ff.

[42] Bod. MS Rawlinson D.892, f. 343.

[43] PRO, PC2/77/160, 170v, 183v, and 185. Bod. MS Carte 78, f. 653. Some of these items are transcribed in Gibson and Brinkworth, *Banbury Records*, pp. 256–59. PRO, KB21/25/178; KB21/26/32v and 36v; and KB29/359/62.

burgesses when four of his foes were out of town. Cooper's absent
opponents immediately sought legal advice, and when the partisan weight
in the assembly was tilted their way by a better attendance, they removed
the two elected by Bailiff Cooper and expelled three others for good
measure.[44]

Parliamentary contests at Chester likewise divided the corporation and
depended on conflicting readings of the recent past, but here as elsewhere,
more was at stake than simply seats in Westminster. Roger Whitley and
George Mainwaring defeated Sir Thomas Grosvenor and Sir Richard
Leving in the contest for Chester's parliamentary seats in early 1689. The
race was close within the corporation, but Whitley and Mainwaring
enjoyed near unanimity among the freemen.[45] Grosvenor and Whitley had
been the gentry leaders of contending corporation parties since the early
1680s, Whitley with his support among the "London whigs," and
Grosvenor among those now called tories.[46] Grosvenor had been the
driving force in gaining Chester's 1685 charter, which named him mayor
and ousted Whitley, Mainwaring, and their friends from the corporation
for nearly four years. Having just been restored, Whitley now bested
Grosvenor for the parliamentary seats. But while Whitley was in
Westminster, Grosvenor soon recovered. The following month, three tory
partisans became aldermen; another two did so before year's end.[47]

Parliamentary elections came around again in early 1690. Whitley's
attempt to hold the vote in Grosvenor's and Leving's absence failed. Then,
just days before the poll, Grosvenor was presented for allegedly speaking
words against King William. Meanwhile, various inhabitants approached
Whitley, promising him their votes if money were given to purchase their
freedoms. Whitley recounted his high-minded refusal in his diary, but must
have felt chagrined when he found Grosvenor's supporters making new
freemen at the pentice, Chester's town hall. The sheriffs began the poll on
March 17. Whitley protested against the new freemen, who voted in droves
for Grosvenor, to no avail. After a confused end to the polling the next day,
one sheriff declared Grosvenor and Leving chosen, while the other
pronounced for Whitley and Mainwaring.[48]

[44] Those expelled made the mistake of getting a single mandamus for all five of them, and thus
it was later disallowed. Hampshire RO, 37M85, 4/MI/5, pp. 36, 45–46, 60–61, 67, 70,
and 84; 37M85, 4/EL/2 and 3. Darrah and Spaul, *Andover*, Andover Local Archives
Committee (1970), pp. 8–10. Spaul, *Andover Archives*, pp. 10–11. *Eng. Rep.*, vol. 88,
p. 1359 (12 Mod. 332), and vol. 91, p. 377 (2 Salk. 433). PRO, KB21/26/9, 12v, 33v, 37,
40, 42v, and 87; KB29/359/34–35.
[45] Whitley Diary, f. 101.
[46] As John Morrill notes, "Organized whig and tory groups were struggling for control of
Chester throughout the 1690s." VCH Cheshire, vol. II, p. 128.
[47] CCRO, AB/3, ff. 20–21v and AF/45a/6. [48] Whitley Diary, ff. 114v–116.

The tories were seated, and remained there after hearings by the Committee of Elections of charges against illegal freemen and a hastily closed poll.[49] All Whitley could do now was rebuild his base and try again. That base was in the freemen. Using them, he would reshape the corporation to suit his needs. Chester's six-part mayoral voting procedure lent itself well to partisan maneuvering. Voters in the first five rounds had two votes each, thus encouraging like-minded candidates to stand in pairs. The fifth round "housed" two men, one of whom would then be chosen mayor by the aldermen. Working together in a partisan pair ensured that the two from whom the final choice would be made were both of the same persuasion. By presenting a pair of the same party, their supporters could choose both at each of the earlier stages. Once that pair was housed, it would not matter who won in the last round since the party would have one of its own in the corporation's head regardless of the outcome. The city's freemen showed remarkable partisan loyalty in mayoral elections in the 1690s. Tory pairs stood against whig pairs. The members of each pair received similar numbers of votes, indicating that their supporters tended to favor both of one side against both of the other, rather than plumping or splitting their votes.

In 1691's mayoral contest, Whitley joined with the Earl of Warrington against Grosvenor's friends, Aldermen William Allen and Henry Bennett. In straight partisan voting by the full assembly in round four, Whitley and Warrington had nineteen votes each, Allen and Bennett twenty-nine apiece. But massive support among the freemen for Whitley and Warrington turned the tide in round five: both were "housed" by a comfortable margin over the tories. Warrington, socially the senior of the pair, won the voting among the aldermen in the last round. Their party controlled the mayor's chair; it hardly mattered which of them should sit in it.[50] Warrington held only one assembly during his year, though he did appear at the county sessions held in the castle in April 1692, where he gave a charge "much in commendation of an elective government."[51]

As early as July 1692, Whitley and George Mainwaring began planning

---

49 The poll was: Grosvenor 498, Leving 494, Whitley 484, and Mainwaring 457. Eaton Hall, Papers of Sir Thomas Grosvenor, 3rd Bart., #14, consulted at the Cheshire RO, and Whitley Diary, ff. 125v–26.

50 Records for the first three rounds of voting do not survive. In the first three rounds, first the senior aldermen, then all the aldermen, and then the aldermen with some of the senior councilmen (former sheriffs) voted. Round four included the entire assembly and round five the assembly and the freemen. Everyone had two votes in each round until the sixth, when the final choice was made by the aldermen from the two chosen in the fifth round. The poll is in CCRO, AF/46a/7. Whitley gives an account in his Diary, f. 137.

51 CCRO, CR99 (diary of Roger Comberbach, of Chester), ff. 60v–61. Henry Booth, second Baron Delamere, was made Earl of Warrington in 1690. He was well known as a whig with populist tendencies. Henning, vol. I, pp. 679–81.

together for the next mayoral election. Partisan tensions were high. In casual meetings at the pentice, in city inns, and in gatherings for dinner or for bowls at Whitley's home at Peele, political speculation and partisan planning must have provided much food for conversation. After hearing a sermon "better fitted to the reign of the late King James," various aldermen gathered "to talk of parties." Tempers flared as the mayoral choice neared, especially when Whitley's friends disturbed a meeting at the home of Alderman Thomas Wilcock, one of Grosvenor's keenest supporters.[52] The election results of 1692 looked much like those of the preceding year: voting within the corporation was close and followed straight partisan lines. And the freemen again "housed" the whig pair by a convincing margin. This time, Whitley was chosen unanimously in round six. Allen and Bennett had again represented the tory interest in 1692, as they would with similar results the following year. Whitley now held the mayoralty, and thus control of the corporation, control he would exercise for four years. His foes would ultimately give up.[53]

Whitley's first meeting in the chair in 1692 dissolved in a "great hurly-burly . . . and indecent expressions" when he took the votes of the sheriffs before some of the aldermen, all of whom were tories. Seniority was a touchy subject since some claimed eminence over others by virtue of different charters: the "ancient" one surrendered in 1684 and resumed in 1688, and "the new" charter of 1685. Those claiming their places by the 1685 charter were all tories. Though James's proclamation of October 17, 1688 had commanded all members restored to the places they held before surrender, Chester's restoration had been incomplete. Whitley would now try to finish it by challenging those tories holding their places by the "new charter."[54] In the spring of 1693, Whitley consulted various allies about certain clauses in their "ancient" charters. He contended that these charters appointed the freemen to make annual elections of the entire common council, though by practice throughout the seventeenth century, the assembly alone had chosen new members as old ones died. Whitley promoted a return to the old method, well aware of the use he could make of the support he enjoyed among the freemen. Richard Leving, his old

---

52 CCRO, CR99, ff. 68v–72v. In early October, three were convicted for drinking seditious healths. All three were elected to the city assembly in 1697, after tories took control from Whitley. John Rylands University of Manchester Library [hereafter Rylands Library], Mainwaring Papers (part 5), #84.
53 CCRO, CR99, ff. 71v–72, and CCRO, AF/46c/1 and 6. Few corporate opponents showed up to vote against him in the mayoral elections of 1694 and 1695: ibid., 20, 21, 38, and 39. P. J. Challinor recounts the same episode: "The Structure of Politics in Cheshire, 1660–1715" (Ph.D., Wolverhampton Polytechnic, 1983), pp. 176–79.
54 Whitley Diary, f. 151. CCRO, AB/3, f. 35, AF/46c/54, and CR99, ff. 73v–74.

parliamentary opponent, feared the consequences of popular elections: "All this bustle and distraction [will] only . . . serve a vile turn."[55]

George Booth and Sir John Mainwaring presented Mayor Whitley with an address subscribed by over 400 citizens in early June, asking that the freemen be allowed to exercise their ancient privilege of electing the council annually. At the same time, a few of the tory aldermen presented a protest signed by seventy-seven, claiming that the city had been prudently managed for generations according to the current usage. Popular elections, they argued, would "dissolve that happy order and tranquillity which have been so long preserved among the citizens by regularity in elections of the common council." Two groups of aldermen arrayed themselves on either side, but with Whitley's group more numerous, a majority voted to hold a council election among the freemen according to the terms of Chester's "ancient charters."[56]

Whitley wrote Secretary of State Sir John Trenchard of his plans the day before the council election in June of 1693. Owing to "the unfortunate dissensions and animosities in this city . . . the well-affected loyal party" could think of no better solution than returning to the ancient mode. He reminded Trenchard of the 1680s. Cestrians had found "that a council modeled or corrupted by Jeffreys . . . is the root and chief cause of our oppression." The new election was meant to purge remnants of the 1685 charter that endured despite the corporation's restoration in 1688. Trenchard expressed concern: "if you should be mistaken in the legal part, the attempt would probably prejudice the party that attempts it."[57] His warning came too late to prevent the elections, which turned out to be anything but prejudicial to Whitley's party. Whitley's manipulation of the process is underscored by his manner of conducting it. No nominations were permitted. Whitley simply presented a list of forty names to the freemen for a single up or down vote. His list omitted twenty names from the current council and added twenty new ones of his own choosing. The freemen approved. One half of the councilmen were now replaced by those Whitley could count on for full support in the assembly's deliberations.[58] Protests against the novel vote availed nothing. For the next four years, eleven of the aldermen who petitioned against the election stayed away from meetings. Appearance by many of the old councilmen who remained was thin, except for those who clearly supported Whitley; the twenty

[55] CCRO, ML4/531 and MF/111, f. 22. Rylands Library, Mainwaring Papers (part 5), #61–67. Leving also feared that if they returned to this old method, it would imply that the method used in recent decades was illegal. Their charters might thus be forfeit for having held illegal elections.
[56] CCRO, AB/3, ff. 36–37 and MF/111, f. 14. Whitley Diary, ff. 158v–59.
[57] Rylands Library, Mainwaring Papers (part 5), #73 and 74.
[58] CCRO, AB/3, f. 37.

newcomers attended meetings consistently to support the regime that brought them into office.[59] Whitley's partisans were exultant, his foes in resigned disarray.

Whitley went to London to answer complaints brought before the Privy Council by those who had lost their places, but the Council left the matter to the law since mandamus proceedings were already under way.[60] The writs were served on Whitley days after his re-election as mayor in October. A deputation of tory aldermen and thirty or forty others came "to demand the restoration of the late common councilmen." Whitley simply said he would answer their demands in court.[61] With these tory aldermen absent from the following meeting, the assembly approved without dissent the returns to the writs prepared by Whitley.[62] When heard in Michaelmas term 1694, the councilmen who lost their places also lost their suit. Sir Thomas Powys – attorney general under James II – served as counsel for the plaintiffs. Oddly enough, it was to Sir William Williams – solicitor general under James II – that Whitley and his allies turned for advice.[63] The justices appreciated well the partisan implications of the case and that those put out would probably have done the same had they had the same legal opportunity. But their decision was made according to a strict reading of the pertinent legal issues.[64]

With the judgment in his favor, Whitley's control was secure. In June 1694, a second annual council election was held before the freemen, who

[59] Thirteen aldermen had been dismissed from the corporation in 1688, a sign of their opposition to dissent and Catholicism. None of these thirteen came to meetings in the four years after the 1692 election, except for William Bennett, who appeared once, and William Ince, who attended meetings irregularly. Eight councilmen also stayed away from meetings. All eight lost their places the following year.

[60] Whitley's successful plea before the Council emphasized the illegality of the charter surrender in 1684 (see above, pp. 230–32), when over 600 citizens had petitioned the corporation to oppose the quo warranto. PRO, PC2/75/190 and 248. CCRO, AB/3, ff. 38–40v. Whitley Diary, ff. 163–64, and Rylands Library, Mainwaring Papers (part 5), #85–87 and 91.

[61] Alderman William Allen was apparently a close runner-up in the mayoral voting, though his supporters may have felt he had won the vote among those they considered the legitimate members of the corporation. Unfortunately, the election record does not include results for the last three rounds. CCRO, AF/46c/6. Whitley Diary, ff. 164v, 165v, 167, and 167v.

[62] Two of the tory aldermen (one in attendance) refused to relinquish their keys to the chest containing the corporate seal in order to prevent sealing the returns to the writs, so the chests were broken open and the job done. *Eng. Rep.*, vol. 90, p. 436 (Comb. 214). CCRO, AB/3, ff. 40v–42.

[63] On Williams's advice to Whitley, and his role in providing access to Secretary of State Trenchard, see Rylands Library, Mainwaring Papers (part 5), #68, 69, 70, 72, and 82.

[64] The justices declared the plaintiffs should have sued separate writs rather than one. As Holt put it: "you cannot all join in one writ, for the election of one is not the election of another." *Eng. Rep.*, vol. 90, pp. 495–96 (Comb. 307), and vol. 87, pp. 487–88 (5 Mod. 11). For the same problem in a case from Andover, see above, n. 44.

ousted the last remaining members unwilling to go along with the new regime. Elections were held at the same time to fill the two vacancies left by death among the aldermen during the year, returning two predictably supportive of Whitley.[65] October 1694 brought Whitley yet a third mayoral win. Another annual council election followed in June 1695, this time making few changes since Whitley's regime was already so well ensconced.[66]

Preparations were soon under way for another parliamentary contest. Sir Thomas Grosvenor initially sought a seat at Newton, having "resolved not to stand a poll at Chester, which will cost £700 or £800," but rumors soon abounded that Grosvenor would make the attempt.[67] With the help of tory aldermen, Grosvenor worked to make an interest with Whitley against Sir William Williams, with whom Whitley was currently joined. Accusations arose that Whitley had abandoned Williams. In the end, Whitley and Grosvenor, formerly arch enemies, were returned to share the city's seats in Westminster. In the meantime, Whitley had also easily won his fourth mayoralty in October 1695. The parliamentary and corporate elections of 1695 suggest how even in the 1690s, the content of partisan allegiances was as much about personal loyalty as about whig and tory ideologies. The freemen were willing to follow Whitley in his apparent apostasy to continue their support of a local regime that did so much to protect their interests. Anyway, Whitley's union with Grosvenor was only a short-term tactical ploy and he was soon "as great as ever with his old friends and favors nobody but them still."[68]

In June 1696, annual council elections were again held before the freemen. Soon thereafter, the assembly ordered that the plaque over the pentice door recounting the grant of the charter of 1685 be taken down, as "containing matter both scandalous and false, and particularly that the new charter was to the general satisfaction of all good men." Further by-laws detailing election procedures passed in October, just before mayoral elections.[69] Whitley's whig-inclined, anti-"new charter" group seemed more dominant than ever. But the political order in Chester was

---

[65] Nine councilmen lost their places in this election, six of whom had petitioned against the elections the preceding year. CCRO, AF/46c/16.

[66] CCRO, AF/46c/20, 21, and 134.

[67] Rylands Library, Letters of Peter Legh the Elder, John Grosvenor to Peter Legh, October 14, 1695. The Newton seat was controlled by Legh, who refused to assist Sir Thomas. Ibid., Sir Thomas Grosvenor to Legh, October 15, 1695, with draft response.

[68] Whitley Diary, ff. 195–98. Grosvenor ended up spending about double his original estimate: £1,444. Eaton Hall, Papers of Sir Thomas Grosvenor, 3rd Bart., #16 and 18, consulted at the Cheshire RO. CCRO, AF/46c/38 and 39. Challinor recounts whig disappointment with Whitley's behavior: "The Structure of Politics in Cheshire," pp. 188–89.

[69] CCRO, AB/3, ff. 51–54. Whitley Diary, f. 205.

soon turned upside down once again, and by none other than the freemen. After four years in the mayor's chair, Whitley did not stand again in October 1696, perhaps owing to poor health. The first four rounds – all within the assembly so beholden to Whitley after the changes of the last four years – went easily for Sir John Mainwaring and Thomas Hand, two of Whitley's chief lieutenants. But the freemen's humor of recent years had changed, and they reversed the results in the fifth round. As Whitley put it so tersely himself: "Mainwaring and Hand were voted on one side, Allen and Bennett on the other; the last two were housed and Bennett was chose [*sic*]."[70]

Mainwaring and Hand were Whitley's strong allies; Peter Bennett and William Allen were equally his foes. All Whitley's successes were soon undone. Under Mayor Bennett, Whitley and eleven of the other aldermen now stayed away from meetings, just as their own enemies had done in the four years the whigs had been ascendant. The aldermen, still divided twelve to twelve, had been made subject to the mood of Chester's hundreds of freemen for four years under Whitley, and would be subject to their very new mood under the opposing regime now installed. Unlike in some towns, Whitley presided over a peaceful transition to his reviled successor, going the day after Bennett's victory to hand over the corporation's plate and regalia. But Whitley did not give up the fight. He attempted in the coming months to use a corporate committee formed to oversee the construction of a new town hall to control city business until his failing health ended his life and his measures prior to the next mayoral election.[71]

Even in his decline, Whitley led a petitioning effort to prevent new elections to the common council by a "tedious poll." Whitley knew that Mayor Bennett planned to end the annual election of council members by electing a new, permanent council, proceeding by voting on each proposed member, one-by-one, rather than using Whitley's method of presenting a full list in a manner that made the whole group an accomplished fact. But Bennett proceeded by his preferred method. The lopsided voting against Whitley's councilmen as their names were called over made clear the reversal they now suffered. Thirty-three of those in the whig-dominated council since 1692 lost their places. Of the newcomers, fifteen had been appointed to the corporation by the 1685 charter – an indication of their tory leanings – and eighteen others had lost their places during Whitley's years.[72] The tories further strengthened their position by repealing the new election by-laws passed the year before and by admitting a slew of new

---

[70] Ibid., f. 210. CCRO, AF/46c/51 and 52.
[71] Whitley Diary, ff. 210, 215, 216, 216v, and 218.
[72] Thirty-six were chosen to the council, including three to replace persons recently deceased. CCRO, AB/3, ff. 54v–57v and AF/46d/1. PRO, PC2/77/22v, 28, 35v, 37v, 46v, 54, and 74.

freemen. The rules made by Whitley's assembly appointing annual, popular council elections were revoked the following July. Days later, Sir Thomas Grosvenor and Peter Shakerley were sent to Parliament with unanimous backing, though two years earlier they had displayed so clearly their political tendencies when they hesitated to sign the Association supporting William III.[73] Grosvenor would be dead in less than two years; perhaps to maintain the political balance, so too would Sir William Williams. But the resurgent tory interest would dominate Chester politics for years to come.

Winning parliamentary elections provided an important incentive for Whitley and Grosvenor to tussle for control of the corporation. But it was not everything. After all, the parliamentary franchise was in the freemen: controlling the corporation meant controlling the returning officers – the sheriffs – but this provided no guarantees about the behavior of the electorate. While party loyalty was strict among corporation members, the freemen apparently could go one way, and then another: witness their abandonment of Whitley's friends in the 1696 mayoral election and the devastating consequences that shift wrought on local whigs' hold on the corporation. The independence of the freemen from their urban leaders was further shown in other mayoral elections, when the corporation voted one way in the first four rounds, and the freemen another way in the fifth. Thus controlling the corporation did not give one the full power over the freemen that was required to win parliamentary elections. More than control of parliamentary seats was needed to inspire Whitley to take the interest he did in corporation politics.

Holding the headship of one of England's most important corporations had a value in and of itself. Whitley proved by his election to the mayoralty four times running, and by using the freemen to elect councilmen to his liking, that he had them in his pocket from 1692 to 1696. This was a force that he then used to bolster his position within the corporation itself, rather than the other way around. His clear support among the freemen was used to elect a common council that would do his bidding. Having a loyal council in turn allowed Whitley to do things for the freemen, thus ensuring their constancy to his leadership. Many of the measures passed by Whitley's assembly arose from an interest in maintaining or restoring the freemen's ancient rights and in protecting their economic privileges. One of his first decrees as mayor barred foreign ale sellers from the city and permitted bakers to reimpose controls on the bread market, thus protecting city bakers from the encroachments of county bakers long supported by tory

---

73 CCRO, AB/3, ff. 59v–61v and 64, and AF/47a/8 and 11. CCRO, MF/113, ff. 23–25. Eaton Hall, Papers of Sir Thomas Grosvenor, 3rd Bart., #25, consulted at the Cheshire RO. On the Association in Chester, see BL, Add. 36,913, f. 266.

gentry.[74] The decision to revert to annual elections of the council by the freemen was likewise a bid to gain support from the freemen whose interest Whitley so studiously cultivated and whose power he wielded with such success.

While partisan affiliations among corporation members remained constant, the freemen's partisan loyalty appears to have been more to the man than to whiggery. They willingly elected Whitley MP, even when he threw over his old associations with the whig Sir William Williams in favor of a short-lived alliance with Grosvenor. It was Whitley the champion of city privileges, not Whitley the whig, that they chose again and again. The reasons behind the freemen's abandonment of the whig interest in 1696 are not altogether clear. But when Whitley decided to drop the burdens of office, his allies in the corporation – who maintained partisan coherence among themselves – proved unable to attract the popular support that had made him such a success. The freemen then went strongly for the tory pair in mayoral voting. The result was that with a tory regime back in corporate power, the most important recent innovation favoring popular interests was reversed, namely the freemen's franchise in annual council elections. Nonetheless, the freemen returned a tory pair to Parliament in 1698, and again and again in the elections following.

Whitley's success, and the demise of his interest among the freemen, underscore the importance of leadership in creating and sustaining corporate partisan groups. Despite partisan cohesion within the corporation, the lack of a strong leader after Whitley left office critically damaged whig support among the freemen. Through careful leadership, and by MP Peter Shakerley's assiduous attention to the city's many needs before Parliament, the tory regime that dominated Chester throughout Anne's reign and beyond served the freemen at least as well as Whitley's more apparently populist government.[75] Freemen held the power in Chester politics, but it was a power that could only be won by one side or the other if partisan leaders wooed them. It was the freemen, led by Whitley, who threw out the tory councilmen in 1693. And it was they who brought those councilmen back again after even mandamus had failed to save them.

Conflict in Chester was stoked by confusion over who held what places by what charter. Whitley manipulated this confusion masterfully, deploying a novel reading of ancient charters for the whigs' great benefit. Conflicts over charters served the interests of parliamentary candidates in towns around the country in the 1690s. Questions about who won seats at

---

[74] CCRO, CR99, ff. 72v–73. Rylands Library, Mainwaring Papers (part 5), #71.

[75] Information on parliamentary elections for Anne's reign, and on Shakerley's efforts, comes from unpublished notes on Chester from the History of Parliament Trust. I am grateful to Dr. David Hayton and Dr. Stuart Handley for permitting me to examine these notes.

Thetford in 1690 depended on answering questions about who was the legal mayor, questions which thus turned on which charter currently had force there. As Thetford's surrender of 1682 was one of the few enrolled, its charter of that year remained their legal constitution despite James's October 1688 proclamation. This did not prevent the Commons' Committee of Elections from finding otherwise. But while the Commons could decide whom to seat in their own body, they could not determine the legality of individual charters. That would be left to the corporation and the court of King's Bench. At Thetford, none other than John Mendham – the same man who had figured so controversially in the charter surrender of 1682 – sued mandamus to be sworn as mayor in 1690, though apparently to no avail.[76] In early 1693, a rump of the corporation agreed to obtain an order in Chancery annulling the charter surrender. Unsurprisingly, Mendham voted against the measure; his foe of the early 1680s, Wormley Hethersett, voted in favor. The old charter was formally restored in 1696 and Hethersett's party was now ascendant.[77] But this did little to end disputes there, disputes in part left over from the 1680s, and in part promoted by troubles surrounding the signing or not signing of the Association in support of William III. Continuing conflict over corporation membership led to more difficulties in the parliamentary choice of 1698, more removals from the corporation, and more writs of mandamus well into Anne's reign. Walter Salter would be removed in 1700 for "creating, encouraging, and promoting divisions and breaches among the members [of the corporation] and suits at law against them." But this was certainly the pot calling the kettle black. Each removal, and each vote on how to respond to the writs brought to reverse the removals, provided occasions for the corporation to split again and again along the same partisan fault lines. Corporation minutes reveal vividly the coherence of partisan groups at Thetford throughout the 1690s and beyond as the competing sides showed remarkable unity from one decision to the next. In Anne's reign, each side would try to unseat the other in back-and-forth rounds of quo warrantos and writs of mandamus. The paradox of partisan politics was alive and well in Thetford.[78]

The Association oath, required by the "Act for the better security of his majesty's royal person" of 1696, imposed yet another loyalty test on the nation's public officials. Those who did not subscribe by August 1, 1696

[76] Thomas Carew, *An Historical Account of the Rights of Election*, 2 vols. (London, 1755), vol. II, p. 197. *CJ*, vol. 10, pp. 358 and 399. PRO, KB21/24/22v and 24v.

[77] Sir Joseph Williamson, still representing Thetford in Parliament, gave £100 to cover costs. Thetford Town Hall, T/C2/6, p. 83. HMC, *Various Collections*, vol. VII, p. 147.

[78] HMC, *Various Collections*, vol. VII, pp. 148–49. *CSPD 1698*, p. 369. Thetford Town Hall, T/C2/6, passim. PRO, KB21/26/2v, 7b, 11v, 18, 42, 47, 49v, 55, 106v, 110, and passim.

were to lose their places, including corporation offices, though unlike the Corporation Act, the "Act appointing the Association" explicitly permitted one's re-election whenever he should subscribe.[79] Though most rallied to the King and signed the Association, another test for office could only provide more matter for controversy in the corporations. Such controversy resulted as much from confusion as from refusal to subscribe. At least two corporations became forfeit in the wake of the Act, their members having neglected to subscribe through ignorance of its provisions: both Eye and Malmesbury received new charters to restore them after such troubles.[80] At Andover, Alexander Daniel was removed, but quickly restored after he proved his due compliance.[81] Elsewhere, accidental neglect of the Association as well as purposeful refusal provided an opportunity for partisans on one side to remove those on the other.[82] But even in the late 1690s, the terms of the Corporation Act, especially the sacrament requirement, continued to provide the most frequently employed justification for controversial corporate purges.[83] This was especially true since it was so easy to neglect taking all the required oaths or the declaration when installed in office and since many – even good church-going Protestants – might not always have the full legal proof required to establish that they had received the sacrament. As we shall see, minor slips in record keeping or in following proper forms could readily be exploited by partisan foes against each other.[84]

James's flight from England in late 1688 left legal and political disarray in the corporations. A few corporations, whether because their surrenders had been enrolled – and they were thereby exempted from James's October 1688 proclamation – or because of willful neglect of the proclamation, continued in turmoil. New charters of the 1690s solved the problems in some cases, though they often did so with a marked partisan bias. And all corporations, regardless of their legal condition and the charter prevailing in them after 1688, became subject to increased pressures for parliamentary seats and thus to partisan struggles conducted largely on whig/tory lines. Parliamentary elections were not the only motivating factor, but unlike before the early 1680s, when corporate partisanship had more to do with

[79] Stat. 7 and 8 William III c. 27.
[80] PRO, PC2/76/287v and 77/41 and 42v–43. *CSPD 1696*, p. 433; and PRO, IND1/4228/213.
[81] Hampshire RO, 37M85, 4/MI/5, pp. 29–30.
[82] Thus Thomas Day lost his place as a portman of Ipswich in 1697. Suffolk RO (Ipswich Branch), C6/1/7, p. 186.
[83] Thus Daniel Love and others at Cambridge were removed for failing to take the sacrament in 1699. Love was re-elected in 1702. Cambridgeshire RO, C/9, pp. 299–301, 309, 313, and 346. PRO, KB21/25/176 and KB21/26/74.
[84] See cases from Abingdon and Oxford: *Eng. Rep.*, vol. 87, pp. 678–80, and vol. 90, pp. 565–66 and 886–87 (5 Mod. 316, Comberbach 419, and Carthew 499).

animosities left over from the Interregnum and the dismissals of the early 1660s than with controlling seats in the Commons, parliamentary election-eering after 1688 had become one of the most prominent components of the problem of partisan politics. Such problems have their solutions, and as before 1688, King's Bench would provide many of them. Perhaps more surprisingly, Parliament too would begin contributing to the court's ability to perform its growing role as the arbiter of corporate political disputes.

SOLUTIONS: KING'S BENCH AND PARLIAMENT

Partisan conflict after 1688 was continuous with conflict before. In the 1690s, corporate contests revolved around different readings of the events of the 1680s, just as in the parliamentary debate over the failed corpora-tions bill of 1690. Similarly, the means for containing corporate conflicts would build upon developments of the previous decades. With the excep-tion of requests for charters, which required an appeal to the monarch, the Privy Council nearly disappeared as a venue for hearing corporate comba-tants' mutual recriminations. King's Bench was busier than ever after 1688 as it became virtually the only arbiter of partisan contests. As before, this development was driven by the initiative of corporate litigants. But in the 1690s and beyond, Parliament too would begin to contribute to the court's ability to supervise the corporations.

The justices of King's Bench set to work immediately in 1688 as ex-corporators from Dunwich gained their mandamuses before James II had fled Whitehall for the last time.[85] More writs followed in 1689 in response to yet another round of corporate purges as townsmen competed to impose conflicting readings of who ruled and by what right after the multiple charters and purges of the 1680s. Surprisingly, the "Act for abrogating the oaths of supremacy and allegiance" (1 William and Mary c. 8) does not seem to have made this problem any worse than it already was. Unlike the Corporation Act, passed almost thirty years earlier, the new loyalty test of 1689 spurred few departures from office.[86] Where failure to take the new oath was used to justify a removal, the judges' decisions tended to focus on

---

[85] PRO, KB21/23/147. Suffolk RO (Ipswich Branch), EE6/1144/13, f. 64. HMC *Various Collections*, vol. VII, p. 104.

[86] An important exception was the case of Alderman Sir James Smith of London, removed after failing to take the oath. This case is of interest less because of its connection to the oath, than because it required the judges to pronounce on London's legal status after the City Restoration Act. The judges (with the exception of Holt) declared corporate seizures on a quo warranto illegal, though all thought individual wrongdoers might be ousted by quo warranto. This doctrine assisted in quo warranto's later revival. *Eng. Rep.*, vol. 87, pp. 258–61, vol. 88, pp. 1135–36, and vol. 89, pp. 562–64 (4 Mod. 53, 12 Mod. 17, and 1 Show. KB, 264). BL, Add. 35,982, ff. 15–24.

other issues such as proper summons to answer charges before dismissal, or precision in the corporation's return to the writ, rather than on the oath itself.[87] Still, business on mandamus grew after 1688, for four reasons. First, there were plenty of partisan dismissals from the corporations. Second, in the 1690s, King's Bench was able to encourage the making of faster returns to the writs and held more expeditious hearings on their merits, thus prompting more to use mandamus. Third, the court, prompted by imaginative litigants, created new uses for mandamus. And fourth and most important, mandamus worked as intended for scores of plaintiffs.

Thus Harris Child, expelled from Bath's common council "for several misdemeanors," compelled the corporation to restore him.[88] Sir Thomas Earle succeeded as well. He had lost his alderman's place at Bristol for allegedly defaming Mayor and MP Sir Richard Hart and others "of the mayor's party [that] were zealous Jacobites." In court, Earle's counsel contended "there cannot be any cause to disfranchise a member of a corporation, unless it be for such a thing done, which works to the destruction of the body corporate . . . and not any personal offense of one member thereof." The justices unanimously agreed. While Earle's words may have wounded Sir Richard personally, it had not presented a challenge to the authority of the corporation itself. Earle won his victory with exemplary haste, the first writ having been obtained in Michaelmas 1690 with the court granting the peremptory order for his restoration in the next term.[89] The fact of serious partisan division in Bristol had created the need for mandamus; putting Earle back in the corporation only allowed him to go on contesting the actions of his partisan foes. The court's use of mandamus continued the pattern developed before 1688: simultaneously dampening the impact of partisan politics by preventing vengeful majorities from expelling foes, while perpetuating partisan competition by returning such foes to the corporations.

The speed of Earle's restoration was matched in other cases in the 1690s. Expeditious proceedings resulted from the court's greater readiness to use its power of attachment to compel performance of its commands, as well as from occasional pronouncements from the bench regulating court proce-

---

[87] Thus at Exeter, Alderman William Glyde allegedly neglected the oaths. But the decision not to grant his mandamus depended on his having moved from the city. Henning, vol. II, pp. 398–99. PRO, KB21/23/207v, 217, and 220, and KB21/24/45, 56v, 63v, 65, and 71. Devon RO, B1/13, f. 68. *Eng. Rep.*, vol. 89, p. 558 (1 Show. KB 257), vol. 87, pp. 245–48 (4 Mod. 33), and vol. 90, p. 992 (Holt, KB 169).

[88] Bath City RO, Council Book 3, pp. 152 and 177. PRO, KB21/24/115v and 120.

[89] *Eng. Rep.*, vol. 90, pp. 705–07 (Carthew 173), and PRO, KB21/23/214 and 222; KB21/24/2v and 7v. Earle may have been right: Hart would be involved in Jacobite plotting in 1695–96, joined by some of his corporate friends. Paul Kleber Monod, *Jacobitism and the English People, 1688–1788* (Cambridge, 1989), pp. 169–70.

dures.[90] But not everyone was as fortunate as Sir Thomas Earle, and despite procedural improvements, most waited much longer to win their peremptory mandamus. Job Slatford's restoration as Oxford's town clerk took five years. Having begun the process in Easter of 1694, he finally won after an unusual detour through the court of Common Pleas in June 1699. But having prevailed there, he would still have to return to King's Bench, for only King's Bench could issue the peremptory writ that would make good the judgment in his favor.[91] In cases involving annual offices – namely mayoralties – lengthy proceedings remained a serious problem in the 1690s and through much of Anne's reign. As we shall see in the following chapter, this problem would at last be addressed in 1711 by legislation that would transform mandamus, and quo warranto too.

Where time was not a problem, enforceability of decisions might be. Orford corporation fell to pieces in the 1690s, dividing into two bodies with mutually excluding claims to legitimacy. An assize verdict and court orders of 1693–95 failed to end election contests and struggles for possession of the charter, assembly books, and the town hall itself. King's Bench justices recognized the partisan import of Orford's troubles in 1701, noting that the outcome would have an "influence on [the] election of Parliament-men, the two factions of whig and tory [being] deeply engaged in it."[92] But Orford's lengthy problems were the exception, not the rule, and the general

---

[90] The argument that there was an increase in the use of attachments is based on a reading of all reports and rule books for the period. See for instance the use of attachments to compel returns to writs of mandamus to Nottingham in 1690, 1693, and 1696: PRO, KB21/23/205, KB21/24/107, and KB21/25/29. Also Radnor, 1692: *Eng. Rep.*, vol. 90, pp. 736–7 (Carthew 227). See too Chief Justice Holt's discussions of attachments in 1698 and 1700: *Eng. Rep.*, vol. 90, pp. 992 and 1142 (Holt KB 170 and 439). For the court's self-regulation to speed process, see PRO, KB21/26/21 and KB21/27/1; the latter rule is described at *Eng. Rep.*, vol. 91, p. 377 (2 Salk. 434). See also Thomas Tapping, *The Law and Practice of the High Prerogative Writ of Mandamus* (London, 1848), pp. 421–23.

[91] One could bring an action on the case – the form of action used to challenge a return to a mandamus – in the other common law courts: this is what Slatford did. But only King's Bench could grant writs of mandamus and thus any peremptory writ that would follow victory on an action for a false return. For Holt's reiteration of this point, see *Eng. Rep.*, vol. 91, p. 372 (2 Salk. 428). On Slatford's case, see PRO, KB21/24/134v, 136v, 138, 140v, 145, 147v, and 163; KB21/25/28, 30v, 33v, and 76. *Eng. Rep.*, vol. 87, pp. 678–80 (5 Mod. 316), and vol. 90, pp. 565–66 (Comberbach 419). Luttrell, *Brief Historical Relation*, vol. IV, pp. 527.

[92] Matters at Orford were only settled in 1704. For court orders and affidavits, see PRO, KB21/24/104v, 144v, and 146; KB21/26/27v; KB29/360/59; and KB33/22/3. *CSPD 1694–95*, pp. 452–53. PRO, PC2/75/472 and 492. *Eng. Rep.*, vol. 88, p. 1487 (12 Mod. 515) and vol. 90, pp. 471–72 (Comberbach 269). The minute books of the competing corporations are at Suffolk RO (Ipswich Branch), EE5/2/3 and EE5/4/3, and are described in HMC, *Various Collections*, vol. IV, pp. 270–71. For a discussion of Orford in the context of county politics, see Murrell, "Suffolk: The Political Behavior of the County," chapter 6.

efficacy of mandamus remained the principal reason for its growing use after 1688.

Mandamus remained the only means for restoration to office. More important, mandamus also began to develop as a way to smooth the transfer of power between successive office holders. Prior to 1688, the most important innovation in the use of mandamus had been to require the swearing of a duly elected officer. By using it for something other than restitution of office, the justices thus began breaking down the conception of mandamus as a device for protecting one's property in an office in favor of a view stressing the proper operation of public institutions by duly constituted public officials. This public rather than private emphasis was strengthened by developments after 1688 when mandamus was used for the first time to require the holding of an election where those in charge tried to prevent one, and as the court increasingly used mandamus to compel the delivery of records or corporate regalia from one officer to his successor. Both of these uses of mandamus would help maintain stable local governance by protecting it at the moment when it was most exposed to potential trouble: when members of opposing partisan groups had to yield power to one another.

The first signs of these uses of mandamus appeared in the early 1690s. Sudbury's outgoing mayor received a mandamus to deliver records and seals to the new mayor in 1690. Bury St. Edmunds required a mandamus in Easter of 1692 to compel them to elect a new town clerk. More writs to Bury followed that summer as two competitors for the office claimed to be the victor of the election held according to the initial writ. One prevailed in the end as his opponent received a mandamus requiring him to deliver the town's records into the hands of the judicially determined office holder. At Radnor, in Wales, one Vaughan prevailed in a mandamus to be sworn as bailiff, but found that office meant little without the corporation's records and seals. He sought and won a second writ requiring his predecessor to hand over both to him. Bossiney too needed a mandamus to compel it to elect a new mayor.[93] By the end of 1693, King's Bench had carved out clear ground for three related uses of mandamus to protect local governance: to compel an election, to install the winner, and to give to him the instruments of his office. By maintaining government at the moment when control moved from one group to their foes, we see the court serving as the guarantor of stability in the provinces.

With new purposes to serve, use of mandamus continued to rise, especially at the end of the decade when hotter national issues and more

---

[93] PRO, KB21/23/202 and 215; KB21/24/61v, 66–v, 69v, 71v, 73v, 114v, 119, 121–v, 126v, and 139. *Eng. Rep.*, vol. 90, pp. 736–37 (Carthew 227).

frequent parliamentary elections sharpened contests for local control.[94]
Abingdon's experience shows well how King's Bench protected the local
polity when it was exposed to potential trouble. James Courteen had
antagonized many at Abingdon since the early 1690s. He had been
dismissed from his burgesship in 1692, only to regain it by mandamus.[95]
Courteen was chosen mayor in 1694 and again in 1698. At the end of his
second term, according to the usual procedure, two principal burgesses –
John Sellwood and John Spinage – were nominated by the commonalty to
stand in election for mayor. Courteen, "being of another party," refused to
proceed to the final choice between them. Sellwood and Spinage thus
sought a mandamus to order Courteen to hold the election. Courteen made
his return that neither of them had received the sacrament according to the
Corporation Act and were thus unqualified for office. Courteen's return –
made against the wishes of most of the corporation – was found faulty, and
in Easter term, a peremptory mandamus issued to order the election.
Spinage was elected; Sellwood succeeded him the year following. Mandamus succeeded in maintaining continuity of governance at Abingdon
amidst partisan conflict. In deciding the matter, the justices had concentrated not on the sacrament requirement, but on questions about the
legality of the means Courteen had used in blocking the vote and later in
making his return to the mandamus.[96] The unintended consequences of this
and other decisions of the 1690s, and especially in Anne's reign, would be
to degrade the impact of the sacrament requirement, though it remained
the law of the land.

Innovations in the use of mandamus happened only because litigants
came before King's Bench proposing new possibilities for the writ's use.
Litigants also drove a more astonishing development: the revival of quo
warranto. After the struggles of the 1680s and the controversies in
Parliament over the corporations bill and the London Restoration Act of
1690, quo warranto stood in ill repute, though more for political than for
legal reasons. The justices' opinions delivered to the House of Lords in
1690 had left open the possibility of surrender in some instances, and thus

---

[94] See for instance a writ requiring election of the two bailiffs at Maldon: *Eng. Rep.*, vol. 91,
pp. 374–75 and 481 (2 Salk. 431 and 1 Lord Raym. 481), and PRO, KB21/25/149, 160,
162v, 164, and 173v. On sharpening party conflict in Parliament and at elections, see
Horwitz, *Parliament, Policy, and Politics*, chapters 11 and 12.

[95] Challenor, *Abingdon*, pp. 180–81. PRO, KB21/24/81, 81v, and 90v.

[96] PRO, KB21/25/176, 178, 179, and 181v; KB21/26/10 and 14; KB29/358/76; and KB29/
359/17v. *Eng. Rep.*, vol. 88, pp. 1340–41 (12 Mod. 308); vol. 90, pp. 886–87 and
1142–43 (Carthew 499 and Holt KB, 440); vol. 91, pp. 375–76, 592, and 1273–75 (2
Salk. 432 and 699, and 1 Lord Raym. 557). Bod., MS Top. Berks. c. 20, f. 103. Legal
arguments turned on the problem of Courteen making a return opposed by the majority of
the corporation, thus raising the still unresolved issue of who could speak for the
corporation. For a similar problem at Norwich, see *Eng. Rep.*, vol. 91, p. 375 (2 Salk. 432).

by implication, the use of quo warranto. The most prominent jurist of the decade – Sir John Holt – defended the possibility of corporate dissolution or seizure on quo warranto though his was a lone voice. Nonetheless, all the judges felt that *individuals* misusing a franchise might be ousted by quo warranto.[97] The possibility of revival thus existed, though now, quo warranto lay dormant.

A broader problem in the use of quo warranto concerned its membership in the suspect category of proceedings by information. Some condemned informations after 1688 because they could be issued on the whim of the attorney general without a previous finding by a grand jury. But in a case heard soon after the Revolution, leading lawyers and judges discussed informations and agreed that though they had been abused in recent years, the abuse of something did not necessarily mean that it should be abandoned. Though the case concerned an information for a riot, the implications of this decision for quo warranto's future were significant. Sir Francis Winnington, who had used informations in the King's name while solicitor general in the 1670s, now condemned such proceedings, claiming that Matthew Hale had declared informations illegal. But Winnington was alone in this position, even though he was in court with some of the most whiggish lawyers of the age. Sir George Treby, now attorney general, declared he had never heard informations challenged before. He reminded the court that there were legitimate uses for informations, including the information in the nature of quo warranto – a curious remark coming from the man who had led London's fight against quo warranto. But given the way quo warranto would develop in Anne's reign, we should note that even in 1683, Treby had suggested that quo warranto informations might be good against individual corporation members doing wrong, if not against the entire body.

Treby was joined in defense of informations by none other than Sir William Williams, ardent advocate of corporate liberties in the 1670s and early 1680s, before becoming James II's solicitor general in late 1687. He had then received a baronetcy for his leading role in the unsuccessful prosecution of the infamous information against the Seven Bishops in 1688. There are few characters of the period around whom revolve more marvelous ironies. Williams himself knew this as he stepped before the bench in 1690 to defend informations. Though he admitted informations had been misused, "the abuse of a thing will not destroy it." Then he made direct reference to the Seven Bishops, and with what must have been a smile on his face, he added, "I will not undertake to justify the proceedings of the late government; we have all done amiss, and must wink at one

[97] They declared this in Smith's case, in 1691. See above, n. 86.

another." We cannot know if the justices winked back, but Holt did say that though Hale had complained about abuses, he had not condemned informations altogether. The other justices joined Holt and Williams in accepting the legality of proceedings on informations.[98] In doing so, they left open the possibility of reviving the most notorious information of them all, the information in the nature of quo warranto.

Parliament soon joined the bench in protecting informations. An act given the royal nod in early 1693 curtailed the possibilities for abusing informations and clarified procedures for their use. The "Act to prevent malicious informations in the Court of King's Bench" required informers entering an information with the master of the Crown Office to provide a £20 recognizance to guarantee they would see the matter through trial. This would prevent the common practice of bringing informations with little or no merit simply to harass the defendants. Should the defendant prevail against an information after the act passed, he would have his costs paid from the recognizance.[99] By creating these safeguards, the act would play an important role in reviving quo warranto five years later, as the corporation of Hertford discovered in late 1698.

In 1692, Hertford's corporation passed a set of by-laws, including among others, new powers for the mayor and aldermen to admit any freemen they liked. As at Dunwich and other corporations whose parliamentary electoral franchise resided in the freemen, the freemanship had become one of the primary objects of contention. By 1696, troubles at Hertford multiplied as a tory dominated corporation struggled to wrest control of the choice of MPs from a whig-dominated freemanship. In March, Deputy Recorder Thomas Dunster's house was searched for arms after suspicions were raised about his loyalty. Then, in the spring of 1698, eighteen freemen, including MP Sir William Cowper, petitioned the King to complain about the corporation's composition and behavior. An investigation by Attorney General Sir Thomas Trevor raised questions about the legality of Dunster's and Town Clerk Charles Fox's hold on office. But this petition was quickly answered in a counter-petition from Dunster, Fox, Recorder Sir Henry Chauncey, most of the corporation, and what they claimed was the majority of the freemen. They condemned their foes as a host of Baptists and Quakers who had refused to sign the Association oath and who spoke abusively to the magistrates. Trevour's further enquiries revealed that Cowper and others had indeed called the corporation a "pack of rogues,"

---

[98] *Eng. Rep.*, vol. 87, pp. 764–67 (5 Mod. 459).

[99] Stat. 4 and 5 William and Mary c. 18. For background on the act and its impact, see John Shortt, *Informations (Criminal and Quo Warranto), Mandamus and Prohibition* (London, 1887), pp. 112–13.

but he concluded that all who had signed the first petition were well affected.[100]

By now, the disgruntled eighteen had already turned elsewhere. By asking King's Bench for help in the autumn of 1698, they were the first to try to use quo warranto since James II ten years earlier. As their counsel explained to the bench: "this [is] no quo warranto in the name or at the prosecution of the King, but only a method to try a right." After several motions, the court granted them leave to file an information in Hilary term 1699 asking by what warrant the corporation claimed the liberty of electing non-resident freemen. Much of the reporting of the case concerns procedural questions, and there were many of these given the clouds around quo warranto's reputation. Most important, what would be the consequences of a guilty verdict? Holt was clear: not seizure, nor dissolution, but only a fine and ouster from the specific franchise concerned. More questions followed over the amount of time the defendants could have to reply to the information. Answering these questions proved important for quo warranto's later use, but in this case, it was for naught. In Easter term, 1700, the corporation moved to quash the information against them because the informers had not given their recognizance in the Crown Office according to the 1693 statute against malicious informations. The plaintiffs insisted that quo warranto was not covered by the statute since it was not mentioned there by name. But the court declared that "every information which in its nature may be vexatious, is within the purview of that statute." The first use of quo warranto after 1688 had failed. But by finding that the 1693 statute covered quo warranto, the bench declared that quo warranto might be used.[101]

The Hertford case was enormously important. Even though it had collapsed, it established a few key points. First, quo warranto was far from dead: the defendants had done nothing to suggest that franchises were not subject to scrutiny by such means. Second, despite its reputation as an

---

[100] Hertfordshire RO, Hertford Corporation Records, vol. 1, #54, 59, 60, and 61, and vol. 33, #52. The record office catalogue misdates these items to 1690, but they clearly belong to disputes of 1696–98. PRO, PC2/77/139v. Ironically, though many of Hertford's dissenters supported whigs, Quakers largely supported the tories. Monod, *Jacobitism and the English People*, p. 157. Henning, vol. I, pp. 270–71, 758–59, and vol. II, pp. 165–66; and Sedgwick, vol. I, pp. 261 and 513–14, and vol. II, pp. 90–91.

[101] *Eng. Rep.*, vol. 88, pp. 1278–79 (12 Mod. 224), vol. 90, p. 888 (Carthew 503), and vol. 91, pp. 325, 591, and 1183 (1 Salk. 374, 2 Salk. 699, and 1 Lord Raym. 426). PRO, KB21/25/154v and KB21/26/8, 13v, 21, 48v, and 49v. The plaintiffs apparently brought another information, but failed, though at one point, Luttrell reported that since the corporation had not appeared to the information, the court would order seizure of their regalia. No such dire consequences followed. Luttrell, *Brief Historical Relation*, vol. IV, p. 539. The corporation continued admitting freemen, and by 1701, both parliamentary seats were in the hands of strong tories.

instrument of arbitrary government, whigs as well as tories appeared ready to use it to win a partisan advantage. Third, quo warranto, like any judicial device, could be, and was, regulated by statute. In this case, statute placed curbs on its use. By preventing malicious informations and by providing costs to victorious defendants, statute actually enhanced its long-term utility by removing some of the taint of arbitrary power from quo warranto. The way was clear for further legislation to make the law ever more useful to competing partisans in containing the consequences of their struggles for corporate control. And this was crucial, especially by the time that the Hertford case was brought, for in the late 1690s, the most serious partisan contentions of the age began as vigorously contested parliamentary elections occurred with even greater frequency. From the late 1690s on, we see an ever greater intersection of developments in the corporations, in King's Bench, and in Parliament as changes in each affected changes in the others.

Historians have rightly been intrigued by party politicking in Parliament and beyond after 1688, especially in the later years of William's reign and throughout Queen Anne's. This interest has focused on contested elections to Parliament and the less than partial role of the Committee of Privileges and Elections in deciding them. There was good reason why the Committee was labeled "the most corrupt council in Christendom."[102] The partisan loyalties of Committee members often had a significant impact on their deliberations. And because election challenges also frequently depended on declaring who legitimately governed in the boroughs, decisions about who would be seated ricocheted back on the corporations concerned, thereby promoting further partisan conflict.

Parliamentary politicking certainly raised the political temperature in the Commons and in towns nationwide. While we have concentrated on this so far, we would also do well to remember Geoffrey Elton's simple yet critical insight about Elizabethan Parliaments – "the function of parliament was to make laws" – and apply it to the analysis of Parliaments a century later.[103] We must be careful not to think of Parliament, even as we enter these years of the "rage of party," as the source of all partisan trouble. Indeed, following Elton, we may go one step further to see Parliament providing solutions to the divisions generated in the corporations, solutions that concentrated on helping King's Bench do the job it had been doing, ever

---

[102] W. A. Speck, "'The Most Corrupt Council in Christendom': Decisions on Controverted Elections, 1702–42," in Clyve Jones, ed., *Party and Management in Parliament, 1660–1784* (Leicester, 1984), p. 107. See also Holmes, *British Politics in the Age of Anne*, pp. 42–44.

[103] Geoffrey Elton, "Parliament in the Sixteenth Century: Functions and Fortunes," *HJ*, 22 (1979), p. 260.

better since 1660. Legislation, like that refining the use of informations, would prove crucial in the coming years to containing corporate partisan conflict.

Remarkably, such legislation was nonetheless effective for actually arising from partisan contests. It is no accident that it was early in 1700, in the wake of contentious decisions about seats for Dartmouth and Newport – decisions that depended on deciding between competitors for corporate offices – that the Commons turned its attention to a variety of matters touching on the stability of corporate government.[104] In February, the House appointed a committee to examine all charters granted since 1689. In a Commons that now had a greater tory showing than in recent years, the enquiry into new charters had a partisan character since many granted in the 1690s had benefited whiggishly inclined groups in the towns. But such charters had resulted less from ministerial manipulation than from the general tendency to read the charters of the 1680s as illegal owing to James II's October 1688 proclamation against them. Charters of the 1690s thus restored pre-surrender charters, which in turn meant restoring surviving members of the corporation in place at the time of surrender. Such men were often of a more whiggish than tory bent: thus the clear partisan victories produced by the charters of Dunwich, Nottingham, and elsewhere. Perhaps because strict legality had been observed in passing these new charters, nothing further came of the Commons' investigation.[105]

But the House continued to work on other related matters. In February 1700, at the same time the controversy over the election at Dartmouth was in consideration, two bills were introduced. First was a bill "for the more speedy and effectual determining the right to offices in corporations," which was intended to speed proceedings on mandamus. By early April, it had been read twice and committed. The bill resulted from complaints made during the Dartmouth enquiry, that though a mandamus had been sought to compel the swearing of the allegedly legal mayor, court hearings on the matter would continue long after the mayoral year in question had ended. Thus the plaintiff would not have his redress, and further corporate elections would be controlled by an ostensibly illegitimate mayor. This in turn meant parliamentary elections might be determined by illegal corporation officers.[106] Despite the effort, and the good reasons for passing it, the bill never made it to the statute books.

At around the same time, the Commons gave leave to bring in a bill

---

[104] Both towns were simultaneously involved in litigation to determine who properly controlled them. PRO, KB21/25/141, 164, 169v, 172v, 176–76v, 178, and 180; KB21/26/3 and 7v; KB29/357/79; KB29/358/44, 74, and 75; and KB29/359/19. *Eng. Rep.*, vol. 88, p. 1296 (12 Mod. 247). *CJ*, vol. 13, pp. 7–8, 164, and 203.

[105] *CJ*, vol. 13, pp. 183, 220, and 224.   [106] Ibid., pp. 267, 276, 304, and 310.

preventing disputes occasioned by failures to sign the Association, which easily ran through the readings. The Lords quickly agreed to the bill and it received the royal assent in April 1700. The "Act to prevent disputes that may arise by officers and members of corporations having neglected to sign the association and taking the oaths in due time" unquestionably helped protect corporate tories.[107] A few undoubtedly had failed to subscribe the Association due to genuine ignorance of the requirement, and this had left them open to attack by local foes who used their failures as a pretext for expelling them from the corporations. But many who had neglected the Association were probably uncomfortable with the requirement it imposed of recognizing William III not only as King *de facto*, but as king *de jure*. Such people were predominantly of the tory persuasion. The Act to Prevent Disputes permitted those who inadvertently neglected the Association, and those who consciously evaded it, to subscribe and thus maintain their offices.

The bill for more speedy determining of offices in corporations never passed, and the Act to Prevent Disputes was certainly meant to favor one partisan group in the towns over the other. But in such legislative efforts, we can see Parliament involving itself in a way that would have beneficial effects over the long term on the functioning of partisan politics in the towns. Statute would become more significant in Anne's reign and after, but in the 1690s, we see the work beginning. That statute was used to control politics in the corporations, and to assist King's Bench in monitoring the corporations, was paralleled in other uses of statute in the 1690s. Statute had restored London's corporation and it had protected the use of informations which, as we shall see in the following chapter, would be of enormous importance to corporate politics in Anne's reign and beyond. Another act of 1693 had simplified proceedings in the Crown Office, through which corporate cases had to pass on their way in and out of King's Bench.[108]

In the 1690s, King's Bench and Parliament began to pursue mutually reinforcing efforts to bolster the court's ability to maintain stability in the corporations. In statutes restricting the use of informations, simplifying Crown Office procedure, or protecting those who neglected the Association from harassing litigation, and even in failed efforts like the bill to speed process on mandamus, Parliament recognized the permanence of partisan politics in the corporations. It also recognized that King's Bench was the proper arbiter of partisan conflict. King's Bench did the same by its allowance of new uses for mandamus, by its readiness to revive quo warranto, and by its own self-regulation. The results were as yet imperfect

---

[107] Ibid., pp. 182, 218, 264, 268, 272, 290, 295, and 305; *LJ*, vol. 16, pp. 557–59, 561–62, and 578. Stat. 11 and 12 William III c. 17.

[108] Stat. 4 and 5 William and Mary c. 22.

– Orford was still vexed by two corporations when William died – but together, King's Bench and Parliament were finding solutions to the problems of the 1690s, problems that were the legacy of corporate partisan politics in the 1680s and before.

ENDURING PARTISAN VERITIES

As dramatic as the events of 1688 had been, they did little to change the intensity, or even the content, of partisan conflict. Whig and tory had briefly become one in their detestation of James II's measures. But once he was gone, they quickly reverted to their opposed positions in towns everywhere. Though a few townsmen had died during the passing years, most of those involved in corporate conflicts in the 1690s were the same as those who had been struggling together since the early 1680s and before: Whitley, Williams, and Grosvenor at Chester; Mendham and Hethersett at Thetford; and the list goes on. Some had surrendered old charters to Charles II; others had been excluded by Charles's new charters. "Surrenderers" and "regulators" – tories and whigs – fought more vigorously than ever after 1688 for local control and typically did so by reference to the events of the 1680s.

But some things did change after 1688. For one thing, the shoe of "loyalty" was now on the other foot. Tory churchmen once thought they had exclusive rights to the label – witness its use by the tory pamphleteer in the corporations bill controversy of 1690 – but now it was they whose "loyalty" might be suspect. Especially after the imposition of the Association oath in 1696, some tories found it difficult to make all the proper outward displays of allegiance, even if they never went so far as to drink the health of a king over the water. But labels of "loyalty" or "faction" were rarely the basis for the retributive, purgative behavior that continued to characterize partisan politics in the 1690s. Instead, the law of corporations provided the language and tools of partisan contest. In the early part of the decade in particular, this meant asking court and Council to determine a corporation's future composition by reference to its past constitutions. Deciding which of many possible charters pertained in various towns necessarily meant deciding who would rule them. By finding again and again that the charters of the 1680s were by law void, political bodies destroyed when they surrendered in the early 1680s were thus revived, as were many of their old members. At Dunwich, at Nottingham, at Plymouth and Plympton, pre-surrender, whig-inclined corporations were reborn.

But relatively few towns received new charters in the 1690s. This left most corporate partisan disputes to the determination of King's Bench. And here, three trends in particular stand out. First, King's Bench continued to make more, better, and faster use of the tools available to it for settling corporate contests. It still could not cure all ills in the body politic, but its remedies were certainly more effective than ever in settling the corporations. Second, its decisions frequently had the unintended consequence of undermining the import of laws meant to exclude dissenters from all access to public life. Successive decisions made by the justices, based often on a consideration of the technical or procedural problems presented in such cases in the 1690s, and more so after 1702, had the effect of permitting those who were not in full communion with the Church of England to remain in the corporations. Third, this simultaneously left unresolved, and slowly tempered, the most vexing question of all in national and local political life: by what doctrinal terms should courts and corporations decide who may and may not participate in local government? By shying away from a strict reading of statutes addressing that question, King's Bench softened the impact of such laws and forced ideological foes to remain and work together. They rarely did so happily, thus the need for mandamuses ordering new elections or the transfer of corporate insignia. But the use of such court instruments was perhaps the best sign of all that partisan politics could be made stable politics by a dynamic society.

9

Partisan conflict and political stability,
1702–1727

Norwich's Mayor Anthony Parmenter could hold no meetings in 1717. "There were of the court of aldermen fourteen of that party or set of gentlemen who distinguish themselves by the name of tories or high Church men"; the ten others, Parmenter among them, were "reputed to be whigs." The mayor summoned five meetings in quick succession, but the tories stayed away, denying him the quorum he needed to conduct business. As one opponent reminded him, when a whig had been mayor, the tories had kept him from convening any assemblies; Parmenter should expect to do no better. Though whigs were ascendant at Westminster, the coordinated action of the "high Church men" stymied the whig mayor of Norwich.

Then Thomas Bubbins, alderman of Mancroft ward, died. Parmenter now faced one less obstacle. Though he would still lack the quorum he needed even if his party gained the seat, the election represented an important opportunity and would be fought with that in mind. So one December night, jailer Peter Harrold moved Robert Beecroft from one end to the other of Norwich's prison. This made a voter of Beecroft. Long an inhabitant of Wymer ward, Beecroft became an inhabitant of Mancroft when he crossed the ward boundary that ran through the jail. Or so suggested his jailer. Beecroft had his doubts that so simple a move changed his official residence, but he went along. Arriving in the Mancroft side of the jail, Beecroft found over 100 men incarcerated in just the last few days. By tradition, prisoners always voted in the elections of their own wards, so everyone went to the poll the following day. Beecroft and the new inmates supported Edward Coleborne, giving him a victory over William Chamberlain by twenty-eight votes. While Beecroft returned to prison, the scores of new prisoners, jailed only on "fobb actions," returned to their homes in every ward but Mancroft.

Chamberlain's tory friends immediately cried foul, arguing that the prisoners' franchise permitted them to vote only in the ward of their normal residence. Spending the night in the Mancroft side of the jail did not make one an inhabitant of the ward. But the mayor declared Coleborne the winner and swore him. As Parmenter put it, "there was then thirteen of the said tory aldermen to eleven of those who always distinguished themselves by their zeal for the present happy succession." Disappointed tories took their arguments to court, to little avail. Parmenter stalled in responding to mandamuses for Chamberlain and others claiming to have been wronged. When the court ordered Parmenter to produce the poll books from the Chamberlain/Coleborne contest, he said they were missing. This did not amuse the justices of King's Bench, so Parmenter spent two years under the court's attachment for his contempt, first in prison, then under a recognizance. Meanwhile, Coleborne continued as an alderman, and served on a committee examining the rights of prospective freemen. Forty new freemen were soon admitted in Mancroft ward in case another vote should be required to confirm Coleborne in his place.[1]

Results in parliamentary elections at Norwich in the early eighteenth century mirrored results nationwide in their swings from one party to the other from one poll to the next. But even after the collapse of the tory parliamentary interest after 1714, Norwich tories remained competitive in city elections, and though Parmenter outmaneuvered them in 1717, the tories generally enjoyed control of the corporation.[2] In 1722, when the parliamentary vote came off for the whig pair without a contest, shrieval and aldermanic choices produced considerable conflict, and ultimately, tory success. Mayor Thomas Newton allegedly turned a blind eye when supporters of tory aldermanic candidate Edward Weld blocked access of his opponents to the polling place, producing a result for Weld. A few weeks later, tories won the sheriff's election too. Since then, tory crowds roamed the city crying "down with the Hanoverians"; "popery" ran amok among the "disaffected party of mal-contents."[3] At least twenty-one corporation elections in all were fought along straight party lines in the 1720s.[4]

Norwich politics had never been a tidy, quiet affair. Just as we saw at Chester in the last chapter, Norwich's freemen again and again proved their independence. This meant that corporate politics remained open to the "high Church men," even as toryism faced one defeat after another in elections to Parliament. In corporations around the country, partisan

[1] This account comes from PRO, KB32/18, part 1: examination on attachment of Andrew Parmenter, November 28, 1718; PRO, KB21/31, passim; and affidavits: PRO, KB1/2 (Part 1): Andrew Parmenter, May 1 and 5, 1719; Robert Beecroft, January 21, 1718; Peter Harrold and John Fransham, May 4, 1719; Robert Snell, April 20, 1719; Edward Weld, April 29, 1719; Edward Mayes and John Jeffreys, April 20 and May 25, 1719; Thomas Hare, September 6, 1718; and Peter Attesley, Thomas Harewood, and Thomas Newton, May 4, 1719.
[2] Speck, *Tory and Whig*, p. 77.
[3] PRO, SP35/32/120 and 164; SP35/33/62; and SP44/122/136–37 and 144–46.
[4] Colley, *In Defiance of Oligarchy*, p. 134. On popular politics in Norwich, see Wilson, *Sense of the People*, chapter 8.

conflict continued long after the historiography has told us that it died. In George I's reign, religion receded as the critical force driving competitive politics. This was owing to the accretion of a number of factors in the four decades after 1688. A string of court decisions permitted occasional conformists – or even nonconformists – to remain in the corporations when challenged, even after the Occasional Conformity Act of 1711 supposedly outlawed the practice so reviled by high churchmen. Legislation made mandamus and quo warranto ever more effective legal instruments for determining the rights and responsibilities of corporate leaders. And further legislation of the late 1710s and 1720s all but ended the formal bars to office put up against Protestant dissenters since the 1660s. The politics of organized groups in competition with one another continued in the towns even though the issues in contention now concerned other things, such as ministerial corruption or the excise. Though the content of partisan division changed, the fact of partisan division did not.

Partisan conflict did not end after 1714. But neither had the "rage of party" of Anne's reign entailed the political instability historians ascribe to it.[5] While political conflict swirled within and about them in the years up to 1714 and well beyond, most corporations continued to do what they were meant to do: manage their property, various local charities, and local courts, and regulate markets, trade, and public spaces. The law had become resilient enough to absorb the blows repeated political contests threw at the corporate body. With mandamus and quo warranto, Queen's Bench established itself as the only inspector of the proper performance of the corporations' public duties, providing a venue where those who complained of illegal treatment by their partisan opponents could have redress. Legislation passed later in Anne's reign and in George I's contributed to the court's ability to do this. In passing such statutes, Parliament recognized the durability of partisan conflict. It also recognized that rules could be made that would moderate its otherwise destabilizing effects, making partisan politics the very essence of politics in a dynamic society.

CORPORATE POLITICS IN THE AGE OF ANNE

At the beginning of the eighteenth century, religious difference continued to provide the organizational and rhetorical center around which corporate parties revolved.[6] Disputes like one over whether or not to seat Thomas Dunch as a Norwich alderman, despite allegations of his failure to receive the sacrament, were the stuff of partisan battle. One side quite happily

---

[5] The phrase is from Plumb, *Growth of Political Stability*, chapter 5.
[6] See for instance Triffitt, "Politics and the Urban Community," chapter 3 and pp. 169–71. Harris, *Politics under the Later Stuarts*, pp. 178–82.

overlooked this shortcoming in order to bring in one they knew was friendly to their interests; the other challenged him, aware that if they could prove a legal disability, they might well replace him with someone amenable to their own interests. But Dunch had his place when Queen's Bench gave him his mandamus.[7] Bridport's town clerk, Thomas Way, removed by local tories for his dissenting tendencies, was also restored by the court.[8] Though the court made decisions like these based on strictly legal considerations – in Dunch's case, because they found the return contradictory – the effect was to water down the meaning of the Corporation Act. But religious sensibilities – in terms of one's readiness to countenance spiritual life outside the established Church and to permit those outside its communion to participate in public life – continued to be politics' first principle. On no other issue – war, taxes, navigation schemes, or other local projects – did one's opinion serve as a statutorily-defined bar to office.

The Toleration of 1689 opened some doors by creating a more permissive atmosphere for dissenters' public participation in certain towns.[9] But the Test and Corporation Acts remained the law of the land, requiring all corporation members to forswear the Covenant and to receive the sacrament regularly. The subscription of the declaration against the Covenant was carefully observed in many towns, but by now, its importance was minimal. Virtually no one remained alive who had ever sworn the Covenant in the 1640s; few now balked at disowning it. This left the sacrament as the chief point of conflict as corporate partisans on one side tried to evade the requirement, and on the other side, tried to use such evasions to expel foes and capture control. The continued growth of occasional conformity – of corporation members who received the sacrament just often enough to qualify and then attended conventicles – suggests a loosening of dissenter consciences about compromise. This made it easier for more of them to take office, and consequently provoked increasing hostility from those who saw in occasional conformity both a blasphemy and a political threat.

Repeated attempts in Anne's reign to proscribe occasional conformity

---

[7] PRO, SP34/6/30, 44, 46, and 49–54. PRO, KB21/26/211v, 213v, 215v, and 220; and KB21/27, ff. 13 and 22. *Eng. Rep.*, vol. 90, p. 1145 (Holt KB, 444), vol. 91, p. 379 (2 Salk 436), and vol. 92, pp. 320–21 (2 Lord Raym. 1244).

[8] Way's case provides another example of an attachment used to compel performance. PRO, KB21/27/85v, 96v, 100, 102v, 109v, and 120v. Short, *A Respectable Society*, pp. 28–29.

[9] Thus Quakers were now permitted to become freemen by giving an affirmation, rather than swearing the traditional oath. See a case at Lincoln in 1698, where a mandamus to make a Quaker a freeman was approved, though later quashed on a legal technicality: *Eng. Rep.*, vol. 87, pp. 731–2 (5 Mod. 403), vol. 91, p. 1121 (1 Lord Raym. 337), and vol. 92, pp. 644–45 (3 Lord Raym. 203).

show the importance of the issue to parliamentary and corporate tories and suggest the political gains they imagined they could make by ending the practice. From 1702 to late 1704, occasional conformity fired some of the hottest controversy at Westminster as tories tried to pass an act outlawing it in the corporations. Three bills came and went, each failing, the last after the rejection of the infamous attempt to "tack" the bill to the land tax. So reports continued to come from towns like Portsmouth, where the mayor had not received the sacrament and allegedly promoted "republican principles." When Mayor Joseph Whitehorn was challenged to show quo warranto he acted as mayor, the justices of Queen's Bench decided that he did not need to show he had taken the sacrament since this requirement was not contained in the town's charter.[10] Incidents like these inspired continued efforts for a statute forbidding corporation officers from associating with dissenting religion. But it took the enthusiasm generated by the high tory sermon of Dr. Henry Sacheverell, his impeachment, and his subsequent "progress" through the towns and villages passed en route to his new parish in Shropshire, to generate the political momentum to pass an act meant to keep men like Whitehorn from office.[11] In 1711, a bill against occasional conformity at last became law, with effect from March 25, 1712.[12]

The title put an innocent face on the act's purposes: "An Act for preserving the Protestant Religion by better securing the Church of England as by Law established and for Confirming the Toleration." It did include a clause confirming the Toleration of 1689, but the operative clauses were elsewhere. The act opened by citing the Corporation and Test Acts, reminding the country that they were still in force, even if leaders in many towns had winked at them in recent years. Any corporation member who attended any place of worship that did not follow the Church of England's liturgy would be fined £40 and be disabled from office holding. One could regain office later if he could show that he had returned to the Church of England for at least one year, had attended no conventicles, and had received the sacrament three times annually. It thus answered the most significant question left unaddressed in the Corporation Act: by what means might those who were removed according to this act's terms qualify themselves again for office?

If the Occasional Conformity Act had been intended as a new Corpora-

---

[10] PRO, SP44/109/253–54 and SP44/110/67–70. *Eng. Rep.*, vol. 88, pp. 627–28 (10 Mod. 64). The parties at Portsmouth continued to challenge each other by quo warrantos: PRO, KB21/28/47v–50, 54, and 61. BL, Add. 35,988, ff. 20–21.

[11] For Sacheverell's reception by Banbury's tories, see *The Banb–y Apes; or, The Monkeys Chattering to the Magpye* (London, 1710).

[12] Stat. 10 Anne c. 6. Holmes, *British Politics in the Age of Anne*, pp. 99–103 and 113.

tion Act, purging all who did not follow the straight and narrow, it failed. No exodus, forced or otherwise, occurred. This may have been due to the need for private prosecutors to ferret out the guilty; or it may have resulted from requirements that charges be brought within ten days of an alleged conventicle visit and that two witnesses confirm the foul deed. With the act hedged round by these restrictions, few occasional conformists quit their posts, aware perhaps that prosecution would be too difficult in most cases.

In Coventry, seven Presbyterians left the corporation soon before the act was to take effect, but it is unclear if they quit because of the act since it was also alleged that they had misappropriated charity funds. Either way, all were replaced by other Presbyterians, so the heavy dissenting influence in Coventry corporation remained largely untouched.[13] Chester, Leicester, and Nottingham each lost one corporation member at the time, all for unspecified reasons.[14] In none of these places was there anything like the intended purge. Nor did the act end the religious/political division at Portsmouth, from which reports came a year later that there were two mayors and two sets of aldermen and burgesses.[15] More surprisingly, crown officers did little to support the act. Five principal burgesses at Thetford were granted royal pardons and kept their offices though they "through inadvertancy neglected" to take the sacrament within one year before their elections. It is difficult to imagine how anyone who meant to be in communion with the Church could accidentally neglect the sacrament for over a year, but royal officers forgave them nonetheless.[16] With support like this from the crown – at the time of a tory regime – the act's impact could not have been great.

Courtroom activity in the Easter and Trinity terms immediately after the Occasional Conformity Act took effect was remarkably slow compared to the rest of the period. Given previous patterns of litigation – for instance in the wake of the Restoration, after the Corporation Act was first imposed, and during efforts to regain places in the 1690s – one would expect numerous courtroom actions of two kinds if the act had had a real impact. First would be writs of mandamus to regain lost places. Second would be quo warrantos brought against individuals to force them to demonstrate

---

[13] Hurwich, "'A Fanatick Town'," p. 30. This corrects Speck, *Tory and Whig*, pp. 51–52, which says sixteen were removed. Speck argues solely from the Coventry example that the Occasional Conformity Act had an important impact. Hurwich reviews the mistakes in the source Speck cites: "'A Fanatick Town'," p. 47, n. 75. The source is T. W. Whitley, *Parliamentary Representation of the City of Coventry* (Coventry, 1894), pp. 139–40.

[14] CCRO, AB/3, f. 195, and AF/49d/22. Leicestershire RO, BRII/1/4, f. 73 (councilman Robert Lowe's name was deleted from an assembly list in June 1712, but no orders were recorded for the assembly ostensibly held that day). *Records of the Borough of Nottingham*, 9 vols. (Nottingham, 1882–1956), vol. VI, p. 54.

[15] PRO, SP34/28/195.   [16] PRO, SP44/357/341–43.

that they held office within the law. Neither occurred. The few years following the act's passage were generally quieter for the court than those immediately before and after, and the court showed no zeal to enforce the act.[17] In one case, the justices reached a conclusion similar to that in the case of Portsmouth's mayor in 1710–11, ordering a mandamus to swear a burgess at Pontefract who allegedly had not received the sacrament according to the Corporation Act.[18] Indeed, in hearings when dissent was alleged, the Corporation Act, not the Occasional Conformity Act, continued as the touchstone for determining the legality of one's hold on office.[19]

The inability to pass an act against occasional conformity before 1711, and the act's negligible impact once passed, left religious/political divisions in many towns unaltered. Local partisans continued throughout Anne's reign to do what they could on their own to force out opponents. Getting a new charter had been the preferred method for excluding foes since Gloucester's charter of 1672. The classic charter case in Anne's reign came in the battle for control of Bewdley. This was in large part a feud between gentlemen trying to win and hold parliamentary seats. Calls for a new charter came as early as 1699 when various burgesses petitioned the King for one to replace the charter of 1685 – gained then "by surprise and undue practices" – under which they still governed.[20] Even by the standards of the times, Bewdley spent the early years of Anne's reign tied up in an extraordinary number of actions and counter-actions on mandamus and quo warranto.

Queen's Bench's decisions in the Bewdley matter turned on determining the validity of the 1685 charter. Bewdley's charter surrender of 1685 was one of those that had been enrolled, so the charter granted then had been excepted from King James's October 1688 proclamation restoring the corporations to their pre-1679 status. Tories led by Salway Winnington favored continuing to act under the 1685 charter; the whigs, arguing that it was void, hoped for a new one to tip the balance their way. The justices found the 1685 charter void as based on an illegal surrender: all those claiming office by it thus did so illegally and usurped on the Queen for

---

[17] PRO, KB21/28. Few mandamuses for restoration to office were granted from 1711 to the end of Anne's reign.

[18] *Eng. Rep.*, vol. 88, pp. 648–49 (10 Mod. 107), and PRO, KB21/28/138. BL, Add. 35,988, ff. 104–10.

[19] See also cases from Aldeburgh and Buckingham: *Eng. Rep.*, vol. 88, p. 645 (10 Mod. 101). BL, Add. 35,988, ff. 46–48. At Aldeburgh, John Sparhawk was removed for not receiving the sacrament. He appears to have failed on his mandamus, but was soon re-elected during a meeting of questionable propriety: Suffolk RO (Ipswich Branch), EE1/F1/1, pp. 52–55, 57, 62, and 63.

[20] PRO, PC2/77/151v, 168v, 176v, 185v, and 188.

acting as if they were members of a non-existent corporation. One person survived from the pre-surrender period, the last time there had been a legal corporation, so the ancient corporation was defunct for lack of sufficient numbers. Only a new charter could correct the situation. But would it be a confirmation, thus essentially maintaining the corporation personnel list as it then stood, or would it be a new grant, providing possibilities for tinkering with that list? Tories contended that since there had been a *de facto* corporation since the surrender, recognizing its deeds would be the easiest method; whigs petitioned for a new grant, and a new list of members. The new charter passed the great seal in April of 1708 on the same day that a writ issued for parliamentary elections. This was no coincidence. The charter virtually excluded the tory interest from the corporation, leaving it open to easy whig control in the parliamentary vote held soon after it arrived in town.[21] Lord Herbert, the driving force behind the new charter, won an easy victory.

Winnington petitioned the Commons to be seated for Bewdley after both the 1708 and 1710 parliamentary elections. Though he failed in the first instance, the tussle in 1710 proved more interesting, depending as it did on his argument that the 1708 charter was illegal and occurring as it did in a now tory-dominated House. The Commons's finding for Winnington in 1710 served as an attack on those who had granted a charter "under arbitrary ministerial power." The debate had been fierce. Bewdley's new grant raised the fear that by altering charters, the ministry of the day could recompose the makeup of Parliament. Speakers quickly recalled the boroughs' dark days in the 1680s:

have you seen the prerogative enlarged and extended farther, I will be bold to say, than it was in the unhappy reign before the Revolution? Every gentleman remembers how highly things of this nature was [*sic*] resented in King James's time, when court arts were used to wheedle and terrify boroughs into a surrender of their charters . . . But this instance now before us is more new and dangerous . . . this is a quicker, a more silent method of doing it . . . If it be in the power of the crown to dissolve old corporations and erect new, in so exorbitant a manner, we may bid adieu to liberty and property.[22]

As in the fight in 1690 over the bill to restore corporations examined in the previous chapter, the comparison with the 1680s was critical to the analysis. Given that this was a tory analysis, it was James's, not Charles's, surrenders that were condemned. But at least the new charters of the 1680s had been entirely legal if politically questionable: "In those times, the forms

---

[21] Styles, "Corporation of Bewdley," pp. 42–70, especially pp. 62–70.
[22] *A Speech Made in the House of Commons upon the Late Ministry's Forcing a New Charter upon the Town of Bewdley* ([London], 1710). A note on the copy of this speech in the Bodleian Library attributes it to Sir John Packington, MP for Worcestershire.

of law at least were observed; quo warrantos [were] brought and judgments obtained against corporations before new charters [were] sent."[23] Not so the charter of 1708. The Commons, now in largely tory hands, resolved that Bewdley's charter had been "imposed on this borough against the consent of the ancient corporation [and] is void, illegal, and destructive of the constitution of parliaments." The resolution directed that the Queen be asked to set it aside.[24] Nothing came of this. The following year, members of the old corporation brought a scire facias in the court of Chancery to repeal the new charter, but this too failed, as did all other efforts to restore the old one.[25]

New charters from the 1670s through the 1690s, and up to Bewdley's in 1708, were used by borough partisans to gain political leverage over one another.[26] But the experience of the 1680s left suspicions that surfaced any time a new charter passed the seals, suspicions that changes in the corporate constitution might affect parliamentary elections. In 1700, the House of Commons had appointed a committee to investigate charges that the charters granted since 1690 had been motivated by just such intentions. The King readily complied in the House's request to see the petitions and other records connected to the new charters of that period, but nothing came of the committee's deliberations, finding as they may well have that none had been granted unduly.[27] Whether owing to this enquiry, or to the political firestorm lit by the Bewdley case, or simply to a general suspicion about charters, few would be granted after 1708.[28] New charters had become too politically volatile to be used to purge borough governments in response to the demands of urban partisans. It would remain entirely up to local partisan competitors to undertake their own efforts to win or hold local power. This they did in court, where the bench continued to respond, as before, with new uses for now well-established legal devices and with procedural changes to improve their usefulness. Most important, Parliament would contribute to this process by passing legislation that

---

[23] This from a tory account of the charter and events leading up to it, in the form of a dialogue: BL, Harl. 6274, f. 209.

[24] Thomas Carew, *An Historical Account of the Rights of Election*, 2 vols. (London, 1755), vol. I, p. 50.

[25] BL, Add. 35,988, ff. 131–32.

[26] A few other charters were granted in Anne's reign, especially in the early years, including new incorporations at Wareham and Glastonbury. Charters went to Salisbury and Leominster to settle differences in each corporation. No one lost his place at Salisbury. Leominster's new charter was opposed by one faction in town, though it is not clear that it did them any harm. PRO, SP44/241/47–51 and 265–68; SP34/35/100; SP44/354/75 and 275; and IND1/4229/32v, 40, 42v, and 51v.

[27] *CJ*, vol. 13, pp. 164, 183, 220, and 224.

[28] Bristol's 1710 charter was the only one passed by Anne after Bewdley's. Three were granted by George I.

would revolutionize the court's procedures, thereby making it ever more effective as the guardian of corporate governance amidst continuing partisan competition.

QUEEN'S BENCH AND PARLIAMENTARY STATUTE

Since few charters would be granted, political competition focused on interpreting rather than rewriting corporate constitutions. As in the 1690s, political combatants continued to rely on Queen's Bench to do this. There they argued over who legally governed under what charters, and about what those charters said about election and oath-taking procedures. Political/legal confrontations grew more common as creative politicians manipulated all the legal possibilities available to them for winning or keeping local control.

Much of corporate litigants' effort was directed at obstructing the transfer of power at the end of the mayoral year. This often took the form of neglecting to hold a new election, a problem that became more frequent in Anne's reign. Charters spelled out electoral procedures in great detail, dictating that elections should occur on a certain date and on no other. Most charters also required a quorum of the electors and the presence of the outgoing mayor for a legal choice. It was thus an easy matter for a mayor who wanted to continue in office not to appear on the appointed day to prevent an election. A well-coordinated majority of electors could also subvert the process by staying away. In either case, election on the 'charter day' would be missed, and with it, any opportunity to hold a mayoral vote for another year.

John Hawkey of Lostwithiel advised Mayor Alexander Johns to stay away from the vote in 1706. So no election was held, and Johns continued in office. At the end of his second year, Johns appeared and a legal election was held at which he received a majority of votes. Johns was sworn for a third year. At Michaelmas 1708, a small group of burgesses, including John Hawkey, "riotously" prevented the election, and Mayor Johns enjoyed a fourth year in the chair. In 1709, Hawkey let it be known he would arrest Johns at his own suit next time he saw him in public, so Johns avoided the election once again. Another "charter day" came and went with no election. In Michaelmas 1710, a mandamus issued from Queen's Bench ordering the corporation to proceed to the election of a new mayor. Even this appears to have failed.[29] It was one of the court's few clear failures to settle matters.

---

[29] PRO, SP44/243/393–94 and KB21/28/27. Affidavits from 1722 suggest that Johns still acted as mayor. KB1/1 (part 1), affidavits of John Tom, Francis Johns, and Samuel Philips, April 11, 1722; Charles Burt, May 11, 1723; John Johns sr. and John Johns jr., May 11, 1723.

Mayor Johns – acting in connivance with Hawkey – took advantage of a seemingly contradictory clause found in most charters: that the mayor should continue for one year, *and* until the next mayor was sworn.[30] Depending on political needs, one could argue that one of two results should follow from a failed mayoral choice: that the current mayor should continue until the next was sworn, in short, until the next legal election could be held, one year hence; or, that the mayor's term ceased at the end of his year, and with no new mayor chosen, the corporation had no head and was therefore forfeit. If one followed the latter reading, a new charter would be required to resurrect the body. Given the political possibilities, many such abortive elections appear to have occurred with precisely this result in mind. But given the reluctance of the crown to grant new charters, most mayors simply continued in office for another year while everyone tried to ignore the legal questions raised by doing so. The crown provided a third possible response to failed elections: granting special writs under the great seal to hold a new election on a day other than that appointed by charter. Strictly speaking, such writs should not have prevented the corporation's legal collapse for breaking one of the critical provisions in its charter. Nonetheless, Penzance received just such a royal order in early 1706 after a double election of mayors the preceding Michaelmas.[31] Though the ensuing vote legitimated William Tonkin's claim to the mayoralty, he still had to get a mandamus from Queen's Bench ordering his opponent John Carveth to hand over the mayor's insignia. Carveth refused, and the same court procedure was required the following year, when the next mayor as well sued mandamus to get the ensigns of authority from Carveth. Not until Easter term of 1707 did a peremptory mandamus come down imposing a conclusive order for Carveth to relinquish the mayor's seal and mace to the judicially approved mayor. A quo warranto prosecuted at the same time found him to be in office illegally. After this loss, Carveth left town.[32] Questionable uses of novel great seal writs notwithstanding, the final solution had to come from Queen's Bench.

Devizes corporation found itself in a similar bind: "being almost equally divided in two opposite parties, one moiety of the capital burgesses constantly keeps away when the other side summons any meeting so that

---

[30] For instance, Leeds's 1661 charter contained this language: "to continue for one whole year . . . until one other of the aldermen . . . shall in due manner be chosen, appointed, and sworn." James Wardell, *The Municipal History of the Borough of Leeds* (London, 1846), appendix, p. lxvii.

[31] PRO, SP44/241/178–79 and SP44/354/155–56. There was precedent for the use of such royal writs after failed shrieval elections in Norwich and York in the 1690s, though their legality occasioned much debate: PRO, PC2/75/494, 79/231, and 81/7.

[32] PRO, KB21/27, ff. 13v, 41, 48v, 62v, and 83v. P. A. S. Pool, *The History of the Town and Borough of Penzance* (Penzance, 1974), pp. 57–59.

for some years last past, the said corporation have not been enabled legally to do any corporate act." Like Penzance, Devizes had essentially two rival groups, one whig, one tory, since a disputed council election in April of 1706. A slew of removals quickly followed. An order to repair broken windows in the council chamber is as good a sign as any of troubles there.[33] After a double mayoral election in 1707, Devizes asked the Queen for a writ ordering a new election, like that sent to Penzance; but this, like most other measures in Devizes, did not end the stalemate. The town continued to be vexed by the presence of not one, but two governments. Rival mayors were chosen again in 1710, though the town settled down after 1711.[34]

Following the same confusing doctrine that the mayor should continue for one year or until his successor was sworn, many tried to prevent the oath taking rather than the election itself. As the case load on mandamus in Queen's Bench grew throughout Anne's reign, most of the added volume came on writs requiring mayors to swear their successors or to hand over the corporation records and insignia that made titular authority real authority. One might be mayor elect, but he did not become mayor until sworn and he could do little then if he did not possess the corporation's records and seals. Virtually all the mandamus business prior to 1688 had been on requests for restoration to office. Use of the writ to swear new mayors and to force the delivery of corporate records and seals now rose rapidly, building on precedents for the same from the 1690s.[35] This suggests how difficult the transfer of power became in many towns after 1688 as partisan conflict within them continued or worsened. But it also signals the court's continued development as the ultimate arbiter of partisan conflict and as the monitor of the proper performance of public duties by corporation officers. At a time when partisan conflict threatened the well-being of many corporations – and thus the well-being of the communities they governed – the court smoothed the transfer of power between groups at odds with one another, thereby providing for the maintenance of effective local governance.

With so much energy focused on controlling the mayoralty, Michaelmas term each year was especially busy for the justices since most towns held their mayoral elections in September. Calls came in from around the

[33] Wiltshire RO, G20/1/19: March and April 1707.
[34] PRO, SP34/9/89 and SP44/243/158–59 and 353–54, and SP44/353/368–69 and 516–17. The writ is at Wiltshire RO, G20/1/19: May 25, 1708; see also G20/1/90/4, 5, and 27. Edward Bradby, "A Deadlock in Eighteenth-Century Devizes," *Wiltshire Archaeological and Natural History Magazine*, 81 (1987), pp. 91–110.
[35] For mandamuses to swear the mayor, see PRO, KB21/28, ff. 65v and 135v: Chichester and Colchester, 1711 and 1712. For mandamuses to deliver the records, seals, or maces, see KB21/28, ff. 73v and 132: Plymouth and Marlborough, 1711 and 1712.

country for judicial orders after failed elections. Rule books for the Michaelmas terms of 1707, 1711, and 1712 show an especially sharp upward spike in courtroom activity. This was particularly true of Michaelmas term 1714, the first of George I's reign, when battles for corporate office were all the more fierce in anticipation of the parliamentary elections that would follow.[36] But hearings on mandamus went on all year long, to restore those illegally removed from office, to command the swearing of duly elected members, and to command corporations to proceed in the election of new town clerks, recorders, or corporation members where the mayor avoided doing so in fear that he could not control the outcome.[37] Corporators everywhere saw mandamus as their protector. As one councilman reminded his brethren at Gloucester: "You may turn me out if you will, but I will bring a mandamus." They did, he did, and he won.[38]

Much if not most of the increased judicial activity by the second half of the age of Anne was on quo warranto rather than mandamus. The parliamentary act of 1690 had deemed the London decision of 1683 illegal; quo warranto stood tainted. But the information once reviled as an instrument of royal repression nonetheless became the legal device of choice for unseating political enemies. The power of what was still very much a royal instrument – quo warranto issued in the monarch's name, though now at the relation of a private subject – knew no detractors of either party. Whigs were as ready as tories to use it; indeed, whigs revived its use at Hertford in 1698, and its first post-1688 use to expel individual corporation members had been made by Bewdley's whig group. The gathering pages of law reports and other writings on corporations thereafter gave renewed strength to pre-1688 notions of the franchisal nature of corporations: that they or their members could commit a wrong for which the entire corporation, or the places of individuals, might be forfeit.[39] It was appropriate that the crown, through the courts, should monitor their behavior and correct their abuses with quo warranto. This notion of judicial oversight of borough governance was now used by corporate partisans against one another.

---

[36] PRO, KB21/28 and 29, passim.

[37] See for instance the mandamus for holding an election of a clerk at Bath in 1704: *Eng. Rep.*, vol. 87, pp. 910–11 (6 Mod. 152). For others, see PRO, KB21/27, f. 12 (Salisbury, to elect a councilman, 1706); KB21/27, ff. 48 and 57 (Thetford, to elect bailiffs, 1706); KB21/28, f. 34 (Norwich, to swear aldermen, 1711); KB21/28, f. 54 (Abingdon, to swear the recorder, 1711). There are scores more examples in the rule books.

[38] *Eng. Rep.*, vol. 88, p. 1034, and vol. 90, pp. 1148–49 (11 Mod. 271 and Holt, KB 450). PRO, KB21/27/138–59, passim.

[39] *Law of Corporations*, chapter 24, is devoted to quo warranto. Chapters 25–27 dealt with the related topics of forfeitures, causes for disfranchisement, and mandamus.

The Bewdley quo warrantos of 1706 – the first since Hertford's eight years earlier – were a new breed of quo warrantos. They followed the precedent of the Worcester case of 1683, not London's, as they were brought by some individuals in the corporation against other individuals to test their claims to office, rather than by the crown to scrutinize the exercise of an entire corporation's privileges. Using quo warranto this way derived from the success of the action against Worcester's whigs in 1681–83, and from repeated pronouncements by the justices in the 1690s that while corporations might not be seized or forfeit on a quo warranto, especially after the London Restoration Act of 1690, quo warranto would still lie against individuals who usurped or abused the King's franchises.[40] Corporation leaders had learned well the legal lessons of the 1680s and 90s. Now they turned them on one another. Competing corporate sides began suing tit-for-tat informations against one another after 1706, each trying to find a legal means for removing the other. Throughout the courtroom battling, both sides remained in office.[41] And this was the key result of quo warranto's revival. Rather than dismiss a foe, which would then be followed by a mandamus battle over the legality of the removal, the legality of one's hold on office could now be tested without first having to remove the intended victim. Quo warranto, as an instrument for purging foes by legal means, may well have prevented purges by illegal means, since it now provided a way to judge claims to office without first inflicting a purge. Court rule books for the reigns of Anne and George I suggest that quo warranto quickly matched or even surpassed mandamus as the legal instrument of choice in corporate partisan conflict.

Despite the sophistication in the use of the law for partisan purposes and the readiness with which it was used, neither mandamus nor quo warranto could cure all political ills. Numerous suits and counter-suits did not stop the trouble at Devizes; Bewdley required a new charter after similar rounds of litigation and even this made matters little better. And the court's orders were occasionally neglected or abused by those receiving them. From Bridgwater came the excuse for ignoring a mandamus that it contained "false Latin."[42] From Nottingham, Thomas Hawkesley admitted he knew no Latin and could make nothing of the court hand in which a mandamus

---

[40] On the judges' support of quo warranto to oust individuals, see Sir James Smith's case: *Eng. Rep.*, vol. 87, pp. 258–61 (4 Mod. 53), vol. 88, pp. 1135–36 (12 Mod. 17), and vol. 89, pp. 569–73 (1 Show. KB 274). BL, Add. 35,982, ff. 15–24.

[41] The numerous back and forth quo warranto and mandamus cases from Bewdley may be followed in KB21/27, passim. Devizes and Thetford experienced similar runs of quo warrantos brought by members of one party against the other; thus those assaulted typically responded in kind: ibid. Extensive legal papers and other matter relating to this survives for Devizes at Wiltshire RO, G20/1/90.

[42] PRO, KB1/1 (part 2), affidavit of Edward Raymond, *et al.*

was written. But the court was little amused when they heard that he had told the clerk who served him the writ to "wipe your arse with it." Hawkesley tried to explain that he used the word "brich," not "arse."[43] Salty language was popular farther north too, where Pontefract alderman Thomas Taylor refused to swear his successor for he "cared not a fart for the said writ of mandamus."[44] James Gully ignored a mandamus, claiming that he had no idea what it was, though dozens of writs had come and gone from his town of Taunton in recent years.[45] In cases like these, writs of attachment conveyed to the ignorant or disrespectful a better understanding of the law's mysteries and a more keen appreciation of its dignity.

Recorder Charles Whitaker of Ipswich went through the usual court rounds to get his place back after dismissal in 1704. First came the mandamus ordering the corporation to restore him or to show cause why they did not. Then came the writ in its alias and pluries forms. Finally, Ipswich made its return and Whitaker could bring his action against the corporation for a false return. After winning the judgment, Whitaker received his peremptory mandamus, ordering the corporation to restore him without further delay. So the corporation obliged. But Whitaker's troubles were not over. Less than three weeks later, the corporation removed him again, forcing Whitaker to begin the same process to regain his place. Since the corporation could show he had been removed by a new order in response to a new cause, they were not technically in contempt of court. Whitaker died before reaching the end.[46] Maidstone's leaders showed similar imagination in keeping out a man they so clearly no longer wanted in their midst, restoring a mayor according to court order, then removing him as a jurat the following year.[47]

Cases like these were less common than might be expected. The real problem with using mandamus lay not in getting back one's place once the peremptory writ came down; rather it lay in reaching that stage. Months or years could go by before the succession of initial, alias, and pluries writs had come and gone, even after procedural improvements of the 1690s.

---

[43] PRO, KB32/18, part 1: examination on an attachment for contempt, 1715.

[44] PRO, SP44/108/205v.

[45] PRO, KB32/18, part 2: examination on attachment for contempt, January 23, 1720.

[46] Suffolk RO (Ipswich Branch), C5/14/6, pp. 43, 56, 59, 74, 130–31, and 145. G. R. Clarke, *The History and Description of the Town and Borough of Ipswich* (London, 1830), pp. 72–78. PRO, KB21/26/187v, 190v, and 192, and KB21/27, ff. 13–13v, 33, 52v, 54v, and 71. J. Wodderspoon, *Memorials of the Ancient Town of Ipswich* (London, 1850), p. 125. *Eng. Rep.*, vol. 90, pp. 1145–46 (Holt, KB 445), and vol. 92, pp. 313–18 and 342 (2 Lord Raym. 1232 and 1283). John Lee, alderman of Canterbury, was also removed – for what the corporation said was a separate offense – after being restored by mandamus: PRO, KB32/17, part 1: examination on an attachment of Edward Tendall and Samuel Johnson, November 28, 1711.

[47] Martin, *Records of Maidstone*, pp. 171–72.

Only after the third writ, the pluries, did the corporation or person receiving it typically make a return. If the aggrieved had not been restored and the corporation made a return giving its reasons why, only then could the plaintiff bring an action for a false return, after which, if he were victorious, he would finally receive a peremptory mandamus ordering that the deed be done with no other options. This long process required money; it also required time. When it involved an order to elect or swear a mayor, the mayoral year might well be over before the matter was settled. In the meantime, the legal mayor had been kept from exercising his office. Similar problems applied in using quo warranto before an annual term of office expired. This would give those holding office illegally time to magnify the wrong by bringing in others of their persuasion. Tories worried about the impact dissenters could have by thus remaining in annual offices, with "proceedings on informations being so long that they can't be well convicted within their year and so may get other dissenters in."[48] Something had to be done.

Relief came by statute. That parliamentary attention turned to mandamus and quo warranto in 1711 suggests something of the importance they had achieved in political and legal usage. This importance had been clear much earlier. As we saw in chapter 8, the Commons considered a bill in 1700 "for the more speedy and effectual determining the right to offices in corporations." But after two readings, the effort disappeared from the parliamentary agenda for over ten years.[49] When it reappeared in January 1711, it moved easily through both Houses. The Commons had addressed the Queen, requesting an account of corporation mandamuses, making particular note of those concerning Devizes, upon which Attorney General Edward Northey duly reported to the House. A draft bill to improve mandamus then passed two readings and was committed, where an amendment was added prohibiting any mayor from serving two successive terms. This measure alone would go a long way toward closing one of the gaps in corporate charters most easily exploited for partisan ends. Another amendment proposed by the committee, permitting corporations to hold elections on days other than those appointed by charter, was rejected by the House. Nonetheless, the bill held out great promise for curing some of the corporations' most enduring woes. The Lords passed the measure with little ado, and the Queen gave it her blessing in May.[50]

The "Act for rendering the proceedings upon writs of mandamus and informations in the nature of quo warranto more speedy and effectual"

---

[48] BL, Add. 35,988, f. 21.   [49] *CJ*, vol. 13, pp. 267, 276, 304, and 310.
[50] Ibid., vol. 16, pp. 450, 463, 472, 515, 534, 545, 617, 626, 659, 662, and 668. *LJ*, vol. 19, pp. 294, 296–97, and 300.

opened with a statement of what by now was evident to all. "Whereas divers persons have of late illegally intruded themselves into . . . the offices . . . of towns corporate," and whereas under current law, it was impossible to try the right to such offices within the year – the only recourse being by mandamus, "the proceedings on which are very dilatory and expensive" – the act commanded that returns be made to all writs in the first instance. From Trinity term 1711 on, all receiving a writ of mandamus would be required either to perform the order or to make a return to the court immediately. Gone were the alias and pluries writs which had spun out the process. Furthermore, if the recipient of a writ made a return, a separate action for a false return would no longer be required to test its validity; the plaintiff suing the writ could have a determination of the truth of the return from the bench without instituting what had essentially been a new set of proceedings. Those suing the writ and winning would receive damages and costs as well as a peremptory mandamus, thus making it easier and more attractive than ever to use. The act effectively removed all the causes of delay inherent in the old process, and gave to winners such recompense that it might make corporation officers in the future think twice before making a questionable return, and instead perform the act required without further delay.

The act also regulated quo warranto. Now it would be easier to bring a quo warranto, though the price of bringing one maliciously rose sharply. The names of those at whose relation the crown brought quo warrantos would now be recorded in the information. To expedite proceedings, informations formerly tried separately against each individual could now be considered together if the court found it proper to do so. For their part, defendants in quo warrantos were now required to make their pleas in the same term rather than put it off by the often interminable procedural maneuvering common before. Whether found against the relator or the defendant, the loser would owe costs to the victor. As was the intention behind new rules for mandamus, those considering a quo warranto might now think again before going ahead with a weak case meant only to harass political foes. Last, the Act made good on promises to prevent mayors succeeding themselves in office by imposing a £100 fine on any who tried to do so.[51]

The judges followed through on the act's intentions. No more alias nor pluries writs appear in the court's rule books from that time forward. Defendants on mandamus now filed their returns in the same term in which

---

[51] Stat. 9 Anne c. 20. This clause also imposed the same fines on any parliamentary returning officer who tried to succeed himself in office, thus affecting sheriffs in corporations that were counties, such as Norwich or Chester.

the writ issued, thus speeding process dramatically.[52] Final judgments took weeks or months instead of years. This did not prevent some, like the mayor of Canterbury, from "paying a mock obedience" to the court's orders.[53] But the court's power to attach such persons for contempt would deter most.

While the Occasional Conformity Act has received much attention, its significance for political life in the corporations was not nearly so great as this act dealing with less sensational but no less important matters of judicial process. In our fascination with parliamentary development and conflicts in high politics, we have overlooked the quieter political and institutional changes that made a divided society a peaceful one. The "Act for rendering proceedings . . . more effectual" – passed easily without a division – signaled an awareness among MPs of the court's importance in softening the impact of partisan politicking. Parliament saw the possibility that statute could assist the growth in the court's role as the overseer of corporation politics. They passed an act which, while not solving all problems, went a long way toward increasing the court's effectiveness in this role.[54] Passed by the same Parliament that later that year gave England the Occasional Conformity Act, the "Act for rendering proceedings . . . more effectual" was a temperate measure in otherwise intemperate times. It did not remove the sources of conflict. Rather, it controlled the way conflict would occur. It was perhaps as good a sign as any that England's political nation was coming to accept the permanence of partisan division, and was now consciously making arrangements to ensure the safe and effective operation of the polity in light of that condition.

More of the same would be needed. A bill for quieting corporations "by limiting [the] time for questioning the rights of [corporate] officers" passed with equal ease through the Commons in the spring of 1714. Amendments made after the second reading would have made quo warranto even more expeditious, though more costly for those who only used it to harass opponents rather than to test truly questionable claims to franchises. Anyone would be permitted to file an information, so long as he also filed a recognizance bond promising to pay all costs if he lost the verdict. Another amendment would have made mandamus less costly. Though the bill

---

[52] See for instance the cases of Chichester and Pontefract in Michaelmas 1711; of Marlborough, Colchester, and Helston in Michaelmas 1712; and Lancaster in Hilary 1713: PRO, KB21/28, *passim*.

[53] BL, Add. 36,117, f. 84.

[54] For general background on the act and its importance in shaping subsequent development of both devices, see James L. High, *A Treatise on Extraordinary Legal Remedies, Embracing Mandamus, Quo Warranto and Prohibition* (Chicago, 1884), chapter 7; Shortt, *Informations*, pp. 112–16; and Tapping, *Law and Practice*, pp. 6–7, 333, 344–46, and 383–89.

passed the Commons, it never became law, instead dying with the Parliament that died with the Queen on August 1, 1714.[55]

THE CORPORATIONS AND THE HOUSE OF HANOVER

Rioting on George I's coronation day in October could not have heartened the new King. Taunton's mayor and other magistrates were active rioters themselves, as were corporation members at Worcester. Reports of disloyal mobs came from numerous towns, including Bristol, Salisbury, Canterbury, and Bath. With cheers of "high Church and Dr. Sacheverell" ringing through the streets of Shrewsbury and "Sacheverell for ever; down with the Roundheads" in Tewkesbury, the high Church, tory leanings of crowds everywhere was unmistakable. Mob use of Interregnum labels to smear the ascendant political order, and attacks on dissenting meeting places in towns around the country the year following, suggest the difficulty the whig victors of the parliamentary elections of 1715 faced as they set about consolidating their political gains.[56] If a tory proscription was the order of the day, that proscription could only go skin deep in a body politic so full of ill humors.

In the wake of the elections of 1715, "Whig leaders went about making the world safe for the Whigs," according to J. H. Plumb.[57] This was done by the time-honored method of purgation, beginning at the heart of royal government: the leading offices of state were taken over by those from one party. For Geoffrey Holmes, toryism was not proscribed, it "committed suicide."[58] Such arguments have been challenged, most notably by Linda Colley, whose work has resuscitated the supposed corpse of tory parliamentary organization and effectiveness.[59] But we can go further still. Even if one accepts the premise of the complete defeat of tories at court or in Parliament, this did not entail the end of toryism, tory partisanship, and partisan conflict in the corporations. Perhaps nowhere else is the survival of effective tory politics more evident after 1715 than in the towns, in many of which holders of the tory political faith remained dominant, or at least served as a check on whig pretensions.

Four interconnected forces sustained partisan conflict and tory politics in the corporations after their supposed demise. First was life tenure. Few corporation members were subject to regular re-election as were the tory

---

[55] *CJ*, vol. 17, pp. 490, 704, 713, 717–18, and 719. *LJ*, vol. 19, p. 748.
[56] PRO, SP35/74/2, 3, 5, 6a, and 6b; SP44/117/58; and SP44/118/150–51. PRO, PC2/85/58v and 71. Monod, *Jacobitism and the English People*, pp. 173–94.
[57] Plumb, *Growth of Political Stability*, p. 161.
[58] Geoffrey Holmes, "Harley, St. John and the Death of the Tory Party," in Holmes, ed., *Britain after the Glorious Revolution, 1689–1714* (London, 1969), p. 235.
[59] Colley, *In Defiance of Oligarchy*.

MPs rejected in the elections of 1715. In most corporations, one only left the council upon death. The same applied to the major offices of recorder or town clerk. Second, over six decades of court cases on mandamus had proved again and again that corporate majorities could not remove from their midst those whose politics they did not like. Good reason had to be shown for dismissals or lost places would be won back again by judicial writ. With the 1711 act for making mandamus more effectual, the power of mandamus to do just that had been increased by raising the penalties on corporations that tried to use false returns to justify unjustifiable removals. Mandamus gave borough partisans something no MP had: judicial protection from the partisan whims of the majority of their respective bodies. When parliamentary politics leaned one way or the other, the outcome of disputed elections was easily foretold. Neither the Committee of Elections nor the full House ever approached the impartiality of King's Bench in deciding electoral disputes. While those with demonstrable electoral majorities were turned away from Westminster by the partisan majority, corporation members who felt unfairly treated had recourse to an institution from which they could reasonably expect fair play.

The third force perpetuating partisan competition was seen in the coronation riots: large sections of popular opinion favored the Church, damned dissent, and occasionally flirted with Jacobite sedition. In towns like Chester, where freemen played an important part in a multi-stage mayoral election process, such opinion imposed itself every year in a way corporation leaders could do little to control. In the more unusual case of Norwich, the freemen not only participated in the choice of mayors, but of councilmen and aldermen too. And below the freemen in Norwich and other towns, a vital political culture bubbled beneath the surface of institutional politicking, thus contributing to the ability of local leaders favored by the populace to withstand pressure from their betters at Westminster and Whitehall.[60] Between life tenure, judicial redress for political wrongs, and popular agitation, there could be nothing like the proscription of tories in the corporations that occurred at Whitehall or Westminster. But fourth, and perhaps most surprising, the power of central government was not turned on corporate tories. There was no centrally-inspired effort to drive them out, probably because when viewed together, the three factors discussed above presented formidable obstacles to the success of any such effort.

The substance of political division in the corporations continued to be largely religious in the first years after 1714. The Corporation, Test, and Occasional Conformity Acts remained in force; the right to participate in

[60] See Wilson, *Sense of the People*, chapter 8.

corporate life was still determined by one's religious proclivities or the willingness of local leaders to overlook them. The name of Dr. Sacheverell continued to raise strong passions too. But partisan rhetoric worked increasingly in a new idiom, the dynastic. In their efforts to remove opponents from their councils, local whigs rarely raised religious themes, as this could well work against them given current law. Instead, they portrayed their conflicts in terms of a struggle between loyalty and sedition. As in the reign of Charles II, when partisan condemnation typically included charges of "disaffection," the rhetorical exchanges of the years after 1714 increasingly included allegations against "anti-Hanoverians." Partisan roles were thus reversed from before. "The Church party" once had exclusive ownership of the tag "the loyal"; now it was they, not their political enemies, whose loyalty would be questioned most often. While there had been intimations of such a rhetorical reversal since 1689, only after 1714 did it become complete.

Given the political leanings of those in favor around the new King, corporate whigs tried unabashedly to use royal power to their advantage, with little regard for the legal propriety of what they proposed. After 1715, they rushed to exploit claims of "loyalty" with the same enthusiasm shown by tories in the 1680s, though arguably with less success now. For instance, clauses requiring royal approbation of town clerks and recorders remained in force in scores of towns still governed by charters granted during the first nineteen years of Charles II's reign. Urban whigs now asked the crown to use this power to their advantage, though in an earlier age, they would have condemned it as an oppression. Labels of disloyalty played an important part in their requests for crown support. But when Leominster chose a "Jacobite" for their new town clerk, he received royal approval nonetheless.[61] Theophilus Levett, Lichfield's choice for town clerk, was approved too despite reports that he wore a white rose on the Pretender's birthday.[62] It would have been quite within the law for the King to disapprove such corporate choices according to whig desires. But there is no sign that crown ministers used the King's continuing power over the selection of corporate officials to prevent the appointment of tories or those allegedly adverse to the prevailing regime, despite the occasionally extreme language used to condemn nominees to corporate office.

Leaders in some towns were even more creative, trying to resurrect the

---

[61] PRO, SP35/9/171 and SP44/360/96–97. On the approbation requirement, see above, pp. 157–60.

[62] Levett was chosen in 1721 but no approbation is recorded before 1726. It is not clear whether he or someone else acted in the interim. PRO, SP/35/27/37 and SP35/28/1, 12, and 68, and SP35/30/17 and 22; SP44/361/471–72. Most towns were careful to get royal approval of new officers according to the terms in their Caroline charters. See PRO, SP44/352–361A, passim, for warrants granting the royal approbation.

long defunct royal power to remove corporate officers appointed in the charters of the 1680s. In early 1717 Lord Stanhope received news from Leeds, a non-parliamentary town, that in the impending choice of a new alderman, "the Jacobite party was very hot for choosing one Wilson who has strangely reflected on our gracious King," while the loyal intended to choose a man active in investigating bonfires lit on the Pretender's birthday. In accordance with current political reality, local dissenters were most likely to help the King, but this was before the repeal of the Occasional Conformity Act and the declaration against the Covenant: "not being qualified by law to serve their country, they are useless." So requests were made for a royal order commanding the election of the "loyal" man and the removal of two aldermen; this and other proposed removals would give the King's party "a power to manage the rest." Only a purge of the tory corporation, which filled each vacancy with "the hottest Jack they can find," could save the loyal.[63] Despite the colorful language, no royal purge of Leeds followed. There was no way in law, without recalling the universally reviled methods of James II, for Whitehall to order the removal of corporation officers.

This did not stop Sir William Lowther, who cited the dubious example of James II when calling for royal orders to remove corporation members at Pontefract. As the owner of sixty burgages in this borough with a burgage franchise, Lowther had a near lock on the parliamentary seats.[64] Controlling the corporation proved another matter altogether. Two vacancies existed on the aldermen's bench in 1717. Instead of holding an election to replace them, which would surely go against him, Lowther proposed that the King turn out two others and then name his own choices to the four empty seats: "this is not without precedent for King James turned out every man in the corporation but the mayor, and when he found the gentlemen would not do what he desired, he turned them out again." The attorney general examined Pontefract's 1685 charter – which according to James II's October 1688 proclamation was void anyway – to see if this were legal. He declared that the King could remove aldermen, but he could not name their replacements: "they cannot be directed who shall be chosen." Anyway, the attorney advised, there was no good case for removing those of whom Lowther complained.[65] Lowther's methods were disreputable, illegal, and unnecessary.

Not long after this disappointing report from the King's chief legal advisor, Lowther's choice lost the mayoral election of 1717. Days later, Lowther endured further outrages when the tories raised a mob at the

---

[63] PRO, SP35/8/47 and 113.   [64] Sedgwick, vol. I, pp. 361–62.
[65] PRO, SP35/9/33, 50, and 58; SP44/120/189–90; and SP44/249/425–26.

market crying "down with the Rump, away with the whigs." So the outgoing mayor, in connivance with Lowther, refused to swear his successor and detained the corporations' records to prevent his tory foe from acting.[66] This led to a mandamus to force the old mayor to relinquish them.[67] The corporation also complained to the King of Lowther's activities. Lowther denied their charges and requested royal assistance in defending the legal action against him. He and others simultaneously petitioned the King for a new charter that would reduce the corporation's size and change the membership, making it easier to manage in his interest. But all Lowther's pleas fell on deaf ears. Solicitor General Nicholas Lechmere recommended that Lowther be left to his own means in defending the suits brought against him. No purge and no new charter would be granted to assist one who claimed to do the King's work in Pontefract.[68]

Lowther's bid to control the corporation continued the following year when he tried to prevent royal approbation of their choice of town clerk and suggested that the King could appoint Lowther's nominee to the office. Once again, the attorney general recommended against Lowther's questionable methods and the clerk chosen by the tory corporation earned the royal nod. Lowther grumbled: "I have not met with so much justice from the great men above as I might have expected."[69] His proposals that the crown use an illegal power to remove or to appoint, that it use a still lawful though controversial power to deny approbation to the corporation's choice of town clerk, or that it use its undoubted authority to grant a new charter to recompose the corporation, had all been rejected. Owning the burgages as he did, Lowther was able to command the parliamentary seats at Pontefract. But the corporation would never be so easily controlled as long as royal advisors refused to use the potential power they had over the corporations to the advantage of Lowther and other local whigs.

Lowther's failure to get a new charter is particularly interesting. After the fracas over the Bewdley charter a decade earlier, it became clear that new charters might provoke more trouble than they were worth, especially when used so blatantly to promote the ends of one local party against another. New charters recalled the political turmoil of the 1680s. Queen Anne granted seven new charters during her reign, a tiny number compared

[66] PRO, SP35/9/160 and 188.
[67] PRO, KB1/1 (part 2), affidavits of Lawrence Fox, January 15, 1718; and Robert Lowther, John Kellam, and Richard Routh, January 19, 1718.
[68] PRO, SP35/10/17, 42, 56, and 62; SP35/74/36(1); and PC2/86/25v and 47v.
[69] PRO, SP44/119/235–36 and SP44/120/354; SP35/12/157 and 167, SP35/17/14, and SP35/18/111. No order for Benezer Hepworth's approbation as town clerk survives, but that he was approved is clear in the order for the approbation of his son as town clerk in 1725: SP44/361A/247–48.

to previous monarchs. George I granted only three during a reign of roughly equal length. One of these, to Banbury, demonstrates the political difficulties associated with new charters and suggests why crown ministers were so reluctant to use their most powerful tool to control the corporations for their political benefit.

Two parties had divided Banbury's corporation since 1688. The tory group held the upper hand during Anne's reign. But after returning Sir Jonathan Cope to Parliament for the town's one seat in January 1715, borough tories found themselves under siege at the mayoral election that autumn. Those trying to topple the tories petitioned the King, charging that the mayoral election had failed as a result of efforts by some to elect one "who had behaved himself with great indecency and disrespect towards your majesty."[70] Alleging that no one had been legally chosen, they argued that the charter was now void since the corporation had no head. The King referred the matter to the attorney general, who suggested that though the corporation was technically in abeyance, another election would be "the most proper means to settle the said corporation on their old foundation."[71] The attorney general clearly wanted to avoid having to grant a new charter.

With the corporation's status so tenuous, no corporate acts were done until the following September when Recorder Shreeve Painton, former Mayor William Box, and other tories proceeded in an election according to the attorney general's recommendation. A majority of votes allegedly went for Box, and he was sworn at Michaelmas.[72] But their opponents preferred the corporation's demise to the measures proposed by the King's chief legal adviser. Seeking their own political advantage, they skipped the election and went to court. Good grounds existed for a quo warranto against all who participated in the 1716 election, if those who stayed away could make a case that the corporation had ceased to exist upon the failure of the mayoral election the year before. If the corporation was forfeit for lack of a mayor in 1715–16, then holding an election in 1716, whatever the attorney general's advice, was a usurpation of royal authority. In short, the quo warrantos brought by Banbury's whigs charged those participating in the election with acting like a corporation when no corporation existed.

Quo warrantos were brought to test the claims to office of Mayor William Box, the recorder and town clerk, four aldermen, two capital

---

[70] The petition is printed in Alfred Beesley, *The History of Banbury* (London, 1841), pp. 514–16. Beesley misdates the petition, and thus the election, to 1717. VCH Oxfordshire, vol. X, p. 75, repeats the error.

[71] PRO, KB1/1 (part 2), affidavits of Richard Burford, and of William Box, Henry Clarson, Timothy Gibbard, John Wyatt, and John Style, dated May 9 and 13, 1717.

[72] Ibid.

burgesses, and two assistants: all part of the tory group.[73] Box and the others quickly disclaimed any malign intent in holding the election, saying that they only followed the suggestions of the attorney general in hopes of sustaining the corporation's life. This was nothing more than what their oaths of office obliged them to do. Such reasonable arguments notwithstanding, judgments came down against six of the defendants in Easter term 1717. The others capitulated the following Michaelmas, submitting to fines imposed by the act of 9 Anne for usurping the King's franchise.[74] The court agreed with the plaintiffs that the corporation no longer existed after the failure of the 1715 elections, so their elections in 1716 were illegal. The only way to restore the defunct body would be with a new charter.[75]

By early 1718, corporators from both sides of the partisan divide came cap in hand before the Privy Council, petitioning for a charter to reconstitute the corporation. The charter they received included a clause permitting the mayor to remain in office until his successor was sworn, thus ending the possibility that the corporation could be forfeit for failure to elect on the proper day.[76] But the new grant did not simply restore the old corporation with a few adjustments in its operating procedures. It also changed the personnel list. While it is difficult to know the full extent of changes made in corporate membership since no lists exist for the years before the breakdown in 1715, some of the most prominent members of the old corporation certainly lost their places. Only one of the tory defendants in the suits of 1715–17 retained his place; three former mayors lost their offices, as did the recorder. Many of those appointed for the first time were non-residents, though the charter proclaimed that all members should be borough inhabitants.[77] The commencement of a new set of corporate records after the charter arrived suggests that the charter achieved the most important goal: providing the town with stable government.

Christchurch corporation went through similar tribulations created by a complex chain of events beginning with the failure to swear a new mayor

[73] PRO, KB21/29, ff. 153v, 157v, 159, 165v–66, 177, 185v, and 188v.

[74] PRO, KB21/30, ff. 4v and 11–12, and KB21/31, ff. 7v and 10v.

[75] *Eng. Rep.*, vol. 88, p. 758 (10 Mod. 346). This report is dated Michaelmas term, 3 George I (autumn, 1716), preceding the affidavits above, and thus does not give the court's final judgment. This report suggests that the court resolved that a new charter would be required to restore the corporation, which is confirmed by the rule book orders cited in the note above.

[76] This second petition for a new charter is at PRO, PC1/14/117; Privy Council hearings are at PRO, PC2/86/47v and 71–2. A copy of the charter is in the Oxfordshire RO, B.B.I/iii/4, a synopsis of which is in Beesley, *Banbury*, pp. 516–18.

[77] Despite the threat of fines for refusal, three appointed by the charter rejected office; others elected in the next few years did likewise. Oxfordshire RO, B.B.XV/i/1, August 1 and 23, 1718, September 5 and October 14, 1719, and passim.

in 1718, followed by an abortive election in 1719, and then the death of two *de facto* mayors. This left confusion as to whether or not any legal corporation continued to exist. The parties there competed in hearings before the attorney and solicitor generals over whether matters might be righted by a writ ordering a new election – citing the examples of Devizes and Penzance – or by a new charter.[78] Despite a finding that a new charter would be best, none was forthcoming. All realized that "in cases of that nature, the granting of a new charter is a matter of nice consideration" as it affected parliamentary elections.[79] Despite this tantalizing possibility, or maybe because of it, the crown passed up a chance to recharter Christchurch. Doing so meant leaving tories in control of the corporation and its parliamentary seats.[80]

The new charter at Banbury, and more so the lack of new charters to Christchurch and other towns with troubled mayoral elections, present a number of puzzles about the intentions and methods of those in control in Whitehall.[81] Charters had long proved the perfect partisan tool, effective for reshaping the constitution and personnel of a governing body to suit the needs of those in power. But Banbury's new charter was only granted after the attorney general tried to provide another method for settling matters there. Only after local partisans forced the issue in court, and after the justices declared that the corporation was dead, did the crown agree to a new charter. Though it resulted in the dismissal of some long-entrenched tories, Banbury's new charter was a measure of last resort, not a device of crown officers eager to use it in the first instance to purge local tories. The Christchurch case presents the same prospect even more vividly. No charter was granted, even after crown legal officers recommended one, and after King's Bench, by finding the mayoralty void on a quo warranto, by implication found the corporation forfeit as well.[82] Given the control over the corporation then exercised by tories, it would seem to have been the perfect opportunity, and a legal one, to refashion the body with a new charter. But this did not happen. By its reluctance to grant new charters, by

---

[78] There were many questions about the legality of such writs. Chief Justice Parker essentially declared against them in the Banbury decision: *Eng. Rep.*, vol. 88, p. 758 (10 Mod. 346). In making their recommendations about Christchurch, the attorney and solicitor generals advised against using such a writ as it had received no judicial support. BL, Add. 36,140, f. 35v.

[79] BL, Add. 36,140, f. 34.

[80] For the legal arguments concerning Christchurch, and the events forcing consideration of the issue, see ibid., ff. 27–36 and Add. 36,134, ff. 34–35 and 41–42. On the constituency, see Sedgwick, vol. I, pp. 249–50. See also PRO, PC2/87/153, 173, 289, and 329–30.

[81] Missed or void mayoral elections at Bodmin, West Looe, and other towns in the 1720s did not lead to new charters, though one was recommended for Bodmin. BL, Add. 36,140, ff. 36–42, and 36,141, f. 42. PRO, PC2/87/97 and SP44/361A/143–46.

[82] PRO, PC2/87/329–30.

its unwillingness to use its power of approbation in the selection of corporation officers, and by its rejection of the extreme measures promoted by the likes of Lowther, the early Hanoverian crown showed little interest in manipulating its legal authority to put the corporations in the hands of those who would do its bidding. This coincides with the findings of Lionel Glassey, that the transformation of the county benches after George I's accession was neither so fast nor so complete as the notion of a "tory proscription" would have us believe.[83] If toryism remained strong in the corporations, this was in large part owing to the forbearance of those who could have used crown powers to refuse tories most any role in the life of the localities.

The corporations were thus left to the law to work out their internal differences, so King's Bench remained the principal and final arbiter of corporation political conflict. Again and again, as in the generations immediately preceding, the court made the decisions that mattered as each side from one town after another simultaneously lay its grievances before the judges. Much of the conflict that generated courtroom business before and after 1715 had resulted from efforts directed toward gaining or retaining a parliamentary seat next time elections came around. This clearly motivated Lowther in Pontefract, and probably inspired the troubles at Banbury. The boroughs of Cornwall provide the most spectacular examples of efforts to control corporate offices in the interest of controlling seats. The post of mayor, as the returning officer, was especially important. Once one captured the mayoralty in Penryn, Helston, Tregony, or other Cornish boroughs, he was loath to give it up. Use of quo warranto in the late 1710s and 1720s was almost constant in a handful of Cornish corporations as each side brought informations against the other. Indeed, by the 1720s, the vast majority of corporation business before King's Bench from one year to the next concerned the towns of Cornwall; in some terms, they were the court's only borough litigants. Extensive affidavits surviving among the records of King's Bench testify to the vitality of such political contests well beyond 1715, and to the ability of relatively humble players to wreck the plans of so-called borough "magnates."[84]

As the parliamentary flap over Bewdley's 1708 charter and other contested returns from the corporations in the early eighteenth century suggest, the liberty of corporations and of Parliaments were closely related. Much of the interest in controlling corporations, and thus much of the conflict within them, resulted from their importance in returning MPs. By deciding writs of mandamus and informations in the nature of quo

---

[83] Glassey, *Politics and the Justices of the Peace*, chapter 8.
[84] Affidavits are in PRO, KB1 and 2.

warranto, the court decided who were legal voters and who were not. Leaders from Calne complained not only to Parliament, but to King's Bench after the election of 1722, contending that persons removed from the corporation by quo warrantos at the end of Anne's reign had voted illegally. The accused, for their part, admitted they were not of the corporation any longer, but they contended that they still possessed the parliamentary franchise by virtue of their common rights in the borough. The case before the bench in 1722–23 thus put the court in the position of figuring out in whom the parliamentary franchise resided, and by what customary or legal means it did so.[85]

Winning and holding corporation parliamentary seats required constant political maneuvering and legal wrangling. As W. A. Speck has written, "where in the counties the party machinery was usually switched on only for an election campaign, in many boroughs it was kept running all the time and demanded frequent overhauling and maintenance."[86] More than anything, this meant controlling who was in the corporation and who rose to its highest offices. Two factors had to be kept in mind in winning a parliamentary seat: gaining votes and controlling the return. Victory might be had with one and not the other; having both put the issue beyond doubt. A pair with the most votes could do little if the mayor or sheriff made a return of their opponents on a questionable franchise, or if he did so willfully ignoring the polling numbers. The return would seat the Members. The only hope would then lie in the lengthy procedure of petition to the Committee of Privileges and Elections. Depending on the political temper of the petitioners and of the new House, polling numbers by the proper franchise might do little to override a return in favor of opponents if the House preferred them.[87] On the other hand, having the return without the numbers could do little to protect seats from a petition to a Committee and House friendly to the petitioners. Having a majority of the recognized voters, and the support of the returning officer, was the goal of all holding or desiring a borough seat. Achieving this required a constant effort to build and protect an urban electoral interest.

In freemen boroughs, getting the numbers meant adding freemen to the rolls. Complaints against the making of new freemen days before an

---

[85] On Calne, see PRO, KB1/2 (part 2), affidavits of Humphrey Townsend and John Hoskins, October 22, 1722; and Humphrey Townsend, John Hoskins, and Simeon Dyer, August 30, 1722. Extensive material from the quo warranto hearings by which many lost their places in 1713–15, and documents concerning complaints in 1722 of their voting for MPs, are at Wiltshire RO, G18/1/11. The judgment of ouster with a fine of 2s 6d each is at PRO, KB21/29/80v–81. See also Sedgwick, vol. I, p. 343.

[86] Speck, *Tory and Whig*, p. 47.

[87] W. A. Speck, "'The Most Corrupt Council in Christendom': Decisions on Controverted Elections, 1702–42," in Jones, *Party and Management*, pp. 107–21.

election were common. Queen Anne herself ordered prosecution of the mayor and two aldermen at St. Albans for making freemen illegally.[88] Anywhere large numbers of freemen were made, especially without the usual admission fines, one could be pretty sure an election was drawing near or an interest was being fortified in anticipation of one. Thus at Cambridge, scores of new freemen were made in the autumn of 1714 prior to the election of the new King's first Parliament.[89] Petitions to Parliament on contested elections were full of reports of illegal freemen made at the last minute. Access to the freedom was closely guarded and actively regulated. Corporations regularly made new rules or rehearsed old ones to protect access to the privilege which not only permitted participation in parliamentary elections in many towns, but corporation elections too, not to mention the right to trade. Any time one party replaced their foes at the head of a corporation, freemen made by their predecessors were often expelled and new ones made. Ninety-six were admitted to the freedom at Colchester by the mayor there without the consent of the corporation two days before the election in 1705; all were removed from the rolls in 1710. The freemanship was also a profit-generating asset. A few years later, Colchester decided "that the freedom of this borough might be sold . . . for raising moneys for defending the rights, and defraying the necessary charges of the corporation."[90]

The work of ongoing party organizing in the corporations was principally done by corporation members, not by national party figures, government officers, or regional magnates. Corporations continued to have political lives that were by and large self-determined. In his study of the corporations of the southwest, John Triffitt has given a useful riposte to the common assumption that major political patrons dictated the course of events in the towns. Triffitt has attacked the "twin myths" of government patronage and gentry power over the towns, stressing instead the independence of their political fortunes from those of interested magnates. We have tended to see such magnates as pulling all the strings because our interest in local politics has concerned its intersection with parliamentary politics. By depending as heavily as we do on the correspondence of major political

[88] PRO, SP44/101/222.
[89] Cambridgeshire RO, Shelf C/9, pp. 531–52, passim. Sedgwick, vol. I, p. 201. See also freemen made at Barnstaple in 1710: Chanter and Wainwright, *Barnstaple Records* (Barnstaple, 1900), vol. I, p. 78. The corporation at Leicester regularly used its power to name freemen to ensure electoral results. R. W. Greaves, *The Corporation of Leicester, 1689–1836* (Oxford, 1939), pp. 87–90. For more examples, see Holmes, *Politics in the Age of Anne*, p. 314.
[90] Philip Morant, *The History and Antiquities of Colchester* (Colchester, 1798), pp. 97–98. See also Woodstock, where the corporation sold the freemanship to make money. Woodstock Town Hall, 86/1, September 27, 1703, October 23, 1705, and March 30 and November 2, 1713.

figures for our view of corporate politics, we accept too uncritically the presumption running through their letters that they could control the events they intended to control. There thus exists what Triffitt terms a "documentary illusion" of actual control.[91] In many ways, these gentlemen were more beholden to the changing political winds from the towns than vice versa: "Instead of lifting political affairs out of the urban context and restricting them to the county community or to Westminster, government departments and gentlemen were drawn into urban conflicts and forced to wait on urban political events."[92]

Not all political activity in the corporations was directed toward getting to Westminster. This is most clearly demonstrated by the fact that conflict in non-parliamentary corporations looked like conflict in parliamentary ones. As we saw above, Penzance endured a double mayoral election in 1705 and two years of litigation to settle it. Doncaster split in 1723 over the advisability of a navigation project. "Heat and violence" characterized the "irregular proceedings"; the mayor even locked some of his opposers in a room in the town hall to force them to back down.[93] Little if anything of whig and tory, and certainly nothing of parliamentary seats, was at stake in the contest. But that combatants should fight so fiercely, and then turn to the law, suggests what local leaders had learned from many decades of partisan dispute in the corporations: that partisan division was a fact of life, and the best way to handle it was by recourse to the law.

Events at Macclesfield a few years earlier demonstrate this all the more clearly. The corporation reeled under the efforts of Henry Booth to build a party around himself. In July 1716, Booth and his friends brandished their swords to frighten off the supporters of his opponent for the recordership. This did the job. Though protests were made against the violence on both sides, and indictments were laid, Booth took office. Perhaps even more important to his victory than the threat of bodily harm had been the mayor's refusal to accept the votes of common burgesses, who according to tradition should have participated, and who, according to general report, would not have supported Booth. But the recorder fracas was simply a noisy prelude to the election of the new mayor and two aldermen in

---

[91] Triffitt, "Politics and the Urban Community," chapter 5, especially pp. 175–76. Most examinations of the boroughs in this period assume that their chief function was to elect MPs, and that they did this according to whichever outside interest gave them the best deal. Thus the History of Parliament volumes for 1715–54 discuss most towns in terms of their "venality" and consider them entirely in terms of who "managed" them. Speck and Holmes operate on the same assumptions to a lesser degree. Speck, *Tory and Whig*, and Holmes, *Politics in the Age of Anne*, passim.

[92] Triffitt, "Politics and the Urban Community," p. 229.

[93] PRO, KB1/1 (part 1), affidavits of Joseph Bayley, May 7 and June 10, 1723; William Eratt, May 7, 1723; and William Broughton, May 13, 1723.

October. By tradition, the common burgesses were to nominate five to stand for mayor, no more and no less. As they polled, Booth required all freemen in his interest to go before the clerk and declare "I vote for the recorder's five," without specifying their names. This denied voters any chance to stray from the pre-established party slate. Those on the other side insisted that each man be allowed to vote freely, according to tradition, speaking the names of each of the five he preferred. Booth "leaped and jumped about, and thumping the table, answered that he cared not for our customs but would proceed whether we would or not." He then stopped the poll and required the clerk to make a return of those nominated so far.[94]

The freemen had given 145 votes to Adam Endor, one of Booth's friends, and 143 votes each to seven others. There were eight mayoral candidates in all, not five as tradition required, with no way to whittle the list without arbitrarily leaving out some of those with equal votes. Fourteen of the corporation members then present were willing to proceed to an election from among these eight, but Booth, outgoing Mayor Roger Boulton, Endor, and four others, refused to join them. Debate raged between those who wanted to choose one from among the eight, and those who preferred to do nothing. Finally, at eleven p.m., with the "charter day" for electing the mayor nearly over, a vote was held by those opposing Booth, who chose John Barber as the new mayor and two others as aldermen. Given that they had proceeded contrary to custom and without the mayor's blessing, the result was immediately challenged. The outgoing mayor, loyal to Booth, refused to swear Barber.[95]

The legal maneuvering that followed the vote was much more intricate than the electoral maneuvering that had preceded it. Burgesses on each side were disfranchised, not as punishment inflicted by opponents, but by their own friends so that they could give depositions on their behalf without the appearance of impropriety. Mayor elect Barber received an information to show by what warrant he claimed the office; informations also went against the two aldermen chosen at the same time. For their part, Barber and his anti-Booth partisans brought writs of mandamus against late Mayor Roger Boulton to swear Barber and the two new aldermen.[96] It was

---

[94] PRO, KB2/1 (part 2), affidavit of Mayor Roger Boulton, October 27, 1716. KB1/1 (part 2), affidavit of Adam Endor. KB1/2 (part 2), November 1716: affidavits of John Smethurst and William Watts; William Clayton; Jasper Hooley; Hugh Hewett; John Blagge; John Barber, Richard Johnson, and Stephen Philips; and Richard Barton and John Partington. Cheshire RO, MF122/1 (microfilm of Macclesfield records in the Birkenhead Public Library), MA/B/IV/9, 10, and 14.

[95] Cheshire RO, MF122/1, MA/B/IV/6 and 14.

[96] Further informations were brought against the JPs for countenancing the rioting at the recorder's election. PRO, KB21/29, ff. 158, 168, and 168v.

a typical example of the kind of legal back and forth that could blow up all at once. Grievances were never felt by one party only. They simultaneously ran in both directions with the result that each side commenced legal proceedings against the other. That both took to the law immediately, rather than pursuing some other mediated solution at the hands of other institutions or persons, points toward the recognition accorded King's Bench as the proper venue for playing out otherwise destabilizing local political differences.

Mayor elect Barber lost his case against the former Mayor Boulton. The court decided that his election had been contrary to custom and was thus void. But this decision did not finally come down until 1720.[97] What became of local governance in the interim is unknown. An effort was made soon after the judgment to get a new charter for Macclesfield, arguments being made that the corporation was now in abeyance in consequence of the void mayoralty. But in keeping with the crown's reluctance to grant new charters, none was forthcoming.[98] Not for a lack of good reasons for one. In arguments reminiscent of the Banbury case, and like those used around the same time for Christchurch, attorneys on one side argued for a new charter to restore a defunct corporation; on the other side, attorneys cited the examples of Devizes and Penzance, and requested a royal writ ordering a new mayoral election.[99] Neither a charter nor a writ was forthcoming. The corporation went into abeyance until 1725 when it was revived by a mandamus out of King's Bench ordering the corporation to elect a new mayor.[100]

That the court could revive a corporation so long dormant was a result not of any self-appointed power, but of legislation expanding its powers. Members of Parliament were as aware as anyone of the troubles the corporations had endured over the last two decades by virtue of abortive elections. Politicking in Cornish corporations seemed largely to concern efforts to prevent mayoral elections in order to maintain an incumbent in his place. In Devon, Tiverton provided a vivid demonstration of the trouble a single corporation member could cause by his non-appearance on a certain day when, in 1723, the election day was missed owing to the mayor's absence. To correct the trouble thus created, the Privy Council

[97] *Eng. Rep.*, vol. 93, pp. 542–43 (1 Strange 314).
[98] As at Christchurch, arguments against a new charter included suggestions that if a failed election were allowed to destroy the corporation, then any mayor might miss an election and destroy the corporation by design. Cheshire RO, MF122/1 and MA/B/IV/15. PRO, PC2/87/224. BL, Add. 36,134, f. 1.
[99] BL, Add. 36,134, ff. 66–67.
[100] PRO, KB21/32, f. 190v. No entries appear in the corporation's minute book from 1716 to 1727. Cheshire RO, LBM/1/1. Earwaker, *East Cheshire*, vol. II, p. 466, says Richard Johnson, an opponent of Booth's, was chosen mayor in 1725.

decided to grant George I's third and last charter in late 1724 to resurrect Tiverton's corporation.[101] Elsewhere the fragility of corporate constitutions had been made clear again and again. As long as their clauses concerning the mayoralty remained contradictory – appointing that the mayor serve for one year or until his successor was sworn – problems would persist. With numerous examples of troubles in towns like Macclesfield and Tiverton immediately before them, the House of Commons began work on a bill to prevent them in the future.

"An Act for preventing the inconveniencies arising for want of elections of mayors or other chief magistrates of boroughs or corporations being made upon the days appointed by charter or usage for that purpose" moved through the Commons without controversy at the same time that Tiverton's charter was prepared for the great seal. It then passed through the Lords without alteration and received the King's blessing in February 1725.[102] It opened by calling attention to the "mischiefs [that] might ensue" upon corporate dissolution and the ease with which that could happen by the accidental or purposeful absence of a single officer on a single day. The act made it lawful for a majority of corporation members to proceed to an election on their appointed day without the mayor. The senior member then present could preside. But to inspire the mayor's participation, the act imposed six months' imprisonment and a permanent disability to hold office on any mayor avoiding a legal election. If the "charter day" still passed without a choice, the vote could be made on another day. Where elections were still not held, King's Bench was empowered to issue writs ordering the corporation to do the same. It was by this clause that the court restored the otherwise defunct corporation of Macclesfield by directing them to choose a mayor for the first time since 1716. This critical piece of legislation saved many corporations from potential demise for lapses in the observance of the details of their charters. It built on the legacy of the statute of 9 Anne for making mandamus and quo warranto more effectual by clarifying the legal rules that had become so important for the conduct of political life.

In addition to such changes in legal practice, the character of partisan conflict changed after 1715 as religion slowly ceased to be the central

---

101 The Privy Council read petitions for and against a new charter. They also considered the precedent of Banbury, where after the court's finding of a void election, both sides acquiesced in a new charter, and precedents like that of Devizes, where a royal order commanded a new election and thus restored the corporation. PRO, PC2/88/334, 354–55, 378–79, 569, 586–93, 596, and 616, and PC2/89/3–6 and 8. PRO, PC1/3/113 and 118, and PC1/4/1. BL, Add. 36,134, ff. 109–10, 116–17, and 204; and BL, Add. 36,135, ff. 30 and 94–229.

102 Stat. 11 George I c. 4. *CJ*, vol. 20, pp. 336, 350, 352, 357, 359, 361–62, 374, and 414. *LJ*, vol. 22, pp. 370–71, 374, 384, 386, 388, and 424.

problem. This too resulted in part from a combination of judicial decisions and legislation. By late 1718, subscribing the declaration against the Covenant remained a requirement for corporation membership, though the declaration had fallen into disuse in many towns. This did not prevent legal scuffles between those who neglected it and those who sought to undermine their opponents' local position by challenging them for such neglect. This happened in Taunton where a quo warranto went against the mayor for holding office without having subscribed. His attorney argued that the act had not been in use there for thirty years; the declaration was "now trumped up to sacrifice the quiet of the whole kingdom to some private pique and revenge." If the judges ruled that the Corporation Act were still in force, so many would be found unqualified for office that many corporations would be dissolved for a lack of sufficient legal members. But the justices disagreed with such arguments from practicality and with contentions that the declaration had been nullified implicitly by the Toleration Act of 1689: "it is too big for this court to repeal and set aside Acts of Parliament."[103]

The judges did not need to set aside the Corporation Act; Parliament did it for them. In the winter of 1718–19, Parliament passed "An Act for strengthening the Protestant interest in these Kingdoms," by another name, a repeal of the Occasional Conformity Act of 1711.[104] Another measure, the "Act for quieting and establishing corporations," passed easily through both Houses in the same months. It abolished the requirement of subscribing the declaration against the Covenant, calling attention to the reality that it had "for several years last past been generally omitted." To end the litigation, the act absolved all currently in office who had not subscribed. Most important, the act indemnified all current corporation members who had not received the sacrament within one year before election to office, the Corporation Act's most important stricture. No one elected in the future who had not received the sacrament prior to election would be liable to removal unless prosecution for non-compliance was begun within six months of his election.[105] Even after these two acts of early 1719, annual receipt of the sacrament technically remained a requirement for holding office. But the test had been virtually nullified by these

---

[103] *Eng. Rep.*, vol. 88, pp. 1051–52, and vol. 93, pp. 422–26 (11 Mod. 297 and 1 Strange 120). In a quo warranto brought from Malmesbury in 1722, the court did not feel that the issue of the oaths could be raised eight years after the defendant had been admitted. The court thus denied the information. PRO, KB21/31/264. *Eng. Rep.*, vol. 88, pp. 45–46 (8 Mod. 55).

[104] Stat. 5 George I c. 4.

[105] Stat. 5 George I c. 6. For its passage, see *CJ*, vol. 19, pp. 39, 41–43, 45–47, 50, and 106; *LJ*, vol. 21, pp. 17, 20–22, 24, 34, 37–38, 43, and 74.

new constraints on it. Occasional conformity was now legal and prosecuting non-compliance with the test was more difficult than ever.

The passage of an Indemnity Act in 1726 simply underscored what had been achieved by the repeal of the Occasional Conformity Act and by the Act for Quieting Corporations. As this first Indemnity Act noted, it was passed in recognition that there were many "zealously affected to [the King's] person and government, and the Protestant succession to his royal house," who had accidentally failed to observe the test. The act did not provide an absolute repeal of the sacramental test. Instead, it pardoned all who were not then in compliance with the Corporation Act's sacrament requirement and gave them eight more months to receive the communion. Passage of further indemnity acts on an almost annual basis thereafter made the sacrament requirement otiose.[106] Most important, one no longer needed to be in full communion with the Church at all times in anticipation of selection for a corporate office, as was the intention of the Corporation Act's requirement that one had to have received the Eucharist within the year *preceding* election. Now one who was of a dissenting persuasion but willing to compromise once or twice to enter public life would need only take the sacrament once after taking a new office.

Gradually, religious sympathies ceased to play the leading role they had played since 1660 in defining who could and could not participate in urban politics. Court decisions throughout the 1690s and Anne's reign began the process, deadening the impact of the test by disallowing it on a number of occasions as a reason for removal from office. The repeal of the Occasional Conformity Act, the passage of the Act for Quieting Corporations, and the indemnity acts passed after 1726 furthered the same process. As explained above in chapter 3, the Corporation Act had for the first time given statutory definition to certain kinds of Protestants who were, by law, to be excluded from public life. This had served as the single most important force perpetuating partisan divisions and conflict since the 1660s. Now, though not actually repealed, the Corporation Act was a dead letter. By killing the Corporation Act with a succession of judicial decisions since the 1690s and a succession of statutes after 1714, religion itself faded as the driving force behind corporate partisan division.[107] Religious conflict had washed over the land and now receded, but partisan conflict remained behind in its wake. Partisan politics outlived the force that first gave it life, in part because of an increasing acceptance of the reality of political

---

[106] K. R. M. Short, "The English Indemnity Acts," *Church History*, 42 (1973), pp. 366–76. Paul Langford, *Public Life and the Propertied Englishman, 1689–1798* (Oxford, 1991), pp. 71–78.

[107] Linda Colley suggests that religion's decline as a disruptive political force began even earlier: *In Defiance of Oligarchy*, p. 13.

division, and in part because the rules governing it had been clarified, thus making it safe for partisan politics to continue.

PARTISAN CONFLICT IN A DYNAMIC SOCIETY

J. H. Plumb's Ford Lectures on the rise of political stability is one of the classics of the political historiography. In vivid strokes, he painted a picture of a troubled society, slowly crafting the institutional means by which it achieved political peace. The seventeenth century was one of political mayhem: "by 1688, violence in politics was an Englishman's birthright." Conflict between two sets of unrestrained partisans created and fed this violence: "party division was real and it created instability; indeed, it was the true reflection of it." By 1700, England had thrown out an absolutist Catholic, "only to succumb to political anarchy." Anarchy prevailed until, in the wake of the death of Queen Anne and the arrival of the Hanoverians, political peace was created by the complete victory of one of these parties over the other: "single party government . . . helped to bring about political stability." Like those who in the Restoration wrote of the political, social, and spiritual horrors attendant on "faction" and "party," Plumb saw only chaos where political competition existed. Thus Plumb's relief upon the establishment of one-party government, and stability, after 1714–15.[108]

But as Linda Colley has pointed out, more borough parliamentary contests occurred in the first six general elections after 1715 than in the six preceding it.[109] Kathleen Wilson too, by looking beyond formal institutions to the press, clubs, and crowds, has found "partisan cultural identities that circulated through a broad cross-section of society."[110] In the three decades after Queen Anne's accession, we can follow a movement in the changing concerns of an ever wider, more energetic political culture from sectarian religious differences, to competing dynastic loyalties, to concerns in the 1730s and after with the excise and "patriotism."[111] Each of these concerns partook of the others as they slowly supplanted one another, but by the end of the process, the religious factor had largely fallen away from political conflict in the corporations, leaving in its wake an enduring form of political practice: partisan politics.

When we look closely, when we move beyond Westminster and probe beneath a political narrative written largely from elite correspondence, we find the new "stable" world was one with a surprising amount of conflict. In the corporations, partisan conflict continued undiminished. This could

---

[108] Plumb, *Growth of Political Stability*, pp. 2, 19, 157, and 172.
[109] Colley, *In Defiance of Oligarchy*, p. 119.
[110] Wilson, *Sense of the People*, p. 106.
[111] On this shift in the content of political difference, see ibid., pp. 116–22.

take many forms: along whig/tory lines in places like Norwich, or around personal groupings as at Macclesfield. Partisan organization not identifiably whig or tory does not mean it was any less partisan. Partisan politics was about well-organized, well-led local groups pursuing common goals. Such local groupings typically arose around the split between whig and tory, but partisan conflict did not need Parliament, nor national questions – "ideological" issues as historians call them – to motivate partisanship. Such conflict was functionally no different from that more clearly whig versus tory. Whatever its stripe, partisan conflict had, by the early Hanoverian period, become the means by which English communities struggled over the most important issues before them.

Did this conflict before and after 1714–15 create instability? "Instability" is one of the touchstones of the historiography. But perhaps the question should not be was English politics unstable; perhaps it should be, what was it that made the English polity – in both national and local manifestations – work? Concentrating on instability makes it impossible to answer this question; indeed the question is assumed to have no meaning. But the polity did work. Corporations around the country continued to lease and maintain property, build water cisterns, and pass regulations about street lighting, even in some of the most hotly contested boroughs. The heaps of assembly minutes, deeds, leases, court books, mayoral correspondence, and other records of activity in corporation muniment chests and guildhall closets serve as a powerful reminder to anyone who might forget that the corporations had a good deal of public business to conduct, and that most of them took care of it. Neo-classical town halls and grand public squares built in the decades after 1688 testify to townsmen's ability to celebrate the vitality, the dynamism, of their world, divided though it may have been.[112] After all, it was the Norwich led by Andrew Parmenter and his generation that lit the city's streets and presided over what Daniel Defoe and others praised as a prosperous regional capital and industrial center.[113]

That even embattled corporations continued to govern was largely the result of changing judicial usage and legislation passed in the reigns of Anne and George I. The court forced the corporations' acceptance of partisan politics by compelling them to retain persons a majority preferred to expel; doing justice to those illegally removed meant requiring political

---

[112] Borsay, *The English Urban Renaissance*, chapter 4 and appendices 1 and 2. For an excellent study of corporate governance in the eighteenth century with an argument for its considerable successes, see Dawson, "Finance and the Unreformed Borough."

[113] Defoe, *A Tour through the Whole Island of Great Britain*, ed. Pat Rogers (Harmondsworth, 1971), pp. 84–86. Borsay, *English Urban Renaissance*, pp. 72–74. Penelope Corfield, "A Provincial Capital in the Late Seventeenth Century: The Case of Norwich," in Clark and Slack, *Crisis and Order*, pp. 263–310.

enemies to live together in the polity. This actually promoted more intense partisan struggle as it made it all the harder for one side to achieve the total victory that the paradox of partisan politics compelled each side to seek. But as each side had recourse to the law if abused by the other, they each saw an institution that appeared impartial and possessed the judicial tools for accommodating their differences. The court also had tools for requiring the performance of the basic obligations of peaceful governors, especially by commanding, where need be, the due transfer of power or the holding of elections to ensure a full complement of corporate officials to do the work of local administration. With such a monitor of the performance of public duties by urban leaders, the divided society of the early eighteenth century was also a dynamic, stable one.

⟪ 10 ⟫

1660, 1688, 1727, and beyond

One King died and another succeeded him; there were parliamentary elections. But 1727 was a year of little significance. So too were most of the other dates we use to separate epochs: 1688, 1714–15, 1722. Much happened in these years. Monarchs came and went, corporations were purged, corporation members sued one another, elections were held. Particularly in 1688–89 and 1714–15, moments marking important turnings in the nation's life, little else changed when the leadership did. Tories certainly fared worse after 1715 in parliamentary and court politics, but tory partisan groups in the corporations, and moreover, toryism among the broader populace, kept partisan competition alive and well beyond Westminster. The tone of political discord softened in the 1720s, and religious identification ceased to be the chief determinant of the right to participate in public life. Partisan conflict was about different things by the late 1720s and 1730s, but partisan conflict endured as the basis of politics in the corporations.[1] It is this continuity in political practice across 1688–89 and 1715 that makes an epoch of the seven or eight decades after 1650 that we otherwise treat as three or four distinct eras.

Partisan politics, born in the maelstrom of civil war, had outlived all the purges and amputations that had been intended to kill it in 1660 and the decades following. Though condemned by all, partisan politics flourished, and nowhere more prominently than in the corporations. It did so because it did not produce the consequences all feared it would. Society did not collapse in a heap of pieces that cut each other as they fell. Instead, through all the rhetoric damning political division and despite all the efforts to end it, partisan politics emerged as a stable means for communities within a dynamic society to make decisions. The success of a political practice so reviled resulted from its being tamed through use, tamed by the law. Thus the significant transformations that occurred in England's political culture

---

[1] As John Triffitt notes, "Almost certainly the pattern [of conflict] was to extend into the 1730s, and perhaps into the forties and fifties as well." "Politics and the Urban Community," p. 229.

in the period 1650–1730 happened less at the points where we usually mark changes of political era, but in gradual developments in between them. Precedent-setting court cases, and after 1688, parliamentary legislation, continually adjusted the legal terms of political conflict. This incremental process accommodated a politics of division against all expectations and with little awareness of what was happening as it unfolded.

Few anticipated this result. William Prynne had warned in 1661 that the Corporation Act would promote the "divisions, contentions, factions, and parties" all prayed the King's return had ended.[2] Implicit in his words was a fear that "factions and parties" represented both a manifestation and a cause of political and social ruin. It was beyond the ken of Prynne and his peers to imagine such a thing as a successful, peaceful partisan politics: hadn't England just fought a civil war? Also behind Prynne's warning lay an assumption that not approving the proposed act would halt the development of "factions and parties." On the other hand, those who promoted the bill did so in the belief that it would prevent the very dangers Prynne foretold. Neither were right. Rejecting the bill would not have prevented the perpetuation of "factions and parties"; nor did passing it.

Partisan politics already had a life of its own, try what measures they might. For the basic principle on which the Corporation Act operated – purgation – had already been at work in the corporations for a number of years. Parliament had ordered the first dismissals from corporate office in 1644, thereby setting the precedent of expulsions directed by central government authority. Urban partisans also undertook purges on their own, purges often more thorough than those ordered from without. Later, the Lord Protector and his major generals commanded more of the same to ensure the safety of their nervous regime. To simplify the task of finding who might remain in the corporations and who could replace those removed, they imposed a series of tests to assess ideological fitness. By sharpening divisions between the "malignant" and those of "good conversation," the turmoil of the 1640s and 50s provided the basis for partisan competition in the corporations in the coming decades. All the devices used by both local partisans and the crown after 1660 had been used in the years before: removals and appointments to office, tests of loyalty, and new charters redefining the terms of local government.

The paradox of partisan politics in these early years was that the assumed means for ending partisan conflict – removing opposition from the polity – would become the most important force promoting it. As partisan groups struggled for control in the corporations, each tried to remove their foes entirely, sometimes by calling in the help of outside authorities. But the

---

[2] [Prynne], *Summary Reasons.*

drive by one side to eradicate partisan politics by excluding partisan enemies only provoked the same measures in return. Thus the removals made from corporate office in the 1640s and 50s were only the first in a host of purges that rolled over the towns in the succeeding years, leaving one set of ins and outs, and then another. The effort after 1660 to restore the nation to some imagined pristine political condition sought to undo what was done in the preceding decades by putting out those brought in and returning those left out during the Interregnum. The work of restoration began even before the King set foot on English soil as erstwhile corporation members got their places back with the help of friends still in the corporation or by court order. The Corporation Act then forced the departure from office of just over one third of England's corporate leaders, putting a bold period to the process of Restoration by exclusion. By using adherence to the ideal of a Presbyterian national church as the test of political fitness, the act fixed religious sensibility as the most important element in political association – and partisan division – for the next two to three generations. The doctrinal lines around Anglican loyalists enclosed the proper political nation; everyone else was "the party," "the factious." But trying to destroy "party" by removing the factious from the polity – whether by the Corporation Act, by judicial writ, or by a corporation's own orders – only left an angry, motivated group outside. In the following years, they would help each other get back many of the places they now lost. The tests established by the Corporation Act – the sacrament and the declaration against the Covenant – promoted political rancor as one side constantly tried to circumvent them, and the other tried to expose such efforts in order to exclude their foes.

Nonetheless, many of those who did not meet these precise qualifications for office found their way back into the corporations in the 1670s. During these years, the King and his advisors seemed little worried by the potential for partisan conflict in the towns, and did little to support the Corporation Act, and at times even discouraged the enforcement of other laws against dissent. In the 1670s, the political climate was such that this rarely endangered political peace, but under the pressure of events from 1679 to 1681, the King learned what a mistake he had made by his complacency. The events of those years prodded the crown to action and galvanized highly motivated urban groups ready to do the King's bidding in curbing suspect political forces. In the corporations, the "tory reaction" took the form of new charters, over 100 of which passed the great seal in the last four years of Charles II's reign. Thus the process of creating local political ins and outs of the early 1660s was repeated. The new charters effected another thorough purge. Groups now identifiably "whig" and "tory" were removed and installed in the most comprehensive reshaping of local government undertaken since the start of the Stuart era. And with clauses permitting the monarch to remove any corporation officer in the future, partisan politics' first principle – purgation – was now enshrined in corporate charters. While the charters of the early to mid-1680s again left an angry group out of corporate life, those brought in or confirmed formed a group large enough and strong enough that they could withstand the pressures of an antagonistic force outside. The political mood of the nation – reflected in the parliamentary elections of 1685 – and the ascendancy of the tory interest in the corporations appeared to foretell their dominance well into the future.

Charles's effort to pass so many new charters succeeded because he made use of extensive political support in the towns. But the new King after 1685 ultimately had very different ambitions. Driven by a vision of religious concord, James II worked with extraordinary energy in 1687 and 1688 to unmake what his brother had made. Thousands of corporation members, many recently installed by Charles's new charters, were ordered to quit their places. Mayhem in the towns ensued as some obeyed the orders and others did not. Replacing them were men with little or no experience of local leadership, men who by their affiliation with dissent and Catholicism were paid little heed by those James intended they should govern. Compounding the trouble was another set of new charters. The effort failed dramatically. James had ignored religious/political realities and was forced from his throne for doing so. Perhaps more than any of his measures, James's attempt to transform corporate government provoked his demise as he succeeded in alienating thousands of leaders in hundreds of urban communities.

As Tim Harris notes, "party strife continued after 1689 precisely because the Revolution did not witness a victory for any one party."[3] Or, to put this another way, it witnessed a victory for both parties. While a few dissenting whigs had actively assisted James, and a few tories had followed the rule of passive obedience and done the King's will, most tories and most whigs in the towns had been rejected by James or had refused to act with him in 1688. The remarkable thing about James's effort was that it attacked nearly everyone who could have been of use to him – of either political tendency – and relied instead on persons with no natural local constituency and little political experience. The interests of whig and tory, generally speaking, were both well served by James's departure and the demise of the upstarts he promoted. The political turnaround that occurred at the end of 1688 did not so much restore either whig or tory to one side's advantage; it restored both, and with them, the status quo ante: partisan competition.

---

[3] Harris, *Politics under the Later Stuarts*, p. 141.

The rapid succession of local constitutions in the years 1679 to 1688, and the various groups of corporation members which came and went according to them, left behind conflicting claims to control of the corporations. These conflicts were compounded by persistent differences over religious qualifications for political participation in the decades after 1688, especially in the years of the "rage of party" in Anne's reign. That rage was most evident in the struggle over occasional conformity. But the Occasional Conformity Act of 1711 had much less impact than all the fuss leading up to its passage foretold. Far more important for corporation politics was the act of the same year for making proceedings on mandamus and quo warranto more effectual. This act proved crucial in determining how politics could be played by determining how political litigation would work and by making such litigation more expeditious. By passing a statute that refined judicial procedure, Parliament recognized and promoted a process long under way: the expansion of the role of King's or Queen's Bench in maintaining political equilibrium in the corporations.[4] In doing so, Parliament also recognized the durability of partisan politics and the possibility that such a politics, if properly monitored, need not entail instability. The courts provided the principal means by which rivalry could occur in a stable society, and this was important, because partisan conflict did not die in 1715, nor in the years following. By the early to mid-1720s, much of the religious rhetoric and anger had fallen away, leaving in place a durable political practice: partisan politics.

Thus at Chester in the early 1730s, a corporation and a pair of parliamentary seats that had been in tory hands since Roger Whitley died suddenly became objects of sharp contest. "Whig" and "tory" were nominally involved, but the real issues centered on the propriety of the Grosvenor family maintaining its powerful influence over city politics, and the wisdom of a proposal to reopen the river Dee. The intensity of organized efforts in 1732 to win the mayoralty, and then during the winter in two parliamentary by-elections, signaled the ease with which political teams formed, identified their goals, and engaged each other in struggles for the stuff of which political strength at Chester was made: the votes of freemen. As had become the custom, the most intractable differences there went to court for a judicial resolution.[5] Such courtroom activity in the

---

[4] The acts of Anne and George I regulating mandamus and quo warranto were followed by more efforts to tighten their use, including an act in 1754 indemnifying corporation members who had not taken the oaths and another act for quieting corporations in 1772. Two attempts to pass the latter had failed in 1767 and 1770. *CJ*, vols. 27, 31, 32, and 33, passim.

[5] On Chester, see Stephen W. Baskerville, "The Management of the Tory Interest in Lancashire and Cheshire, 1714–1747" (D.Phil., University of Oxford, 1976), pp. 183–223. For reports of the legal actions that grew out of this, in part over the issues from the 1690s concerning

1730s suggests partisan conflict continued beyond 1715 and the 1720s, and that law remained the chief means by which its effects were moderated.[6] Participants in the legal actions in the decades after Anne died would have been surprised to hear either that partisan conflict had ended with the advent of one-party government at Whitehall, or that such conflict in any way threatened the stability of nation or town.

Corporations were created by the monarch and existed only in law. As such, only the law could provide the means for controlling what went on within them. Sir William Blackstone noted later in the eighteenth century that one of the greatest advances in the law since 1688 was "the protection of corporate rights by the improvements in the writs of mandamus and informations in nature of quo warranto."[7] It was ironic that quo warranto, once denounced as the scourge of corporate privileges, had become their protector. But partisan politics, by its very nature, required the active presence of an external authority to inspect, control, and correct the corporations. Quo warranto, along with mandamus, provided the King's court with the means for doing this. In arguments on mandamus, one's success depended on defining the public good that the corporation existed to serve and on explaining how the performance of public duties was damaged by the action the writ would redress.[8] Quo warranto also imposed on the corporations clearer notions about public duties and provided the means for competing corporators to raise questions about each other's hold on office without first resorting to an illegal purge. By ordering corporations to accept in their midst those they tried to exclude, and by protecting the proper transfer of power between competing groups, the court did not resolve conflict, rather they forced locals to accommodate it. The impact of years of court decisions was at last to break the paradox of partisan politics by convincing local political leaders that it was now impossible, and unnecessary, to create unity by purging their foes.

King's Bench was very much a part of the King's government. If the courts were the King's, and if they were the chief instrument by which political behavior in the localities was to be monitored, then this puts royal authority in a different light. We can see more clearly now how local and

---

the proper mode of choosing corporation members, see *Eng. Rep.*, vol. 87, pp. 1187–88 and 1202–05 (7 Mod. 198, 220, and 223).

[6] See for instance cases from New Romney, Hastings, Evesham, Shrewsbury, and Liverpool from the 1730s: Howell, *State Trials*, vol. XVII, pp. 801–924, and *Eng. Rep.*, vol. 87, pp. 1167–70, 1184, 1184–85, and 1190–91 (7 Mod. 166, 169, 193, 194, and 201).

[7] Blackstone, *Commentaries*, vol. IV, p. 441.

[8] As a recent student of public law notes, "the modern doctrine of limited judicial review is foreshadowed in these early mandamus cases . . . In a period of administrative diversity and disorder, mandamus was therefore essential for the carrying on of effective government . . . almost the entire law of public duties has grown out of mandamus." Harding, *Public Duties*, pp. 85 and 131.

national judicial and administrative institutions were increasingly integrated over the period 1660–1727, and in particular, we can see how this integration was driven from the margins, not from the center of the polity. From Geoffrey Elton's "Tudor revolution" to John Brewer's "sinews of power," the story of state building has been recounted largely as the evolution of institutions at Whitehall.[9] Less well known, though more significant, is the way in which units of local government were knit into the fabric of a sovereign national state. Today we take for granted that organs of the state should superintend the behavior of local governors. In particular, we accept the role of national courts to review the decisions of courts and councils in the localities, and on occasion, to correct and punish abuses there. In this way, we see institutions of the central government as guarantors of various freedoms, protecting citizens from the oppressions of local governors. But modern interpretations of crown authority in the seventeenth century focus on a struggle between the threat of "absolutism" posed by Stuart monarchs and the hope for "liberty" expressed by autonomy-loving leaders in the provinces. Getting from one view to the other remains a problem, but it is one that we can solve if we shift our assumptions about what the crown and courts were doing in the localities after 1660 and about who was driving their involvement. We must modify our ideas of a crown interested in "absolutism" and explore the wider implications of legal and institutional changes like those recounted in the chapters above. By appreciating how the courts were institutions of royal government, by seeing how their role changed dramatically in this period – even supplanting the King's Council – and by understanding how this change happened in response, not in opposition, to local demands, we gain a completely different perspective on the relationship between national and provincial institutions. Partisan politics, by dividing urban communities, made a national institution crucial to stability in the provinces. Townsmen understood this better than anyone else as they encouraged the development of such a national institution by coming again and again before the King's court with their grievances.

As partisan politics emerged, it propelled a process by which the paradox of partisan politics was broken, by which the cycle of retributive purges wrought in hopes of imposing unity was undone. By studying the corporations, we have seen not only where and how the politics of partisan competition emerged, we have also seen how other forces accommodated its growth. Analyses concentrating on instability, by stressing conflict and not its containment, have overlooked the means by which this happened.

[9] Geoffrey Elton, *The Tudor Revolution in Government* (Cambridge, 1953). John Brewer, *The Sinews of Power: War, Money and the English State, 1688–1783* (New York, 1989).

The rhetoric of corporateness and loyalty insisted on the impossibility of a workable partisan political practice. But corporate political opponents and the courts slowly worked to compose solutions to the problems created by this new and persistent form of political practice. What is so impressive about partisan politics as it dismembered the body politic is not the threat that it posed to society, but the way in which a dynamic society found the means to absorb that threat, despite all the insistence that it could not.

Appendix A: Royal charters of incorporation, 1660–1727

This is a list of the 284 English borough charters that passed the great seal between 1660 and 1727, compiled from PRO, IND1/4227–30 (great seal dockets) and C66 (patent rolls index). Charters of confirmation, new incorporation, or reincorporation are included; exemplifications – copies of earlier charters lost or destroyed – are not. Liverpool charters marked "*" were granted under the seal of the Duchy of Lancaster, not the great seal.

Falmouth	5 Oct. 1661	York	3 June 1664
Leeds	2 Nov. 1661	Chester	6 June 1664
Hull	3 Dec. 1661	Grantham	10 June 1664
Newport, I.o.W.	9 Dec. 1661	Oxford	23 June 1664
Preston	22 Mar. 1662	Shrewsbury	6 July 1664
Wigan	16 May 1662	Newbury	11 July 1664
Maidenhead	12 Mar. 1663	St. Albans	27 July 1664
London	24 June 1663	Sudbury	27 July 1664
Norwich	26 June 1663	Sutton Coldfield	27 July 1664
Wallingford	1 July 1663	Higham Ferrers	4 Aug. 1664
Lancaster	4 July 1663	Newcastle under Lyme	4 Aug. 1664
Coventry	6 July 1663	Woodstock	23 Aug. 1664
Colchester	3 Aug. 1663	Stratford-upon-Avon	31 Aug. 1664
Northampton	3 Aug. 1663	Warwick	13 Oct. 1664
Beverley	15 Sept. 1663	Lichfield	5 Nov. 1664
High Wycombe	16 Nov. 1663	Gloucester	16 Nov. 1664
Abingdon	3 Dec. 1663	Leicester	20 Jan. 1665
Morpeth	30 Dec. 1663	Ipswich	17 Feb. 1665
Yarmouth	8 Jan. 1664	King's Lynn	9 Mar. 1665
Bedford	9 Feb. 1664	Shaftesbury	22 Mar. 1665
Windsor	9 Feb. 1664	Harwich	14 Apr. 1665
Newcastle upon Tyne	13 Feb. 1664	Ludlow	14 Apr. 1665
Tamworth	17 Feb. 1664	Stafford	14 Apr. 1665
Stamford	19 Feb. 1664	Nottingham	25 Apr. 1665
Albrighton	17 Mar. 1664	Leominster	6 June 1665
Carlisle	9 Apr. 1664	Bridport	15 Aug. 1666
Bristol	22 Apr. 1664	Poole	24 Nov. 1666
Doncaster	2 May 1664	Macclesfield	31 Dec. 1666
Derby	21 May 1664	Congleton	14 Feb. 1667
Hedon	27 May 1664	Plymouth	20 Feb. 1667

Reading	20 Aug. 1667	Bury St. Edmunds	2 July 1684
Yarmouth	10 Feb. 1668	Yarmouth	3 July 1684
Richmond	14 Mar. 1668	Ipswich	8 July 1684
Bury St. Edmunds	5 June 1668	King's Lynn	9 July 1684
Cinque Ports	23 Dec. 1668	Richmond	9 July 1684
Camelford	24 July 1669	Bedford	12 July 1684
Christchurch	25 Aug. 1670	Dartmouth	12 July 1684
Gloucester	18 Apr. 1672	Buckingham	25 July 1684
Bedwyn	23 Jan. 1673	Scarborough	2 Aug. 1684
Newark	13 Jan. 1674	Dover	7 Aug. 1684
Oswestry	13 Jan. 1674	Oxford	29 Sept. 1684
Stratford-upon-Avon	27 Aug. 1674	Totnes	2 Oct. 1684
Daventry	2 Feb. 1675	Barnstaple	22 Oct. 1684
Salisbury	13 Feb. 1675	Exeter	22 Oct. 1684
Pontefract	20 Feb. 1677	Wallingford	27 Oct. 1684
Newark	4 Apr. 1677	Canterbury	8 Nov. 1684
Liverpool*	18 July 1677	Colchester	8 Nov. 1684
Taunton	13 Sept. 1677	Macclesfield	19 Nov. 1684
Saltash	11 Feb. 1678	Tiverton	20 Nov. 1684
Corfe	12 Feb. 1679	Carlisle	3 Dec. 1684
Garstang	6 Aug. 1679	Helston	10 Dec. 1684
Wootton Bassett	2 Dec. 1679	Leicester	10 Dec. 1684
Chesterfield	21 July 1680	Lincoln	17 Dec. 1684
Hertford	29 Nov. 1680	Lancaster	22 Dec. 1684
Chipping Sodbury	10 Feb. 1681	Lyme Regis	23 Dec. 1684
Thetford	6 Mar. 1682	Leeds	24 Dec. 1684
Hereford	28 Mar. 1682	South Molton	24 Dec. 1684
Tavistock	29 July 1682	Bath	31 Dec. 1684
Portsmouth	18 Aug. 1682	Cambridge	3 Jan. 1685
Andover	2 Sept. 1682	Newcastle upon Tyne	5 Jan. 1685
Derby	5 Sept. 1682	Preston	14 Jan. 1685
Nottingham	28 Sept. 1682	Kendal	15 Jan. 1685
Maidstone	26 Oct. 1682	Leominster	15 Jan. 1685
Norwich	22 Mar. 1683	Chester	4 Feb. 1685
Chard	29 June 1683	Hedon	18 Feb. 1685
Northampton	20 Sept. 1683	Worcester	18 Feb. 1685
Coventry	31 Oct. 1683	Grantham	25 Feb. 1685
Saltash	27 Nov. 1683	Southwold	25 Feb. 1685
Bridgwater	8 Dec. 1683	Wigan	25 Feb. 1685
Warwick	18 Dec. 1683	Newark	28 Feb. 1685
Banbury	9 Jan. 1684	High Wycombe	3 Mar. 1685
Wells	10 Jan. 1684	Launceston (Dunheved)	3 Mar. 1685
Higham Ferrers	18 Feb. 1684	Stamford	3 Mar. 1685
Newport, I.o.W.	5 Mar. 1684	Bridport	4 Mar. 1685
Sandwich	5 Mar. 1684	Orford	7 Mar. 1685
Shaftesbury	10 Apr. 1684	Salisbury	7 Mar. 1685
Bristol	2 June 1684	Boston	9 Mar. 1685
Okehampton	4 June 1684	Beverley	11 Mar. 1685
Evesham	12 June 1684	Dunwich	11 Mar. 1685
Plymouth	26 June 1684	Chippenham	13 Mar. 1685

Truro	13 Mar. 1685	Guildford	14 Apr. 1686
Liskeard	16 Mar. 1685	Huntingdon	9 July 1686
Newcastle under Lyme	16 Mar. 1685	Lichfield	9 July 1686
St. Albans	16 Mar. 1685	Berwick	17 Sept. 1636
Devizes	17 Mar. 1685	Grimsby	4 Nov. 1686
Penryn	17 Mar. 1685	Brackley	11 Nov. 1686
Shrewsbury	17 Mar. 1685	Ripon	12 Jan. 1687
Plympton	21 Mar. 1685	Maldon	4 Mar. 1687
Pontefract	23 Mar. 1685	Gravesend	16 Mar. 1687
Windsor	23 Mar. 1685	Exeter	10 Mar. 1688
Doncaster	25 Mar. 1685	Totnes	9 Apr. 1688
Sudbury	26 Mar. 1685	Queenborough	10 July 1688
Bodmin	27 Mar. 1685	Newcastle upon Tyne	24 July 1688
Chichester	27 Mar. 1685	Tamworth	3 Aug. 1688
Fowey	28 Mar. 1685	Hertford	27 Aug. 1688
Looe, East	28 Mar. 1685	Woodstock	27 Aug. 1688
Looe, West	28 Mar. 1685	Nottingham	1 Sept. 1688
Ludlow	28 Mar. 1685	Wells	1 Sept. 1688
Malmesbury	28 Mar. 1685	Buckingham	11 Sept. 1688
St. Ives	28 Mar. 1685	Salisbury	11 Sept. 1688
Tregony	28 Mar. 1685	Calne	12 Sept. 1688
Retford, East	1 Apr. 1685	Evesham	12 Sept. 1688
Camelford	4 Apr. 1685	Tiverton	12 Sept. 1688
Grampound	4 Apr. 1685	Barnstaple	15 Sept. 1688
Liverpool*	4 Apr. 1685	Bishop's Castle	15 Sept. 1688
Tintagell	4 Apr. 1685	Boston	15 Sept. 1688
Godmanchester	6 Apr. 1685	Bridport	15 Sept. 1688
Honiton	6 Apr. 1685	Chester	15 Sept. 1688
Lostwithiel	6 Apr. 1685	Colchester	15 Sept. 1688
Bradninch	10 Apr. 1685	Grantham	15 Sept. 1688
Harwich	10 Apr. 1685	Hull	15 Sept. 1688
Mitchell	10 Apr. 1685	Ipswich	15 Sept. 1688
Calne	18 Apr. 1685	King's Lynn	15 Sept. 1688
Bewdley	4 May 1685	Leicester	15 Sept. 1688
Newbury	14 May 1685	Marlborough	15 Sept. 1688
Hull	9 June 1685	Morpeth	15 Sept. 1688
Maidenhead	15 June 1685	Norwich	15 Sept. 1688
Stafford	8 July 1685	Oxford	15 Sept. 1688
Saffron Walden	29 July 1685	Poole	15 Sept. 1688
York	29 July 1685	Southampton	15 Sept. 1688
Appleby	31 July 1685	Taunton	15 Sept. 1688
Kingston upon Thames	28 Aug. 1685	Winchester	15 Sept. 1688
Callington	10 Oct. 1685	Brackley	18 Sept. 1688
Faversham	3 Dec. 1685	Grimsby	18 Sept. 1688
Romney	3 Feb. 1686	London	3 Oct. 1688
Hastings	11 Feb. 1686	Winchester	6 Nov. 1688
Torrington	24 Feb. 1686	Doncaster	10 Nov. 1688
Abingdon	26 Feb. 1686	Poole	8 Dec. 1688
Reading	26 Feb. 1686	Fowey	28 Apr. 1690
Tewkesbury	12 Mar. 1686	Nottingham	19 Oct. 1692

Ludlow	19 Dec. 1692	Romsey	25 July 1698
Plympton	10 Feb. 1693	Deal	13 Oct. 1699
Warwick	18 Mar. 1693	Yarmouth	11 Mar. 1703
Colchester	27 July 1693	Wareham	23 Aug. 1703
Dunwich	28 Apr. 1694	Leominster	16 Mar. 1705
Saffron Walden	26 Dec. 1694	Glastonbury	23 June 1705
Liverpool	26 Sept. 1695	Salisbury	14 June 1707
Malmesbury	14 Nov. 1695	Bewdley	20 Apr. 1708
Plymouth	8 Dec. 1696	Bristol	24 July 1710
Hereford	14 June 1697	Banbury	16 July 1718
Eye	11 Oct. 1697	Henley	22 Sept. 1722
Tewkesbury	13 July 1698	Tiverton	4 Dec. 1724

Appendix B: Enforcement of the Corporation Act, 1662–1663

Thirty-six towns are studied here. Column A gives numbers dismissed from each rank in the corporation: mayor (or other head officer, including bailiffs, where there are two), aldermen (or those in a senior body by another name), councilmen (or those in a junior body by another name), and assistants (or those in a third body found in some towns). "Other" includes town clerks, recorders, and high stewards. Because the percentage of removals is critical, the number of members at each rank in the corporation according to its charter is given in column B. Column C gives the percentage of those dismissed from each rank.

The commissioners did not always note their reasons for removing officers; where known, these are given in the two right-hand columns: total removals for each reason in the first, and the percentage of those removed for each reason of all for whom the reason for removal is known. In row 1 are those removed for refusing to subscribe the declaration against the Covenant. In row 2 are those whom the commissioners removed arbitrarily, "for public safety." In row 3 are those removed for refusing the declaration or one of the other oaths, the distinction being unclear in the evidence. In row 4 are those dismissed after failing to appear when the commissioners came to town. A statistical summary for all towns is presented at the end, followed by a list of sources consulted.

		A Removed (#)	B On corp. (#)	C Removed (%)	Reason for removal	(#)	(%)
Abingdon	Mayor	0	1				
	Aldermen	4	12	33	Declaration	2	66.7
	Councilmen	5	16	31	Arbitrary	0	0.0
	Assistants				Oath/decl.	1	33.3
	Other	0	2		Absence	0	0.0
	Total	9	31	29			
Banbury	Mayor	0	1				
	Aldermen	0	6	0	Declaration		0.0
	Councilmen	0	30	0	Arbitrary		0.0
	Assistants				Oath/decl.		0.0
	Other	0	2		Absence		0.0
	Total	0	39	0			

Barnstaple	Mayor	0	1				
	Aldermen	0	2	˙ 0	Declaration	3	100.0
	Councilmen	3	22	14	Arbitrary	0	0.0
	Assistants				Oath/decl.	0	0.0
	Other	0	2		Absence	0	0.0
	Total	**3**	**27**	**11**			
Bedford	Mayor	0	1				
	Aldermen	2	11	18	Declaration		?
	Councilmen	0	13	0	Arbitrary		?
	Assistants				Oath/decl.		?
	Other	0	2		Absence		?
	Total	**2**	**27**	**7**			
Beverley	Mayor	0	1				
	Aldermen	6	12	50	Declaration	0	0.0
	Councilmen				Arbitrary	6	100.0
	Assistants				Oath/decl.	0	0.0
	Other	0	2		Absence	0	0.0
	Total	**6**	**15**	**40**			
Bewdley	Mayor	0	1				
	Aldermen	5	12	42	Declaration	20	95.2
	Councilmen	16	25	64	Arbitrary	1	4.8
	Assistants				Oath/decl.	0	0.0
	Other	0	1		Absence	0	0.0
	Total	**21**	**39**	**54**			
Boston	Mayor	1	1				
	Aldermen	8	12	67	Declaration		?
	Councilmen	8	18	44	Arbitrary		?
	Assistants				Oath/decl.		?
	Other	0	2		Absence		?
	Total	**17**	**33**	**52**			
Bristol	Mayor	0	1				
	Aldermen	0	11	0	Declaration	2	100.0
	Councilmen	2	31	7	Arbitrary	0	0.0
	Assistants				Oath/decl.	0	0.0
	Other	0	2		Absence	0	0.0
	Total	**2**	**45**	**4**			
Bury St. Edmunds	Mayor	0	1				
	Aldermen	0	4	0	Declaration	1	100.0
	Councilmen	1	12	8	Arbitrary	0	0.0
	Assistants	0	24	0	Oath/decl.	0	0.0
	Other	0	2		Absence	0	0.0
	Total	**1**	**43**	**2**			

(*cont.*)

Table (*cont.*)

		A Removed (#)	B On corp. (#)	C Removed (%)	Reason for removal	(#)	(%)
Cambridge	Mayor	1	1				
	Aldermen	7	12	58	Declaration	11	55.0
	Councilmen	12	24	50	Arbitrary	1	5.0
	Assistants				Oath/decl.	0	0.0
	Other	0	2		Absence	8	40.0
	Total	20	39	51			
Canterbury	Mayor	0	1				
	Aldermen	2	12	17	Declaration	0	0.0
	Councilmen	7	24	29	Arbitrary	3	30.0
	Assistants				Oath/decl.	7	70.0
	Other	1	2		Absence	0	0.0
	Total	10	39	26			
Chester	Mayor	0	1				
	Aldermen	11	23	48	Declaration	0	0.0
	Councilmen	21	40	53	Arbitrary	1	2.9
	Assistants				Oath/decl.	33	97.1
	Other	2	2		Absence	0	0.0
	Total	34	66	52			
Chesterfield	Mayor	1	1				
	Aldermen	4	6	67	Declaration	11	91.7
	Councilmen	4	6	67	Arbitrary	0	0.0
	Assistants	7	12	58	Oath/decl.	0	0.0
	Other	0	1		Absence	1	8.3
	Total	16	26	62			
Coventry	Mayor	0	1				
	Aldermen	1	10	10	Declaration		?
	Councilmen	10	25	40	Arbitrary		?
	Assistants				Oath/decl.		?
	Other	0	2		Absence		?
	Total	11	38	29			
Devizes	Mayor	0	1				
	Aldermen	6	12	50	Declaration		?
	Councilmen	10	24	42	Arbitrary		?
	Assistants				Oath/decl.		?
	Other	1	2		Absence		?
	Total	17	39	44			

Exeter	Mayor	0	1				
	Aldermen	5	11	46	Declaration	10	83.3
	Councilmen	7	24	29	Arbitrary	2	16.7
	Assistants				Oath/decl.	0	0.0
	Other	0	2		Absence	0	0.0
	Total	**12**	**38**	**32**			
Gloucester	Mayor	0	1				
	Aldermen	11	11	100	Declaration	3	12.5
	Councilmen	24	35	69	Arbitrary	21	87.5
	Assistants				Oath/decl.	0	0.0
	Other	1	2		Absence	0	0.0
	Total	**36**	**49**	**74**			
Henley	Mayor	0	1				
	Aldermen	0	11	0	Declaration		?
	Councilmen	0	24	0	Arbitrary		?
	Assistants				Oath/decl.		?
	Other	0	1		Absence		?
	Total	**0**	**37**	**0**			
Kingston upon Thames	Mayor	0	2				
	Aldermen	3	8	38	Declaration	4	80.0
	Councilmen	4	12	33	Arbitrary	1	20.0
	Assistants	0	15	0	Oath/decl.	0	0.0
	Other	0	3		Absence	0	0.0
	Total	**7**	**40**	**18**			
Leicester	Mayor	0	1				
	Aldermen	15	24	63	Declaration		?
	Councilmen	25	48	52	Arbitrary		?
	Assistants				Oath/decl.		?
	Other	0	3		Absence		?
	Total	**40**	**76**	**53**			
Liverpool	Mayor	1	1				
	Aldermen	5	8	63	Declaration	13	92.9
	Councilmen	7	24	29	Arbitrary	1	7.1
	Assistants				Oath/decl.	0	0.0
	Other	1	2		Absence	0	0.0
	Total	**14**	**35**	**40**			
Maidenhead	Mayor	1	1				
	Aldermen	0	2	0	Declaration	3	100.0
	Councilmen	2	8	25	Arbitrary	0	0.0
	Assistants				Oath/decl.	0	0.0
	Other	0	2		Absence	0	0.0
	Total	**3**	**13**	**23**			

(*cont.*)

Table (*cont.*)

		A Removed (#)	B On corp. (#)	C Removed (%)	Reason for removal	(#)	(%)
Maidstone	Mayor	0	1				
	Aldermen	6	12	50	Declaration	16	100.0
	Councilmen	16	32	50	Arbitrary	0	0.0
	Assistants				Oath/decl.	0	0.0
	Other	0	2		Absence	0	0.0
	Total	22	47	47			
Maldon	Mayor	1	2				
	Aldermen	4	6	67	Declaration	15	100.0
	Councilmen	10	18	56	Arbitrary	0	0.0
	Assistants				Oath/decl.	0	0.0
	Other	0	2		Absence	0	0.0
	Total	15	28	54			
Marlborough	Mayor	1	1				
	Aldermen	9	11	82	Declaration		?
	Councilmen	17	37	46	Arbitrary		?
	Assistants				Oath/decl.		?
	Other				Absence		?
	Total	27	49	55			
Newcastle under Lyme	Mayor	0	1				
	Aldermen	1	2	50	Declaration	0	0.0
	Councilmen	11	24	46	Arbitrary	3	25.0
	Assistants				Oath/decl.	9	75.0
	Other	0	2		Absence	0	0.0
	Total	12	29	41			
Norwich	Mayor	0	1				
	Aldermen	4	24	17	Declaration		?
	Councilmen	0	60	0	Arbitrary		?
	Assistants				Oath/decl.		?
	Other	0	2		Absence		?
	Total	4	87	5			
Plymouth	Mayor	1	1				
	Aldermen	6	12	50	Declaration	15	100.0
	Councilmen	13	24	54	Arbitrary	0	0.0
	Assistants				Oath/decl.	0	0.0
	Other	1	2		Absence	0	0.0
	Total	21	39	54			

Reading	Mayor	1	1				
	Aldermen	7	12	58	Declaration	5	35.7
	Councilmen	6	12	50	Arbitrary	9	64.3
	Assistants				Oath/decl.	0	0.0
	Other	0	2		Absence	0	0.0
	Total	**14**	**27**	**52**			
Shrewsbury	Mayor	1	1				
	Aldermen	9	23	39	Declaration	0	0.0
	Councilmen	12	48	25	Arbitrary	1	100.0
	Assistants				Oath/decl.	0	0.0
	Other	1	2		Absence	0	0.0
	Total	**23**	**74**	**31**			
Stratford-upon-Avon	Mayor	0	1				
	Aldermen	3	12	25	Declaration		?
	Councilmen	3	14	21	Arbitrary		?
	Assistants				Oath/decl.		?
	Other	0	2		Absence		?
	Total	**6**	**29**	**21**			
Wallingford	Mayor	1	1				
	Aldermen	5	7	71	Declaration		0.0
	Councilmen	9	12	75	Arbitrary	15	100.0
	Assistants				Oath/decl.		0.0
	Other	0	2		Absence		0.0
	Total	**15**	**22**	**68**			
Walsall	Mayor	0	1				
	Aldermen	14	24	58	Declaration	2	100.0
	Councilmen				Arbitrary		0.0
	Assistants				Oath/decl.		0.0
	Other	1	2		Absence		0.0
	Total	**15**	**27**	**56**			
Warwick	Mayor	1	1				
	Aldermen	1	12	8	Declaration	3	100.0
	Councilmen	1	12	8	Arbitrary	0	0.0
	Assistants				Oath/decl.	0	0.0
	Other	0	2		Absence	0	0.0
	Total	**3**	**27**	**11**			
Windsor	Mayor	0	1				
	Aldermen	4	9	44	Declaration		?
	Councilmen	0	13	0	Arbitrary		?
	Assistants	0	18	0	Oath/decl.		?
	Other	0	2		Absence		?
	Total	**4**	**43**	**9**			

(*cont.*)

Appendix B

Table (*cont.*)

		A Removed (#)	B On corp. (#)	C Removed (%)	Reason for removal	(#)	(%)
Woodstock	Mayor	1	1				
	Aldermen	4	23	17	Declaration		?
	Councilmen				Arbitrary		?
	Assistants				Oath/decl.		?
	Other	1	1		Absence		?
	Total	6	25	24			

Summary

Total members of the corporations studied	1,387
Total remaining in office	919 (66.26%)
Total dismissed	468 (33.74%)

Reasons for dismissals known
1. Declaration	139	52.9%
2. Arbitrary	65	24.7%
3. Oath or declaration	50	19.0%
4. Absence	9	3.4%
Total known reasons for dismissal	263	100%
Reason for dismissal unknown	205	

Sources consulted for enforcement of the Corporation Act

Please see the Bibliography for full citations of the items below.

Abingdon: Challenor, *Abingdon*, pp. 147–49. Berkshire RO, T/F41, ff. 190v–93, and A/AOza and b.
Banbury: Gibson and Brinkworth, *Banbury Records*, p. 211.
Barnstaple: Chanter and Wainwright, *Barnstaple Records*, vol. I, pp. 230–31.
Bedford: Parsloe, *Minute Book of Bedford*, p. 146.
Beverley: Dennett, *Beverley Records*, pp. 103–04.
Bewdley: Styles, "Corporation of Bewdley," pp. 46–47.
Boston: Bailey, *Minutes of Boston*, vol. III, pp. 386–87.
Bristol: Latham, *Bristol Charters*, p. 39.
Bury St. Edmunds: Suffolk RO (Bury Branch), D14/1.
Cambridge: Palmer, "Reformation of the Corporation of Cambridge," pp. 75–136.
Canterbury: Canterbury City and Cathedral Archives, CC/AC/5, ff. 55–62v.
Chester: CCRO, AB2/135–37v.
Chesterfield: Yeatman, *Chesterfield*, p. 138. Riden and Blair, *Chesterfield*, p. 92.
Coventry: Hurwich, "'A Fanatick Town'," p. 19. F. J. Routledge, ed., *Calendar of the Clarendon State Papers Preserved in the Bodleian Library*, vol. V (Oxford, 1970), p. 255.
Devizes: Cunnington, *Devizes*, pp. 133–34.

Exeter: Devon RO, B1/10, pp. 356–61.

Gloucester: Austin, "Gloucester and the Regulation," pp. 257–74.

Henley: Oxfordshire RO, A.V.6.

Leicester: record of the commissioners' work at Leicester does not survive, but may be inferred from surviving evidence: Stocks, *Records*, pp. 606–07. These lists compare perfectly with lists from the last full meeting before and right after their visit: Leicestershire RO, BRII/18/30, f. 244, and BRII/1/3, ff. 774–76.

Liverpool: Muir and Platt, *Liverpool*, p. 101. Picton, *Liverpool Records*, pp. 238–40.

Maidenhead: Berkshire RO, M/AC1/1/1, second pagination, pp. 49 and 51.

Maidstone: Martin, *Records of Maidstone*, pp. 145–46.

Maldon: Bod., MS. Top. Essex e.6/11, ff. 13v and 75v–79.

Marlborough: Waylen, *Marlborough*, pp. 330–31. Stedman, *Marlborough*, p. 156.

Newcastle under Lyme: Pape, *Newcastle-under-Lyme*, pp. 16–23.

Norwich: Francis Blomefield, *An Essay Towards a Topographical History of the County of Norfolk*, 11 vols. (London, 1805–10), vol. III, pp. 403–05.

Plymouth: HMC 9, app. 1, p. 284. Worth, *Records of Plymouth*, pp. 5–6.

Reading: Sacret, "Reading," pp. 18–42.

Shrewsbury: HMC 15, app. 10, p. 41. Owen and Blakeway, *Shrewsbury*, pp. 483–84.

Stratford: VCH, Worcestershire, vol. III, p. 250.

Wallingford: Berkshire RO, W/AC1/1/2, ff. 25v–27.

Walsall: Homeshaw, *Walsall*, pp. 45–46. Walsall RO, 277/66/3 and 277/235.

Warwick: Styles, "Warwick," pp. 25 and 30.

Windsor: Bond, *Hall Book of Windsor*, vol. I, pp. 11–12.

Woodstock: Woodstock Town Hall, 76/1, ff. 4v–6v.

SELECT BIBLIOGRAPHY

MANUSCRIPT SOURCES

BODLEIAN LIBRARY, OXFORD

Carte Manuscripts
Clarendon Manuscripts
MS Add.c.303: Dolben Papers
MS Eng. Hist. c.711: Diary of Col. Roger Whitley, 1684–97
MS Film 53: Diary of Sir Thomas Mainwaring, 1648–88
MS Top. Berks.c.20: Papers concerning Abingdon
MS Top. Essex.e.6/11: Corporation Act commissioners' orders, Maldon (transcript)
MS Top. Northants.c.9: Northampton notes by Henry Lee
MS Top. Oxon.c.351: a collection of antiquities of Woodstock
Rawlinson Manuscripts
Tanner Manuscripts

BRITISH LIBRARY, LONDON

Additional Manuscripts:
   23,215 and 25,124–25: Coventry Papers
   28,875, 28,879–81: Ellis Papers
   32,518–20: Guilford Papers
   34,222: Earl of Westmorland, lieutenancy letter book, 1660–65
   34,653: Dunwich collections
   35,980, 35,982, 35,984, 35,988–90, 36,134–35, and 36,140–41: Hardwicke
     Papers
   37,157: Herbert of Cherbury Papers
   41,605: Aldeburgh Letter Book, 1625–68
   41,803–05 and 41,823: Middleton Papers
Egerton Manuscripts:
   868: notes on Southampton mayors
   3329–31, 3336, and 3348: Leeds Papers
Harleian Manuscripts:
   6846: Humphrey Wanley Papers
Stowe Manuscripts:
   745–48: Dering correspondence, 1667–1759

FOLGER SHAKESPEARE LIBRARY, WASHINGTON, DC

V.b.294: Papers of Edward Southwell, 1678–1718
LC: Newdigate Newsletters, 1674–1715

HOUSE OF LORDS RECORD OFFICE, LONDON

MS5/H/3/1: Lords' Committee minute book, 1660–64
MS5/E/7/1/13: House of Lords' minutes

HUNTINGTON LIBRARY, SAN MARINO, CALIFORNIA

Hastings Letters (on microfilm: *The Aristocracy, the State and the Local Community: The Hastings Collection of Mss from the Huntington Library*, Brighton, 1986)

JOHN RYLANDS UNIVERSITY OF MANCHESTER LIBRARY, MANCHESTER

Legh of Lyme Papers
Mainwaring Papers

PUBLIC RECORD OFFICE, KEW

Assizes:
  ASSI2 and 4: Oxford Circuit, crown and process books
  ASSI22 and 24: Western Circuit, minute and miscellaneous books
Chancery:
  C66: patent rolls index
  C75: surrender rolls
  C93: Charity Commissions, inquisitions and reports
  C181: Crown Office, Entry Books of Commissions (including commissions of the peace to boroughs)
  C203/5: certificates, including surrenders, 1680s
  C231/7–10: Crown Office, great seal docket books, 1660–1746
  IND1/4227–30: Patent Office warrants for great seal, docket books, 1660–1729
King's Bench:
  KB1 and 2: affidavits
  KB21: crown side rule books
  KB29: controlment rolls
  KB32: interrogatories on contempt
  KB33: precedents in mandamus and quo warranto
Privy Council:
  PC1: petitions and papers
  PC2/55–89: Privy Council registers, 1660–1727
State Papers:
  SP9: Sir Joseph Williamson's Papers
  SP29: State Papers, temp. Charles II
  SP31: State Papers, temp. James II
  SP34: State Papers, temp. Anne
  SP35: State Papers, temp. George I
  SP38: dockets

SP44: entry books of letters, warrants, and petitions
SP46: State Papers, supplementary

MANUSCRIPT SOURCES, LOCAL RECORD OFFICES

BATH CITY RECORD OFFICE

Council Books, numbers 1–3: 1631–1711

BERKSHIRE RECORD OFFICE, READING

Abingdon:
  A/AOz: removals from office, 1662/3 and 1687
  T/F41: corporation minutes, 1591–1686
Maidenhead:
  M/AC1/1/1: minute book, 1636–1761
  M/IC5 and 8: charters, 1663 and 1685
Reading:
  R/AC1/1/6–21: corporation diaries, 1655–1730
  Uncatalogued corporation documents
Wallingford:
  W/AC1/1/1 and 2: corporation minute books, 1507–1683 and 1648–1766
  W/AO4: corporation lists, 1678 and 1689

CAMBRIDGESHIRE RECORD OFFICE, CAMBRIDGE

Shelf C/8 and 9: Cambridge corporation common day books, 1647–1722

CANTERBURY CITY AND CATHEDRAL ARCHIVES

CC/AC/5 and 6: burghmote minutes, 1658–1684

CHESHIRE RECORD OFFICE, CHESTER

DCH: Cholmondeley of Cholmondeley Papers
Grosvenor Papers (held at Eaton Hall)
Shakerley Collection
Macclesfield:
  Items on microfilm MF122/1:
    MA/B/14: notes on 1716 mayoral election
    MA/B/IV: notes on mayoral election, 1716–17
    MA/B/VI/10: charter surrender, 1684
    MA/B/VI/13 and 15: Privy Council orders, 1688
  LBM/1/1: borough minutes, 1619–1744
  LBM/2703/66: mayors' accounts, 1708–1809

CHESTER CITY RECORD OFFICE, CHESTER

CR99: Diary of Roger Comberbach, 1692

Chester:
AB/2, 3, and 4: assembly books, 1624–85, 1685–1725, and 1725 and following
AF: assembly files
G/Mc.9: petition to Judge Jeffreys concerning Chester charter (1683–84)
MB: mayors' books
MF: mayors' files
ML: mayors' letters

DEVON RECORD OFFICE, EXETER

Exeter:
B1/10, 11, and 13: chamber act books, 1651–1730

NORTH DEVON RECORD OFFICE, BARNSTAPLE

Barnstaple:
B1/615: minute of charter surrender, 1684
B1/1119, 1121: mandamus and order restoring alderman, 1663
B1/1998–99: documents concerning the Corporation Act

GLOUCESTERSHIRE RECORD OFFICE, GLOUCESTER

Gloucester:
GBR/B3/3: minute book, 1656–88
GBR/B3/4: draft minute book, 1668–73
GBR/C8/1: Corporation Act subscription register
GBR/F5: stewards' account books

HAMPSHIRE RECORD OFFICE, WINCHESTER

Andover: 37M85/
2/JC/2: sessions books
4/EL: documents concerning removals from corporation, 1698–99
4/MI/3 and 5: town minutes, 1678/9 and 1693–1713
4/OD: oath subscriptions, 1696–1700, and letters
Lymington: 27M74/
DBC2: accounts and minutes
DBC283: orders of the Corporation Act commissioners, 1662
Winchester:
W/B1/5–7: books of ordinances, 5–7, 1647–1707
W/B2/4: first proposal book, 1663–1704

HEREFORD AND WORCESTER RECORD OFFICE, WORCESTER (ST.
HELEN'S)

Worcester:
Shelf A.10, Boxes 3 and 4: accounts, 1660–92
Shelf A.14, no box: chamber order book, 1650–76
Shelf A.14, Box 2: chamber order book, 1669–1721
Shelf C.2, Box 1: charters

HERTFORDSHIRE RECORD OFFICE

Berkhamsted:
 D/EX/652/22: minutes, 1628–62
 D/EX/652/13, 15–17, 32–35: records in quo warranto, and charter petition, etc.,
  1663–64
Hertford:
 Volume 1: charters
 Volume 30: corporation elections, 1609–1846
 Volume 33: corporation minutes, 1574–1837
 Volume 36: corporation matters, 1702–1893

HULL CITY RECORD OFFICE

BRL and BRS: corporation correspondence and other papers

LEICESTERSHIRE RECORD OFFICE, LEICESTER

Leicester:
 14D32: Huntingdon letters
 BRI/2/48: Attorney's bills, 1665
 BRII/1/3–6: hall books, 1587–1736
 BRII/5: letters
 BRII/8: papers concerning town lands
 BRII/18/30–39: hall papers, bound, 1660–1709
 BRII/19: working papers
 BRIII/2/86–98 and 109: chamberlains' accounts, 1660–1726
 BRIII/8: financial records
 BRIV/9: legal papers
 O.S.88: "Catalogue of documents in the charter chest" [1708?]

NORTHAMPTONSHIRE RECORD OFFICE, NORTHAMPTON

Brackley:
 Br.14 and 16: charters, 1686 and 1688
Northampton:
 3/2: second assembly book, 1629–1744

OXFORDSHIRE RECORD OFFICE, OXFORD

Banbury:
 B.B.I/iii/4: charter, 1718
 B.B.XV/i: borough journal extracts, 1718–69
 B.B.XV/ii/1: borough journal extracts, 1722–61
 B.B.XVII/i: town book, 1561–1741
Henley:
 A.I.6: papers concerning 1722 charter
 A.V.6–8: assembly minutes, 1624–1799

SHAKESPEARE BIRTHPLACE TRUST, STRATFORD-UPON-AVON

Stratford:
  BRU2/4: council minute book, 1657–95
  BRU15: miscellaneous documents

SHROPSHIRE RECORDS AND RESEARCH SERVICE, SHREWSBURY

Bridgnorth:
  4001/Admin/3/1: common hall book, 1634–86
Ludlow:
  LB/1/18: letter of Charles II, 1680
  LB/1/19: petition to William and Mary
  LB2/1/2: minute book, 1648–80
  LB2/3/8: by-laws, 1663
Shrewsbury:
  3365/2718: roll of admissions of aldermen and assistants, 1694–1738

SUFFOLK RECORD OFFICE, BURY ST. EDMUNDS BRANCH

Bury St. Edmunds:
  D1/6/10: charter, 1668
  D4/1/2: corporation book, 1652–91
  D10/3: items in Chancery suit, 1661–62
  D11/11/2 and 3: books of subscriptions of Corporation Act, 1663–1718
  D14/1: orders of Corporation Act commissioners, 1662
Sudbury:
  EE501/2/7: borough court book, 1639–72
  EE501/2/8: book of orders, 1658–85
  EE501/6/170: charter surrender and petition, 1685

SUFFOLK RECORD OFFICE, IPSWICH BRANCH

Aldeburgh:
  EE1/C5/3: Corporation Act commissioners' orders, 1662
  EE1/E1/2: order book, 1643–1746
  EE1/F1/1: order book, 1697–1817
  EE1/D1/1: register and formula book, 1611–1739
Dunwich:
  EE6/1144/13 and 14: assembly books, 1676–1790
  EE6/1144/20: voting list for bailiff, 1710
  EE6/1144/23/5: order removing recorder, 1694
  EE6/1144/29: writ of mandamus, 1726
Eye:
  EE2/D5/1: state of the case of George Walsh
  EE2/I/2: assembly book, 1670–90
  EE2/K/5/5: notes [of parliamentary debate], January 22, 1689/90
  EE2/K/5/22: notes on the case of Daniel Hoar of Hull, 1680
Ipswich:
  C5/14/5: general court book, 1680–1703

C5/14/6: great court book, 1703–1710
C6/1/7: assembly book, 1680–1726
HD36/A: miscellaneous letters
Orford:
  EE5/2/2 and 3: Corporation Act books, 1579–1701
  EE5/4/3: assembly act book, 1693–1736

SURREY RECORD OFFICE, KINGSTON-UPON-THAMES

Kingston upon Thames:
  KA3/2: surrenders and letters concerning charter, 1685
  KB1/1: assembly book, 1680–1725
  KB9/1: patents of appointment to corporation offices
  KB12/1: papers concerning elections and declarations against the Covenant
  KB13/1: Corporation Act commissioners' orders
  KD5/1/2: chamberlains' accounts, 1638–1710

EAST SUSSEX RECORD OFFICE, LEWES

Rye 1/17 and 3/22: minute books

THETFORD TOWN HALL

T/C1/11: miscellaneous manuscripts
T/C1/19: by-laws, 1668
T/C2/6 and 7: assembly minute book, 1682–1771

WALSALL LOCAL HISTORY CENTRE, WALSALL

Acc276: leases and other documents, feoffees of town lands
Acc277/
  8: documents in law suits
  13: mayors' accounts
  66 and 86: corporation commissioners' orders and papers in Privy Council
    enquiry, 1668
  84, 94, 112: papers concerning feoffees of town lands
  235: book of entries, 1647–1749

WILTSHIRE RECORD OFFICE, TROWBRIDGE

Calne:
  G18/1/1: guild stewards' book, 1561–1814
  G18/1/3: election memoranda
  G18/1/11: papers in elections and legal matters
Devizes:
  G20/1/18: entry book, 1660–81
  G20/1/19: common council minute book, 1688–1749
  G20/1/90: miscellaneous papers
Marlborough:
  G22/1/7: corporation's case against surrender, 1682

G22/1/54: quo warranto and documents in *Rex* v. *Williams*, 1715
G22/1/91: memorial of corporation to King, 1680
G22/1/22–29: entry books, 1646–1730
Salisbury:
G23/1/4: ledger book, 1640–1723
G23/1/17: council minute book, 1683–1708
G23/1/38: letters, 1569–1692
G23/1/42: miscellaneous documents
Wilton:
G25/1/17–19: petition for a charter, and other papers, 1684–1710
G25/1/21: general entry book, 1454–1705
G25/1/87: writ of mandamus, 1701
G25/1/181: return to quo warranto, temp. Charles II
G25/1/186: town clerk's papers

WOODSTOCK TOWN HALL

76/1 and 2, and 86/1 and 87/1: council acts, 1661–1746
96: lists of freemen and inhabitants, 1611–1748
149: charter, 1664

SEVENTEENTH- AND EIGHTEENTH-CENTURY BOOKS, PAMPHLETS, AND SERMONS

An Account of the Surrender of the Old Charter of Northampton . . . and the Manner of their Receiving their New Charter. [1683].

Allen, William. *A Sermon Preach't in Bridgewater, The Next Day After the Election of Burgesses.* London, 1681.

The Banb–y Apes: or, The Monkeys Chattering to the Magpie. London, 1710.

Barksdale, Clement. *A Sermon Preached upon the Fifth of November, 1679, in the Cathedral Church at Gloucester.* Oxford, 1680.

Blackstone, William. *Commentaries on the Laws of England,* 15th edn., 4 vols. London, 1809; reprint, Abingdon, 1982.

Blake, Martin. *An Earnest Plea for Peace and Moderation in a Sermon, Preached at Barnstaple.* London, 1661.

Bradford, Samuel. *A Sermon Preach'd . . . At the Election of the Lord Mayor.* London, 1700.

Brady, Robert. *An Historical Treatise of Cities and Burghs.* London, 1690.

Burnet, Gilbert. *An Exhortation to Peace and Union: A Sermon Preached . . . at the Election of the Lord-Mayor.* London, 1681.

The Case between the Mayor and Aldermen of Canterbury, and Mr. Serjeant Hardres their Late Recorder. 1681.

The Case of Daniel Hoar, Merchant, Alderman of . . . Kingston-upon-Hull. London, 1682.

The Case of the Burgesses of Nottingham, in Reference to the Surrendering of their Charters. London, 1682.

The Case of the Charter of London Stated. London, 1683.

The Case of the City of Oxford: Shewing How Far the Said City is Concerned to Oppose the Confirmation of the Charters, and Pretended Privileges of the University by Parliament. 1687.

The Charter of London's Answer to a Scurrilous Libel, Entitled, Its Last Will and Testament. London, 1683.

The Charter: A Comical Satire. London, 1682.

The Citizen's Loss when the Charter of London Is Forfeited, or Given Up. London, 1683.

Conold, Robert. *A Sermon Preached before the Maior of the City of Norwich.* London, 1675.

Ellison, Nathanael. *The Magistrates Obligation to Punish Vice: A Sermon Preach'd before . . . the mayor . . . of Newcastle upon Tyne.* London, 1700.

Fowler, Edward. *A Discourse of Offences. Delivered in Two Sermons . . . in the Cathedral Church of Gloucester.* London, 1683.

The Great Wickedness and Mischievous Effects of Slandering. London, 1685.

A Sermon Preached at the General Meeting of Gloucestershire-Men. London, 1685.

A Sermon Preached before the Judges, etc., In the time of the Assizes in the Cathedral Church at Gloucester. London, 1681.

Glover, Henry. *An Exhortation to Prayer for Jerusalems Peace. In a Sermon Preached at Dorchester.* London, 1663.

Griffith, John. *A Sermon Preached at St. Lawrence Church in Reading in the County of Berks . . . [on] the Day on which the Mayor was Sworn.* London, 1693.

Hale, Sir Matthew. *The Prerogatives of the King.* Ed. by D. E. C. Yale. Selden Society, vol. 92. London, 1975.

Hunt, Thomas. *A Defence of the Charter, and Municipal Rights of the City of London. And the Rights of Other Municipal Cities and Towns of England.* London, [1683].

Jackson, Christopher. *The Magistrate's Duty in a Sermon, Preached . . . in the City of York . . . Immediately after the Reception of the Charter, and the Swearing of the Lord Mayor.* York, 1685.

Jeffrey, John. *A Sermon Preached in the Cathedral Church of Norwich, at the Mayor's Guild.* London, 1693.

The Kingdoms Intelligencer of the Affairs Now in Agitation in England, Scotland, and Ireland. London, 1660–63.

The Last Will and Testament of the Charter of London. London, 1683.

The Law of Corporations: Containing the Laws and Customs of All the Corporations and Inferior Courts of Record in England. London, 1702.

L'Estrange, Sir Roger. *The Lawyer Outlaw'd; or a Brief Answer to Mr. Hunt's Defence of the Charter.* [London], 1683.

A Letter Concerning the Disabling Clauses, Lately Offered to the House of Commons, for Regulating Corporations. London, 1690.

London's Lamentation for the Loss of their Charter. London, 1683.

Long, Thomas. *The Original of War: Or, The Causes of Rebellion. A Sermon Preached in the Castle of Exon.* London, 1684.

Madox, Thomas. *Firma Burgi, or an Historical Essay Concerning the Cities, Towns and Buroughs of England.* London, 1726.

March, John. *A Sermon Preached Before the Right Worshipful, The Mayor, Recorder, Aldermen, Sheriff &c. of . . . Newcastle upon Tyne.* London, 1677.

Sermons Preach'd on Several Occasions. London, 1699.

Newberry, William, and William Edmunds. *A Letter to Dr. Fowler in Answer to his Late Vindicatory Preface.* 1685.

North, Roger. *Examen; Or, An Enquiry into the Credit and Veracity of a Pretended Complete History.* London, 1740.

The Power of the Kings of England to Examine the Charters of Particular Corporations and Companies. London, 1684.

The Proceedings of the Citizens of Hereford in the Delivery up of their Charter and Renewing of it. London, 1682.

[Prynne, William]. *Summary Reasons, Humbly Tendered to the Most Honorable House of Peers . . . against the New Intended Bill for Governing and Reforming Corporations.* [London, 1661].

Pudsey, Sir George. *The Speech of Sir George Pudsey, Serjeant-at-Law, Recorder of the City of Oxford . . . at the Swearing the New Mayor.* [London], 1685.

Reflections on the City-Charter, and Writ of Quo Warranto. London, 1682.

Reflections upon that Act of the Gloucester Common-Council: Which Occasioned Dr. Fowler's Printing his Discourse of Offenses. London, 1683.

Richardson, Joshua. *A Sermon Preach'd before the Right Honourable the Lord Mayor and Aldermen of the City of London.* London, 1682.

Rively, B. *A Sermon Preach'd at the Cathedral of Norwich upon the Annual Solemnity of the Mayors Admission to his Office.* London, 1679.

Shepheard, William. *Of Corporations, Fraternities and Guilds.* London, 1659.

A Speech Made in the House of Commons upon the Late Ministry's Forcing a New Charter upon the Town of Bewdley. [London], 1710.

Strengfellow, William. *A Sermon Preach'd before the Right Honourable the Lord Mayor, Aldermen and Livery-Men of the City of London . . . At the Election of the Lord Mayor for the Year Ensuing.* London, 1693.

The True Friends to Corporations Vindicated, in Answer to A Letter Concerning the Disabling Clauses Lately Offered to the House of Commons for Regulating Corporations. London, 1690.

Whitby, Daniel. *A Sermon Preached at the Election of the Mayor of Sarum.* London, 1685.

Williams, John. *A Sermon Preached at St. Lawrence Jewry . . . At the Election of the Lord Mayor.* London, 1695.

Williams, William. *The Necessity & Extent of the Obligation, with the Manner and Measures of Restitution, in a Sermon Preached . . . Before the Corporation of Haverford West.* London, 1682.

Religion Exprest by Loyalty: In a Sermon Preach'd before the Right Worshipful Samuel Swift Esq., Mayor of . . . Worcester, the First Sunday after his Inauguration. London, 1685.

Wroe, Richard. *The Beauty of Unity, in a Sermon Preached at Preston in Lancashire, at the Opening of the Guild-Merchant.* London, 1682.

GENERAL PRINTED SOURCES

Calendar of State Papers, Domestic.

Calendar of Treasury Books.

The English Reports, vols. 77–93. London, 1907–09. Reprint, Abingdon, 1979–86.

Historical Manuscripts Commission, *Reports.*

Howell, T. B. *A Complete Collection of State Trials.* 34 vols. London, 1816.

Luttrell, Narcissus. *A Brief Historical Relation of State Affairs from September 1678 to April 1714.* 6 vols. Oxford, 1857.

Routledge, F. J., ed. *Calendar of the Clarendon State Papers Preserved in the Bodleian Library*, vol. V. Oxford, 1970.

TOWN HISTORIES AND PRINTED TOWN RECORDS

Abram, William Alexander. *Memorials of the Preston Guilds*. Preston, 1882.

Ashford, L. J. *The History of the Borough of High Wycombe from its Origins to 1880*. London, 1960.

Atkyns, Sir Robert. *The Ancient and Present State of Glostershire*. London, 1712; reprint, Wakefield, 1974.

Austin, Roland. "The City of Gloucester and the Regulation of Corporations, 1662–63." *Transactions of the Bristol and Gloucestershire Archaeological Society*, 58 (1936): 257–74.

An Authentic Copy of the Charter and Bye-Laws of the City of Rochester. London, 1809.

Bailey, John F. *Transcription of the Minutes of the Corporation of Boston*. 5 vols. Boston, 1980–93.

Beesley, Alfred. *The History of Banbury*. London, 1841.

Bennett, James. *The History of Tewkesbury*. Tewkesbury, 1830.

Biden, W. D. *The History and Antiquities of the Ancient and Royal Town of Kingston-upon-Thames*. Kingston, 1852.

Birch, Walter de Gray. *The Royal Charters of the City of Lincoln*. Cambridge, 1911.

Bond, Shelagh, ed. *The First Hall Book of the Borough of New Windsor, 1653–1725*. Windsor Borough Historical Records Publications, vol. 1. Windsor, 1968.

Boyle, J. R. *Charters and Letters Patent Granted to Kingston-upon-Hull*. Hull, 1905.

Bradby, Edward. "A Deadlock in Eighteenth-Century Devizes." *Wiltshire Archaeological and Natural History Magazine*, 81 (1987): 91–110.

Brand, J. *The History and Antiquities of . . . Newcastle-Upon-Tyne*. London, 1789.

A Brief Description of the Borough and Town of Preston and its Government and Guild. Preston, 1818.

Brown, Cornelius. *A History of Newark-on-Trent*. Newark, 1907.

Bunce, C. R. *A Translation of the Several Charters Granted . . . to the Citizens of Canterbury*. Canterbury, 1791.

A Calendar to the Records of the Borough of Doncaster. Doncaster, 1899–1902.

Canning, Richard. *The Principal Charters which have been Granted to the Corporation of Ipswich*. London, 1754.

Challenor, Bromley, ed. *Selections from the Municipal Chronicles of the Borough of Abingdon*. Abingdon, 1898.

Chanter, J. R., and Thomas Wainwright, eds. *Reprint of the Barnstaple Records*. 2 vols. Barnstaple, 1900.

The Charter of the Borough of Sudbury of Charles II. Sudbury, 1830; reprint, Sudbury, 1989.

"Charter of Totnes." *Transactions of the Devon Association*, 56 (1924): 215–47.

The Charters and Letters Patent Granted to the Borough [of Colchester]. Colchester, 1904.

Clark, J. G. *The Court Books of the Leeds Corporation: First Book, January 1662 to August 1705*. Thoresby Society, vol. 34. Leeds, 1933.

Clarke, G. R. *The History and Description of the Town and Borough of Ipswich.* London, 1830.

Clarkson, Christopher. *History of Richmond in the County of York.* Richmond, 1814.

Collier, C., and R. H. Clutterbuck. *The Archives of Andover.* Andover, 1889.

Cooper, Charles Henry. *Annals of Cambridge.* Cambridge, 1845.

Copies of the Charters and Grants to the Town of Ludlow. Ludlow.

"Cromwell's Charter, High Wycombe." *Records of Buckinghamshire,* 7 (1987): 11.

Cruden, Robert Pierce. *The History of the Town of Gravesend.* London, 1843.

Cunnington, B. Howard. *The Orders, Decrees and Ordinances of the Borough and Town of Marlborough.* Devizes, 1929.

Some Annals of the Borough of Devizes. Devizes, 1925.

Darrah, M. J., and J. E. H. Spaul. *The Corporation of Andover.* Andover Local Archives Committee. 1970.

Dennett, J., ed. *Beverley Borough Records, 1575-1821.* Yorkshire Archaeological Society Record Series, vol. 84. Wakefield, 1932.

Dibben, A. A. *Coventry City Charters.* The Coventry Papers, vol. 2. Coventry, 1969.

Drake, Francis. *Eboracum: or, The History and Antiquities of the City of York.* London, 1736.

Earwaker, J. P. *East Cheshire: Past and Present, or A History of the Hundred of Macclesfield.* 2 vols. London, 1877–80.

East, Robert. *Extracts from the Records in the Possession of the Municipal Corporation of the Borough of Portsmouth.* Portsmouth, 1891.

Edie, Carolyn. "Charles II, the Commons, and the Newark Charter Dispute: The Crown's Last Attempt to Enfranchise a Borough." *JBS,* 10 (1970): 49–68.

Edwards, G. "Shrewsbury Corporation Orders." *Transactions of the Shropshire Archaeological and Natural History Society,* 11 (1888): 153–210.

Evans, John T. *Seventeenth-Century Norwich: Politics, Religion, and Government, 1620–1690.* Oxford, 1979.

Farrington, E. *The Charter and also the Constitutions Granted to the Inhabitants of the Town of St. Albans.* St. Albans, 1813.

Ferguson, R. S. *The Royal Charters of the City of Carlisle.* Publications of the Cumberland and Westmorland Antiquarian and Archaeological Society. Carlisle, 1894.

Ferguson, R. S., and William Nanson. *Some Municipal Records of the City of Carlisle.* Westmorland Antiquarian and Archaeological Society. London, 1887.

Fosbrooke, Thomas Dudley. *An Original History of the City of Gloucester.* London, 1819.

Gauci, Perry. *Politics and Society in Great Yarmouth, 1660–1722.* Oxford, 1996.

Gibson, J. S. W., and E. R. C. Brinkworth, eds. *Banbury Corporation Records: Tudor and Stuart.* Banbury Historical Society, vol. 15. Banbury, 1977.

Gidden, H. W., ed. *The Charters of the Borough of Southampton.* Publications of the Southampton Record Society, vol. 2. Southampton, 1910.

Greaves, R. W. *The Corporation of Leicester, 1689–1836.* Oxford, 1939.

"The Earl of Huntingdon and the Leicester Charter of 1684." *Huntington Library Quarterly,* 15 (1952): 371–91.

Greaves, R. W., ed. *The First Ledger Book of High Wycombe.* Buckinghamshire Record Society, vol. 11. 1947.

Griffith, Edward. *A Collection of Ancient Records Relating to the Borough of Huntingdon.* London, 1827.

Groome, A. N. *Borough of Higham Ferrers: Charters and Insignia.* 1961.
Hall, Hubert, ed. "The Salisbury Commonwealth Charter." *Camden Miscellany,* 11 (Camden Society, 3rd series, vol. 13, 1907): 163–64.
Harrison, William. *Ripon Millenary Record.* Ripon, 1892.
Hay, Alexander. *The History of Chichester.* Chichester, 1804.
Hedges, John Kirby. *The History of Wallingford.* 2 vols. London, 1881.
Hewitson, W. "The Appleby Charters." *Transactions of the Cumberland and Westmorland Antiquarian and Archaeological Society,* 11 (1890): 279–85.
Hill, J. W. F. *Tudor and Stuart Lincoln.* Cambridge, 1956.
Hillen, Henry J. *History of the Borough of King's Lynn.* Norwich, 1907.
The History of Guildford. Guildford, 1801.
The History of Ripon. London, 1806.
Hobson, M. G., and H. E. Salter. *Oxford Council Acts, 1626–1665.* Oxfordshire Historical Society, vol. 95. Oxford, 1933.
Holmes, Richard. *The Book of Entries of the Pontefract Corporation.* Pontefract, 1882.
Homeshaw, Ernest James. *The Corporation of the Borough and Foreign of Walsall.* Walsall, 1960.
Howell, Roger. *Newcastle-on-Tyne and the Puritan Revolution: A Study of the Civil War in North England.* Oxford, 1967.
Hudson, William, and John Cottingham Tingey. *Records of the City of Norwich.* 2 vols. Norwich, 1906–10.
Hunter, Joseph. *South Yorkshire: The History and Topography of the Deanery of Doncaster.* 2 vols. London, 1828–31.
Hurwich, Judith, "'A Fanatick Town': The Political Influence of Dissenters in Coventry, 1660–1720." *Midland History,* 4 (1977): 15–48.
Hutton, William. *The History of Derby.* London, 1817.
James, William Roberts. *The Charters and Other Documents Relating to the King's Town and Parish of Maidstone.* London, 1825.
Jenkins, Alexander. *History and Description of the City of Exeter and its Environs.* Exeter, 1806.
Jones, W. A. B. *Hadleigh Through the Ages.* Ipswich, 1977.
Keast, John. *A History of East and West Looe.* Chichester, 1987.
The Story of Fowey. Trewolsta, Cornwall, 1987.
Kirby, Joan. "Restoration Leeds and the Aldermen of the Corporation, 1661–1700." *Northern History,* 22 (1986): 123–74.
Latham, R. C., ed. *Bristol Charters, 1509–1899.* Bristol Record Society, vol. 12. Bristol, 1947.
Leighton, S. "The Records of the Corporation of Oswestry." *Transactions of the Shropshire Archaeological Society,* 4 (1881): 1–52.
Lingard, J. *The Charters Granted by Different Sovereigns to the Burgesses of Preston.* Preston, 1821.
Mabbs, A. W. *Guild Stewards' Book of the Borough of Calne, 1561–1688.* Wiltshire Archaeological and Natural History Society, vol. 7. Devizes, 1951.
Macray, W. D. *Catalogue of and Index to Manuscripts . . . Selected from the Municipal Archives of the City of Hereford.* Hereford, 1894.
Maitland, Frederick William, and Mary Bateson. *The Charters of the Borough of Cambridge.* Cambridge, 1901.
Markham, Christopher, and John Charles Cox, eds. *The Records of the Borough of Northampton.* 2 vols. Northampton, 1898.

Marsh, A. E. W. *A History of the Borough and Town of Calne*. Calne, 1904.

Martin, G. H. *The Royal Charters of Grantham, 1463–1688*. Leicester, 1963.

Martin, K. S., ed. *Records of Maidstone*. Maidstone, 1926.

Mayo, Charles Herbert. *The Municipal Records of the Borough of Dorchester, Dorset*. Exeter, 1908.

The Municipal Records of the Borough of Shaftesbury. Sherborne, 1889.

Morant, Philip. *The History and Antiquities of Colchester*. Colchester, 1798.

Muir, Ramsey, and Edith M. Platt. *A History of Municipal Government in Liverpool*. Liverpool, 1906.

Mullett, Michael. "Conflict, Politics, and Elections in Lancaster, 1660–1688." *Northern History*, 19 (1983): 61–86.

"'Deprived of our Former Place': The Internal Politics of Bedford, 1660–1688." *Publications of the Bedfordshire Historical Record Society*, 59 (1980): 1–42.

"'To Dwell Together in Unity': The Search for Agreement in Preston Politics, 1660–1690." *Transactions of the Historic Society of Lancashire and Cheshire*, 125 (1974): 61–81.

"'Men of Knowne Loyalty': The Politics of the Lancashire Borough of Clitheroe, 1660–1680." *Northern History*, 21 (1985): 108–36.

"The Politics of Liverpool, 1660–1688." *Transactions of the Historic Society of Lancashire and Cheshire*, 124 (1973): 31–56.

Murrell, Patricia E. "Bury St. Edmunds and the Campaign to Pack Parliament, 1687–88." *Bulletin of the Institute for Historical Research*, 54 (1981): 188–206.

Noall, Cyril. *The Book of Penzance*. Buckingham, 1983.

Owen, H. and J. B. Blakeway. *History of Shrewsbury*. London, 1825.

Palmer, Charles Ferrers. *The History of the Town and Castle of Tamworth*. Tamworth, 1845.

Palmer, W. M. "The Reformation of the Corporation of Cambridge." *Proceedings of the Cambridge Antiquarian Society*, 17 (1912–13): 75–136.

Pape, T. *The Charters of the City of Lancaster*. Lancaster, 1952.

The Restoration Government and the Corporation of Newcastle-under-Lyme. Manchester, 1940.

Park, Godfrey Richard. *The History of the Ancient Borough of Hedon*. Hull, 1895.

Parker, John. *The Early History and Antiquities of Wycombe*. High Wycombe, 1878.

Parkes, Joseph. *The Governing Charter of the Borough of Warwick*. London, 1827.

Parkin, Charles. *The History and Antiquities of the City of Norwich*. Lynn, 1783.

Parsloe, C. G. "The Corporation of Bedford, 1647–1664." *TRHS*, 4th ser., 29 (1947): 151–66.

"The Growth of a Borough Constitution: Newark-on-Trent, 1549–1688." *TRHS*, 4th ser., 22 (1940): 171–98.

Parsloe, Guy. *The minute book of Bedford Corporation, 1647–64*. Bedfordshire Historical Record Society, vol. 26. Streatley, 1944–45.

Picton, James A. *City of Liverpool: Selections from the Municipal Archives and Records*. Liverpool, 1883.

Poulson, George. *Beverlac: Or the Antiquities and History of the Town of Beverley*. London, 2 vols. 1829.

Radford, G. H. "Charter of Tavistock." *Transactions of the Devon Association*, 46 (1914): 176–80.

Records of the Borough of Nottingham, 9 vols. (London, 1882–1956).

Riden, Philip, and John Blair, eds. *History of Chesterfield*. Records of the Borough of Chesterfield and Related Documents, 1204–1835, vol. 5. Chesterfield, 1980.

Riland Bedford, W. K. *History of Sutton Coldfield*. Birmingham, 1891.

Roots, George. *The Charters of the Town of Kingston-Upon-Thames*. London, 1797.

Round, J. H. "Colchester during the Commonwealth." *EHR*, 15 (1900): 641–64.

Rudge, Thomas. *The History and Antiquities of Gloucester*. Gloucester, 1811.

Sacret, J. H. "The Corporation Act Commissioners in Reading." *The Berks, Bucks and Oxon Archaeological Journal*, 30 (1926): 18–42.

St. Barbe, Charles. *Records of the Corporation of Lymington, in the County of Southampton*. London, 1849.

Scandal on the Corporation: Royalist and Puritans in Mid-17th Century Kingston, from the Kingston Borough Archives. Kingston, 1982.

A Schedule of the Records and Other Documents of the Corporation of Bedford. Bedford, 1883.

Scott, John. *Berwick-Upon-Tweed: The History of the Town and Guild*. London, 1888.

Sheahan, James Joseph. *History of the Town and Port of Kingston-upon-Hull*. Beverley, 1866.

Shilton, Dorothy O., and Richard Holworthy. *Wells City Charters*. Somerset Record Society, vol. 46. [London], 1932.

Short, Basil. *A Respectable Society: Bridport, 1593–1835*. Bradford-on-Avon, 1976.

Simpson, Robert. *A Collection of Fragments Illustrative of the History and Antiquities of Derby*. 2 vols. Derby, 1826.

Sinclair, David. *The History of Wigan*. 2 vols. London, 1882.

Spaul, J. E. H. *Andover Archives: The Bailiwick, 1599–1835*. Andover Local Archives Committee. 1971.

Speck, W. A. "Brackley: A Study in the Growth of Oligarchy." *Midland History*, 3 (1975): 30–41.

Stanewell, L. M. *Calendar of . . . the Archives of the Corporation [of Hull]*. Kingston upon Hull, 1951.

Stedman, A. R. *Marlborough and the Upper Kennet Country*. Marlborough, 1960.

Stevenson, W. H. *Calendar of the Records of the Corporation of Gloucester*. Gloucester, 1893.

Stevenson, W. H., ed. *Royal Charters Granted to the Burgesses of Nottingham*. London, 1890.

Stocks, Helen, ed. *Records of the Borough of Leicester, 1603–1688*. Cambridge, 1923.

Stokes, Ethel, and Lilian Redstone. "Calendar of the Muniments of the Borough of Sudbury." *Proceedings of the Suffolk Institute of Archaeology and Natural History*, 13 (1909): 259–310.

Stoyle, Mark. *From Deliverance to Destruction: Rebellion and Civil War in an English City*. Exeter, 1996.

Styles, Philip. "The Corporation of Bewdley under the Later Stuarts." In *Studies in Seventeenth-Century West Midlands History* (Kineton, 1978).

"The Corporation of Warwick, 1660–1835." *Transactions of the Birmingham Archaeological Society*, 59 (1935): 9–122.

Swinden, H. *The History and Antiquities of the Ancient Burgh of Great Yarmouth*. Norwich, 1772.

Sydenham, John. *The History of the Town and County of Poole.* London, 1839; reprint, Poole, 1986.

Thomas, R. *History and Description of the Town and Harbour of Falmouth.* Falmouth, 1827.

Tighe, Robert Richard, and James Edward Davis. *Annals of Windsor.* London, 1858.

Tindal, William. *The History and Antiquities of the Abbey and Borough of Evesham.* Evesham, 1794.

Tomlinson, John. *Doncaster from the Roman Occupation to the Present Time.* Doncaster, 1887.

Toulmin, Joshua. *The History of Taunton.* Taunton, 1822.

Toy, Spencer H. *The History of Helston.* Oxford, 1936.

Turnor, Lewis. *History of the Ancient Town and Borough of Hertford.* Hertford, 1830.

Underdown, David. *Fire from Heaven: Life in an English Town in the Seventeenth Century.* New Haven, 1992.

Wardell, James. *The Municipal History of the Borough of Leeds.* London, 1846.

Warner, Richard. *The History of Bath.* Bath, 1801.

Waylen, James. *A History, Military and Municipal, of the Town of Marlborough.* London, 1854.

Wilcockson, I. *Authentic Records of the Guild Merchant of Preston.* Preston, 1822.

Willis, Browne. *The History and Antiquities of the Town, Hundred and Deanery of Buckingham.* London, 1755.

Wodderspoon, J. *Memorials of the Ancient Town of Ipswich.* London, 1850.

Worth, R. N. *Calendar of the Municipal Records of Plymouth.* Plymouth, 1893.

Yeatman, John Pym. *Records of the Borough of Chesterfield.* Chesterfield, 1894.

GENERAL WORKS CONSULTED

Barry, Jonathan, ed. *The Tudor and Stuart Town: A Reader in English Urban History, 1530–1688.* London, 1990.

Borsay, Peter. *The English Urban Renaissance: Culture and Society in the Provincial Town, 1660–1770.* Oxford, 1989.

Borsay, Peter, ed. *The Eighteenth-Century Town: A Reader in English Urban History, 1688–1820.* London, 1990.

Braddick, Michael. "State Formation and Social Change in Early Modern England: A Problem Stated and Approaches Suggested." *Social History,* 16 (1991): 1–17.

Brown, Jethro. "The Personality of the Corporation and the State." *Law Quarterly Review,* 21 (1905): 365–79.

Browning, Andrew. "Parties and Party Organization in the Reign of Charles II." *TRHS,* 4th ser., 30 (1948): 21–36.

Carr, C. T. *The General Principles of the Law of Corporations.* Cambridge, 1905.

Challinor, P. J. "Restoration and Exclusion in the County of Cheshire." *Bulletin of the John Rylands University Library,* 64 (1982): 360–85.

Clark, Peter, ed. *The Transformation of English Provincial Towns, 1600–1800.* London, 1984.

Clark, Peter, and Paul Slack. *English Towns in Transition, 1500–1700.* Oxford, 1976.

Clark, Peter, and Paul Slack, eds. *Crisis and Order in English Towns, 1500–1700: Essays in Urban History.* Toronto, 1972.

Coleby, Andrew. *Central Government and the Localities: Hampshire, 1649–1689.* Cambridge, 1987.

Colley, Linda. *In Defiance of Oligarchy: The Tory Party, 1714–1760.* Cambridge, 1982.

Cromartie, Alan. *Sir Matthew Hale, 1609–1676: Law, Religion and Natural Philosophy.* Cambridge, 1995.

Davis, John P. *Corporations: A Study of the Origin and Development of Great Business Combinations and of their Relation to the Authority of the State.* 2 vols. New York, 1905; reprint, Buffalo, 1986.

DeKrey, Gary Stuart. "The First Restoration Crisis: Conscience and Coercion in London, 1667–73." *Albion,* 25 (1993): 565–80.

A *Fractured Society: The Politics of London in the First Age of Party, 1688–1715.* Oxford, 1985.

de Smith, S. A. *Judicial Review of Administrative Action,* 4th edn., by J. M. Evans. London, 1980.

Duckett, Sir George, ed. *Penal Laws and Test Act: Questions Touching their Repeal Propounded in 1687–88 by James II.* London, 1883.

Eaton, Amasa M. "The First Book in English on the Law of Incorporation." *Yale Law Journal,* 12 (1903): 259–86 and 364–79.

Fletcher, Anthony. "The Enforcement of the Conventicle Acts, 1663–1679." In W. S. Sheils, ed., *Persecution and Toleration.* Oxford, 1984.

Reform in the Provinces: The Government of Stuart England. New Haven, 1986.

Forster, G. C. F. "Government in Provincial England under the Later Stuarts." *TRHS,* 5th ser., 33 (1983): 29–48.

Garrett-Goodyear, Harold. "The Tudor Revival of Quo Warranto and Local Contributions to State Building." In Morris S. Arnold, *et al,* eds., *On the Laws and Customs of England: Essays in Honor of Samuel E. Thorne.* Chapel Hill, 1981.

George, R. H. "The Charters Granted to English Parliamentary Corporations in 1688." *EHR,* 55 (1940): 47–56.

Glassey, Lionel K. J. *Politics and the Appointment of Justices of the Peace, 1675–1720.* Oxford, 1979.

Greaves, Richard L. *Deliver us from Evil: The Radical Underground in Britain, 1660–63.* Oxford, 1983.

"Great Scott! The Restoration in Turmoil, or, Restoration Crises and the Emergence of Party." *Albion,* 25 (1993): 605–18.

Halliday, Paul D. "'A Clashing of Jurisdictions': Commissions of Association in Restoration Corporations." *Historical Journal* (forthcoming, 1998).

Harding, A. J. *Public Duties and Public Law.* Oxford, 1989.

Harris, Tim. *London Crowds in the Reign of Charles II: Propaganda and Politics from the Restoration until the Exclusion Crisis.* Cambridge, 1987.

"Party Turns? Or, Whigs and Tories Get Off Scott Free." *Albion,* 25 (1993): 581–90.

Politics under the Later Stuarts: Party Conflict in a Divided Society, 1660–1715. London, 1993.

Harris, Tim, Paul Seaward, and Mark Goldie, eds. *The Politics of Religion in Restoration England.* Oxford, 1990.

Havighurst, A. F. "The Judiciary and Politics in the Reign of Charles II." *Law Quarterly Review,* 66 (1950): 62–78 and 229–252.

Hazeltine, H. D., G. Lapsley, and P. H. Winfield, eds. *Maitland: Selected Essays.* Cambridge, 1936.

Henderson, B. L. K. "The Commonwealth Charters." *Transactions of the Royal Historical Society*, 3rd ser., 6 (1912): 129–62.
Henderson, Edith G. *Foundations of English Administrative Law: Certiorari and Mandamus in the Seventeenth Century*. Cambridge, Mass., 1963.
Henning, Basil Duke, ed. *The House of Commons, 1660–1690*. 3 vols. London, 1983.
High, James L. *A Treatise on Extraordinary Legal Remedies, Embracing Mandamus, Quo Warranto and Prohibition*, Chicago, 1884.
Holmes, Geoffrey. *British Politics in the Age of Anne*. Revised edn., London, 1987.
Politics, Religion, and Society in England, 1679–1742. London, 1986.
Holmes, Geoffrey, and W. A. Speck, eds. *The Divided Society: Parties and Politics in England, 1694–1716*. London, 1967.
Horwitz, Henry. *Parliament, Policy, and Politics in the Reign of William III*. Newark, 1977.
Hosford, David H. *Nottingham, Nobles, and the North: Aspects of the Revolution of 1688*. Studies in British History and Culture, vol. 4. Hamden, Conn., 1976.
Howell, Robert H. "An Historical Account of the Rise and Fall of Mandamus." *Victoria University of Wellington Law Review*, 15 (1985): 127–45.
Howell, Roger N. "The Structure of Urban Politics in the English Civil War." *Albion*, 11 (1979): 111–27.
Hutton, Ronald. *The Restoration: A Political and Religious History of England and Wales, 1658–1667*. Oxford, 1985.
Impey, Walter J. *A Treatise on the Law and Practice of the Writ of Mandamus*, London, 1826.
Jenks, Edward. "The Prerogative Writs in English Law." *Yale Law Journal*, 32 (1923): 523–34.
Jones, Clyve, ed. *Britain in the First Age of Party, 1680–1750: Essays Presented to Geoffrey Holmes*. London, 1987.
Party and Management in Parliament, 1660–1784. Leicester, 1984.
Jones, J. R. *Charles II: Royal Politician*. London, 1987.
The First Whigs: The Politics of the Exclusion Crisis, 1678–1683 (Oxford, 1961).
"James II's Whig Collaborators." *HJ*, 3 (1960): 65–73.
The Restored Monarchy, 1660–1688. Totowa, N. J., 1979.
The Revolution of 1688 in England. New York, 1972.
Kishlansky, Mark. "The Emergence of Adversary Politics in the Long Parliament." *Journal of Modern History*, 49 (1977): 617–40.
Parliamentary Selection: Social and Political Choice in Early Modern England. Cambridge, 1986.
Knights, Mark. *Politics and Opinion in Crisis, 1678–1681*. Cambridge, 1994.
Lacey, Douglas R. *Dissent and Parliamentary Politics in England, 1661–1689: A Study in the Perpetuation and Tempering of Parliamentarianism*. New Brunswick, 1969.
Landau, Norma. *Justices of the Peace, 1679–1760*. Berkeley, 1984.
Lee, Colin. "'Fanatic Magistrates': Religious and Political Conflict in Three Kent Boroughs, 1680–1684." *HJ*, 35 (1991): 43–61.
Leigh, L. H. *The Criminal Liability of Corporations in English Law*. London, 1969.
Lemmings, David. *Gentlemen and Barristers: The Inns of Court and the English Bar, 1680–1730*. Oxford, 1990.
Levin, Jennifer. *The Charter Controversy in the City of London, 1660–1688*. London, 1969.

Maitland, Frederick William. *Township and Borough*. Cambridge, 1897.
Matthews, Nancy. *William Sheppard, Cromwell's Law Reformer*. Cambridge, 1984.
Merewether, H. A., and A. J. Stephens. *The History of the Boroughs and Municipal Corporations of the United Kingdom, from the Earliest to the Present Time*. London, 1835.
Miller, John. "The Crown and the Borough Charters in the Reign of Charles II." *EHR*, 100 (1985): 53–84.
James II: A Study in Kingship. Revised edn. London, 1989.
Popery and Politics in England, 1660–1688. Cambridge, 1973.
"The Potential for 'Absolutism' in Later Stuart England." *History*, 69 (1984): 187–207.
Monod, Paul Kleber. *Jacobitism and the English People, 1688–1788*. Cambridge, 1989.
Nenner, Howard. *By Colour of Law: Legal Culture and Constitutional Politics in England, 1660–1689*. Chicago, 1977.
Norrey, P. J. "The Restoration Regime in Action: The Relationship between Central and Local Government in Dorset, Somerset, and Wiltshire, 1660–1678." *HJ*, 31 (1988): 789–812.
Patterson, Catherine. "Conflict Resolution and Patronage in Provincial Towns, 1590–1640," *JBS* (forthcoming, 1998).
"Leicester and Lord Huntingdon: Urban Patronage in Early Modern England." *Midland History*, 16 (1991): 45–62.
Plumb, J. H. *The Growth of Political Stability in England, 1675–1725*. London, 1967.
Pollock, Frederick. "Has the Common Law Received the Fiction Theory of Corporations?" *Law Quarterly Review*, 27 (1911): 219–35.
Richardson, R. C., ed. *Town and Countryside in the English Revolution*. Manchester, 1992.
Roberts, Clayton. *The Growth of Responsible Government in Stuart England*. Cambridge, 1966.
Roberts, S. K. *Recovery and Restoration in an English County: Devon Local Administration, 1646–1670*. Exeter, 1985.
Roy, Ian. "The English Republic, 1649–1660: The View from the Town Hall," in H. G. Koenigsberger and Elisabeth Müller-Luckner, *Republiken und Republikanismus im Europa der Frühen Neuzeit*. Munich, 1988.
Sacret, J. H. "The Restoration Government and Municipal Corporations." *EHR*, 45 (1930): 232–59.
Scott, Jonathan. *Algernon Sidney and the Restoration Crisis, 1677–1683*. Cambridge, 1991.
"Restoration Process. Or, if This Isn't a Party, We're Not Having a Good Time." *Albion* 25 (1993): 619–37.
Seaward, Paul. *The Cavalier Parliament and the Reconstruction of the Old Regime, 1661–67*. Cambridge, 1989.
Sedgwick, Romney, ed. *The House of Commons, 1715–1754*. 2 vols. New York, 1970.
Shortt, John. *Informations (Criminal and Quo Warranto), Mandamus and Prohibition*, London, 1887.
Speck, W. A. *Tory and Whig: The Struggle in the Constituencies, 1701–1715*. London, 1970.

Spurr, John. *The Restoration Church of England, 1646–1689*. New Haven, 1991.
Tapping, Thomas. *The Law and Practice of the High Prerogative Writ of Mandamus, as it Obtains both in England and in Ireland*, London, 1848.
Webb, Beatrice, and Sidney Webb. *English Local Government from the Revolution to the Municipal Corporations Act: The Manor and the Borough*. London, 1908; reprint, Hamden, Conn., 1963.
Weinbaum, Martin. *British Borough Charters, 1307–1660*. Cambridge, 1943.
The Incorporation of the Boroughs. Manchester, 1937.
Western, J. R. *Monarchy and Revolution: The English State in the 1680s*. London, 1985.
Willman, Robert. "The Origins of 'Whig' and 'Tory' in English Political Language." *HJ*, 17 (1974): 247–64.
Wilson, Kathleen. *The Sense of the People: Politics, Culture and Imperialism in England, 1715–1785*. Cambridge, 1995.

THESES AND DISSERTATIONS

Allen, David Frank. "The Crown and the Corporation of London in the Exclusion Crisis, 1678–1681." Ph.D., University of Cambridge, 1977.
Beaver, Dan. "Symbol and Boundary: Religion, Family, and Community in Northern Gloucestershire, 1590–1690." Ph.D., University of Chicago, 1991.
Challinor, P. J. "The Structure of Politics in Cheshire, 1660–1715." Ph.D., Wolverhampton Polytechnic, 1983.
Davis, James R. "Colchester, 1600–1662: Politics, Religion and Officeholding in an English Provincial Town." Ph.D., Brandeis University, 1980.
Dawson, Elizabeth June. "Finance and the Unreformed Borough: A Critical Appraisal of Corporate Finance, 1660 to 1835, with Special Reference to the Boroughs of Nottingham, York and Boston." Ph.D., University of Hull, 1978.
Halliday, Paul D. "Partisan Conflict and the Law in the English Borough Corporation, 1660–1727." Ph.D., University of Chicago, 1993.
Johnson, A. M. "Some Aspects of the Political, Constitutional, Social and Economic History of the City of Chester, 1550–1662." D.Phil., University of Oxford, 1971.
Marlowe, Nicholas. "Government and Politics in the West Country Incorporated Boroughs, 1642–1662." Ph.D., University of Cambridge, 1986.
Murrell, Patricia E. "Suffolk: The Political Behavior of the County and its Parliamentary Boroughs from the Exclusion Crisis to the Accession of the House of Hanover." Ph.D., University of Newcastle upon Tyne, 1982.
Norrey, P. J. "The Relationship between Central Government and Local Government in Dorset, Somerset and Wiltshire, 1660–1688." Ph.D., Bristol University, 1988.
Patterson, Catherine F. "Urban Patronage in Early Modern England: Corporate Boroughs, the Landed Elite, and the Crown, 1580–1640." Ph.D., University of Chicago, 1994.
Pickavance, Robert. "The English Boroughs and the King's Government: A Study of the Tory Reaction, 1681–85." D.Phil., University of Oxford, 1976.
Schilling, W. A. H. "The Central Government and the Municipal Corporations in England, 1642–1663." Ph.D., Vanderbilt University, 1970.
Sinner, Robert John. "Charles II and Local Government: The Quo Warranto Proceedings, 1681–1685." Ph.D., Rutgers University, 1976.

Triffitt, John M. "Politics and the Urban Community: Parliamentary Boroughs in the Southwest of England, 1710–1730." D.Phil., University of Oxford, 1985.

Williams, James Richard. "County and Municipal Government in Cornwall, Devon, Dorset and Somerset, 1649–1660." Ph.D., University of Bristol, 1981.

Index

Abingdon, 48, 49, 51n, 75, 78, 94, 95n, 96, 99, 100n, 143, 169, 246, 279n, 290n, 295, 316n, 354
absolutism, *see* state, development of
addresses to monarch, 78, 152, 202, 226, 229, 230n, 242–43, 247–48, 261
Albemarle, Christopher Monck, Duke of, 235
Aldeburgh, 97, 116, 267, 310n
Allen, William, 281, 282, 284n, 286
Andover, 17, 52, 123–24, 218, 220, 241n, 251n, 279–80, 284n, 290
Anne, Queen, 17, 312, 322, 326, 332, 339
Appleby, 251n
appointment, royal power of, *see* nomination, royal power of in charters
approbation, royal power of in charters, 66–67, 150, 153–54, 157–61, 166, 168, 171, 172, 173, 183–88, 191–92, 212, 214, 215, 220, 222, 226, 259, 275, 324, 326, 330
Arundel, 99, 164–65
associated justices, *see* commissions of association
Association Oath, 287, 289–90, 297, 301, 302
Atkyns, Sir Edward, 274, 276n
Atkyns, Sir Robert, 32, 41
attachments for contempt, *see* King's or Queen's Bench, attachments for contempt
attendance at corporation meetings, 42–43
attorney general, 130, 132, 138–39, 143, 149, 154, 158, 163, 164, 165, 166, 172, 173–76, 198, 200, 203, 206, 219, 230, 237, 266, 296, 325, 326, 327, 328, 329

Bagge's Case, 68–69
Banbury, 100, 125, 255n, 279, 308n, 327–29, 330, 335, 336n, 354

Barnstaple, 48, 49, 96, 102n, 166, 235, 249n, 252n, 253–54, 322n, 355
Barrington, Henry, 71, 74
Basingstoke, 248
Bath, John Grenville, Earl of, 227, 250, 256, 259
Bath, 61, 77, 82–83, 86, 102, 103n, 143, 167, 292, 316n, 322
Beaufort, Duke of, *see* Somerset, Henry
Bedder, Edward, 119–20
Bedford, 38n, 126, 128n, 261, 355
Bennett, Henry, 281, 282
Bennett, Peter, 286
Berkhamsted, 63, 165, 168
Bermuda Company, quo warranto against, 200
Bernardiston, Arthur, 71, 142n
Berwick, James Fitzjames, Duke of, 256
Berwick, 38n, 165, 198, 228, 234, 237–40, 241
Beverley, 39n, 97, 100, 127n, 158n, 217n, 355
Bewdley, 111, 114, 217n, 310, 312n, 316, 317, 326, 330, 355
bills, *see* Parliament, bills in
Bishop's Castle, 251n, 253n
Blackstone, Sir William, 26, 32n, 163, 199n, 347
Blagrave, Daniel, 71–72, 74, 142n
Bodmin, 175, 329n
body politic, idea and language of, *see* corporations, idea and language of
Booth, Henry, 333–35
Bossiney, 70, 137n, 279n, 294
Boston, 38n, 40, 78, 79n, 97, 101, 125, 242n, 252n, 268, 355
Brackley, 251n, 252n, 253n
Brafield, John, 106–08
Brandon, Charles Gerard, Lord, 154
Bridgnorth, 251n
Bridgwater, 217n, 317

Bridport, 115–16, 158n, 248n, 252n, 253n, 307
Bristol, 61, 77, 92, 94, 96, 98, 99, 100, 144, 159, 174, 175–76, 228n, 236n, 241n, 242n, 249n, 292, 312n, 322, 355
Brooke, Fulke Greville, Lord, 227
Buckingham, 38n, 73n, 241n, 251n, 310n
Bulstrode, Richard, 71–72, 74
Burnet, Gilbert, 13, 20
Bury St. Edmunds, 98, 109–11, 122, 125, 152, 294, 355
by-laws, *see* corporations, by-laws of

Calamy, Benjamin, 12
Calne, 228, 331
Cambridge, 38n, 52n, 78, 100, 116, 167, 243, 247, 258, 290n, 332, 356
Canterbury, 39n, 76, 79, 101, 103, 122n, 126, 128n, 135n, 141, 166, 176n, 218n, 242n, 318n, 321, 322, 356
certiorari, writ of, 137
Chancery, court of, 110, 199, 312
Chard, 99
Charles I, 59–60, 61, 63, 74, 155n
Charles II, 3, 18, 19, 29, 39, 57, 73, 75, 77, 88, 92, 118, 128, 133, 149, 157, 158, 164, 165, 170, 180, 183, 184, 185, 193, 204, 222, 234, 236, 237, 238–39, 240, 241, 245, 251, 260–62, 265, 271, 302, 311, 324, 344
  letters of to corporations, 58, 79–83, 99
  moderation of toward corporations, 81–85, 99, 117, 159, 161–62, 177–78, 195
  moderation of toward corporations ends, 124, 130–31, 136, 145, 192, 196, 203
"charter day" for elections, 36, 313, 334, 336
charter forfeiture, 83–84, 90, 115, 151–52, 162, 170, 180, 183, 198, 205–08, 251, 327–28, 335
  see also charter surrenders; dissolution or seizure of corporate franchises; quo warranto
charter surrenders, 83, 171–73, 180, 182, 183, 189–90, 192, 197–98, 202, 203, 208–34 *passim*, 240, 251, 253, 261, 265, 268, 270, 271, 273–75, 277, 278, 289, 290, 295, 302, 310, 311
  effects of, 171, 172–73, 182n, 217–20, 231
  enrollment of, 182, 214, 215, 216–18, 258, 265, 266, 278, 289, 290, 310
  legality of, 217, 273–75, 278
  policies concerning, 171–73, 187, 209, 216–20, 240, 251
  types of, 213, 215, 218–19

see also charter forfeiture; dissolution or seizure of corporate franchises; quo warranto
charters of incorporation, 7, 17, 19, 33–41, 148–252 *passim*, Appendix A
  1650s, 18, 63, 64–67, 73–76, 151
  1660s, 83–85, 87, 89–90, 98, 115–16, 149–61, 193
  1670s, 117, 177–87, 193
  1682–85, 19, 20, 145, 189–236 *passim*, 260, 265, 268, 271, 273, 302, 311–12, 344
  1685–88, 19, 129–30, 193, 237–62 *passim*, 268, 302, 345
  post-1688, 266–68, 277–79, 290, 300, 302, 310–13, 326–30
  contents and language of, 29–30, 32, 33–41, 45, 72, 77, 78, 79, 80, 122, 142–43, 150, 160–61, 167–68, 83–87, 182, 220–23, 225–26, 235–36, 252, 277–78, 313–14, 328; *see also* approbation, royal power of in charters; displacement, royal power of in charters; mortmain restrictions; nomination; non-intromittant clauses; *non obstante* clauses
  forfeiture of, *see* charter forfeiture
  historiography of, 161–62, 193–96
  local initiative in seeking charters, 150–51, 152, 154, 156, 167, 188, 192, 195, 212, 214, 220, 223
  numbers of over time, 152–53, 155–56, 177, 192, 312, 326–27, Appendix A
  purges by new charters, 19, 153, 158, 182, 192, 214, 215, 226, 232, 233–34, 251–60, 266–68, 279, 311, 326, 328–30
  royal policies concerning, 36, 39–40, 83–85, 89–90, 138, 152, 155, 156–58, 160–77 *passim*, 187–88, 195–201, 212–23, 235–36, 252, 255, 257–58, 260–61, 300, 312, 329–30; *see also* charter surrenders; James II, proclamation of October 17, 1688; quo warranto
  see also corporations, creation of
Chester, 37, 42–43, 44, 46n, 48n, 50, 51, 60, 62, 75, 94, 96, 97, 100, 125, 133, 139, 160, 170, 227, 242, 249n, 254, 260, 280–88, 302, 305, 309, 320n, 323, 346, 356
  1685 charter, 230–32, 233, 234, 280, 282, 283
Chesterfield, 38n, 52n, 95n, 96, 97, 125, 185, 356
Chichester, 218n, 248n, 315n, 321n
Chipping Sodbury, 185

Christchurch, 81, 328–29, 335
Cinque Ports, 127, 133
Civil War, xiii, 18, 30, 40, 59–61, 69, 108, 235
Clarendon, Edward Hyde, 1st Earl of, 9, 78–79, 80, 92, 159, 166n, 173
Clarendon, Henry Hyde, 2nd Earl of, ii, 249
Coke, Sir Edward, 31, 32, 34, 68, 73, 199n, 205n, 206, 207
Colchester, 50, 51, 64–65, 66, 70, 71, 74, 96, 97, 117, 159, 218n, 235, 236n, 251n, 252n, 278, 315n, 321n, 332
Colley, Linda, 21, 23, 322, 338n, 339
commissions of association, 123, 159, 162, 169–70, 171, 173, 177, 182, 185, 188, 190–91, 194, 195, 196–97, 221, 236, 237, 241n, 261
    see also corporations, judicial powers of; magistracy, royal concern for
Common Pleas, court of, 293
concession theory of corporations, 32n, 211
    see also corporations, creation of; corporations, law of; franchises, idea and law of
Corfe, 185
corporate criminality, 31, 204–06
corporate personality, 29–30, 31–32, 34, 42, 206–07, 208, 209, 211
Corporation Act, *see* statutes, Corporation Act
Corporation Act commissioners, 19, 107, 110n, 115, 132, 141, 149, 158, 164, 181, 183, 255
    appointment of, 85–86, 90, 92–94
    implementation of Act, 1662–63, 95–101
    powers of, 90–92, 102, 103–04
    see also statutes, Corporation Act
corporations
    by-laws of, 47–54, 332; specific by-laws concerning: elections and voting, 48, 50–51, 52–53, 285–87, fines, 51, meetings, 3–4, 47–51, records, 51–52
    creation of, xii, xiv, 29–30, 32–34, 66, 205, 211, 221; *see also* charters of incorporation; concession theory of corporations; franchises, idea and law of
    dissolution of, *see* dissolution or seizure of corporate franchises
    elections in, *see* elections in corporations
    as fictional persons, *see* corporate criminality; corporate personality
    functions and operation of, 7, 29–30, 33–46 *passim*, 306, 340
    idea and language of, xii–xiv, 3–4, 28, 29–30, 30–33, 54–55, 57–58, 205–06, 208, 209–10, 349; *see also* corporate

criminality; corporate personality; paradox of partisan politics; public and private, ideas concerning
    independence of, 28, 54, 84–85, 87–88, 208
    judicial powers of, 37–39, 46, 87–88, 123–24, 150, 154–55, 159, 161, 168–69, 182, 185–86, 221–22; *see also* commissions of association; royal concern for; non-intromittant clauses
    law of, 31–33, 42, 205, 209–10, 276, 302; *see also* charters of incorporation; franchises, idea and law of; King's or Queen's Bench; mandamus; quo warranto
    members and officers of, 35–37, 42–46; *see also* approbation, royal power of in charters; displacement, royal power of in charters; nomination, royal power of in charters
    offices in as property, 42, 68–69, 102, 140–42, 294; *see also* corporations, law of; public and private, ideas concerning
    property of, 44–45, 218–19, 231; *see also* feoffments and trusts; mortmain restrictions
    records of, 35n, 37, 50–52, 125–26, 180n, 326, 340; *see also* mandamus, to surrender records or regalia
    resignations from 43n, 44n, 63, 75–76, 98, 242n, 246, 309
Coventry, Henry, 184–85, 187
Coventry, 46n, 100, 112n, 114, 158n, 173, 227, 234, 236n, 259, 309, 356
criminality, corporate, *see* corporate criminality
"crisis," idea of in historiography, 22–24
    see also dynamic society, idea of; stability, political
Cromwell, Oliver, 62, 64–65, 66, 73, 151, 343
Cromwell, Richard, 73
Crouch, Thomas, 132–35
Crown Office, *see* King's or Queen's Bench, Crown Office
crown relations with corporations, xii, xiv, 28, 40, 44, 45–46, 54–55, 78–79, 89–90, 196, 323, 329–30
    see also charters of incorporation, royal policies concerning; corporations, creation of; franchises, idea and law of; magistracy, royal concern for; Privy Council; quo warranto

Danby, Thomas Osborne, Earl of, 9, 224

Dartmouth, George Legge, Lord, 228
Dartmouth, 279n, 300
Daventry, 186n
declaration against the Covenant, *see* Solemn
    League and Covenant, declaration
    against
Declarations of Indulgence
    1672, 19, 118, 129
    1687, 242
    1688, 247, 248, 261
Defoe, Daniel, 340
Denbigh, 152n
Derby, Charles Stanley, Earl of, 82, 98–99,
    154
Derby, 217–18, 220, 241n, 251n, 279n
Devizes, 99, 116, 167, 258, 314–15, 317,
    319, 329, 335, 336n, 356
disabling clause, *see* Sacheverell clause
displacement, royal power of in charters, 19,
    63, 133, 153, 184, 191–92, 220,
    222–23, 236, 241–42, 345
    numbers displaced, 1687–88, 248
    resistance to royal orders, 246–50,
    253–54, 255, 260–62
    use of, 238, 241–42, 243–50, 255–56,
    261, 324–25; *see also* regulators
dissolution or seizure of corporate franchises,
    162–64, 199–200, 207–11, 251, 254,
    274, 298, 317, 327–29, 335–36
    see also charter forfeiture; charter
    surrenders; quo warranto
Dolben, William, 138, 274n
Doncaster, 152, 248, 251n, 333
Dorchester, 78, 114, 164, 251n
Dorney, John, 117, 178, 181
Dover, 75, 118, 127, 130
Droitwich, 255n
Dunwich, 128, 228, 246, 251n, 265–68, 278,
    291, 300, 302
Durham, 96
dynamic society, idea of, xv, 24, 27–28, 268,
    303, 306, 339–41, 349
    see also "crisis," idea of in historiography;
    law, idea and role of; stability, political

elections in corporations, 35–37, 43, 48, 50,
    52–53, 60, 61, 75, 80, 114, 186,
    258–59, 280–88, 323, 325
    disputed and failed elections, 48, 53,
    82–83, 106–07, 115–16, 118–24,
    132–34, 159–60, 179–80, 212–13, 224,
    226, 230, 279–80, 294–95, 304–05,
    313–16, 327–29, 333–36
Elizabeth I, 3, 39
Elliot, Henry, 119–20, 121
Engagement, the, 62

Evesham, 47, 48, 49, 157n, 248n
Exchequer, court of, 107, 201
Exclusion Crisis, 19, 22n, 43, 108, 124, 185
Exeter, 59n, 63, 72, 241, 248n, 252, 256,
    259, 292n, 357
Eye, 118–19, 128, 136n, 142, 290
Eyre, Sir Giles, 274, 276n

faction, idea and language of, *see* party, idea
    and language of
Falmouth, 153
feoffments and trusts, 18, 109–11, 121, 190,
    219, 254n
    see also corporations, property of
Finch, Sir Heneage (later Lord Nottingham),
    87–89, 138, 143, 171, 174–77, 180,
    182n, 187, 217n
Finch, Heneage the younger, 199, 205–07,
    209n, 213n, 251–52
Fowey, 250
Fowler, Edward, 13, 16
franchises, idea and law of, 27, 30, 33,
    162–63, 169, 205, 207, 211, 274, 275,
    316
    see also charters of incorporation;
    concession theory of corporations;
    corporations, creation of; quo warranto
Friend, John, 107–08

George I, 312n, 322, 327, 330, 336, 342
Glastonbury, 312n
Glorious Revolution, *see* Revolution of 1688
Gloucester, 12, 16, 23n, 39n, 47, 50, 51, 98,
    117, 125, 158n, 165n, 178–82, 186,
    187, 188, 197–98, 214, 245, 310, 316,
    357
Glynn, Sir John, 81
Godmanchester, 218n, 251n
Goldie, Mark, 10, 17
Grampound, 241
Grantham, 14, 35, 39n, 45, 81, 166, 251n,
    252n
Gravesend, 240n, 241, 251n, 252, 253n
Greaves, William, 226, 278
Gregory, Sir William, 274
Grimsby, 251n, 252n, 253n
Grosvenor, Sir Thomas, 232–33, 235, 280,
    281n, 282, 285, 287, 288, 302
Guildhall, 142, 240n
Guilford, Sir Francis North, Lord, 51, 119,
    138, 162, 169, 174, 177, 187, 217, 218,
    221–22, 228, 235

Hadleigh, 165n
Hale, Sir Matthew, 30, 31, 32–33, 141,
    162–63, 205n, 209, 296, 297

Harris, Tim, 10, 11, 345
Harwich, 77, 235, 242n, 251n
Haverfordwest, 14
Havering, 158n
Hedon, 158n
Helston, 218n, 321n, 330
Hemel Hempstead, 165n
Henley, 42–43, 44, 45n, 47, 51, 100, 357
Herbert, Lord, *see* Somerset, Henry
Hereford, 70n, 77, 215–16, 218, 251n
Hertford, 39n, 60, 185, 251n, 253n, 257, 258, 297–99, 316, 317
Hethersett, Wormley, 212–13, 214, 289, 302
High Wycombe, 65, 66, 75, 98, 119–20, 121
Hoar, Daniel, 128–30, 136n, 253, 254n
Hobbes, Thomas, 28
Holmes, Geoffrey, 20, 322
Holt, Sir John, 42n, 138n, 209n, 237, 274–75, 276n, 278, 284n, 291n, 293n, 296–97, 298
Howell, John, 138
Hull, *see* Kingston upon Hull
Hume, David, 8, 9, 12
Hunt, Thomas, 210–11, 225n
Huntingdon, Theophilus Hastings, Earl of, 189–91, 193, 217n, 227, 232, 234, 235, 242, 247n
Huntingdon, 126
Hyde, Sir Robert, 61, 77, 114, 119
Hythe, 134

informations, 296–99, 300
  see also quo warranto
instability, *see* stability, political
Interregnum, 18, 40, 62–67, 69–73, 83–84, 291, 322, 344
Ipswich, 159, 168, 248n, 251n, 252n, 259, 290n, 318
Irish corporations, 162, 170–73, 177, 186, 187, 197, 200, 236

James II, xii, 19–20, 23, 130, 139, 193, 234, 236, 237–62 *passim*, 265, 273, 277, 278, 296, 298, 302, 311, 325, 345
  as Duke of York, 19, 88, 123, 124, 189, 229
  proclamation of October 17, 1688, 239, 257–59, 260, 265, 266, 268, 277, 279, 282, 290, 291, 300, 310, 325
Jeffreys, Sir George, 135n, 138, 139, 213n, 219, 224, 226, 228, 230, 232, 237, 244, 283
Jenkins, Sir Leoline, 114, 126, 127, 136, 212–13, 214n, 225n, 227, 229
Jones, J. R., 9, 239, 245, 249, 260–61
Jones, Sir William, 138, 143n

judges of the royal courts, 274–75, 295–96
  see also King's or Queen's Bench, justices of
justices of the peace, corporate, *see* corporations, judicial powers of

King's or Queen's Bench (also Upper Bench), court of, xi–xv, 21, 24–28, 30, 54–55, 56–57, 67–73, 76–78, 101–03, 105, 107, 176, 186, 201–10, 212–14, 224, 228, 232, 251, 268, 276, 278, 289, 291–302, 302–03, 307, 308, 309–10, 313–22, 330, 346–48
  see also law, idea and role of; mandamus; quo warranto
  affidavits, xiv, 18, 313n, 330
  attachments for contempt, 68, 101n, 137, 174, 213, 214, 292, 293n, 305, 307n, 318, 321
  Crown Office, 163, 165, 297, 298, 301
  justices of, 25, 53, 68–69, 72–73, 137–39, 141–43, 176, 251, 274–75, 320–21
  process, speed of, 68, 73, 135–36, 144–45, 292–94, 300, 301, 317–22
  records of, xiv, 69–70, 164, 316, 330
  supplants Privy Council as arbiter of corporation disputes, 24, 108–09, 131–43, 143–44, 277, 291
Kingston upon Hull, 29–30, 36, 39n, 62, 78, 99, 128–30, 136n, 152, 153, 157, 228, 251n, 252n, 253, 254
Kingston upon Thames, 44n, 51, 56–59, 67, 70, 78n, 84, 94, 96, 98, 142n, 219, 235, 243, 248, 258, 259, 357
Kirkby Kendal, 218n, 251n
Kishlansky, Mark, 6, 11, 12n
Knights, Mark, 10, 11

Lancaster, 38n, 167, 246, 321n
language of party, *see* party, idea and language of
Launceston, 218n
law, idea and role of, xiii, xiv–xv, 24–28, 42, 53, 105, 136–43, 291, 302–03, 306, 313, 323, 330, 336–39, 346–48
  and political stability, xiii, xv, 25–28, 30, 54–55, 73, 105, 136, 139–40, 143–45, 268, 276, 294, 303, 306, 315–16, 321, 335, 340–41, 342–43, 347–48
  see also statute, role of
Lechmere, Sir Nicholas, 274n, 326
Leeds, 32, 39n, 44n, 98, 153, 157, 227n, 314n, 324
Leicester, 35, 42–43, 44n, 45, 46n, 50, 52n, 78, 97, 101, 125, 126, 167, 242, 245, 247–48, 249n, 252n, 255, 258, 309, 332n, 357

Leicester (*cont.*)
  charter, 1665, 149–51, 158n
  charter, 1684, 189–91, 217n, 232, 234
Leominster, 77, 229, 234, 312n
L'Estrange, Roger, 23, 211n
Leving, Sir Richard, 280, 281n, 282, 283n
Levinz, Sir Creswell, 126, 138n
Lichfield, 39n, 240n, 259n, 324
Lincoln, 77, 80n, 251n, 307n
Lindsey, Montague Bertie, Earl of, 78
Liverpool, 33n, 38n, 48, 94, 95n, 96, 97,
  167, 357
London, 64, 77, 86, 92, 130, 164, 256, 270,
  271, 274, 291n, 296, 301
  quo warranto against, 26–27, 163,
  200–01, 203–12, 214, 216, 223, 225,
  274, 316–17
Looe, West, 329n
Lostwithiel, 250, 313–14
Lovelace, John Lovelace, Lord, 99, 100
Lowther, Sir William, 325–26, 330
Ludlow, 40, 127, 128n, 159, 198, 217, 217n,
  277–78
Luttrell, Narcissus, 245, 298n
Lyme Regis, 97, 112
Lymington, 52–53, 98, 125, 251n

Macclesfield, 20, 46n, 125, 158n, 248, 251n,
  333–35, 336, 340
magistracy, royal concern for, 39, 123–24,
  155, 159, 168–69, 185–88, 194,
  221–22, 236
  see also commissions of association;
  corporations, judicial powers of; non-
  intromittant clauses
Maidenhead, 94, 155, 357
Maidstone, 18, 39n, 60, 72, 76, 79, 80, 96,
  115, 160, 166, 220, 222, 241n, 358
Mainwaring, George, 280, 281
Mainwaring, Sir John, 283, 286
Maldon, 97, 115n, 176n, 295n, 358
Malmesbury, 290, 337n
Manchester, Edward Montagu, Earl of,
  57–58, 107
mandamus, writ of, xv, 14n, 26, 27, 53,
  56–57, 67–73, 105, 177, 202, 256n,
  276, 280n, 289, 301, 306, 317–19, 323,
  330, 347
  college fellows' use of, 70, 140
  definition of, 67–68
  development and judicial doctrine of,
  68–73, 139–43, 144–45, 292–95,
  315–16, 319–22, 335–36, 347
  to hold elections, 268, 279, 294, 303,
  313–16, 335, 336
  and partisan politics, 20, 56–57, 71–73,

77, 105, 139–40, 145, 212–13, 224,
  279–80, 284, 289, 291–95, 305, 307,
  313–16, 334–35
  peremptory writ, 68, 71, 133, 137, 213,
  292, 293, 295, 314, 318, 319, 320
  returns to, 68, 71–72, 102–03, 142–43,
  213, 292, 295, 307, 318, 319, 320
  to surrender records or regalia, 52n, 141,
  267n, 268, 279, 294, 303, 314, 315, 326
  to swear newly elected officers, 70, 141,
  294, 315, 316
  types of writs, 67–68, 137, 318–19, 320
  use of, 1650s, 56–57, 67, 69–73, 76–77
  use of, 1662–63, 101–03
  use of, 1660s to 1680s, 76–77, 107,
  114–15, 119, 133–43, 176, 212–13, 224
  use of, after 1688, 267, 268, 279–80, 284,
  289, 291–95, 300–02, 305, 307,
  309–10, 313–16, 317–19, 326, 334,
  335–36
  see also King's or Queen's Bench; law, idea
  and role of; quo warranto
Marlborough, 53, 66, 116, 127, 251n, 252n,
  253n, 315n, 321n, 358
Matthew, St., Gospel of, xi, 13
Maynard, Sir John, 71–72, 81
mediation and mediators in settling
  corporation disputes, 5, 56–58, 59, 69,
  80–82, 143–44, 335
  see also Charles II, moderation of toward
  corporations
Mendham, John, 136–37, 212–14, 223, 250,
  289, 302
Middleton, Charles Middleton, Lord, 256
Miller, John, 87n, 88, 113n, 124n, 194–95
Monmouth, James Scott, Duke of, 16n, 230
Monmouth, 70n, 251n
Mordaunt, John Mordaunt, Viscount, 57–58,
  100, 169
Morpeth, 251n, 253n
mortmain restrictions, 39–40, 109n, 160,
  235
  see also corporations, property of
Much Wenlock, 175, 251n
Mulgrave, John Sheffield, Earl of, 273

Newark, 15n, 81, 157n, 160, 186, 187, 218n
Newbury, 99, 165, 169, 175, 248n
Newcastle, John Holles, Duke of, 225, 226,
  237
Newcastle, William Cavendish, Marquess of,
  54, 84–85, 87n, 156
Newcastle under Lyme, 38n, 39n, 93, 94,
  101, 158n, 166, 219, 245, 358
Newcastle upon Tyne, 13, 60, 75, 80, 99,
  126, 252n

Newport, Isle of Wight, 38n, 153, 279n, 300
Newtown, Isle of Wight, 132, 136n
Nicholas, Edward, 82, 98–99
nomination, royal power of in charters, 153, 155, 156–58, 166, 183, 252, 275, 325
non-intromittant clauses, 38–39, 150, 161, 186
non obstante clauses, 252, 270n
Norfolk, Henry Howard, Duke of, 257
North, Sir Francis, *see* Guilford, Lord
North, Roger, 12n, 16–17, 174, 213n
Northampton, 46n, 106–08, 109, 122, 125, 131, 135, 136, 139, 143, 176n, 183, 233, 242n, 258
Northey, Edward, 319
Norwich, 14, 61, 62n, 63n, 64, 65, 75, 76, 98, 115n, 158n, 159, 222–23, 223–24, 252n, 254, 295n, 304–06, 306–07, 314n, 316n, 320n, 323, 340, 358
Nottingham, 34, 78, 92, 102n, 244, 248n, 274, 293n, 300, 302, 309, 317–18
    1682 charter, 217n, 220, 224–27, 234, 241n, 278

oaths, *see* tests for office holding
occasional conformity, 111–12, 114, 120, 128–30, 269, 306, 307–10, 346
    see also partisan politics, and religious identity; statutes, Occasional Conformity Act
Okehampton, 251n
Orford, 267, 293, 302
Ormonde, James Butler, Duke of, 83, 170
Oswestry, 186
Oxford, 38n, 59, 100, 116, 165, 228n, 233, 234, 254, 290n, 293

Palmer, Sir Geoffrey, 57–58, 79n, 88–89, 153, 154, 174, 183, 200
paradox of partisan politics, xii, xiii, 6, 28, 64, 65, 145, 233–34, 289, 341
    definition of, xii, 15
    and impulse to purge foes, xii, 6, 14–15, 18, 26, 30, 58, 64–65, 87, 103–04, 104–05, 108, 154, 227, 234, 267–68, 343–44
    and rhetoric of "party," 11–18, 30, 86–87; *see also* partisan politics; party, idea and language of
Parliament, 6–10, 20, 22, 27, 60–63, 74–75, 78, 84, 85–90, 112–13, 192, 193–94, 196, 198, 203, 226, 239, 241, 243, 261, 269–71, 273–76, 291–302, 308, 310–11, 321, 331, 336–38, 343
    bills in: comprehension (1689), 269; corporations bills (1662 and 1663),

112–13; for more speedy determining the rights to offices in corporations (1700), 300, 301, 319; for quieting corporations (1714), 321–22; to repeal the Corporation Act, 130, 197, 269, 276; to restore corporations (1689–90), 270–75, 276n, 291, 295, 311
    elections to, 19, 20–21, 106, 118–21, 122–24, 132, 201–02, 243, 255, 265, 267, 277, 279–81, 285, 288, 291, 295, 299, 305, 311, 312, 316, 323, 327, 330–33, 339, 345, 346
    see also statute, role of; statutes
Parmenter, Andrew, 304, 305, 340
partisan politics, xi–xiv, 57, 58, 92, 104–05, 136, 137, 139, 192, 223, 233–34, 261–62, 291, 301, 305–06, 322–25, 331, 336–37, 339–40, 342–43, 346–49, and *passim*
    and by-laws, 52–54
    and charters, 17, 153–54, 177–87, 223–34, 234–36, 266–68, 279, 300, 310–13
    contrasted with "party," xi–xii, 5–11
    definition of, xi–xii, 5–6, 57
    and mandamus, 26, 56–57, 71–73, 77, 105, 119, 139–40, 145, 212–13, 224, 279–80, 284, 289, 291–95, 305, 307, 313–16, 334–35
    in non-parliamentary corporations, 20, 121, 325, 333–35; *see also* individual towns by name
    organization and leadership in corporations, xiii, 5–6, 64, 71, 82–83, 108, 110–11, 115–16, 118, 119–24, 132, 132–35, 154, 201–03, 212–13, 224–26, 232, 265–67, 279–87, 288, 304–06, 313–14, 331–33, 333–35
    origins of in corporations, xi–xiii, 6–8, 10–11, 30, 58, 59–62, 64, 67, 104, 108, 122–23, 342–43
    and religious identity, xiii–xiv, 17–18, 18–19, 61, 64, 92, 103–04, 110–14, 117–18, 119–23, 272–73, 306–10, 322, 323–24, 336–39, 346; *see also* occasional conformity; Solemn League and Covenant, declaration against; statutes, Occasional Conformity Act
    and rhetoric, role of, 11–18, 67
    see also charters of incorporation, purges by new charters; paradox of partisan politics; party
party
    historiography of, xi, 8–11, 11–12, 339
    idea and language of, 3–4, 8, 10, 11–18, 24, 57, 60, 83, 84–85, 107, 120, 121,

party (*cont.*)
    126, 132, 134–35, 178, 203, 224–27,
    229–30, 232–33, 272–73, 277, 304, 322,
    324, 325, 343, 344; in sermons, 12–16
    labels, types of, 15–18
    see also, paradox of partisan politics;
    partisan politics
Patterson, Catherine, 5, 12n
Pemberton, Sir Francis, 126
Penryn, 330
Penzance, 314, 315, 329, 333, 335
peremptory mandamus, *see* mandamus,
    peremptory writ
personality, corporate, *see* corporate
    personality
Pickavance, Robert, 194–95, 212, 214n, 234
Pickmer, Francis, 106–08
Plumb, J. H., 21–22, 24, 322, 339
    see also stability, political
Plymouth, Thomas Windsor, Earl of, 202,
    228
Plymouth, 68, 72, 96, 278, 279n, 302, 315n,
    358
Plympton, 183, 218n, 302
Pollexfen, Sir Henry, 138n, 139, 198, 205,
    207–08, 210, 223, 226, 237, 258, 274,
    276n
Pontefract, 50, 94, 97, 186, 318, 321n,
    325–26, 330
Poole, 38n, 101, 252n
"Popish Plot," 9, 124, 192, 204
Portland, Jerome Weston, Earl of, 88–89
Portsmouth, 220, 251n, 308, 309, 310
Powys, Sir Thomas, 252, 284
Preston, 3–4, 49, 50, 79, 98, 112n, 227n,
    246
    charter, 1662, 4, 38–39, 153–54, 158n
Privy Council, 80–83, 89, 92, 99, 107–08,
    115–17, 118–21, 123, 125–31, 164,
    166, 172, 177, 180, 183–84, 186, 213,
    230, 244, 253, 254, 255, 277–78, 284,
    328, 335–36
    supplanted by King's Bench as arbiter of
    corporation disputes, 24, 108–09,
    131–43, 143–44, 277, 291
Prynne, William, 61, 77, 82–83, 102–03, 105
    Summary Reasons, 12, 86–87, 102, 272n,
    343
public and private, ideas concerning, 41–42,
    45, 46, 68–69, 102, 137, 140–41, 221,
    294, 347
    see also corporate personality;
    corporations, offices in as property
purgation, idea and language of, *see* paradox
    of partisan politics, and impulse to purge
    foes

Queenborough, 251n, 253n
Queen's Bench, *see* King's Bench
quo warranto, information in the nature of,
    xv, 20, 53, 86, 126–27, 149, 160, 188,
    191, 269, 270, 271, 274, 275, 276, 301,
    306, 309, 310, 312, 319, 347
    to compel charter surrender, 187, 189–90,
    192–93, 197–98, 212, 215, 216, 224,
    227–32, 233, 234, 237, 251, 252, 253,
    265
    definition and development of, 26–27,
    162–64, 175–77, 192–93, 195,
    198–210, 295–99, 316–17, 320–22
    resistance to, 228–32, 237, 251, 265; *see
    also* London, quo warranto against;
    Worcester, quo warranto against
    use of, 1660s, 164–69, 174, 183
    use of, 1670s, 170, 175–76
    use of, 1681–85, 196–236 *passim*, 237
    use of, 1687–88, 237, 251–54, 257
    use of after 1688, 289, 296, 297–99,
    314–17, 327, 329, 330, 331, 334, 337
    see also charter forfeiture; charter
    surrenders; dissolution or seizure of
    corporate franchises; franchises, idea
    and law of

Radnor, 293n, 294
Reading, 13, 52n, 65, 71–72, 73, 74, 99,
    100, 101, 111n, 137n, 139, 140n, 160,
    169, 248n, 359
regulators, 1687–88, 244–50, 253, 256, 269,
    270, 271, 273
    see also displacement, royal power of in
    charters; the three questions
religion, *see* partisan politics, and religious
    identity
restitution, writ of, *see* mandamus
Restoration, 18, 43, 56, 57, 73–85, 309
Revolution of 1688, 19–20, 23, 259–62, 290,
    296, 302, 311, 345
rhetoric of "party," *see* party, idea and
    language of
Richmond, Charles Stuart, Duke of, 78
Richmond, 102n, 139
Ripon, 38n, 142, 251n
Rochester, 47, 48, 121, 177–78, 188, 198,
    199
Rokeby, Thomas, 274n
Romsey, 116n
royal government, *see* charters of
    incorporation, royal policies concerning;
    crown relations with corporations; Privy
    Council
Rye, 17, 132–35, 139, 143, 145, 164–65,
    229

Sacheverell, Dr. Henry, 308, 322, 324
Sacheverell, William, 224, 226, 244, 269,
    271, 272, 274, 275
Sacheverell clause, 270–72, 275
sacramental test, 111–12, 113, 122–23,
    128–30, 252, 269, 270, 278n, 290, 295,
    306–10, 337–38
    see also occasional conformity; statutes,
    Corporation Act, Occasional
    Conformity Act, Test Act
Sacret, J. H., 88, 156n, 193–95
Saffron Walden, 38n, 235n, 248n
St. Albans, 48, 49n, 51, 60, 158n, 332
Salisbury, 40, 60, 66, 74, 77, 78, 80, 251,
    312n, 316n, 322
Saltash, 136n, 186
Sandwich, 126
Saunders, Sir Edmund, 138n, 206, 208
Sawyer, Sir Robert, 205–07, 209n, 210,
    213n, 215, 217n, 229, 252
Scarborough, 219n
scire facias, 198, 199, 200, 312
Scott, Jonathan, 9–10
Scroggs, Sir William, 138n, 139
seizure, corporate, see dissolution or seizure
    of corporate franchises
Shaftesbury, Anthony Ashley Cooper, Earl of,
    9, 22, 23, 186, 189, 271
Shakerley, Sir Geoffrey, 230n, 231n, 232
Shakerley, Peter, 287, 288
Sheppard, William, 66, 205n
    Of Corporations, 29, 32, 34n, 42, 66
Shrewsbury, 94, 165, 322, 359
Sinner, Robert, 193–95
Solemn League and Covenant, declaration
    against, 90–92, 95–97, 100, 103–04,
    252, 269, 275, 307, 325, 337
    observance and neglect of, 111–14,
    117–18, 125–27, 129–30, 136, 178,
    198, 202, 213, 215, 246–47, 252–53,
    258, 290, 307, 337; see also occasional
    conformity; statutes, Corporation Act
solicitor general, 138–39, 158, 165, 173–74,
    266, 329
Somerset, Henry, Lord Herbert, Marquess of
    Worcester, and Duke of Beaufort, 98–99,
    180–81, 229
South Molton, 251n
Southampton, Thomas Wriothesley, Earl of,
    88–89
Southampton, 92, 94, 165, 168, 251, 251n,
    252n, 253n
Speck, W. A., 21, 331
stability, political, xi, xiii, xv, 4, 21–28, 30,
    47, 54–55, 73, 136, 268, 294, 303, 306,
    315, 322, 339–41, 342, 346, 347–49

see also dynamic society, idea of; law, idea
    and role of; statute, role of
Stafford, 15, 139, 165, 250
Stamford, 34n, 158n, 251n
state, development of, xi, xii, 25, 40, 347–38
statute, role of, 268, 276, 291–301, 306,
    312–13, 319–22, 335, 336–39, 340–41,
    343, 346
statutes
    Association, Act appointing the (7 and 8
        William III c. 27), 289–90; see also
        statutes, Disputes, Act to Prevent
    Conventicle Acts, 111n, 117–18, 122
    Corporation Act (13 Charles II st. II c. 1),
        17, 18, 83n, 120, 131, 135, 136–37,
        140, 145, 150, 151, 152, 155, 193, 197,
        198, 215, 291, 295, 307, 308, 309, 310,
        323, 337, 338, 343, 344, and Appendix
        B; contents of, 90–92; enquiry into
        enforcement (1668) 116–17, (1680)
        124–31, 132, 196, 253; failure of,
        109–17, 120, 123, 124–31, 132–33,
        178; impact of, 1662–63, 95–101,
        103–04, 106, 109, 177; implementation
        of, 1662–63, 92-104; legislative history,
        85–90; and partisan politics, 92,
        103–04, 113, 117, 130, 178; renewal
        efforts, 1662–63, 112–13; repeal efforts,
        130, 197, 269, 276; see also
        Corporation Act commissioners;
        Parliament, bills in
    Disputes (for failure to sign the
        Association), Act to Prevent (11 and 12
        William III c. 17), 301
    Engagement (1650), Act for Subscribing
        the, 62
    Indemnity Acts (1726 and following), 338
    Indemnity and Free Pardon (1659), Act of,
        74, 76, 83
    Indemnity and Oblivion (12 Charles II c.
        11), 83, 151
    informations, Act to prevent malicious (4
        and 5 William and Mary c. 18), 297,
        298, 300, 301
    judicial proceedings, Act for confirming
        (12 Charles II c. 12), 83
    London Restoration Act (2 William and
        Mary c. 8), 27, 275–76, 291n, 295, 301,
        316, 317
    mandamus and quo warranto, Act for
        rendering proceedings upon . . . more
        effectual (9 Anne c. 20), 319–21, 323,
        328, 336, 346
    mayors, Act for preventing inconveniences
        for want of electing (11 George I c. 4),
        336

statutes (*cont.*)
  oaths of supremacy and allegiance, Act for
    abrogating (1 William and Mary c. 8),
    269, 291
  Occasional Conformity Act (10 Anne c. 6),
    306, 308–10, 321, 323, 325, 346
  Occasional Conformity Act, repeal of the
    (5 George I c. 4), 337–38
  Quieting Corporations, Act for (5 George I
    c. 6), 337–38
  Settling Ireland, Act for (Irish statute),
    170
  Test Act (25 Charles II c. 2), 122, 307,
    308, 323
  Toleration Act (1 William and Mary c. 18),
    307, 308, 337
Stockbridge, 176n
Stratford-upon-Avon, 73n, 116, 139, 143n,
  158n, 166, 170, 176, 182n, 183, 359
Street, Thomas, 201, 203
Sudbury, 37, 49, 66, 70n, 75, 116, 125, 152,
  159, 167, 294
Sunderland, Robert Spencer, Earl of, 255,
  256
surrenders, *see* charter surrenders
Sutton Coldfield, 39n, 161n

Tamworth, 251n, 253n
Taunton, 38n, 99, 164, 183–85, 186, 187,
  252n, 318, 322, 337
Tavistock, 220, 241n
tests for office holding, 17, 62–63, 91–92,
  104, 197, 244, 269, 323–24, 337–38,
  343, 344
  see also Association Oath; the
    Engagement; sacramental test; Solemn
    League and Covenant, declaration
    against; statutes, Corporation Act; the
    three questions
Tewkesbury, 73n, 79, 217n, 219, 245, 322
Thetford, 12, 38n, 136–37, 167, 250, 251n,
  289, 302, 309, 316n, 317n
  1682 charter, 212–14, 215, 216, 217n,
    218, 220, 223, 250
three questions, the, 244, 246; *see also*
  regulators
Tiverton, 198, 335–36
toleration, 238, 239–40, 242, 243
Torrington, 77, 251n
tory proscription, idea of questioned,
  322–23, 329–30
Totnes, 72, 175, 235, 242, 248n, 252
Tournay, Thomas, 17, 132–35, 136, 145,
  229
Treby, Sir George, 138, 139, 205–07, 209n,
  210, 278, 296

Tregony, 330
Trenchard, Sir John, 283
Trevor, Sir Thomas, 297–98
Truro, 241
Turton, John, 274n
Twisden, Thomas, 60n, 71–72, 141–43,
  176

Upper Bench, *see* King's and Queen's Bench

Ventris, Peytron, 274, 276n

Wallingford, 81, 99–100, 117, 157, 169,
  359
Walpole, Sir Robert, 21
Walsall, 93, 97, 111n, 121, 359
Wareham, 312n
Warrington, Henry Booth, Earl of, 281
Warwick, 38n, 46n, 95, 96, 114, 127, 157,
  227, 234, 254, 359
Wells, 235, 248n
Westcombe, Thomas, 123–24
Weymouth, 251n
Whitley, Col. Roger, 44, 230, 231n, 232,
  260n, 280–88, 302, 346
Wigan, 38n, 82n, 154–55, 157
Wilde, Sir William, 138
William, Prince of Orange and King of
  England, 19–20, 259, 260, 268, 280,
  287, 289, 297, 301, 302
Williams, Sir William, 133, 138–39, 224,
  229, 230–32, 252, 257, 284, 285, 287,
  288, 296–97, 302
Williamson, Sir Joseph, 178, 214, 289n
Wilson, Kathleen, 21, 339
Wilton, 249–50, 251n
Wimbledon, William, 17, 123–24
Winchelsea, 126, 127
Winchester, 35n, 50, 62, 70, 76, 114–15,
  251n, 254, 260n
Windham, Wadham, 141
Windsor, 46, 99, 100, 158n, 159–60, 169,
  359
Winnington, Sir Francis, 138, 139, 201–02,
  204, 296
Winnington, Salway, 310, 311
Woodstock, 38n, 42–43, 44n, 45n, 46n, 94,
  100, 101n, 137n, 139, 158n, 166, 242,
  252, 252n, 253n, 332n, 360
Worcester, Marquess of, *see* Somerset,
  Henry
Worcester, 63, 69, 77, 80n, 98, 170, 242n,
  246, 249, 322
  quo warranto against, 26–27, 126–27,
    195, 200–04, 206, 211, 212, 216, 223,
    234, 317

writs, royal, for ordering corporate elections, 314, 315, 329, 335

Yarmouth, Robert Paston, Earl of 224
Yarmouth, Norf., 35, 59n, 70n, 75, 78, 79, 100, 112n, 116n, 158–59, 167, 235
York, Duke of, *see* James II
York, 15, 61, 80, 139, 164, 228, 250, 251n, 255, 257, 314n

Titles in the series

The Common Peace: Participation and the Criminal Law in Seventeenth-Century England*
CYNTHIA B. HERRUP

Politics, Society and Civil War in Warwickshire, 1620–1660
ANN HUGHES

London Crowds in the Reign of Charles II: Propaganda and Politics from the Restoration to the Exclusion Crisis*
TIM HARRIS

Criticism and Compliment: The Politics of Literature in the England of Charles I*
KEVIN SHARPE

Central Government and the Localities: Hampshire, 1649–1689
ANDREW COLEBY

John Skelton and the Politics of the 1520s
GREG WALKER

Algernon Sidney and the English Republic, 1623–1677
JONATHAN SCOTT

Thomas Starkey and the Commonwealth: Humanist Politics and Religion in the Reign of Henry VIII
THOMAS F. MAYER

The Blind Devotion of the People: Popular Religion and the English Reformation*
ROBERT WHITING

The Cavalier Parliament and the Reconstruction of the Old Regime, 1661–1667
PAUL SEAWARD

The Blessed Revolution: English Politics and the Coming of War, 1621–1624
THOMAS COGSWELL

Charles I and the Road to Personal Rule
L. J. REEVE

George Lawson's 'Politica' and the English Revolution
CONAL CONDREN

Puritans and Roundheads: The Harleys of Brampton Bryan and the Outbreak of the Civil War
JACQUELINE EALES

An Uncounselled King: Charles I and the Scottish Troubles, 1637–1641
PETER DONALD

Cheap Print and Popular Piety, 1550–1640*
TESSA WATT

The Pursuit of Stability: Social Relations in Elizabethan London
IAN W. ARCHER

Prosecution and Punishment: Petty Crime and the Law in London and Rural Middlesex, c. 1660–1725
ROBERT B. SHOEMAKER

Algernon Sidney and the Restoration Crisis, 1677–1683
JONATHAN SCOTT

Exile and Kingdom: History and Apocalpyse in the Puritan Migration to America
AVIHU ZAKAI

The Pillars of Priestcraft Shaken: The Church of England and its Enemies, 1660–1730
J. A. I. CHAMPION

Steward, Lords and People: The Estate Steward and his World in Later Stuart England
D. R. HAINSWORTH

Civil War and Restoration in the Three Stuart Kingdoms: The Career of Randal MacDonnell, Marquis of Antrim, 1609–1683
JANE H. OHLMEYER

The Family of Love in English Society, 1550–1630
CHRISTOPHER W. MARSH

The Bishops' Wars: Charles I's Campaign against Scotland, 1638–1640*
MARK FISSEL

John Locke: Resistance, Religion and Responsibility*
JOHN MARSHALL

Constitutional Royalism and the Search for Settlement, c. 1640–1649
DAVID L. SMITH

Intelligence and Espionage in the Reign of Charles II, 1660–1685
ALAN MARSHALL

The Chief Governors: The Rise and Fall of Reform Government in Tudor Ireland, 1536–1588
CIARAN BRADY

Politics and Opinion in Crisis, 1678–1681
MARK KNIGHTS

Catholic and Reformed: The Roman and Protestant Churches in English Protestant Thought, 1604–1640
ANTHONY MILTON

Sir Matthew Hale, 1609–1676: Law, Religion and Natural Philosophy
ALAN CROMARTIE

Henry Parker and the English Civil War: The Political Thought of the Public's 'Privado'
MICHAEL MENDLE

Protestantism and Patriotism: Ideologies and the Making of English Foreign Policy, 1650–1668
STEVEN C. A. PINCUS

Gender in Mystical and Occult Thought: Behmenism and its Development in England
  B. J. GIBBONS

William III and the Godly Revolution
  TONY CLAYDON

Law-Making and Society in Late Elizabethan England: The Parliament of England, 1584–1601
  DAVID DEAN

Conversion, Politics and Religion in England, 1580–1625
  MICHAEL C. QUESTIER

Politics, Religion and the British Revolutions: The Mind of Samuel Rutherford
  JOHN COFFEY

King James VI and I and the Reunion of Christendom
  W. B. PATTERSON

The English Reformation and the Laity: Gloucestershire, 1540–1580
  CAROLINE LITZENBERGER

Godly Clergy in Early England: The Caroline Puritan Movement, c. 1620–1643
  TOM WEBSTER

Prayer Book and People in Elizabethan and Early Stuart England
  JUDITH MALTBY

Sermons at Court, 1559–1629: Religion and Politics in Elizabethan and Jacobean Preaching
  PETER E. MCCULLOUGH

Dismembering the Body Politic: Partisan Politics in England's Towns, 1650–1730
  PAUL D. HALLIDAY

*Also published as a paperback

Learning Resources
Centre

Printed in the United Kingdom
by Lightning Source UK Ltd.
9729000001B/265-270